Introduction to the Philosophy of Science

Introduction
to the
Philosophy of Science

ARTHUR ZUCKER

Ohio University

PRENTICE HALL
Upper Saddle River, New Jersey 07458

Library of Congress Cataloging-in-Publication Data

Zucker, Arthur (date)
    Introduction to the philosophy of science / Arthur Zucker.
       p. cm.
    Includes bibliographical references (p.).
    ISBN 0-02-432104-4 (pbk.)
    1. Science—Philosophy. I. Title.
Q175.Z82 1995
501—dc20
                                    95–20631
                                          CIP

Acquisitions editor: Ted Bolen
Editorial/production supervision: Karen Trost
Interior design: Joan Greenfield
Copy editor: Bruce Emmer
Buyer: Lynn Pearlman
Editorial assistant: Meg McGuane
Cover design: Bruce Kenselaar
Cover photo: "Collage with Two Profiles," Fred Otnes
The Stock Illustration Source, Inc.

Acknowledgments for text selections appear as footnotes on the first page of each selection, which constitute a continuation of the copyright page.

Printed in the United States of America
10 9 8 7 6 5 4 3 2 1

ISBN 0-02-432104-4

Prentice-Hall International (UK) Limited, *London*
Prentice-Hall of Australia Pty. Limited, *Sydney*
Prentice-Hall Canada Inc., *Toronto*
Prentice-Hall Hispanoamericana, S.A., *Mexico*
Prentice-Hall of India Private Limited, *New Delhi*
Prentice-Hall of Japan, Inc., *Tokyo*
Simon & Schuster Asia Pte. Ltd., *Singapore*
Editora Prentice-Hall do Brasil, Ltda., *Rio de Janeiro*

Contents

CONTENTS

CHAPTER 3
Confirmation 141

CHAPTER 4
Realism and Antirealism 202

CHAPTER 5
Can Medicine Be a Science? 240

CHAPTER 6

Can There Be a Science of Dreams? 288

CHAPTER 7

Science and Gender 349

CHAPTER 8

Further Readings from Chemistry, Biology, Physics, and the Sociology of Medicine 393

CONTENTS

Preface

Introduction to the Philosophy of Science is aimed primarily at students taking their first course in the philosophy of science. Usually such students have a mixed background in philosophy but are similar in having little preparation in science or the history of science. Chapter 1 as well as the first reading in Chapter 2 constitute an attempt to make up for deficiencies in these areas. The text presumes no background in philosophy. The introductions to the chapters and to the individual selections attempt to provide some general philosophical background for beginning philosophy students.

Each chapter begins with a general introduction. Each article has a fairly detailed introduction. These introductions serve to: summarize the main arguments; make connections among authors, positions, and topics; and, as noted above, give some of the background in the philosophy of science (and philosophy in general) necessary for a fuller understanding of the issues discussed. The selections with the most detailed introductions are those in the first four chapters. This is because these chapters—which cover traditional topics, cases from the history of science, explanation, confirmation, and realism/anti-realism—provide the material necessary for application in Chapters 5–7.

Chapters 5 and 6 ask the students to apply what they have learned in order to answer some traditional philosophical questions posed by philosophers of science about the disciplines of medicine and psychology. Chapter 7 is devoted to feminist philosophy of science. Many of the views represented in Chapter 7 will conflict with the more traditional positions taken in previous chapters. This should encourage critical reflection on the part of students. For instructors who find this topic too untraditional, Chapter 7 need not be assigned.

The various topics (reductionism, holism, realism, instrumentalism, etc.) are introduced and discussed in detail as they arise in the readings. They are discussed, in other words, when needed. In this sense, the book follows the method of discovery. My experience is that students do very well with this method.

Despite the relatively lengthy introductions, there is still much leeway for instructors to pursue in greater breadth and depth any particular topic, philosopher, area of science, or episode from the history of science. At the end of each chapter, there are five study questions that are meant to help students tie issues together, see a bit further, and do some critical thinking on their own.

Although physics *is* represented throughout the text, examples from biology (especially genetics), medicine, and psychology are used frequently, as most students find such examples much less daunting than those taken from physics or chemistry.

The last chapter, entitled "Further Readings," offers more science and history of science selections as fodder for the philosophy of science. I have not given detailed introductions to the articles in this chapter for two reasons: (1) students who seek out supplementary reading should have the rewarding experience of "getting it" on their own; (2) the material in this section can be used for assignments such as take-home exams. I have made every effort to choose these selections so that enterprising students can work through the material on their own.

I would like to thank Maggie Barbieri, for encouraging me to submit the original proposal, and Ted Bolen, for helping to see it to completion. The following Prentice Hall staff also deserve thanks: Jennifer Weinberg, Marketing, and Meg McGuane, editorial assistant for Philosophy and Religion. Karen Trost supervised production with great expertise. The initial copy editing was done with great skill and care by Bruce Emmer, and Lisbeth Isaacs did the final proofreading. Malaysia T. Smith, my undergraduate research assistant here at Ohio University, and Paul O. Donnell, my graduate research assistant, combined to do a great deal of the "drudgework" connected with the book. Stephanie Bethel and Glen Matthews used some of their work-study time to help with the project. Alice Donohoe and Christina Dalesandry, who already do the brunt of the department work at Ohio University, gave generously of their time. My colleague here in the department, Ed Slowik, read and commented on the chapter dealing with realism. My daughter, Elena, read and made many helpful comments on an earlier version of the manuscript. My wife, Laurie, was supportive, understanding, and helped tremendously with the final proofreading.

Contributors

HELEN BERMAN, Department of Chemistry, Rutgers the State University of New Jersey.

MAY BRODBECK (1917–1983) was a member of the University of Minnesota faculty from 1947 to 1974, president of the American Philosophy Association from 1970 to 1971, and Carver Professor Emerita at the University of Iowa in 1983, where she had been Dean of Faculty beginning in 1974.

MARTIN BUNZL, Department of Philosophy, Rutgers the State University of New Jersey.

ARTHUR L. CAPLAN, Director of the Center for Bioethics and Professor of Philosophy, University of Pennsylvania.

RUDOLF CARNAP (1891–1970) was one of the leaders of the "positivist" schools in philosophy. He wrote numerous works devoted to logic, epistemology, and the philosophy of science. He taught at the University of Chicago.

JAMES D. CARNEY, Department of Philosophy, Arizona State University.

NANCY CARTWRIGHT, Department of Philosophy, London School of Economics and Political Science, University of London.

K. DANNER CLOUSER, Department of Humanities, Pennsylvania State University College of Medicine.

JACK S. COHEN, Department of Pharmacology, Georgetown University Medical Center.

CHARLES DARWIN (1809–1882) was a British naturalist who expounded the theory of evolution by natural selection in *On the Origin of Species* (1859).

JOHN EARMAN, Department of Philosophy, Department of History and Philosophy of Science, University of Pittsburgh.

EDWARD ERWIN, Department of Philosophy, University of Miami.

EDUARD FARBER (1892–?) was a German-American organic chemist who wrote many articles on the history of chemistry.

PAUL FEYERABEND (1924–1994) was Professor Emeritus of Philosophy at the University of California, Berkeley, since 1990. He also taught at Yale, University College of London, and the Federal Institute of Technology in Zurich.

ARTHUR FINE, Department of Philosophy, Northwestern University.

JANE FLAX, Department of Political Science, Howard University.

SIGMUND FREUD (1856–1939) is often considered the founder of psychoanalysis.

RUTH GINZBERG, Department of Philosophy, Wesleyan University.

SAMUEL GOROVITZ, Department of Philosophy, Syracuse University.

ADOLF GRÜNBAUM, Department of Philosophy, Department of History and Philosophy of Science, University of Pittsburgh.

IAN HACKING, Department of Philosophy, Victoria College—University of Toronto.

CARL G. HEMPEL, Department of Philosophy, Princeton; Department of History and Philosophy of Science, University of Pittsburgh.

MARY HESSE, Department of History and Philosophy of Science, Cambridge University.

J. ALLAN HOBSON, Psychiatrist, Massachusetts Mental Health Hospital.

FREDERICK HOLMES, History of Medicine, Yale University Medical School.

ROBERT HOOKE (1635–1703) was an English philosopher, physicist, chemist, and inventor.

ALISON JAGGAR, Department of Philosophy, University of Colorado, Boulder.

CARL G. JUNG (1875–1961), initially a student of Freud, was one of the founders of psychoanalysis. He later broke with Freud.

FRIEDRICH AUGUST KEKULÉ (1829–1896) was a German chemist and founder of structural organic chemistry.

EVELYN FOX KELLER, Professor of Rhetoric, Women's Studies, and the History of Science, University of California, Berkeley.

PHILIP KITCHER, Department of Philosophy, University of California, San Diego.

PETER KOSSO, Department of Philosophy, Northern Arizona University.

THOMAS KUHN, Department of Linguistics and Philosophy, Massachusetts Institute of Technology.

IMRE LAKATOS (1922–1974) was a prominent philosopher of mathematics and science. He taught at the University of London after leaving his native Hungary.

LARRY LAUDAN, Department of Philosophy, University of Hawaii at Manoa.

HENRY LEICESTER (1906–1991) was an historian of chemistry who taught at University Pacific Dental School in San Francisco from 1962 until his death in 1991.

HELEN E. LONGINO, Department of Philosophy, University of Minnesota.

ROBERT W. MCCARLEY, Professor of Psychiatry, Harvard University Medical School.

ALASDAIR MACINTYRE, Department of Philosophy, University of Notre Dame.

NORMAN MALCOLM (1911–1990) was an American philosopher who helped introduce the philosophy of Ludwig Wittgenstein into America. Malcolm was Susan Linn Sage Professor of Philosophy at Cornell.

ROBERT MATTHEWS is a freelance science writer who lives in England.

CAROLYN MERCHANT, Department of Conservation and Resource Studies, University of California, Berkeley.

H. CLARK METCALFE is a high school physics teacher.

E. A. MURPHY, Professor of Biostatistics, Medicine, and Biology, Johns Hopkins University Medical School.

ROBERT OLBY, Philosophy Department, University of Leeds.

PAUL OPPENHEIM (1885–1977) earned his doctorate in chemistry at the University of Giessen, but was primarily interested in the philosophy and methodology of science. He was not affiliated with any academic institution.

SIR KARL POPPER (1902–1994) was a professor of logic and scientific method at the London School of Economics from 1949 to 1969 and wrote numerous books, including *The Open Society and Its Economics* and *The Poverty of Historicism.*

FRANKLIN H. PORTUGAL, Biochemist, National Cancer Institute.

KENNETH F. SCHAFFNER, Department of Philosophy and College of Medicine, George Washington University.

RICHARD K. SCHEER, Department of Philosophy, Kansas State University.

MICHAEL SCRIVEN, Department of Philosophy, Western Michigan University.

PAUL STARR, Department of Sociology, Princeton University.

SHIRLEY STRUM, Department of Anthropology, University of California, San Diego.

GEORGE E. THIBAULT, Physician, Massachusetts General Hospital.

FREDERICK TRINKLEIN is a high school physics teacher.

BAS C. VAN FRAASSEN, Department of Philosophy, Princeton University.

JOHN WILLIAMS is a high school physics teacher.

ARTHUR ZUCKER, Department of Philosophy, Ohio University.

Introduction

Philosophers ask questions. In ethics, philosophers might ask, "What is the 'good' life? What does 'good' mean?" As philosophers get answers to these questions, related concepts get clarified. In the case of ethics, these concepts would include good and bad, right and wrong, rights and duties, obligations and responsibility, selfishness and altruism, and many others. One could therefore say that philosophy and philosophers deal with *concepts*. In a discussion of art, a philosopher might ask for a careful examination of concepts such as beautiful, work of art, unity, intention, and meaning.

There is, however, another way to view the task of philosophers. Their goal is to ferret out crucial assumptions that are not explicit in arguments or in disciplines and then to analyze them. Having identified the assumptions, a philosopher might ask, "What do the important terms in them mean? Are the assumptions true or even reasonable? How do the assumptions interrelate? Is there any independent support for the assumptions?"

Let us clarify this with an example that will give some idea of what the philosophy of science might be. Suppose that someone says that your real reason for studying philosophy is that you have a compulsive personality. Here are some of the assumptions behind this statement:

That there is a distinction between real and apparent reasons

That there is a way to distinguish the real from the apparent

That the real reasons are not always obvious to the people who are acting because of them

That some behavior can be characterized as compulsive

That hidden reasons can be the motives (driving forces) behind our actions

Terms that require definitions are *real, apparent, obvious, motive,* and, of course, *compulsive*. Identifying these terms and these assumptions would be a part of what is usually called the philosophy of psychology. One could consider the philosophy of psychology a branch of the philosophy of science. Notice, however, that as we characterized these terms, we would also be creating some version of a psychological theory about why people do what they do. Part of what this example has shown is that the boundary between the philosophy of science (the philosophy of psychology) and science (psychology) is thin. We might, of course, also ask, "Is psychology a science?"

Just as we applied the methodology of philosophy to psychology, we could turn philosophy on any science or any part of a science. We might ask, "How good a theory is the neo-Darwinian account of evolution? Do explanations in Newtonian mechanics differ from those in quantum mechanics? Why does meteorology have such a difficult time making good predictions?" Notice that in this last question, we are using an expression, "good prediction," that needs clarification.

Our examples so far have been relatively specific. However, the philosophy of science also hopes to come to some general conclusions about science. For example, what is a scientific theory, what is a good scientific theory, what is the difference between a scientific explanation and any explanation (assuming that there *is* an important difference), what counts as a prediction (rather than a guess), what is causality, what is probability, what is the best characterization of scientific laws and do they differ from discipline to discipline? In general, is there a scientific method to be found, one that is guaranteed to give correct answers, no matter what the specific discipline, if only it is properly used?

These questions are important because the promise of science is to get at the truth about how the world really is. For at least a century, it has seemed that if any group of people really knew what they were talking about, it was scientists. So it makes sense to look into science to find a trustworthy path to knowledge.

That is what this book does. It explores science in a philosophical manner. It brings to light for analysis what a number of philosophers have had to say about some important issues in the philosophy of science, taking an approach that is a bit different from others.

For example, we begin in Chapter 1 with an initial discussion of the history of science. From Aristotle, we proceed through the important changes wrought by Galileo and the new science of the seventeenth century and end with examples of science into the late nineteenth and early twentieth centuries. Many of the technical terms of the philosophy of science are introduced in Chapter 1. Although they are defined in the introductions to the anthologized works, they are also used by the authors in the articles in ways that clarify and amplify their definitions. In this way, you can learn both terms and philosophy as you need them. This manner of introducing terms is used throughout the book.

Chapters 2 and 3 focus on the related problems of explanation and confirmation in science. One of those problems is, "Just how theoretical can a theory be?" Chapter 4, on realism and anti-realism, deals with this very important issue of current interest.

Chapters 5 and 6 also make this anthology different from many others, for they examine the realms of medicine and dreams. Using the conceptual tools developed in Chapters 1, 2, and 3, we ask first whether medicine is in fact a science and then whether the interpretation of dreams can be considered a science (or part of a science). The philosophy of psychology is a long-standing philosophical area. Texts in the philosophy of science often have sections devoted to psychology in general. No current text, however, focuses on dreams and their possible meanings. The philosophy of medicine is a relatively new philosophical area, gaining in interest as medical ethics gains in popularity. Even so, philosophical analysis of medicine as a problem-solving discipline is new territory for philosophy of science anthologies.

There is even more to our look at the philosophy of science. One of the implications of the historical approach to it is that science is not easily divorced from social and political factors. That is, we are led to question the assumption that one can (and should) distinguish between what scientists literally do as scientists and the outside influences that affect them. Because the distinction between the two is often seen as the basis for what is claimed to be the objectivity of science, the claim that science is totally objective is being called into question. In other words, if science is in part a function of social and political factors, then our usual claim that science is objective, in the sense of being free of such value-laden influences, must be scrutinized carefully.

Objectivity has been challenged even further by people who point out that the traditional story of Western science is a story about men written primarily by men. It may be that our picture of science is just a man's (androcentric—sometimes the word *phallocentric* is used) picture of how to get knowledge. It may be that what we think is a true look at the world is just the way it looks to men. Perhaps if women had been in charge, our entire idea of science and what is true about the world would be different. We would then have a gynocentric view of the world. The claim that knowledge itself is gender-related is disconcerting, to say the least. This specific issue is discussed in Chapter 7. By the time you have completed the readings, the philosophical questions that can be asked of scientific explanation and confirmation will have been raised within a larger set of questions about science, history, and gender.

Articles in Chapter 8 supplement the readings in Chapters 1 through 7 by offering more details on examples used in these previous chapters. To take three examples, Portugal and Cohen discuss Mendelian genetics in Chapter 1, and in Chapter 3, Thomas Kuhn mentions the theory of phlogiston and Kitcher analyzes Darwin on biogeography. Three of the selections in Chapter 8 focus on just these points.

1

Case Studies from the History of Science

It is impossible to study the philosophy of science without discussing some actual science. In this chapter, we will look at well-researched examples from the history of science. The point is not to learn all the details of these episodes so much as to get a general picture of how some scientists have done their work. Each of these case studies exemplifies in its own way much of what will be studied in greater depth throughout the book.

The experiment related by Hooke is considered the ideal form of both an experiment and an experimental report. Clear, concise, precise—we know what hypothesis is being tested and how. We know what will support the hypothesis and what will count against it. Hooke even tells us what he will report on next. From Hooke's account, we can come to understand what a scientific experiment is and what a scientific experiment assumes about methodology. It will also require us to discuss causality as well as what is known as the problem of induction.

The series of experiments on the mechanism of digestion is equally classic in approach. By analyzing a series of experiments designed around a single question, Holmes reveals the history of the question as well as various answers. To understand fully Tiedemann and Gmelin's research into digestion, we will have to deal with the concepts of reductionism, holism, and vitalism.

Kekulé's discovery of the structure of benzene and Farber's account of dreaming and visions in the history of chemistry seem to show that discoveries in science are not always the result of logic. Can this be? Again, what does this say about objectivity in science? It might say nothing. For this to be the case, we would need a distinction between discovery and the validation of discovery, being careful to mean by "science" the validation of discoveries. We will see the distinction made by some authors and challenged by others.

Strum was one of the first to make crucial observations about baboons. But she was not the first person to study baboons. Her success forces us to question much that scientists assume about the nature of objectivity. We get a glimpse of how the gender of an investigator may actually affect the manner of investigation and, therefore, the knowledge gained. Portugal and Cohen discuss Mendel's classic set of experiments on peas that led to the formation of the discipline of genetics.

Merchant does not so much tell us about experiments as provide us with a philosophical interpretation of the history of science. She begins with Aristotle and takes us to contemporary times. Her goal is to show how science and philosophy are related. She is trying to show that pursuing science is part of a general worldview that includes the values one holds, a claim to which we will return in Chapter 7. Notice that Merchant does more than merely present a list of facts in chronological order. Indeed, history is always more than just a listing of what happened when. Even in their brief history of genetics, Portugal and Cohen speculate about how the "rediscovery" of Mendel's work may really have happened. History often presents facts against a background of ideas. Sometimes this approach is called intellectual history or the history of ideas. In reviewing the history of science, one must have some idea of what to include as science. Even if one decides to include whatever was called "science" in any period of history, this decision by the historian makes the history more than just a list of facts. Thus to write a history of science requires that one decide what science is and how far to stray from the simplest list of facts.

The philosophy of science was characterized by example in the Introduction to the Book. Now let us ask, "How should one study the philosophy of science?" Obviously, one answer is, "By studying the history of science." The following are some other approaches.

Science can be studied as a subset of some particular theory of knowledge. (Knowledge theory, also known as epistemology, is a branch of philosophy.) First one gets a general theory of what counts as knowledge, and then one uses that to study the disciplines regarded as scientific. This procedure can be evaluative by holding some piece of science up to the standard established by a theory of knowledge.

Science can be studied as if it were a subset of logic and mathematics. One establishes foundations for logic and mathematics and then uses those foundations to study science. Again, this procedure can be evaluative by comparing some example of science to the foundations of logic or mathematics.

Science can also be studied by making a careful description of what scientists actually do. Of course, one might have to appeal to history to decide which scientists to study. If this method is followed, there will be no evaluations, only descriptions. However, if there is an attempt to study only the "greatest" scientists, comparison to the resulting standards will be tempting and, of course, will result in evaluative philosophy of science.

As you read through this book, watch for the interplay of these various ways to approach history and the philosophy of science.

CAROLYN MERCHANT, "THE WORLD AN ORGANISM"

Merchant points out that until about the time of Galileo (1564–1642), explanations were given in terms of the four causes identified by Aristotle (384–322 B.C.) in his

Metaphysics (bk. 5, chap. 2). Consider the making of a statue. In Aristotelian terms, its *material cause* is the marble block, its *efficient cause* is the movement of the chisel in the hand of the artist against the marble block (Aristotle said, "The maker [is] a cause of the thing made"), its *formal cause* is the plan in the sculptor's mind or the preliminary sketch (what Aristotle referred to as the "definition of the essence"), and its *final cause* is the reason for making the statue—money, fame, to dazzle the world with beauty, to please the Gods, or the like.

The question "How was the statue made?" was considered best answered by asking, "*Why* was the statue made?" Thus the best answer was always couched in terms of final cause. The world, according to Merchant, should be viewed primarily in terms of reasoning things and not in terms of mechanical action—explanation should be given in terms of final causes. Go back to the statue example. The statue must be seen as an integral part of a system composed of the marble block, the chisel, and the sculptor if its best explanation is in terms of final cause. This is how nature must be seen—as part of a reasoning system—if final causes are to be used. According to Merchant, nature was portrayed as a reasoning organism, a living unit organized in a hierarchical fashion intended to reach goals. This sort of explanation is called teleological.

Merchant points out that there was a shift to mechanism and efficient cause at about the time of Galileo. When she asks why, her answer is that philosophy was getting nowhere, but physics was. Physics as practiced by Galileo and Newton assumed that matter was dead (never living) stuff acting mechanically. It required explanation in terms of material and efficient causes if it was to be understood. This can be put in another way. The world was regarded as a machine—a clock or a pump; no longer was it considered a living entity. Merchant refers to this new way of seeing the world as the death of nature. Matter was no longer an active thing with its own ability to move from within. By Newton's time, force was external to matter, and matter was "dead." Matter and nature were passive. So ethically, nature could be manipulated.

In the organic world, order was defined as fitting into the hierarchy. In the mechanical world, order was defined as rational predictability based on mathematically stated laws. The world for the new science is clearly rational at its basis. (We will see this assumption brought to light and challenged in Chapter 2 by Nancy Cartwright. She refers to it as the "tidy universe assumption.") Merchant wants us to see the death of nature as the most far-reaching effect of the scientific revolution.

Corpuscularianism, the overall view of Pierre Gassendi (1592–1655) and Thomas Hobbes (1588–1679), was an early scientific worldview—what Thomas Kuhn would call a paradigm. This view was a form of atomism:

1. *Corpuscles are the basic building blocks of all things.* Corpuscles are hard and "massy." They have shape, and they move. Their motion and their shape together account for things like perceived color and sound. Perceived color and

sound are caused by the shape and motion of the corpuscles. The properties of the corpuscles are real and called primary; properties such as color and sound are less real and referred to as secondary. This distinction between primary and secondary qualities is usually attributed to Galileo.

2. *No occult qualities exist.* This is a way of saying that all qualities are either the primary qualities of the corpuscles or reducible to them. There are no hidden qualities. By definition, any other kind of quality would be called occult.

3. *Every effect has a cause.* Nothing just happens. Whatever does happen has corpuscles in motion as an explanation.

4. *No action can occur at a distance.* This is a way to define causality. For one thing to cause a change in another requires that they touch or communicate through a medium such as air.

5. *No scientific knowledge is known for certain.* Scientific knowledge is factual knowledge. All factual knowledge is probabilistic. Only mathematical knowledge is certain knowledge. This part of corpuscularianism is a clear break with Descartes (1596–1650), who believed that knowledge that was not certain was not worthy of the name knowledge. The Cartesian view, an example of what is termed rationalism, can be considered a form of reductionism.

In France, the rise of mechanism and the rise of centralized government go together. Hobbes can also be seen as a mix of science and social philosophy. Hobbes gave a mechanistic account of society, which made it easy to support the need for royalty and a strong police force.

How did life and its motions come about in a dead universe? Both Leibniz (1646–1716) and Newton (1642–1727) had answers. Newton claimed that matter is passive and that force is active and external to matter; but matter has intrinsic properties (such as inertia). Newton's examples of intrinsic active principles included gravity and fermentation.

Leibniz took a different tack. He argued that matter doesn't even exist; only energy exists. The world is made of points of energy called monads. The best explanations for the behavior of monads are teleological. For Leibniz, the real world is not mechanical. The real world is a world permeated with the tiny perceptions of monads.

Merchant ends with a thumbnail sketch of her version of the philosophy known as positivism, logical positivism, or logical empiricism. Positivists, she claims, depend on mathematical formalism as the criterion for rationality. They use what they take to be facts of nature as the criteria for empirical validity. They view modern science as objective and value free. This is shown by the ability to reduce everything to mathematical-mechanical models. (Models will be discussed in the introduction to the article by Mary Hesse in Chapter 2. For now, they can be considered synonymous with "a way, pictorial or mathematical, to understand.") Carnap, who will be read in Chapter 3, holds logical positivist views. Hempel, appearing

7

in Chapter 2, has positivist leanings. Brodbeck (also in Chapter 2) can also be considered a clear example of a positivist. After reading these three authors, go back to Merchant and see how good a characterization she has given of positivism.

Very few, if any, contemporary philosophers of science will admit to being positivist in any of its forms. This is due in part to its being subjected to many trenchant criticisms and in part to the fact that positivism now carries with it—unfairly—the negative connotation of old-fashioned, wrong, almost silly. No matter how some of the articles in this book may shape your views, it is crucial not to let a word such as *positivism* become a term of abuse, signaling obviously wrongheaded views. Philosophy is about rigorous argument, not name-calling.

In later passages (not quoted here), Merchant cites the rise of interest in systems theory and holism as recent counters to the views of positivism. She points out that holism is supported by ecology in the sense that ecology cannot be studied except holistically. Thus to be a scientific environmentalist, one must also be a holist. Any nonholistic approach leads all too easily to destroying the environment. Merchant therefore favors holism as a general approach to science.

The World an Organism

CAROLYN MERCHANT

The Scientific Revolution of the sixteenth and seventeenth centuries has been treated by most historians as a period of intellectual enlightenment in which a new science of mechanics and a mechanical world view laid the foundation for modern scientific, technological, and social progress. But, in the face of the current crisis over the depletion of natural resources, Western society is once more beginning to appreciate the environmental values of the premechanical "world we have lost." Today the ecological consequences of exploitative attitudes toward the four elements—earth, air, water, and fire—the ancient sources of life and energy, are beginning to be fully recognized.

Along with current challenges to mechanistic technology, holistic presuppositions about nature are being revived in ecology's premise that everything is connected to everything else and in its emphasis on the primacy of interactive processes in nature. All parts are dependent on one another and mutually affect each other and the whole. Each portion of an ecological community, each niche, exists in a dynamic relationship with the surrounding ecosystem. The organism occupying any particular niche affects and is affected by the entire web of living and nonliving environmental components. Ecology, as a philosophy of nature, has roots in organicism—the idea that the cosmos is an organic entity, growing and developing from within, in an integrated unity of structure and function.

Organismic thought contributed the rudimentary philosophical framework out of which ecological science and the conservation of natural resources developed. The Romantics of the early nineteenth century, reacting against the mechanism of the Scientific Revolution and the Enlightenment, turned back to the organismic idea of a vital animating principle binding together the whole created world. American Romantics such as Emerson looked to wildness as a source of spiritual insight, while Thoreau found evidence of a vital life permeating the rocks, ponds, and mountains in pagan and American Indian animism. Such influences were an inspiration to the preservation movement led by John Muir in the late nineteenth century, and to such early ecologists as Frederick Clements, whose theory of plant succession held that a plant community grew, developed, and matured much like an individual organism.[1]

Variations of the organic framework of the Renaissance shared certain presuppositions about nature. The Renaissance cosmos was a living unit, of which all parts were interconnected in a tightly organized system. The orthodox view inherited from the medieval interpretation of Aristotle was an earth-centered hierarchical cosmos extending upward from the four inanimate elements, which were mixed together to form the minerals, vegetables, and animals found in the sublunar region of change, to the unchanging ether-filled spheres of the seven planets, with their associated hierarchies of angels, above the moon. Beyond the planets was the sphere of the *primum mobile*, source of the daily rotation of the heavens, then the sphere of the fixed stars and zodiacal constellations, and finally the Empyrean heaven of God. Together they comprised a living chain of being, each member a step in a stable, ordered, spherically-enclosed world, each member sharing some particular feature with the steps below and above, yet excelling in some unique characteristic. Man was linked to the animal world below,

with which he shared sensation, and to the angels above, with whom he shared rationality. Each part of his body was governed by one of the zodiacal signs, so that as a microcosm, he was a miniature replica of the celestial spheres, or macrocosm. Human society, as discussed in the preceding chapter, was also stratified according to status, with peasants at the bottom, the king and pope at the apex, and women below the men of their particular status group. Nature as the involuntary agent of God was the immanent manifestation of God's law in the world. . . .

As cultural developments challenged Aristotelian authority and economic changes undermined the established social order, more radical organic philosophies emerged, stressing change over structure and force over form. Naturalists including Bernardino Telesio (1509–1588), Tommaso Campanella (1568–1639), and Giordano Bruno (1548–1600) unified the world's soul and spirit into a single all-pervasive living entity, distinct from matter but coeternal with it, while asserting change as the dialectical opposition of contraries. The vitalist view put forward somewhat earlier by Paracelsus (1490–1541) further reduced the explanation of change to a monistic unity of vital spirit and phenomenal matter. Neoplatonism and naturalism thus made a distinction between matter and its activity, while vitalism unified matter and spirit into single, active evolving substances.

But the cluster of ecological, commercial, technological, and social changes evolving during the sixteenth and seventeenth centuries continued to differentiate among these philosophies, with the result that some of the above assumptions about the organic world were criticized and transformed by the emerging mechanical philosophy of the mid-seventeenth century, while others were rendered implausible and rejected. Mechanism, which superseded the organic framework, was based on the logic that knowledge of the world could be certain and consistent, and that the laws of nature were imposed on creation by God. The primacy of organic process gave way to the stability of mathematical laws and identities. Force was external to matter rather than immanent within it. Matter was corpuscular, passive, and inert; change was simply the rearrangement of particles as motion was transmitted from one part to another in a causal nexus. Because it viewed nature as dead and matter as passive, mechanism could function as a subtle sanction for the exploitation and manipulation of nature and its resources. By the late seventeenth century, however, the organicism of the Renaissance had begun to achieve a new synthesis with the mechanical philosophy of the mid-century, resulting in a managerial perspective concerning the future use of resources.

This mechanical philosophy and its managerial point of view have also contributed to the science of ecology. The concept of the ecosystem, which by the 1950s had replaced the idea of the biotic community (rejected as being too anthropomorphic), is based on the mathematical modeling of nature. Data are abstracted from the organic context in the form of information bits and then manipulated according to a set of differential equations, allowing the prediction of ecological change and the rational management of the ecosystem and its resources as a whole. The organic and mechanical philosophies of nature cannot, therefore, be viewed as strict dichotomies, nor can most philosophers be placed solidly in one camp or the other. The tensions between these two perspectives on nature have continued to be influential ever since the Scientific Revolution. . . .

———

The fundamental social and intellectual problem for the seventeenth century was the problem of order. The perception of disorder, so important to the Baconian doctrine of dominion over nature, was also crucial to the rise of mechanism as a rational antidote to the disintegration of the organic cosmos. The new mechanical philosophy of the mid-seventeenth century achieved a reunification of the cosmos, society, and the self in terms of a new metaphor—the machine. Developed by the French thinkers Mersenne, Gassendi, and Descartes in the 1620s and 1630s and elaborated by a group of English émigrés to Paris in the 1640s and 1650s, the new mechanical theories emphasized and reinforced elements in human experience developing slowly since the late Middle Ages, but accelerating in the sixteenth century.

New forms of order and power provided a remedy for the disorder perceived to be spreading throughout culture. In the organic world, order meant the function of each part within the larger whole, as determined by its nature, while power was diffused from the top downward through the social or cosmic hierarchies. In the mechanical world, order was redefined to mean the predictable behavior of each part within a rationally determined system of laws, while power derived from active and immediate intervention in a secularized world. Order and power together constituted control. Rational control over nature, society, and the self was achieved by redefining reality itself through the new machine metaphor.

As the unifying model for science and society, the machine has permeated and reconstructed human consciousness so totally that today we scarcely question its validity. Nature, society, and the human body are composed of interchangeable atomized parts that can be repaired or replaced from outside. The "technological fix" mends an ecological malfunction, new human beings replace the old to maintain the smooth functioning of industry and bureaucracy, and interventionist medicine exchanges a fresh heart for a worn-out, diseased one.

The mechanical view of nature now taught in most Western schools is accepted without question as our everyday, common sense reality—matter is made up of atoms, colors occur by the reflection of light waves of differing lengths, bodies obey the law of inertia, and the sun is in the center of our solar system. None of this was common sense to our seventeenth-century counterparts. The replacement of the older, "natural" ways of thinking by a new and "unnatural" form of life—seeing, thinking, and behaving—did not occur without struggle. The submergence of the organism by the machine engaged the best minds of the times during a period fraught with anxiety, confusion, and instability in both the intellectual and social spheres.

The removal of animistic, organic assumptions about the cosmos constituted the death of nature—the most far-reaching effect of the Scientific Revolution. Because nature was now viewed as a system of dead, inert particles moved by external, rather than inherent forces, the mechanical framework itself could legitimate the manipulation of nature. Moreover, as a conceptual framework, the mechanical order had associated with it a framework of values based on power, fully compatible with the directions taken by commercial capitalism.

. . . Gassendi's mechanical philosophy supposed the unchanging constituents of reality to be solid, impenetrable, corporeal atoms that retained their identity through change. They had the properties of extension, shape, weight, and an internal force of motion. Although the atoms and corpuscles of later mechanists were inert and passive, Gassendi's atoms, like those of Epicurus, were endowed with an "internal energy" and were therefore active and in motion.

For Gassendi, however, this principle of motion was material, not incorporeal and vital, as were the elements and seeds of Paracelsus and Van Helmont. Leucippus, Democritus, and Epicurus, he wrote, "did not consider atoms the matter of all things to be inert or motionless, but rather as most active and mobile."[2] Quoting Lucretius on "matter's teeming bodies . . . driven with what movement endowed to scoot across the great void," Gassendi concluded that "the internal principle of action that works in second causes is not some incorporeal substance [such as the forms and species assumed by the Aristotelians and scholastics] but a corporeal one." The atoms were self-moving, least parts of matter activated by an inherent corporeal principle. But they were created by an incorporeal Christian God who "pervade[s] and support[s] the universal machine of the world." The atoms were material, not the incorporeal parts of God's substance "pulled apart as it were and cut into little pieces which become the individual souls, or forms," of men, beasts, plants, metals, stones, and "every single thing."

Although the atomic particles of matter were inherently active, the cumulative effect of their individual motions was such that gross visible bodies obeyed the principle of inertia. In a larger corporeal body, "atoms may indeed be restrained until they do not move, but not to the point that they do not strain and endeavor to disentangle themselves and renew their motion." The motion of gross bodies occurred through a nexus of efficient physical causes rather than through the tensions between sympathies and antipathies, attractions and repulsions assumed by the naturalists. Occult qualities could be explained by that universal law governing the whole natural world—the law of causality. Every effect had a cause, no cause acted without motion, and no cause acted at a distance.

Using political metaphor, Gassendi argued that God was not the soul of the world inherent within it, but its governor or director. The earth could not be said to be animated by a soul, as could plants, animals, or men. There was no place for spontaneity in nature itself, nor could it be sanctioned in the human soul. Spontaneous action was not to be confused with freedom of action. Spontaneity was an impulse of nature, of passion. Free action depended on man's reason, examination, judgment, and choice.[3] . . .

In France, the rise of the mechanical world view was coincident with a general tendency toward central governmental controls and the concentration of power in the hands of the royal ministers. The rationalization of administration and of the natural order was occurring simultaneously. Rational management in the social and economic spheres helps to explain the appeal of mechanism as a rational order created by a powerful sovereign deity. As Descartes wrote to Mersenne in 1630, "God sets up mathematical laws in nature as a king sets up laws in his kingdom."[4]

In France by the seventeenth century, the centralized control and management of industry and natural resources was well under way. The king controlled large-scale industry (principally gunpowder, saltpeter, and salt) and claimed ownership of all metals and ores. Concessions were granted for mining and milling in return for revenue. The regulation of industry was conducted by salaried administrators who fixed the prices of products and prescribed manufacturing methods. Royal authority thus tended to discourage private industrial enterprises while strengthening state control. Under the rationalizing tendencies emerging in the governments of strong nation-states such as France and England, nature came to be viewed as a resource to be subjected to control with human beings as her earthly managers.[5] . . .

Already in his "Little Treatise" of 1630, Hobbes had developed a mechanical explanation of sensation based on the motion of contiguous particles of matter. Sensations, he held, were not in the objects but purely subjective. Thus the sound was not in the bell, for only its parts were in motion; or in the air, for only its parts were in motion. Nor was it in the ear, for the parts of the ear only moved the animal spirits in the nerves and brain. Sensation was therefore only the subjective experience of local motion in the brain. No initiating principle of motion was contained in the soul, the brain, the will, the appetite, or the animal spirits. But in the "Little Treatise," Hobbes had not yet resolved the important question of whether matter had some inherent form of motion (or species) that produces the motion of the medium on which sensation is based. The issue was whether matter itself was active and therefore sent out the "species" whose motion produced sensation. "Whatsoever moveth another moveth it either by active power inherent in itself, or by motion received from another. . . . Agents send out their species continually. For seeing the agent hath power in itself to produce such species, and is always applied to the patient, . . . it shall produce and send out species continually."[6]

During the early 1640s, Hobbes—probably influenced by Gassendi, with whose work on Epicurus he was acquainted—assumed that matter was composed of small, invisible parts or atoms in a vacuum. In a 1645 letter, Charles Cavendish reported that Hobbes believed that all change occurred as the result of the motions of invisible parts of bodies. The following year, Hobbes admitted the existence of vacuity, in a draft of his "optical treatise." A 1648 letter from Hobbes to Mersenne stated, "There exist very small spaces now here, now there, in which there is no body." Bodies are set in motion by collision with neighboring bodies, "an action which necessarily results in certain void spaces."[7] It is not clear, however, whether Hobbes, like Gassendi, assumed the atoms to be self-active through a material cause. . . .

In *De Corpore,* Hobbes introduced the concept of endeavor or *conatus,* which in the hands of philosopher Gottfried Wilhelm von Leibniz (1646–1716) would become the basis for dynamics. Endeavor, however, was not an inherent, vital, spontaneous function of matter, but an impulse toward motion, a *conatus,* "made in less space and time than can be given," propagated through the surrounding medium by contact with continuous bodies, *ad infinitum.* Impetus was a measure of the velocity of its propagation.

In animals, endeavor was the beginning of animal motion but was nevertheless mechanical motion, an appetite. Sensation or the transmission of mechanical motion by the animal spirits either excited or slowed the action of the heart's motion, resulting in pleasure or pain. Found even in the embryo, endeavor was the first response of the animal to pleasure or pain, the first impulse toward motion "for the avoiding of what troubleth it, or the pursuing of what pleaseth it," the two being called *aversion* and *appetite.* In both man and beast, appetite was the result of a prior necessary cause— that is, motion—and was not free. Similarly, liberty was not freedom and spontaneity, but simply the power to carry out what previously had been willed.[8]

Mechanism thus reordered the world in terms of a new metaphor, the machine. The cosmos was operated from the outside by God, the bodily machine by the human soul, or, as for Hobbes, by the mechanical transfer of motion among material particles. To this restructuring of reality, Hobbes added, as a third essential ingredient, a mechanistic analysis of society. The body politic was composed of equal atomistic beings united by contract out of fear and governed from above by a powerful sovereign. . . .

————

The world in which we live today was bequeathed to us by Isaac Newton and Gottfried Wilhelm von Leibniz. Twentieth-century advances in relativity and quantum theory notwithstanding, our Western commonsense reality is the world of classical physics. The legacy left by Newton was the brilliant synthesis of Galilean terrestrial mechanics and Copernican-Keplerian astronomy; that of Leibniz was dynamics— the foundation for the general law of conservation of energy. Both contributions are fundamental in generality; they describe and extend over the entire universe. Classical physics and its philosophy structure our consciousness to believe in a world composed of atomic parts, of inert bodies moving with uniform velocity unless forced by another body to deviate from their straight line paths, of objects seen by reflected light of varying frequencies, and of matter in motion responsible for all the rich variations in colors, sounds, smells, tastes, and touches we cherish as human beings. In our daily lives, most of us accept these teachings as givens, without much critical reflection on their origins or associated values. To Newton, Leibniz, and their followers, however, the situation was not so straightforward. They saw their mechanics, their philosophies, and their own beliefs about God and nature as deeply divergent from each other.

The problem that the mechanization of the world raised for the generation after . . . Hobbes was the very issue of the "death of nature." If the ultimate principles were matter and motion, as they were for the first generation of mechanists, or even matter, motion, void space, and force as they became for Newton, this left unresolved the central issue of explaining the motion of life forms in a dead cosmos. . . .

Hobbes' monistic materialism, which further reduced the will and mind to material motion, raised the specter of atheism. Nor . . . could Newton entertain the pantheistic assumption that God was immanent in matter, together with its associated radical intellectual and social implications. He specifically argued against this position in his queries to the Latin edition of his *Opticks* in 1706: "And yet we are not to consider the world as the body of God, or the several parts thereof, as the parts of God."[9] God was neither a living animal-writ-large nor the soul of the world.

Yet as the most powerful synthesis of the new mechanical philosophy, Newton's *Philosophiae Naturalis Principia Mathematica* (*The Mathematical Principles of Natural Philosophy*, 1687) epitomized the dead world resulting from mechanism. Throughout the complex evolution of his thought, Newton clung tenaciously to the distinguishing feature of mechanism—the dualism between the passivity of matter and the externality of force and activity. But he refined this ontology in significant ways. The *Principia* and *Opticks* transformed the mechanical philosophy into a mechanical science, counterposing a fourfold ontology of matter, motion, force, and void space to the simpler plenum of matter in motion postulated by . . . Hobbes.

. . . Newton departed from the strict passivity this earlier mechanical philosophy had assigned to matter by associating with it a complex, overlapping set of passive forces, while nevertheless maintaining the basic assumption that "matter is a passive principle and cannot move itself."[10] By its *vis insita* (innate force) a body continued in its state of rest or uniform motion, a state that could be altered only with difficulty. The *vis inertiae* (force of inertia) was the force of corporeal matter by which a body resisted an externally impressed force. The innate *vis conservans* (conserving force) maintained a body's forward direction by a succession of impulses.[11]

. . . Newton viewed changes in motion as external in origin, rather than as the internal activity central to organicism. His *vis impressa* (impressed force) was an external impressed force acting on the body so as to change its state of motion or rest. Likewise external to matter were various active principles such as gravity, fermentation, and cohesion necessary for explaining changes and activity not produced by impact. Gravitational force, unlike the impressed contact forces, acted at a distance, attracting all particles of matter toward each other according to the inverse square of the distance between them ($1/r^2$).

The mathematization of the world picture presented in the *Principia*, based on the dualism between the passivity of matter and the externality of force, epitomized the success of the mechanical analysis of nature. Mechanism eliminated from the description of nature concepts of spatial hierarchy, value, purpose, harmony, quality, and form central to the older organic description of nature, leaving material and efficient causes—matter and force. Motion was not an organic process but a temporary state of a body's existence relative to the motion or rest of other bodies. The mathematizing tendencies in Newtonian thought which emphasized not the process of change, but resistance to change, the conservation of a body's motion, and the planets and satellites as ideal spheres and point sources of gravitational force were manifestations of the mechanical philosophers' concern with geometrical idealization, stability, structure, being, and identity, rather than organic flux, change, becoming, and process. In mechanism the primacy of process was thus superseded by the stability of structure.

Completely consistent with this restructuring of the cosmos as passive matter and external force was the division of matter into atomic parts separated by void space. The book of nature was no longer written in symbols, signs, and signatures, but in corpuscular characters. The atomic analysis of matter ultimately became an exemplar for the atomic division of data, problems, and events on a global scale. . . .

Leibniz likewise developed a mechanical philosophy of nature as one component of his thought. His world of corporeal phenomena, governed by efficient causes and mechanical laws imposed initially by a rational creator, like Newtonian mechanics, held implications for the rational management of nature from which human progress would result.

Leibniz's dynamics, developed during the years 1686–1695, defined the "force" of a body in motion to be the product of its quantity of matter and the distance through which it fell under acceleration. This living force, or *vis viva* (mv^2 or mass times velocity squared; now, as $1/2\ mv^2$, called kinetic energy), was conserved in all elastic impacts. In semielastic and inelastic collisions it was temporarily stored in the small parts of the body's matter and therefore not lost to the universe.[12]

For Leibniz, "force" was the foundation for an understanding of both the phenomenal and spiritual universes. Primitive active force, an activity or striving toward a future state, (later defined as the essence of his monad) was a true substance, while derivative force (mv^2) observed in impacts between corporeal bodies, was not fully real, but was grounded in primitive force and subject to the laws of nature. Corporeal objects were not substances, but collections of confused minds (monads), perceived to be extended bodies. The properties of these ostensibly extended bodies—size, shape, inertia, impenetrability, and motion—were "well-founded" in the states of existence of the monads which constituted them. Leibniz thus assigned extension, which for Descartes was a substance, to the world of well-founded phenomena *(phenomena bene fundata)*, arguing that extension and motion were merely attributes of phenomenal bodies, while force, on the other hand, was real. Inertness or passivity, an essential property of matter for Descartes and Newton, was for Leibniz simply an expression of the limitation placed on the monad because of the accommodation of its life to the unfolding lives and activities of all the other monads. Mechanical phenomena obeyed the laws of efficient causation, whereas monads or true substances were governed by final causes.[13] . . .

Newton's answer to the problem of the revitalization of the cosmos was to replenish its motion through "active principles" such as gravity and fermentation:

Seeing . . . the variety of motion which we find in the world is always decreasing, there is a necessity of conserving and recruiting it by active principles, such as are *the cause of gravity*, by which planets and comets keep their motions in their orbs, and bodies acquire great motion in falling; and *the cause of fermentation*, by which the heart and blood of animals are kept in perpetual motion and heat . . . for we meet with very little motion in the world, besides what is owing to these active principles.[14]

Without these active principles, Newton warned, "the bodies of the earth, planets, comets, sun, and all things in them would grow cold and freeze, and become inactive masses . . . and the planets and comets would not remain in their orbs."[15] For Newton, fermentation thus furnished an antidote to the "death of nature" implicit in a mechanical universe, a universe founded on passivity and having an inherent tendency towards decay, decline, and eventual death. Unsatisfied with the mechanistic analysis of phenomena, he, like Leibniz, was searching for the causes and laws that would unify biological processes, just as his gravitational theory had synthesized physical interactions. . . .

Between 1500 and 1700 an incredible transformation took place. A "natural" point of view about the world in which bodies did not move unless activated, either by an inherent organic mover or a "contrary to nature" superimposed "force," was replaced by a non-natural non-experiential "law" that bodies move uniformly unless hindered. The "natural" perception of a geocentric earth in a finite cosmos was superseded by the "non-natural" common-sense "fact" of a heliocentric infinite universe. A subsistence economy in which resources, goods, money, or labor were exchanged for commodities was replaced in many areas by the open-ended accumulation of profits in an international market. Living animate nature died, while dead inanimate money was endowed with life. Increasingly capital and the market would assume the organic attributes of growth, strength, activity, pregnancy, weakness, decay, and collapse obscuring and mystifying the new underlying social relations of production and reproduction that make economic growth and progress possible. Nature, women, blacks, and wage laborers were set on a path toward a new status as "natural" and human resources for the modern world system. Perhaps the ultimate irony in these transformations was the new name given them: rationality.[16]

In 1500 the parts of the cosmos were bound together as a living organism; by 1700 the dominant metaphor had become the machine. Although machines and the cosmic *machina mundi* had been parts of the ancient and medieval worlds, the organic conception of nature had been sufficiently integrative as a framework to override changes and discrepancies within it. Similarly, although the mechanistic analysis of reality has dominated the Western world

since the seventeenth century, the organismic perspective has by no means disappeared. It has remained as an important underlying tension, surfacing in such variations as the Romantic reaction to the Enlightenment, American transcendentalism, the ideas of the German *Naturphilosophen*, the early philosophy of Karl Marx, the nineteenth-century vitalists, and the work of Wilhelm Reich. The basic tenets of the organic view of nature have reappeared in the twentieth century in the theory of holism of Jan Christiaan Smuts, the process philosophy of Alfred North Whitehead, the ecology movements of the 1930s and 1970s, alternative analyses in nuclear physics (the "bootstrap" model), and developmental theories in psychology. Some philosophers have argued that the two frameworks are fundamentally incommensurable. Although such a perception of the dichotomy is too extreme, as the fusions between the two perspectives discussed in previous chapters have shown, a reassessment of the values and constraints historically associated with the organic world view may be essential for a viable future.[17]

The mechanistic view of nature, developed by the seventeenth-century natural philosophers and based on a Western mathematical tradition going back to Plato, is still dominant in science today. This view assumes that nature can be divided into parts and that the parts can be rearranged to create other species of being. "Facts" or information bits can be extracted from the environmental context and rearranged according to a set of rules based on logical and mathematical operations. The results can then be tested and verified by resubmitting them to nature, the ultimate judge of their validity. Mathematical formalism provides the criterion for rationality and certainty, nature the criterion for empirical validity and acceptance or rejection of the theory.

The work of historians and philosophers of science notwithstanding, it is widely assumed by the scientific community that modern science is objective, value-free, and context-free knowledge of the external world. To the extent to which the sciences can be reduced to this mechanistic mathematical model, the more legitimate they become as sciences. Thus the reductionist hierarchy of the validity of the sciences first proposed in the nineteenth century by French positivist philosopher August Comte is still widely assumed by intellectuals, the most mathematical and highly theoretical sciences occupying the most revered position.

The mechanistic approach to nature is as fundamental to the twentieth-century revolution in physics as it was to classical Newtonian science, culminating in the nineteenth-century unification of mechanics, thermodynamics, and electromagnetic theory. Twentieth-century physics still views the world in terms of fundamental particles—electrons, protons, neutrons, mesons, muons, pions, taus, thetas, sigmas, pis, and so on. The search for the ultimate unifying particle, the quark, continues to engage the efforts of the best theoretical physicists.

NOTES

1. For a recent critique of the mechanical, reductionist, scientific methodology as applied to the environmental deterioration of the four ancient elements, see Barry Commoner, *The Closing Circle* (New York: Knopf, 1972), esp. Chaps. 1–6, 10. For a critique of holism, see D. C. Phillips, *Holistic Thought in Social Science* (Stanford, Cal.: Stanford University Press, 1976). On the historical roots of ecology, their origins in organismic philosophies, and the systems approach of the new ecology, see Donald Worster, *Nature's Economy* (San Francisco: Sierra Club Books, 1977), esp. Chaps. 3, 4, 14. On romanticism and American preservationism, see Roderick Nash, *Wilderness and the American Mind*

(New Haven, Conn.: Yale University Press, 1967), Chaps. 3–8. For an analysis of the philosophical differences and points of overlap between the organic and mechanical philosophies of nature, see Steven Pepper, *World Hypotheses* (Berkeley: University of California Press, 1970), esp. Chaps. 9, 11. A more recent discussion arguing for the incommensurability of these world systems is William Overton and Hayne Reese, "Models of Development: Methodological Implications," in John R. Nesselroade and Hayne Reese, eds., *Life Span Developmental Psychology* (New York: Academic Press, 1973), pp. 65–86.

2. Pierre Gassendi, "Syntagma Philosophicum" (first published 1658), *Opera*, vol. 1. Quotations from P. Gassendi, *The Selected Works of Pierre Gassendi*, trans. Craig B. Bush (London: Johnson Reprint, 1972), pp. 380–434, quotations on pp. 411–22, 417.

3. Gassendi, "Syntagma Philosophicum" in *Opera*, vol. 1, pp. 158, 450; vol. 2, pp. 3, 822–23; Sortais, pp. 121–22, 154.

4. Descartes, "Lettre à Mersenne," April 15, 1630, *Oeuvres*, vol. 1, p. 145.

5. John U. Nef, *Industry and Government in France and England, 1540–1640* (Philadelphia: American Philosophical Society, 1940), pp. 10, 24, 72.

6. Thomas Hobbes, "A Short Tract on First Principles" (known as the "Little Treatise"), in Ferdinand Tönnies, ed., *The Elements of Law* (New York: Barnes & Noble, 1969), appendix 1, pp. 193–201.

7. "Hobbes to R. Mersenne," 17 February 1648, quoted in R. Kargon, *Atomism in England* (Oxford: Clarendon Press, 1966), p. 58. Hobbes was widely viewed in England as holding Epicurean ideas concerning a materialist formation of the world from a chaos of atoms. See Thomas Franklin Mayo, *Epicurus in England, 1650–1725* (Dallas, Tex.: Southwest Press, 1934), Chap. 8. On the differences between Hobbes and Epicurus, see Charles T. Harrison, "Bacon, Hobbes, Boyle and the Ancient Atomists," *Harvard Studies and Notes in Philology and Literature* 15 (1933): 191–218, and "The Ancient Atomists and English Literature of the Seventeenth Century," *Harvard Studies in Classical Philology* 45 (1934): 1–79.

8. Hobbes, *English Works*, vol. 1 (London: John Bohn, 1839), pp. 206–7, 216, 389–90, 477, 407, 409; Brandt, pp. 300–301, Howard Bernstein, "Conatus, Hobbes, and the Young Leibniz," *Studies in History and Philosophy of Science* 9 (1979); J. N. Watkins, *Hobbes' System of Ideas* (London: Hutchinson University Library, 1965), pp. 120–37.

9. Isaac Newton, *Optice sive de Reflexionibus, Refractionibus, Inflexionibus Lucis* (London, 1706). Citations refer to I. Newton, *Opticks*, 4th ed., 1730

CAROLYN MERCHANT

(reprinted New York: Dover, 1952; first published 1704), see p. 403.

10. Newton, University Library, Cambridge, England, Additional Manuscripts 3970, folio 619^r.

11. Isaac Newton, *Philosophiae Naturalis Principia Mathematica* (London, 1687). Citations refer to I. Newton, *Mathematical Principles of Natural Philosophy*, trans. A. Motte, 1729, rev. Florian Cajori (Berkeley: University of California Press, 1934), Definition III, p. 2. For a discussion of Newton's modification of the Cartesian ontology, see Ernan McMullin, *Newton on Matter and Activity* (South Bend, Ind.: University of Notre Dame Press, 1978), pp. 33–43. On Newton's transformation of Cartesianism, see Richard Westfall, *Force in Newton's Physics* (London: Macdonald, 1971); Alexandre Koyré, "The Significance of the Newtonian Synthesis," in *Newtonian Studies* (Chicago: University of Chicago Press, 1965), pp. 3–24. Alan Gabbey, "Force and Inertia in Seventeenth Century Dynamics," *Studies in History and Philosophy of Science* 2 (May 1971): 1–67.

12. Gottfried Wilhelm von Leibniz, "Brevis demonstratio erroris memorabilis Cartesii et aliorum circa legem naturalem, secundum quam volunt a Deo eandem semper quantitatem motus conservari; quo et in re mechanica abutuntur," *Acta Eruditorum* (1686): 161–63. English translation: Gottfried Wilhelm Leibniz, *Philosophical Papers and Letters*, trans. Leroy E. Loemker, 2 vols. (Chicago: Univ. of Chicago Press, 1956), vol. 1, pp. 455–63. G. W. Leibniz, *Discours de métaphysique* (written 1686), in *Die Philosophischen Schriften von Gottfried Wilhelm Leibnitz*, ed. C. I. Gerhardt, 7 vols. (Berlin, 1875–1890), vol. 4, pp. 442, 443. English translation in Loemker, vol. 1, pp. 464–506. G. W. Leibniz, "Essay de dynamique sur les loix du mouvement, ou il est monstre, qu'il ne se conserve pas la même quantite de mouvement, mais la même force absolue, ou bien la même quantité de l'action motrice," *Mathematische Schriften*, pp. 215–31. English translation: G. W. Leibniz, *New Essays Concerning Human Understanding*, ed. and trans. A. G. Langley (La Salle: Open Court, 1949), appendix pp. 657–70. On the development of Leibniz's dynamics, see Carolyn [Merchant] Iltis, "Leibniz and the *Vis Viva* Controversy," *Isis* 62 (1970): 21–35, and Pierre Costabel, *Leibniz et la Dynamique: Les Textes de 1692* (Paris: Hermann, 1960).

13. G. W. Leibniz, "Specimen Dynamicum," *Mathematische Schriften*, vol. 4, pp. 234–54; *Philosophical Papers 2nd Letters*, vol. 2, pp. 714–18. See also Gerd Buchdahl, *Metaphysics and the Philosophy of Science* (Oxford, England: Blackwell, 1969), pp. 393, 410, 414, 417, 420, 422–23; C. D.

Broad, *Leibniz: An Introduction* (Cambridge, England: Cambridge University Press, 1975), Chap. 4, pp. 87–129; George Gale, "The Physical Theory of Leibniz," *Studia Leibnitiana*, vol. 2, no. 2 (1970): 114–27.

14. Newton, *Opticks,* p. 399; italics added. On gravitation see J. E. McGuire, "Force, Active Principles and Newton's Invisible Realm," *Ambix* 15 (1968): 154–208; and P. M. Heimann, "'Nature is a Perpetual Worker': Newton's Aether and Eighteenth-Century Natural Philosophy," *Ambix* 20 (March 1973): 1–25; P. M. Heimann and J. E. McGuire, "Newtonian Forces and Lockean Powers: Concepts of Matter in Eighteenth-Century Thought," *Historical Studies in the Physical Sciences* 3 (1971): 233–306; David Kubrin, "Newton and the Cyclical Cosmos: Providence and the Mechanical Philosophy, *Journal of the History of Ideas* 28 (July–September 1967): 325–46.

15. Newton, *Opticks*, pp. 399–400, subsequent quotations in order on pp. 380, 401, 403. For more on the vegetative spirit and fermentation see I. Newton, University Library, Cambridge, England, Add. 3970 fol. 237^r "De Vita et Morte Vegetabili."

16. On the transformation in cosmology see Koyré, "The Significance of the Newtonian Synthesis," in *Newtonian Studies*; and Koyré, *From the Closed World to the Infinite Universe* (New York: Harper & Row, 1958). On the transformation in economic values from those of Aristotle to those of Adam Smith and the endowment of money with organic properties see Michael Taussig, "The Genesis of Capitalism Amongst a South American Peasantry: Devil's Labor and the Baptism of Money," *Comparative Studies in Society and History* 19 (April 1977): 130–53.

17. The impact of Newton and Leibniz on subsequent history is complex. On Newtonianism in the eighteenth century, see A. Thackray, *Atoms and Powers* (Cambridge: Harvard University Press, 1970); Heimann and McGuire, "Newtonian Forces and Lockean Powers"; Robert Schofield, *Mechanism and Materialism: British Natural Philosophy in an Age of Reason* (Princeton, N.J.: Princeton University Press, 1970); Guerlac, *Essays and Papers*. On Leibniz, see W. H. Barber, *Leibniz in France from Arnauld to Voltaire: A Study in French Reactions to Leibnizianism, 1670–1760* (Oxford, 1955); Carolyn [Merchant] Iltis, "The Decline of Cartesianism in Mechanics: The Leibnizian-Cartesian Debates," *Isis* 64 (1973): 356–73; C. [M.] Iltis, "The Leibnizian-Newtonian Debates," *British Journal of the History of Science* 6 (1973): 343–377; C. [M.] Iltis, "Madame du Châtelet's Metaphysics and Mechanics," *Studies in History and Philosophy of Science* 8 (1977): 29–40; C.

[M.] Iltis "D'Alembert and the *Vis Viva* Controversy," *Studies in History and Philosophy of Science* 1 (1970): 134–35; Joseph Needham, *Science and Civilization in China* (Cambridge, Mass.: Harvard University Press, 1959), vol. 2, pp. 291–343, 496–505. On the "bootstrap model" in particle physics see Fritjof Capra, *The Tao of Physics* (Berkeley, Cal.: Shambala, 1975). On the incommensurability of the mechanical and organic world views and its implication for developmental psychology, see Willis F. Overton and Hayne W. Reese, "Models of Development: Methodological Implications" in John R. Nesselroade and Hayne W. Reese, eds., *Life Span Developmental Psychology*

(New York: Academic Press, 1973). On organismic perspectives on nature see L. R. Wheeler, *Vitalism: Its History and Validity* (London: Witherby, 1939); Alfred North Whitehead, *Process and Reality* (Cambridge, England: Cambridge University Press, 1929); Dorothy Emmet, *Whitehead's Philosophy of Organism*, 2nd ed. (London: Macmillan, 1966); Howard L. Parsons, ed., *Marx and Engels on Ecology* (Westport, Conn.: Greenwood Press, 1977); Wilhelm Reich, *The Discovery of the Orgone* (New York: Orgone Institute Press, 1942); for a critique, see D. C. Phillips, *Holistic Thought in Social Science* (Stanford, Cal.: Stanford University Press, 1976).

ROBERT HOOKE, "PRESERVING ANIMALS ALIVE BY BLOWING THROUGH THEIR LUNGS WITH BELLOWS"

Hooke (1635–1703) performed this experiment in 1667. It is considered a classic of scientific experimentation. He asks a question whose answer will be the result of manipulating some variables while holding others constant. He understands exactly what equipment is needed to perform the experiment. And to ensure objectivity, he performs the experiment in front of others.

Hooke says that he has done the first part of this experiment before. However, since others had not been able to duplicate it, he is redoing it. This shows that Hooke believes that no scientific experiment is worth accepting unless others are able to repeat it. Making sure that the method of gaining information is open to all is one way of guaranteeing objectivity in science. Put another way, we might say that one meaning of the statement "science is objective" is that its experiments and results must be replicable. This implies that scientific information be freely available or, at the very least, that if someone wanted to repeat the experiment and had full details, it could be replicated.

Hooke had shown that bellows, properly attached to a dog's lungs, could keep it alive, as long as the bellows was pumping air. This led to the hypothesis that the motion of the lungs is necessary for life. This is the hypothesis that Hooke set out to test. Hooke showed that when the lungs do not move but the bellows blows air, the dog remains alive. Thus he demonstrated that it is not motion of the lungs that is necessary for life but rather air. He also showed that as long as air was forced through the lungs, blood circulates through the lungs' cells, whether the lungs move or not.

In contemporary language, we would say that Hooke falsified one hypothesis and confirmed another. This will be discussed in Chapter 3.

Hooke controlled for the air flow to the dog, varying the motion of the lungs. When the lungs were moving and air was flowing, the dog lived. When the lungs were not moving and air was flowing, the dog also lived. When the air stopped flowing, the dog clearly was about to die. This indicated that motion of the lungs is not necessary for the dog to be living.

Hooke says that the immediate cause of death of the dog when the experiment was stopped was lack of fresh air. Obviously, Hooke is making a distinction between immediate cause and less immediate cause. What would be a less than immediate cause? Suppose a pedestrian crosses a busy street against the light and is killed by an automobile. What is the cause of death, the crash or some biological function that the crash caused to be disrupted? The death certificate of such a person would state that death was due to, say, internal bleeding secondary to trauma. This means that the accident is considered the primary cause, the primary contributor to the death. It is not just that the accident came before the internal bleeding because the decision to cross the street against the light also came before both the accident and the internal bleeding.

This sense of immediate cause is not what Hooke means by "immediate cause." For Hooke, the immediate cause in the pedestrian case would be the internal bleeding. Notice that the more we know, the more "immediate causes" we can list. In the pedestrian case, we might say that internal bleeding caused a loss in blood pressure that led to heart failure and that heart failure led to lack of oxygen in the brain, which led to depressed respiration, and so on.

The fact that we can give such a list of causes may mean that finding a cause is not like finding some particular entity. Rather, finding a cause means deciding on a cause, and deciding on a cause depends on what we know. Put another way, deciding what to call a cause is a function of our theoretical knowledge about the subject matter under investigation. As we will see in Chapter 2, trying to be clear on how to interpret causality is a bone of contention between Michael Scriven and May Brodbeck. Thomas Kuhn, in Chapter 3, will suggest that when the concept of cause changes, so does our way of seeing the world.

Hooke has made an important assumption in his experiment. He claims to have shown that motion of the lungs is not necessary for life. Strictly speaking, however, what he should have said is, "For this dog, in my laboratory, today, motion of the lungs is not necessary for life." The assumptions made are, first, that this dog not only represents any dog but that any dog represents any animal (any mammal) and, second, that when the experiment is done, where it is done, and by whom it is done, has no relevance to the outcome. The second set of assumptions is built in to the nature of a properly performed scientific experiment. The first set of assumptions needs some support. It might turn out that beagle lungs are different from Doberman lungs. It might be that this dog is different from all other dogs, having been born with strange lungs. It is also possible that in some mammals, respiration can be accomplished by other means when the lungs are not working properly.

That assumptions are made is not necessarily a weakness of science. It just shows that gaining knowledge requires that some assumptions be made. It also indicates that in an experimental situation, not every factor can be varied at the same time. It may be that a factor we do not vary actually would make a difference. The usual claim made by defenders of the traditional scientific method is that if the scientific method is used properly, it will reveal any incorrect assumptions.

But why trust the scientific method? That it has worked in the past is not evidence that it will work in the future without the assumption that the future will be like the past. But what evidence do we have that the future will be like the past, except that it always has been? In the eighteenth century, the philosopher David Hume (1711–1776) pointed out that very circularity in defense of induction as a method. He felt that he had shown that the use of induction was not defensible by reason, even though it is readily explainable by appeal to what he termed habit and custom. The problem raised by Hume is called the problem of induction. "Induction" here refers to any method that uses facts as evidence (as Hooke did) to support further factual claims. Consider a worst-case Humean scenario: motion of the lungs may not be necessary for life today, but perhaps tomorrow it will. Even worse, perhaps tomorrow, the color of the experimenter's smock will change the results of the experiment.

Preserving Animals Alive by Blowing through Their Lungs with Bellows

ROBERT HOOKE

This Noble Experiment came not to the Publisher's *hands, till all the preceding Particulars were already sent to the Press, and almost all Printed off, (for which cause also it could not be mentioned among the* Contents: *(And it might have been reserved for the next opportunity, had not the considerableness thereof been a motive to hasten its Publication. It shall be here annexed in the Ingenious* Author *his own words, as he presented it to the* Royal Society, October. 24. 1667. *the Experiment it self having been both repeated (after a former successful trial of it, made by the same hand a good while agoe) and improved the week before, at their* publick Assembly. *The Relation it self follows;*

I did heretofore give this *Illustrious Society* an account of an Experiment I formerly tryed of keeping a Dog alive after his *Thorax* was all display'd by the cutting away of the *Ribs* and *Diaphragme;* and after the *Pericardium* of the Heart also was taken off. But divers persons seeming to doubt of the certainty of the Experiment (by reason that some Tryals of this matter, made by other hands, failed of success) I caus'd at the last Meeting the same Experiment to be shewn in the presence of this *Noble Company,* and that with the same success, as it had been made by me at first;

the Dog being kept alive by the Reciprocal blowing up of his Lungs with *Bellowes*, and they suffered to subside, for the space of an hour or more, after his *Thorax* had been so display'd, and his *Aspera arteria* cut off just below the *Epigolotis* and bound on upon the nose of the Bellows.

And because some Eminent Physicians had affirm'd, that the *Motion of the Lungs* was necessary to Life upon the account of promoting the Circulation of the Blood, and that it was conceiv'd, the Animal would immediately be suffocated as soon as the Lungs should cease to be moved, I did (the better to fortifie my own *Hypothesis* of this matter, and to be the better able to Judge of several others) make the following additional Experiment; *viz.*

The Dog having been kept alive, (as I have now mentioned) for above an hour, in which time the Tryal hath often been repeated, in suffering the dog to fall into *Convulsive* motions by ceasing to blow the Bellows, and permitting the Lungs to subside and lye still, and of suddenly reviving him again by renewing the blast, and consequently the motion of the Lungs: This I say, having been done, and the Judicious Spectators fully satisfied of the reality of the former Experiment; I caused another pair of Bellows to be immediately joyn'd to the first, by a contrivance, I had prepar'd, and pricking all the outercoat of the Lungs with the slender point of a very sharp pen-knive, this second pair of Bellows was mov'd very quick, whereby the first pair was always kept full and always blowing into the Lungs; by which means the Lungs also were always kept very full, and without any motion, there being a continual blast of Air forc'd into the Lungs by the first pair of Bellows, supplying it as fast, as it could find its way quite through the Coat of the Lungs by the small holes pricked in it, as was said before. This being continued for a pretty while, the dog, as I expected, lay still, as before, his eyes being all the time very quick, and his Heart beating very regularly: But, upon ceasing this blast, and suffering the Lungs to fall and lye still, the Dog would immediately fall into Dying convulsive fits; but be as soon reviv'd again by the renewing the fulness of his Lungs with the constant blast of fresh Air.

Towards the latter end of this Experiment a piece of the Lungs was cut quite off; where 'twas observable, that the Blood did freely circulate, and pass thorow the Lungs, not only when the Lungs were kept thus constantly extended, but also when they were suffered to subside and ly still. Which seem to be Arguments, that as the *bare* Motion of the Lungs *without fresh* Air contributes nothing to the life of the Animal, he being found to survive as well when they were not mov'd, as when they were; so it was not the subsiding or movelessness of the Lungs that was the immediate cause of Death, or the stopping the Circulation of the Blood through the Lungs, but the *want* of a sufficient *supply of fresh Air*.

I shall shortly further try, whether the suffering the Blood to circulate through a vessel, so as it may be openly exposed to the fresh Air, will not suffice for the life of an Animal; and make some other Experiments, which, I hope, will throughly discover the *Genuine use of Respiration;* and afterwards consider of what benefit this may be to Mandkind.

FREDERICK HOLMES, "THE INVESTIGATION OF DIGESTION, 1750–1830"

FREDERICK HOLMES, "THE INVESTIGATION OF DIGESTION, 1750–1830"

Holmes details work of the early eighteenth century on digestion. Initially, the question to be answered was "Is digestion mechanical grinding, or is it some sort of chemical solvent action?" The answer, shown by an unambiguous experiment, was that it had to be both. The question then became, "What is the nature of the chemical action? Is it simple dissolving, or is it something more complex? And what is the solvent?" If the solvent were nothing more than a simple acid, the whole view of vitalism would be challenged.

Vitalists held that living things differ in kind from nonliving things, that living, organic entities are made of different sorts of things and work on principles different from those that govern nonliving things. In other words, to understand how a human arm works, one would need more than just a knowledge of chemistry, levers, and pulleys. Exactly what this more would be was never entirely clear.

Sometimes it was held that even if the components of the living and the nonliving were the same, something had to account for the difference between them. There had to be a special life-giving and life-organizing principle—a vital principle, which was dubbed *élan vital* or entelechy. The view that the living and the nonliving run according to the same principles and are made of the same basic components is called materialistic mechanism or physicalistic mechanism. The view that the principles of the living can be fully explained by the principles that govern inanimate chemicals is one sense of what is called reductionism. Thus we can interpret Holmes's point that chemical development had reached the stage where chemical investigation of biological phenomena was possible as a claim that a reduction (of biology to chemistry) was taking place.

What is reduction in science? There are at least eight senses of reductionism.

1. *Ontological reductionism.* This is based on the claim that big things are made of smaller things and that the properties of those smaller things account for the properties of the bigger things.

2. *Mathematical reductionism.* In genetics and evolution, mathematical models are central to contemporary research. The Punnett square used to illustrate simple genetic crosses is an example of a mathematical model. The introduction to the article by Portugal and Cohen later in this chapter discusses such a use of the Punnett square.

3. *Shift in the objects of study.* The shift from relatively large organisms like corn and fruit flies to microorganisms such as bacteria is a trend that began in the early 1930s. Another example would be the interest in a biophysical model for the gene, which also began in the 1930s.

4. *Mechanical reductionism.* This hinges on that all explanations should be put in mechanical terms.

5. *Monistic reductionism.* This holds that there is only one basic explanatory principle. Note that vitalism is reductionistic in this sense.

6. *Translatability.* If one theory is reducible to another, then the laws of the reduced science must be translatable without remainder into laws of the reducing science. Hence if Holmes is claiming the reduction of biology to chemistry, he would be committed to the view that the laws of biology are translatable with no remainder into the laws of chemistry.

7. *Deducibility.* If one theory is reducible into another, then the reduced theory must be derivable from the reducing theory or from a close version of it. The importance of logical derivation to science will be explored in greater detail in Chapter 2.

8. *Methodological reductionism.* An object of study, such as a human being, almost always has levels of organization. A person has organs, tissues, cells, genes, and other components and exhibits gross behavior. The levels of these are ranked in terms of size and composition. Often, each level has a distinctive method of study. When a method of study used for a lower level replaces one used on a higher level, a methodological reduction has taken place. Such a replacement usually occurs when the lower-level method is easier than the higher-level one or gives better results. For example, studying some diseases genetically can give a better picture of who has the disease than the traditional upper-level diagnosis based on a history and a physical in a doctor's office.

Each of these forms of reductionism is logically distinct; no one form entails any other. If these distinctions are not kept firmly in mind, it is easy to slide from one sense of reduction to another, thereby making unwarranted claims. Notwithstanding this logical independence, however, historically, as ontological reduction takes place, methodological reductionism tags along with it.

Chemical research offered a methodological reduction of some biological processes. Consequently, more insight into the nature of chemistry as a tool was needed. Prior to the late eighteenth century, the main tool of chemists was distillation. Chemists of the late eighteenth century felt that there was a problem with distillation. It required heat, and heat, it was feared, might actually change the properties of the chemicals. This meant that the main experimental technique might be changing what was experimented on. Hooke, in his experiment, had assumed that what he learned about a dog whose thorax was cut open also held for dogs and other animals whose thoraxes were intact. Chemists felt much safer using methods that did not require the addition of great heat. This shows that theories interact. Chemists feared possible chemical contamination by heat because of what they held heat to be. Another theory of heat might not have led them to believe in possible contamination.

Defining substances or kinds of substances in terms of an experimental operation is called an operational definition. Holmes gives us an example of such a definition. Rouelle (1703–1770), Holmes tells us, "defined categories of plant constituents on the basis of their solubility properties." A simpler example would be defining an acid by whether it turns blue litmus paper red. An operational definition of acid tells us that this is all that we mean by acid and all that we have to mean. That is, for the purposes of our understanding, given everything else we know, this definition of acid is enough. In the experiments related to us by Holmes, Tiedemann and Gmelin used operational definitions for starch and for sugar.

The concept of the scientific paradigm will be introduced in Chapter 3 in the article by Thomas Kuhn. Part of its definition is an accepted set of methods (and instruments) used for solving the problems of interest. According to Holmes, what we see in the early study of physiology is a paradigm made of a group of chemical procedures. No one procedure was *the* procedure. This had been the case when distillation was just about the only method used.

Another point that will be made in the Kuhn article is that in the study of science, science itself cannot be separated from the study of the social setting of science. We see an example of this interplay with digestion: The French Academy's offer of a prize for the best work on digestion spurred a great deal of research in that area.

The work of Friedrich Tiedemann (1781–1861) and Leopold Gmelin (1788–1853) was reductionistic. One way to see this is that they duplicated outside the stomach the mechanism of digestion by gastric acid as it occurs inside the living stomach. A vitalist would have been sure that this could not be done. To a vitalist, it would be certain that true digestion can take place only in a living stomach. Whatever takes place outside the stomach may simulate digestion, but it cannot really *be* digestion. In his critique of the REM interpretation of dreams in Chapter 6, Norman Malcolm will make a similar point. He will argue that a *dream* as we use the word cannot also be a *dream* as the REM researchers use the word. The vitalists would say that *digestion* means what goes on in a living stomach to break down food. It cannot also be applied to what goes on in a test tube. Thus it was important when Tiedemann and Gmelin showed that starch is transformed to sugar in the body just as it is in the laboratory. Holmes refers to their having produced *direct* evidence. What do you think he means by "direct"? What would be "indirect" evidence? Is this use of *direct* similar to what Hooke meant by *immediate*?

Tiedemann and Gmelin proposed a theory of digestion. What makes it a theory is what makes any attempted explanation a theory.

The following characteristics of theory are meant to be general enough to include what are termed theories in many different disciplines. It might turn out that what is termed theory in one discipline, such as theoretical physics, is not at all like what is termed theory in another discipline, such as animal behavior. Exactly what makes a scientific theory is open to question. It could be an entire topic itself. Instead of dealing with it fully here, only some suggestions will be made. Of the characteristics of a theory listed here, the fourth is the most contentious.

1. It is provisional and conjectural.

2. It offers a mechanism.

3. Some of its terms refer to entities that are not readily observable.

4. It makes some use of a previously understood mechanism as a model.

5. It contains laws.

6. Trivially, it contains many statements. One provisional and conjectural claim is better referred to as a hypothesis.

Tiedemann and Gmelin's mechanism is rough in the sense that they did not know all its parts. The missing parts would have been the less than readily observable entities. Yet having all the chemical parts might not have been enough for them. They state that "digestion is a vital process, an event conditioned by the life of the animal." Functions such as digestion, they claimed, "take place through the connection and interactions of the stomach with the entire living organism." This view that ties one function of an organism (or system) to the entire organism (or system) is called holism. Holism need not be vitalistic. Its basic claim is that any particular part of an integrated system—and an organism is an integrated system—cannot be understood without understanding the fit between the part and the whole. In other words, to understand the part requires an understanding of the whole. This is holism in a nutshell. Often holism is expressed as the belief that the whole (of an integrated system) is greater than the sum of its parts. This is merely a picturesque way of making the same claim. In any case, holism is always antireductionistic.

The Investigation of Digestion, 1750–1830

FREDERICK HOLMES

The general approaches to the investigation of the digestive action of the stomach upon which physiologists relied during the 1840's can be traced back to experiments performed nearly one hundred years before by the versatile French scientist René Antoine Ferchault de Réaumur. Réaumur had taken up a question debated for a long time previously, whether digestion consists of a mechanical grinding of food into small particles or a special solvent action. His own work demonstrated that neither theory was exclusively correct, for both processes occur. He showed that the muscular stomachs of birds with gizzards could exert such force as to crush strong metal cylinders. The thin-walled stomachs of other types of birds, however, could not produce such effects. They contained, on the other hand, a very

Reprinted by permission of the publishers from Frederick Holmes, *Claude Bernard and Animal Chemistry* (Cambridge, Mass.: Harvard University Press, 1974), pp. 141–159. Copyright © 1979 by the President and Fellows of Harvard College.

active solvent, a conclusion he established using his well-known buzzard, a bird which swallows all parts of its prey and afterward regurgitates the indigestible components. Réaumur suspended pieces of meat on a thread running through a metal tube, which he then wrapped with more thread so that only fluids might penetrate to the food. He then forced the bird to swallow the tube. A day or so later, when the bird had thrown the tube up, Réaumur found the meat reduced to a fraction of its original size and weight. It no longer resembled meat in color or consistency, but was soft and grayish, and felt unctuous. Even bone, which he similarly fed to the animal, was softened and lost a considerable part of its weight. Grains and other vegetable foods which are not part of the buzzard's ordinary diet were, however, little altered.[1] . . .

Spallanzani found that the quantity and properties of gastric juice varied according to the conditions under which he obtained it. That derived from fasting animals seemed "purer" and more transparent than that from a stomach containing food, so whenever possible he procured the former. The juice found in the stomach cavity differed, he thought, from that discharged from the lining of the esophagus or a particular portion of the stomach. He regarded the active solvent, therefore, as a mixture of these and of bile regurgitated from the small intestine.[2]

Despite the comprehensiveness of Spallanzani's demonstration of the digestive action of gastric juice, doubts and disagreements with his conclusions were common during the next fifty years. Some people continued to defend the theory of fermentation, contending that a mere process of solution was inadequate to account for the conversion of the widely diverse foods animals eat into the uniform, bland end product of digestion known as chyle. Others debated over whether gastric juice was neutral or acid, and

if it were the latter, what the nature of the acid was. Some questioned more basically the whole theory that gastric juice is the agent of digestion. Experiments which A. Jenin de Montegre reported to the French Institute in 1812 enhanced such skepticism. Using his own gastric juice, obtained by vomiting, Montegre found that it acted just like saliva, having no special solvent properties corresponding to those of the stomach itself. These results encouraged a growing school of vitalists in France who denied that digestion is a chemical process at all.[3]

Meanwhile, methods for isolating and identifying organic substances had been undergoing a gradual but fundamental change. This development had now reached the point at which a new kind of investigation of the chemical aspects of biological phenomena was becoming possible. The tests which Scopoli did for Spallanzani represented the traditional basis for analyzing animal or vegetable matter. Since the sixteenth-century, herbalists and chemists had customarily sought to separate these materials into their constituent substances by operations oriented around distillations of the gross matter. The limitations of these methods became increasingly evident during the seventeenth-century, however, and several generations of analysts sought for ways to avoid the disruptions of the substances thought to be due to the fire. By the early eighteenth-century they were turning increasingly to extraction by means of the solvents water and alcohol in order to separate constituents which had not lost their distinctive properties. The first person to portray this approach as a new general "order of analysis" was the popular French teacher of chemistry, Guillaume-François Rouelle. By avoiding the destructive agent fire, Rouelle claimed, one could attain by these methods "a true idea of the composition of plants." Typically, he applied a double extraction procedure. First he would digest pieces of the plant in alcohol, then evaporate the alcohol to leave whatever had dissolved in it as a residue, or precipitate substances by adding water to the alcoholic solution. The materials soluble in alcohol but insoluble in water he called resin. Then he extracted from the remaining plant material the substances soluble in water and called them "extractive matter." He discovered a third type of substance soluble in both alcohol and water, which he named "extracto-resinous." Thus Rouelle defined the categories of plant constituents on the basis of their solubility properties. With such methods he was able to isolate the "green matter" from plants, by extraction in alcohol.[4]

Rouelle's method did not dominate the analysis of vegetable matter in the same way that distillation formerly had, because chemical investigation was becoming too progressive for any simple orthodox set of operations to remain unaltered. In mineral chemistry, the application of methods for separating and identifying acids and bases by forming soluble and insoluble salts was expanding rapidly. Carl Wilhelm Scheele introduced these methods into the study of vegetable acids with such spectacular success as to overshadow the achievements made with Rouelle's extraction procedure. Nevertheless, Rouelle's approach strongly influenced his successors. The solvent method was soon broadened by the addition of ether, a liquid whose preparation and properties were just becoming known. . . .

By the 1820's this progress in methods of organic analysis suggested that the time was ripe for new investigations of the chemical phenomena of digestion. Such reasoning motivated the French Academy to propose in 1823 a prize for whoever could determine "by a series of chemical and physiological experiments what are the phenomena which follow one another in the digestive organs, during the act of diges-

tion." Competitors were to examine first the changes which simple "immediate principles," such as "gelatin, albumin, sugar, etc." undergo, then to deal with the more complex ordinary foods in which these are combined.[5] The ability of the Academy to pose the problem in these terms was itself an outcome of the recent developments in chemistry which had made it possible to consider individually some of the immediate principles comprising alimentary matter.

Two memoirs were submitted for the prize. One was by the Frenchmen François Leuret and Louis Lassaigne. The other came from two German colleagues at the University of Heidelberg, the physiologist Friedrich Tiedemann, and the chemist Leopold Gmelin. The Academy did not award the prize to either, but offered to each a portion of the prize money as an encouragement to further effort. Of the two memoirs, however, that of Tiedemann and Gmelin was more complete and more significant in its influence on further developments.

Unlike some contemporaries, Tiedemann and Gmelin did not question Spallanzani's general assertion that gastric juice produces digestion in the stomach. They sought rather to extend his conclusion by a more specific chemical description of the process. They retained the three basic approaches which had emerged from Réaumur's memoirs: that is, they fed animals aliments and examined their condition in the digestive system a few hours afterward; they duplicated digestion with gastric juice outside of the stomach; and they analyzed gastric juice chemically. They did not limit their concern to the stomach, but extended some of the same procedures to the events in the small intestines associated with the secretion of bile, pancreatic juice, and the glands of the intestinal wall. They also investigated salivation, the changes which occur lower in the intestines, and absorption of aliments into the lacteal vessels and the blood.

Of these approaches, that to which they gave least attention was artificial digestion. They devoted only two pages to it out of a report totaling nearly seven hundred, and concluded merely that they had "confirmed" Spallanzani's assertion.[6] They expended, on the other hand, far more effort to analyze the digestive juices. One of the principal obstacles they saw to a determination of the changes which individual alimentary materials undergo was the uncertainty over whether the substances they found along the digestive tract derived from the aliment or from the digestive fluids. Consequently, they analyzed the latter in meticulous detail, hoping that by comparing these results with the contents of the stomach or intestines during digestion they could ascertain what part of those contents had come from each source.[7]

To collect each digestive juice in a pure state was a difficult problem in itself. For gastric juice, pancreatic juice, and the intestinal secretions they had to "devise and carry out new ways of proceeding." When they opened the stomach of a fasting dog, for example, they found only a small amount of a salty fluid, which was almost entirely neutral in its reaction with litmus. After forcing another animal to swallow quartz stones, however, they obtained a "copious" and strongly acidic fluid. The stomach therefore must only secrete gastric juice, they inferred, when it is mechanically or chemically stimulated. They had not only a procedure for procuring gastric juice, but an explanation for the divergence of opinion among their predecessors over whether it is acid.[8] According to Johannes Müller, it was this work which "finally settled the question."[9] Tiedemann and Gmelin similarly observed during their investigations that pancreatic juice, bile, and intestinal mucus seemed to be secreted in response to

excitation by the chyme entering the small intestine.[10] . . .

Tiedemann and Gmelin ascertained that the gastric juice of dogs and horses contained no albumin. It did yield osmazome, a substance soluble in alcohol, and "salivary matter," insoluble in alcohol but soluble in water. Having settled that there is a free acid in gastric juice, they attempted to determine its nature. By distilling the juice from a horse they found one acidic fraction which produced a precipitate with silver nitrate, so that they inferred that the juice contained hydrochloric acid. They confirmed its existence in the stomach by feeding a dog calcareous stones. Afterward they observed large quantities of calcium chloride, which they attributed to a neutralization reaction between the ingested calcium carbonate and hydrochloric acid in the digestive fluid. . . .

After analyzing the gastric juice itself, Tiedemann and Gmelin were ready to try to follow the changes which various aliments undergo along the digestive tract. Using dogs, they waited in each case for a certain time after feeding, then killed the animal, opened up its stomach and intestines, and analyzed the materials they found in the different portions. They utilized in turn, as "simple" aliments, liquid albumin, coagulated albumin, fibrin, gelatin, butter, cheese (casein), starch, and gluten. They then tried "composed" nutrients, including milk, raw meat, cooked meat, meat and bread, bones, and other combinations.[11] After completing these experiments on dogs they repeated some of them for comparison on cats, horses, cows, and sheep. They also did similar experiments with birds, reptiles, and fish. From all of these painstaking efforts Tiedemann and Gmelin seem at first sight to have derived relatively sparse general conclusions about the chemical nature of digestion. They themselves pointed out that the task set by the French Academy was so enormous that they might be excused if they could often reach "only conjectures in place of definite conclusions, and had in some cases abstained even from the former."[12] In the case of the complex nutrients they could do little more than describe the visible changes during the stages of digestion. . . .

In one crucial case, however, they were able to establish more precisely the chemical nature of the transformation involved. Starch was the only simple aliment they used for which there was a distinctive identification test, applicable even when the material was mixed with a variety of other organic substances. When reacted with iodine it produced a characteristic blue or violet color not easily confused with any effect which a constituent of the digestive juices might cause.

After they had fed a dog starch for several days and opened its intestinal tract about three hours after its last meal, they found starch in the stomach and intestine, but not in the chyle, blood, or urine. Somewhere during digestion, they inferred, starch disappears.[13] They knew immediately what to look for in its place, for one of the few chemical transformations of an important organic nutrient substance into another which had at this time been clearly demonstrated was the conversion of starch to sugar. Gottlieb Sigismund Kirchhoff, the director of the imperial apothecary in St. Petersburg, Russia, had shown in 1812 that such a change can be produced by means of sulfuric acid. . . .

With this knowledge available to them in 1823, it is not surprising that after their first experiment, in which starch appeared not to be absorbed in its original state, Tiedemann and Gmelin undertook another one "in order to ascertain if the starch was transformed into sugar or into 'starchgum' (dextrin)."[14] This time they waited five hours after feeding before killing the animal, and then they found that the starch had disappeared even from the stomach. Next they undertook a "search for sugar." They evaporated to dryness portions of the fluid contents of the stomach and of the intestines, chyle, urine, blood from the portal vein and from the vena cava. The residues they extracted with alcohol, in which any sugar present should dissolve. After evaporating these solutions they placed the remaining solid matter from each fluid in a pneumatic flask over mercury, added yeast, and observed substantial fermentation from each. Therefore, they concluded, "as soon as starch dissolves in the digestive juices, it loses its property of turning iodine blue and is transformed, at least in part, into sugar."[15]

This discovery by Tiedemann and Gmelin was a special landmark in the history of animal chemistry. It must have been one of the first occasions on which anyone had produced direct evidence that a substance had undergone within the animal body a specific chemical transformation which had also been demonstrated in the laboratory with the same substance isolated from any organism. When Claude Bernard set out twenty years later to follow inside the animal the reactions which chemists inferred theoretically to occur there, he had at least one clear precedent to guide him.

After recounting their experiments, Tiedemann and Gmelin presented a "theory of digestion" based on them. The most persuasive and general conclusion to be drawn, they felt, was that "simple as well as composed ailments are undeniably dissolved and converted to chyme by the gastric juice."[16] Unlike many earlier physiologists, however, they did not envision all manner of foods being reduced somehow to a single uniform chyme or chyle; they noted carefully the variations in these fluids corresponding with the digestion of different nutrients, implying that the composition of the former depends upon the nature of the particular types of nutrient which are dissolved to form it. They wished also to go beyond what those before them had done by asking what the constituent of the gastric juice is that dissolves nutrients. For this they could only speculate, but here again they displayed the significance of distinguishing between the processes which might occur with different alimentary substances. They did not assume that there was one universal agent, but sought explanations based on the solubility properties of the various "immediate principles." Since uncoagulated albumin, gelatin, osmazome, sugar, gum, and cooked starch were soluble in water, the water content of gastric juice might suffice for these. Coagulated albumin, fibrin, coagulated casein, gluten, and similar substances, on the other hand, were insoluble in water but soluble in acid. It was natural to suppose, therefore, that the acid whose presence they had established in gastric juice was the solvent for them. To test the latter theory they placed some of the materials in this category in acetic acid and hydrochloric acid, but the results were not satisfactory and they did not comment on them.[17] Afterward Johannes Müller did similar experiments with several acids, none of which dissolved meat or albumin. Consequently he had to conclude that "we do not know the active principle."[18] Tiedemann and Gmelin believed that besides solution a "special decomposition" occurred in the stomach, for other substances probably underwent transformations similar to that of starch. They conjectured that the organic constituents of gastric juice, "salivary matter" or osmazome, might contribute to such conversions, since (as Kirchhoff had shown), gluten exerts such an action on starch.[19] Inconclusive though Tiedemann and Gmelin's theories of digestion were, they were searching and suggestive. . . .

Tiedemann and Gmelin were after a chemical explanation of nutritional phenomena, and their work contributed substantially toward that goal. Gastric juice, they said, owes its action to its chemical composition, and "its effect upon aliments is a chemical one." Nevertheless, they maintained, "digestion is a vital process, an event conditioned by the life of the animal." For it to operate, the stomach must be in such a condition that it can respond to stimuli by secreting gastric juice; it must be able to separate an acid fluid from alkaline blood, and it must dispatch digested material from the stomach into the intestine so that undigested portions can be exposed to the chemical action of gastric juice. These functions can only take place through the connection and interactions of the stomach with the entire living organism. Since antiquity, they noted, it had been clear that the pneumogastric nerves influence digestion, and recent experiments had indicated many ways in which disruption of the nervous system affected digestion. The sectioning of the pneumogastric nerves was thought to slow it down primarily by stopping the motions of the stomach. By their own vivisection experiments on dogs Tiedemann and Gmelin found that after these nerves are severed the stomach no longer becomes acidic, even when the animal has swallowed food. They believed, therefore, that the secretion of gastric juice also is under the influence of nervous action.[20]

In his general treatise on human physiology Tiedemann supported a rather mild form of vitalism.[21] When he and Gmelin insisted upon the vital aspects of digestion in the foregoing situation, however, they were not invoking an ultimate philosophical principle; they were espousing the importance of dealing experimentally with events which involve a higher level of organization in the animal than chemical means of analysis alone can treat.

NOTES

1. Réaumur, "Sur la digestion des oiseaux. Premier Mémoire," *Hist. Acad.*, 1752 [1756], pp. 266–307; Réaumur, "Sur la digestion des oiseaux. Second Mémoire," ibid., pp. 461–495.

2. Spallanzani, Lazzaro, *Dissertations Relative to the Natural History of Animals & Vegetables*. Trans. anon., London, 1784, I, 48, 76–77.

3. This paragraph follows the discussion of those topics in Bates, Donald G., "The Background to John Young's Thesis on Digestion." *Bull. Hist. Med.* 1962, *36:* 341–361; and in Bylebyl, Jerome J., "William Beaumont, Robley Dunglison, and the 'Philadelphia Physiologists.'" *J. Hist. Med.* 1970, *25:* 3–21.

4. Holmes, Frederic L., "Analysis by Fire and Solvent Extraction: The Metamorphosis of a Tradition." *Isis* 1971, *62:* 141–148.

5. Tiedemann, Friedrich, and Gmelin, Leopold, *Recherches experimentales, physologiques et chimiques, sur la digestion*. Trans. A.J.L. Jourdan, Paris, 1826–1827, I, v–vii.

6. Tiedemann and Gmelin, *Die Verdauung nach Versuchen*. Heidelberg, 1826–1827, I, 306. Tiedemann and Gmelin, *Sur la digestion*, 227–229, 344. References to both the German and French editions of this book are given because I have translated from the German and followed it when they differ in emphasis, but the French edition was most likely that with which Bernard and other French scientists were familiar. The pages in the French edition will in the following references be given in parentheses following the reference to the German.

7. Tiedemann and Gmelin, *Verdauung*, I, 2 (Fr. pp. ix–x, 2).

8. Ibid., "Introduction" (paginated separately), p. 3, pp. 143–149 (Fr. pp. viii, 160–165).

9. Müller, Johannes, *Handbuch der Physiologie des Mensches für Verlesungen*. 3rd edition, Coblenz, 1838, I, 511.

10. Tiedemann and Gmelin, *Verdauung*, I, 156 (This paragraph is not present in the French edition. See Fr., p. 171).

11. Tiedemann and Gmelin, *Verdauung*, I, 162–286. (Fr., pp. 176–325).

12. Ibid., "Intro.," p. 5 (Fr., p. x).

13. Ibid., pp. 180–183 (Fr., pp. 199–201).

14. Tiedemann and Gmelin, *Verdauung*, I, 183 (Fr., p. 201). Kirchhoff had found in addition to sugar a residue insoluble in alcohol but soluble in water, which he considered to be "modified starch which has not yet completely changed to sugar." Kirchhoff, *J. Pharm.*, 1816, 2:253. Tiedemann and Gmelin also found besides sugar a substance soluble in water which they regarded as "a starch approaching gum" and which no longer reacted with iodine as starch does. Their substance was not the same as that of Kirchhoff, however, for that found by the latter did not form a precipitate with infusion of gall-nuts, while theirs did. Tiedemann and Gmelin, *Verdauung*, pp. 185–186. The nature of these intermediary products, named dextrin shortly afterward by Biot, because they rotated polarized light strongly to the right, was partially clarified in 1833 by Payen and Persoz.

15. Tiedemann and Gmelin, *Verdauung*, I, 185 (Fr., p. 202).

16. Ibid., p. 305 (Fr., p. 343). See also p. 327 (Fr., p. 363).

17. Ibid., pp. 330–333 (Fr., pp. 366–368).

18. Müller, *Handbuch*, I, 543–544.

19. Tiedemann and Gmelin, *Verdauung*, I, 333 (Fr., pp. 368–369).

20. Ibid., pp. 336–341 (Fr., pp. 371–375).

21. Tiedemann, Friedrich, *Traité complet de physiologie de l'homme*. Trans. A.J.L. Jourdan, Paris, 1831, I, 131–136; II, 415–416, 420–422.

FRIEDRICH AUGUST KEKULÉ, "ORIGIN OF THE BENZENE AND STRUCTURAL THEORY"

We are not so much interested in what Kekulé (1829–1896) means by theory or what the structure of benzene really is; what concerns us here is methodology. How did the idea of benzene's structure come to Kekulé? Notice that Hooke does not tell us how the idea came to him that the motion of the lungs might not be necessary for life. Perhaps it came to him only as he did the experiment. Perhaps he refused even to consider any such idea until he had tested it experimentally. We simply do not know. But with Kekulé, we do know because he tells us what has become one of the most famous stories in the history of science: He dreamed it. Of course, what he dreamed was not the explicit answer. What he dreamed (what Freud would call the manifest content of the dream) had to be interpreted.

Kekulé asks if hard drudging work can lead to discovery in science. He answers that great discoveries are not likely to be made only by studying the texts and journals of the time. Such study is necessary, but it should be done only because it is the surest way to develop insight—the insight required to go beyond the ordinary scientist.

The positivist-leaning Hempel, Oppenheim, and Brodbeck, whose readings are in Chapter 2, would assume that dreaming is part of what they would call the context (or logic) of discovery. When it comes to discovering a new idea, anything goes. The scientific method is the demonstration that the dreamed discovery is actually true. Notice that Kekulé says that when he awoke, he spent the rest of the night working out the consequences of his dreamed hypothesis. This working out is what Hempel, Oppenheim, and Brodbeck would refer to as the context (or logic) of justification. I call this the "two-contexts distinction." This distinction is crucial for positivists, for it keeps us focused on science and not extraneous factors. According to the positivistic view, social, political, economic, personal, and historical influences are extraneous to the philosophy of science. These factors are interesting and worth studying, positivists believe; however, they do not make up the philosophy of science. The philosophy of science should limit its subject matter to what Kekulé called working out. The other factors will only cloud the questions that have to be answered if one is to understand fully what makes science such a trustworthy finder of information.

To the positivists, the philosophy of science, in trying to find the true scientific method, is trying ultimately to set the standards for how to gather knowledge. To positivists, the philosophy of science, then, is not merely describing what scientists do and why, for this would mix the two contexts. Rather, the philosophy of science first locates the best examples of science and then finds the context of justification for each example. From this point, there are two methods to pursue. One would be to look for similarities in the contexts. Another would be to compare each context to a philosophically determined "correct method."

Writers such as Scriven (Chapter 2), Kuhn (Chapter 3), and most of the feminist philosophers of science deny that the two-contexts distinction can ever be made without distorting science. To these philosophers, making the two-contexts distinction will not yield a true picture of science as a human enterprise.

Origin of the Benzene and Structural Theory

FRIEDRICH AUGUST KEKULÉ

The following passages are abstracted from the 25th anniversary celebration of Kekulé's benzene theory, held in the Berlin City Hall, in 1890. Kekulé spoke about his idea in 1858 that carbon atoms form chains and his proposal seven years later that carbon atoms can also form rings. The complete speech can be found in the Journal of Chemical Education 35, no. 21 (1958).

We all stand on the shoulders of our predecessors; is it then surprising that we can see further than they? If we follow the roads built by our predecessors and effortlessly reach places which they had attained only after overcoming countless obstacles, what special merit is it if we can penetrate further into the unknown?

It was said that the benzene theory appeared like a meteor in the sky, absolutely new and unheralded. Gentlemen! The human intellect does not operate that way. Something absolutely new has never been thought, certainly not in chemistry. Our present opinions do not, as has frequently been asserted, stand on the ruins of earlier theories. A seed here and there may have lain in the ground without germinating; but everything that grew came from the seed that had been previously sown. In a like manner, my views also have grown out of those of my predecessors and are based on them.

One summer evening during my stay in London when I was returning home by the last bus, I fell into a reverie, and lo, the atoms were gamboling before my eyes. I saw how, frequently, two smaller atoms united to form a pair; how a larger one embraced the two smaller ones; how still larger ones kept hold of three or even four

of the smaller; whilst the whole kept whirling in a giddy dance. I saw how the larger ones formed a chain, dragging the smaller ones after them but only at the ends of the chain. I spent a part of the night in putting on paper sketches of these dream forms. This was the origin of the "structural theory."

Something similar happened with the benzene theory. During my stay in Ghent I was sitting writing at my textbook, but the work did not progress; my thoughts were elsewhere. I turned my chair to the fire and dozed. Again the atoms were gamboling before my eyes. This time the smaller groups kept modestly in the background. I could now distinguish larger structures of manifold conformations—long rows, sometimes more closely fitted together all twining and twisting in snakelike motion. Then one of the snakes seized its own tail, and the form whirled mockingly before my eyes. This time also I spent the rest of the night in working out the consequences of the hypothesis. . . .

One cannot explore new countries in express trains, nor will the study of even the best textbooks qualify a man to become a discoverer. By following well laid paths some forgotten flower may be gathered, but nothing essentially new will be found. True, whoever wishes to train himself as an investigator must study the traveller's original works, but, so thoroughly that he is able to read between the lines—to divine the

From *Chemistry* 38 (1965): 9. This article in a longer version originally appeared in *Berichte der Deutschen Chemischen Gesellschaft*, 1890, 68, 1302.

author's unexpressed thought and follow the same path; he must note every footprint, every bent twig, every fallen leaf. Then, standing at the destination of his predecessors, it will be easier to perceive where the foot of a new pioneer may find solid ground.

EDUARD FARBER, "DREAMS AND VISIONS IN A CENTURY OF CHEMISTRY"

Farber tries to dignify the role of dreams and visions in chemistry. He includes them as a reputable part of the methodology of science. They are more than just delightful stories. Farber quotes a positivist-leaning philosopher of science, Philipp Frank, who clearly implies that the origin of what Frank terms "principles" is of no concern to what should be considered the work of scientists.

Farber considers the use of models and analogies in science to be akin to visions and dreams. Hesse, as will be clear from her article in Chapter 2, would certainly disagree. Since almost no philosopher of science will deny the importance of models and analogies in scientific reasoning, Farber's claim, if true, would make dreams and visions an integral part of scientific thought. Farber's most general example of a model in science is that of the macrocosm in the microcosm (the structure of the entire world as a whole is pictured in the structure of any part of the entire world, as discussed by Merchant). It is one of the most ancient of all concepts used to picture the world.

In the appendix to his article, Farber criticizes an account that tries to explain why Kekulé had the dream that he did. Farber prefers his explanation of the dream: that Kekulé was remembering an alchemist symbol. Farber suggests that any dream of a circle might have done the trick. We know from Kekulé's testimony that it took this particular dream, at this particular time, to show him what to do. After reading Chapter 6, "Can There Be a Science of Dreams?" ask yourself why the dream of the snake was so potent for Kekulé. Then after reading Chapter 6, ask yourself whether Farber is committed to some sort of Jungian view about science and knowledge in general.

Dreams and Visions in a Century of Chemistry

EDUARD FARBER

In addition to accidental observations, analogies, and inferences by close reasoning, dreams and visions had an important part in the progress of chemistry. Four classes of progress can be distinguished: (1) symbolization and construction of models: Kekulé, van't Hoff, J. J. Thompson; (2) extrapolation in quantity: Wöhler, Sabatier, Kurnakow; (3) projection in time: Kuhlmann, Le Bon, Aston; (4) generalizations: Clausius, Le Chatelier, Ostwald. This list is incomplete and leaves out the failures. Not all those with dreams and visions were as careful as Kekulé was to check and test before publishing. The courage to persist must be combined with a critical evaluation of the facts, and this is especially necessary when solutions are achieved primarily in broad jumps rather than small steps.

We need Kekulé's testimony today as a powerful reminder that chemistry advances not by experiments alone but by a process in which dreams and visions can play an important role. Chemists seem to be particularly inclined to disparage anything that is not experiment; perhaps they still have a guilt complex about alchemy and the speculative periods of the 17th and 18th centuries. In an attitude of defense against speculation, J. C. Poggendorff refused to publish Robert Mayer's paper about "forces in inanimate nature" (1842). This defensive position was fortified by scientific standards of verification, but it also contained an element of prejudice that has been harmful. Results of experimental work were rejected when they would have required a change in cherished assumptions. A prominent example was the measurement by Hermann Helmholtz that the propagation of impulses in nerves takes time and is not, as generally believed, instantaneous (1850).

Kekulé took his dreamlike vision seriously enough to work on it for years, but it had no place in his scientific paper of 1865; he described it at the celebration of this paper 25 years later. While many dreams and visions may never have found their way into the scientific literature, others were mentioned in biographies and letters; all of them should be recognized for their significance in the history and methodology of science. Usually, accounts of such visions

delight us as anecdotes, as individual acts that, while too complex for scientific analysis, yet are significant features of scientific progress. Because of this apparent ambiguity, they are not dignified enough to be included in the philosophy of science. For example, Philipp Frank writes:

Thus the work of the scientist consists of three parts: (1) setting up principles; (2) making logical conclusions from these principles in order to derive observable facts about them; (3) experimental checking of these observable facts.[1]

Frank here omits the fact that the "principles" are often replaced by symbols or models, and all of them have their particular origins, sometimes in dreams and visions. Yet, he certainly was familiar with a report like that by Sir William Rowan Hamilton:

The Quaternions started into life, or light, full grown, on the 16th of October, 1843, as I was walking with Lady Hamilton to Dublin, and came up to Brougham Bridge, which my boys have since called Quaternion Bridge, that is to say, I then and there felt the galvanic circuit of thought close, and the sparks which fell from it were the fundamental equations between i, j, k, exactly such as I have used them ever since.[2]

Frank also knew how Henri Poincaré solved the problem of Fuchsian functions during a sleepless night:

I felt them knocking against each other ... until two of them hung together, as it were, and formed a stable combination. In the morning, I had established the existence of a class of Fuchs-functions. The results were set down in a few hours.

Occurrences like these two selected from the history of mathematics are frequent enough in the history of science to be accepted as influential, and if they cannot be "explained," they can at least be classified according to distinguishing features. I propose to do just that for 12 instances from the last 100 years in chemistry.[3]

CLASS I: SYMBOLS TO MODELS

What Kekulé saw in his dream was a snake which "seized hold of its own tail." The picture of a snake in this position was familiar to historians; it was a symbolic reality for alchemists who called it Ouroboros. Had Kekulé seen it in one of the later reproductions? It appears on the title page of a chemical book published in 1690 . . . [and] on a portrait of Thomas Wright painted in 1740.[4] Injecting the concept of the tetravalent carbon atom, Kekulé turned the ancient symbol into a modern model.

Kekulé had to interpret what he saw in his dream; Poincaré had to take a similar step to understand the symbolic language of the dream. Jacobus Henricus van't Hoff's vision was much more direct; it showed him the tetrahedron as the model for the carbon atom in organic compounds. The complete vision occurred to him, as it did on an entirely different subject to Hamilton, while he was taking a walk. The tetrahedron was not a new model in notions of substance, and Kekulé himself had come close to it seven years before van't Hoff in a publication of 1867:

The four units of affinity of the carbon atom, instead of being placed in one plane, radiate from the sphere representing the atom . . . so that they end in the faces of a tetrahedron. . . .[5]

Thus, the extension of formulas into space, from two to three dimensions, had already been seen as desirable before van't Hoff proved that it was necessary and solved the problem of the isomeric lactic acids. However, it was a new approach to use the model to represent asymmetry in organic compounds. What Pasteur had

explained as derived from the general asymmetry of the universe was now reduced to a structure of the molecule. The vision was elaborated into a theory, but Hermann Kolbe would perhaps not have attacked it so violently if he had felt that it was only a theory.

Models representing the structure of the atom began to be developed in 1840. The somewhat childish drawings of Dalton and their elaboration by Marc Antoine Augustin Gaudin in 1833 were far exceeded in the new visions of the atom as a vortex by Rankine, Helmholtz, William Thomson (Lord Kelvin), and J. J. Thomson[6] or as a planetary system with a central sun. We may question whether these models really were the results of visions—were they not merely analogies? The answer is that all analogies, especially when they combine greatly different things, contain something visionary. The planetary model, in particular, is related to the ancient vision of an analogy between microcosm and macrocosm.

The foregoing three dreams and visions have one aspect in common—they led to the construction or design of models. Kekulé considers his model symbolic; the others can be called ikonic, accepting the definitions given by Frey, although after making the distinction Frey also introduces the "ikonic-symbolic" model for "a symbolic model for which there is also a completely representational (vollständig abbildendes) ikonic model."[7] In the engineering sciences, a model is most often a small object reproducing essential features of a larger one—e.g., the model of a ship or of a distillation column. In chemistry (and physics) models are enlargements—idealizations that enable us to visualize and to design experiments.

CLASS II: EXTRAPOLATIONS

Like analogies, extrapolations of a wide range belong to this story also. The first example for a visionary extrapolation comes from a letter which Friedrich Wöhler wrote to his friend Liebig on June 25, 1863:

I live completely in the laboratory, busy with the new silicium compound which is generated from silicium-calcium and is deep orange-yellow when pure. I become more and more convinced that it [the yellow compound] is composed in the manner of organic compounds in which carbon is replaced by silicium. Its entire behavior is analogous. In the dark, even in water, it remains quite unchanged; in sunlight, however, it develops, in a kind of fermentation, hydrogen gas and turns snow-white. . . . On dry distillation the yellow silicone, as I shall call it, behaves like an organic compound. One obtains hydrogen gas, silicium-hydride gas, brown amorphous silicium (corresponding to coal) and silicium dioxide (corresponding to carbon dioxide).[8]

In my translation I have used the German form of the name for the element silicon, particularly because silicium is more distinctly different from the new word silicon(e), coined by Wöhler.

In contrast to Wöhler's vision, note the conclusion Frederick Stanley Kipping (1863–1949) reached after intensive work on silicones:

Most if not all the known types of organic derivatives of silicon base have now been considered, and it may be seen how few they are in comparison with those which are entirely organic; as moreover the few which are known are very limited in their reactions, the prospect of any immediate and important advance in this section of organic chemistry does not seem to be very hopeful.[9]

He stated this in 1936. Five years later, important advances began at General Electric Co. and the Dow Chemical Co.

Nikolai Semonowitsch Kurnakow (1860–1941) introduced the distinction between Daltonides and Berthollides. He extrapolated from studies of the thallium-bismuth system in combination with (a) the concept of phase according to Gibbs, (b) thoughts about the definite proportions in chemical compounds, published by Franz Wald and supported by Wilhelm Ostwald, (c) the work on variable compositions of minerals by Friedrich Rinne, and (d) other information concerning relationships between properties and composition. Kurnakow designated as "Dalton points" the singular points on diagrams for the relationship of composition to properties (melting points, electric conductivities, etc.): "the composition that corresponds to this point remains constant when the factors of equilibrium change." Besides the Daltonides there is a class of variable compounds comprising the large number of Berthollides: "Before our eyes, a new and unexplored field opens up, attracting the scientist by its freshness, and promising him rich yields."[10]

In his work on hydrogenations and dehydrogenations with metals as catalysts, Paul Sabatier (1854–1941) encountered many difficulties. The catalysts would sometimes refuse to act. It took time and persistence before the disappointments were explained by a poisoning of the catalysts, especially by sulfur or arsenic. One great idea kept him going:

This idea of an intermediary, unstable combination [between catalyst and reagent] has been the beacon that directed all my research on catalysis. Its light will perhaps be extinguished in the future when more powerful new brightnesses will unexpectedly arise; nonetheless, what the beacon has shown will remain as established facts.[11]

In his book on catalysis in organic chemistry Sabatier repeated these words; they were not just a rhetorical embellishment in a speech at a solemn meeting.

Hermann von Helmholtz (1821–1894) described a similar personal experience when he reminisced about his work on an "eye-mirror" at the celebration of his 70th birthday:

Without the assured theoretical conviction that it should be feasible, I would perhaps not have persisted. Since I was in the uncomfortable position quite frequently of having to wait for helpful intuitions, I have gained some experience when and how they arrive which may perhaps become useful for others. Often enough, such intuitions sneak in gently into the thinking, and their significance is not recognized at the start; later on it may be only an accidental circumstance that serves to realize when and under which conditions they have come; otherwise, they are just there and we do not know whence. In other situations they step in suddenly, without effort, as if by association. As far as my experience goes, they never come to the tired brain and not at the writing desk. I always had to turn my problem around and around so much that I had a survey of all its contortions and complications in my head and was able to follow them freely without any writing.[12]

What Sabatier calls idea and Helmholtz calls intuition is not very different from vision, particularly when this is based on extrapolation.

CLASS III: PREDICTIONS

Predictions made from an established system of facts and for a near future are a normal part of science. A visionary element enters when predictions are ventured from a small factual basis and for a distant future. Three examples follow.

Frédéric Kuhlmann (1803–1881) concluded from a long study of ammonia and nitric acid:

The ease with which I have been able to transform ammonia into nitric acid indicates that Europe will some day be placed in the condition of the greatest inadequacies from overseas relations for its supply of nitrates; and if the calamities of war were to place us again under the conditions of a blockade, France would get along without India or Peru for assurance of war munitions, for France would always possess animal matter and manganese dioxide.[13]

The vision of a Europe inadequately supplied with nitrates from overseas and the prediction of a France under blockade and having to produce nitric acid for ammunition by oxidizing ammonia came true following the events of 1914, although neither animals nor MnO_2 were used in the process.

In his book on the evolution of matter, Gustave Le Bon (1841–1931) visualized far-reaching consequences; among them:

Force and matter are two different forms of one and the same thing. The power to dissociate matter freely would put at our disposal an infinite source of energy and would render unnecessary the extraction of that coal the provision whereof is rapidly becoming exhausted.[14]

At the end of his Nobel Prize lecture in 1922, Francis William Aston (1877–1945) explained that 1 gram of hydrogen would release the equivalent of 200,000 kw-hours if it were completely converted into helium and then added this vision of what could happen:

Should the research worker of the future discover some means of releasing this energy in a form which could be employed, the human race will have at its command powers beyond the dream of scientific fiction. . . .

If, however, the reaction should get out of control, it would be "published at large to the universe as a new star."[15]

CLASS IV: UNIVERSAL GENERALIZATIONS

In the year in which Kekulé published his benzene formula Rudolf Clausius expressed the basic laws of the universe which correspond respectively to the two laws of the mechanical theory of heat in the following simple form:

1. The energy of the universe is constant
2. The entropy of the universe aspires to a maximum.[16]

Clausius uses the verb *strebt . . . zu*, which is more adequately rendered by *aspires* than by the usual translation *tend toward*. He coined the word entropy for the quantity:

$$S = S_o + \int \frac{dQ}{T}$$

Previously, he had called *verwandelt* the heat transferred from high to low temperature in the Carnot cycle. I assume he selected the letter *S* because the letters on both sides of it, *Q, R, T, U,* and *V* already had found their definite meanings in thermodynamics by a generally accepted convention. Entropy stands for the "transformation content" (*Verwandlungsinhalt*), and its maximum meant a minimum in the possibility of further "transformation."

With this universal generalization Clausius went beyond anything that can be called theory and even beyond the generalization William Thomson (1822–1907) had reached in 1852: "There is at present in the material world a universal tendency to the dissipation of mechanical energy."

Josiah Willard Gibbs used the two Clausius sentences as a motto and placed them in front of his lengthy paper "On the Equilibrium of Heterogeneous Substances."

The vision of a general tendency recurs in the law which Henri Louis Le Chatelier published in 1884:

Every system in stable chemical equilibrium, submitted to the influence of an exterior force which tends to cause variation either of its temperature or its condensation . . . , can undergo only those interior modifications which, if they occurred alone, would produce a change of temperature, or of condensation, of a sign contrary to that resulting from the exterior force.[17]

This law of an interior counteraction against an exterior force was of great help to Walter Nernst and to Fritz Haber when they designed the optimum conditions for combining nitrogen with hydrogen in synthesizing ammonia.

In the spring of 1890, Wilhelm Ostwald (1853–1932) left Leipzig to persaude a friend in Berlin to write a textbook of physics from the standpoint of energetics. A long discussion, joined by others, extended far into the night:

I . . . slept for a few hours, then suddenly awoke immersed in the same thought and could not go back to sleep. In the earliest morning hours I went from the hotel to the Tiergarten, and there, in the sunshine of a glorious spring morning, I experienced a real Pentecoste, an outpouring of the spirit over me. . . . This was the actual birth-hour of energetics. What a year before, at that first, sudden sensation in my brain that was the conception of the thought, had confronted me as rather strange, even with the taint of frightening newness, now it proved to belong to myself, so much so that it was a life-supporting part of my being. . . . At once everything was there, and my glance only had to glide from one place to the other in order to grasp the whole new creation in its perfection.[18]

When Ostwald wrote this, he was unaware of what Helmholtz had said about his "intuitions" almost 40 years before. Ostwald had gone through other experiences of "lightning-like" visions, but this was the most important because it was the most universal generalization he could reach.

Though the thought was completely subjective—"a life-important part of my being"—it embraced an objective totality. The apparent paradox recurs in all dreams and visions; it is especially great in the universal generalizations.

CONCLUSION

Many more examples could have been cited, extending from recent chemistry to dreams and visions at other times, on different subjects, starting with Johannes Kepler's dream of a trip to the moon, mentioning René Descartes, continuing with

Emanuel Swedenborg, and ending with Arnold Toynbee.[19] The classification could have been based on the kind of visualized picture or on the scientific consequences, and the psychological conditions would have formed the best basis if only the biographical information were available in sufficient depth. The classification I used has more the function of an aid to the memory than the character of a deeply unifying system. In addition, there is a certain increase in range in the progression from the first class to the fourth.

The main conclusion is that dreams and visions deserve to be recognized, without ridicule or pretense, as having an important place, even in modern chemistry. They must be treated with critical respect. Danger looms as much in their presence as in their absence. Imagine what might have happened if Otto Hahn and his group had not stuck to the "false trans-uranium elements" which they later found to be a scientific error: "A completely unexpected reaction, forbidden by physics, the break-up of the highly charged element uranium into barium and . . . krypton"[20] opened a new era to those who had the vision, though they were not the first to carry out the experiment.

In describing the "how and when," Helmholtz tried to arrive at a prescription for inviting "intuitions." These prescriptions, together with the experiences cited, lead to a further conclusion—they required a relaxed patience that nevertheless was charged with the vital tension necessary to solve a problem, followed by a critical objectivity towards the vision. This is entirely different from a "crash program" that diverts mental functions from the problem to pretentious and premature communications.

Dreams and visions are necessary, but they are not sufficient. Drawing attention to the rightful place of a component should never imply that it is more than a part, and certainly it is not identical with the whole.

Great advances in chemistry have come through improved experimental skill and accuracy. Increased reliability of analysis led to the discovery of lithium and of the first three "nationalistic" elements: scandium, gallium, and germanium. Greater precision in measuring optical emission spectra was instrumental in finding several new elements and atomic structures. The complementary nature that exists between visions and experimental skills does not mean that they must be distributed over different personalities; the same man can use one or the other at different times in his work.

APPENDIX: KEKULÉ AND THE SERPENT

In the book resulting from the Kekulé Symposium in London, 1958, P. E. Verkade writes:

On the other hand, it is to be noted that the snake biting its own tail had also played a part early in Kekulé's life. In 1847 he appeared as a witness in a trial for the murder of Countess Görlitz, who lived next door to his father at Darmstadt; this murder was coupled with a theft of jewelry, including a ring that consisted of two intertwined metal snakes biting their own tails. The incident in question made a deep impression on Kekulé and may have led to the famous dream.[21]

In this account the facts are inaccurate, and the conclusions are no less arbitrary than my conjecture of a connection with the ancient symbol of Ouroboros. In 1847 Kekulé saw the fire in his neighbor's house, and he was therefore called in as an eye witness in the murder trial, which took place in Darmstadt, March 11 to April 11, 1850. The expert witness at the trial was Justus Liebig. Richard Anschütz describes the events from the sources available to him and adds:

Bei der Erzählung der Aufstellung der Benzoltheorie werden wir Kekulé das Bild von der Schlange, die sich in den Schwanz beisst, auf die Kohlenstoff-Kette anwenden sehen, die sich zum Ringe schliesst.[22]

There is no hint here that Kekulé saw the ring or that he knew about its form. Those who are sensitive to form and logic in historiography will notice with distress that Anschütz reverses the relationships between "the carbon chain . . . which closes in on itself to a ring" and "the picture of the snake which bites its own tail."

After this incidental remark I return to our problem. Finger rings with various forms of special emphasis on the "return into itself" were not unusual; several of them are shown in a relatively recent book on jewelry design.[23] If Kekulé had continued to have "a deep impression" of any of these rings, including that of the Countess, would he not have mentioned it in the story he leisurely told about his dream? The snake and its magic position did not have any function after the dream. Could not the picture of any ring, in fact of any circle, have served to initiate his thoughts about the benzene "ring"? We could imagine that it might have happened this way, but the historical reality was different. The action Kekulé saw in his dream showed him what to do.

NOTES

1. Frank, P., *Philosophy of Science: The Link between Philosophy and Science* (Englewood Cliffs, NJ: Prentice Hall, 1957), p. 43.
2. Graves, R. P., *Life of Hamilton*, vol. 2 (Dublin, 1882), p. 434.
3. Poincaré, H., *Science and Method* (New York: Dover, 1913), p. 52.
4. Paneth, F., *Durham Univ. J.* 2 (1941): 111; reprinted in H. Dingle and G. R. Martin (eds.), *Chemistry and Beyond* (New York: Wiley Interscience, 1965), p. 95.
5. Kekulé, F. A., *Z. Chem.* 3 (1867): 217.
6. Ihde, A. J., *The Development of Modern Chemistry* (New York: Harper & Row, 1964), p. 475.
7. Frey, G. *Proc. Colloq. Div. Phil. Sci., Dordrecht* (1961): 96.
8. Hofmann, A. W., *Zur Erinnerung an vorangegangene Freunde*, vol. 2 (Brunswick, Germany: Vieweg, 1888), p. 99.
9. Kipping, F. S., *Proc. Roy. Soc.* A159 (1936): 147.
10. Kauffmann, G. B., and Beck, A., *J. Chem. Ed.* 39 (1962): 44; Kurnakow, N. S., *Anorg. Chem.* 88 (1914): 109.
11. Sabatier, P., *Ber.* 44 (1911): 2001.
12. Helmholtz, H., *Vorträge und Reden*, 5th ed., vol. 1 (Brunswick, Germany: Vieweg, 1902), pp. 12, 15.
13. Kuhlmann, F., *Ann.* 20 (1847): 223; Mittasch, A., *Salpetersäure aus Ammoniak* (Weinheim, Germany: Verlag Chemie, 1953), p. 15.
14. Le Bon, G., *The Evolution of Matter*, trans. F. Legge, 2nd ed. (London and New York: Walter Scott, 1907), pp. 8, 51; Farber, E., *Chymia* 9 (1964): 198.
15. Farber, E., *Nobel Prize Winners in Chemistry* (New York: Abelard-Schuman, 1963), p. 90.
16. Clausius, R., *Pogg. Ann.* 125 (1865): 353; Koenig, F. C., *Men and Moments in the History of Science*, ed. E. M. Evans (Seattle: University of Washington Press, 1959), p. 57.
17. Le Chatelier, H. L., *Compt. Rend.* 99 (1884): 786; trans. in H. M. Leicester, and H. S. Klickstein, *A Source Book in Chemistry* (New York: McGraw-Hill, 1952), p. 481.
18. Ostwald, W., *Lebenslinien: Eine Selbstbiographie*, vol. 2 (Berlin: Velhagen & Klasing, 1933), p. 160.
19. Rosen, E., *Proc. 10th Intern. Congr. History Sci., Ithaca* (1962): 81; Meyer-Lune, I., *Swedenborg: Eine Studie über seine Entwicklung* (Leipzig, 1922); Stroh, A. H., and Ekelof, G., *Isis* 23 (1935): 459, 520; Toynbee, A. J., *A Study of History*, vol. 10 (Oxford: Oxford University Press, 1954), p. 139.
20. Hahn, O., *Naturw. Rundschau* 15 (1962): 43; *Naturw. Rundschau* 18 (1955): 90.
21. Verkade, P. E., *Theoret. Org. Chem.*, *Papers Kekulé Symposium, London, 1958* (1959): xvi.
22. Anschütz, R., *August Kekulé*, vol. 1 (Berlin: Verlag Chemie, 1925), p. 19. "With the recounting of the structure of benzene, we already see Kekulé using the picture of the snake which bites its own tail for the carbon chain which closes in on itself to a ring." (Tr. by Algis Mickunas)
23. Jossic, Y. F., *1050 Jewelry Designs* (Philadelphia: Lampe, 1946), plate 17-2.

SHIRLEY STRUM, "STARTING OUT"

Why study baboons? One answer is that they may present the best model for understanding human behavior. Another related answer is that what had been known about baboons may not have been accurate. Baboon behavior had been studied, but what had in fact been studied was the behavior of male baboons. Perhaps if females had been studied as carefully, a different picture of baboon behavior might have emerged.

There is a difference in style between Hooke and Strum in recounting their work. Hooke tells us nothing of his background. To him, it would have been irrelevant. Strum evidently thinks that it is part of her story about baboon behavior that she tell us about herself. She describes the animals as graceful, wondrously camouflaged, magnificent, appalling, ugly. Hooke never once mentions the kind of dogs he used or how he felt about them.

Once in the field, Strum is warned not to get out of the van. Danger is everywhere. The baboons are not really accustomed to people; they are accustomed to the van. She probably wondered how baboons could be studied from a van. She tried and felt like a voyeur. She saw much from the van while at the same time sensing that she was missing just as much. She realized after some time that she had to join the troop, getting as close to her subjects as possible. Distance (literal or figurative) from one's experimental subjects does not always work to one's advantage. In the case of primate behavior, it seems a crucial error. Is this because of the nature of primate behavior, or is it true of all scientific methodology? Perhaps animal behavior (ethology) as a discipline is quite different from something like the study of digestion, even though both animal behavior and physiology are parts of biology.

Strum thinks to herself that Matt, the graduate student she was to replace, was embarrassed by the baboons. They make us feel uncomfortable because they force us to realize that they are like us. As Strum found out, it was only when she acted normally in front of the baboons that they really accepted her.

Being autobiographical and being psychoanalytic are two marks of feminist philosophy of science. They are also important characteristics of feminist theory in general.

Starting Out

SHIRLEY STRUM

... I was jerked awake. My driver announced that it was time for some fresh air. Once I was out of the van, the Great Rift Valley of Kenya stretched before me; I could see for at least forty miles in both directions. There were no buildings, no people, just endless vistas. In the distance were the extinct craters of Longonot and Suswa, rising from the floor of the Rift. The scene was daunting. Not even the Pacific had prepared me for the dimensions of the African savannah. This was the Africa I had imagined, not the steaming jungles of common fantasy nor the clog of humanity we had just experienced, but vast grasslands teeming with wildlife. This was the landscape of human evolution. Some say the savannah's special opportunities—its wildlife—attracted our earliest ancestors from the forest. Others suggest that humans were forced out of our original forest home by more successful competitors: monkeys and apes. But it doesn't matter whether we were bright opportunists or desperate fugitives. The feat was monumental. How had the earliest humans managed? Vulnerable and primitive, they had only rudimentary tools, no language and a brain not much bigger than a chimpanzee's. We know a lot about their bodies and their anatomy, but the real key to their survival was their behavior. What was it like? How had they overcome the challenges of their new environment?

This was more than an academic question. We, today, are their descendants, products of an experiment that began three or four million years ago. We have inherited both their talents and their shortcomings. If, in this modern world, we hope to realize our human potential, maximizing strengths and circumventing limitations, we have to know what is in our evolutionary heritage.

It was this quest that had brought me to Africa. In recent years, science has begun to tackle the problem of human origins. Paleoanthropologists have studied and interpreted our predecessor's fossils. Anthropologists, zoologists and psychologists have examined the behavior of our closest living relatives, the nonhuman primates.

Already some scientists felt they had discovered answers about our past. Humans began with an aggressive society that was tight and cohesive. It had to be; there was safety in numbers. But protection went beyond density. Aggressive, powerful males provided a formidable defense against large savannah predators. There was bound to be aggression and competition within the group among the many males as well. Male jostling created a dominance hierarchy in which every male had and knew his place. This hierarchy prevented constant aggressive contests. Size, brute force and dominance status created male leaders who determined where the group went and what it did.

Females played their part. They were the mothers, bearing children and caring for them. But their attention was always focused on the males, the critical core of the group. Females didn't need male political skills since they had little to do with group protection or leadership.

These ideas had impressed more than the scientists. Robert Ardrey and others told the lay public that modern humans were not far removed from our primeval days. A killer ape still lurked inside each of us. Men and women were naturally different in abilities. Even if we wanted a society with greater sexual equality, we might not be able to overcome millions of years of biology.

What if they were right? Worse still, what if they were wrong and we believed them? As a student in the new field of primate behavior, I was in Kenya to study olive baboons, *Papio anubis*. Like the early humans, baboons have met the challenges of savannah life. Few other primates have. Watching baboons might help us understand the problems early humans may have faced and the solutions they found. Baboons are not relics of our human past, yet comparing the options open to two primates on the savannah is more productive than making comparisons between humans and elephant, wildebeest and lion.

If these weren't reasons enough to study baboons, there was another critical one. The model of an aggressive human society controlled by powerful males was an *extrapolation* from the first studies of baboon behavior. Could we really make the link so simply between baboons and humans? Apes are more closely related to us in their biology and anatomy than are monkeys. Which species should we take as our template, chimpanzees or baboons?

I agreed with those who had selected baboons. The human adventure began with our shift to the savannah. It was almost unique in primate history. Almost. Baboons took that fateful step and survived. What could chimpanzees or gorillas or orangutans tell us about what it must have meant?

Although I sided with baboons, I wondered whether baboon society was really governed by aggression, dominance and males. There were grounds for doubt. The pioneering first studies had their shortcomings. They identified only the few adult males, gave them names and watched them carefully as individuals. Females and youngsters were shortchanged, lumped together by age and gender. Perhaps these individuals were more interesting, complex and important than they seemed. I expected so, based on what had been learned about the variety and complexity of behavior in other closely related monkeys and apes in the years since those first baboon studies.

What are baboons really like? How useful are they in our quest to understand ourselves? This was what I hoped to discover.

As we walked back to the van, I was told we were not far from Kekopey, my destination. Kekopey was a 45,000-acre cattle ranch, the home of "my" troop of baboons. These wild animals had already become accustomed to humans. Three years earlier, Bob Harding, the first graduate student to watch them, had christened them the Pumphouse Gang, after the Tom Wolfe book. The name stuck. Like their human namesakes, they spent a lot of time around a pumphouse situated near one of their sleeping sites.

I hung on for dear life as we bumped along toward Kekopey. I was tired and excited. I was also beginning to worry. Now that I was here, armed with my burning intellectual questions, could I really accomplish my task? The realization that I was an unlikely person for such a job was finally sinking in. I was properly trained, with lots of ideas. But what about the rest? Was there anything in my past that indicated I could manage a study of wild baboons?

I was a city girl, born and bred. To make matters worse, I was not athletic or physically active. I'd been camping only once in my life and the first night had been a disaster; I let my imagination run away with fantasies of dangerous beasts about to attack. I'd been a rather isolated only child, always looking for a connection with something bigger. History provided a tangible link to the past for me. I had felt it most strongly when, at the age of eleven, I was taken to the Acropolis. I had experimented with religion too, first a Jewish cultural heritage going back five thousand years and then other religions: Taoism and Buddhism. But it was not until I reached Berkeley as an undergraduate in September 1965 that I finally found my niche. As I lived through the Free Speech movement and the Vietnam War protests, I found myself confronting, over and over again, questions about human nature, about what was innate and impossible to modify and what was flexible and worth changing.

For a while I toyed with abnormal psychology, then sociology. But it was my first cultural anthropology class that finally convinced me: here was the right approach. The course looked at human behavior from a cross-cultural perspective. One class led to another: I decided to major in anthropology.

Then the other shoe dropped. I sat with a thousand other students, mesmerized, as Sherwood Washburn traced the human inheritance back further and further, to the earliest prosimians, those least progressive primates of sixty million years ago. As Washburn held the fossil of a tiny prosimian in his hand for the class to see, I marveled that this minute creature had experienced the world, when it was alive, more the way I did than my own dear cat, Crazy. Like me, it perceived its surroundings in depth and in color. Its delicate primate hands already had finger pads and nails, and its brain had changed and grown to control them. I felt linked not only to a few thousand years of art or culture, but to millions of generations, to something bigger than I had ever imagined existed. . . .

I had originally wanted to study these [patas monkeys] beautiful animals. Patas intrigued me. They live in small groups with only one adult male in each group, and although the males are more than twice the size of the females, they do not dominate group life. Groups are led by the females, who also act as the policers. The male's role is to be on the lookout for possible predators. Taking as high a vantage point as he can find in a tree or bush, he alerts the group of danger, then puts on a diversionary display to attract the predator's attention and runs as fast as he can in the direction opposite to that of the group. Meanwhile the rest of the troop remain silent and motionless in the tall grass, hoping to escape detection. This would be a foolhardy defense if it weren't for a special patas adaptation: male patas are remarkable runners, probably the fastest primates in the world.

Patas survived life on the savannah in a manner completely opposed to the described life-style of baboons. They seemed an anomaly. Why did savannah living produce one set of behaviors in baboons and another in patas? What would it have taken to make our human ancestors more pataslike and less baboonlike? These were questions I proposed to answer in the patas study I wanted to do. At that time, only one brief study of the patas, by Ronald Hall, existed, and I felt optimistic that my proposal would be well received.

Finally, Washburn called me to his office. I could tell by the expression on his face what was about to follow; still, I was shocked. He rejected my idea totally. Patas had been done! There was nothing of great note left to learn, he proclaimed. I agreed that Hall's work was superb, but he had watched patas for only six months. We now considered one thousand hours of observation the minimum standard. Hall had raised important questions, but we still lacked many of those answers. I thought I had produced a convincing case.

By the time I had enough courage to see Washburn again, to ask for his suggestions, I was feeling very low indeed.

BABOONS! I couldn't believe my ears. What did he mean, baboons? They were the *most* studied species of primates. They were the basis of the existing model of early hominids, the one I was dubious about. I couldn't think what else there was to learn about baboons.

Given the situation, there was only one avenue left to me. I decided to salvage the ideas I would have explored in the patas study and adapt them to baboons.

I never learned why Washburn accepted baboons and not patas, but I doubted that even he realized what a productive avenue my baboon study would prove to be.

At the time, though, I wasn't thrilled. I knew about baboons already, from the classes I had taken. The baboons I had seen in films and at the zoo had not impressed me. They had none of the appealing attractiveness of the patas. In fact, in medieval literature, baboons represented the repulsive—the evil spirits, not the good ones. Even today to call someone a baboon is a grave insult. In Kenya, and elsewhere in Africa, baboons are not thought of as wildlife or as valued and protected animals. Legally they are vermin. But I had to admit that this attitude was actually a tribute to their success as a species. Until recently, there were many more baboons than people in Africa, some said. No matter the exact figures, baboons were numerous. I could admire their success, but wondered whether I could ever feel more positive toward them.

Since I was interested in intellectual issues, not cuddly animals, it shouldn't matter, I told myself. Often in my life, even as a child, I'd used intellectual pleasures to transform an unpleasant, difficult or threatening situation. Maybe it would be the same with studying baboons.

Excitement returned as I wrote up my proposal. Whatever imperfections there were in our understanding of baboons,

these animals were of critical importance to interpretations of human evolution. I wanted to "test" the baboon model again, to see whether baboons were as they had been described.

How was I going to do this? I had two tools. The first was to apply new observation techniques to studying the species. These were more rigorous and systematic than the methods Washburn and the others had thought necessary in the era of the first baboon studies. I would also identify all the individuals in the group, not just the adult males, as the early baboon watchers had done. By identifying all the individuals, watching a representative sample of them, giving females equal time with males and using the new observation techniques, I hoped to eliminate any selective biases that might unconsciously have been incorporated into the previous picture of baboon society. Perhaps I would learn something more about how males and females functioned in the group.

Washburn felt that observation alone was not enough. If I wanted to find out how important the males were to the group and what roles females played, I'd have to experiment. At the end of my observational study, I had decided to trap all the males and temporarily hold them captive. That way I could see what the remaining, untrapped females would do. Who would lead, police, protect the troop? Where would the group go, and how would they fare with the neighboring baboons?

As the VW bounced closer and closer to Kekopey, I only hoped that The National Science Foundation, the agency that was funding my project, knew what they were doing with their money. I had with me all the necessary study tools: binoculars, tape recorder, cameras, books about primates and papers describing the previous baboon studies. But would that be enough? In retrospect, I see that it was a strange combination of intellectual fervor, naïveté and a complete ignorance of what it meant to live in Africa that made the whole process of getting to Kekopey merely another turn of the academic grindstone.

———

This was September, the end of the winter months which are cold, dry and overcast. Today the clouds were large billows of white, partially obscuring the intense blue sky. Even the filtered light made me squint in my bath.

I thought about Matt.[1] I had known him only casually in graduate school. He seemed as unlikely a field worker as I was, being a raconteur and a gourmet cook; his interest was primate communication.

Tim and I depended on Matt for our introduction to the Pumphouse Gang. It had taken us this whole week to find them. Only then did I really understand Matt's assurance that the troop, having been observed and followed by two graduate students since 1970, was now accustomed to being observed.

"You want to get *out?*" he had asked incredulously. "Out? Of the *van?*" It was the white VW van the monkeys accepted, not people. According to Matt, danger lurked everywhere. There were poisonous snakes, vicious warthogs who would rather gore you with their tusks than look at you; crazed male buffalo harboring resentment along with stray bullets, ready to take their revenge on any human; there were even large predators. Matt was firm. We must not leave the van.

———

At first I thought it was real concern for our safety that had made us so cautious as we drove around Kekopey looking for the baboons. I didn't mind much; I was distracted by the beauty of the place and by the animals. I had gradually begun to see them more readily—herds of zebra, Thomson's gazelles, impala and eland. To begin with I could spot only the largest animals and had trouble telling different species apart. During the last day or two of this week I had begun to spot the smaller, more secretive creatures: foot-high dik-dik and slightly larger rufous steinbok; bat-eared foxes and blackbacked jackals; reebok and klipspringer—both wondrously camouflaged among the gray granite cliffs. There were also warthogs, hyrax, mongooses and another kind of reebok among the more common animals. I saw very few cows; if it weren't for the water troughs and wire fences, this could be wild Africa, not a commercial ranch.

The sky was alive with birds, not the little brown ones that had bored me in California but brilliantly colored ones, the smallest and the largest I had ever seen. Green-white-orange bee-eaters, orange-black-white hoopoes and lilac-turquoise-white rufous rollers were the first I recognized. Even the starlings were beautiful. Magnificent birds of prey soared on thermals and nested on rocky cliff ledges. There were ugly birds as well: giant ground hornbills, their appalling red wattles resting on sinister black chests, and marabou storks, whose bald heads, heavy bills and pendulous neck pouches were set off by the beautiful neck and shoulder feathers that were used to make fancy boas for 1920s flappers. . . .

. . . [W]e had finally tracked down the Pumphouse Gang. Of course I didn't know one baboon from another, but even I could tell the difference in this troop's tolerance. All the other baboons had fled at the mere sight of the van. As the three of us began to watch, it was as if I ceased to exist. Matt directed all of his comments to Tim, although I was the one about to take over the baboon work. Finally I asked Matt a direct question: Couldn't we move the van a bit closer? The troop was forty yards away and from that distance they looked like dozens of brown bumps spread out over the grassland.

Oh, we could get closer without the troop running off, he'd said, but who knows what the animals might do. To the van? I wondered.

I resigned myself to the distance. While Matt told Tim anecdotes of African dangers narrowly avoided, I sat and watched baboons with my binoculars. I had the eerie feeling of being a Peeping Tom, invading the baboons' privacy and spying on their most intimate behaviors without their permission. The Pumphouse Gang moved from one activity to the next in an orderly way. Daily life seemed to follow a definite routine: sleep, then socializing, followed by feeding, resting, more feeding and more resting. Social activities were interposed, particularly during the midday rest period and just before the day ended at the sleeping cliffs.

Each type of activity was itself composed of many parts, and I began to see just how complicated each one really was. Eating took up the most time. I had expected to be bored—how absorbing is a cow grazing in a field?—but the baboons were fascinating eaters. Now I saw what Washburn had meant about the versatility of the primate hand. The baboons' nimble fingers were into everything, plucking grass blades, digging up roots, selecting the tiniest herb peeking out of the ground cover. Flowers, buds, shoots, berries, seeds and pods all fell victim to these voracious monkeys. They seemed to be eating everything from the ground up. Only later would I discover how selective they really were, how good at choosing the most nutritious part each plant had to offer in each season. Their hands had both power and precision; the opposability of the thumb and fingers was as essential here on the savannah as it had been millions

of years ago when tiny ancestral primates climbed into the forest canopy. Some foods had to be excavated from rock-hard ground; others had to be peeled or seeded. The monkeys used their teeth to help, usually ending up with a litter of debris scattered on the ground and hanging from their long facial hairs.

Their feeding postures varied. Sitting in one place was easiest, but only if there was lots of food within arm's reach. Often the baboons shuffled along on their bottoms from one patch of food to another. Grass heads were more easily harvested from a standing position. Walking from one spot to another was seldom a waste of time, since there was usually something to eat along the way.

Some variations on these basic themes were comical. One medium-sized youngster seemed too lazy to sit up. He lay on his stomach, chin resting on the earth, plucking the grass from in front of his eyes. Unfortunately when he tried to put the food into his mouth, he had to move his whole head up and down, since his jaw rested on solid ground. Many of the baboons had a Groucho Marx crouch, freeing both hands to feed. Double-fisted feeding was common. I didn't know whether this was because of the appeal of the particular food, the sheer bulk that was needed or fear that a more dominant animal would grab the place.

The monkeys didn't appear to share food with one another, not even a mother with her baby. Taking a closer look, I saw little that could be shared: a blade of grass, a small piece of fruit, a flower, even a root just wasn't big enough.

Along with eating came resting. Resting postures were more idiosyncratic than feeding positions. Chin on chest, knees pulled up and hands folded calmly in the lap was a popular position. Sometimes a monkey sat back and leaned against a rock or tree, almost reclining. Big males occasionally found a rock in the shade and lay down on their backs. They looked particularly vulnerable in this position, with chin, neck, belly and genitals exposed. Mothers rested with their babies cradled in their laps, both arms gently wrapped around them for support. Resting often occurred in clusters; several baboons sat with sides or backs touching, or making tentative but neighborly contact with hands, tails or toes.

While many rested, others socialized. Youngsters took the opportunity, when the troop wasn't moving, to play. Grooming was also common. Even my inexperienced eye could see in fact what I had been taught in theory: grooming was intense and had several functions. The first was hygiene. The groomer removed insects, grass burrs, dirt, scabs. Grooming helped wounds to stay clean and open so that they healed more rapidly, and kept the thick, coarse hair from becoming an uncomfortable matted mess. Baboons will groom themselves, but when they can, they get someone else to do it. Far from being a disgusting habit, as it has been viewed by many humans from medieval times until the present, grooming is essential to good health when you live in the wild.

But grooming is also a major social activity, an excuse for individuals to be close to one another, a way to establish or reinforce positive feelings about others. A look at any grooming pair illustrated why. The animal being groomed was completely relaxed, often nearly asleep, luxuriating in the monkey equivalent of a good massage. If attention needed to be paid to some particular spot, it was thrust in the groomer's face. Often an extended arm or leg or a tilted head revealed the next spot that needed grooming. Grooming was usually reciprocal, but how this reciprocity worked wasn't yet obvious to me. It seemed that nearly everyone had someone to groom, and in turn had someone to groom him or her.

I began to realize that I was missing a lot by being inside the van. It was impossible to hear all the sounds, to catch all the subtle gestures or to know whether smells played a role in baboon interactions. It was impossible to follow any individual if he moved far through the troop or went out of sight behind a bush, a ridge or up the cliffs.

What did Matt think about the difficulty of watching baboons from the van? Was he confident that he could really study communication this way? I wanted to talk to him about other things as well. After a year with the troop, did he understand the complexities of what went on? Who decided where the troop went or what it would eat? How did the grooming pairs match up? Why didn't the baboons share their food?

. . . I decided then that Matt was not the person to ask. I wondered if he simply didn't like baboons. Perhaps he wanted to keep his distance, not from fear, but because, somehow, baboons make us all feel uncomfortable. Intellectually we recognize that we are linked to these animals, through their behavior and through the evolution of our biology. While we are fascinated and challenged by them, we are also embarrassed and threatened, as much today as in Victorian times, when Darwin confronted the world with his new set of "facts." . . .

Pumphouse was currently a troop of sixty animals: six adult males, seventeen adult females and thirty-seven immature baboons. There were other baboon troops on Kekopey, but Matt didn't seem to know either how many or how big they were.

My developing skills led me to have even more doubts about Matt. Several times I was sure he was wrong in his identifications. That was not Beth but Harriet, not Marcia but Frieda. To begin with I thought *I* was wrong. It was Dieter, the infant male that Matt pointed out to me, who helped me gain confidence in myself. Where, I wondered, was Dieter's penis? I knew that infant penises were not difficult to see; a bunch of black infants running around all had what looked like a pink fifth leg. Finally I spoke privately with Tim, who, after a few minutes with the binoculars, verified my suspicions. Tim and I changed Dieter's name to Dierdre, but never said anything to Matt.

In retrospect, I see that Matt did me a great service. Left alone, I concentrated on the baboons and began to form my own independent impressions. Given what I saw, or didn't see, I was even more convinced that I had to walk among the baboons in order to do a good study; Matt's performance confirmed this. His timidity made my rudimentary courage seem more subtantial. All in all, comparing myself to Matt, I gained confidence that I could manage, that I *could* study wild baboons. . . .

. . . I had slowly, almost imperceptibly . . . moved into the midst of the troop. I was always careful about how I moved and where I stepped, making sure it wasn't on an infant, who could be sitting half hidden in the grass. I was also always careful at whom I looked; when I came face to face with one of the animals, I'd lower my eyes or turn away my head. It was for this reason that I was unable to wear sunglasses, despite the wind and the blinding light; the first animals to catch a glimpse of me wearing them ran off in obvious terror. Small wonder: to them, the glasses not only covered my own eyes, obliterating important visual communication, but presented them with the biggest, wide-eyed threat they'd ever seen. Above all, I had to be especially careful about exactly where I interposed my body—never between two animals in any kind of interaction. . . .

. . . I followed other individuals, always being careful not to press anyone too closely. I had been warned by other field workers to dress drably and always to wear the same clothes. This was more of a prob-

lem than I had anticipated. We were two degrees south of the equator, at an altitude of nearly 7,000 feet. The wind brought some relief, but added its own burden to my already abused skin. Since the temperature ranged from frigid in the shadow of the sleeping cliffs in the early morning to blistering in the midday sun, I had to dress in layers and peel off. Tank top covered by turtleneck covered by sweatshirt made a bulky but practical outfit. There was no problem with the sweatshirt, but my underlayers were by chance of different colors; I couldn't wear the same dirty clothes day after day.

The baboons seemed not to care what I wore, what color it was or how different I looked from one day to the next, as long as I peeled the layers off slowly, not scaring them by any abrupt movements. They knew me by now, and I shouldn't have been surprised that they did, considering that they could recognize different makes of vehicles from as far as a mile away. . . .

So, pink-nosed and squinting, I became the intrepid baboon watcher, going wherever the troop went, juggling tape recorder, clipboard and binoculars—observing, taking notes, thinking. I finally became comfortable enough to attempt a feat I'd been contemplating for days. It is not only baboons that have to answer the call of nature. At first I'd retreat behind the VW to relieve myself, but now the van was often miles away, and I hated to leave and miss something.

I decided I would pee on the spot. Trying not to move too quickly, I lowered my shorts. So far, so good. Suddenly every baboon around stopped dead in its tracks. They stared at me in wonder as the sound reached them. I thought I understood what was going on; up until then, I'd arrived, watched and left. They hadn't seen me eat, rest, drink or sleep. They hadn't been fooled into thinking I was a baboon. They knew I was human, but they had never been so close to one before and maybe they thought humans didn't have to pee. They stared, but not one ran away, and when I pulled up my shorts, they lost interest. The next time, they didn't react at all. As the baboons relaxed around me, I gradually relaxed around them. But even so, I was determined to preserve my role as a nonentity within the troop, never to interact with the animals, to be simultaneously tolerated but unobtrusive. It was natural that I found myself constantly wanting to reach out to them, to touch an infant, return the play invitation of a juvenile, groom a new baby, but to interact would change the nature of the study. Although I could learn a lot about the animals from their behavior toward humans, the approach that I championed insisted that the most important insights would come if their human observer always let the baboons be baboons, allowing them to remain as unaffected in their life with one another as possible.

I must admit it was a little different with Ray. I suppose that in his eyes, as in mine, we had a special relationship. We had both entered the troop at the same time, with the same patience and caution. Certainly our acceptance within it showed a number of parallels. One day, Ray surprised me. Socially speaking, he was at the end of a rather long losing streak. I was dutifully recording his bluffing interaction with Big Sam and Sumner when, without warning, he turned and rushed at me. I was more baffled than alarmed; none of the baboons had ever been aggressive toward me, even when they were being aggressive with one another. This, I had reasoned, was another benefit of not interacting with the troop: I was neither friend nor foe.

Yet here was Ray, making straight for me. There was no mistaking what he meant, and it took me only a few long seconds to figure out what was happening. Ray wasn't threatening me; he was soliciting my help. He wanted me to support him against the other males!

I checked his gestures quickly to make sure. There was no doubt about it: he was slapping the ground with his hand, looking first at me, then staring at the two males, then back at me to see what I was going to do.

This handsome, powerful male struggling to become part of the troop spoke strongly to something in me. I badly wanted to help him, but I couldn't. I signaled this by turning away completely, leaving Ray to handle the situation on his own. Suddenly I realized how far I had come from those early days . . . I was tougher, leaner, braver, but the biggest change had been in my attitude toward the animals. Ray won his struggle alone, but I shall never forget how honored I felt by the compliment he paid me.

The day ended as so many had ended before, with the fading light signaling that it was time for the animals to return to their sleeping cliffs. There was nothing different about the day; I was different. My mind was full of new questions and my heart of new emotions.

NOTES

1. Matt and Tim were graduate students from Berkeley. [Ed. note]

FRANKLIN H. PORTUGAL AND JACK S. COHEN, "THE EVOLUTION OF MODERN GENETICS"

In Chapter 2, we will explore the logical-positivist philosophy of science in the works of Hempel, Oppenheim, and Brodbeck. Logical positivism, as we have seen in our discussion of Kekulé, makes a distinction between the context (logic) of discovery and the context (logic) of justification. But there are other important aspects of the positivist philosophy of science.

The positivist views science as gradually approaching the truth by means of a self-corrective method. The details of this method, positivists remind us, are yet to be worked out. In principle, it is self-corrective, in large part because its claims are objective. An objective claim is quantitative and, to some extent because of this, is intersubjectively verifiable or intersubjectively falsifiable. That is, scientists can agree on the truth and falsity of the claims. (The distinction between verifiable and falsifiable will be discussed in Chapter 3, especially in the selections from Carnap and Popper.)

What exactly does *quantitative* mean? The usual sense is "able to be put into (or expressed by) numbers." What makes something expressible in or by numbers is measurement. If something can be measured in a manner that is accurate (gives the right answer) and precise (gives the same answer when the measurement is repeated), it is measurable in a way that is suitable to science. Notice that an object such as a table can be measured over and over with a very similar result. Any differences in measurement can be attributed to a flaw in our ability to measure or in the measuring system (yardstick, our eyes, our ability to lay the yardstick down just at the right place) itself. We assume that what is measured stays the same. This is a crucial assumption for science. It can be put another way. We assume that the measuring system does not affect what is measured. Without these assumptions, we would need a different sense for *quantitative*.

There are different ways to measure. Each way to measure is also a way to classify things. Here are five different ways to measure.

1. We can count members in a group to find out how many there are if the members are recognizably the same over time and differ from one another in a way that we can recognize. Counting is usually not considered measurement, but it does give us a measure of how many objects are in a group.

2. We might measure (classify) everything to determine weight. Everything would be either 1 gram or not 1 gram. This would result in what is called a dichotomous classification. (Although not done by traditional measuring, the dichotomy between living things and nonliving things made by vitalists is an example of such a measurement.)

3. Suppose that we showed a picture of a rainbow to a person known to have a finely honed ability to discriminate among shades of colors. We tell that person to list seven and only seven distinct shades from most red to most yellow.

The items on the resulting list will be distinct. No two will overlap, and no item will be listed more than once. This sort of measuring scale is called nominal.

4. Another sort of measuring scale is called ordinal. A good example of an ordinal scale is the one used to classify wind force, the Beaufort scale. Hurricanes are given a 12; strong breezes, a 6; and calm, a zero. Hurricanes have more force than a calm breeze; strong breezes, however, are not half the strength of a hurricane.

5. The interval scale is the one used most often in science. Weighing objects on a balance results in an interval scale. Objects have weights that are different, but the weights can be very, very close to each other, differing by mere thousandths of a gram; the weights on this scale are said to be continuous. An object weighing 4 grams is twice as heavy as an object weighing 2 grams. We can also adjust our balance to make it as precise as we like.

According to some positivistic philosophers, what science does is best seen as taking ordinary experience, subjecting it to some form of measurement so that a scale is created, and then finding numerical relationships within that scale and between that scale and other scales.

To a positivist, claims such as the following would be examples of claims that are not quantifiable enough to be intersubjectively verified or falsified:

There are houses haunted by ghosts.

My grandmother's cure for headaches always works.

Many people have been abducted and then returned by visitors from outer space.

Beethoven is a better composer than Mozart.

Claims such as the following would be accepted by positivists as either intersubjectively verifiable or intersubjectively falsifiable:

My car is brown.

The earth is smaller than Jupiter.

The age of reptiles was brought to an end by a large extraterrestrial object smashing into the earth.

The claim about Beethoven is often seen as a claim about a person's musical preferences and not about anything objective in the music. The theory about the death of the dinosaurs was initially the theory of just a few scientists. But they were able to convince other scientists that the theory was very likely correct. They did it by appealing to facts that were available to all. No one would have claimed, as with the statement comparing Beethoven and Mozart, that their beliefs reflected only their preferences and not something that happened in the world.

Objectivity, in the positivist view, is guaranteed by the scientific method's avoiding the vagaries of external factors. (We will see this in Brodbeck's spirited defense of the deductive model of explanation in Chapter 2.) The positivists point out that no matter how scientific theories are built, they are tested against facts, and either they help to predict accurately or they do not. When they do predict accurately, they are accepted, and when they do not, they are rejected. (This is roughly the view presented by Carnap in Chapter 3.) The details of theory construction and prediction and rules for claiming that a prediction is "good enough" remain to be worked out by a thorough examination of science, philosophy, logic, and, to a lesser extent, the history of science. Thus the positivist sets the program for future work in the history and philosophy of science.

With this firmly in mind, we can move on to Portugal and Cohen's brief look at part of the history of genetics.

To begin, let us examine one set of experiments, published in 1866 by Mendel (1822–1884). He crossed tall pea plants that had bred true for tall, that is, bred only tall plants for many generations, with short plants that had bred true for short. Let us represent this cross as tall × short. All the resulting plants were tall. When Mendel then crossed these tall plants with themselves, that is, tall × tall (called selfing), the resulting ratio of tall to short plants was three tall plants to one short plant. When Mendel took these short plants and crossed them with other short plants (called a testcross—when a testcross is made with the actual parents, it is called a backcross), he got all short plants, all of which then bred true. A similar testcross of the talls yielded a ratio of two tall plants to one short plant, and *not* all of the tall plants bred true.

Mendel explained these crosses using three hypotheses that employed some technical terms. We have already used the expression "breeds true." In addition, Mendel refers to "dominant," "recessive" and "hybrid." Mendel knew from experiments that tall plants when crossed with short plants never yielded more short than tall plants. He also knew that smooth peas crossed with wrinkled peas never yielded more wrinkled than smooth peas. Mendel used the term *dominant* for the traits that usually predominated in number. The traits that were not dominant he called *recessive*. Thus tall was dominant over short, and short was recessive to tall. Mendel, and others, noted that while some tall plants when crossed with other tall plants gave only tall plants ("breeding true"), some tall plants, when crossed with other tall plants, yielded some short plants. These sorts of tall plants with the ability to yield short plants were called *hybrids*. They did not breed true. This observation held true for all the dominant traits. Hence smooth plants might or might not breed true, yellow might or might not breed true, and so on.

Now let us examine Mendel's hypotheses.

No blending occurs. Mendel assumed that the traits of peas were best described as either tall or short, its seeds' textures either smooth or wrinkled, its cotyledons (seed covers) green or yellow, and so on. In other words, for the purposes of his experiment, the traits of peas could be considered mutually exclusive (no medium-sized plants, no chartreuse plants). Nor did the factors of inheritance themselves blend.

The factors of inheritance are particulate and maintain their integrity. Mendel assumed that each trait, such as height, was determined by a *pair* of factors and that one factor was contributed by the male and one factor was contributed by the female. The sex of the contributor made no difference to how the factor worked. They worked side by side in pairs and not by combining in any physical way. (An analogy is that when young children play, they play next to each other, not truly *with* each other, even though somehow a house of blocks may get built.)

Probability governs the inheritance of the traits examined. If we represent the two factors determining height as *T* and *t*, then according to Mendel, there would be two ways for the factors to combine to make a plant tall. A plant could have the factors *TT*, or a plant could have the factors *Tt*. There was only one way to be short, *tt*. (Since about 1909, the factors referred to by Mendel have been called genes; what we have symbolized as *TT*, *Tt*, or *tt* has been known as the genotype; and the trait of the plant, the way it looks to us, has been called the phenotype.) Mendel realized that he could correctly predict the ratios he found in his crosses by using the assumption that in a cross, the factors assorted randomly, following the laws of random distribution. Hence for any cross, one got all the possible combinations of factors. Thus if one crossed a *Tt* pea plant with another *Tt* pea plant (both would look tall), one would get some plants that were *TT*, some that were *Tt*, and some that were *tt*. The ratios of *TT* to *Tt* to *tt* were determined only by chance. In the cross just proposed, the ratio would be one *TT* to two *Tt* to one *tt*. This is easy to illustrate.

A male *Tt* plant makes two sorts of pollen. One kind is *T*, and the other is *t*. A female plant makes two kinds of eggs. One kind is *T*, and the other is *t*. The meeting of pollen types and egg types is governed by chance. So there will be four possibilities:

1. Male *T* meeting female *t*

2. Male *t* meeting female *T*

3. Male *T* meeting female *T*

4. Male *t* meeting female *t*

There are two ways for a plant to become *Tt*—(1) and (2). There is only one way for a plant to become *TT* or *tt*—(3) or (4). Thus one would expect that there would be twice as many *Tt* plants as *TT* or *tt*. Therefore, since *TT* plants and *Tt* plants both look tall, one would expect three times as many tall plants as short plants as a result of this cross. One might have assumed that a *T* female meeting a *t* male would yield a different result from *T* male meeting a *t* female. In the case of peas and height (and other factors), this turns out not to be true.

As to what the actual *physical* mechanism governing heredity was, Mendel was mum. He was satisfied with his ability to predict the results of crosses by using the laws of probability. Whatever the physical mechanism behind heredity would turn out to be, it would have to account for why the rather simple laws of probability worked to give such good predictions. The success of Mendel's hypothesis showed that one did not need to know much about factors of heredity to use them to predict the results of crosses, that is, to have a successful theory. For example, neither the chemical composition of the factors nor where, precisely, the factors were located mattered if being able to predict the results of crosses was the criterion for a successful theory.

Whether Mendel failed to *explain* the crosses depends on what we take a scientific explanation to be. This question will be addressed in Chapter 2. Naturally, what remained for parties interested in a full account of heredity was to find out exactly what the factors were and how they worked.

Mendel continued assuming that the factors were contributed equally and randomly by the two sexes of the plants under consideration. Thus when he began to work on a plant that developed by apomixis (the embryo forms from female tissue alone without meiosis or fertilization), Mendel falsely believed that *he* was controlling the fertilization. It is no wonder that he could not account for the results and could not convince others he had discovered general laws of heredity.

Mendel's results are often put in the form of two laws:

1. *The law of segregation:* Genes exist in pairs in individuals. In the formation of gametes (eggs or sperm), each gene separates (segregates) from the other member of the pair, passing into a different gamete. Thus each gamete has only one of each kind of gene. Which kind of gene it gets is determined by chance alone.

2. *The law of independent assortment:* The distribution of one pair of genes into gametes is independent from the distribution of any other pair of genes.

Thus in a cross between plants with wrinkled green seeds and smooth yellow seeds, the factors for wrinkled/smooth separate independently from the factors for green/yellow. If one had the factors *wwgg* for wrinkled green and *WWGG* for smooth yellow, this would yield the following kinds of gametes: for wrinkled green; *wg,* for smooth yellow, *WG;* for smooth green, *Wg;* and for wrinkled yellow, *wG.* If there were *not* independent assortment, one might get only *WG* for smooth yellow or only *wg* for wrinkled green. The explanation for that state of affairs would probably be quite complicated.

Two things are worth noting about the laws. They nicely summarize what takes a long time to say in narrative form. It is even easier to express the laws and the narrative in a mathematical form. You are probably all familiar with the Punnett square. Here are representations of two of Mendel's crosses:

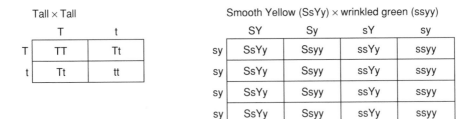

Tall × Tall

	T	t
T	TT	Tt
t	Tt	tt

Smooth Yellow (SsYy) × wrinkled green (ssyy)

	SY	Sy	sY	sy
sy	SsYy	Ssyy	ssYy	ssyy
sy	SsYy	Ssyy	ssYy	ssyy
sy	SsYy	Ssyy	ssYy	ssyy
sy	SsYy	Ssyy	ssYy	ssyy

These are pictorial representations of probabilities. They indicate that mathematically stated laws are concise and clear. It is no wonder many scientists consider them to be the ultimate in scientific explanation.

Now let us return to Portugal and Cohen's history of genetics. Their quotation from Bateson makes the point that the goal of genetics was to find the physical basis of heredity. Mendelian factors were mere abstractions until they could be tied to the reality of chromosomes. In current terminology, the sorts of things that Mendel called hereditary units or factors we call theoretical entities. The terms we use to refer to these entities we call theoretical terms. Theoretical entities play an important role in scientific explanation—indeed, in all explanation.

An example will help make this plain. Suppose that your office is in a basement, has no windows, and is insulated very well against outside noises. You look up and notice that one of your co-workers, George, has just come in and is dripping wet. You assume that it is raining out. Put somewhat inflatedly, you have explained a fact, George's being soaked to the skin, using a theoretical term, *rain,* which refers to the theoretical entity rain. You may object that rain is not an abstraction. You are partly right. There are circumstances when rain is perfectly visible. In this case, it is not—and this is very important. Whether something is theoretical or not is a function of circumstance and the language we use given those circumstances.

To continue with our story, you could go outside and see the rain. It would be as if you made a prediction: "If I am right and rain is the explanation for George's dripping clothes, then if I go outside, I will see rain." This would be the check on the theoretical explanation that it is rain that explains the wet co-worker. Notice that even if we would never put such a situation in these words, we do, in fact, do these sorts of things. And these sorts of things are basically what the positivists say that scientists do in a very orderly and logical (methodical) fashion.

At the turn of the twentieth century, Mendel's units were still theoretical. Cytology was able to suggest that these units were real. There was nothing abstract about cytology. So if cytological advances suggested that hereditary units were parts of chromosomes, there was no reason to doubt that the units were real even if they could not yet be seen. What were the cytological advances? Two scientists, William Sutton and Theodore Boveri, working independently (about 1902), realized that if Mendel's factors were assumed to be on chromosomes, this would explain the random assorting seen (or, more accurately, inferred) in many cross-ing experiments because in mitosis and meiosis, the destination of any particular chromosome is random. Portugal and Cohen refer to Sutton as having given a mechanical explanation for the transmission of hereditary traits.

By the 1920s, genetics was a well-established discipline in large part because of the ability to tie Mendel's abstractions to visible reality. Theoretical terms were now given a realistic interpretation. Whether or not such interpretations are nec-essary or, for that matter, even possible is an issue of current interest in the phi-losophy of science. The question is often put, "How realistic must scientific theo-ries be?" To answer this question, we need some background on realism.

Realism is a family of views:

1. That the world is the way that we see it—this is often called naive or direct real-ism.

2. That only some of the world (what have come to be called the primary quali-ties—defined by Merchant) is the way that we experience it. The hardness of a table is real. The color of a table is not real. The hardness is a property of the table. The color is a property of us. This view is often called representational realism.

3. That theoretical terms cannot serve their function in theories if they are not assumed to refer to things in the world. This sense of realism sets research for science: Find the referents of theoretical terms. Genetics is often interpreted as a discipline that became realistic in its research of the gene.

The denial of the third position has recently come to be called antirealism.

Realism fits better with giving mechanisms as the goal of science. Refer to the list of senses for reduction and see which best fits realism. It is possible to claim that the job of science is mere prediction, that explanation is the job of philosophy. Such a view is called instrumentalism. This view means that one does not have to be concerned with the existence of theoretical entities because the need for refer-ence is generated by a need for explanation. If prediction is all that is needed for science, then whether entities mentioned in theories actually exist is not a relevant question. In fact, according to instrumentalism, scientific theories do not consist of meaningful statements. What makes up any scientific theory is just a collection of calculating (predicting) devices. To an instrumentalist, the only question worth asking is, "Does the theory make accurate predictions?" Operationalism, a view similar to instrumentalism, holds that scientific theories are made up of statements whose meanings are given by operational definitions, which we explained in our discussion of Tiedemann and Gmelin. How we make predictions, especially where mathematics is required, will vary with the sophistication of our mathematics. Also, what we accept as good enough predictions may vary from era to era. These are two senses of the position known as conventionalism. A third sense is men-tioned below in the discussion of antirealism.

Looking for the biochemical basis of genetics, as in researching the structure of DNA, would also be a reductionistic approach. The history of genetics seems to begin with abstraction and lead to the principles of biochemistry.

Antirealism and approaches to explanation that stress understanding via contextual framework go well together. If theoretical terms need not refer to anything, then very likely what makes an explanation acceptable must be what it does for us in terms of allaying discomfort that comes with lack of knowledge. If we see the power of an explanation in its psychological effect in minimizing discomfort, we will place less emphasis on the requirement that the theoretical entities used by the theory actually exist.

If theories are not grounded in reality by the existence of their theoretical terms, accepting one theory instead of a competitor may be based solely on psychological grounds—which theory makes us feel better about dealing with the data. Since what makes people "feel better" is often culturally relative, antirealism lends itself to a relativistic view of science. That is, which theory we accept, how we view science, may reflect nothing more than the accepted conventions of a society. This is a third sense of conventionalism, although all three senses dovetail. Con-ventionalism, instrumentalism, and antirealism are a closely related family of views.

In Chapter 4, we will focus in detail on the contemporary debate between realism and antirealism.

The Evolution of Modern Genetics

FRANKLIN H. PORTUGAL AND JACK S. COHEN

... The start of the twentieth century marked the beginning of an intensive period of investigation into the mechanisms of heredity. Interest in the processes by which parents transmit characteristics to offspring had, as we have seen, arisen much earlier. But it was only at the turn of the century that a sufficiently broad base of information in diverse areas had been established, enabling geneticists to construct theories that are still accepted today.

From Franklin H. Portugal and Jack S. Cohen, *A Century of DNA* (Cambridge, MA: MIT Press, 1977), pp. 109–116. Copyright © 1977 by The Massachusetts Institute of Technology.

What was commonplace during the earlier period was the development of ideas about heredity that were difficult to prove. How, for example, would it be possible to show clearly that the "tension" of a postulated idioplasm resulted in the transmission of specific characteristics? In those cases where experiments were possible, the results were negative, such as Galton's testing of the gemmule concept by the transfusion of animal blood. Yet these early theories had value, for they helped focus attention on extremely fundamental biological processes.

Progress on important scientific problems may come from unexpected quarters. When this happens, however, it frequently takes longer for contemporary scientists to recognize the significance of the work and to accept it. One of the most outstanding examples of such a situation was the discovery of a predictable transfer of characteristics from parents to offspring by a relatively obscure Moravian priest named Gregor Mendel. It was this discovery with plants that laid the groundwork for the intensive studies in genetics in the early part of the twentieth century.

Gregor Johann Mendel was born in 1822 in the village of Heinzendorf in northern Moravia. At the time, this area was part of Austria; today it is the part of Czechoslovakia that borders on Poland. Though Mendel was the only son of a family of peasants, he was able to gain a thorough education. His intelligence was obvious even to his first schoolteacher, Thomas Makytta, as well as to the village priest, Johann Schreiber. Mendel's later studies in natural sciences at the Philosophical Institute at Olomouc and agricultural sciences at the Philosophical Institute at Brno also gained attention. When his family became unable to support any further school studies, Mendel did the only thing possible at that time to continue them: he applied in 1843 for admission as a novice to the Augustinian Monastery. Four years later he became a priest. Despite Mendel's promise as a student, his scholastic record was uneven. In 1850, for example, he failed an examination for a teaching certificate. From 1851 to 1853, Mendel spent four terms at the University of Vienna where his performance was not outstanding.

Animal and plant breeding attracted great interest in Moravia, a predominantly agricultural region. In 1840, the Congress of German Agriculturalists and Foresters had taken place there, attended by 383 representatives from twelve European countries.

Details of the congress were published in 1841, and the one hundred topics presented in the book attest to the level of knowledge in these areas in the first half of the nineteenth century. Of particular interest is the fact that one of the organizers of the congress was F. C. Napp, the abbot of the Augustinian Monastery, Mendel's superior, and a member of the Agricultural Society, who fully supported and encouraged Mendel's interest in heredity. F. Diebl, who published a book on the breeding (hybridization) of plants in 1835, also had a considerable influence on Mendel: The students of the Brno Philosophical Institute where Professor Diebl provided the lectures on agriculture and pomiculture, studied Diebl's textbook in four volumes. Among those students in 1846 was also Gregor Mendel. Diebl described plant breeding in detail. He explained how a plant breeder obtained cultured forms of wild plants. According to him, the improvement was achieved through artificial pollination first of all. He also described the crossing technique and the blossom anatomy. After pollination, selection was described, followed by the description of multiplication of seeds.[1]

With this interest in hybridization established, we find that at the University of Vienna Mendel mainly studied plant sciences and physics. In the plant sciences, he was fortunate to have F. Unger as a lecturer. The latter's lectures entitled "Anatomy and Physiology of Plants and Practices with Microscope and Organization of Experiments in Physiology" were published in 1855. This book was considered one of the best available at the time. Unger's lectures began with the teachings of Matthias Schleiden and Theodor Schwann who emphasized the cellular nature of both plant and animal tissue. Unger was influenced by the modern developments in chemistry and, in turn, relayed this interest to his students.

But most of all, Unger was involved in the concepts of hybrid formation. In 1846, he had written in reference to hybrids that "embryo formation determined from both sides (i.e., both parents) represents the middle way."[2] Later he further emphasized,

Without dispute the greatest influence upon the production and improvement of cultural plants was exerted by the sexual crossing of closely related culture species and varieties of one or different species. Through these the middle forms were created, which thereupon with the mixture of paternal characters produced the one-sided formation of one part of the plant or the other, enabling in this way greater usefulness.[3]

But Unger also noted that the mechanisms by which species changes occurred and hybrids were produced remained unknown. In 1854, after returning to Brno, Mendel began his now classical experiments on pea breeding and the formation of hybrids, which were eventually published in 1866.

Mendel noted,

Among all the numerous experiments made, not one has been carried out to such an extent and in such a way as to make it possible to determine the number of different forms under which the offspring of hybrids appear, or to arrange these forms with certainty according to their separate generations, or definitely to ascertain their statistical relations.[4]

He undertook studies using artificial fertilization of pea plants. He chose these plants for several reasons: they had certain constant traits that were easily distinguishable, the hybrids were perfectly fertile, the plants were resistant to interference by foreign pollen, they were easily cultivated, there was only a short growth period, and, most important, artificial fertilization almost always succeeded. The traits that Mendel selected to follow included differences in seed shape, seed coloration, pod shape and color, flower position, and stem length.

Basically what Mendel did was to cross fertilize a plant carrying one trait, such as smooth seed, with another variety carrying a different trait for the same character, such as wrinkled seed (Figure 1). The offspring obtained, whether as the seed or the plant, was called the F_1 generation. For each of the characters selected, Mendel obtained an F_1 generation that was always of one type. Thus, the F_1 generation for the seed experiment above always gave a smooth seed. When the plants from these seeds were allowed to self-fertilize, a second generation was produced (F_2) in which 75 percent of the seeds were smooth and only 25 percent were wrinkled. Thus, Mendel had demonstrated two points that held true for the other characteristics he investigated. First, in the formation of the hybrid generation, one parental trait (or factor) remained hidden. In the F_2 generation, this factor reappeared. Second, it was possible to predict and quantitate the number of offspring in the F_2 generation with each specific factor. Mendel wrote,

Those traits that pass into hybrid association entirely or almost entirely unchanged, thus themselves representing the traits of the hybrid, are termed dominant, and those that become latent in the association, recessive. The word "recessive" was chosen because the traits so designated recede or disappear entirely in the hybrids, but reappear unchanged in their progeny. . . .[5]

Thus, Mendel demonstrated that the hybrid offspring from parents that possessed different traits for the same characteristic produced germ cells in which the parental traits segregated (separated). In the second generation, the particular trait carried by each of the two germ cells that formed the offspring, in turn, determined what the character would be. This was to be termed the *principle of segregation.*

The publication of Mendel's work in the *Proceedings of the Society of Natural Sciences* in Brno attracted little attention. Certainly

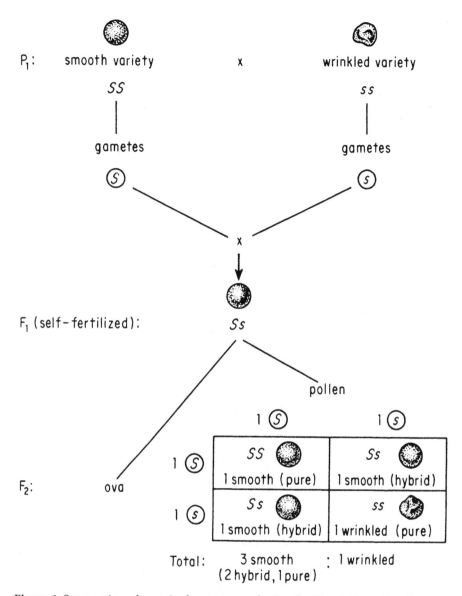

Figure 1 Segregation of genetic characters producing the Mendelian ratios. *Source:* Strickberger, M., *Genetics,* 3d ed., p. 106. © 1985. Reprinted by permission of Prentice Hall, Upper Saddle River, New Jersey.

no relationship between the phenomenon Mendel observed for pea plants and nuclein (or DNA) was noted. Mendel corresponded for several years with Karl Nägeli about his work, but this correspondence also evoked little response. In part, the correspondence failed because Mendel chose to discuss fur-

ther experiments with the hawkseed, *Hieracium.* Unfortunately, Mendel had no way of knowing that this plant produced embryos by an exceptional process and therefore did not adhere to his predictions based on the studies with pea plants. It is probable that one main reason for the failure of Mendel's work to gain attention arose from the fact that too little was known about the nucleus, the chromosomes, and fertilization. Until this information was firmly established through the efforts of many investigators in the latter half of the nineteenth century, it was not possible to evaluate properly the significance of Mendel's work.

At the turn of the century, three botanists reported findings that verified Mendel's studies. The three were Carl Correns, Erich von Tschermak, and Hugo De Vries. Each claimed to have carried out his studies independently of the others and without the knowledge of Mendel's earlier studies. Correns, for example, stated,

I thought that I had found something new. But then I convinced myself that the Abbot Gregor Mendel in Brünn, had, during the sixties, not only obtained the same result through extensive experiments with peas, which lasted for many years, as did De Vries and I, but had also given exactly the same explanation, as far as that was possible in 1866.[6]

De Vries wrote in a letter,

After finishing most of these experiments I happened to read L. H. Bailey's "Plant Breeding" of 1895. In the list of literature of this book, I found the first mention of Mendel's now celebrated paper, and looked it up and studied it.[7]

The process by which Mendel's earlier studies were brought to light by these three scientists has been termed by historians the "rediscovery" of Mendel. In this respect it is interesting, therefore, to mention the following points: Correns was a graduate student with Nägeli, with whom Mendel corresponded about the hybridization studies. Eric von Tschermak was the grandson of Eduard Fenzl with whom Mendel had studied botany and who, in 1861, along with Unger, had been elected to honorary membership in the Natural Science Society—the same one that published Mendel's paper.

While no specific documentation has been found, it does not appear unlikely that Correns and von Tschermak might have heard of Mendel earlier. Nevertheless, what is important is that Mendel's experiments were confirmed and the significance of the work was recognized after more than thirty years' delay.

Within a few years after this verification of Mendel's work, the relationship between the chromosomes (but not DNA) and Mendelian genetics was established. In 1891, Hermann Henking had reported an unusual chromatinlike element that lagged behind the other chromosomes when they separated during mitosis.[8] By 1902, this chromatin particle was identified as an important accessory chromosome that was thought to determine the sex of offspring.[9] In the same year, these initial observations linking one hereditary determinant to the chromosomes were generalized and extended by W. S. Sutton, a graduate student with E. B. Wilson at Columbia. Sutton never finished his graduate work but eventually received an M.D. degree and later went on to become a practicing surgeon. His work depended on many separate observations on the cytology and histology of the cell made by previous investigators, and it succeeded due to the careful choice of cell material for study—the spermatocytes of *Brachystola magna* (the great "lubber" grasshopper). These cells contain eleven pairs of easily distinguishable chromosomes together with the unpaired sex-determining chromosome. As a result, Sutton could readily follow the stages of meiosis or reduction division as they occurred in the cells. In answer to Bateson's statement, "We want to know the whole truth of the matter: we want to know the physical basis, the inward and essential nature, the causes as they are sometimes called, of heredity. We want also to know the laws which the outward and visible phenomena obey."[10] Sutton declared from his studies that hybrid formation resulted from the mechanics of chromosome separation.[11] Perhaps the most important point with regard to Mendel's observations on hybrid formation was that "many points were discovered which strongly indicate that the position of the bivalent chromosomes . . . is purely a matter of chance . . . and hence that a large number of different combinations of maternal and paternal chromosomes are possible in the mature germ-product of an individual."[12] The union of germ cells, during fertilization, each with half the normal number of chromosomes and containing different proportions of maternal and paternal chromosomes, produced the different combinations of characteristics that Mendel had observed. In other words, Sutton provided a mechanical explanation, based on cytological examination, for the transmission of hereditary characteristics. Sutton then continued, "The constant size differences observed in the chromosomes of *Brachystola* early led me to the suspicion . . . that the individual chromosomes . . . play different roles in development. . . . Accepting this conclusion we should be able to find an exact correspondence between the behavior in inheritance of any chromosome and that of the characters associated with it in the organism."[13] Anticipating the work of geneticists over the next decade or two, Sutton maintained,

We have not before inquired whether an entire chromosome or only a part of one is to be regarded as the basis of a single allelomorph [unit character]. The answer must unquestionably be in favor of the latter possibility, for otherwise the number of distinct characters possessed by an individual could not exceed the number of chromosomes in the germ-products, which is undoubtedly contrary to fact. . . . It is conceivable that the chromosome may be divisible into smaller entities (somewhat as Weismann assumes) . . . and may be dominant or recessive independently.[14]

NOTES

1. V. Orel, J. Rod, and M. Vavra, "Animal and Plant Breeders in Moravia before Mendel," *Folia Mendeliana* 6 (1971): 38.
2. V. Orel, "Mendel and New Scientific Ideas at the Vienna University," *Folia Mendeliana* 7 (1972): 33.
3. Ibid., 34.
4. A. H. Sturtevant, *A History of Genetics*, (New York: Harper & Row, 1965), p. 12.
5. C. Stern and E. R. Sherwood, *Origin of Genetics* (San Francisco, Freeman, 1966), p. 9.
6. Ibid., p. 120.
7. Ibid., p. 133.
8. H. Henking, "Über Spermatogenese bei *Pyrrhocoris apterus*," *Zeit. Wissen. Zool.* 51 (1891): 685–736.
9. C. E. McClung, "Notes on the Accessory Chromosome," *Anat. Anz.* 20 (1901): 220–226.
10. W. Bateson, "Problems of Heredity as a Subject for Horticultural Investigation," *J. Roy. Hort. Soc.* 24 (1900): 2.
11. W. S. Sutton, "On the Morphology of the Chromosome Group in *Brachystola magna*," *Biol. Bull.* 4 (1902): 24–39.
12. W. S. Sutton, "The Chromosomes in Heredity," *Biol. Bull.* 4 (1903): 233.
13. Ibid., 235.
14. Ibid., 240.

EXERCISES

1. Which of the articles gives the best version of the scientific method? Are different methods being used? Do they vary from time period to time period? Or is the variation more a function of what is being studied?
2. What are objectivity and subjectivity? Give examples from the articles.
3. Compare Portugal and Cohen's history to Merchant's.

4. Suppose that Farber is right in thinking that dreams and visions have played an important role in the history of chemistry. Would that make chemistry any less a science than physics? Suppose that another historian, Shmarber, comes along and shows that dreams and visions played an important role in the history of physics, and so on. Would we then lose what is distinctive about science?

5. Take any of the philosophical concepts defined in this chapter (realism, reductionism, measurement, and so on), and apply it to some episode in a science not mentioned here—for example, William Harvey on blood flow, Snow on discovering the cause of cholera, or Leverier on the discovery of Uranus. Then do the same for a social science.

2

Scientific Explanation

Why is heart disease such a killer? How can we determine the age of a tree? How do computers work? These are all examples of questions with scientific answers. The answers will count as scientific explanations. Science seems to do so much and so much so well that it makes sense to understand what, if anything, separates science from other ways of knowing and other ways of answering questions.

What are some answers to why heart disease is such a killer? Too many people eat foods high in saturated fats. Too many people fail to exercise properly. Too many people smoke.

We all have enough information to know that these answers are acceptable as far as they go. But we all know that to be truly scientific, they should go further.

In this chapter, we will look at a number of answers to the question "What are the marks of a scientific explanation?" None of the answers proposed will tell us what counts as the right scientific explanation. In other words, we have to distinguish the question "What is a scientific explanation?" from the question "What is the right (or acceptable) scientific explanation?" This latter question will be the topic of Chapter 3, confirmation.

As we examine the various answers offered, we will see that the question about scientific explanation is tied to other concepts that play crucial roles in science. Among them are prediction, law, context, model, and probability. The chapter is basically a series of replies and rejoinders to the positivist claim that scientific explanation is best seen as deduction. This is the view of Hempel and Oppenheim in their article "The Logic of Explanation." May Brodbeck tries to expand their view in order to defend it against criticisms leveled against it by Michael Scriven. The same sorts of criticisms made by Scriven are refined and revised by Nancy Cartwright and Bas van Fraassen. Mary Hesse is critical of the positivist position primarily for its failure to see the proper role of metaphor in scientific explanation.

As you read, you will almost assuredly be led to conclude that no matter where we started, we would be led to the same concepts. Because of this interconnectedness, there is no sharp distinction among any of the topics used in this book. Therefore, an article under "explanation" might be just as fitting under "confirmation" or "history" or "gender." So do not think you have missed something because you cannot see exactly why an article appears under one heading and not another.

Here is another warning: Do not get the impression that articles are arranged in order of goodness, with the best saved for last. The articles should be seen as building on each other in such a way that each article has something worth adding to the total edifice. To continue the metaphor, sometimes more is torn down than kept; sometimes there is smoothing over, with a bit of replacement; and still other times something is put back. Perhaps in the end, it is difficult to achieve agreement because it is not easy to decide exactly what sort of building one wants.

JAMES D. CARNEY AND RICHARD K. SCHEER, "PATTERNS OF EXPLANATION"

James Carney and Robert Scheer, in their book, *Fundamentals of Logic,* suggest that there are two general forms of scientific explanation: deductive and probabilistic. They cite the following as examples of these types of explanation:

1. *Newton's explanation of why a stone dropped from the mast of a moving ship falls at the foot of the mast and not at some point behind the mast.* Briefly, the law governing the free fall of bodies (from Galileo) combined with the laws of motion and inertia (from Newton) *logically entail*—allow us to *deduce*—that the stone will fall at the foot of the mast.

2. *The explanation for why there are so few cities with competing daily newspapers.* Here the explanation is in terms of *probabilistic* statements such as "Advertisers usually prefer larger papers because they reach more customers at lower cost per line of advertising."

According to Carney and Scheer, these two types of scientific explanation are mutually exclusive.

As noted in the introduction to this chapter, we will focus on the strengths and weaknesses of the view that scientific explanation is best pictured as deduction. Part of the discussion will bear on the claim that probabilistic explanations are not (and cannot be) truly deductive.

What follows is a set of thirteen explanations taken from various disciplines. They are meant to help by giving you specific examples against which to test the general philosophical claims made by each of the authors in this, and following, chapters.

Patterns of Explanation

JAMES D. CARNEY AND RICHARD K. SCHEER

1. Why are tornadoes so destructive? A tornado destroys property and causes loss of life because the low pressures lead to the explosion of closed buildings and vehicles and the strong winds blow away whatever lies in their path.

"The reasons for the explosions are well known. The pressure in a tornado may cause a drop of atmospheric pressure by 8 per cent or more in a matter of seconds. Suppose the pressure inside a house is normal atmospheric, about 15 pounds per square inch. If a tornado moves over the house, the pressure outside may suddenly drop by 8 per cent to 13.8 pounds per square inch. Since the pressure inside the house will drop fairly slowly, especially if all the doors and windows are closed, the force on each square inch of wall and ceiling may amount to 1.2 pounds or about 170 pounds per square foot. If the house had a ceiling space 20 by 40 feet in area, the force exerted on the roof would be about 68 tons. This suddenly applied force can blow the roof off the house as if an explosion had occurred. This is especially true for dwellings, because in most houses the roof is held on mainly by its own weight. And it is evident, too, that few walls will survive 170 pounds of force per square foot."

The strong winds associated with the tornado are capable of picking up and moving the entire house. Cars, trucks, trailers, and other heavy objects are frequently carried away. The velocity of these winds has been estimated at 500–700 miles per hour.[1]

From James D. Carney and Richard K. Scheer, *Fundamentals of Logic* (New York: Macmillan, 1964), pp. 402–409. Courtesy of the Authors.

2. How is light energy converted into chemical energy? Nature set herself the task to catch in flight the light streaming towards the earth, and to store this, the most evasive of all forces, by converting it into an immobile form. To achieve this, she has covered the earth's crust with organisms, which while living take up the sunlight and use its force to add continuously to a sum of chemical difference.

These organisms are the plants: the plant world forms a reservoir in which the volatile sun rays are fixed and ingeniously laid down for later use; a providential economic measure, to which the very physical existence of the human race is inexorably bound.[2]

3. Why does great display of wealth no longer occur in the United States? John Galbraith in his book *The Affluent Society* gives this explanation:

Such display is now passé. There was an adventitious contributing cause. The American well-to-do have long been curiously sensitive to fear of expropriation—a fear which may be related to the tendency for even the mildest reformist measures to be viewed, in the conservative conventional wisdom, as the portents of revolutions. The depression and especially the New Deal gave the American rich a serious fright. One consequence was to usher in a period of marked discretion in personal expenditure. Purely ostentatious outlays, especially on dwellings, yachts, and females, were believed likely to incite the masses to violence. They were rebuked as unwise and improper by the more discreet. It was much wiser to take on the protective coloration of the useful citizen, the industrial statesman, or even the average guy.

However, deeper causes were at work. Increasingly in the last quarter century the display of expensive goods, as a device for suggesting wealth, has been condemned as vulgar. The term is precise. Vulgar means: "Of or pertaining to the common people, or to the common herd or crowd." And this explains what happened. Lush expenditure could be afforded by so many that it ceased to be useful as a mark of distinction. A magnificent, richly upholstered, and extremely high-powered automobile conveys no impression of wealth in a day when such automobiles are mass-produced by the thousands. A house in Palm Beach is not a source of distinction when the rates for a thousand hotel rooms in Miami Beach rival its daily upkeep. Once a sufficiently impressive display of diamonds could create attention even for the most obese and repellent body, for they signified membership in a highly privileged caste. Now the same diamonds are afforded by a television star or a talented harlot. Modern mass communications, especially the movies and television, insure that the populace at large will see the most lavish comparisoning on the bodies not of the daughters of the rich but on the daughters of coal miners and commercial travelers, who struck it rich by their own talents or some facsimile thereof. In South America, in the Middle East, to a degree in socialist India, and at Nice, Cannes, and Deauville, ostentatious display by the rich is still much practiced. This accords with expectations. In these countries most people are still, in the main, poor and unable to afford the goods which advertise wealth. Therefore ostentation continues to have a purpose. In not being accessible to too many people it has not yet become vulgar.[3]

4. In the early 1930's, while the world struggled to escape from the great depression that was shaking capitalism to its foundations, the classically trained economists wrestled to fit facts to orthodox theory. Public policy was in disarray. Classical theory had taught that when demand fell, prices and wages should fall and resources would once again be employed. But the actual effects of the drastic fall in prices on farmers was a disastrous fall in income! . . .

Gardiner Means and other economists were struck by the fact that some prices were more classical than others, that while farm prices had fallen sharply, many industrial prices—those in the great corporate industries—had fallen very little. Working for the Department of Agriculture, Means studied the behavior of 747 prices. This led him to his second major advance, the notion of administered prices.

There are, he found, two principal kinds of prices. One price is set in competitive markets and changes frequently in response to changes in demand. The other is set by administrative action and held constant for varying periods of time, despite changes in demand. Farm prices are typical market prices. Cement prices are typically administered.

In an administered market, an increase in demand leads to an increase in output. When demand falls, as it did during the great depressions, the price is largely held and output is slashed. This characteristic of rigid prices, Means concluded, was the basic cause of the depression's depth. As demand fell, output instead of price was cut; men were thrown out of work, and their loss of income further reduced total demand.[4]

5. Consider the pre–Civil War clash of convictions on slavery in the United States. By and large, the prevailing opinion in the North was that slavery was morally wrong, and in the South that it was morally right. In the debate that raged in those days, both sides appealed to the highest moral authority in support of their respective views. Such a clear-cut division of moral senti-

ments on geographical lines is most remarkable. It could not have happened by chance and must be explained.

Today most of us would accept the explanation that the different convictions derived from the existence of different institutions. Slavery was a fact in the South. It was woven into the very fabric of southern life. Therefore, a disturbance of slavery meant for southerners a profound change in their way of life. Under the supposition that man usually resists profound changes of established ways (except when the established ways become unbearable), we see that the southern support of slavery was understandable.

But the Marxists wish to delve deeper. . . .

Underlying the clash of conceptions of what is morally right, according to the Marxists, were the clashing economic interests of the ruling classes of the North and the South, respectively. In the South, the ruling class, that is, the owners of the large plantations, derived their incomes and therefore their power, by exploiting agricultural labor. In those days, agricultural labor required no skill and could best be controlled if the laborers were kept in complete ignorance. Slavery, therefore, filled the bill. In the North, however, a new ruling class was emerging—the industrialists, who controlled the means of production in manufacture. Now the increasing importance of machinery made slave labor unfit in factories. The industrial worker had to be at least somewhat literate. More than that, he had to be motivated in a way that a slave could not be. Finally, it was in the interest of the manufacturer to have a fluid labor force, a labor market, a reservoir, from which labor could be recruited and on which it could be dumped when not needed. . . . the industrialist did not buy the whole worker: he bought only the worker's labor. . . .

An ambition to extend the industrial system to the South would therefore be coupled with a conviction that slavery must be replaced by a free labor force. Since high sounding ideals are easier to defend (to oneself as well as to others) than economic self-interest, it is easy to see how the real aim, freedom of contract, became translated quite sincerely into "freedom of person."[5]

6. Freud, in his *General Introduction to Psychoanalysis,* recounts how he was called upon to explain why a fifty-three year old happily married woman had *delusions of jealousy.* A young girl, clearly out of jealousy, sent a letter to the woman telling that another young girl was having an affair with her husband. Though the woman clearly saw the accusation was false, she was prostrated by the letter. She suffered as much as she would have if the charges were well-founded. What caused this suffering?

Freud first found out that the letter was provoked by the patient herself. She had said to the young lady, who was then her housemaid, that nothing could be more awful than to hear that her husband was having an affair. During the interview with the patient, Freud found that she had an infatuation for her son-in-law which she was not fully aware of, and she disguised it as harmless tenderness.

From these two observations, Freud provided this explanation for the woman's illness: such a monstrous infatuation was an impossible thing and could not come to her conscious mind. Some sort of relief had to be found since it "persisted" and "unconsciously exerted a heavy pressure." ". . . the simplest alleviation lay in that mechanism of displacement which so regularly plays its part in the formation of delusional jealousy. If not merely she, old woman that she was, were in love with a young man, but if only her old husband too were in love with a young mistress, then her torturing conscience would be absolved from infidelity."

Relief came to her by her "projecting" her own state of mind onto her husband.

7. When the group norms are no longer binding or valid in an area or for a population subgroup—... deviant behavior becomes more frequent.... In a stable community a child is born and raised in a context of established norms which are supported by a social consensus. He tends to interiorize these norms, and they contribute to the establishment of his psychological field of needs, goals and motivations. Generally, the child acts to satisfy his needs in a manner which has the approval of society. If he acts in a deviant fashion, formal and informal controls—including his own ego with its interiorized norms—act to deter the child from further deviant conduct. Unstable community conditions and the consequent weakening of social controls that are congruent with the dominant culture provide fertile ground for the emergence of variant norms and group standards.[6]

8. Why does it appear that man will not always dominate the planet? In the words of Edward Drinker Cope, the great American naturalist: "The highly developed, or specialized types of one geological period have not been the parents of the types of succeeding periods but ... the descent has been derived from the less specialized of preceding ages." The highly and narrowly adapted flourish, but they move in a path which becomes ever more difficult to retrace or break away from as their adaptation becomes perfected. Their proficiency may increase, their numbers may grow. But their perfect adaptation, so necessary for survival, can become a euphemism for death. Man's specialization has introduced a new kind of life into the universe—one capable within limits of ordering its own environment and transmitting that order through social rather than biological hered-

ity. Nevertheless his physical modifications appear to be at an end, or close to an end, and sooner or later, Cope's law of the unspecialized will have its chance once more.[7]

9. To understand how chelation works we must examine the nature of a chemical bond. According to the modern theory of valence, the atoms in a molecule are bound together by electrons, the charged particles that surround every atom. The bond may be established in one of two ways. An atom may transfer one of its electrons to its neighbor. In that case the atom that loses the electron also loses its electrical neutrality and becomes positively charged, while the atom that receives the electron becomes negatively charged. These two "ions" then are held together by the electrical attraction of their opposite charges. The other way in which two atoms may be bound together is by sharing a pair of electrons—as if two persons were held together by a pair of ropes that belonged not exclusively to either individual but to both together. This is called a covalent bond: the chemist represents it by a single line joining the two atoms. Usually each of the two joined atoms supplies one of the two binding electrons. But sometimes one atom supplies both, and that kind of link is called a co-ordinate bond. The chemist's symbol for such a bond is an arrow pointing toward the atom which has received the electrons. Now a chelate ring is simply a group of atoms linked into a ring with one or more co-ordinate bonds. The atoms that donate the electrons are usually oxygen, nitrogen or sulfur; the acceptor atom, grasped in the claw of arrows, is nearly always a metal. In such a ring the metal atom is gripped more firmly than if it were merely attached to atoms in independent molecules. Another way of saying this is that a metal atom is much more prone to unite with two donor atoms in a ring-forming molecule than with the same atoms in

two separate molecules. The mechanics of the situation make clear why this is so. To become attached to two separate molecules, the metal atom must capture a donor atom in each molecule separately, and this depends on chance contacts. But when the metal atom becomes attached to one end of a molecule that can form a ring around it, it easily links up with the other end, for the latter is tethered and cannot range far ahead.[8]

10. We know that the substances extracted from plants ferment when they are abandoned to themselves, and disappear little by little in contact with the air. We know that the cadavers of animals undergo putrefaction and that soon only their skeletons remain. This destruction of dead organic matter is one of the necessities of the perpetuation of life.

If the remnants of dead plants and animals were not destroyed, the surface of the earth would soon be encumbered with organic matter, and life would become impossible because the cycle of transformation . . . could no longer be closed.

It is necessary that the fibrin of our muscles, the albumin of our blood, the gelatine of our bones, the urea of our urine, the ligneus matter of plants, the sugar of their fruits, the starch of their seeds . . . be progressively converted into water, ammonia and carbon dioxide so that the elementary principles of these complex organic substances be taken up again by plants, elaborated anew, to serve as food for new living beings similar to those that gave birth to them, and so on *ad infinitum* to the end of the centuries.[9]

11. The theory [Clark L. Hull's Learning Theory] is introduced by an anecdotal experiment. The subject is a six-year-old child who likes candy and is hungry for it. While she is out of the room a piece of her favorite candy is hidden under the edge of the center book in the lower shelf of a bookcase of several shelves. She is brought into the room, told there is candy hidden under one of the books, and asked if she wants to try to find it. She does, so she proceeds to look for the candy, after she is told that she must replace each book after looking under it, and that she may eat the candy when she finds it. She finds the candy after spending 210 seconds and examining 37 books. The next time she goes right to the lower shelf, and it takes her only 87 seconds and she looks under only 12 books. The next time she finds the candy under the second book examined, and it has taken her only 11 seconds. The next time she doesn't do so well. She starts at the other end of the shelf and works back. The authors speculate that she either was just lucky the time before, or introduced some other notion as a result of her previous experience with hiding games, such as, "He'll probably change the place now that I know it." Thereafter she continues to do better until on the ninth and tenth trials she goes right to the correct book and gets the candy.

According to some psychologists, there are four facts in learning: drive, cue, response, and reward. A *drive* is a strong stimulus which impels to action. The child's drives were a complex of hunger, a cultivated appetite for candy, and secondary drives related to social participation and social approval. Responses are elicited by *cues*. Cues determine "when he will respond, where he will respond, and which response he will make." The child was given a great many cues. She was told that the candy was under a book, and that she would be permitted to eat it when she found it. Drive impels the individual to *respond* to certain cues. Only if the response occurs can it be rewarded and learned, and one of the tasks of training is so to arrange the situation that the desired response will occur. The little girl was impelled to begin picking up books by her appetite for candy and her knowledge that candy was to be found under a book. Responses made to cues in the presence of drives will be learned if they are *rewarded*. If they are not rewarded, the tendency to repeat them will be weakened. Rewards produce reduction in drives; drive-reduction is, in fact, what makes them rewarding. That is why it is rewarding to be relieved from pain, to drink when thirsty, to eat when hungry. In the case of the little girl, eating the candy was rewarding.[10]

12. The reason why religion is necessary is apparently to be found in the fact that human society achieves its unity primarily through the possession by its members of certain ultimate values and ends in common. Although these values and ends are subjective, they influence behavior, and their integration enables the society to operate as a system. Derived neither from inherited nor from external nature, they have evolved as a part of culture by communication and moral pressure. They must, however, appear to the members of the society to have some reality, and it is the role of religious belief and ritual to supply and reinforce this appearance of reality. Through belief and ritual the common ends and values are connected with an imaginary world symbolized by concrete sacred objects, which world in turn is related in a meaningful way to the facts and trials of the individual's life. Through the worship of the sacred objects and the beings they symbolize, and the acceptance of supernatural prescriptions that are at the same time codes of behavior, a powerful control over human conduct is exercised, guiding it along lines sustaining the institutional structure and conforming to the ultimate ends and values.[11]

13. What is the nature of the forces that hold together the protons and neutrons in an atomic nucleus? In 1935 the Japanese physi-

cist Hideki Yukawa suggested that a new kind of field, consisting of quanta of energy which might take the form of particles of a certain mass, might account for these forces. He pointed out that electrical and gravitational forces, the two chief forces previously known, could be explained in terms of the emission and reabsorption of light quanta and gravitational quanta respectively. Since the nuclear forces were of a completely different type—not only more powerful but acting over much smaller distances than electrical or gravitational forces—it seemed reasonable to Yukawa to introduce a new type of field which would be responsible for the nuclear forces. . . . Yukawa estimated that the mass of the field quanta exchanged between two nucleons would be about 200 to 300 times that of the electron. He called these field quanta mesons. The mesons were thought of as the nuclear glue binding together the neutrons and protons in the nucleus. Since there were three types of equally strong bonds in the nucleus (neutron-proton, proton-proton, and neutron-neutron) it was assumed that there would be three kinds of mesons, namely, positive, negative and neutral.[12]

NOTES

1. Louis J. Battan, *The Nature of Violent Storms* (New York: Anchor/Doubleday, 1961).
2. Julius Robert von Mayer, 1845.
3. John Kenneth Galbraith, *The Affluent Society* (Boston: Houghton Mifflin, 1958), pp. 91–93. Copyright © 1958 by John Kenneth Galbraith. Reprinted by permission.
4. Bernard Nossiter, "The World of Gardiner Means," *New Republic*, May 7, 1962. Copyright © 1962 by *The New Republic*. Reprinted by permission.
5. Anatol Rapoport, *Fights, Games and Debates* (Ann Arbor: University of Michigan Press, 1960). Copyright © 1960 by the University of Michigan. Reprinted by permission.
6. Bernard Lander, *Towards an Understanding of Juvenile Delinquency* (New York: Columbia University Press, 1954).
7. Adapted from Loren C. Eiseley, "Is Man Here to

Stay?" in *Scientific American Reader* (New York: Simon & Schuster, 1953), pp. 483–489.

8. Harold F. Walton, "Chelation," in *New Chemistry* (New York: Simon & Schuster, 1957). Copyright © 1957 by Scientific American, Inc. Reprinted by permission.

9. René Dubos, *Pasteur and Modern Science* (Garden City, N.Y. Anchor Books/Doubleday, 1960), pp. 74–75.

10. Adapted from Ernest L. Hilgard, *Theories of*

Learning (New York: Appleton-Century-Crofts, 1948), pp. 77–79.

11. Kingsley Davis and Wilbert E. Moore, "Some Principles of Stratification," in *American Sociological Review*, vol. 10, pp. 244–245. Reprinted by permission.

12. Robert E. Marskak, "The Multiplicity of Particles," in *Scientific American Reader* (New York: Simon & Schuster, 1953), p. 109. Copyright © 1953 by Scientific American, Inc. Reprinted by permission.

CARL G. HEMPEL AND PAUL OPPENHEIM, "THE LOGIC OF EXPLANATION"

Despite its awesome and intimidating-sounding name, the deductive-nomological (D-N) model of explanation is based on a simple idea. "Deductive" refers to the fact that explanations are really arguments, made of premises that lead to conclusions. What we want to explain (the *explanandum*) is the conclusion of an argument, the premises of which (the *explanans*) lead to the conclusion and force us to accept it.

Consider the following premises:

All A is B.

All B is C.

What is the inevitable conclusion? One needs no formal course in logic to see that the conclusion, what follows, is

All A is C.

To accept the premises and to reject the conclusion leads to a contradiction.

Suppose we accept as true the premises

All horses are mammals.

All mammals have four-chambered hearts.

What deductively follows is

All horses have four-chambered hearts.

If we denied the truth of all horses having four-chambered hearts, while accepting the truth of the premises, it would mean that there might be a horse without a four-chambered heart. But by the premise, which we have accepted, all mammals have four-chambered hearts, this horse would not be a mammal. If this horse is not a mammal, then by the premise that all horses are mammals, this horse could not be a horse. There is our contradiction in accepting the premises and rejecting the conclusion.

Taking scientific explanation as deduction means that we will know when we have the right explanation. It will be when we have premises that force us to derive the conclusion. What is the nature of the premises according to the deductive-nomological model? Here is where "nomological" plays a role. *Nomological* means "according to law." Thus for Hempel and Oppenheim, the premises must contain at least one scientific law. We will discuss laws in some detail later. For now, the important point about scientific laws is that they are general. Laws according to Hempel and Oppenheim are general statements of causal regularities. These sorts of laws are referred to as "covering laws."

Here are some examples of scientific laws:

All cats purr.

All living things reproduce using either DNA or RNA.

Any object at rest tends to remain at rest unless acted on by an external object.

Scientific explanations are explanations about particular events (or things). Obviously, laws alone will not be able to explain particular things. In the example that follows, we will use "All cats purr" as if it were a scientific law. It is a generalization that is easy to understand. It makes the point that Hempel and Oppenheim want to make about explanation and prediction. It does not have the "look" of a scientific law. However, it is deducible from, or could be considered part of, a large body of information about felines, their breathing and vocalizations. Suppose that we wanted to know why Sinbad, my cat, is purring. Merely saying that all cats purr is not enough. We have to be specific and add that Sinbad is a cat. Then the explanation looks like this:

All cats purr.

Sinbad is a cat.

Sinbad purrs.

The statement "Sinbad is a cat" is a way of bringing the generalization down to earth, of giving it some particularity. The technical name for statements such as "Sinbad is a cat" is *initial condition*. Notice that we have to be specific and say, "Sinbad is a cat." It is a strength of this model for explanation that the premises in the argument must be carefully and explicitly stated. Strictly speaking, for Hempel and Oppenheim, unstated assumptions are not allowed. (If you are thinking that "All cats purr" should be amended to read "All cats purr, but only when they are content," you have anticipated some of the points that will be made by Nancy Cartwright.)

The D-N model does more than just explain. According to Hempel and Oppenheim, a completed D-N explanation will yield all the predictions necessary to make an explanation acceptable. Once told that my pet is a cat, you would, by means of the law "All cats purr," be able to predict that I have a pet that purrs. In a complete D-N explanation, the only difference between the explanation and a prediction made from it is temporality; that is, in an explanation, we are given an event and we then explain it, whereas in a prediction, we first predict an event and then the event either occurs or does not. For example, the reason a person smells baking bread all the time is explained by the presence of a rare brain tumor. If we know that a person has this tumor, we can correctly predict that this person will smell baking bread all the time. The view that complete D-N explanation and prediction are logically equivalent is called the symmetry thesis.

A D-N explanation must satisfy two sorts of conditions, logical and empirical. The empirical condition is that the premises must be true. The logical conditions are these:

That the premises must entail the conclusion

That the generalization used is a real scientific law

That the laws must be testable in the usual scientific manner

Clearly, then, Hempel and Oppenheim will be concerned with the nature of scientific laws and what counts as testable. They do not discuss what it is to be true because they have a well-known theory of truth to which they subscribe. They do not discuss entailment because to them it is a well-understood notion from logic. We will not pursue the philosophical ins and outs of either truth or entailment in this book.

The D-N model is meant to capture the essence of scientific explanation, which according to Hempel and Oppenheim means causal explanation. They do not tell us what they mean by "causal." A clear example of what they mean by a causal explanation would be explaining the motion of a billiard ball by pointing out that it was hit by another billiard ball or the cue stick. Are some explanations immune from being cast in the form of the D-N model because they do not appeal to this sense of causality? We often say things like "I went to the store because I needed bread" or "because I wanted frozen yogurt." Human behavior is explained in terms of motives, desires, and goals. Such explanations are often referred to as teleological. Hempel and Oppenheim point out that even teleological explanations ("I went to the store because I wanted bread") can be shown to make implicit appeal to laws such as "Whenever people want an object that is readily available, they will take measures to get that object." Such explanations are incomplete until the laws are explicitly stated.

Hempel and Oppenheim realize that these sorts of explanations in terms of goals seem odd because the goal is in the future and causes cannot be in the future. This is only apparent, they point out, for it is not the future goal but the present desire and belief that is the cause. In the D-N model, we must try to translate goals and purposes into physiological functions, which are causes in the usual sense. This does not mean that explanations such as "That plant turned in order to face the sun" do not serve a heuristic (helpful teaching) function.

Can unique events be explained using the D-N model? For example, can we explain, using a law, why Caesar crossed the Rubicon, a unique and unrepeatable event? Hempel and Oppenheim argue that kinds of events can be used to subsume what appears to be unique. What they mean is this: Caesar's crossing the Rubicon is just an example of a certain kind of despot in a certain kind of situation acting in a certain kind of way. Thus for them, laws needed for the D-N model can be used in historical explanation.

Laws play a central role in understanding science. So laws must be understood. According to Hempel and Oppenheim, laws can be characterized in the following ways.

1. *They must be true, not just highly confirmed.* If "All cats purr" is to be taken as a law, we must be able to say that it is true; just as true as is the claim "Zucker's cat is brown and white." For Hempel and Oppenheim, "highly confirmed" means there is a great deal of favorable evidence. Of course, a claim can be highly confirmed and still be wrong. This is not good enough for laws.

2. *They must be more than just lawlike.* The statement "All the books in my office have 'philosophy' in the title" is true (not just highly confirmed). Yet we would not be tempted to claim that this statement about the books in my office is a scientific law. Laws are statements of patterns found in nature. There are patterns that are true of my office. It is clear that these patterns are not patterns of nature. This point is often made by saying that the sorts of patterns found in my office are contingently true—meaning that they are true only of my office, not of offices in general.

3. *They often have a universal form but are often stated conditionally.* In logic, "All cats purr" can be restated as "If a thing is a cat, then it will purr." The conditional refers to the "if . . . then" formulation. Notice that "All trespassers will be shot," when translated into its conditional form, "If anyone does trespass, then that person will be shot," shows us that the statement can be true even if no one actually ever trespasses. This is part of the force of the "if." Another aspect is that the conditional statement represents a counterfactual claim. In other words, "All cats purr" really makes the very wide claim that if anything, anywhere were to be a cat, then it would have to purr. To use another example not from science, when you say, "If only I could fly to the moon, then I would be an astronaut," you are making a counterfactual claim. Here are some other counterfactual claims: "If cows could fly, then we would need very strong umbrellas." "If you pass this course, I will eat my entire head."

4. *Laws refer to an open class, not particulars.* "All cats purr" refers to anything that is a cat. This is another way of saying that "All cats purr" is really a conditional statement. It does not refer to just those cats that we know about now. It refers to all cats, past, present, and future.

5. *Laws are sometimes fundamental and sometimes derivative.* In the usual versions of Euclidean geometry, that the interior angles of a triangle equal two right angles is derived from definitions of line, triangle, right angle, and so on. These definitions are the basic assumptions of Euclidean geometry. They themselves are not derived. This is the distinction Hempel and Oppenheim are making here. In the introduction to the article by Schaffner in Chapter 5, there is a more extended example from Euclidean geometry.

6. *Laws do not designate particulars.* In stating the law "All cats purr," no particular cat is mentioned. "Tabby purrs" would not be a law because it mentions a particular cat. In the language of Hempel and Oppenheim, Tabby designates a particular cat and occurs essentially. By "essentially," they mean that the statement would have a different meaning if Tabby were to be replaced by another term, such as Boots, and that it might even become false.

7. *Laws have purely qualitative predicates.* In the sentences "My cup is red," "Fred is tall," and "My cup is full," the words "is red," "is tall," and "is full" are predicates. Assuming normal color vision and no odd lighting conditions, deciding that the cup is red and not another color can be done at a glance. This is an easy way to understand what Hempel and Oppenheim mean by a purely qualitative predicate. By contrast, deciding that Fred is tall is not easily determined if Fred's height is 6 feet. If Fred stands 7 feet high, it seems much clearer that "Fred is tall" is true. But in the land of pygmies, Fred might measure 5 feet 5 inches and be tall. Thus "is tall" is not a purely qualitative predicate. Again, it is clearer that in "My shirt is red," "is red" is closer to being a purely qualitative predicate than "is soluble" in "That sugar cube is soluble." The example of the 5-foot-5 giant in the land of pygmies makes it plain that the concept of a purely qualitative predicate is not as clear as Hempel and Oppenheim would like it to be.

8. *Laws need a formal language of expression if they are to be fully understood.* The requirements for being a law are very difficult to meet using ordinary language. Even using the language of science, it is unclear, for example, whether "All cats purr" is truly universal. After all, so far as we know, cats exist only on earth, and so mention of earth is perhaps essential in the statement of the law. Because of this sort of problem, Hempel and Oppenheim suggest that a specialized language be invented just for science so that in this language what was and what was not a law would be very clear. What would such a formal language be like? It would have to be abstract, since it would have to apply to all sciences. It would have to list its basic terms and show how to form sentences from those terms. It would have to list rules of inferences—ways of making derivations from the basic statements. Such a formal language has yet to be constructed.

9. *Laws may be probabilistic.* Consider the statement "Ninety percent of Buicks are sedans." Given this law and the fact that a car is a Buick, what follows? We can say either "This is a sedan with 90 percent certainty" or "This car has a 90 percent

probability of being a sedan." The latter certainly seems to follow deductively from the law about Buicks being sedans. Hempel and Oppenheim prefer this way of interpreting probabilistic laws. May Brodbeck will give this same interpretation.

The Logic of Explanation

CARL G. HEMPEL AND PAUL OPPENHEIM

§1. Introduction

To explain the phenomena in the world of our experience, to answer the question "why?" rather than only the question "what?" is one of the foremost objectives of all rational inquiry; and especially, scientific research in its various branches strives to go beyond a mere description of its subject matter by providing an explanation of the phenomena it investigates. While there is rather general agreement about this chief objective of science, there exists considerable difference of opinion as to the function and the essential characteristics of scientific explanation. In the present essay, an attempt will be made to shed some light on these issues by means of an elementary survey of the basic pattern of scientific explanation and a subsequent more rigorous analysis of the concept of law and of the logical structure of explanatory arguments.

The elementary survey is presented in Part I of this article; Part II contains an analysis of the concept of emergence; in Part III, an attempt is made to exhibit and to clarify in a more rigorous manner some of the peculiar and perplexing logical problems to which the familiar elementary analysis of explanation gives rise.[1]

From Carl Hempel and Paul Oppenheim (1948). "Studies in the Logic of Explanation," *Philosophy of Science* 15: 135–175. Courtesy of Williams & Wilkins.

PART I. ELEMENTARY SURVEY OF SCIENTIFIC EXPLANATION

§2. Some Illustrations

A mercury thermometer is rapidly immersed in hot water; there occurs a temporary drop of the mercury column, which is then followed by a swift rise. How is this phenomenon to be explained? The increase in temperature affects at first only the glass tube of the thermometer; it expands and thus provides a larger space for the mercury inside, whose surface therefore drops. As soon as by heat conduction the rise in temperature reaches the mercury, however, the latter expands, and as its coefficient of expansion is considerably larger than that of glass, a rise of the mercury level results.— This account consists of statements of two kinds. Those of the first kind indicate certain conditions which are realized prior to, or at the same time as, the phenomenon to be explained; we shall refer to them briefly as antecedent conditions. In our illustration, the antecedent conditions include, among others, the fact that the thermometer consists of a glass tube which is partly filled with mercury, and that it is immersed into hot water. The statements of the second kind express certain general laws; in our case, these include the laws of the thermic expansion of mercury and of glass, and a statement about the small thermic conductivity of glass. The two sets of statements, if adequately and completely formulated, explain the phenomenon under consideration: They entail the consequence that the mercury will first drop, then rise. Thus, the event under discussion is explained by subsuming it under general laws, i.e., by showing that it occurred in accordance with those laws, by virtue of the realization of certain specified antecedent conditions.

Consider another illustration. To an observer in a row boat, that part of an oar which is under water appears to be bent upwards. The phenomenon is explained by means of general laws—mainly the law of refraction and the law that water is an optically denser medium than air—and by reference to certain antecedent conditions—especially the facts that part of the oar is in the water, part in the air, and that the oar is practically a straight piece of wood.—Thus, here again, the question "*Why* does the phenomenon happen?" is construed as meaning "according to what general laws, and by virtue of what antecedent conditions does the phenomenon occur?"

So far, we have considered exclusively the explanation of particular events occurring at a certain time and place. But the question "Why?" may be raised also in regard to general laws. Thus, in our last illustration, the question might be asked: Why does the propagation of light conform to the law of refraction? Classical physics answers in terms of the undulatory theory of light, i.e. by stating that the propagation of light is a wave phenomenon of a certain general type, and that all wave phenomena of that type satisfy the law of refraction. Thus, the explanation of a general regularity consists in subsuming it under another, more comprehensive regularity, under a more general law.—Similarly, the validity of Galileo's law for the free fall of bodies near the earth's surface can be explained by deducing it from a more comprehensive set of laws, namely Newton's laws of motion

and his law of gravitation, together with some statements about particular facts, namely the mass and the radius of the earth.

§3. The Basic Pattern of Scientific Explanation

From the preceding sample cases let us now abstract some general characteristics of scientific explanation. We divide an explanation into two major constituents, the explanandum and the explanans.[2] By the explanandum, we understand the sentence describing the phenomenon to be explained (not that phenomenon itself); by the explanans, the class of those sentences which are adduced to account for the phenomenon. As was noted before, the explanans falls into two subclasses; one of these contains certain sentences $C_1, C_2, \ldots, C_k$ which state specific antecedent conditions; the other is a set of sentences $L_1, L_2, \ldots, L_r$ which represent general laws.

If a proposed explanation is to be sound, its constituents have to satisfy certain conditions of adequacy, which may be divided into logical and empirical conditions. For the following discussion, it will be sufficient to formulate these requirements in a slightly vague manner; in Part III, a more rigorous analysis and a more precise restatement of these criteria will be presented.

I. *Logical conditions of adequacy*

    (R1) The explanandum must be a logical consequence of the explanans; in other words, the explanandum must be logically deducible from the information contained in the explanans, for otherwise, the explanans would not constitute adequate grounds for the explanandum.

    (R2) The explanans must contain general laws, and these must actually be required for the derivation of the explanandum.—We shall not make it a necessary condition for a sound explanation, however, that the explanans must contain at least one statement which is not a law; for, to mention just one reason, we would surely want to consider as an explanation the derivation of the general regularities governing the motion of double stars from the laws of celestial mechanics, even though all the statements in the explanans are general laws.

(R3) The explanans must have empirical content; i.e., it must be capable, at least in principle, of test by experiment or observation.—This condition is implicit in (R1); for since the explanandum is assumed to describe some empirical phenomenon, it follows from (R1) that the explanans entails at least one consequence of empirical character, and this fact confers upon it testability and empirical content. But the point deserves special mention because, as will be seen in §4, certain arguments which have been offered as explanations in the natural and in the social sciences violate this requirement.

II. *Empirical condition of adequacy*

(R4) The sentences constituting the explanans must be true. That in a sound explanation, the statements constituting the explanans have to satisfy some condition of factual correctness is obvious. But it might seem more appropriate to stipulate that the explanans has to be highly confirmed by all the relevant evidence available rather than that it should be true. This stipulation however, leads to awkward consequences. Suppose that a certain

phenomenon was explained at an earlier stage of science, by means of an explanans which was well supported by the evidence then at hand, but which had been highly disconfirmed by more recent empirical findings. In such a case, we would have to say that originally the explanatory account was a correct explanation, but that it ceased to be one later, when unfavorable evidence was discovered. This does not appear to accord with sound common usage, which directs us to say that on the basis of the limited initial evidence, the truth of the explanans, and thus the soundness of the explanation, had been quite probable, but that the ampler evidence now available made it highly probable that the explanans was not true, and hence that the account in question was not—and had never been—a correct explanation. (A similar point will be made and illustrated, with respect to the requirement of truth for laws, in the beginning of §6.)

Some of the characteristics of an explanation which have been indicated so far may be summarized in the following schema:

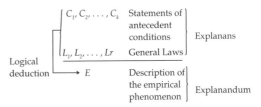

Let us note here that the same formal analysis, including the four necessary conditions, applies to scientific prediction as well as to explanation. The difference between the two is of a pragmatic character.

If E is given, i.e. if we know that the phenomenon described by E has occurred, and a suitable set of statements $C_1, C_2, \ldots, C_k, L_1, L_2, \ldots, L_r$ is provided afterwards, we speak of an explanation of the phenomenon in question. If the latter statements are given and E is derived prior to the occurrence of the phenomenon it describes, we speak of a prediction. It may be said, therefore, that an explanation is not fully adequate unless its explanans, if taken account of in time, could have served as a basis for predicting the phenomenon under consideration.[3]— Consequently, whatever will be said in this article concerning the logical characteristics of explanation or prediction will be applicable to either, even if only one of them should be mentioned.

It is this potential predictive force which gives scientific explanation its importance: only to the extent that we are able to explain empirical facts can we attain the major objective of scientific research, namely not merely to record the phenomena of our experience, but to learn from them, by basing upon them theoretical generalizations which enable us to anticipate new occurrences and to control, at least to some extent, the changes in our environment.

Many explanations which are customarily offered, especially in pre-scientific discourse, lack this predictive character, however. Thus, it may be explained that a car turned over on the road "because" one of its tires blew out while the car was travelling at high speed. Clearly, on the basis of just this information, the accident could not have been predicted, for the explanans provides no explicit general laws by means of which the prediction might be effected, nor does it state adequately the antecedent conditions which would be needed for the prediction.—The same point may be illustrated by reference to W. S. Jevons's view that every explanation consists in pointing out a resemblance between facts, and that in some cases this process may require no reference to laws at all and "may involve nothing more than a single identity, as when we explain the appearance of shooting stars by showing that they are identical with portions of a comet."[4] But clearly, this identity does not provide an explanation of the phenomenon of shooting stars unless we presuppose the laws governing the development of heat and light as the effect of friction. The observation of similarities has explanatory value only if it involves at least tacit reference to general laws.

In some cases, incomplete explanatory arguments of the kind here illustrated suppress parts of the explanans simply as "obvious"; in other cases, they seem to involve the assumption that while the missing parts are not obvious, the incomplete explanans could at least, with appropriate effort, be so supplemented as to make a strict derivation of the explanandum possible. This assumption may be justifiable in some cases, as when we say that a lump of sugar disappeared "because" it was put into hot tea, but it is surely not satisfied in many other cases. Thus, when certain peculiarities in the work of an artist are explained as outgrowths of a specific type of neurosis, this observation may contain significant clues, but in general it does not afford a sufficient basis for a potential prediction of those peculiarities. In cases of this kind, an incomplete explanation may at best be considered as indicating some positive correlation between the antecedent conditions adduced and the type of phenomenon to be explained, and as pointing out a direction in which further research might be carried on in order to complete the explanatory account.

The type of explanation which has been considered here so far is often referred to as causal explanation. If E describes a particular event, then the antecedent circumstances described in the sentences $C_1, C_2, \ldots, C_k$

may be said jointly to "cause" that event, in the sense that there are certain empirical regularities, expressed by the laws $L_1, L_2, \ldots, L_r$, which imply that whenever conditions of the kind indicated by $C_1, C_2, \ldots, C_k$ occur, an event of the kind described in E will take place. Statements such as $L_1, L_2, \ldots, L_r$, which assert general and unexceptional connections between specified characteristics of events, are customarily called causal, or deterministic laws. They are to be distinguished from the so-called statistical laws which assert that in the long run, an explicitly stated percentage of all cases satisfying a given set of conditions are accompanied by an event of a certain specified kind. Certain cases of scientific explanation involve "subsumption" of the explanandum under a set of laws of which at least some are statistical in character. Analysis of the peculiar logical structure of that type of subsumption involves difficult special problems. The present essay will be restricted to an examination of the causal type of explanation, which has retained its significance in large segments of contemporary science, and even in some areas where a more adequate account calls for reference to statistical laws.[5]

§4. Explanation in the Non-Physical Sciences. Motivational and Teleological Approaches

Our characterization of scientific explanation is so far based on a study of cases taken from the physical sciences. But the general principles thus obtained apply also outside this area.[6] Thus, various types of behavior in laboratory animals and in human subjects are explained in psychology by subsumption under laws or even general theories of learning or conditioning; and while frequently, the regularities invoked cannot be stated with the same generality and precision as in physics or chemistry, it is clear,

at least, that the general character of those explanations conforms to our earlier characterization.

Let us now consider an illustration involving sociological and economic factors. In the fall of 1946, there occurred at the cotton exchanges of the United States a price drop which was so severe that the exchanges in New York, New Orleans, and Chicago had to suspend their activities temporarily. In an attempt to explain this occurrence, newspapers traced it back to a large-scale speculator in New Orleans who had feared his holdings were too large and had therefore begun to liquidate his stocks; smaller speculators had then followed his example in a panic and had thus touched off the critical decline. Without attempting to assess the merits of the argument, let us note that the explanation here suggested again involves statements about antecedent conditions and the assumption of general regularities. The former include the facts that the first speculator had large stocks of cotton, that there were smaller speculators with considerable holdings, that there existed the institution of the cotton exchanges with their specific mode of operation, etc. The general regularities referred to are—as often in semi-popular explanations—not explicitly mentioned; but there is obviously implied some form of the law of supply and demand to account for the drop in cotton prices in terms of the greatly increased supply under conditions of practically unchanged demand; besides, reliance is necessary on certain regularities in the behavior of individuals who are trying to preserve or improve their economic position. Such laws cannot be formulated at present with satisfactory precision and generality, and therefore, the suggested explanation is surely incomplete, but its intention is unmistakably to account for the phenomenon by integrating it into a general pattern of economic and socio-psychological regularities.

We turn to an explanatory argument taken from the field of linguistics.[7] In Northern France, there exist a large variety of words synonymous with the English "bee," whereas in Southern France, essentially only one such word is in existence. For this discrepancy, the explanation has been suggested that in the Latin epoch, the South of France used the word "apicula," the North the word "apis." The latter, because of a process of phonologic decay in Northern France, became the monosyllabic word "é"; and monosyllables tend to be eliminated, especially if they contain few consonantic elements, for they are apt to give rise to misunderstandings. Thus, to avoid confusion, other words were selected. But "apicula," which was reduced to "abelho," remained clear enough and was retained, and finally it even entered into the standard language, in the form "abbeille." While the explanation here described is incomplete in the sense characterized in the previous section, it clearly exhibits reference to specific antecedent conditions as well as to general laws.[8]

While illustrations of this kind tend to support the view that explanation in biology, psychology, and the social sciences has the same structure as in the physical sciences, the opinion is rather widely held that in many instances, the causal type of explanation is essentially inadequate in fields other than physics and chemistry, and especially in the study of purposive behavior. Let us examine briefly some of the reasons which have been adduced in support of this view.

One of the most familiar among them is the idea that events involving the activities of humans singly or in groups have a peculiar uniqueness and irrepeatability which makes them inaccessible to causal explanation because the latter,—with its reliance upon uniformities, presupposes repeatability of the phenomena under consideration.

This argument which, incidentally, has also been used in support of the contention that the experimental method is inapplicable in psychology and the social sciences, involves a misunderstanding of the logical character of causal explanation. Every individual event, in the physical sciences no less than in psychology or the social sciences, is unique in the sense that it, with all its peculiar characteristics, does not repeat itself. Nevertheless, individual events may conform to, and thus be explainable by means of, general laws of the causal type. For all that a causal law asserts is that any event of a specified kind, i.e. any event having certain specified characteristics, is accompanied by another event which in turn has certain specified characteristics; for example, that in any event involving friction, heat is developed. And all that is needed for the testability and applicability of such laws is the recurrence of events with the antecedent characteristics, i.e. the repetition of those characteristics, but not of their individual instances. Thus, the argument is inconclusive. It gives occasion, however, to emphasize an important point concerning our earlier analysis: When we spoke of the explanation of a single event, the term "event" referred to the occurrence of some more or less complex characteristic in a specific spatio-temporal location or in a certain individual object, and not to *all* the characteristics of that object, or to all that goes on in that space-time region.

A second argument that should be mentioned here[9] contends that the establishment of scientific generalizations—and thus of explanatory principles—for human behavior is impossible because the reactions of an individual in a given situation depend not only upon that situation, but also upon the previous history of the individual.—But surely, there is no *a priori* reason why generalizations should not be attainable which take into account this dependence of behavior on the past history of the agent. That indeed the given argument "proves" too much, and is therefore a *non sequitur*, is made evident by the existence of certain physical phenomena, such as magnetic hysteresis and elastic fatigue, in which the magnitude of a specific physical effect depends upon the past history of the system involved, and for which nevertheless certain general regularities have been established.

A third argument insists that the explanation of any phenomenon involving purposive behavior calls for reference to motivations and thus for teleological rather than causal analysis. Thus, for example, a fuller statement of the suggested explanation for the break in the cotton prices would have to indicate the large-scale speculator's motivations as one of the factors determining the event in question. Thus, we have to refer to goals sought, and this, so the argument runs, introduces a type of explanation alien to the physical sciences. Unquestionably, many of the—frequently incomplete—explanations which are offered for human actions involve reference to goals and motives; but does this make them essentially different from the causal explanations of physics and chemistry? One difference which suggests itself lies in the circumstance that in motivated behavior, the future appears to affect the present in a manner which is not found in the causal explanations of the physical sciences. But clearly, when the action of a person is motivated, say, by the desire to reach a certain objective, then it is not the as yet unrealized future event of attaining that goal which can be said to determine his present behavior, for indeed the goal may never be actually reached; rather—to put it in crude terms—it is (a) his desire, present before the action, to attain that particular objective, and (b) his belief, likewise present before the action, that such and such a course of action is most

likely to have the desired effect. The determining motives and beliefs, therefore, have to be classified among the antecedent conditions of a motivational explanation, and there is no formal difference on this account between motivational and causal explanation.

Neither does the fact that motives are not accessible to direct observation by an outside observer constitute an essential difference between the two kinds of explanation; for also the determining factors adduced in physical explanations are very frequently inaccessible to direct observation. This is the case, for instance, when opposite electric charges are adduced in explanation of the mutual attraction of two metal spheres. The presence of those charges, while eluding all direct observation, can be ascertained by various kinds of indirect test, and that is sufficient to guarantee the empirical character of the explanatory statement. Similarly, the presence of certain motivations may be ascertainable only by indirect methods, which may include reference to linguistic utterances of the subject in question, slips of the pen or of the tongue, etc.; but as long as these methods are "operationally determined" with reasonable clarity and precision, there is no essential difference in this respect between motivational explanation and causal explanation in physics.

A potential danger of explanation by motives lies in the fact that the method lends itself to the facile construction of ex-post-facto accounts without predictive force. It is a widespread tendency to "explain" an action by ascribing it to motives conjectured only after the action has taken place. While this procedure is not in itself objectionable, its soundness requires that (1) the motivational assumptions in question be capable of test, and (2) that suitable general laws be available to lend explanatory power to the assumed motives. Disregard of these requirements frequently deprives alleged motivational explanations of their cognitive significance.

The explanation of an action in terms of the motives of the agent is sometimes considered as a special kind of teleological explanation. As was pointed out above, motivational explanation, if adequately formulated, conforms to the conditions for causal explanation, so that the term "teleological" is a misnomer if it is meant to imply either a non-causal character of the explanation or a peculiar determination of the present by the future. If this is borne in mind, however, the term "teleological" may be viewed, in this context, as referring to causal explanations in which some of the antecedent conditions are motives of the agent whose actions are to be explained.[10]

Teleological explanations of this kind have to be distinguished from a much more sweeping type, which has been claimed by certain schools of thought to be indispensable especially in biology. It consists in explaining characteristics of an organism by reference to certain ends or purposes which the characteristics are said to serve. In contradistinction to the cases examined before, the ends are not assumed here to be consciously or subconsciously pursued by the organism in question. Thus, for the phenomenon of mimicry, the explanation is sometimes offered that it serves the purpose of protecting the animals endowed with it from detection by its pursuers and thus tends to preserve the species.—Before teleological hypotheses of this kind can be appraised as to their potential explanatory power, their meaning has to be clarified. If they are intended somehow to express the idea that the purposes they refer to are inherent in the design of the universe, then clearly they are not capable of empirical test and thus violate the requirement (R3) stated in §3. In certain cases, however, assertions about the purposes of biological characteristics may be translatable into statements in non-teleological terminology which assert that those characteristics function in a specific manner which is essential to keeping the organism alive or to preserving the species.[11] An attempt to state precisely what is meant by this latter assertion—or by the similar one that without those characteristics, and other things being equal, the organism or the species would not survive—encounters considerable difficulties. But these need not be discussed here. For even if we assume that biological statements in teleological form can be adequately translated into descriptive statements about the life-preserving function of certain biological characteristics, it is clear that (1) the use of the concept of purpose is not essential in these contexts, since the term "purpose" can be completely eliminated from the statements in question, and (2) teleological assumptions, while now endowed with empirical content, cannot serve as explanatory principles in the customary contexts. Thus, e.g., the fact that a given species of butterflies displays a particular kind of coloring cannot be inferred from—and therefore cannot be explained by means of—the statement that this type of coloring has the effect of protecting the butterflies from detection by pursuing birds, nor can the presence of red corpuscles in the human blood be inferred from the statement that those corpuscles have a specific function in assimilating oxygen and that this function is essential for the maintenance of life.

One of the reasons for the perseverance of teleological considerations in biology probably lies in the fruitfulness of the teleological approach as a heuristic device: Biological research which was psychologically motivated by a teleological orientation, by an interest in purposes in nature, has frequently led to important results which can be stated in non-teleological terminology and which increase our scientific knowledge of the causal connections between biological phenomena.

Another aspect that lends appeal to teleological considerations is their anthropomorphic character. A teleological explanation tends to make us feel that we really "understand" the phenomenon in question, because it is accounted for in terms of purposes, with which we are familiar from our own experience of purposive behavior. But it is important to distinguish here understanding in the psychological sense of a feeling of empathic familiarity from understanding in the theoretical, or cognitive, sense of exhibiting the phenomenon to be explained as a special case of some general regularity. The frequent insistence that explanation means the reduction of something unfamiliar to ideas or experiences already familiar to us is indeed misleading. For while some scientific explanations do have this psychological effect, it is by no means universal: The free fall of a physical body may well be said to be a more familiar phenomenon than the law of gravitation, by means of which it can be explained; and surely the basic ideas of the theory of relativity will appear to many to be far less familiar than the phenomena for which the theory accounts.

"Familiarity" of the explicans is not only not necessary for a sound explanation—as we have just tried to show—, but it is not sufficient either. This is shown by the many cases in which a proposed explicans sounds suggestively familiar, but upon closer inspection proves to be a mere metaphor, or an account lacking testability, or a set of statements which includes no general laws and therefore lacks explanatory power. A case in point is the neovitalistic attempt to explain biological phenomena by reference to an entelechy or vital force. The crucial point here is not—as it is sometimes made out to be—that entelechies cannot be seen or otherwise directly observed; for that is true

also of gravitational fields, and yet, reference to such fields is essential in the explanation of various physical phenomena. The decisive difference between the two cases is that the physical explanation provides (1) methods of testing, albeit indirectly, assertions about gravitational fields, and (2) general laws concerning the strength of gravitational fields, and the behavior of objects moving in them. Explanations by entelechies satisfy the analogue of neither of these two conditions. Failure to satisfy the first condition represents a violation of (R3); it renders all statements about entelechies inaccessible to empirical test and thus devoid of empirical meaning. Failure to comply with the second condition involves a violation of (R2). It deprives the concept of entelechy of all explanatory import; for explanatory power never resides in a concept, but always in the general laws in which it functions. Therefore, notwithstanding the flavor of familiarity of the metaphor it invokes, the neovitalistic approach cannot provide theoretical understanding.

The preceding observations about familiarity and understanding can be applied, in a similar manner, to the view held by some scholars that the explanation, or the understanding, of human actions requires an empathic understanding of the personalities of the agents.[12] This understanding of another person in terms of one's own psychological functioning may prove a useful heuristic device in the search for general psychological principles which might provide a theoretical explanation; but the existence of empathy on the part of the scientist is neither a necessary nor a sufficient condition for the explanation, or the scientific understanding, of any human action. It is not necessary, for the behavior of psychotics or of people belonging to a culture very different from that of the scientist may sometimes be explainable and predictable in terms of general principles even though the scientist who establishes or applies those principles may not be able to understand his subjects empathically. And empathy is not sufficient to guarantee a sound explanation, for a strong feeling of empathy may exist even in cases where we completely misjudge a given personality. Moreover, as the late Dr. Zilsel has pointed out, empathy leads with ease to incompatible results; thus, when the population of a town has long been subjected to heavy bombing attacks, we can understand, in the empathic sense, that its morale should have broken down completely, but we can understand with the same ease also that it should have developed a defiant spirit of resistance. Arguments of this kind often appear quite convincing; but they are of an *ex post facto* character and lack cognitive significance unless they are supplemented by testable explanatory principles in the form of laws or theories.

Familiarity of the explanans, therefore, no matter whether it is achieved through the use of teleological terminology, through neovitalistic metaphors, or through other means, is no indication of the cognitive import and the predictive force of a proposed explanation. Besides, the extent to which an idea will be considered as familiar varies from person to person and from time to time, and a psychological factor of this kind certainly cannot serve as a standard in assessing the worth of a proposed explanation. The decisive requirement for every sound explanation remains that it subsume the explanandum under general laws. . . .

PART III. LOGICAL ANALYSIS OF LAW AND EXPLANATION

§6. Problems of the Concept of General Law

From our general survey of the characteristics of scientific explanation, we now turn to

a closer examination of its logical structure. The explanation of a phenomenon, we noted, consists in its subsumption under laws or under a theory. But what is a law, what is a theory? While the meaning of these concepts seems intuitively clear, an attempt to construct adequate explicit definitions for them encounters considerable difficulties. In the present section, some basic problems of the concept of law will be described and analyzed; in the next section, we intend to propose, on the basis of the suggestions thus obtained, definitions of law and of explanation for a formalized model language of a simple logical structure.

The concept of law will be construed here so as to apply to true statements only. The apparently plausible alternative procedure of requiring high confirmation rather than truth of a law seems to be inadequate: It would lead to a relativized concept of law, which would be expressed by the phrase "sentence S is a law relatively to the evidence E." This does not seem to accord with the meaning customarily assigned to the concept of law in science and in methodological inquiry. Thus, for example, we would not say that Bode's general formula for the distance of the planets from the sun was a law relatively to the astronomical evidence available in the 1770s, when Bode propounded it, and that it ceased to be a law after the discovery of Neptune and the determination of its distance from the sun; rather, we would say that the limited original evidence had given a high probability to the assumption that the formula was a law, whereas more recent additional information reduced that probability so much as to make it practically certain that Bode's formula is not generally true, and hence not a law.[13]

Apart from being true, a law will have to satisfy a number of additional conditions. These can be studied independently of the factual requirement of truth, for they refer, as it were, to all logically possible laws, no matter whether factually true or false. Adopting a convenient term proposed by Goodman,[14] we will say that a sentence is lawlike if it has all the characteristics of a general law, with the possible exception of truth. Hence, every law is a lawlike sentence, but not conversely.

Our problem of analyzing the concept of law thus reduces to that of explicating the meaning of "lawlike sentence." We shall construe the class of lawlike sentences as including analytic general statements, such as "A rose is a rose", as well as the lawlike sentences of empirical science, which have empirical content.[15] It will not be necessary to require that each lawlike sentence permissible in explanatory contexts be of the second kind; rather, our definition of explanation will be so constructed as to guarantee the factual character of the totality of the laws—though not of every single one of them—which function in an explanation of an empirical fact.

What are the characteristics of lawlike sentences? First of all, lawlike sentences are statements of universal form, such as "All robins' eggs are greenish-blue," "All metals are conductors of electricity," "At constant pressure, any gas expands with increasing temperature." As these examples illustrate, a lawlike sentence usually is not only of universal, but also of conditional form; it makes an assertion to the effect that universally, if a certain set of conditions, C, is realized, then another specified set of conditions, E, is realized as well. The standard form for the symbolic expression of a lawlike sentence is therefore the universal conditional. However, since any conditional statement can be transformed into a non-conditional one, conditional form will not be considered as essential for a lawlike sentence, while universal character will be held indispensable.

But the requirement of universal form is not sufficient to characterize lawlike sentences. Suppose, for example, that a certain basket, b, contains at a certain time t a number of red apples and nothing else.[16] Then the statement

(S_1) Every apple in basket b at time t is red

is both true and of universal form. Yet the sentence does not qualify as a law; we would refuse, for example, to explain by subsumption under it the fact that a particular apple chosen at random from the basket is red. What distinguishes S_1 from a lawlike sentence? Two points suggest themselves, which will be considered in turn, namely, finite scope, and reference to a specified object.

First, the sentence S_1 makes, in effect, an assertion about a finite number of objects only, and this seems irreconcilable with the claim to universality which is commonly associated with the notion of law.[17] But are not Kepler's laws considered as lawlike although they refer to a finite set of planets only? And might we not even be willing to consider as lawlike a sentence such as the following?

(S_2) All the sixteen ice cubes in the freezing tray of this refrigerator have a temperature of less than 10 degrees centigrade.

This point might well be granted; but there is an essential difference between S_1 on the one hand and Kepler's laws as well as S_2 on the other: The latter, while finite in scope, are known to be consequences of more comprehensive laws whose scope is not limited, while for S_1 this is not the case.

Adopting a procedure recently suggested by Reichenbach,[18] we will therefore distinguish between fundamental and derivative laws. A statement will be called a derivative law if it is of universal character and follows from some fundamental laws. The concept of fundamental law requires further clarification; so far, we may say that fundamental laws, and similarly fundamental lawlike sentences, should satisfy a certain condition of non-limitation of scope.

It would be excessive, however, to deny the status of fundamental lawlike sentence to all statements which, in effect, make an assertion about a finite class of objects only, for that would rule out also a sentence such as "All robins' eggs are greenish-blue," since presumably the class of all robins' eggs—past, present, and future—is finite. But again, there is an essential difference between this sentence and, say, S_1. It requires empirical knowledge to establish the finiteness of the class of robins' eggs, whereas, when the sentence S_1 is construed in a manner which renders it intuitively unlawlike, the terms "basket b" and "apple" are understood so as to imply finiteness of the class of apples in the basket at time t. Thus, so to speak, the meaning of its constitutive terms alone—without additional factual information—entails that S_1 has a finite scope.—Fundamental laws, then, will have to be construed so as to satisfy what we have called a condition of non-limited scope; our formulation of that condition however, which refers to what is entailed by "the meaning" of certain expressions, is too vague and will have to be revised later. let us note in passing that the stipulation here envisaged would bar from the class of fundamental lawlike sentences also such undesirable candidates as "All uranic objects are spherical," where "uranic" means the property of being the planet Uranus; indeed, while this sentence has universal form, it fails to satisfy the condition of non-limited scope.

In our search for a general characterization of lawlike sentences, we now turn to a second clue which is provided by the sentence S_1. In addition to violating the condi-

tion of non-limited scope, this sentence has the peculiarity of making reference to a particular object, the basket b; and this, too, seems to violate the universal character of a law.[19] The restriction which seems indicated here, should however again be applied to fundamental lawlike sentences only; for a true general statement about the free fall of physical bodies on the moon, while referring to a particular object, would still constitute a law, albeit a derivative one.

It seems reasonable to stipulate, therefore, that a fundamental lawlike sentence must be of universal form and must contain no essential—i.e., uneliminable—occurrences of designations for particular objects. But this is not sufficient; indeed, just as this point, a particularly serious difficulty presents itself. Consider the sentence

(S_3) Everything that is either an apple in basket b at time t or a sample of ferric oxide is red.

If we use a special expression, say "x is ferple", as synonymous with "x is either an apple in b at t or a sample of ferric oxide," then the content of S_3 can be expressed in the form

(S_4) Everything that is ferple is red.

The statement thus obtained is of universal form and contains no designations of particular objects, and it also satisfies the condition of non-limited scope; yet clearly, S_4 can qualify as a fundamental lawlike sentence no more than can S_3.

As long as "ferple" is a defined term of our language, the difficulty can readily be met by stipulating that after elimination of defined terms, a fundamental lawlike sentence must not contain essential occurrences of designations for particular objects. But this way out is of no avail when "ferple," or another term of the kind illustrated by it, is a primitive predicate of the language under consideration. This reflection indicates that certain restrictions have to be imposed upon those predicates—i.e., terms for properties or relations,—which may occur in fundamental lawlike sentences.[20]

More specifically, the idea suggests itself of permitting a predicate in a fundamental lawlike sentence only if it is purely universal, or, as we shall say, purely qualitative, in character; in other words, if a statement of its meaning does not require reference to any one particular object or spatio-temporal location. Thus, the terms "soft," "green," "warmer than," "as long as," "liquid," "electrically charged," "female," "father of" are purely qualitative predicates, while "taller than the Eiffel Tower," "medieval," "lunar," "arctic," "Ming" are not.[21]

Exclusion from fundamental lawlike sentences of predicates which are not purely qualitative would at the same time ensure satisfaction of the condition of non-limited scope; for the meaning of a purely qualitative predicate does not require a finite extension; and indeed, all the sentences considered above which violate the condition of non-limited scope make explicit or implicit reference to specific objects.

The stipulation just proposed suffers, however, from the vagueness of the concept of purely qualitative predicate. The question whether indication of the meaning of a given predicate in English does or does not require reference to some one specific object does not always permit an unequivocal answer since English as a natural language does not provide explicit definitions or other clear explications of meaning for its terms. It seems therefore reasonable to attempt definition of the concept of law not with respect to English or any other natural language, but rather with respect to a formalized language—let us call it a model language, L,—which is governed by a well-determined system of logical rules, and in which every term either is characterized as primitive or is introduced by an explicit definition in terms of the primitives.

This reference to a well-determined system is customary in logical research and is indeed quite natural in the context of any attempt to develop precise criteria for certain logical distinctions. But it does not by itself suffice to overcome the specific difficulty under discussion. For while it is now readily possible to characterize as not purely qualitative all those among the defined predicates in L whose definiens contains an essential occurrence of some individual name, our problem remains open for the primitives of the language, whose meanings are not determined by definitions within the language, but rather by semantical rules of interpretation. For we want to permit the interpretation of the primitives of L by means of such attributes as blue, hard, solid, warmer, but not by the properties of being a descendant of Napoleon, or an arctic animal, or a Greek statue; and the difficulty is precisely that of stating rigorous criteria for the distinction between the permissible and the non-permissible interpretations. Thus the problem of setting up an adequate definition for purely qualitative attributes now arises again; namely for the concepts of the meta-language in which the semantical interpretation of the primitives is formulated. We may postpone an encounter with the difficulty by presupposing formalization of the semantical meta-language, the meta-meta-language, and so forth; but somewhere, we will have to stop at a non-formalized meta-language, and for it a characterization of purely qualitative predicates will be needed and will present much the same problems as non-formalized English, with which we began. The characterization of a purely qualitative predicate as one whose meaning can be made explicit without reference to any one particular object points to the intended meaning but does not explicate it precisely, and the problem of an adequate definition of purely qualitative predicates remains open.

There can be little doubt, however, that there exists a large number of property and relation terms which would be rather generally recognized as purely qualitative in the sense here pointed out, and as permissible in the formulation of fundamental lawlike sentences; some examples have been given above, and the list could be readily enlarged. When we speak of purely qualitative predicates, we shall henceforth have in mind predicates of this kind. . . .

NOTES

1. Only portions of Parts I and III are reprinted here.
2. These two expressions, derived from the Latin *explanare,* were adopted in preference to the perhaps more customary terms "explicandum" and "explicans" in order to reserve the latter for use in the context of explication of meaning, or analysis. On explication in this sense, cf. Carnap [Concepts], p. 513.—Abbreviated titles in brackets refer to the references at the end of this selection.
3. The logical similarity of explanation and prediction, and the fact that one is directed towards past occurrences, the other towards future ones, is well expressed in the terms "postdictability" and "predictability" used by Reichenbach in [Quantum Mechanics], p. 13.
4. [Principles], p. 533.
5. The account given above of the general characteristics of explanation and prediction in science is by no means novel; it merely summarizes and states explicitly some fundamental points which have been recognized by many scientists and methodologists.

    Thus, e.g., Mill says: "An individual fact is said to be explained by pointing out its cause, that is, by stating the law or laws of causation of which its production is an instance", and "a law of uniformity in nature is said to be explained when another law or laws are pointed out, of which that law itself is but a case, and from which it could be deduced." ([Logic], Book III, Chapter XII, section 1.) Similarly, Jevons, whose general characterization of explanation was critically discussed above, stresses that "the most important process of explanation consists in showing that an observed fact is one case of a general law or tendency." ([Principles], p. 533.) Ducasse states the same point

as follows: "Explanation essentially consists in the offering of a hypothesis of fact, standing to the fact to be explained as case of antecedent to case of consequent of some already known law of connection." ([Explanation], pp. 150–51.) A lucid analysis of the fundamental structure of explanation and prediction was given by Popper in [Forschung], section 12, and, in an improved version, in his work [Society], especially in Chapter 25 and in note 7 referring to that chapter.—For a recent characterization of explanation as subsumption under general theories, cf., for example, Hull's concise discussion in [Principles], chapter I. A clear elementary examination of certain aspects of explanation is given in Hospers [Explanation], and a concise survey of many of the essentials of scientific explanation which are considered in the first two parts of the present study may be found in Feigl [Operationism], pp. 284 ff.

6. On the subject of explanation in the social sciences, especially in history, cf. also the following publications, which may serve to supplement and amplify the brief discussion to be presented here: Hempel [Laws]; Popper [Society]; White [Explanation]; and the articles *Cause* and *Understanding* in Beard and Hook [Terminology].
7. The illustration is taken from Bonfante [Semantics], section 3.
8. While in each of the last two illustrations, certain regularities are unquestionably relied upon in the explanatory argument, it is not possible to argue convincingly that the intended laws, which at present cannot all be stated explicitly, are of a causal rather than a statistical character. It is quite possible that most of all of the regularities which will be discovered as sociology develops will be of a statistical type. Cf., on this point, the suggestive observations by Zilsel in [Empiricism] section 8, and [Laws]. This issue does not affect, however, the main point we wish to make here, namely that in the social no less than in the physical sciences, subsumption under general regularities is indispensable for the explanation and the theoretical understanding of any phenomenon.
9. Cf., for example, F. H. Knight's presentation of this argument in [Limitations], pp. 251–52.
10. For a detailed logical analysis of the character and the function of the motivation concept in psychological theory, see Koch [Motivation].—A stimulating discussion of teleological behavior from the standpoint of contemporary physics and biology is contained in the article [Teleology] by Rosenblueth, Wiener and Bigelow. The authors propose an interpretation of the concept of purpose which is free from metaphysical connotations,

and they stress the importance of the concept thus obtained for a behavioristic analysis of machines and living organisms. While our formulations above intentionally use the crude terminology frequently applied in philosophical arguments concerning the applicability of causal explanation to purposive behavior, the analysis presented in the article referred to is couched in behavioristic terms and avoids reference to "motives" and the like.

11. An analysis of teleological statements in biology along these lines may be found in Woodger [Principles], especially pp. 432 ff.; essentially the same interpretation is advocated by Kaufmann in [Methodology], chapter 8.

12. For a lucid brief exposition of this idea see Feigl [Operationism], pp. 284–288.

13. The requirement of truth for laws has the consequence that a given empirical statement S can never be definitely known to be a law; for the sentence affirming the truth of S is logically equivalent with S and is therefore capable only of acquiring a more or less high probability, or degree of confirmation, relatively to the experimental evidence available at any given time. On this point, cf. Carnap [Remarks].—For an excellent non-technical exposition of the semantical concept of truth, which is here applied, the reader is referred to Tarski [Truth].

14. [Counterfactuals], p. 125.

15. This procedure was suggested by Goodman's approach in [Counterfactuals].—Reichenbach, in a detailed examination of the concept of law, similarly construes his concept of nomological statement as including both analytic and synthetic sentences; cf. [Logic], chapter VIII.

16. The difficulty illustrated by this example was stated concisely by Langford ([Review]), who referred to it as the problem of distinguishing between universals of fact and causal universals. For further discussion and illustration of this point, see also Chisholm [Conditional], especially pp. 301f.—A systematic analysis of the problem was given by Goodman in [Counterfactuals], especially part III.—While not concerned with the specific point under discussion, the detailed examination of counterfactual conditionals and their relation to laws of nature, in Chapter VIII of Lewis's work [Analysis], contains important observations on several of the issues raised in the present section.

17. The view that laws should be construed as not being limited to a finite domain has been expressed, among others, by Popper ([Forschung], section 13) and by Reichenbach ([Logic], p. 369).

18. [Logic], p. 361.—Our terminology as well as the definitions to be proposed later for the two types

of law do not coincide with Reichenbach's, however.

19. In physics, the idea that a law should not refer to any particular object has found its expression in the maxim that the general laws of physics should contain no reference to specific space-time points, and that spatio-temporal coordinates should occur in them only in the form of differences or differentials.

20. The point illustrated by the sentences S_3 and S_4 above was made by Goodman, who has also emphasized the need to impose certain restrictions upon the predicates whose occurrence is to be permissible in lawlike sentences. These predicates are essentially the same as those which Goodman calls projectible. Goodman has suggested that the problems of establishing precise criteria for projectibilty, of interpreting counterfactual conditionals, and of defining the concept of law are so intimately related as to be virtually aspects of a single problem. (Cf. his articles [Query] and [Counterfactuals].) One suggestion for an analysis of projectibility has recently been made by Carnap in [Application]. Goodman's note [Infirmities] contains critical observations on Carnap's proposals.

21. That laws, in addition to being of universal form, must contain only purely universal predicates was clearly argued by Popper ([Forschung], sections 14, 15).—Our alternative expression "purely qualitative predicate" was chosen in analogy to Carnap's term "purely qualitative property" (cf. [Application]).—The above characterization of purely universal predicates seems preferable to a simpler and perhaps more customary one, to the effect that a statement of the meaning of the predicate must require no reference to particular objects. For this formulation might be too exclusive since it could be argued that stating the meaning of such purely qualitative terms as "blue" or "hot" requires illustrative reference to some particular object which has the quality in question. The essential point is that no one specific object has to be chosen; any one in the logically unlimited set of blue or of hot objects will do. In explicating the meaning of "taller than the Eiffel Tower," "being an apple in basket b at the time t," "medieval," etc., however, reference has to be made to one specific object or to some one in a limited set of objects.

REFERENCES

The abbreviated titles in brackets are used for reference throughout the selection.

Beard, Charles A., and Hook, Sidney. [Terminology] "Problems of Terminology in Historical Writing." In

Theory and Practice in Historical Study: A Report of the Committee on Historiography. New York: Social Science Research Council, 1946, chap. IV.

Bonfante, G. [Semantics] "Semantics, Language." In P. J. Harriman (ed.), *The Encyclopedia of Psychology,* New York: Philosophical Library, 1946.

Carnap, Rudolf. [Concepts] "The Two Concepts of Probability." *Philosophy and Phenomenological Research* 5 (1945): 513–532.

———. [Remarks] "Remarks on Induction and Truth." *Philosophy and Phenomenological Research* 6 (1945): 590–602.

———. [Application] "On the Application of Inductive Logic." *Philosophy and Phenomenological Research* 8 (1947): 133–147.

Chisolm, Roderick M. [Conditional] "The Contrary-to-Fact Conditional." *Mind* 55 (1946): 289–307.

Ducasse, C. J. [Explanation] "Explanation, Mechanism, and Teleology." *Journal of Philosophy* 22 (1925): 150–155.

Feigl, Herbert. [Operationism] "Operationism and Scientific Method." *Psychological Review* 52 (1945): 250–259, 284–288.

Goodman, Nelson. [Query] "A Query on Confirmation." *Journal of Philosophy* 43 (1946): 383–385.

———. [Counterfactuals] "The Problem of Counterfactual Conditionals." *Journal of Philosophy* 44 (1947): 113–128.

———. [Infirmities] "On Infirmities of Confirmation Theory." *Philosophy and Phenomenological Research* 8 (1947): 149–151.

Hempel, Carl G. [Laws] "The Function of General Laws in History." *Journal of Philosophy* 39 (1942): 35–48.

Hospers, John. [Explanation] "On Explanation." *Journal of Philosophy* 43 (1946): 337–356.

Hull, Clark L. [Variables] The problem of intervening variables in molar behavior theory. *Psychological review,* vol. 50 (1943), pp. 273–291.

———. [Principles] Principles of behavior. New York, 1943.

Jevons, W. Stanley. [Principles] The principles of science. London, 1924. (1st ed. 1874.)

Kaufmann, Felix. [Methodology] Methodology of the social sciences. New York, 1944.

Knight, Frank H. [Limitations] The limitations of scientific method in economics. In Tugwell, R., ed., The trend of economics. New York, 1924.

Koch, Sigmund. [Motivation] "The Logical Character of the Motivation Concept." *Psychological Review* 48 (1941): 15–38, 127–154.

Langford, C. H. [Review] "Review." *Journal of Symbolic Logic* 6 (1941): 67–68.

Lewis, C. I. [Analysis] *An Analysis of Knowledge and Valuation.* La Salle, IL, 1946.

Mill, John Stuart. [Logic] *A System of Logic.*

Popper, Karl. [Forschung] *Logik der Forschung.* Vienna, 1935.

———. [Society] *The Open Society and Its Enemies.* London, 1945.

Reichenbach, Hans. [Logic] *Elements of Symbolic Logic.* New York, 1947.

Rosenblueth, A., Wiener, N., and Bigelow, J. [Teleology] "Behavior, Purpose, and Teleology." *Philosophy of Science* 10 (1943): 18–24.

Tarski, Alfred. [Truth] "The Semantical Conception of Truth and the Foundations of Semantics." *Philosophy and Phenomenological Research* 4 (1944): 341–376.

White, Morton G. [Explanation] "Historical Explanation." *Mind* 52 (1943): 212–229.

Woodger, J. H. [Principles] *Biological Principles* New York, 1929.

Zilsel, Edgar. [Empiricism] "Problems of Empiricism." In *International Encyclopedia of Unified Science,* vol. II, no. 8. Chicago: University of Chicago Press, 1941.

———. [Laws] "Physics and the Problem of Historico-sociological Laws." *Philosophy of Science* 8 (1941): 567–579.

MICHAEL SCRIVEN, "EXPLANATIONS, PREDICTIONS, AND LAWS"

Scriven argues that the D-N model is committed to the view that there are no complete explanations because we can never get all the necessary grounds to make the deduction. To show this, Scriven uses the example of the knocked-over ink bottle. Imagine that he has just knocked over a bottle of ink and the carpet is stained. According to Scriven, the explanation for the stain on the carpet is nothing more than "I knocked over the ink bottle." The context as outlined by Scriven makes this an acceptable explanation. If we tried to get enough information to satisfy the D-

N model, we would go on forever collecting data and never get to the explanation. Think of what would be entailed in making a strict deduction. First, just what is being explained? Why is the stain just where it is and not just a bit to the left? Why does it have the precise shape it has? Why is the stain just the shade that it is here and slightly different there? The laws required to answer these questions would be incredibly difficult to state. Second, and perhaps worse, the initial conditions for these laws would be close to impossible to determine, thus making it equally close to impossible to go from the law to the actual particular (stain) being explained.

Strictly speaking, Scriven points out, even the examples used by Hempel and Oppenheim do not and cannot satisfy their own criteria for being complete explanations. He focuses on the very first example offered by Hempel and Oppenheim. They give the example of a mercury thermometer rapidly immersed in hot water. First the mercury column drops, and then it rises. Their explanation for this falling and rising is that first the temperature change affects the glass tube; the tube expands, and the mercury column falls. Then the mercury expands faster than the glass, resulting in the column's rising. Scriven replies that what Hempel and Oppenheim have said is literally false. The mercury begins to expand almost immediately because of radiation effects from the heat, and the glass of the tube is not so perfect that it expands evenly throughout its length. Again, it is not clear what is to be explained. If it is the precise rising and falling of the mercury column, then the laws required will be extraordinarily complex and the antecedent conditions virtually impossible to find.

Scriven stresses that the major mistake of the D-N model is the assumption that scientific explanations are context free, that scientific explanations are just examples of deductive logic. Deduction is just a question of following rules of logic. Deduction is context free. According to Scriven, no explanation is context free. All questions make presuppositions about what is known, and it is these presuppositions that supply the context of the answer. Scientific explanations are just specific kinds of explanations. Here, both he and van Fraassen agree. But of course, Hempel and Oppenheim would disagree with Scriven.

Scriven offers criteria by which to judge the adequacy of any explanation. Explanations should be accepted when they are (1) correct/accurate (are true), (2) complete/adequate (give the appropriate causal connection), and (3) relevant/appropriate/proper (cite the appropriate context).

Scriven offers the following characterization of a scientific explanation. It is topically unified—that is, it satisfies points 2 and 3. It imparts understanding. It does this by meeting all three criteria. Scriven goes on to tell us a bit about understanding. Understanding is organized knowledge—knowing how things actually do relate to each other. Ultimately, explanations—if they are to work—must take us back to what Scriven calls "the most fundamental features of our knowledge." Although he does not state it in this selection, Scriven believes that one of the fundamental features of our knowledge is the ability to understand the notion of a cause. Thus for Scriven, our ability to give causal explanations precedes any scientific knowledge. If this were not so, Scriven could not claim—as he has—that scientific (causal) explanation is really no different from any other kind of explanation.

Explanations, Predictions, and Laws

MICHAEL SCRIVEN

THE LAST TWO CONDITIONS AND A SUMMARY OF DIFFICULTIES

It is stated that the explanation "must contain general laws, and these must actually be required for the derivation. . . ." And finally, it is said that the derivation must be deductive, ". . . for otherwise the [explanation] would not constitute adequate grounds for [the proposition describing the phenomenon]."[1] We now have a general idea of Hempel and Oppenheim's model of explanation, which I have elsewhere christened, for obvious reasons, "the deductive model."[2] I wish to maintain against it the following criticisms in particular, and some others incidentally;

1. It fails to make the crucial logical distinctions between explanations, grounds for explanations, predictions, things to be explained, and the description of these things.
2. It is too restrictive in that it excludes their own examples and almost every ordinary scientific one.
3. It is too inclusive and admits entirely nonexplanatory schema[s].
4. It requires an account of cause, law,

From Herbert Feigl and Grover Maxwell (eds.), *Minnesota Studies in the Philosophy of Science*, vol. 3 Minneapolis: Univ. of Minnesota Press 1962, pp. 170–230. Copyright © 1962 by the University of Minnesota.

and probability which are basically unsound.

5. It leaves out of account three notions that are in fact essential for an account of scientific explanation: context, judgment, and understanding.

These objections are not wholly independent, and I have already dealt with some of them. . . .

When we say that a perfectly good explanation of one event, e.g., a bridge collapsing, may be no more than an assertion about another event, e.g., a bomb exploding, might it not plausibly be said that this can only be an explanation if some laws are assumed to be true, which *connect* the two events? After all, the one is an explanation of the other, not because it came before it, but because it *caused* it. In which case, a full statement of the explanation would make explicit these essential, presupposed laws.

The major weakness in this argument is the last sentence; we can put the difficulty again by saying that, if completeness requires not merely the existence but the quoting of all necessary grounds, there are no complete explanations at all. For just as the statement about the bomb couldn't be an explanation of the bridge collapsing unless there was some connection between the two events, it couldn't be an explanation unless it was true. So, if we must include a statement of the relevant laws to justify our belief in the connection, i.e., in the soundness of the explanation, then we must include a statement of the relevant data to justify our belief in the claim that a bomb burst, on which the soundness of the explanation also depends."[3]

Certainly in putting forward one event as an explanation of another in the usual cause-seeking contexts, we are committed to the view that the first event caused the second, and we are also committed to the view that the first took place. Of course, we may be wrong about either view and then we are wrong in thinking we have given the explanation. But it is a mistake to suppose this error can be eliminated by quoting further evidence (whether laws or data); it is merely that the error may be then located in a more precise way—as due to a mistaken belief in such and such a datum or law. The function of deduction is only to shift the grounds for doubt, though doubts sometimes get tired and give up after a certain amount of this treatment.

Perhaps the most important reason that Hempel and Oppenheim have for insisting on the inclusion of laws in the explanation is what I take to be their belief (at the time of writing the paper in question) that only if one had such laws in mind could one have any rational grounds for putting forward one's explanation. This is simply false as can be seen immediately by considering an example of a simple physical explanation of which we can be quite certain. If you reach for a cigarette and in doing so knock over an ink bottle which then spills onto the floor, you are in an excellent position to explain to your wife how that stain appeared on the carpet, i.e., why the carpet is stained (if you cannot clean it off fast enough). You knocked the ink bottle over. This is the explanation of the state of affairs in question, and there is no nonsense about it being in doubt because you cannot quote

the laws that are involved, Newton's and all the others; in fact, it appears one cannot here quote any unambiguous true general statements, such as would meet the requirements of the deductive model.

The fact you cannot quote them does not show they are not somehow *involved*, but the catch lies in the term "involved." Some kind of connection must hold, and if we say this *means* that laws are involved, then of course the point is won. The suggestion is debatable, but even if true, it does not follow that we will be able to state a law that guarantees the connection. The explanation requires that there be a connection, but not any particular one—just one of a wide range of alternatives. Certainly it would not be the explanation if the world was governed by *antigravity*. But then it would not be the explanation if you had not knocked over the ink bottle—and you have just as good reasons for believing that you did knock it over as you have for believing that knocking it over led to (caused) the stain. Having reasons for causal claims thus does not always mean being able to quote laws. We shall return to this example later. For the moment, it is useful mainly to indicate that (i) there is a reply to the claim that one cannot have good reasons for a causal ascription unless one can quote intersubjectively verifiable general statements and (ii) there is an important similarity between the way in which the production of an appropriate law supports the claim that one event explains another, and the way in which the production of further data (plus laws) to confirm the claim that the prior event occurred supports the same claim. They are defenses against two entirely different kinds of error or doubt, indeed, but they are also both support for the same kind of claim, viz., the claim that one event (state, etc.) explains another.

This is perhaps obscured by the fact that when we make an assertion our claim is in full view, so to speak, whereas when we put forward an assertion as an explanation, its further role is entirely derived from the context, e.g., that it is produced in answer to a request for an explanation, and so its further obligations seem to require explicit statement. This is a superficial view. All that we actually identify in the linguistic entity of a 'declarative statement' is the subject, predicate, tense, etc. We have no reason at all, apart from the context of its utterance, for supposing it to be asserted, rather than proposed for consideration, pronounced for a grammatical exercise, mouthed by an actor, produced as an absurdity, etc.[4] That it is asserted to be true we infer from the context just as we infer that it is proffered as the explanation of something else; and for both these tasks it may need support. We may concede that assertion is the *primary* role of indicative sentences without weakening this point.

It is in fact the case that considerations of context, seen to be necessary even at the level of identifying assertions and explanations themselves, not only open up another dimension of error for an explanation, that of pragmatic inappropriateness, but simultaneously offer a possible way of identifying *the* explanation of something, where this notion is applicable.

A particular context—such as a discussion between organic chemists working on the same problem—may make one of many deductively acceptable explanations of a biochemical phenomenon entirely inappropriate, and make another of exactly the right type. (Of course, I also wish to reject the criteria of the deductive model; but even if one accepted it, the consideration of context turns out to be *also* necessary. So its importance is not only apparent in dealing with alternative analyses.)

We may generalize our observations in the following terms. An explanation is sometimes said to be incorrect or incom-

plete or improper. I suggest we pin down these somewhat general terms along with their slightly more specific siblings as follows. If an explanation explicitly contains false propositions, we can call it *incorrect* or *inaccurate*. If it fails to explain what it is supposed to explain because it cannot be 'brought to bear' on it, e.g., because no causal connection exists between the phenomenon as so far specified and its alleged effect, we can call it *incomplete* or *inadequate*. If it is satisfactory in the previous respects but is clearly not the explanation required in the given context, either because of its difficulty or its field of reference, we can call it *irrelevant, improper,* or *inappropriate.*

Corresponding to these possible failings there are types of defense which may be relevant. Against the charge of inaccuracy, we produce what I shall call *truth-justifying grounds.* Against the charge of inadequacy, we produce *role-justifying grounds,* and against the complaint of inappropriateness, we invoke *type-justifying grounds.* To put forward an explanation is to commit oneself on truth, role, and type, though it is certainly not to have explicitly considered grounds of these kinds in advance, any more than to speak English in England implies language-type consideration for a life-long but polylingual resident Englishman. . . .

COMPLETENESS IN EXPLANATIONS

The possibility of indefinitely challenging the successive grounds of an explanation has suggested to some people—*not* Hempel and Oppenheim—that a complete explanation cannot be given within science. Such people are adopting another use of "complete"—even less satisfactory than Hempel and Oppenheim's—according to which the idea of a complete explanation becomes not only foreign to science but in fact either wholly empty, essentially teleological, or capable of completion by appeal to a self-caused cause. Interesting though this move is in certain respects, it essentially requires saying that we can better understand something in the world by ultimately ascribing its existence and nature to the activities of a mysterious entity whose existence and nature cannot be explained in the same way, than by relating it to its proximate causes or arguing that the world has existed indefinitely. I shall only add that we are supposed to be studying scientific explanations, and if none of them are complete in this sense, we may as well drop this sense while making a note of the point—which is equivalent to the point that the causal relation is irreflexive and hence rather unexciting—for there is an important and standard use of "complete" which does apply to some suggested scientific explanation, and not to others, and is well worth analyzing.

Now, if some scientific explanations are complete—and think how a question in a physics exam may ask for a complete explanation of, for example, the effects noticed by Hertz in his experiments to determine whether electromagnetic waves existed—it cannot be because there is a last step in the process of challenging grounds, for there is no stage at which a request for further proof could not make sense. But *in any given context* such requests eventually become absurd, because in any scientific context certain kinds of data are taken as beyond question, and there is no meaning to the notions of explanation and justification which is not, directly or indirectly, dependent on a context. This situation is of a very familiar kind of logic. It makes perfectly good sense to ask for the spatial location of any physical object; and perfectly proper and complete answers will involve a reference to the location of some other physical objects. Naturally we can, and often do, go on to ask the further question concerning where these other objects are ("Where's Carleton

College?" "In Northfield." "But where's Northfield?"). And no question in a series of this kind is meaningless, unless one includes the question "Where is the universe, i.e., everything?" as of this kind. If one does include this question (which is the analogue of "Where did the universe *come from?*"), then the impossibility of answering it only shows something about the notion of position, and nothing about the incompleteness of our knowledge. If one excludes this question, the absence of a last stage in such a series does not show our inability to give anyone complete directions to the public library but only that the notion of completeness of such descriptions involves context criteria. . . .

Having distinguished the types of difficulty an explanation may encounter, one can more easily see there is no reason for insisting that it is complete only if it is armed against them in advance, since (i) to display in advance one's armor against *all* possible objections is impossible and (ii) the value of such a requirement is adequately retained by requiring that scientific explanations be such that scientifically sound defenses of the several kinds indicated *be available for* them though not necessarily *embodied in* them. Since there is no special reason for thinking that true first-level role-justifying assumptions are any more necessary for the explanation than any others, it seems quite arbitrary to require that they should be included in a complete explanation; and it is quite independently an error to suppose they must take the form of laws.

Hempel and Oppenheim's[5] . . . mistake, then, lies in the supposition that by subsumption under a generalization one has automatically explained *something,* and that queries about this "explanation" represent a request for *further* and *different* explanation. Sometimes these queries merely echo the original puzzlement, and it is wholly illicit to argue that the original matter has been explained. It is as if I asked the way to the town hall from the post office and you replied, "It's in the same relation to the post office as town halls always are"; and upon my indicating dissatisfaction you were to say, "Ah! What you *really* wanted to know (what you now want to know) is the geographic relation of all town halls to their post offices." This was not at all what I wanted to know, though in the light of the facts an answer to this will provide me with the answer I seek. You have produced an interesting regularity related to my question, but you have not, in this case, adequately done what I asked you to do. . . .

THE RELATION BETWEEN DEDUCTION FROM TRUE PREMISES AND SOUND INFERENCE

By requiring deduction from true premises, Hempel and Oppenheim impose a pair of conditions which exclude their own examples and most scientific explanations of events. The reasons for this are, I think, clear and interesting. Deduction looks as if it is the only watertight connection between the premises and the conclusion, and it appears obvious that a watertight connection must be insisted on. But the matter is much more complicated, and eventually we must abandon even the idea that they are proposing a useful *ideal* for explanation.

I want to begin with the explanation of events and only then go on to the explanation of laws. Hempel and Oppenheim never deal with the explanation of a particular event instance, but only with events of a certain *kind;* naturally success in this task will enable one to explain particular events of this kind, but it is worth remembering that a degree of generality is already present which is absent in the case of many scientific explanations, e.g., of the formation of the earth, the emergence of Homo sapiens, and the extinction of the dinosaurs. This

degree of generality in their examples is one of the factors which lends what I take to be spurious plausibility to their explanation-prediction correlation. For an explanation of events of *kind* X is necessarily couched timelessly and hence may more reasonably be thought applicable prospectively as well as retrospectively.

Turning to the example with which they begin, and which they give in more detail than any other, we read, "A mercury thermometer is rapidly immersed in hot water; there occurs a temporary drop of the mercury column, which is then followed by a swift rise. How is this phenomenon to be explained? The increase in temperature affects at first only the glass tube of the thermometer; it expands and thus provides a larger space for the mercury inside, whose surface therefore drops. As soon as by heat conduction the rise in temperature reaches the mercury, however, the latter expands, and as its coefficient of expansion is considerably larger than that of glass, a rise of the mercury level results."[6] What can be said about this example in the terms of their analysis?

In the first place, it undoubtedly does represent a certain kind of scientific explanation. Not only is what is given, to the best of my knowledge, an explanation of the phenomenon described, but it could often perfectly well be called *the* explanation of it, since the appropriate contextual conditions for that description are usually met. Hence, an analysis of it will have some claim to be an analysis of scientific explanation. However, it is equally indubitable that it contains false statements, some of them being the alleged laws, and that the statements given do not entail the desired consequence. Their example therefore violates all three of their own criteria (one trivially, since general statements are "essentially" involved even if they are not true and hence not laws). This rather extraordinary situation was not altogether unnoticed by the authors. Referring to the deduction requirement, they say of the explanation as they give it that "if adequately and completely formulated," it would "entail the consequence that the mercury will first drop, then rise," which implies that the formulation given will *not* do this.

I shall not elaborate in detail the various physical errors in this and their other examples.[7] An example or two will suffice, since I do not take these errors to invalidate the explanation, only the deductivist analysis of it. There are two kinds of error in their explanation. First, they say: "The increase in temperature affects at first only the glass tube of the thermometer; it expands and thus . . ." No physicist would be willing to accept this as literally true. Radiation effects reach the mercury at the speed of light and are causing it to expand while the slower conduction effects are expanding the glass; but even these reach the mercury long before the glass has expanded enough to produce a visible drop in the mercury column. Second, they do not allow for the fact that glass itself is a physically unique substance, with highly anisotropic *multiple* coefficients of expansion, the relationship between them being dependent upon the minutiae of its chemical composition and details of the annealing process, which vary even from batch to batch of the closely controlled thermometer glass.

Surely these complaints are not serious; a little research or rewording would take care of them, would it not? They are not serious for the explanation: it is correct. But they are serious for the analysis because it requires literal truth. The only way in which literal truth could be salvaged here would be by invoking an extremely complicated inequality, involving all the coefficients mentioned, the specific heats, the radiation rates, energy distribution factors, upper limits obtained from the heat-transfer equa-

tions, and so on. And with every complication at the theoretical level—as we try to employ laws that are exactly correct—there is a corresponding complication at the experimental end, since new measurements are required in order to apply the more complex theory.

The upshot of this is not merely that Hempel and Oppenheim's example is "incomplete" according to their own criteria of completeness; it is that it is not an explanation at all, on their analysis. Now could the situation be redeemed by turning to some textbook and using the more complex relationships referred to above? A serious research effort would be required to obtain the material, and it has certainly never been done. That is, there *is* as yet no "complete" explanation of this simple phenomenon, on their criterion of completeness. All we have are "explanation sketches," which they think are characteristic of the *social* sciences, by *contrast* with physics. But in physics, just as in economics, virtually all the explanations given are of this kind, and they are usually just as "complete" as they should be, i.e., as complete as is necessary to attain the requisite degree of reliability. Hempel and Oppenheim have an oversimple logical model: an explanation that fails to measure up to its standards may be a great deal more complete than one that does, i.e., it may identify the relevant effective variables and ignore the ineffective ones, as does their example in this case. Other processes are going on here, but nobody asked for a complete description of the thermodynamic process; they asked for the explanation of a particular effect. Giving an explanation requires *selecting* from among the variables that are involved those whose activities are unknown to the inquirer and crucial for the phenomenon; it does not involve dragging in or constructing *all* the relations of these variables to the others involved. The explanation won't be an explanation unless the variables selected are crucial. To *show* they are would thus be appropriate only if the explanation were challenged in this respect. . . .

Can we explain why bodies near the earth's surface fall according to the law $s = kt^2$? According to Hempel and Oppenheim, who use this example, this is done "by deducing it from a more comprehensive set of laws, namely Newton's laws of motion and his law of gravitation, together with some statements about particular facts namely the mass and radius of the earth."[8] There would be circumstances under which this would be a satisfactory explanation, though there are others where it would be hopeless (e.g., where the explanation is "Atmospheric density varies less than 10% over the earth's surface, and $s = 16t^2$ when measured from the top of the campanile at Pisa"). But the points to be made here are that (1) the Newtonian laws are known to be in error, and (2) even if true, they would not entail $s = kt^2$, since (a) the actual relationship varies from point to point and height to height, so no such formula is derivable, and (b) the premises quoted are inadequate for the proposed deduction anyway (the earth has no single radius, air resistance is not considered,[9] etc.).

I conclude that, where it is appropriate to invoke Newton's laws for this explanation, the point is not *at all* that deduction from these as true premises is possible, but that these relations are the crucial factors for this inquiry, in this context, i.e., the only *important* ones (with respect to the degree of accuracy judged appropriate from the context, and the level of knowledge of the inquirer(s)). We know this to be true, and we could even go out and do the experiments to show it is true. It does not follow from the claim that we know it and that we have to be able to show it true by deduction from true premises now in our possession . . .

THE ALTERNATIVE ANALYSIS

What is a scientific explanation? It is a topically unified communication, the content of which imparts understanding of some scientific phenomenon. And the better it is, the more efficiently and reliably it does this, i.e., with less redundancy and a higher *over-all* probability. What is understanding? Understanding is, roughly, organized knowledge, i.e., knowledge of the relations between various facts and/or laws. These relations are of many kinds—deductive, inductive, analogical, etc. (Understanding is deeper, more thorough, the greater the span of this relational knowledge.) It is for the most part a perfectly objective matter to test understanding, just as it is to test knowledge,[10] and it is absurd to identify it with a subjective feeling, as have some critics of this kind of view. So long as we give examinations to our students, we think we can test understanding objectively. (On the other hand, it is to be hoped and expected that the subjective feeling of understanding is fairly well *correlated with* real understanding as a result of education.)

Explanation is not "reduction to the familiar," partly because the familiar is often not understood (rainbows, memory, the appeal of music) and partly because we may understand the unfamiliar perfectly well (pure elements, the ideal gas, absolute zero). On the other hand, (i) we do understand much of what is familiar and so much explanation *is* reduction to the familiar. And (ii) "familiar" *can* be taken as synonymous with "explained," in which case this slogan comes nearer the truth, though by using the tautology route. Finally, (iii) there is the great truth implicit in this view that at a particular stage in explanations of a certain kind, there is very little more to understanding besides familiarity. We do come to accept facts and relations which we at first viewed as wholly incomprehensible; we come to accept gravity and to reject Newton's vituperative condemnation of the view that it is inherent in matter and can act through a vacuum without mediation. The stage at which we do this is the last stage in an explanation, and the explanations which lead us to this kind of last stage are those which take us back to the most fundamental features of our knowledge.

NOTES

1. Hempel, Carl and Oppenheim, Paul, "The Logic of Explanation," in H. Feigl and M. Brodbeck (eds.), *Readings in the Philosophy of Science* (New York: Appleton-Century Crofts, 1953), p. 321.
2. "Certain Weaknesses in the Deductive Model of Explanation," paper presented at the Midwestern Division of the American Philosophical Association, May 1955.
3. Their model requires the truth of the asserted explanation, but it doesn't require the inclusion of evidence for this. Instead of similarly requiring a causal connection, it actually requires the inclusion of one special kind of evidence for this. If it treated both requirements equitably, the model would be either trivial (causal explanations must be true and causally relevant) or deviously arbitrary (... must include *deductively* adequate grounds for the truth of any assertions and for the causal connection).
4. See Max Black's "Definition, Presupposition, and Assertion," in his *Problems of Analysis* (London: Routledge and Kegan Paul, 1954).
5. I attribute this to the joint authors on the basis of exegetical discussion by Hempel alone; the point is not made in their article.
6. Hempel and Oppenheim, *op. cit.*, p. 320.
7. See pp. 255–350 of my "Explanations," D. Phil. thesis, Oxford, 1956, microfilmed by the University of Illinois library.
8. Hempel and Oppenheim, *op. cit.*, p. 321.
9. Hempel and Oppenheim refer to "Galileo's Law for the free fall of bodies," not $s = kt^2$. In the *Dialogue concerning Two New Sciences* (Third Day), it is made clear that $s = kt^2$ is intended, and that it is held to apply to motion in air. (Details are in my "Explanations," p. 346.)
10. Knowledge stands in relation to understanding rather as explanations do to theories. We know the date of our birthday, but we understand the calendrical system: we know the items and the relations which, combined, make up understanding.

NANCY CARTWRIGHT, "THE TRUTH DOESN'T EXPLAIN MUCH"

Hempel and Oppenheim's D-N model requires the use of causal laws, laws that state causal regularities in general terms. These sorts of laws (as noted in the introduction to the Hempel-Oppenheim article) are called "covering laws." Cartwright argues that the D-N model cannot work because there really are no covering laws. According to Hempel and Oppenheim, covering laws must be totally general and true. Cartwright claims that all the laws of physics are *ceteris paribus* laws (*ceteris paribus* means "other things being equal"); that is, they hold only given certain assumptions. If we leave out the *ceteris paribus* conditions, the laws are literally false. If we do not leave them out, the laws are much more restricted than Hempel and Oppenheim are willing to admit. The restrictive *ceteris paribus* conditions come dangerously close to being mentions of particulars, something that Hempel and Oppenheim claim true laws cannot have.

Go back to the example of a law used previously, "All cats purr." As stated, there are no *ceteris paribus* conditions. What would they be? Most simply, suppose that our cat is asleep. Does it purr? No. Suppose that we found a catlike animal that did not ever purr. Would it be a cat? How we answer this question is a function of why cats purr. What we call purring is the sound of a cat's breathing when the animal is relaxed. If a catlike animal had a slightly different throat structure, the sound made when relaxed might be more like a rasp. If our catlike animal was like other cats in all other ways except for rasping instead of purring and we could explain the lack of purring, then, yes, we could classify this nonpurring animal as a cat. Thus the true *ceteris paribus* condition for "All cats purr" is something like "given this particular respiratory system." Notice that this condition is derived from a rather sophisticated group of theories about physiology and acoustics. What this shows—and it is implicit in Cartwright's approach to understanding laws—is that laws cannot be understood independent from the theory with which they are associated. Of note here is that Hempel and Oppenheim have a similar view. They claim that strictly speaking, scientific explanations are done by the appropriate theories. The laws we actually do cite, as in their examples, are proxies for the full theoretical explanation.

Cartwright examines a well-known law from optics, Snell's law. Snell's law can be stated as a covering law: The ratio of the angle of incidence to the angle of refraction is a constant. But this is not strictly true for cases where the two media are anisotropic, that is, have properties (e.g., density) that are not distributed equally in all directions. Since actually all naturally occurring liquids do have density (and temperature) gradients, Snell's law must be modified. In Hempel and Oppenheim's example of the bent oar, the law used would have to be amended to take into account the density gradients of the water. Thus the law would not quite have the general scope that Hempel and Oppenheim demand, and finding the actual antecedent conditions—the values for the density gradients at just the time required—would be close to impossible. This criticism of the D-N model made by Cartwright is very similar to the one made by Scriven when he pointed out that the Hempel-Oppenheim explanation of the mercury thermometer really did not work. Cartwright and Scriven clearly agree that Hempel and Oppenheim have oversimplified the nature of scientific laws.

Cartwright has two other critiques of the D-N model of explanation.

1. The D-N model assumes that the universe is tidy, that at rock bottom, the laws that govern "everything" are really quite simple. However, this may not be true. There may be no laws at all for complex happenings. Even if there are such laws, they may be very messy laws. They may be just chock full of all sorts of *ceteris paribus* clauses. Of course, we can state them simply. But this just gets us back to problem of *ceteris paribus* laws. And laws that are literally true are so restricted by their *ceteris paribus* conditions that they would not explain much. If not restricted, then they are literally false. (Hesse will handle this point by claiming that laws of science are not meant to be taken literally.)

2. Often there is no one clean law to use. Cartwright uses an example from cooking. We know that potatoes cook faster in salted water and slower at high altitudes. The law for each of these cases has to do with how water boils and, of

course, what it means to cook a potato. But there is no law telling us how potatoes will cook in salted water at high altitudes. This is not to say that we could not discover laws for this case. But this case is easy. For the truly complex cases of science, the intersection of laws creates a jumble, unlikely, in Cartwright's opinion, to be mastered by the finding of one simple law.

Cartwright tells of planting camellias in rich, hot soil. Camellias like rich but cool soil. Despite her excellent care, many of the flowers died. Her explanation? The soil was too warm. Of course, other factors (e.g., the lack of some trace element) may have been involved. Yet given what she knew, her explanation is quite reasonable. Her point is that this explanation does not use a true covering law. There is no such law stating that when camellias just like the ones she used, planted in soil with just the richness and heat of hers, cared for in just the manner that she did, will yield just what her garden did. Her guess is that there never could be such a law. Her overall point is that our understanding of causality precedes our scientific ability to cite laws and give sophisticated scientific explanations. This is precisely the same point made by Scriven when he pointed out that our knowledge of causality is a fundamental feature of what we know.

For Cartwright, laws do not function as pure descriptions but rather as suggestions about which patterns in nature we ought to look at. If there are generalizations that are literally true, it is unlikely that they will be very good at organizing knowledge. The generalizations that will be good at organizing will almost assuredly not be literally true. Here, Cartwright may be approaching the ideas of Mary Hesse, who will make the connection between laws and metaphors.

The Truth Doesn't Explain Much

NANCY CARTWRIGHT

0. INTRODUCTION

Scientific theories must tell us both what is true in nature, and how we are to explain it. I shall argue that these are entirely different functions and should be kept distinct. Usually the two are conflated. The second is commonly seen as a by-product of the first.

Scientific theories are thought to explain by dint of the descriptions they give of reality. Once the job of describing is done, science can shut down. That is all there is to do. To describe nature—to tell its laws, the values of its fundamental constants, its mass distributions—is *ipso facto* to lay down how we are to explain it.

This is a mistake, I shall argue; a mistake that is fostered by the covering-law model of explanation. The covering-law model supposes that all we need to know are the laws of nature—and a little logic, perhaps a little probability theory—and then we know which factors can explain which others. For example, in the simplest deductive-nomological version,[1] the covering-law model says that one factor explains another just in case the occurrence of the second can be deduced from the occurrence of the first given the laws of nature.

But the D-N model is just an example. In the sense which is relevant to my claims here, most models of explanation offered recently in the philosophy of science are covering-law models. This includes not only Hempel's own inductive statistical model,[2] but also Patrick Suppes's probabilistic model of causation,[3] Wesley Salmon's statistical relevance model,[4] and even Bengt Hanson's contextualistic model.[5] All these accounts rely on the laws of nature, and just the laws of nature, to pick out which factors we can use in explanation.

A good deal of criticism has been aimed at Hempel's original covering-law models. Much of the criticism objects that these models let in too much. On Hempel's account it seems we can explain Henry's failure to get pregnant by his taking birth control pills, and we can explain the storm by the falling barometer. My objection is quite the opposite. Covering-law models let in too little. With a covering-law model we can explain hardly anything, even the things of which we are most proud—like the role of DNA in the inheritance of genetic characteristics, or the formation of rainbows when sunlight is refracted through raindrops. We cannot explain these phenomena with a covering-law model, I shall argue, because we do not have laws that cover them. Covering laws are scarce.

Many phenomena which have perfectly good scientific explanations are not covered by any laws. No true laws, that is. They are at best covered by *ceteris paribus* generalizations—generalizations that hold only under

special conditions, usually ideal conditions. The literal translation is "other things being equal"; but it would be more apt to read *ceteris paribus* as "other things being *right.*"

Sometimes we act as if this does not matter. We have in the back of our minds an 'understudy' picture of *ceteris paribus* laws: *ceteris paribus* laws are real laws; they can stand in when the laws we would like to see are not available and they can perform all the same functions, only not quite so well. But this will not do. *Ceteris paribus* generalizations, read literally without the *"ceteris paribus"* modifier, are false. They are not only false, but held by us to be false: and there is no ground in the covering-law picture for false laws to explain anything. On the other hand, with the modifier the *ceteris paribus* generalizations may be true, but they cover only those few cases where the conditions are right. For most cases, either we have a law that purports to cover, but cannot explain because it is acknowledged to be false, or we have a law that does not cover. Either way, it is bad for the covering-law picture.

1. *CETERIS PARIBUS* LAWS

When I first started talking about the scarcity of covering laws, I tried to summarize my view by saying "There are no exceptionless generalizations." Then a friend asked, "How about 'All men are mortal'?" She was right. I had been focusing too much on the equations of physics. A more plausible claim would have been that there are no exceptionless quantitative laws in physics. Indeed not only are there no exceptionless laws, but in fact our best candidates are known to fail. This is something like the Popperian thesis that *every theory is born refuted.* Every theory we have proposed in physics, even at the time when it was most firmly entrenched, was known to be deficient in specific and detailed ways. I think this is also true for every precise quantitative law within a physics theory.

But this is not the point I had wanted to make. Some laws are treated, at least for the time being, as if they were exceptionless, whereas others are not, even though they remain "on the books." Snell's law (about the angle of incidence and the angle of refraction for a ray of light) is a good example of this latter kind. In the optics text I use for reference,[6] it first appears on page 21, and without qualification:

Snell's Law: At an interface between dielectric media, there is (also) *a refracted ray* in the second medium, lying in the plane of incidence, making an angle θ_t with the normal, and obeying Snell's law:

$$\sin \theta / \sin \theta_t = n_2 / n_1$$

where v_1 and v_2 are the velocities of propagation in the two media, and $n_1 = (c/v_1)$, $n_2 = (c/v_2)$ are the indices of refraction.

It is only some 500 pages later, when the law is derived from the "full electromagnetic theory of light," that we learn that Snell's law as stated on page 21 is true only for media whose optical properties are *isotropic.* (In anisotropic media, "there will generally be *two* transmitted waves.") So what is deemed true is not really Snell's law as stated on page 21, but rather a refinement of Snell's law:

Refined Snell's Law: For any two media which are optically isotropic, at an interface between dielectrics there is a refracted ray in the second medium, lying in the plane of incidence, making an angle θ_t with the normal, such that:

$$\sin \theta / \sin \theta_t = n_2 / n_1$$

The Snell's law of page 21 in Klein's book is an example of a *ceteris paribus* law, a law that holds only in special circumstances—in this case when the media are both isotropic. Klein's statement on page 21 is clearly not to be taken literally. Charitably, we are

inclined to put the modifier *"ceteris paribus"* in front to hedge it. But what does this *ceteris paribus* modifier do? With an eye to statistical versions of the covering-law model (Hempel's I-S picture, or Salmon's statistical relevance model, or Suppes's probabilistic model of causation) we may suppose that the unrefined Snell's law is not intended to be a universal law, as literally stated, but rather some kind of statistical law. The obvious candidate is a crude statistical law: *for the most part,* at an interface between dielectric media there is *a* refracted ray ... But this will not do. For *most* media are optically anisotropic, and in an anisotropic medium there are *two* rays. I think there are no more satisfactory alternatives. If *ceteris paribus* laws are to be true laws, there are no statistical laws with which they can generally be identified.

2. WHEN LAWS ARE SCARCE

Why do we keep Snell's law on the books when we both know it to be false and have a more accurate refinement available? There are obvious pedagogic reasons. But are there serious scientific ones? I think there are, and these reasons have to do with the task of explaining. Specifying which factors are explanatorily relevant to which others is a job done by science over and above the job of laying out the laws of nature. Once the laws of nature are known, we still have to decide what kinds of factors can be cited in explanation.

One thing that *ceteris paribus* laws do is to express our explanatory commitments. They tell what kinds of explanations are permitted. We know from the refined Snell's law that in any isotropic medium, the angle of refraction can be explained by the angle of incidence, according to the equation $\sin \theta / \sin \theta_t = n_2 / n_1$. To leave the unrefined Snell's law on the books is to signal that the same kind of explanation can be given even for some anisotropic media. The pattern of explanation derived from the ideal situation is employed even where the conditions are less than ideal; and we assume that we can understand what happens in *nearly* isotropic media by rehearsing how light rays behave in pure isotropic cases.

This assumption is a delicate one. . . . For the moment I intend only to point out that it *is* an assumption, and an assumption which (prior to the "full electromagnetic theory") goes well beyond our knowledge of the facts of nature. We *know* that in isotropic media, the angle of refraction is due to the angle of incidence under the equation $\sin \theta / \sin \theta_t = n_2 / n_t$. We *decide* to explain the angles for the two refracted rays in anisotropic media in the same manner. We may have good reasons for the decision; in this case if the media are nearly isotropic, the two rays will be very close together, and close to the angle predicted by Snell's law; or we believe in continuity of physical processes. But still this decision is not forced by our knowledge of the laws of nature.

Obviously this decision could not be taken if we also had on the books a second refinement of Snell's law, implying that in any anisotropic media the angles are quite different from those given by Snell's law. But laws are scarce, and often we have no law at all about what happens in conditions that are less than ideal.

Covering-law theorists will tell a different story about the use of *ceteris paribus* laws in explanation. From their point of view, *ceteris paribus* explanations are elliptical for genuine covering law explanations from true laws which we do not yet know. When we use a *ceteris paribus* "law" which we know to be false, the covering-law theorist supposes us to be making a bet about what form the true law takes. For example, to retain Snell's unqualified law would be to bet that the (at the time unknown) law for anisotropic media will entail values "close enough" to those derived from the original Snell law.

I have two difficulties with this story. The first arises from an extreme metaphysical possibility, in which I in fact believe. Covering-law theorists tend to think that nature is well-regulated; in the extreme, that there is a law to cover every case. I do not. I imagine that natural objects are much like people in societies. Their behaviour is constrained by some specific laws and by a handful of general principles, but it is not determined in detail, even statistically. What happens on most occasions is dictated by no law at all. This is not a metaphysical picture that I urge. My claim is that this picture is as plausible as the alternative. God may have written just a few laws and grown tired. We do not know whether we are in a tidy universe or an untidy one. Whichever universe we are in, the ordinary commonplace activity of giving explanations ought to make sense.

The second difficulty for the ellipsis version of the covering-law account is more pedestrian. Elliptical explanations are not explanations: they are at best assurances that explanations are to be had. The law that is supposed to appear in the complete, correct D-N explanation is not a law we have in our theory, not a law that we can state, let alone test. There may be covering-law explanations in these cases. But those explanations are not our explanations: and those unknown laws cannot be our grounds for saying of a nearly isotropic medium, "$\sin \theta_t \approx k \ (n_2/n_1)$ *because* $\sin \theta = k$."

What then are our grounds? I assert only what they are not: they are not the laws of nature. The laws of nature that we know at any time are not enough to tell us what kinds of explanations can be given at that time. That requires a decision; and it is just this decision that covering-law theorists make when they wager about the existence of unknown laws. We may believe in these unknown laws, but we do so on no ordinary grounds: they have not been tested, nor are they derived from a higher level theory. Our grounds for believing in them are only as good as our reasons for adopting the corresponding explanatory strategy, and no better.

3. WHEN LAWS CONFLICT

I have been maintaining that there are not enough covering laws to go around. Why? The view depends on the picture of science that I mentioned earlier. Science is broken into various distinct domains: hydrodynamics, genetics, laser theory, . . . We have many detailed and sophisticated theories about what happens within the various domains. But we have little theory about what happens in the intersection of domains. . . . For example, (ceteris paribus) adding salt to water decreases the cooking time of potatoes; taking the water to higher altitudes increases it. Refining, if we speak more carefully we might say instead, "Adding salt to water while keeping the altitude constant decreases the cooking time; whereas increasing the altitude while keeping the saline content fixed increases it." . . . But neither of these tells what happens when we both add salt to the water and move to higher altitudes.

Here we think that probably there is a precise answer about what would happen, even though it is not part of our common folk wisdom. But this is not always the case. I discuss this in detail in the next essay. Most real life cases involve some combination of causes; and general laws that describe what happens in these complex cases are not always available. Although both quantum theory and relativity are highly developed, detailed, and sophisticated, there is no satisfactory theory of relativistic quantum mechanics. A more

detailed example from transport theory is given in the next essay. The general lesson is this: where theories intersect, laws are usually hard to come by.

4. WHEN EXPLANATIONS CAN BE GIVEN ANYWAY

So far, I have only argued half the case. I have argued that covering laws are scarce, and that ceteris paribus laws are no true laws. It remains to argue that, nevertheless, ceteris paribus laws have a fundamental explanatory role. But this is easy, for most of our explanations are explanations from ceteris paribus laws.

Let me illustrate with a humdrum example. Last year I planted camellias in my garden. I know that camellias like rich soil, so I planted them in composted manure. On the other hand, the manure was still warm, and I also know that camellia roots cannot take high temperatures. So I did not know what to expect. But when many of my camellias died, despite otherwise perfect care, I knew what went wrong. The camellias died because they were planted in hot soil.

This is surely the right explanation to give. Of course, I cannot be absolutely certain that this explanation is the correct one. Some other factor may have been responsible, nitrogen deficiency or some genetic defect in the plants, a factor that I did not notice, or may not even have known to be relevant. But this uncertainty is not peculiar to cases of explanation. It is just the uncertainty that besets all of our judgements about matters of fact. We must allow for oversight; still, since I made a reasonable effort to eliminate other menaces to my camellias, we may have some confidence that this is the right explanation.

So we have an explanation for the death of my camellias. But it is not an explanation from any true covering law. There is no law that says that camellias just like mine, planted in soil which is both hot and rich, die. To the contrary, they do not all die. Some thrive; and probably those that do, do so *because* of the richness of the soil they are planted in. We may insist that there must be some differentiating factor which brings the case under a covering law: in soil which is rich and hot, camellias of one kind die; those of another thrive. I will not deny that there may be such a covering law. I merely repeat that our ability to give this humdrum explanation precedes our knowledge of that law. On the Day of Judgment, when all laws are known, these may suffice to explain all phenomena. But in the meantime we do give explanations; and it is the job of science to tell us what kinds of explanations are admissible.

In fact I want to urge a stronger thesis. If, as is possible, the world is not a tidy deterministic system, this job of telling how we are to explain will be a job which is still left when the descriptive task of science is complete. Imagine for example (what I suppose actually to be the case) that the facts about camellias are irreducibly statistical. Then it is possible to know all the general nomological facts about camellias which there are to know—for example, that 62 percent of all camellias in just the circumstances of my camellias die, and 38 percent survive.[7] But one would not thereby know how to explain what happened in my garden. You would still have to look to the *Sunset Garden Book* to learn that the *heat* of the soil explains

the perishing, and the *richness* explains the plants that thrive.

5. CONCLUSION

Most scientific explanations use *ceteris paribus* laws. These laws, read literally as descriptive statements, are false, not only false but deemed false even in the context of use. This is no surprise: we want laws that unify; but what happens may well be varied and diverse. We are lucky that we can organize phenomena at all. There is no reason to think that the principles that best organize will be true, nor that the principles that are true will organize much.

NOTES

1. C. G. Hempel, "Scientific Explanation," in C. G. Hempel (ed.), *Aspects of Scientific Explanation* (New York: Free Press, 1965).
2. Ibid.
3. Patrick Suppes, *A Probabilistic Theory of Causality* (Amsterdam: North-Holland, 1970).
4. Wesley Salmon. "Statistical Explanation," in Wesley Salmon (ed.), *Statistical Explanation and Statistical Relevance* (Pittsburgh: University of Pittsburgh Press, 1971).
5. Bengt, Hanson, *Explanations—or What?* (mimeograph, Stanford University, 1974).
6. Miles V. Klein, *Optics* (New York: Wiley, 1970), p. 21; italics added. θ is the angle of incidence.
7. Various writers, especially Suppes (note 3) and Salmon (note 4), have urged that knowledge of more sophisticated statistical facts will suffice to determine what factors can be used in explanation. I do not believe that this claim can be carried out. . . .

MAY BRODBECK, "EXPLANATION, PREDICTION, AND 'IMPERFECT' KNOWLEDGE"

Brodbeck defends the deductive model. In this selection, she is aiming at many of the arguments against the deductive model that were made by Scriven.

She points out that why or how one holds a premise is quite different from whether or not the premise actually entails the conclusion. Many of us believe what we do for psychological, sociological, or political reasons. Sometimes we refuse to believe something if it is also believed by someone we dislike or do not trust. Often we believe something because we have it on the authority of someone we do trust. These are all examples of what logic books refer to as informal fallacies. If we fail to look for the logical connections in scientific arguments, preferring instead "something less," we will be doomed to accepting some fallacious arguments in science. This clearly will not, and should not, do. It is the prime insight of the D-N model to focus our attention on the logical relations between premises and conclusion.

Brodbeck also stresses a difference between types of disciplines. Some disciplines present us with perfect knowledge, and others do not; they yield only imperfect knowledge. Theories that deal with closed systems and are complete yield perfect knowledge. What is a closed system? First, we must answer "What is a system?" A system is any group of events that has a specifiable border. To have a system requires that we be able to differentiate the events taking place within the borders of the system from events taking place outside the borders of the system. To have a closed system, it must be true that the events outside the borders do not affect the events within the borders of the system. Brodbeck calls the laws governing such systems process laws. An example will help clarify the concept of a closed system.

The ideal gas law, which would be a process law, according to Brodbeck, states that

$$PV = nRT$$

where P is pressure, V is volume, n is the amount of gas, R is a constant, and T is temperature.

The pressure, volume, temperature, and amount of gas are the only variables needed to use the law. The law holds for the closed system of a gas in a container. Think of the container as a thermos bottle. The container obviously has borders and cannot have holes in it. We usually think of a container as rigid. The actual requirement is that we be able to measure pressure against the sides. Rigidity makes this easy but is not necessary. If the container had holes in it, some molecules of gas would escape, making measurement of volume inaccurate. The law is ideal in that no container can be kept totally free from registering minute changes in temperature from the outside. For most purposes, these changes can be ignored. This is what is meant by saying that the events outside the borders do not affect the events within the borders of the system. The claim is not literally true; rather, it is true for our purposes. That the claim is not literally true will be picked up by Hesse. That the claim is true for our purposes, or true within certain limits, is a way of making Cartwright's point that all laws are *ceteris paribus* laws.

If you have trouble picturing the ideal gas law, just think of a thermos used for keeping liquids hot or cold. The thermos is not much good if it has holes in it or does not insulate the contents from the outside temperature. We all know that while some thermoses are much better than others, none is truly perfect. If you wait a few days or a few hours, the hot coffee or cold soda will be lukewarm. The limitations (they might be stated on the label) are the *ceteris paribus* conditions. If we need the thermos to work only for an hour or so, then we can say that it will work "perfectly."

Brodbeck points out that the D-N model is meant for perfect knowledge and not for imperfect knowledge. She admits that Hempel and Oppenheim cannot fill in all the details to get a deductive explanation in the cases they cite. For her, however, this is not a problem with the D-N model. She points out that the D-N model is a philosophical analysis of scientific explanation. As such, it need only show the principles involved. The details are not a part of the philosophy. Here we see a very basic difference between Scriven and Cartwright on the one hand and Hempel and Oppenheim and Brodbeck on the other. Brodbeck (and to a lesser extent, Hempel and Oppenheim) sees the philosophy of science as a philosophy telling science what it ought to be doing.

This approach is called the normative or evaluative philosophy of science. It is done against the backdrop of philosophy, which writers like Brodbeck take to be a given. Scriven and Cartwright, by contrast, are more interested in describing what scientists do and telling that to philosophers in philosophical language. The goal of science, as Brodbeck sees it, is to advance from imperfect to perfect knowledge. Neither Scriven nor Cartwright would want to say what the goal of science should be.

Only some areas of physics are examples of perfect knowledge. Some areas of biology and, especially, the social sciences exemplify what Brodbeck takes to be imperfect knowledge.

In Chapters 5 and 6, we will examine medicine, psychology, and biology. These would be examples, according to Brodbeck, of disciplines whose laws are statistical and so yield only imperfect knowledge. We will see that these disciplines do differ from certain areas within physics. Whether Brodbeck has adequately characterized that difference is something that we must decide.

Laws in areas of imperfect knowledge are statistical as opposed to universal. Sometimes the terms in the laws are vague. For example, what counts as a boom in trade or as inflation is not precisely spelled out. If terms in an argument are vague, the argument commits a fallacy and must be rejected. (Brodbeck's claim that "All men are mortal" is also vague because from it we cannot explain or predict a particular person's death. Cartwright used this as an example of the only true non–*ceteris paribus* law.) Not all statistical laws are vague. Thus Brodbeck asks, can we have deduction if laws are statistical? Her answer is yes.

Brodbeck interprets statistical generalizations as universal because they make a claim about the distribution of a property over an entire class. She asserts that the conclusion of a statistical deduction is known with certainty. She uses lung cancer and smoking as an example. Here is another, simpler example to make the same point. Suppose that we have an urn with 60 red balls and 40 green balls. We randomly draw a ball from the urn. From the premises "There is a 60 percent chance of drawing a red ball" and "You picked a ball," one of two conclusions follows deductively: "The probability that you chose a red ball is 60 percent," and "The probability that you chose a green ball is 40 percent."

Using another example and other words, according to Brodbeck, from the premises "90 percent of swans are white" and "This bird is a swan," it can be asserted with certainty that "This bird has a 90 percent chance of being white."

Scriven, by contrast, would say that from "90 percent of swans are white" and "This bird is a swan," nothing may be asserted with certainty. The best we can say is that with about 90 percent assuredness, the bird in question is a swan. Or, going back to the urn example, Scriven would say that from the premises as stated, it follows with 60 percent probability that you drew a red ball and 40 percent probability that you drew a green ball. For Brodbeck, the probability is asserted of the conclusion; the premises for her logically entail the conclusion. For Scriven, the probability is asserted of the connection between the premises and the conclusion. The premises do not logically entail the conclusion if the premises are statistical.

It might help to draw a distinction between inductive and epistemic probability. Inductive probability is a property of arguments and not individual statements. The inductive probability of an argument is the probability that its conclusion is true, given that its premises are true. The argument, "There is a live *Tyrannosaurus rex* in Toledo. Therefore, there is a live reptile in Toledo weighing over 500 pounds" has a high inductive probability, for if the premise is true, it is highly likely that the conclusion will also be true. (Remember that the *T. rex* might be newly hatched.)

Epistemic probability is the probability of a particular statement. In the above argument, the epistemic probability of the premise and the epistemic probability of the conclusion are extremely low. Are Brodbeck and Scriven referring to epistemic or inductive probability?

Scriven (in an article not reprinted here) had used two examples against the symmetry thesis of the D-N model. One concerns a flood in a forest. Scriven's point was that although we can explain after the flood why particular animals survived, we could not have predicted which particular animals would have survived before the flood happened. The best we could do, said Scriven, is to use a law such as "If there is a flood, animals with better swimming ability will tend to survive." This law, Scriven pointed out, is statistical and so does not allow the sort of deduction required for prediction. Brodbeck counters that the law is about types of animals and kinds of situations. It allows us to deduce that more aquatic animals than terrestrial animals will survive. There is no reason to think that we should be able to predict exactly which particular animals would survive (e.g., Bambi or Mr. Limpet). Moreover, according to Brodbeck, the symmetry thesis still holds. Both explanation and prediction concern types of animals.

In a more famous example, Scriven refers to the medical condition called paresis, a kind of paralysis that is caused only by syphilis. Because only about 10 percent of syphilis cases ever advance to paresis, if we see a case of paresis, we explain it by citing syphilis as the cause. But if we have a case of syphilis, we must predict that there will (very likely) be no paresis. Again, claimed Scriven, here we have an asymmetry between explanation and prediction. Brodbeck replies in two ways. First, she points out that from the premise "Only 10 percent of syphilis cases develop into paresis," we can make no prediction about an individual case because the law refers only to types and not to individuals. Second, in real medical cases, we have to make some prediction (to set up a regimen of treatment), and to do so, according to Brodbeck, we implicitly use the assumption that an event with a 10 percent probability will likely not occur. Once we make explicit appeal to such a law, we make the prediction a logical deduction.

Brodbeck continues her attack on Scriven's paresis example by showing that his claim that paresis is explained by appeal to syphilis is not correct. A particular case of paresis is not explained by an appeal to syphilis unless we add the rider "and there is no other cause for paresis." Again, once we do this, we have a deduction from the premises "This is a case of paresis" and "Nothing else causes paresis except syphilis" to the conclusion "This was caused by syphilis." Brodbeck asks of claims such as "X causes Y," what do we mean by "cause"? Her answer is that the use of causality presupposes some lawlike connection between X and Y. Thus anytime we use a causal claim such as "Syphilis is the only cause of paresis," we are presupposing that syphilis and paresis are related by law. Thus again, there seems no way around admitting that explanation and prediction can be analyzed in terms of deduction. Her point is that any time one uses a statement of causality, one is really using a law. And once one uses a law in an explanation, one has a deduction. Scriven and Brodbeck have another serious disagreement here. Even if Brodbeck's analysis of the use of causal claims is correct, Scriven would deny that presuppositions ought to be counted as hidden premises, any more than any of our background knowledge (e.g., in the flood example, we have as background knowledge that some fish have scales) ought to be brought forward to count as a premise. Scriven recognizes that there is such background knowledge; he refers to it as the grounds for the explanation. He denies that such grounds must be cited in the explanation and that we actually do consciously appeal to such grounds. Brodbeck would reply that whether we do appeal to them is irrelevant. What counts is logic. Logic demands that the grounds, if they are logically needed, be brought forward and cited.

Explanation, Prediction, and "Imperfect" Knowledge

MAY BRODBECK

. . . If the generalizations and individual statements of fact serving as premises are accepted as true, then, because of the tautological connection, the conclusion *must* be true. This and this alone is the virtue of deductive explanation. Once such terms as "must," "guarantees," and "logically implies" are clarified, then it is clear why deduction and deduction alone "justifies" the conclusion. At the same time, it is also clear why any other kind of explanation of individual facts cannot possess this conclusiveness. Either the explanation is deductive or else it does not justify what it is said to explain.

All this is not to "set limits" to what may constitute a sound explanation, but to explicate *one* sense of sound "explanation" which is the only one that is conclusive for the reasons just mentioned. For the philosopher concerned with language as description, the task is to show what, so to speak, in the facts themselves, or, to be accurate, *in the statements asserting them*, rather than in the mind or behavior of a particular person or group of persons, makes one or more statements a "reason," in a precise logical sense of reason, for one or more others. What in the statements themselves makes one statement a prediction from others, one confirm a general hypothesis, another refute it? Deductive explanation is the only answer to this question, insofar as language is used to speak, not just about how we speak, but about the world.

From Herbert Feigl and Grover Maxwell (eds.), *Minnesota Studies in the Philosophy of Science*, vol. 3 (Minneapolis: Univ. of Minnesota Press, 1962), pp. 231–272. Copyright © 1962 by the University of Minnesota.

One particular appeal to ordinary usage to bolster the claim that scientific explanation is not deductive verges on the bizarre. Reading "deductive" to mean "syllogistic" in the Aristotelian sense, it is concluded that scientific explanation, since not syllogistic in form, is not deductive.[1] Explanation in science is indeed not syllogistic, at least in the most interesting cases, namely, those involving quantification, relations, or both. But I think it may be said safely that however the half-educated plain man may use the term, no scientist since Galileo has so narrowly conceived "deduction" and certainly no logician for almost a century. Yet, insofar as these critics concede a correlate to strict deduction in ordinary speech, including science, they perceive it to mean something like Barbara. Hence, if not Barbara, then not deductive. Words do mean only what we say they mean. But one use of a term hardly justifies the assertion that nothing corresponds to another and different use of that same term.

Like "deductive," the word "explain" has, as we saw, many uses. To assail the deductive model because it does not apply to all these uses is irrelevant at best, puerile punning at worst.[2] Deduction is not put forward as the model for those uses of "explain" when we speak, say, of explaining (i.e., describing) the structure of the Egyptian ruling class, a symbolism, or how to play chess. The model is proposed for only one but one very important use of "explain." In particular, the occurrence of certain events, like an eclipse or an earthquake, can, upon the model, sometimes in practice and always in principle be explained and predicted deductively.

Practically, we can both explain and predict the occurrence of an eclipse. We can only explain the earthquake after it happens. The critics' most plausible case rests, of course, on such all-too-common "earthquake" situations. But they are not content to rest on such cases. Though conceding at one place that Newton "did achieve a large number of mathematically precise and scientifically illuminating deductions [sic!] from his theory," this is, to put it moderately, not the prevailing tenor of the argument.[3] What one hand gives, the other snatches away. Or perhaps it was only Newton himself who could accomplish the feat of deduction. In any case, the claim is that not even in physics do we really have deductive explanation. Apart from the untenable, because false, appeal to usage, the argument has, so to speak, two facets or takes two different forms. The first grants that laws *do* play a role in some explanations, but such explanations are allegedly still not really deductive. The other holds that explanation of an individual fact is always by other such facts without the intermediary in any way of laws. After a few preliminary comments about the structure of classical physical theory, I shall discuss these two different arguments in the order mentioned.

"PERFECT" KNOWLEDGE AND DEDUCTIVE EXPLANATION

Celestial mechanics is a paradigm of what has usefully been called "perfect knowledge."[4] Nonatomic thermodynamics is another. In the first theory, mass, velocity, and distance are variables that interact only with each other; in the second, volume, temperature, pressure, and a few other variables of this sort do the same. In each case, no variables that in fact make a difference have been omitted from the expressions of the theory. These theories are *complete*. Nothing that happens at any other time or

place than that being considered affects the behavior of the properties with which the theory is concerned, or, at worst, we know how to take account of these outside influences in our predictions or computations. The system, in other words, is *closed*. The laws of these theories are *process laws*, that is, the values of *any* one variable at any time can be computed by means of the laws from the values of *all* the others at any other time. We can predict the future course of all our variables or compute their entire past history; we know how changes in any one variable produce changes in any other; we know to what extent by tinkering with the system we can bring about desired changes, to what extent we are powerless.

Such knowledge may, not unreasonably, be called "perfect," for there is clearly nothing else we could possibly want to know, as far as these variables are concerned. Nor is there any unreasonable sense of "perfection" implied by this notion. Every measurement has its limits of accuracy. Inductive generalization may be overgeneralization, as indeed we now know about the Newtonian law of gravitation. These frailties are common to all empirical science and do not affect the nature of the deductions we can make from such theories, when we assume that the laws are true and that our measurements are accurate.

From the Newtonian law of gravitation in conjunction with the positions of the sun and the planets at any one time, we can predict or postdict their position at any other time. Thus we can deductively predict future eclipses or explain present and past ones. The laws of Newton may be applied, of course, to a vast number of vastly different situations, terrestrial as well as celestial. If we know enough about the initial conditions, then we can predict what will happen. Using these laws, we can predict how long it will take an elephant to slide down a green, grassy hill, if we know only his mass, the angle of inclination of the hill, and the coefficient of friction. Or we can predict where and when a cannon ball will land, if we know but a few relevant variables. In some cases, where we fail to predict, as when a bridge collapses under a certain load, we could have done so, if we had taken the trouble to find out the state of the system, that is, the initial conditions, before the catastrophe. If we did not take the trouble or if it was too complicated to do so, then, after the event, we deductively explain it by reference to the laws and to what the conditions must have been to make the bridge give way.

"CERTAINTY" OF PREMISES VS. DEDUCTIVE VALIDITY

How, then, in the light of all this can the critics nevertheless maintain that explanations in physics are not deductive? The physicist, it is pointed out, might be wrong either in deciding that a particular universal law applies to a given set of conditions—whether or not they are within the scope of the law—or in describing the initial conditions. The physicist must, therefore, like the historian, use "judgment" and even "empathy" rather than formal deduction in making his inferences.[5] Or so the argument goes.

However, the choice of premises, or even the use of false ones, is not in the strict sense a logical matter and does not affect the validity of a deduction. The validity of the deduction itself is here confused with the error of using, say, a first approximation like Boyle's law where only a more general gas law would do, or in believing that the effects of friction are negligible when in fact they are not. Once the scientist has used his "judgment," which is indeed a psychological matter dependent on his skill and training, then the deduction follows. The explanation *is* deductive, whether or not we are

"certain" about the premises, either the law or the initial conditions. A prediction in the same circumstances is also deductive. The scientist, in fact, tests his judgment by deductively inferring what *must* be the case if what he believes to be the applicable laws and the true initial conditions really are so. Premises deductively imply a conclusion no matter how certain or unsure we may be about their truth. Logical entailment (or inconsistency) is a property of the statements themselves, not of our knowledge about them. If the prediction were not deductive, then there would be no reason why its failure should cast doubt upon the premises. In fact, it shows that at least one of them is false. In theoretical science, when a prediction fails, this generally, though not necessarily, casts doubt upon the laws. In engineering or applied science, on the other hand, the initial conditions become suspect. Far from requiring "exact truth" for its premises, all that the deductive model requires is exact *statement* of a hypothesis about their truth. The hypothesis is then tested by the "exact deduction" which, I am sorry to have to repeat, does not mean and never has meant only the syllogistic deduction with which the critics sometimes equate it.

Hempel's careful statement of the deductive model unfortunately uses an illustration that, from the point of view of the principle involved, is inadequate. Understandably, for expository purposes, trying to avoid the mathematical complications of those areas where perfect or near-perfect knowledge exists, he uses a homely, everyday illustration, the breaking of a car's radiator in freezing weather. Hempel's so-called failure here is not one of deduction, but a failure of complete knowledge. He cannot state all the initial conditions that will permit him to deduce that the radiator broke. If one appreciates that philosophical explication is explication of the principles involved, this is no failure at all. Once again, only because there is a deductive connection between the laws of physics and, among other things, the state of the weather and insufficient antifreeze in the radiator, have we any good reason to assert that the cold rather than the sparrows who daily perch upon the hood explains the breakage. The physicist does not judge "inductively . . . what the explanation is."[6] Correctly stated, he makes an inductive judgment about the premises. And to make this correction is not, as is claimed, to "convert" either the premises or the judgment into a deduction. We want to know whether a given statement is deductively entailed by certain others. This is a logical question. To import considerations about what the scientist happens to know, certainly or otherwise, or even, if knowing, what he happens to assert explicitly or to "quote," is to doubly muddy the waters by first introducing irrelevant psychological factors and then confusing context-bound sentences and complete statements. . . .

"IMPERFECT" KNOWLEDGE AND DEDUCTIVE EXPLANATION

Perfect knowledge is the ideal, actualized only in certain branches of physical science. Elsewhere, as in biology, economics, sociology, psychology, and the social sciences generally, knowledge is conspicuously "imperfect." We do not know all the variables that affect, say, a person's resistance to disease, or his behavior under certain circumstances, or the price fluctuations of certain commodities. Our theories in these areas are not complete, nor do we know fully the conditions for closure of such systems. Since we do not know all the factors that make a difference to the variables with which we are concerned, we also have no process laws. From the values of the variables at any *one* time, we cannot predict

their value at *all* other times. Yet, the social and biological sciences have developed techniques to compensate for lapses in closure and completeness. The most important of these techniques is the use of statistical concepts. Which face will turn up when a die is cast is determined by numerous causes—the center of gravity of the die, the force with which it is thrown, and so on. An attempt to calculate the results of each throw by means of the laws of mechanics is practically hopeless because of the difficulty in precisely measuring all the initial conditions. Instead, we represent, as it were this multiplicity of causes by a probability distribution for the attribute in question. The use of the statistical concept marks our ignorance of all the influencing factors, a failure in either completeness or closure or, usually, both. Similarly, the social scientist, deliberately selecting for study fewer factors than actually influence the behavior in which he is interested, shifts his goal from predicting individual events or behaviors to predicting the frequency with which this kind of behavior occurs in a large group of individuals possessing the circumscribed number of factors. This use of statistical concepts, due to lapses in closure and completeness, differs from their use for errors of measurement. Even assuming perfect observation, they would still be necessary.

Statistical knowledge is not the only kind of imperfect knowledge. We also have non-quantified imperfection. Any law, whether it be about physical objects, persons, or societies, is "imperfect" if it does not permit us to compute (predict or postdict) the state of the system, either an individual or a group, at any moment from its state at one moment. Consider the assertion that a boom in trade is always followed by slump and depression. This is imprecise with respect to time, for it does not tell us exactly when the later events will follow the earlier one, nor how long each will last. Moreover, its concepts have a fringe of vagueness that make it difficult to tell precisely when we have instances of the kinds of events mentioned. In psychology, the laws of learning that make essential use of the past history of a person in order to predict his future behavior are also imperfect. The equilibrium laws of physics, whose concepts are not vague, are nevertheless imperfect because though they tell us that under certain conditions no change in certain respects will occur, they do not tell us what will happen if these conditions are not fulfilled. To be sure, the equilibrium laws of physics are derivable from the process laws of the theory, but for those of economics no such perfect laws are available. In general, imperfect laws are indefinite with respect to time, or hedged in by qualification, or they are statistical.

The inadequacies of such "imperfect" knowledge do not affect the possibility of deduction. Not only do we sometimes know enough to deduce some of these laws, like the law of the lever or certain statistical laws of physics, from process laws, but all kinds of deductions can be made *from the imperfect laws themselves,* whether or not they are in turn deducible from something else. An explanation utilizing imperfect laws as premises is not the same as Hempel's "explanation sketch." The latter he describes as "a more or less vague indication of the laws and initial conditions considered as relevant, and it needs "filling out" in order to turn into a full-fledged explanation."[7] Imperfect laws, as here defined, need not be vague or, as explicit premises from which deductions can be made, incomplete. For instance, "All men are mortal," though universal, is imperfect by our criterion, since from it we can neither explain nor predict a man's death at a particular time. But such nonquantitative universal generalizations, as well as many laws of the biological and social sciences or statistical laws generally, are not necessarily

"vague." Nor do they necessarily need "filling out" before they can be used for significant deductions or "full-fledged" explanations.

On the other hand, it is indeed true, as I illustrate later, that we often have to make guesses as to the appropriate imperfect laws, about either individuals or groups of individuals, that will permit us to explain or predict a given event. However, the deductive model by no means requires that premises be the deterministic process laws of perfect knowledge. Once this is grasped, the admitted difficulty in formulating so-called universal laws, of which the critics make so much, no longer appears insuperable. They set a demand that is not logically required by the model. After all, deductive inference was with us centuries before Newton formulated the first process laws.

"The criterion of deduction must be abandoned if the criterion of universal (nonstatistical) hypotheses is abandoned." Moreover, if we only have statistical knowledge, then though we cannot predict, we can use such knowledge to explain with "certainty" the occurrence of individual events.[8] Neither of these claims, as I have just suggested, is justified. A statistical law asserts that if each member of a certain class has a certain attribute, then a certain fraction or percentage of them will have another attribute. For instance, "60 percent of all cigarette smokers develop lung cancer." This is a generalization or universal statement, for it says of all cigarette smokers, past, present, and future, those observed and those as yet unobserved, that 60 percent of this group will suffer from cancer of the lungs.[9] Like all statistical generalizations, the evidence for it is a finite number of cases. The statement asserts, however, that in the class of all individuals of a certain kind, a particular attribute will turn up with a specified frequency. In this respect, a statistical generalization is as "universal" as a so-called deterministic or nonstatistical law stating that each and every individual having a certain character will also have another. In both cases, the law goes far beyond the evidence. If it did not, but was just a summary of observations, it would have neither explanatory nor predictive power. The difference between them is not that one permits prediction while the other does not, but in the nature of what can be predicted or, what amounts to the same, in how they are tested.

From a deterministic law, given the initial conditions, we can predict an individual event. From a statistical law and its initial conditions (the occurrence of a large group of cigarette smokers), we can predict only a so-called mass event, that is, the frequency with which an attribute will be distributed in the given class. If an unbiased coin is tossed a large number of times, then the frequency with which heads will turn up is 50 percent. This says something about the class of *all tosses* of a coin, though it says nothing about what will happen in any particular toss. Similarly, the lung-cancer generalization says nothing about any particular cigarette smoker, though it says a good deal about the class of all cigarette smokers. From a statistical law, then, nothing can be predicted about an individual event. On the other hand, neither can we explain an individual event by reference to such a law.

It is embarrassing to rehearse these elementary matters. But the critics force such rehearsal upon one, for they argue to the contrary. Consider the nonquantified, implicitly statistical statement that Scriven calls a "hypothetical probability prediction," namely, that if a flood occurs, then animals who can swim will be more likely to survive than those who cannot.[10] Scriven notes that unless we can predict the flood, we cannot predict which animals will survive. However, he believes that, in retrospect, "we can *explain why* certain animals

and plants have survived even when we could not have *predicted that* they would." In fact, given such a law, even if we could have predicted the flood, we could not have predicted anything about individual animals. We could have predicted only that more animals who can swim would survive than those who could not, that is, an implicit frequency distribution. By the same token, we cannot explain why a particular animal happened to survive. For, as Scriven says, there may be many other unknown factors besides swimming ability that contribute to survival. Our knowledge is incomplete. That, indeed, is why we can only state a "hypothetical probability prediction" or statistical law. In other words, though we can explain and, moreover, explain deductively why more fishes than chipmunks survive, we *cannot* explain why a particular fish survived. Since many do not, the "explanation" in terms of swimming alone is clearly inconclusive, far from "certain," no matter how plausible it may appear.

From statistical generalizations, we do not deduce "with probability" that a certain event will occur, rather we deduce exactly the relative frequency or "probability" with which an event will occur in a certain group. Similarly, contrary to what Scriven maintains, both statistical and deterministic laws are falsified if the prediction fails.[11] The difference is only in the falsifying event. In the statistical case, the failure, not of an individual event, but of an attribute to occur with a certain frequency in a "mass event" falsifies the law. If our generalization is not quantified and says merely that one event is "more likely" than another, then if in other large samples that event does not turn up more times, the law is falsified. If of a specified large group of cigarette smokers, satisfying certain conditions, only 50 per cent develop lung cancer before their death, then the "law" has been falsified. The use of statistical hypotheses does not, therefore, require abandoning deduction. Quite the contrary. Just as in the deterministic case, without deduction we could neither test statistical hypotheses nor, for that matter, have any rational grounds for, say, recommending a decrease in cigarette smoking or, to change the example, to innoculate our children against poliomyelitis. No doubt we would much prefer to know that each and every child receiving a certain vaccine is immune to the disease, or the exact conditions under which cancer develops in a particular person. Yet, statistical knowledge is not to be scorned though it is imperfect rather than perfect. It is far from valueless to know the factors statistically correlated to the frequency of occurrence of an event. And it is the exact deductions from such knowledge that make it valuable.

Scriven's claim that statistical premises nondeductively permit us to explain individual events rests on no firmer foundation than converting a specious plausibility into a "certainty." But he also maintains that we can explain individual events without recourse to laws at all. In particular, an appeal to laws is held to be "wholly unnecessary" for identifying the causes of an event. Let us see.

EXPLANATION BY "CAUSES" VS. EXPLANATION BY LAWS

"We can explain but not predict whenever we have a proposition of the form 'The only cause of X is A,' for example, 'The only cause of paresis is syphilis.' "[12] Given A, we cannot predict X, for only a few cases of A develop X. Only A in conjunction with certain unknown conditions is followed by X. Therefore, Scriven maintains, given a case of A, "on the evidence" we must predict that X will not occur. He is mistaken. "On the evidence" we are in no position to predict any such thing. No such prediction is logically justified, no matter how soothing or useful it may be, any more than we can predict of any particular cigarette smoker that he will or will not get cancer. To make his prediction, Scriven explicitly uses the premise that only a few A's develop X. Now, if we make the decision, as is customary when action is necessary, always to assume that the statistically more likely case will occur, then of course we can predict that X will not occur. But, then, having made that assumption, the prediction of the nonoccurrence of X follows deductively from these premises. True, we cannot predict, under the hypothesis given, that X will occur, but when it does we can explain it. However, as we shall see, the deductive model can account for this practical asymmetry.

The sentence "The only cause of X is A" needs considerable unpacking. Scriven, believing that "cause" is an unanalyzable concept that everyone just naturally understands, denies any need for unpacking. He can therefore maintain that such sentences present instances where we can "explain what we could not have predicted, even if we had had the information about the antecedent conditions." Or, as he goes on to say, "sometimes the kind of correlation we need for prediction is absent, but a causal relationship can be identified."[13] The only way Scriven persuades himself that he can explain an event that could not even in principle be predicted is by leaving "causal" statements wholly unanalyzed. Despite the confident use of the causal idiom in everyday speech, we may still significantly ask under what conditions statements like "C is a cause of E" are true or false. I shall not take the time here to exhibit the problematic nature of the notion of "cause." Nor do I believe that to most this needs exhibiting. How then must the statement be unpacked?

To say "The only cause of X is A" is at least to affirm the law that X never occurs without A. In other words, A is a necessary condition for X, or "Whenever we have X, then we also have A." It is also, however, to say *more,* namely, that there is a complex of conditions, of which A is always one, under which X occurs; that is, certain other factors, b, c, d, *and* A are sufficient for X. In other words, A is a necessary condition and also one of several jointly sufficient conditions. This indeed is a situation in which we speak of one event as the "cause" of another. As is obvious, this causal imputation is far from being independent of any laws, known or surmised. By hypothesis, we do not know the other sufficient conditions. If we knew them, then deductive explanation *and* prediction would follow directly from a statement of the necessary and sufficient conditions. However, since we do not know the sufficient conditions, how do we account for the fact that actually we would normally explain X by A? Our only justification, and in fact the only way anyone, including Scriven, does justify doing this, is by implicitly adding to our knowledge of the necessary-condition law, our "guess" about the sufficient-condition law. Knowing that both X and A have occurred, we assume the presence of the unspecifiable b, c, and d. The explanation of X then follows deductively. That is *why* we accept A as an explanation of X. In order to predict X from A, the unknown factors must also be specified and this we cannot do. The asymmetry exists in practice, but not in principle. Nor is this an "unhelpful" sense of "in principle." For only by exhibiting the form of the argument that would, if we knew b, c, and d, permit the prediction, can we clarify why the purported explanation really does state "why" X occurred.

This explanation implicitly assumed that certain unspecifiable events had occurred. Even more frequently, perhaps, the implicit premise is that certain easily specifiable events did *not* occur. We explain a man's death as due to his being struck by an auto-

mobile. This is not because we grasp the meaning of the term "cause,"[14] but because we know a law to the effect that if anyone is struck by a car, then he will be either killed or badly hurt. This is imperfect because, among other things, it does not tell us *which* alternative will occur. We therefore cannot predict the death from the law and the fact that he was hit by a car. But knowing it and, therefore, knowing also that the second alternative (or whatever others there may be) did not occur, the death follows deductively from the law, the initial conditions, and the denial of the alternative. The explanation of the event is conclusive because, given the explicit and *implicit* premises, it must have occurred. Clearly, if we knew the implicit premise before the event, it could be predicted. In very many cases where we know such "disjunctive" laws, we can in fact also eliminate all but one of the alternatives. . . .

REFERENCES

1. M. Scriven, in P. Gardiner (ed.), *Theories of History* (Glencoe, Ill.: Free Press, 1959), p. 462; S. Toulmin, *Philosophy of Science* (London: Hutchinson, 1953), p. 25.
2. Scriven, in Gardiner, pp. 463, 468.
3. M. Scriven, "Explanation and Prediction in Evolutionary Theory," *Science* 130 (1959): 477.
4. The distinction between "perfect" and "imperfect" knowledge is Bergmann's. For a thorough discussion, see G. Bergmann, *Philosophy of Science* (Madison: University of Wisconsin Press, 1957).
5. Scriven, in Gardiner, pp. 459, 462.
6. Scriven, in Gardiner, p. 457.
7. Hempel, in Gardiner, p. 351.
8. Scriven, in Gardiner, pp. 457, 464; and in *Science* 130: 479, 480.
9. For the sake of an illustration, I have stated the hypothesis in this very alarming way, just as one might say that 60 percent of all Norwegians are blond. Realistically, the actual lung-cancer hypothesis is a bit less terrifying, asserting a comparison between smokers and nonsmokers and that a higher percentage of the former than the latter will develop lung cancer. The relevant logic of the situation is identical in either case. See the examples that follow.

10. Scriven, in *Science* 130: 478.
11. Just as deterministic laws cannot be conclusively *verified,* statistical laws, by their nature, cannot be conclusively *falsified.* Accepting an observed frequency in a sample as the true probability requires an induction that this frequency will persist for indefinitely large samples; this may not be correct. Lack of conclusiveness, however, does not mean that we may not have good evidence either for accepting a deterministic law or for rejecting a statistical one. Conclusiveness, again, is not required of the premises but only of the connection between premises and conclusion.
12. Scriven, in *Science* 130: 480.
13. Scriven, in *Science* 130: 480.
14. Scriven, in *Science* 130: 480.

BAS C. VAN FRAASSEN, "THE PRAGMATIC THEORY OF EXPLANATION"

There is a well-known counterexample to the symmetry thesis of the D-N model. We can predict (determine) the height of a tree using as premises the length of the tree's shadow and the angle the tree makes with the sun. It hardly makes sense, however, to explain the height of the tree from the length of the tree's shadow and the angle the tree makes with the sun. We need the right law, not just any law from which the derivation can be made. This is a way of saying that we need the appropriate context. In the case of trees, we need to know the factors that go into tree growth—light, water, soil type, and so forth.

Van Fraassen begins his account of explanation with a story about a tower whose height *is explained* by the length of its shadow. This shows the power of context in explanation. The D-N model made scientific explanation context free. Scriven criticized this, claiming that it made explanations just about impossible. He offered a context-bound sense for explanation. Cartwright characterized laws in such a way that they depended on *ceteris paribus* conditions, which is a way of saying that laws are not context free. Van Fraassen further develops the importance of context to explanation.

To van Fraassen, explanations are answers to why questions. He asks, "What counts as an answer to a why question?" As an example, he takes the question, "Why is this conductor warped?" He offers three concepts in his analysis:

1. The topic of concern—this is the warped conductor.

2. For every topic of concern, there is a contrast class. The contrast class is not in this case merely all other conductors but rather all other conductors relevantly like this one that have gone through similar histories. (In technical terms, the contrast class is not simply the complementary class of the topic class.)

3. Explanatory relevance—there might be different reasons for asking. We might know for example, that normally the conductor does not begin to melt when it is used. So our question is, "What went wrong?" We might already know what went wrong and be asking, "Why was this allowed to happen?"

Van Fraassen's topic of concern and explanatory relevance make explanation what Scriven referred to as unified communication.

Van Fraassen also agrees with Scriven that scientific explanations are just explanations. Context is just as important in science as in ordinary situations. If you go by my house and notice that the porch light is still on at 11 P.M., you might ask, "Why?" There are many possible correct answers. Here are some:

My daughter is not home yet from her first date.

I am looking for a paper I think I dropped on the porch.

I am testing the light.

I am signaling passing cars that there is a speed trap ahead.

Electrical current is flowing through the circuits.

The last answer in one sense is always correct, yet often inappropriate and would be considered no answer at all by my wife, who called down to me, "Why is that light still on?" Both Scriven and van Fraassen would agree that my answer to this question in this context in terms of electrical circuitry would be no answer at all and so no explanation at all. To a proponent of the D-N model, such an answer, properly filled out, would always be a correct explanation, even if not much of an answer. This is because the D-N model assumes a sharp distinction between everyday affairs and science. Philosophers such as Scriven, Cartwright, van Fraassen, and, as we shall see, Hesse, think it a mistake to separate everyday life from a philosophical analysis of science.

"Why is this conductor warped" need not refer to matters of electricity. Context would determine whether the word *conductor* referred to a piece of metal, a train's ticket taker, or an orchestra leader. We might be asking why the person in front of the symphony orchestra was leading the orchestra with a hockey stick.

The Pragmatic Theory of Explanation

BAS C. VAN FRAASSEN

"THE TOWER AND THE SHADOW"

During my travels along the Saône and Rhône last year, I spent a day and night at the ancestral home of the Chevalier de St. X——, an old friend of my father's. The Chevalier had in fact been the French liaison officer attached to my father's brigade

© Bas C. van Fraassen 1980. Reprinted from *The Scientific Image* by Bas C. van Fraassen by permission of Oxford University Press.

in the first war, which had—if their reminiscences are to be trusted—played a not insignificant part in the battles of the Somme and Marne.

The old gentleman always had *thé à l'Anglaise* on the terrace at five o'clock in the evening, he told me. It was at this meal that a strange incident occurred; though its ramifications were of course not yet perceptible when I heard the Chevalier give his simple explanation of the length of the shadow which encroached upon us there on the terrace. I had just eaten my fifth piece of bread and butter and had begun my third cup of tea when I chanced to look up. In the dying light of that late afternoon, his profile was sharply etched against the granite background of the wall behind him, the great aquiline nose thrust forward and his eyes fixed on some point behind my left shoulder. Not understanding the situation at first, I must admit that to begin with, I was merely fascinated by the sight of that great hooked nose, recalling my father's claim that this had once served as an effective weapon in close combat with a German grenadier. But I was roused from this brown study by the Chevalier's voice.

"The shadow of the tower will soon reach us, and the terrace will turn chilly. I suggest we finish our tea and go inside."

I looked around, and the shadow of the rather curious tower I had earlier noticed in the grounds, had indeed approached to within a yard from my chair. The news rather displeased me, for it was a fine evening; I wished to remonstrate but did not well know how, without overstepping the bounds of hospitality. I exclaimed, "Why must that tower have such a long shadow? This terrace is so pleasant!"

His eyes turned to rest on me. My question had been rhetorical, but he did not take it so.

"As you may already know, one of my ancestors mounted the scaffold with Louis XVI and Marie Antoinette. I had that tower erected in 1930 to mark the exact spot where it is said that he greeted the Queen when she first visited this house, and presented her with a peacock made of soap, then a rare substance. Since the Queen would have been one hundred and seventy-five years old in 1930, had she lived. I had the tower made exactly that many feet high."

It took me a moment to see the relevance of all this. Never quick at sums, I was at first merely puzzled as to why the measurement should have been in feet; but of course I already knew him for an Anglophile. He added drily, "The sun not being alterable in its course, light traveling in straight lines, and the laws of trigonometry being immutable, you will perceive that the length of the shadow is determined by the height of the tower." We rose and went inside.

I was still reading at eleven that evening when there was a knock at my door. Opening it I found the housemaid, dressed in a somewhat old-fashioned black dress and white cap, whom I had perceived hovering in the background on several occasions that day. Courtseying prettily, she asked, "Would the gentleman like to have his bed turned down for the night?"

I stepped aside, not wishing to refuse, but remarked that it was very late—was she kept on duty to such hours? No, indeed, she answered, as she deftly turned my bed covers, but it had occurred to her that some duties might be pleasures as well. In such and similar philosophical reflections we spent a few pleasant hours together, until eventually I mentioned casually how silly it seemed to me that the tower's shadow ruined the terrace for a prolonged, leisurely tea.

At this, her brow clouded. She sat up sharply. "What exactly did he tell you about this?" I replied lightly, repeating the story about Marie Antoinette, which now sounded a bit far-fetched even to my credulous ears.

"The *servants* have a different account," she said with a sneer that was not at all becoming, it seemed to me, on such a young and pretty face. "The truth is quite different, and has nothing to do with ancestors. That tower marks the spot where he killed the maid with whom he had been in love to the point of madness. And the height of the tower? He vowed that shadow would cover the terrace where he first proclaimed his love, with every setting sun—that is why the tower had to be so high."

I took this in but slowly. It is never easy to assimilate unexpected truths about people we think we know—and I have had occasion to notice this again and again.

"Why did he kill her?" I asked finally.

"Because, sir, she dallied with an English brigadier, an overnight guest in this house." With these words she arose, collected her bodice and cap, and faded through the wall beside the doorway.

I left early the next morning, making my excuses as well as I could.

A MODEL FOR EXPLANATION

I shall now propose a new theory of explanation. An explanation is not the same as a proposition, or an argument, or list of propositions; it is an *answer*. (Analogously, a son is not the same as a man, even if all sons are men, and every man is a son.) An explanation is an answer to a why-question. So, a theory of explanation must be a theory of why-questions. . . .

Questions

We must now look further into the general logic of questions. There are of course a number of approaches: I shall mainly follow that of Nuel Belnap, though without committing myself to the details of his theory.[1]

A theory of questions must needs be based on a theory of propositions, which I shall assume given. A *question* is an abstract entity; it is expressed by an *interrogative* (a piece of language) in the same sense that a proposition is expressed by a declarative sentence. Almost anything can be an appropriate response to a question, in one situation or another; as "Peccavi" was the reply telegraphed by a British commander in India to the question how the battle was going (he had been sent to attack the province of Sind).[2] But not every response is, properly speaking, an answer. Of course, there are degrees; and one response may be more or less of an answer than another. The first task of a theory of questions is to provide some typology of answers. As an example, consider the following question, and a series of responses:

> Can you get to Victoria both by ferry and by plane?
>
> (a) Yes.
>
> (b) You can get to Victoria both by ferry and by plane.
>
> (c) You can get to Victoria by ferry.
>
> (d) You can get to Victoria both by ferry and by plane, but the ferry ride is not to be missed.
>
> (e) You can certainly get to Victoria by ferry, and that is something not to be missed.

Here *(b)* is the "purest" example of an answer: it gives enough information to answer the question completely, but no more. Hence it is called a *direct answer*. The word "Yes" *(a)* is a *code* for this answer.

Responses *(c)* and *(d)* depart from that direct answer in opposite directions: *(c)* says properly less than *(b)*—it is implied by *(b)*—while *(d)*, which implies *(b)*, says more. Any proposition implied by a direct answer is called a *partial answer* and one which implies a direct answer is a *complete answer*. We must resist the temptation to say that therefore an answer, *tout court*, is any combination of a partial answer with further information, for in that case, every proposition would be an answer to any question. So let us leave *(e)* unclassified for now, while noting it is still "more of an answer" than such responses as "Gorilla!" (which is a response given to various questions in the film *Ich bin ein Elephant, Madam*, and hence. I suppose, still more of an answer than some). There may be some quantitative notion in the background (a measure of the extent to which a response really "bears on" the question) or at least a much more complete typology (some more of it is given below), so it is probably better not to try and define the general term "answer" too soon.

The basic notion so far is that of direct answer. In 1958, C. L. Hamblin introduced the thesis that a question is uniquely identifiable through its answers.[3] This can be regarded as a simplifying hypothesis of the sort we come across for propositions, for it would allow us to identify a question with the set of its direct answers. Note that this does not preclude a good deal of complexity in the determination of exactly what question is expressed by a given interrogative. Also, the hypothesis does not identify the question with the disjunction of its direct answers. If that were done, the clearly distinct questions

Is the cat on the mat?

 direct answers: The cat is on the mat.

      The cat is not on the mat.

Is the theory of relativity true?

 direct answers: The theory of relativity is true.

      The theory of relativity is not true.

would be the same (identified with the tautology) if the logic of propositions adopted were classical logic. Although this simplifying hypothesis is therefore not to be rejected immediately, and has in fact guided much of the research on questions, it is still advisable to remain somewhat tentative towards it.

Meanwhile we can still use the notion of direct answer to define some basic concepts. One question Q may be said to *contain* another, Q', if Q' is answered as soon as Q is—that is, every complete answer to Q is also a complete answer to Q'. A question is

empty if all its direct answers are necessarily true, and *foolish* if none of them is even possibly true. A special case is the *dumb* question, which has no direct answers. Here are examples:

1. Did you wear the black hat yesterday or did you wear the white one?
2. Did you wear a hat which is both black and not black, or did you wear one which is both white and not white?
3. What are three distinct examples of primes among the following numbers: 3, 5?

Clearly 3 is dumb and 2 is foolish. If we correspondingly call a necessarily false statement foolish too, we obtain the theorem *Ask a foolish question and get a foolish answer.* This was first proved by Belnap, but attributed by him to an early Indian philosopher mentioned in Plutarch's *Lives* who had the additional distinction of being an early nudist. . . .

A THEORY OF WHY-QUESTIONS

There are several respects in which why-questions introduce genuinely new elements into the theory of questions.[4] Let us focus first on the determination of exactly what question is asked, that is, the contextual specification of factors needed to understand a why-interrogative. After that is done (a task which ends with the delineation of the set of direct answers) and as an independent enterprise, we must turn to the evaluation of those answers as good or better. This evaluation proceeds with reference to the part of science accepted as "background theory" in that context.

As [an] example, consider the question "Why is this conductor warped?" The questioner implies that the conductor is warped, and is asking for a reason. Let us call the proposition that the conductor is warped the *topic* of the question (following Henry

Leonard's terminology, "topic of concern"). Next, this question has a *contrast-class*, as we saw, that is, a set of alternatives. I shall take this contrast-class, call it X, to be a class of propositions which includes the topic. For this particular interrogative, the contrast could be that it is *this* conductor rather than *that* one, or that this conductor has warped rather than retained its shape. If the question is "Why does this material burn yellow?" the contrast-class could be the set of propositions: this material burned (with a flame of) colour x.

Finally, there is the respect-in-which a reason is requested, which determines what shall count as a possible explanatory factor, the relation of *explanatory relevance*. In the first example, the request might be *for events "leading up to" the warping*. That allows as relevant an account of human error, of switches being closed or moisture condensing in those switches, even spells cast by witches (since the evaluation of what is a good answer comes later). On the other hand, the events leading up to the warping might be well known, in which case the request is likely to be for the standing conditions that made it possible for those events to lead to this warping: the presence of a magnetic field of a certain strength, say. Finally, it might already be known, or considered immaterial, exactly how the warping is produced, and the question (possibly based on a misunderstanding) may be about exactly what function this warping fulfils in the operation of the power station. Compare "Why does the blood circulate through the body?" answered (1) "because the heart pumps the blood through the arteries" and (2) "to bring oxygen to every part of the body tissue."

In a given context, several questions agreeing in topic but differing in contrast-class, or conversely, may conceivably differ further in what counts as explanatorily relevant. Hence we cannot properly ask what is relevant to this topic, or what is relevant to this contrast-class. Instead we must say of a given proposition that it is or is not relevant (in this context) to the topic with respect to that contrast-class. For example, in the same context one might be curious about the circumstances that led Adam to eat the apple rather than the pear (Eve offered him an apple) and also about the motives that led him to eat it rather than refuse it. What is "kept constant" or "taken as given" (that he ate the fruit; that what he did, he did to the apple) which is to say, the contrast-class, is not to be dissociated entirely from the respect-in-which we want a reason. . . .

NOTES

1. Belnap's theory was first presented in *An analysis of questions: preliminary report* (Santa Monica, Cal.: System Development Corporation, technical memorandum 7–1287–1000/00, 1963), and is now more accessible in N. D. Belnap Jr. and J. B. Steel, Jr., *The Logic of Questions and Answers* (New Haven: Yale University Press, 1976).

2. I heard the example from my former student Gerald Charlwood. Ian Hacking and J. J. C. Smart told me that the officer was Sir Charles Napier.

3. C. L. Hamblin, "Questions," *Australasian Journal of Philosophy* 36 (1958), 159–68.

4. In the book by Belnap and Steel (see n. 1 above), Bromberger's theory of why-questions is cast in the general form common to elementary questions. I think that Bromberger arrived at his concept of "abnormic law" (and the form of answer exhibited by" 'Grünbaum' is spelled with an umlaut because it is an English word borrowed from German, and no English words are spelled with an umlaut except those borrowed from another language in which they are so spelled"), because he ignored the tacit *rather than* (contrast-class) in why-interrogatives, and then had to make up for this deficiency in the account of what the answers are like.

MARY HESSE, "THE EXPLANATORY FUNCTION OF METAPHOR"

Hesse offers a fuller account of Scriven's and van Fraassen's idea of context. She takes the D-N model to be a model for theoretical explanation. Theoretical explanation is scientific explanation where mention of theoretical entities is necessary at some point. Such explanation is, according to Hesse, metaphorical redescription of the domain of the explanandum (what is to be explained).

She uses some ideas from the contemporary philosopher Max Black, who wrote extensively on models. The interaction view is that metaphors must be understood in terms of primary and secondary systems—where each is a literal language. The primary system is the domain of explanandum—it is the language of observation. The secondary system provides the explanation; for example, the explanation of sound (primary) in terms of waves (secondary). In this view, metaphors, models, explanandum, explanans, and theory are all linguistic entities.

Hesse stresses metaphors. Because metaphors can themselves serve as models, we shall use them interchangeably. Briefly, a model (or metaphor) is any way to represent some set of facts. The goals are usually to help in understanding, help in predicting, or make more vivid. One can represent the movements of a swimmer during a race with computerized pictures. One can represent a person by painting a likeness or photographing the person. One can represent a real airplane by building a much smaller version of it "to scale." One can represent an economic situation by using mathematical equations. One can say things like "the boulevard of broken dreams." This would be referred to as a metaphor rather than a model. For a model or metaphor to help in understanding or in making more vivid, it must bear some relation to what it models or is about. Models and metaphors are like analogies. They are never perfect. As with even the best analogies, there will be disanalogies, so with even the best models and metaphors, there will be points of disconnection. In this regard, think of fashion models. They represent men and women, but only vaguely. Their points of connection with the literal world are not so much with the men and women they represent but rather with what makes the clothes they wear look best to consumers.

The language of observation blends into the language of explanation. Usually, however, the language used to express observation is better understood than the explaining language. When using a mathematical model to help with understanding the genetics of populations, the frequency of the traits in the population (e.g., the frequency of blue versus brown eyes) would be the observation language. It is clearer to most people than equations in the form of binomial expansions. Neither language need be totally accurate. To be useful, a metaphor requires some antecedent similarity. It is not the case that anything goes. All the similarity is not created by the use of the metaphor. Black, Hesse points out, suggests otherwise. This may be so in literature. But in science, this is not accurate. For example, heat as a fluid did not work as a usable metaphor. No metaphor can be reduced to a literal description. Metaphors work by transferring associated ideas: They select, emphasize, suppress, and so on. This goes in both directions. When we say, "It's a jungle out there," we come to see people more like wild animals and wild animals as more like people.

Hesse notes a problem with her idea of explanation in terms of metaphor. What do the terms in a metaphorical redescription refer to? If you say, "It is raining cats and dogs," that might be a good explanation for why you are so wet. What can the "cats" and "dogs" refer to? Certainly not real cats and dogs falling out of the sky! She says that the primary system is the best answer to what is the referent of a metaphor. It is not simple identification because some identifications can be meaningless. Moreover, identifications can be false. In this regard, scientific metaphors and models are not like poetic or everyday metaphors. Rather, scientific metaphors are meant to be worked on, quantified, and used to suggest further work. Yet if she is right, science is unlikely to be translatable into any formalized language as Hempel and Oppenheim (as well as Carnap in Chapter 3) think possible and helpful.

The D-N model assumes that as science develops, terms keep their meanings. This is called the thesis of meaning invariance. Meaning invariance is needed if one wants to hold that the laws of older theories are deducible from newer theories. If there is meaning invariance, we can explain why Max von Pettenkofer (1818–1901, a disbeliever in the idea that cholera was caused by drinking water infected with cholera germs) was able to drink a vial of water infected with cholera germs and not get cholera. We can give our explanation by deducing what was known in the germ theory of the late nineteenth century from what we now know about germs (and cholera).

Hesse's claim, however, is that as our knowledge changes by means of metaphor, so do the meanings of the terms. This means that no deduction is possible unless it commits what is known as the fallacy of equivocation (having one term mean two different things). In the example used, she would claim that *germ* and *cholera* have changed their meanings. Kuhn (Chapter 3) agrees with Hesse. His views entail the falsity of the thesis of meaning invariance.

Hesse says that her ideas should be used to supplement and modify the D-N model. Here she may be too modest. Her views are far closer to destroying the D-N model than to modifying it. We have seen the D-N model criticized by Scriven and Cartwright for failing to meet its own standards. They have pointed out that the closest we can get to a covering law is an approximation to a covering law. Hesse suggests why that is so. It is because the important laws come from theories that can be seen as metaphorical approximations. The critics of the D-N model all point out in one way or another that deduction is not really the focus of scientific explanation. Hesse agrees, saying that the focus should be on how the metaphor connects to the primary system.

The Explanatory Function of Metaphor

MARY HESSE

The thesis of this paper is that the deductive model of scientific explanation should be modified and supplemented by a view of theoretical explanation as metaphoric redescription of the domain of the explanandum. This raises two large preliminary questions: first, whether the deductive model requires modification, and second, what is the view of metaphor presupposed by the suggested alternative. I shall not discuss the first question explicitly. Much recent literature in the philosophy of science has answered it affirmatively,[1] and I shall refer briefly at the end to some difficulties tending to show that a new model of explanation is required, and suggest how the conception of theories as metaphors meets these difficulties.

The second question, about the view of metaphor presupposed, requires more extensive discussion. The view I shall present is essentially due to Max Black, who has developed in two papers, entitled respectively "Metaphor" and "Models and Archetypes,"[2] both a new theory of metaphor, and a parallelism between the use of literary metaphor and the use of models in theoretical science. I shall start with an exposition of Black's *interaction view* of metaphors and models, taking account of modifications suggested by some of the subsequent literature on metaphor.[3] It is still unfortunately necessary to argue that metaphor is more than a decorative literary device, and that it has cognitive implications whose nature is a proper subject of philosophic discussion. But space forces me

From Mary Hesse, *Revolutions and Reconstructions in the Philosophy of Science* (Bloomington: Indiana University Press, 1980), pp. 111–124. Courtey of the author and Harvester Press.

to mention these arguments as footnotes to Black's view, rather than as an explicit defence *ab initio* of the philosophic importance of metaphor.

THE INTERACTION VIEW OF METAPHOR

1. We start with two systems, situations, or referents, which will be called respectively the primary and secondary systems. Each is described in literal language. A metaphoric use of language in describing the primary system consists of transferring to it a word or words normally used in connection with the secondary system: for example, "Man is a wolf," "Hell is a lake of ice." In a scientific theory the primary system is the domain of the explanandum, describable in observation language; and the secondary is the system, described either in observation language or the language of a familiar theory, from which the model is taken: for example, "sound (primary system) is propagated by wave motion (taken from a secondary system)"; "gases are collections of randomly moving massive particles."

Three terminological remarks should be inserted here. First, "primary" and "secondary system," and "domain of the explanandum" will be used throughout to denote the referents or putative referents of descriptive statements; and "metaphor," "model," "theory," "explanans" and "explanandum" will be used to denote linguistic entities. Second, use of the terms "metaphoric" and "literal," "theory" and "observation," need not be taken at this stage to imply a pair of irreducible dichotomies. All that is intended is that the "literal" and "observation" languages are assumed initially to be well understood and unproblematic, whereas the "metaphoric" and "theoretical" are in need of analysis. The third remark is that to assume initially that the two systems are "described" in literal or observation language does not imply that they are exhaustively or accurately described or even that they could in principle be so in terms of these languages.

2. We assume that the primary and secondary systems each carry a set of associated ideas and beliefs that come to mind when the system is referred to. These are not private to individual language-users, but are largely common to a given language community and are presupposed by speakers who intend to be understood in that community. In literary contexts the associations may be loosely knit and variable, as in the wolf-like characteristics which come to mind when the metaphor "Man is a wolf" is used; in scientific contexts the primary and secondary systems may both be highly organized by networks of natural laws.

A remark must be added here about the use of the word "meaning." Writers on metaphor appear to intend it as an inclusive term for reference, use, and the relevant set of associated ideas. It is, indeed, part of their thesis that it has to be understood thus widely. To understand the meaning of a descriptive expression is not only to be able to recognize its referent, or even to use the words in the expression correctly, but also to call to mind the ideas, both linguistic and empirical, which are commonly held to be associated with the referent in the given language community. Thus a shift of meaning may result from a change in the set of associated ideas, as well as in change of reference or use.

3. For a conjunction of terms drawn from the primary and secondary systems to constitute a metaphor it is necessary that there should be patent falsehood or even absurdity in taking the conjunction literally. Man is not, literally, a wolf; gases are not in the usual sense collections of massive particles. In consequence some writers have denied that the referent of the metaphoric expression can be identified with the primary system without falling into absurdity or contradiction. I shall return to this in the next section.

4. There is initially some principle of assimilation between primary and secondary systems, variously described in the literature as "analogy," "intimations of similarity," "a programme for exploration," "a framework through which the primary is seen." Here we have to guard against two opposite interpretations, both of which are inadequate for the general understanding of metaphors and scientific models. On the one hand, to describe this ground of assimilation as a *programme* for exploration, or a *framework* through which the primary is seen, is to suggest that the secondary system can be imposed *a priori* upon the primary, as if *any* secondary can be the source of metaphors or models for *any* primary, provided the right metaphor-creating operations are subsequently carried out. Black does indeed suggest that in some cases "it would be more illuminating . . . to say that the metaphor creates the similarity than to say it formulates some similarity antecedently existing" (p. 37), and he also points out that some poetry creates new metaphors precisely by itself developing the system of associations in terms of which "absurd" conjunctions of words are to be metaphorically understood. There is however an important distinction to be brought out between such a use of metaphor and scientific models, for, whatever may be the case for poetic use, the suggestion that *any* scientific model can be imposed *a priori* on *any* explanandum and function fruitfully in its explanation must be resisted. Such a

view would imply that theoretical models are irrefutable. That this is not the case is sufficiently illustrated by the history of the concept of a heat fluid, or the classical wave theory of light. Such examples also indicate that no model even gets off the ground unless some antecedent similarity or analogy is discerned between it and the explanandum.

But here there is a danger of falling into what Black calls the *comparison* view of metaphor. According to this view the metaphor can be replaced without remainder by an explicit, literal statement of the similarities between primary and secondary systems, in other words, by a simile. Thus, the metaphor "Man is a wolf" would be equivalent to "Man is like a wolf in that . . . ," where follows a list of comparable characteristics; or, in the case of theoretical models, the language derived from the secondary system would be wholly replaced by an explicit statement of the analogy between secondary and primary systems, after which further reference to the secondary system would be dispensable. Any interesting examples of the model-using in science will show, however, that the situation cannot be described in this way. For one thing, as long as the model is under active consideration as an ingredient in an explanation, we do not know how far the comparison extends—it is precisely in its extension that the fruitfulness of the model may lie. And a more fundamental objection to the comparison view emerges in considering the next point.

5. The metaphor works by transferring the associated ideas and implications of the secondary to the primary system. These select, emphasize, or suppress features of the primary; new slants on the primary are illuminated; the primary is "seen through" the frame of the secondary. In accordance with the doctrine that even literal expressions are understood partly in terms of the

set of associated ideas carried by the system they describe, it follows that the associated ideas of the primary are changed to some extent by the use of the metaphor, and that therefore even its original literal description is shifted in meaning. The same applies to the secondary system, for its associations come to be affected by assimilation to the primary; the two systems are seen as more like each other; they seem to interact and adapt to one another, even to the point of invalidating their original literal descriptions if these are understood in the new, post-metaphoric sense. Men are seen to be more like wolves after the wolf-metaphor is used, and wolves seem to be more human. Nature becomes more like a machine in the mechanical philosophy, and actual, concrete machines themselves are seen as if stripped down to their essential qualities of mass in motion.

This point is the kernel of the interaction view, and is Black's major contribution to the analysis of metaphor. It is incompatible with the comparison view, which assumes that the literal descriptions of both systems are and remain independent of the use of the metaphor, and that the metaphor is reducible to them. The consequences of the interaction view for theoretical models are also incompatible with assumptions generally made in the deductive account of explanation, namely that descriptions and descriptive laws in the domain of the explanandum remain empirically acceptable and invariant in meaning to all changes of explanatory theory. I shall return to this point.

6. It should be added as a final point in this preliminary analysis that a metaphoric expression used for the first time, or used to someone who hears it for the first time, is intended to be *understood*. Indeed it may be said that a metaphor is not metaphor but nonsense if it communicates nothing, and that a genuine metaphor is also capable of

communicating something other than was intended and hence of being *mis*understood. If I say (taking two words more or less at random from a dictionary page) "A truck is a trumpet" it is unlikely that I shall communicate anything; if I say "He is a shadow on the weary land," you may understand me to mean (roughly) "He is a wet blanket, a gloom, a menace," whereas I actually meant (again roughly) "He is a shade from the heat, a comfort, a protection."

Acceptance of the view that metaphors are meant to be intelligible implies rejection of all views which make metaphor a wholly non-cognitive, subjective, emotive, or stylistic use of language. There are exactly parallel views of scientific models which have been held by many contemporary philosophers of science, namely that models are purely subjective, psychological, and adopted by individuals for private heuristic purposes. But this is wholly to misdescribe their function in science. Models, like metaphors, are intended to communicate. If some theorist develops a theory in terms of a model, he does not regard it as a private language, but presents it as an ingredient of his theory. Neither can he, nor need he, make literally explicit all the associations of the model he is exploiting; other workers in the field "catch on" to its intended implications, indeed they sometimes find the theory unsatisfactory just because some implications which the model's originator did not investigate, or even think of, turn out to be empirically false. None of this would be possible unless use of the model were intersubjective, part of the commonly understood theoretical language of science, not a private language of the individual theorist.

An important general consequence of the interaction view is that it is not possible to make a distinction between literal and metaphoric descriptions merely by asserting that literal use consists in the following of linguistic rules. Intelligible metaphor also implies the existence of rules of metaphoric use, and since in the interaction view literal meanings are shifted by their association with metaphors, it follows that the rules of literal usage and of metaphor, though they are not identical, are nevertheless not independent. It is not sufficiently clear in Black's paper that the interaction view commits one to the abandonment of a two-tiered account of language in which some usages are irreducibly literal and others metaphoric. The interaction view sees language as dynamic: an expression initially metaphoric may become literal (a "dead" metaphor), and what is at one time literal may become metaphoric (for example the Homeric "he breathed forth his life," originally literal, is now a metaphor for death). What is important is not to try to draw a line between the metaphoric and the literal, but rather to trace out the various mechanisms of meaning-shift and their interactions. The interaction view cannot consistently be made to rest on an initial set of absolutely literal descriptions, but rather on a relative distinction of literal and metaphoric in particular contexts. I cannot undertake the task of elucidating these conceptions here (an interesting attempt to do so has been made by K. I. B. S. Needham),[4] but I shall later point out a parallel between this general linguistic situation and the relative distinctions and mutual interactions of theory and observation in science.

THE PROBLEM OF METAPHORIC REFERENCE

One of the main problems for the interaction view in its application to theoretical explanation is the question what is the *referent* of a model or metaphor. At first sight the referent seems to be the primary system, which we choose to describe in metaphoric rather than literal terms. This, I believe, is in the end the right answer, but the process of metaphoric description is such as to cast doubt on any simple identification of the metaphor's reference with the primary system. It is claimed in the interaction view that a metaphor causes us to "see" the primary system differently, and causes the meanings of terms originally literal in the primary system to shift towards the metaphor. Thus "Man is a wolf" makes man seem more vulpine, "Hell is a lake of ice" makes hell seem icy rather than hot, and a wave theory of sound makes sound seem more vibrant. But how can initial similarities between the objective systems justify such changes in the meanings of words and even, apparently, in the things themselves? Man does not in fact change because someone uses the wolf-metaphor. How then can we be justified in identifying what we see through the framework of the metaphor with the primary system itself? It seems that we cannot be entitled to say men *are* wolves, sound *is* wave motion, in any identificatory sense of the copula.

Some recent writers on metaphor[5] have made it the main burden of their argument to deny that any such identification is possible. They argue that if we allow it we are falling into the absurdity of conjoining two literally incompatible systems, and the resulting expression is not metaphoric but meaningless. By thus taking a metaphor literally we turn it into a *myth*. An initial misunderstanding may be removed at once by remarking that "identification" cannot mean in this context identification of the referent of the metaphoric expression, taken in its *literal* sense, with the primary system. But if the foregoing analysis of metaphor is accepted, then it follows that metaphoric use is use in a different from the literal sense, and furthermore it is use in a sense not replaceable by any literal expression. There remains the question what it is to identify the referent of the metaphoric expression or model with the primary system. As a preliminary to answering this question it is important to point out that there are two ways, which are often confused in accounts of the "meaning of theoretical concepts," in which such identification may fail. It may fail because it is in principle meaningless to make any such identification, or it may fail because in a particular case the identification happens to be *false*. Instances of false identification, e.g. "heat is a fluid" or "the substance emitted by a burning object is phlogiston," provide no arguments to show that other such identifications may not be both meaningful and true.

Two sorts of argument have been brought against the view that metaphoric expressions and models can refer to and truly describe the primary system. The first depends on an assimilation of poetic and scientific metaphor, and points out that it is characteristic of good poetic metaphor that the images introduced are initially striking and unexpected, if not shocking; that they are meant to be entertained and savoured for the moment and not analyzed in pedantic detail nor stretched to radically new situations; and that they may immediately give place to other metaphors referring to the same subject matter which are formally contradictory, and in which the contradictions are an essential part of the total metaphoric impact. Any attempt to separate these literal contradictions from the nexus of interactions is destructive of the metaphor, particularly on the interaction view. In the light of these characteristics there is indeed a difficult problem about the correct analysis of the notion of metaphoric "truth" in poetic contexts. Scientific models, however, are fortunately not so intractable. They do not share any of the characteristics listed above which make poetic metaphors peculiarly subject to formal contradictoriness. They may initially be unexpected, but it is not their chief aim to shock; they are meant to be exploited energetically and often in extreme quantitative detail and in quite novel observational domains; they are meant to be internally tightly knit by logical and causal interrelations; and if two models of the same primary system are found to be mutually inconsistent, this is not taken (*pace* the complementarity interpretation of quantum physics) to enhance their effectiveness, but rather as a challenge to reconcile them by mutual modification or to refute one of them. Thus their truth criteria, although not rigorously formalizable, are at least much clearer than in the case of poetic metaphor. We can perhaps signalize the difference by speaking in the case of scientific models of the (perhaps unattainable) aim to find a "perfect metaphor," whose referent is the domain of the explanandum, whereas literary metaphors, however adequate and successful in their own terms, are from the point of view of potential logical consistency and extendability often (not always) intentionally imperfect. . . .

Secondly, if the interaction view of scientific metaphor or model is combined with the claim that the referent of the metaphor is the primary system (i.e. the metaphor is true of the primary system), then it follows that the thesis of meaning-invariance of the literal observation-descriptions of the primary system is false. For, the interaction view implies that the meaning of the original literal language of the primary system is changed by adoption of the metaphor. Hence those who wish to adhere to meaning-invariance in the deductive account of explanation will be forced to reject either the interaction view or the realistic view that a scientific model is putatively true of its primary system. Generally they reject both. But abandonment of meaning-invariance, as in many recent criticisms of the deductive model of explanation, leaves room for adoption of both the interaction view, and realism, as I shall now try to spell out in more detail.

EXPLANATION AS METAPHORIC REDESCRIPTION

The initial contention of this paper was that the deductive model of explanation should be *modified* and *supplemented* by a view of theoretical explanation as metaphoric redescription of the domain of the explanandum. First, the association of the ideas of "metaphor" and of "explanation" requires more examination. It is certainly not the case that all explanations are metaphoric. To take only two examples, explanation by covering-law, where an instance of an A which is B is explained by reference to the law "All A's are B's," is not metaphoric, neither is the explanation of the working of a mechanical gadget by reference to an actual mechanism of cogs, pulleys, and levers. These, however, are not examples of *theoretical* explanation, for it has been taken for granted that the essence of a theoretical explanation is the introduction into the explanans of a new vocabulary or even of a new language. But introduction of a metaphoric terminology is not in itself explanatory, for in literary metaphor in general there is no hint that what is metaphorically described is also thereby explained. The connection between metaphor and explanation is therefore neither that of necessary nor sufficient condition. Metaphor becomes explanatory only when it satisfies certain further conditions.

The orthodox deductive criteria for a scientific explanans[6] require that the explanandum be deducible from it, that it contain at least one general law not redundant to the deduction, that it be not empirically falsified up to date, and that it be predictive. We cannot simply graft these requirements on to the account of theories as metaphors without investigating the consequences of the interaction view of metaphor for the notions of "deducibility," "explanandum," and "falsification" in the orthodox account. In any case, as has been mentioned already, the requirement of deducibility in particular has been subjected to damaging attack, quite apart from any metaphoric interpretation of theories. There are two chief grounds for this attack, both of which can be turned into arguments favourable to the metaphoric view.

In the first place it is pointed out that there is seldom in fact a deductive relation strictly speaking between scientific explanans and explanandum, but only relations of approximate fit. Furthermore, what counts as sufficiently approximate fit cannot be decided deductively, but is a complicated function of coherence with the rest of a theoretical system, general empirical acceptability throughout the domain of the explanandum, and many other factors. I do not propose to try to spell out these relationships in further detail here, but merely to make two points which are relevant to my immediate concern. First, the attack on deducibility drawn from the occurrence of approximations does not imply that there are *no* deductive relations between explanans and explanandum. The situation is rather this. Given a descriptive statement D in the domain of the explanandum, it is usually the case that the statement E of an acceptable explanans does not entail D, but rather D', where D' is a statement in the domain of the explanandum only "approximately equivalent" to D. For E to be acceptable it is necessary both that there be a deductive relation between E and D', and that D' should come to be recognized as a *more acceptable* description in the domain of the explanandum than D. The reasons why it might be more acceptable—repetition of the experiments with greater accuracy, greater coherence with other acceptable laws, recognition of disturbing factors in arriving at D in the first place, metaphoric

shifts in the meanings of terms in D consequent upon the introduction of the new terminology of E, and so on—need not concern us here. What is relevant is that the non-deducibility of D from E does not imply total abandonment of the deductive model unless D is regarded as an invariant description of the explanandum, automatically rendering D' empirically false. That D cannot be so regarded has been amply demonstrated in the literature. The second point of contact between these considerations and the view of theories as metaphors is now obvious. That explanation may modify and correct the explanandum is already built into the relation between metaphors and the primary system in the interaction view. Metaphors, if they are good ones, and *ipso facto* their deductive consequences, do have the primary system as their referents, for they may be seen as correcting and replacing the original literal descriptions of the same system, so that the literal descriptions are discarded as inadequate or even false. The parallel with the deductive relations of explanans and explananda is clear: the metaphoric view does not abandon deduction, but it focuses attention rather on the interaction between metaphor and primary system, and on the criteria of acceptability of metaphoric descriptions of the primary system, and hence not so much upon the deductive relations which appear in this account as comparatively uninteresting piece of logical machinery.

Finally, a word about the requirement that an explanation be predictive. It has been much debated within the orthodox deductive view whether this is a necessary and sufficient condition for explanation, and it is not appropriate here to enter into that debate. But any account of explanation would be inadequate which did not recognize that, in general, an explanation is required to be predictive, or, what is closely connected with this, to be falsifiable.

Elsewhere[7] I have pointed out that, in terms of the deductive view, the requirement of predictivity may mean one of three things:

(i) That general laws already present in the explanans have as yet unobserved instances. This is a trivial fulfilment of the requirement, and would not, I think, generally be regarded as sufficient.

(ii) That further general laws can be derived from the explanans, *without* adding further items to the set of correspondence rules. That is to say, predictions remain within the domain of the set of predicates already present in the explanandum. This is a weak sense of predictivity which covers what would normally be called *applications* rather than extensions of a theory (for example, calculation of the orbit of a satellite from the theory of gravitation, but not extension of the theory to predict the bending of light rays).

(iii) There is also a strong sense of prediction in which new observation predicates are involved, and hence, in terms of the deductive view, additions are required to the set of correspondence rules.

. . . I have argued that on the metaphoric view, . . . since the domain of the explanandum is redescribed in terminology transferred from the secondary system, it is to be expected that the original observation language will both be shifted in meaning and extended in vocabulary, and hence that predictions in the strong sense will become possible. They may not of course turn out to be *true*, but that is an occupational hazard of

any explanation or prediction. They will however be rational, because rationality consists just in the continuous adaptation of our language to our continually expanding world, and metaphor is one of the chief means by which this is accomplished.

NOTES

1. See, for example, P. K. Feyerabend, "An Attempt at a Realistic Interpretation of Experience," *Proc. Arist. Soc.* 58 (1957): 143; *idem*, "Explanation, Reduction, and Empiricism," in *Minnesota Studies in the Philosophy of Science*, ed. H. Feigl and G. Maxwell, Minneapolis, 1962; T. S. Kuhn, *The Structure of Scientific Revolutions*, Chicago, 1962; W. Sellars, "The Language of Theories," in *Current Issues in the Philosophy of Science*, ed. H. Feigl and G. Maxwell, New York, 1961.
2. M. Black, *Models and Metaphors*, Ithaca, 1962.
3. See M. C. Beardsley, *Aesthetics*, New York, 1958; D. Berggren, "The Use and Abuse of Metaphor," *Rev. Met.* 16 (1962): 237, 450; M. A. McCloskey, "Metaphors," *Mind* 73 (1964): 215; D. Schön, *The Displacement of Concepts*, London, 1963; C. Turbayne, *The Myth of Metaphor*, New Haven, 1962.
4. K. I. B. S. Needham, *Synonymy and Semantic Classification*, unpublished Ph.D. thesis, Cambridge, 1964.
5. Bergren, McCloskey, and Turbayne, in the works cited above.
6. For example, C. G. Hempel and P. Oppenheim, "The Logic of Explanation," in *Readings in the Philosophy of Science*, ed. H. Feigl and M. Brodbeck, New York, 1953, p. 319.
7. M. Hesse, *Models and Analogies in Science*, London, 1963; see also *idem*, "A New Look at Scientific Explanation," *Rev. Met.* 17 (1963): 98.

EXERCISES

1. Which examples from the selection by Carney and Scheer best fit the deductive-nomological model? Which examples are hardest to fit to the D-N model? What makes them easier or more difficult to fit?
2. What important similarities among Scriven, Cartwright, van Fraassen, and Hesse lead the four of them to disagree with Hempel and Oppenheim? Are there important differences among the four?

3. Cartwright has written a book, *How the Laws of Physics Lie.* How would Hesse argue that the laws of physics do not lie?

4. Read a brief discussion of the philosophy of pragmatism or something on the thoughts of William James, C. S. Peirce, or John Dewey. Why does van Fraassen refer to his theory of explanation as "pragmatic"?

5. How would Brodbeck and Scriven each compare the selections by Hooke and Strum from Chapter 1?

3

Confirmation

In the introduction to Chapter 2, we asked how science would explain the high rate of heart disease in the United States. We pointed out that knowing what counted as a scientific explanation would not tell us what counted as the correct explanation. That is the job of what is sometimes called confirmation theory. When an explanation is accepted, it is usually because it is confirmed at least to some degree. This means that there is evidence that supports the explanation. How much evidence is needed to support a claim, how well that evidence supports the claim, what counts as evidence—these are questions to be answered by confirmation theory.

Let us look at a relatively simple case. If my car's radiator is cracked in the morning, it might be due to vandalism, insufficient antifreeze on a particularly cold night, or a defect in the metal of the radiator. If there has been similar vandalism in my neighborhood and if I know that I just filled the radiator with antifreeze and defective radiators are very rare, the vandalism explanation will be more highly confirmed than either of the other two options. Notice that I have to assume that the antifreeze was truly antifreeze as stated on the container. If there has not been similar vandalism in the neighborhood and if I have a trustworthy new car, the antifreeze is the likely culprit, especially if I am forgetful. It is important to see that the best-supported explanation may not be the right explanation. For example, it might be that two extremely sharp-toothed raccoons, annoyed that my garbage lids are on too tight for them to remove, decide to eat a hole in my car's radiator.

This example of the cracked automobile radiator models scientific confirmation. There are competing explanations: vandalism, no antifreeze, metal defect. Evidence for each is gathered and then compared. One of the competing explanations is chosen because it is better supported by the evidence. Yet the explanation accepted is always accepted only provisionally because as with the raccoons, new evidence might surface, forcing us to realize that we might have chosen the wrong explanation. In the case of the cracked radiator, what counts as evidence and more (or less) support is much clearer than it often is in cases of theoretical science.

Sometimes only one explanation is offered. Even in the absence of competing explanations, we must gather evidence to support the explanation. We may accept an explanation with a lower degree of confirmation because we have only one explanation, as a practical consideration, out of some sort of psychological need for order. Making confirmation, even in part, a function of psychological need makes it subjective. Many people feel that that sacrifices much, if not all, of what is unique to science—its objectivity.

If we need an explanation and have only one, what choice do we have but to accept it? Think of the gambler's adage: "When do you play in a crooked game? When it's the only one in town." The saying assumes that gambling under any circumstances is better than not gambling at all.

The question is, how badly do we need an explanation, and its corollary, how serious will it be if we choose the wrong explanation? If choosing the wrong explanation has very serious consequences and we do not have to choose, then rather than accept an explanation with a low degree of confirmation only because it is the only explanation, we would probably just bide our time and wait for a better-confirmed explanation.

In the readings in this chapter, you will encounter differing views on confirmation (Carnap, Popper, Kuhn, Lakatos, Laudan, and Kitcher) as well as a renegade opinion (Feyerabend) claiming that scientific reasoning is nothing like it is claimed to be, that both scientists and philosophers of science have totally mischaracterized the nature of science and its method. The chapter ends with a brief selection from John Earman's book *Bayes or Bust*. He will suggest how Popper, Kuhn, Lakatos, Laudan, and Feyerabend have all gone astray.

There is a logical and historical progression in the series of readings in this chapter. They are logical in that the articles focus on similar points. The historical sequence is obvious. Seeing issues developed this way makes them easier to grasp. The reason for the series of articles is therefore heuristic, that is, to help with teaching. Do not get the idea that the sequence of articles necessarily shows development from wrong to right or even from worst to best. In fact, the relativistic views of Kuhn and the anarchic version of Feyerabend, though once very popular and still central to what some term postmodernist philosophy, are now being severely questioned. Many of the philosophers coming down on the side of realism in the realism/antirealism debate (discussed in Chapter 4) find realism attractive because it brings with it an objectivity that is an antidote to the relativism of Kuhn and Feyerabend (and the postmodernists). In fact, Kuhn is presently working on a less relativistic version of his own views.

RUDOLF CARNAP, "TESTABILITY AND MEANING"

Carnap distinguishes between verification and confirmation. Verification establishes, once and for all, the truth of claims. Confirmation is the testing of claims to see how true they are, how close they come to being true. For a claim to be testable, we must know how to test it, and for a claim to be confirmable, we must know when the claim would be confirmed. Therefore, a claim's confirmation is always relative to the tests made. Test results must always be observable. Strictly speaking, no factual claim is ever verified because there might always appear some evidence to show that it is false. Carnap therefore focuses on confirmation.

Carnap's basic picture of confirmation can be seen from the example he uses. To verify the claim that there is a white piece of paper on my desk, we examine sentences we infer from the one in question. From "This is a piece of paper," we infer that if we do certain tests on the material, we will get certain results indicative of paper and not nylon or polished oak. These sentences that we infer are predictions.

A scientific law, such as "All acids turn blue litmus red," is also confirmed by making predictions. From this law, we would predict that if a liquid in question is an acid, then when we dip blue litmus into it, the litmus will turn red.

(There is a logical problem here. Let "All acids turn blue litmus red" be represented by "If any liquid is an acid, then it will turn blue litmus red" and this as "If L, then R." Then we are arguing as follows: From "If this liquid is an acid, then this liquid will turn blue litmus red" and "This liquid turned blue litmus red" to "This liquid is an acid." It seems to make sense. But the form of this argument is not valid. Its form is

If L, then R.

R.

Therefore, L.

To see that the argument is not valid, substitute as follows: L = "That animal is a horse"; R = "That animal is a mammal." Then we get

If that animal is a horse, then that animal is a mammal.

That animal is a mammal.

But "That animal is a horse" certainly does not follow from "That animal is a mammal" and "If that animal is a horse, then that animal is a mammal."

After all, there are many mammals other than horses.

This form of confirmation therefore commits a logical fallacy known as affirming the consequent. The lesson to be drawn may be that this is not how confirmation works or that simple logic cannot be used to capture the way confirmation works.)

Carnap (like Hempel-Oppenheim) realizes that he must explain what it is to be observable; otherwise, his attempt to clarify confirmation in terms of testing will not make sense. A property is observable if a normal observer, in usual circumstances, feels satisfied that he or she can determine the presence or absence of the property quickly, at a glance. The standard example is something like this: I can tell at a glance whether your shirt is red or green quickly and to my satisfaction. Determining whether it is midnight blue or black would take me some time. I might want to check on the lighting. I might want to look at a color wheel to refresh my memory of these shades.

Confirmation requires that tests be set up such that the results are observationally interpretable at a glance. Carnap puts a rider on this claim, requiring only that there be possible observations that would confirm a claim if we could make the appropriate test. This is a way of saying that confirmability can be based on counterfactual claims. Recall that Hempel and Oppenheim (Chapter 2) gave a counterfactual twist to the interpretation of scientific law. Carnap is doing the same for confirmation. A claim such as "The last surviving giant redwood will be cut down on a Tuesday" is confirmable by possible observations. If we were there to observe we would see the tree being cut and know the day of the week. Carnap is concerned that if confirmability is limited to actual observation, much of theoretical science will fail to be confirmable.

Carnap raises four issues in the philosophy of science that we will not pursue in detail. They are, however, important.

1. To Carnap, testability and meaning are almost identical. He says, "The meaning of a sentence is in a certain sense identical with the way we determine its truth or falsehood [and we do this through testing]." Confirmation through testing, which is the heart of science according to Carnap, is the key to understanding literal meaning. Put another way, if one began by looking for a theory of literal meaning, one would be led to confirmation and testability. As we will see, Popper will make clear that this is not how his interest in the philosophy of science was piqued.

2. Is there a clear distinction between observable and theoretical properties? Carnap answers that there is only a gradation between the two. Seeing a red shirt is seeing a clearly observable physical thing, according to Carnap; seeing a cold front moving in is not. For seeing a cold front is really seeing clouds move, feeling wind, noting that it is getting colder, and making an inference from these observations. "Cold front" is referred to as a theoretical term because the inference we make is based on some theory. To say, as some philosophers do, that all observation is theory-laden is to say that all observation requires some background knowledge. To see scientific things such as electrons, viruses, and cold fronts requires that the background knowledge be a scientific theory. Some philosophers think that only some observation is theory-laden. Those who hold that only some observations are theory-laden believe that there are what might be termed "brute facts." Holding that there are these brute facts is a way out of the following regress. Knowledge requires observation. Observation requires background knowledge. The background knowledge itself must be based on observation, which is based on background knowledge, based on observation, based on background knowledge, and so on, *ad infinitum.*

3. Carnap points out that whether or not we accept a claim as true is more than just a function of the tests that have been done. Some claims are so important that we will require many tests before we feel comfortable in accepting or rejecting the claims. Western-trained physicians were much slower to accept the claims of acupuncture than they were claims about the dangers of cigarette smoking. Carnap refers to this difference as practical or conventional. He is quick to point out that this does not mean that testing is conventional. Is this just the two-contexts distinction in another form? Richard Rudner (a portion of whose 1950 article on science and values will be quoted in the introduction to Helen Longino's article in Chapter 7) believed that the distinction as made by Carnap will not hold up to scrutiny. In effect, this means that the literal doing of science and practical values cannot be separated. As Rudner puts it, the scientist, as scientist, makes value judgments.

4. Carnap talks about reducibility of the terms of scientific language to the terms of the physical language. By this he means that it must be possible to know how to translate via testability (given the appropriate theory) whatever can meaningfully be asserted in the sciences to claims about what can easily be observed. For example, to say in genetics that the gene for tallness in pea plants is dominant to its allele for shortness becomes via testability (and the theory of genetics) "If you cross tall peas and short peas, you will get either all tall peas or an equal ratio of tall to short peas in the next generation." That these ratios are present is easily observed, although one does have to count. There are other meanings for the term *reduction*, as we have already seen.

Testability and Meaning

RUDOLF CARNAP

I. INTRODUCTION

1. Our Problem: Confirmation, Testing and Meaning

Two chief problems of the theory of knowledge are the question of meaning and the question of verification. The first question asks under what conditions a sentence has meaning, in the sense of cognitive, factual meaning. The second one asks how we get to know something, how we can find out whether a given sentence is true or false. The second question presupposes the first one. Obviously we must understand a sentence, i.e. we must know its meaning, before we can try to find out whether it is true or not. But, from the point of view of empiricism, there is a still closer connection between the two problems. In a certain sense, there is only one answer to the two questions. If we knew what it would be for a given sentence to be found true then we

From R. Carnap, "Testability and Meaning," *Philosophy of Science* 3: 419–471. Courtesy of Williams & Wilkins.

would know what its meaning is. And if for two sentences the conditions under which we would have to take them as true are the same, then they have the same meaning. Thus the meaning of a sentence is in a certain sense identical with the way we determine its truth or falsehood; and a sentence has meaning only if such a determination is possible.

If by verification is meant a definitive and final establishment of truth, then no (synthetic) sentence is ever verifiable, as we shall see. We can only confirm a sentence more and more. Therefore we shall speak of the problem of *confirmation* rather than of the problem of verification. We distinguish the *testing* of a sentence from its confirmation, thereby understanding a procedure—e.g. the carrying out of certain experiments—which leads to a confirmation in some degree either of the sentence itself or of its negation. We shall call a sentence *testable* if we know such a method of testing for it; and we call it *confirmable* if we know under what conditions the sentence would be confirmed. As we shall see, a sentence may be confirmable without being testable; e.g. if we know that our observation of such and such a course of events would confirm the sentence, and such and such a different course would confirm its negation without knowing how to set up either this or that observation.

2. Confirmation Instead of Verification

If verification is understood as a complete and definitive establishment of truth then a universal sentence, e.g. a so-called law of physics or biology, can never be verified, a fact which has often been remarked. Even if each single instance of the law were supposed to be verifiable, the number of instances to which the law refers—e.g. the space-time-points—is infinite and therefore can never be exhausted by our observations

which are always finite in number. We cannot verify the law, but we can test it by testing its single instances i.e. the particular sentences which we derive from the law and from other sentences established previously. If in the continued series of such testing experiments no negative instance is found but the number of positive instances increases then our confidence in the law will grow step by step. Thus, instead of verification, we may speak here of gradually increasing *confirmation* of the law.

Now a little reflection will lead us to the result that there is no fundamental difference between a universal sentence and a particular sentence with regard to verifiability but only a difference in degree. Take for instance the following sentence: "There is a white sheet of paper on this table." In order to ascertain whether this thing is paper, we may make a set of simple observations and then, if there still remains some doubt, we may make some physical and chemical experiments. Here as well as in the case of the law, we try to examine sentences which we infer from the sentence in question. These inferred sentences are predictions about future observations. The number of such predictions which we can derive from the sentence given is infinite; and therefore the sentence can never be completely verified. To be sure, in many cases we reach a practically sufficient certainty after a small number of positive instances, and then we stop experimenting. But there is always the theoretical possibility of continuing the series of test-observations. Therefore here also *no complete verification is possible* but only a process of gradually increasing *confirmation*. We may, if we wish, call a sentence disconfirmed[1] in a certain degree if its negation is confirmed in that degree.

The impossibility of absolute verification has been pointed out and explained in detail by *Popper*.[2] In this point our present views are, it seems to me, in full accordance with *Lewis*[3] and *Nagel*.[4]

Suppose a sentence S is given, some test-observations for it have been made, and S is confirmed by them in a certain degree. Then it is a matter of practical decision whether we will consider that degree as high enough for our acceptance of S, or as low enough for our rejection of S, or as intermediate between these so that we neither accept nor reject S until further evidence will be available. Although our decision is based upon the observations made so far, nevertheless it is not uniquely determined by them. There is no general rule to determine our decision. Thus the acceptance and the rejection of a (synthetic) sentence always contains a *conventional component*. That does not mean that the decision—or, in other words, the question of truth and verification—is conventional. For, in addition to the conventional component there is always the non-conventional component—we may call it, the objective one—consisting in the observations which have been made. And it must certainly be admitted that in very many cases this objective component is present to such an overwhelming extent that the conventional component practically vanishes. For such a simple sentence as e.g. "There is a white thing on this table" the degree of confirmation, after a few observations have been made, will be so high that we practically cannot help accepting the sentence. But even in this case there remains still the theoretical possibility of denying the sentence. Thus even here it is a matter of decision or convention. . . .

EMPIRICAL ANALYSIS OF CONFIRMATION AND TESTING

Observable and Realizable Predicates

. . . In what follows we shall deal with *empirical methodology*. Here also we are concerned with the questions of confirming and testing sentences and predicates. These considerations belong to a theory of language just as the logical ones do. But while the logical analysis belongs to an analytic theory of the formal, syntactical structure of language, here we will carry out an empirical analysis of the application of language. Our considerations belong, strictly speaking, to a biological or psychological theory of language as a kind of human behavior, and especially as a kind of reaction to observations. We shall see, however, that for our purposes we need not go into details of biological or psychological investigations. In order to make clear what is understood by empirically testing and confirming a sentence and thereby to find out what is to be required for a sentence or a predicate in a language having empirical meaning, we can restrict ourselves to using very few concepts of the field mentioned. We shall take two descriptive, i.e. non-logical, terms of this field as *basic terms* for our following considerations, namely *"observable"* and *"realizable."* All other terms, and above all the terms "confirmable" and "testable," which are the chief terms of our theory, will be defined on the basis of the two basic terms mentioned; in the definitions we shall make use of the logical terms defined in the foregoing chapter. The two basic terms are of course, as basic ones, not defined within our theory. Definitions for them would have to be given within psychology, and more precisely, within the behavioristic theory of language. We do not attempt such definitions, but we shall give at least some rough explanations for the terms, which will make their meaning clear enough for our purposes.

Explanation 1. A predicate "P" of a language L is called *observable* for an organism (e.g. a person) N, if, for suitable arguments, e.g. "b," N is able under suitable circumstances to come to a decision with the help of few observations about a full sentence, say "P(b)," i.e. to a confirmation of either "P(b)" or "~ P(b)" of such a high degree that he will either accept or reject "P(b)."

This explanation is necessarily vague. There is no sharp line between observable and non-observable predicates because a person will be more or less able to decide a certain sentence quickly, i.e. he will be inclined after a certain period of observation to accept the sentence. For the sake of simplicity we will here draw a sharp distinction between observable and non-observable predicates. By thus drawing an arbitrary line between observable and non-observable predicates in a field of continuous degrees of observability we partly determine in advance the possible answers to questions such as whether or not a certain predicate is observable by a given person. Nevertheless the general philosophical, i.e. methodological question about the nature of meaning and testability will, as we shall see, not be distorted by our over-simplification. Even particular questions as to whether or not a given sentence is confirmable, and whether or not it is testable by a certain person, are affected, as we shall see, at most to a very small degree by the choice of the boundary line for observable predicates.

According to the explanation given, for example the predicate "red" is observable for a person N possessing a normal colour sense. For a suitable argument, namely a space-time-point c sufficiently near to N, say a spot on the table before N, N is able under suitable circumstances—namely, if there is sufficient light at c—to come to a decision about the full sentence "the spot c is red" after few observations—namely by looking at the table. On the other hand, the predicate "red" is not observable by a colour-blind person. And the predicate "an electric field of such and such an amount" is not observable to anybody, because, although we know how to test a full sen-

tence of this predicate, we cannot do it directly, i.e. by a few observations; we have to apply certain instruments and hence to make a great many preliminary observations in order to find out whether the things before us are instruments of the kind required.

Explanation 2. A predicate "P" of a language L is called *"realizable"* by N, if for a suitable argument, e.g. "b," N is able under suitable circumstances to make the full sentence "P(b)" true, i.e. to produce the property P at the point b.

When we use the terms "observable," "realizable," "confirmable," etc. without explicit reference to anybody, it is to be understood that they are meant with respect to the people who use the language L to which the predicate in question belongs.

Examples. Let "$P_1(b)$" mean: "the space-time-point b has the temperature 100°C." "P_1" is realizable by us because we know how to produce that temperature at the point b, if b is accessible to us.—"$P_2(b)$" may mean: "there is iron at the point b." "P_2" is realizable because we are able to carry a piece of iron to the point b if b is accessible.—If "$P_3(b)$" means: "at the point b is a substance whose index of light refraction is 10," "P_3" is not realizable by anybody at the present time, because nobody knows at present how to produce such a substance. . . .

Confirmability

. . . If confirmation is to be feasible at all, this process of referring back to other predicates must terminate at some point. The reduction must finally come to predicates for which we can come to a confirmation directly, i.e. without reference to other predicates. According to Explanation 1, the observable predicates can be used as such a basis. This consideration leads us to the following definition of the concept "confirmable." . . . A *sentence* S is called *confirmable* (or completely confirmable, or incompletely confirmable) if the confirmation of S is reducible (or completely reducible, or incompletely reducible, respectively) to that of a class of observable predicates. . . .

When we call a sentence S confirmable, we do not mean that it is possible to arrive at a confirmation of S under the circumstances as they actually exist. We rather intend this possibility under some *possible circumstances,* whether they be real or not. Thus e.g. because my pencil is black and I am able to make out by visual observation that it is black and not red, I cannot come to a positive confirmation of the sentence "My pencil is red." Nevertheless we call this sentence confirmable and moreover completely confirmable for the reason that we are able to indicate the—actually non-existent, but possible—observations which would confirm that sentence. Whether the real circumstances are such that the testing of a certain sentence S leads to a positive result, i.e. to a confirmation of S, or such that it leads to a negative result . . . is irrelevant for the questions of confirmability, testability and meaning of the sentence. . . .

NOTES

1. O. Neurath, "Pseudorationalismus der Falsifikation," *Erkenntniss* 5 (1935).
2. K. Popper, "Empirische Methode," in *Congress Logik der Forschung,* Vienna, 1935.
3. C. I. Lewis, with C. H. Langford, *Symbolic Logic,* New York, 1932; "Experience and Meaning," *Philos. Review* 43 (1934); *An Analysis of Knowledge and Valuation,* La Salle, IL, 1946; "Prof. Chisholm and Empiricism," *Journal of Philosophy* 45 (1948).
4. E. Nagel, "Verifiability, Truth, and Verification," *Journal of Philosophy* 31 (1934); "Impressions and Appraisals of Analytic Philosophy in Europe," *Journal of Philosophy* 33 (1936).

KARL POPPER, "SCIENCE: CONJECTURES AND REFUTATIONS"

Popper tells us that he found himself comparing Marxism and psychological theories to physics. Physics, he felt, was clearly a science. What about Marxism and Freudian psychoanalysis? Is there a clear line of demarcation between what is science and what is not science? Popper decided that there was such a line and that it was falsifiability. Popper makes his case using examples from Freud and Adler, comparing their theories to Einstein's theory of relativity. Popper began his inquiry looking for the line of demarcation and not for a theory of meaning.

In brief, Popper found that Sigmund Freud (1856–1939) and Alfred Adler (1870–1937) differed on what they took to be basic for explaining human behavior. Where Freud might see an unresolved Oedipus complex, Adler would see an inferiority complex. Popper also found that nothing seemed to count as clear evidence that one was right and the other wrong. While both theories had no trouble pointing to confirming instances, neither theory made it clear how to construct a test that would show it to be wrong. Popper says that any piece of human behavior could be interpreted in a Freudian manner or in an Adlerian manner. No clear bit of evidence could ever say which was right and which was wrong.

This was not so with Albert Einstein (1879–1955). His theory made a risky prediction in the sense that it could be tested and the results would make clear whether it tested out for Einstein or against him. This sort of test Popper would call "severe."

Popper saw this making of risky predictions as the mark of science. Prior to Popper, the emphasis had been on confirmation through positive instances, where an explanation was confirmed to the extent that its predictions were borne out. What Popper realized is that confirmation in this sense is easy—much too easy. Stressing this version of confirmation leads to the situation where there is no way to distinguish the goodness of one theory (Freud's) from another (Adler's). Hence Popper suggests a shift—ask how easy an explanation makes it for itself to be wrong. For Popper, the better of two competing explanations is the one that makes it clear how to falsify it and manages to survive the attempts at falsification. Where there is no competitor, Popper would advise constructing an explanation that is easily falsifiable.

Popper is not saying that the best explanations are the ones that are wrong. He is saying that to be good science, an explanation must make plain how it might (in the counterfactual sense) be wrong and therefore rejected. Notice how this compares to Carnap. Carnap had basically attempted to define confirmation and meaningfulness in terms of tests. Popper is trying to characterize the line of demarcation between science and pseudoscience. Popper suggested that we use the word *confirmation* to refer to positions other than his and use *corroboration* for his view, which makes the acceptability of a scientific claim a function of its falsifiability.

Here is another example of what Popper had in mind. Astrology is a theory that explains human behavior on the basis of the position of the heavenly bodies at the time of one's birth. How good is the theory? Popper would say that astrology is as good as the predictions it makes. If a prediction is not borne out, astrologers can always say that they needed a more precise time of birth. This reply is built into the theory. It makes the theory unfalsifiable. We cannot even imagine a test because one can always ask for a more precise time on the grounds that instants in time are infinitesimally small. If the reply "I need a more precise time of birth" were not part of the theory, it would have been added to save the theory. When such assumptions, in this case concerning what is meant by "time of birth," are added to protect a theory, Popper refers to them as *ad hoc*, Latin for "to this [end]." That is, the assumption is added only because it helps the proponents of the theory get over this particular problem. The hypothesis is added for no other reason; it does no work other than to save the theory. Lakatos will suggest that it is difficult to decide just what is *ad hoc* and what is acceptable.

Here is an astrological prediction (horoscope):

> You could be seeking attention in all the wrong places. Stay closer to home. Romance is unpredictable; focus on building trust.

How could one take issue with this bit of advice, which is really the prediction that if you are a Scorpio, this advice will fit you today? What counts as "seeking attention," "closer to home," "romance," "trust"? Moreover, "could be" makes the claim so weak that anything done (writing this chapter, walking my dog) could count as "seeking attention." Could home be my birthplace or my present house or my office, which I call my home away from home? Could romance refer to a sexual relationship, a platonic relationship, or just a deep and caring feeling toward the book that I am writing? What counts as building trust? Is letting someone share your table at a cafeteria building trust? Does building trust require that I do something like lend money to a stranger?

Popper concluded from this sort of criticism that astrology is not a science. He referred to disciplines such as astrology as pseudosciences. They had the look of science about them, but on close examination, they fail to be falsifiable. Popper included under pseudoscience Freudian psychology, alchemy, Marxist interpretations of history, and, at one time, the neo-Darwinian theory of evolution.

Science: Conjectures and Refutations

KARL POPPER

Mr. Turnbull had predicted evil consequences, . . . and was now doing the best in his power to bring about the verification of his own prophecies. —Anthony Trollope

I

When I received the list of participants in this course and realized that I had been asked to speak to philosophical colleagues I thought, after some hesitation and consultation, that you would probably prefer me to speak about those problems which interest me most, and about those developments with which I am most intimately acquainted.[1] I therefore decided to do what I have never done before: to give you a report on my own work in the philosophy of science, since the autumn of 1919 when I first began to grapple with the problem, *"When should a theory be ranked as scientific?"* or *"Is there a criterion for the scientific character or status of a theory?"*

From Karl Popper, *Conjectures and Refutations* (New York: Basic Books, 1962), pp. 33–41, 52–59. Copyright © 1962 by Karl R. Popper.

The problem which troubled me at the time was neither, "When is a theory true?" nor, "When is a theory acceptable?" My problem was different. I *wished to distinguish between science and pseudo-science;* knowing very well that science often errs, and that pseudo-science may happen to stumble on the truth.

I knew, of course, the most widely accepted answer to my problem: that science is distinguished from pseudo-science—or from "metaphysics"—by its *empirical method*, which is essentially *inductive*, proceeding from observation or experiment. But this did not satisfy me. On the contrary, I often formulated my problem as one of distinguishing between a genuinely empirical method and a non-empirical or even a pseudo-empirical method—that is to say, a method which, although it appeals to observation and experiment, nevertheless does not come up to scientific standards. The latter method may be exemplified by astrology, with its stupendous mass of empirical evidence based on observation—on horoscopes and on biographies.

But as it was not the example of astrology which led me to my problem I should perhaps briefly describe the atmosphere in which my problem arose and the examples by which it was stimulated. After the collapse of the Austrian Empire there had been a revolution in Austria: the air was full of revolutionary slogans and ideas, and new and often wild theories. Among the theories which interested me Einstein's theory of relativity was no doubt by far the most important. Three others were Marx's theory of history, Freud's psycho-analysis, and Alfred Adler's so-called "individual psychology."

There was a lot of popular nonsense talked about these theories, and especially about relativity (as still happens even today), but I was fortunate in those who introduced me to the study of this theory. We all—the small circle of students to which I belonged—were thrilled with the result of Eddington's eclipse observations which in 1919 brought the first important confirmation of Einstein's theory of gravitation. It was a great experience for us, and one which had a lasting influence on my intellectual development.

The three other theories I have mentioned were also widely discussed among students at that time. I myself happened to come into personal contact with Alfred Adler, and even to co-operate with him in his social work among the children and young people in the working-class districts of Vienna where he had established social guidance clinics.

It was during the summer of 1919 that I began to feel more and more dissatisfied with these three theories—the Marxist theory of history, psycho-analysis, and individual psychology; and I began to feel dubious about their claims to scientific status. My problem perhaps first took the simple form, "What is wrong with Marxism, psycho-analysis, and individual psychology? Why are they so different from physical theories, from Newton's theory, and especially from the theory of relativity?"

To make this contrast clear I should explain that few of us at the time would have said that we believed in the *truth* of Einstein's theory of gravitation. This shows that it was not my doubting the *truth* of those other three theories which bothered me, but something else. Yet neither was it that I merely felt mathematical physics to be more *exact* than the sociological or psychological type of theory. Thus what worried me was neither the problem of truth, at that stage at least, nor the problem of exactness or measurability. It was rather that I felt that these other three theories, though posing as sciences, had in fact more in common with primitive myths than with science; that they resembled astrology rather than astronomy.

I found that those of my friends who were admirers of Marx, Freud, and Adler, were impressed by a number of points common to these theories, and especially by their apparent *explanatory power*. These theories appeared to be able to explain practically everything that happened within the fields to which they referred. The study of any of them seemed to have the effect of an intellectual conversion or revelation, opening your eyes to a new truth hidden from those not yet initiated. Once your eyes were thus opened you saw confirming instances everywhere: the world was full of *verifications* of the theory. Whatever happened always confirmed it. Thus its truth appeared manifest; and unbelievers were clearly people who did not want to see the manifest truth; who refused to see it, either because it was against their class interest, or because of their repressions which were still "un-analysed" and crying aloud for treatment.

The most characteristic element in this situation seemed to me the incessant stream of confirmations, of observations which "verified" the theories in question; and this point was constantly emphasized by their adherents. A Marxist could not open a newspaper without finding on every page confirming evidence for his interpretation of history; not only in the news, but also in its presentation—which revealed the class bias of the paper—and especially of course in what the paper did *not* say. The Freudian analysts emphasized that their theories were constantly verified by their "clinical observations." As for Adler, I was much impressed by a personal experience. Once, in 1919, I reported to him a case which to me did not seem particularly Adlerian, but which he found no difficulty in analysing in terms of his theory of inferiority feelings, although he had not even seen the child. Slightly shocked, I asked him how he could be so sure. "Because of my thousandfold experience," he replied; whereupon I could not help saying: "And with this new case, I suppose, your experience has become thousand-and-one-fold."

What I had in mind was that his previous observations may not have been much sounder than this new one; that each in its turn had been interpreted in the light of "previous experience," and at the same time counted as additional confirmation. What, I asked myself, did it confirm? No more than that a case could be interpreted in the light of the theory. But this meant very little, I reflected, since every conceivable case could be interpreted in the light of Adler's theory, or equally of Freud's. I may illustrate this by two very different examples of human behaviour: that of a man who pushes a child into the water with the intention of drowning it; and that of a man who sacrifices his life in an attempt to save the child. Each of these two cases can be explained with equal ease in Freudian and in Adlerian terms. According to Freud the first man suffered from repression (say, of some component of his Oedipus complex), while the second man had achieved sublimation. According to Adler the first man suffered from feelings of inferiority (producing perhaps the need to prove to himself that he dared to commit some crime), and so did the second man (whose need was to prove to himself that he dared to rescue the child). I could not think of any human behaviour which could not be interpreted in terms of either theory. It was precisely this fact—that they always fitted, that they were always confirmed—which in the eyes of their admirers constituted the strongest argument in favour of these theories. It began to dawn on me that this apparent strength was in fact their weakness.

With Einstein's theory the situation was strikingly different. Take one typical instance—Einstein's prediction, just then confirmed by the findings of Eddington's expedition. Einstein's gravitational theory had led to the result that light must be attracted by heavy bodies (such as the sun), precisely as material bodies were attracted. As a consequence it could be calculated that light from a distant fixed star whose apparent position was close to the sun would reach the earth from such a direction that the star would seem to be slightly shifted away from the sun; or, in other words, that stars close to the sun would look as if they had moved a little away from the sun, and from one another. This is a thing which cannot normally be observed since such stars are rendered invisible in daytime by the sun's overwhelming brightness; but during an eclipse it is possible to take photographs of them. If the same constellation is photographed at night one can measure the distances on the two photographs, and check the predicted effect.

Now the impressive thing about this case is the *risk* involved in a prediction of this kind. If observation shows that the predicted effect is definitely absent, then the theory is simply refuted. The theory is *incompatible with certain possible results of observation*—in fact with results which everybody before Einstein would have expected.[2] This is quite different from the situation I have previously described, when it turned out that the theories in question were compatible with the most divergent human behaviour, so that it was practically impossible to describe any human behaviour that might not be claimed to be a verification of these theories.

These considerations led me in the winter of 1919–20 to conclusions which I may now reformulate as follows.

1. It is easy to obtain confirmations, or verifications, for nearly every theory—if we look for confirmations.
2. Confirmations should count only if they are the result of *risky predictions;* that is to say, if, unenlightened by the theory in question, we should have expected an event which was incompatible with the theory—an event which would have refuted the theory.
3. Every "good" scientific theory is a prohibition: it forbids certain things to happen. The more a theory forbids, the better it is.
4. A theory which is not refutable by any conceivable event is non-scientific. Irrefutability is not a virtue of a theory (as people often think) but a vice.
5. Every genuine *test* of a theory is an attempt to falsify it, or to refute it. Testability is falsifiability; but there are degrees of testability: some theories are more testable, more exposed to refutation, than others; they take, as it were, greater risks.
6. Confirming evidence should not count *except when it is the result of a genuine test*

of the theory; and this means that it can be presented as a serious but unsuccessful attempt to falsify the theory. (I now speak in such cases of "corroborating evidence.")
7. Some genuinely testable theories, when found to be false, are still upheld by their admirers—for example by introducing *ad hoc* some auxiliary assumption, or by re-interpreting the theory *ad hoc* in such a way that it escapes refutation. Such a procedure is always possible, but it rescues the theory from refutation only at the price of destroying, or at least lowering, its scientific status. (I later described such a rescuing operation as a *"conventionalist twist"* or a *"conventionalist stratagem."*)

One can sum up all this by saying that *the criterion of the scientific status of a theory is its falsifiability, or refutability, or testability.*

II

I may perhaps exemplify this with the help of the various theories so far mentioned. Einstein's theory of gravitation clearly satisfied the criterion of falsifiability. Even if our measuring instruments at the time did not allow us to pronounce on the results of the tests with complete assurance, there was clearly a possibility of refuting the theory.

Astrology did not pass the test. Astrologers were greatly impressed, and misled, by what they believed to be confirming evidence—so much so that they were quite unimpressed by any unfavourable evidence. Moreover, by making their interpretations and prophecies sufficiently vague they were able to explain away anything that might have been a refutation of the theory had the theory and the prophecies been more precise. In order to escape falsification they destroyed the testability of their theory. It is a typical soothsayer's trick to predict things so vaguely that the predictions can hardly fail: that they become irrefutable.

The Marxist theory of history, in spite of the serious efforts of some of its founders and followers, ultimately adopted this soothsaying practice. In some of its earlier formulations (for example in Marx's analysis of the character of the "coming social revolution") their predictions were testable, and in fact falsified.[3] Yet instead of accepting the refutations the followers of Marx reinterpreted both the theory and the evidence in order to make them agree. In this way they rescued the theory from refutation; but they did so at the price of adopting a device which made it irrefutable. They thus gave a "conventionalist twist" to the theory; and by this stratagem they destroyed its much advertised claim to scientific status.

The two psycho-analytic theories were in a different class. They were simply non-testable, irrefutable. There was no conceivable human behaviour which could contradict them. This does not mean that Freud and Adler were not seeing certain things correctly: I personally do not doubt that much of what they say is of considerable importance, and may well play its part one day in a psychological science which is testable. But it does mean that those "clinical observations" which analysts naïvely believe confirm their theory cannot do this any more than the daily confirmations which astrologers find in their practice.[4] And as for Freud's epic of the Ego, the Super-ego, and the Id, no substantially stronger claim to scientific status can be made for it than for Homer's collected stories from Olympus. These theories describe some facts, but in the manner of myths. They contain most interesting psychological suggestions, but not in a testable form.

At the same time I realized that such myths may be developed, and become testable; that historically speaking all—or very nearly all—scientific theories originate from myths, and that a myth may contain important anticipations of scientific theories. Examples are Empedocles' theory of evolution by trial and error, or Parmenides' myth of the unchanging block universe in which nothing ever happens and which, if we add another dimension, becomes Einstein's block universe (in which, too, nothing ever happens, since everything is, four-dimensionally speaking, determined and laid down from the beginning). I thus felt that if a theory is found to be non-scientific, or "metaphysical" (as we might say), it is not thereby found to be unimportant, or insignificant, or "meaningless," or "nonsensical."[5] But it cannot claim to be backed by empirical evidence in the scientific sense—although it may easily be, in some genetic sense, the "result of observation."

(There were a great many other theories of this pre-scientific or pseudo-scientific character, some of them, unfortunately, as influential as the Marxist interpretation of history; for example, the racialist interpretation of history—another of those impressive and all-explanatory theories which act upon weak minds like revelations.)

Thus the problem which I tried to solve by proposing the criterion of falsifiability was neither a problem of meaningfulness or significance, nor a problem of truth or acceptability. It was the problem of drawing a line (as well as this can be done) between the statements, or systems of statements, of the empirical sciences, and all other statements—whether they are of a religious or of a metaphysical character, or simply pseudo-scientific. Years later—it must have been in 1928 or 1929—I called this first problem of mine the *problem of demarcation.* The criterion of falsifiability is a solution to this problem of demarcation, for it says that statements or systems of statements, in order to be ranked as scientific, must be capable of conflicting with possible, or conceivable, observations. . . .

V

The belief that science proceeds from observation to theory is still so widely and so firmly held that my denial of it is often met with incredulity. I have even been suspected of being insincere—of denying what nobody in his senses can doubt.

But in fact the belief that we can start with pure observations alone, without anything in the nature of a theory, is absurd; as may be illustrated by the story of the man who dedicated his life to natural science, wrote down everything he could observe, and bequeathed his priceless collection of observations to the Royal Society to be used as inductive evidence. This story should show us that though beetles may profitably be collected, observations may not.

Twenty-five years ago I tried to bring home the same point to a group of physics students in Vienna by beginning a lecture with the following instructions: "Take pencil and paper; carefully observe, and write down what you have observed!" They asked, of course, *what* I wanted them to observe. Clearly the instruction, "Observe!" is absurd.[6] (It is not even idiomatic, unless the object of the transitive verb can be taken as understood.) Observation is always selective. It needs a chosen object, a definite task, an interest, a point of view, a problem. And its description presupposes a descriptive language, with property words; it presupposes similarity and classification, which in its turn presupposes interests, points of view, and problems. "A hungry animal," writes Katz, "divides the environment into edible and inedible things. An animal in flight sees roads to escape and hiding places. . . . Generally speaking, objects change . . . according to the needs of the ani-

mal."[7] We may add that objects can be classified, and can become similar or dissimilar, *only* in this way—by being related to needs and interests. This rule applies not only to animals but also to scientists. For the animal a point of view is provided by its needs, the task of the moment, and its expectations; for the scientist by his theoretical interests, the special problem under investigation, his conjectures and anticipations, and the theories which he accepts as a kind of background: his frame of reference, his "horizon of expectations."

The problem "Which comes first, the hypothesis *(H)* or the observation *(O)*," is soluble; as is the problem, "Which comes first, the hen *(H)* or the egg *(O)*." The reply to the latter is, "An earlier kind of egg"; to the former, "An earlier kind of hypothesis." It is quite true that any particular hypothesis we choose will have been preceded by observations—the observations, for example, which it is designed to explain. But these observations, in their turn, presupposed the adoption of a frame of reference: a frame of expectations: a frame of theories. If they were significant, if they created a need for explanation and thus gave rise to the invention of a hypothesis, it was because they could not be explained within the old theoretical framework, the old horizon of expectations. There is no danger here of an infinite regress. Going back to more and more primitive theories and myths we shall in the end find unconscious, *inborn* expectations.

The theory of inborn *ideas* is absurd, I think; but every organism has inborn *reactions* or *responses*; and among them, responses adapted to impending events. These responses we may describe as "expectations" without implying that these "expectations" are conscious. The new-born baby "expects," in this sense, to be fed (and, one could even argue, to be protected and loved). In view of the close relation between expectation and knowledge we may even speak in quite a reasonable sense of "inborn knowledge." This "knowledge" is not, however, *valid a priori*; an inborn expectation, no matter how strong and specific, may be mistaken. (The newborn child may be abandoned, and starve.)

Thus we are born with expectations; with "knowledge" which, although not *valid a priori*, is *psychologically or genetically a priori*, i.e. prior to all observational experience. One of the most important of these expectations is the expectation of finding a regularity. It is connected with an inborn propensity to look out for regularities, or with a *need* to *find* regularities, as we may see from the pleasure of the child who satisfies this need.

This "instinctive" expectation of finding regularities, which is psychologically *a priori*, corresponds very closely to the "law of causality" which Kant believed to be part of our mental outfit and to be *a priori* valid. One might thus be inclined to say that Kant failed to distinguish between psychologically *a priori* ways of thinking or responding and *a priori* valid beliefs. But I do not think that his mistake was quite as crude as that. For the expectation of finding regularities is not only psychologically *a priori*, but also logically *a priori*: it is logically prior to all observational experience, for it is prior to any recognition of similarities, as we have seen; and all observation involves the recognition of similarities (or dissimilarities). But in spite of being logically *a priori* in this sense the expectation is not valid *a priori*. For it may fail: we can easily construct an environment (it would be a lethal one) which, compared with our ordinary environment, is so chaotic that we completely fail to find regularities. . . .

To sum up . . . we may consider the idea of building an induction machine. Placed in a simplified "world" (for example, one of sequences of coloured counters) such a

machine may through repetition "learn," or even "formulate," laws of succession which hold in its "world." If such a machine can be constructed (and I have no doubt that it can) then, it might be argued, my theory must be wrong; for if a machine is capable of performing inductions on the basis of repetition, there can be no logical reasons preventing us from doing the same.

The argument sounds convincing, but it is mistaken. In constructing an induction machine we, the architects of the machine, must decide *a priori* what constitutes its "world"; what things are to be taken as similar or equal; and what *kind* of "laws" we wish the machine to be able to "discover" in its "world." In other words we must build into the machine a framework determining what is relevant or interesting in its world: the machine will have its "inborn" selection principles. The problems of similarity will have been solved for it by its makers who thus have interpreted the "world" for the machine.

NOTES

1. This was originally a lecture given at Peterhouse, Cambridge, in the summer of 1953 as part of a course on developments and trends in contemporary British philosophy organized by the British Council; it was first published under the title "Philosophy of Science: A Personal Report" in *British Philosophy in Mid-Century*, ed. C. A. Mace, 1957.
2. This is a slight oversimplification, for about half of the Einstein effect may be derived from the classical theory, provided we assume a ballistic theory of light.
3. See, for example, my *Open Society and Its Enemies*, chap. 15, sec. iii, and notes 6 and 7.
4. "Clinical observations," like all other observations, are *interpretations in the light of theories;* and for this reason alone they are apt to seem to support those theories in the light of which they were interpreted. But real support can be obtained only from observations undertaken as tests (by "attempted refutations"); and for this purpose *criteria of refutation* have to be laid down beforehand: it must be agreed which observable situations, if actually

observed, mean that the theory is refuted. But what kind of clinical responses would refute to the satisfaction of the analyst not merely a particular analytic diagnosis but psycho-analysis itself? And have such criteria ever been discussed or agreed upon by analysts? Is there not, on the contrary, a whole family of analytic concepts, such as "ambivalence" (I do not suggest that there is no such thing as ambivalence), which would make it difficult, if not impossible, to agree upon such criteria? Moreover, how much headway has been made in investigating the question of the extent to which the (conscious or unconscious) expectations and theories held by the analyst influence the "clinical responses" of the patient? (To say nothing about the conscious attempts to influence the patient by proposing interpretations to him, etc.) Years ago I introduced the term *Oedipus effect* to describe the influence of a theory or expectation or prediction *upon the event which it predicts* or describes: it will be remembered that the causal chain leading to Oedipus' parricide was started by the oracle's prediction of this event. This is a characteristic and recurrent theme of such myths, but one which seems to have failed to attract the interest of the analysts, perhaps not accidentally. (The problem of confirmatory dreams suggested by the analyst is discussed by Freud, for example in *Gesammelte Schriften*, III (1925), where he says on p. 314: "If anybody asserts that most of the dreams which can be utilized in an analysis . . . owe their origin to [the analyst's] suggestion, then no objection can be made from the point of view of analytic theory. Yet there is nothing in this fact," he surprisingly adds, "which would detract from the reliability of our results.")

5. The case of astrology, nowadays a typical pseudo-science, may illustrate this point. It was attacked, by Aristotelians and other rationalists, down to Newton's day, for the wrong reason—for its now accepted assertion that the planets had an "influence" upon terrestrial ("sublunar") events. In fact Newton's theory of gravity, and especially the lunar theory of the tides, was historically speaking an offspring of astrological lore. Newton, it seems, was most reluctant to adopt a theory which came from the same stable as for example the theory that "influenza" epidemics are due to an astral "influence." And Galileo, no doubt for the same reason, actually rejected the lunar theory of the tides; and his misgivings about Kepler may easily be explained by his misgivings about astrology.

6. See sec. 30 of Karl Popper, *The Logic of Scientific Discovery* (New York: Basic Books, 1959).

7. D. Katz, *Animals and Men* (New York: Longmans Green, 1937).

THOMAS KUHN, "THE STRUCTURE OF SCIENTIFIC REVOLUTIONS"

Kuhn attacks the philosophy of science as most philosophers practiced it when he first began to write in the early 1960s. He points out that what was then the current philosophy of science was based on what he calls "finished scientific achievements." That is, the history of science had not been given appropriate attention. Too many philosophers of science had considered that paying attention to the history of science meant focusing on the context of discovery to the exclusion of the context of justification. Naturally, history was interesting—but the study of history alone would never reveal the logic of science, the logic of justification. When history is ignored, the picture of science that emerges is of a discipline that is slowly but surely approaching the truth, a method that works in increments, piling truth upon truth.

Of course, no philosopher of science had ever totally ignored the history of science, and Kuhn knew this. The problem was that it was all too easy to view the history of science as either a list of simple facts—who did what when, where, and with whom—or as a place to find cases to bolster one's existing positions in the philosophy of science.

Kuhn convinced most philosophers of science that if they were to take a fuller (less philosophically biased) look at the history of science, they would see the following pattern. First, there is what Kuhn terms the "arbitrary element." By this he means that at any given time during the development of a science, there is a consensus (often unstated) among scientists about which problems ought to be studied, the ways to study them, and the range of acceptable answers. These things are themselves determined by assumptions about what sorts of things exist and what we take to be well-founded knowledge. Taken together, these make up what Kuhn calls a "paradigm." When there is such a paradigm, science seems to flourish. This part of a science's development Kuhn calls "normal science."

There are times, however, when normal science is not up to answering certain questions. Such questions come about when some discoveries conflict with the paradigm. These discoveries Kuhn calls "anomalies." (A current anomaly being discussed is some prehistoric bone tissue that may indicate that dinosaurs were warmblooded.) Anomalies are at first suppressed in some way because they compromise the paradigm in use. Real anomalies, however, will not go away. They continue to appear until it is clear that a new paradigm is needed. This will mean giving up the normal science that is in place. When, as a result of this process, a new paradigm is accepted, Kuhn says that there has been a "scientific revolution." The paradigm shift entails a whole new way of looking at the world. It is analogous to looking at a line drawing of a cube and first seeing it go into the paper and then seeing it come out of the paper. Kuhn's major point is that paradigm shifts are neither rational nor irrational. They just occur when they do for a whole host of reasons that cannot be reduced to simple logic or some simple ideas about confirmation or falsification.

Kuhn makes it plain that in his view, science does not "progress" by increments but rather by total revolution. Paradigms so control the way we approach the world and are so different that they cannot be compared to one another. This is called the "incommensurability thesis." Kuhn is actually saying that the idea of scientific progress makes no sense. That is why in the sentence that began this paragraph, "scare quotes" were used around the word *progress*. Paradigms require consensus. Since Kuhn claims to have shown that getting consensus is never only a logical procedure, the sociological, psychological, and economic factors, ignored by positivist philosophers, become important to a Kuhnian view of science. Kuhn says that there are almost always holdouts—scientists who refuse to give up the old for the new paradigm. A new paradigm is not fully accepted until the holdouts for the old paradigm die. Dying always happens, whereas seeing the world differently may not.

Scientific knowledge is always relative to some paradigm in use. Normal science therefore can never really answer the question "Is there a better method?" Kuhn sees this as a fact he has discovered about science (and knowledge in general) and not as a weakness of his view or a weakness in science.

Kuhn mentions Lavoisier's ideas on chemistry. Larry Laudan, a critic of Kuhn, also mentions Lavoisier (1743–1794) and his rival, Joseph Priestley (1733–1804). In Chapter 8, there is a discussion of the issue that divided Lavoisier and Priestley. It had to do with the explanation for combustion.

The Structure of Scientific Revolutions

THOMAS KUHN

History, if viewed as a repository for more than anecdote or chronology, could produce a decisive transformation in the image of science by which we are now possessed. That image has previously been drawn, even by scientists themselves, mainly from the study of finished scientific achievements as these are recorded in the classics and, more recently, in the textbooks from which each new scientific generation learns to practice its trade. Inevitably, however, the aim of such books is persuasive and pedagogic; a concept of science drawn from them is no more likely to fit the enterprise that produced them than an image of a national culture drawn from a tourist brochure or a language text. This essay attempts to show that we have been misled by them in fundamental ways. Its aim is a sketch of the quite different concept of science that can emerge from the historical record of the research activity itself.

Even from history, however, that new concept will not be forthcoming if historical data continue to be sought and scrutinized mainly to answer questions posed by the unhistorical stereotype drawn from science texts. Those texts have, for example, often seemed to imply that the content of science

is uniquely exemplified by the observations, laws, and theories described in their pages. Almost as regularly, the same books have been read as saying that scientific methods are simply the ones illustrated by the manipulative techniques used in gathering textbook data, together with the logical operations employed when relating those data to the textbook's theoretical generalizations. The result has been a concept of science with profound implications about its nature and development.

If science is the constellation of facts, theories, and methods collected in current texts, then scientists are men who, successfully or not, have striven to contribute one or another element to that particular constellation. Scientific development becomes the piecemeal process by which these items have been added, singly and in combination, to the ever growing stockpile that constitutes scientific technique and knowledge. And history of science becomes the discipline that chronicles both these successive increments and the obstacles that have inhibited their accumulation. Concerned with scientific development, the historian then appears to have two main tasks. On the one hand, he must determine by what man and at what point in time each contemporary scientific fact, law, and theory was discovered or invented. On the other, he must describe and explain the congeries of error, myth, and superstition that have

From Thomas Kuhn, *The Structure of Scientific Revolutions*, in *International Encyclopedia of Unified Science*, vol. 2, no. 2, ed., Otto Neurath (Chicago: University of Chicago Press, 1974), pp. 1–22. Copyright © 1962, 1970 by The University of Chicago.

inhibited the more rapid accumulation of the constituents of the modern science text. Much research has been directed to these ends, and some still is.

In recent years, however, a few historians of science have been finding it more and more difficult to fulfill the functions that the concept of development-by-accumulation assigns to them. As chroniclers of an incremental process, they discover that additional research makes it harder, not easier, to answer questions like: When was oxygen discovered? Who first conceived of energy conservation? Increasingly, a few of them suspect that these are simply the wrong sorts of questions to ask. Perhaps science does not develop by the accumulation of individual discoveries and inventions. Simultaneously, these same historians confront growing difficulties in distinguishing the "scientific" component of past observation and belief from what their predecessors had readily labeled "error" and "superstition." The more carefully they study, say, Aristotelian dynamics, phlogistic chemistry, or caloric thermodynamics, the more certain they feel that those once current views of nature were, as a whole, neither less scientific nor more the product of human idiosyncrasy than those current today. If these out-of-date beliefs are to be called myths, then myths can be produced by the same sorts of methods and held for the same sorts of reasons that now lead to scientific knowledge. If, on the other hand, they are to be called science, then science has included bodies of belief quite incompatible with the ones we hold today. Given these alternatives, the historian must choose the latter. Out-of-date theories are not in principle unscientific because they have been discarded. That choice, however, makes it difficult to see scientific development as a process of accretion. The same historical research that displays the difficulties in isolating individual interventions and discoveries gives ground for profound doubts about the cumulative process through which these individual contributions to science were thought to have been compounded.

The result of all these doubts and difficulties is a historio-graphic revolution in the study of science, though one that is still in its early stages. Gradually, and often without entirely realizing they are doing so, historians of science have begun to ask new sorts of questions and to trace different, and often less than cumulative, developmental lines for the sciences. Rather than seeking the permanent contributions of an older science to our present vantage, they attempt to display the historical integrity of that science in its own time. They ask, for example, not about the relation of Galileo's views to those of modern science, but rather about the relationship between his views and those of his group, i.e., his teachers, contemporaries, and immediate successors in the sciences. Furthermore, they insist upon studying the opinions of that group and other similar ones from the viewpoint—usually very different from that of modern science—that gives those opinions the maximum internal coherence and the closest possible fit to nature. Seen through the works that result, works perhaps best exemplified in the writings of Alexandre Koyré, science does not seem altogether the same enterprise as the one discussed by writers in the older historio-graphic tradition. By implication, at least, these historical studies suggest the possibility of a new image of science. This essay aims to delineate that image by making explicit some of the new historiography's implications.

What aspects of science will emerge to prominence in the course of this effort? First, at least in order of presentation, is the insufficiency of methodological directives, by themselves, to dictate a unique substantive conclusion to many sorts of scientific

THOMAS KUHN

questions. Instructed to examine electrical or chemical phenomena, the man who is ignorant of these fields but who knows what it is to be scientific may legitimately reach any one of a number of incompatible conclusions. Among those legitimate possibilities, the particular conclusions he does arrive at are probably determined by his prior experience in other fields, by the accidents of his investigation, and by his own individual makeup. What beliefs about the stars, for example, does he bring to the study of chemistry or electricity? Which of the many conceivable experiments relevant to the new field does he elect to perform first? And has aspects of the complex phenomenon that then results strike him as particularly relevant to an elucidation of the nature of chemical change or of electrical affinity? For the individual, at least, and sometimes for the scientific community as well, answers to questions like these are often essential determinants of scientific development. We shall note, for example, in Section II that the early developmental stages of most sciences have been characterized by continual competition between a number of distinct views of nature, each partially derived from, and all roughly compatible with, the dictates of scientific observation and method. What differentiated these various schools was not one or another failure of method—they were all "scientific"—but what we shall come to call their incommensurable ways of seeing the world and of practicing science in it. Observation and experience can and must drastically restrict the range of admissible scientific belief, else there would be no science. But they cannot alone determine a particular body of such belief. An apparently arbitrary element, compounded of personal and historical accident, is always a formative ingredient of the beliefs espoused by a given scientific community at a given time.

That element of arbitrariness does not, however, indicate that any scientific group could practice its trade without some set of received beliefs. Nor does it make less consequential the particular constellation to which the group, at a given time, is in fact committed. Effective research scarcely begins before a scientific community thinks it has acquired firm answers to questions like the following: What are the fundamental entities of which the universe is composed? How do these interact with each other and with the senses? What questions may legitimately be asked about such entities and what techniques employed in seeking solutions? At least in the mature sciences, answers (or full substitutes for answers) to questions like these are firmly embedded in the educational initiation that prepares and licenses the student for professional practice. Because that education is both rigorous and rigid, these answers come to exert a deep hold on the scientific mind. That they can do so does much to account both for the peculiar efficiency of the normal research activity and for the direction in which it proceeds at any given time. When examining normal science in Sections III, IV, and V, we shall want finally to describe that research as a strenuous and devoted attempt to force nature into the conceptual boxes supplied by professional education. Simultaneously, we shall wonder whether research could proceed without such boxes, whatever the element of arbitrariness in their historic origins and, occasionally, in their subsequent development.

Yet that element of arbitrariness is present, and it too has an important effect on scientific development, one which will be examined in detail in Sections VI, VII, and VIII. Normal science, the activity in which most scientists inevitably spend almost all their time, is predicated on the assumption that the scientific community knows what the world is like. Much of the success of the

162

enterprise derives from the community's willingness to defend that assumption, if necessary at considerable cost. Normal science, for example, often suppresses fundamental novelties because they are necessarily subversive of its basic commitments. Nevertheless, so long as those commitments retain an element of the arbitrary, the very nature of normal research ensures that novelty shall not be suppressed for very long. Sometimes a normal problem, one that ought to be solvable by known rules and procedures, resists the reiterated onslaught of the ablest members of the group within whose competence it falls. On other occasions a piece of equipment designed and constructed for the purpose of normal research fails to perform in the anticipated manner, revealing an anomaly that cannot, despite repeated effort, be aligned with professional expectation. In these and other ways besides, normal science repeatedly goes astray. And when it does—when, that is, the profession can no longer evade anomalies that subvert the existing tradition of scientific practice—then begin the extraordinary investigations that lead the profession at last to a new set of commitments, a new basis for the practice of science. The extraordinary episodes in which that shift of professional commitments occurs are the ones known in this essay as scientific revolutions. They are the tradition-shattering complements to the tradition-bound activity of normal science.

The most obvious examples of scientific revolutions are those famous episodes in scientific development that have often been labeled revolutions before. Therefore, in Sections IX and X, where the nature of scientific revolutions is first directly scrutinized, we shall deal repeatedly with the major turning points in scientific development associated with the names of Copernicus, Newton, Lavoisier, and Einstein. More clearly than most other episodes in the history of at least the physical sciences, these display what all scientific revolutions are about. Each of them necessitated the community's rejection of one time-honored scientific theory in favor of another incompatible with it. Each produced a consequent shift in the problems available for scientific scrutiny and in the standards by which the profession determined what should count as an admissible problem or as a legitimate problem-solution. And each transformed the scientific imagination in ways that we shall ultimately need to describe as a transformation of the world within which scientific work was done. Such changes, together with the controversies that almost always accompany them, are the defining characteristics of scientific revolutions.

These characteristics emerge with particular clarity from a study of, say, the Newtonian or the chemical revolution. It is, however, a fundamental thesis of this essay that they can also be retrieved from the study of many other episodes that were not so obviously revolutionary. For the far smaller professional group affected by them, Maxwell's equations were as revolutionary as Einstein's, and they were resisted accordingly. The invention of other new theories regularly, and appropriately, evokes the same response from some of the specialists on whose area of special competence they impinge. For these men the new theory implies a change in the rules governing the prior practice of normal science. Inevitably, therefore, it reflects upon much scientific work they have already successfully completed. That is why a new theory, however special its range of application, is seldom or never just an increment to what is already known. Its assimilation requires the reconstruction of prior theory and the reevaluation of prior fact, an intrinsically revolutionary process that is seldom completed by a single man and never overnight.

163

No wonder historians have had difficulty in dating precisely this extended process that their vocabulary impels them to view as an isolated event.

Nor are new inventions of theory the only scientific events that have revolutionary impact upon the specialists in whose domain they occur. The commitments that govern normal science specify not only what sorts of entities the universe does contain, but also, by implication, those that it does not. It follows, though the point will require extended discussion, that a discovery like that of oxygen or X-rays does not simply add one more item to the population of the scientist's world. Ultimately it has that effect, but not until the professional community has re-evaluated traditional experimental procedures, altered its conception of entities with which it has long been familiar, and, in the process, shifted the network of theory through which it deals with the world. Scientific fact and theory are not categorically separable, except perhaps within a single tradition of normal-scientific practice. That is why the unexpected discovery is not simply factual in its import and why the scientist's world is qualitatively transformed as well as quantitatively enriched by fundamental novelties of either fact or theory.

This extended conception of the nature of scientific revolutions is the one delineated in the pages that follow. Admittedly the extension strains customary usage. Nevertheless, I shall continue to speak even of discoveries as revolutionary, because it is just the possibility of relating their structure to that of, say, the Copernican revolution that makes the extended conception seem to me so important. The preceding discussion indicates how the complementary notions of normal science and of scientific revolutions will be developed in the nine sections immediately to follow. The rest of the essay attempts to dispose of three remaining central questions. Section XI, by discussing the textbook tradition, considers why scientific revolutions have previously been so difficult to see. Section XII describes the revolutionary competition between the proponents of the old normal-scientific tradition and the adherents of the new one. It thus considers the process that should somehow, in a theory of scientific inquiry, replace the confirmation or falsification procedures made familiar by our usual image of science. Competition between segments of the scientific community is the only historical process that ever actually results in the rejection of one previously accepted theory or in the adoption of another. Finally, Section XIII will ask how development through revolutions can be compatible with the apparently unique character of scientific progress. For that question, however, this essay will provide no more than the main outlines of an answer, one which depends upon characteristics of the scientific community that require much additional exploration and study.

Undoubtedly, some readers will already have wondered whether historical study can possibly effect the sort of conceptual transformation aimed at here. An entire arsenal of dichotomies is available to suggest that it cannot properly do so. History, we too often say, is a purely descriptive discipline. The theses suggested above are, however, often interpretive and sometimes normative. Again, many of my generalizations are about the sociology or social psychology of scientists; yet at least a few of my conclusions belong traditionally to logic or epistemology. In the preceding paragraph I may even seem to have violated the very influential contemporary distinction between "the context of discovery" and "the context of justification." Can anything more than profound confusion be indicated by this admixture of diverse fields and concerns?

Having been weaned intellectually on

these distinctions and others like them, I could scarcely be more aware of their import and force. For many years I took them to be about the nature of knowledge, and I still suppose that, appropriately recast, they have something important to tell us. Yet my attempts to apply them, even *grosso modo*, to the actual situations in which knowledge is gained, accepted, and assimilated have made them seem extraordinarily problematic. Rather than being elementary logical or methodological distinctions, which would thus be prior to the analysis of scientific knowledge, they now seem integral parts of a traditional set of substantive answers to the very questions upon which they have been deployed. That circularity does not at all invalidate them. But it does make them parts of a theory and, by doing so, subjects them to the same scrutiny regularly applied to theories in other fields. If they are to have more than pure abstraction as their content, then that content must be discovered by observing them in application to the data they are meant to elucidate. How could history of science fail to be a source of phenomena to which theories about knowledge may legitimately be asked to apply?

———

In this essay, "normal science" means research firmly based upon one or more past scientific achievements, achievements that some particular scientific community acknowledges for a time as supplying the foundation for its further practice. Today such achievements are recounted, though seldom in their original form, by science textbooks, elementary and advanced. These textbooks expound the body of accepted theory, illustrate many or all of its successful applications, and compare these applications with exemplary observations and experiments. Before such books became popular early in the nineteenth century (and

until even more recently in the newly matured sciences), many of the famous classics of science fulfilled a similar function. Aristotle's *Physica*, Ptolemy's *Almagest*, Newton's *Principia* and *Opticks*, Franklin's *Electricity*, Lavoisier's *Chemistry*, and Lyell's *Geology*—these and many other works served for a time implicitly to define the legitimate problems and methods of a research field for succeeding generations of practitioners. They were able to do so because they shared two essential characteristics. Their achievement was sufficiently unprecedented to attract an enduring group of adherents away from competing modes of scientific activity. Simultaneously, it was sufficiently open-ended to leave all sorts of problems for the redefined group of practitioners to resolve.

Achievements that share these two characteristics I shall henceforth refer to as "paradigms," a term that relates closely to "normal science." By choosing it, I mean to suggest that some accepted examples of actual scientific practice—examples which include law, theory, application, and instrumentation together—provide models from which spring particular coherent traditions of scientific research. These are the traditions which the historian describes under such rubrics as "Ptolemaic astronomy" (or "Copernican"), "Aristotelian dynamics" (or "Newtonian"), "corpuscular optics" (or "wave optics"), and so on. The study of paradigms, including many that are far more specialized than those named illustratively above, is what mainly prepares the student for membership in the particular scientific community with which he will later practice. Because he there joins men who learned the bases of their field from the same concrete models, his subsequent practice will seldom evoke overt disagreement over fundamentals. Men whose research is based on shared paradigms are committed to the same rules and standards for scientific practice. That commitment and the apparent consensus it produces are prerequisites for normal science, i.e., for the genesis and continuation of a particular research tradition.

Because in this essay the concept of a paradigm will often substitute for a variety of familiar notions, more will need to be said about the reasons for its introduction. Why is the concrete scientific achievement, as a locus of professional commitment, prior to the various concepts, laws, theories, and points of view that may be abstracted from it? In what sense is the shared paradigm a fundamental unit for the student of scientific development, a unit that cannot be fully reduced to logically atomic components which might function in its stead? . . . Answers to these questions and to others like them will prove basic to an understanding both of normal science and of the associated concept of paradigms. That more abstract discussion will depend, however, upon a previous exposure to examples of normal science or of paradigms in operation. In particular, both these related concepts will be clarified by noting that there can be a sort of scientific research without paradigms, or at least without any so unequivocal and so binding as the ones named above. Acquisition of a paradigm and of the more esoteric type of research it permits is a sign of maturity in the development of any given scientific field.

If the historian traces the scientific knowledge of any selected group of related phenomena backward in time, he is likely to encounter some minor variant of a pattern here illustrated from the history of physical optics. Today's physics textbooks tell the student that light is photons, i.e., quantum-mechanical entities that exhibit some characteristics of waves and some of particles. Research proceeds accordingly, or rather according to the more elaborate and math-

ematical characterization from which this usual verbalization is derived. That characterization of light is, however, scarcely half a century old. Before it was developed by Planck, Einstein, and others early in this century, physics texts taught that light was transverse wave motion, a conception rooted in a paradigm that derived ultimately from the optical writings of Young and Fresnel in the early nineteenth century. Nor was the wave theory the first to be embraced by almost all practitioners of optical science. During the eighteenth century the paradigm for this field was provided by Newton's *Opticks,* which taught that light was material corpuscles. At that time physicists sought evidence, as the early wave theorists had not, of the pressure exerted by light particles impinging on solid bodies.[1]

These transformations of the paradigms of physical optics are scientific revolutions, and the successive transition from one paradigm to another via revolution is the usual developmental pattern of mature science. It is not, however, the pattern characteristic of the period before Newton's work, and that is the contrast that concerns us here. No period between remote antiquity and the end of the seventeenth century exhibited a single generally accepted view about the nature of light. Instead there were a number of competing schools and sub-schools, most of them espousing one variant or another of Epicurean, Aristotelian, or Platonic theory. One group took light to be particles emanating from material bodies; for another it was a modification of the medium that intervened between the body and the eye; still another explained light in terms of an interaction of the medium with an emanation from the eye; and there were other combinations and modifications besides. Each of the corresponding schools derived strength from its relation to some particular metaphysic, and each emphasized, as paradigmatic observations, the particular cluster of optical phenomena that its own theory could do most to explain. Other observations were dealt with by *ad hoc* elaborations, or they remained as outstanding problems for further research.[2]

At various times all these schools made significant contributions to the body of concepts, phenomena, and techniques from which Newton drew the first nearly uniformly accepted paradigm for physical optics. Any definition of the scientist that excludes at least the more creative members of these various schools will exclude their modern successors as well. Those men were scientists. Yet anyone examining a survey of physical optics before Newton may well conclude that, though the field's practitioners were scientists, the net result of their activity was something less than science. Being able to take no common body of belief for granted, each writer on physical optics felt forced to build his field anew from its foundations. In doing so, his

choice of supporting observation and experiment was relatively free, for there was no standard set of methods or of phenomena that every optical writer felt forced to employ and explain. Under these circumstances, the dialogue of the resulting books was often directed as much to the members of other schools as it was to nature. That pattern is not unfamiliar in a number of creative fields today, nor is it incompatible with significant discovery and invention. It is not, however, the pattern of development that physical optics acquired after Newton and that other natural sciences make familiar today. . . .

NOTES

1. Joseph Priestley, *The History and Present State of Discoveries Relating to Vision, Light, and Colors* (London, 1772), pp. 385–90.
2. Vasco Ronchi, *Histoire de la lumière*, trans. Jean Taton (Paris: Colin, 1956), chaps. i–iv.

IMRE LAKATOS, "FALSIFICATION AND THE METHODOLOGY OF SCIENTIFIC RESEARCH PROGRAMMES"

Lakatos thinks that Popper has oversimplified the actual method used by scientists in deciding whether or not to accept a theory. Lakatos sees theories as entities existing over time. They get changed as new information is gathered. Theories are readjusted to fit the facts as the facts are obtained. What this means to Lakatos is that theories are not rejected when a tested prediction fails. Instead, the theory is fixed in order to account for the failure. The idea that there can be a crucial experiment, one that yields a result that will tell us which of two competing theories is correct, is a myth. He uses the following example to show what he means.

Suppose that a physicist, P, in the late eighteenth century uses Newtonian mechanics to derive the orbit of a newly discovered planet, L. Astronomers find that L deviates from the path predicted for it by P. Has Newtonian mechanics been falsified? Should it be given up? Not at all. Instead, physicist P postulates the existence of planet M, which is the cause of the deviation. P is able to use Newtonian mechanics to predict exactly where M will be. However, M is so small that contemporary telescopes cannot find it. So opticians have to build better telescopes. Better telescopes do not reveal planet M. Should P now give up Newtonian mechanics? Not at all. P claims that there is some cosmic dust interfering with the telescopes. Now we can continue the story into present times. We send a satellite into space to confirm the existence of the dust. The satellite, however, finds no dust. Perhaps a magnetic field or some new kind of radiation is affecting the instruments of the satellite. There is no way, according to Lakatos, for just one fact to refute a theory.

But then, won't all scientific theories be pseudoscience, like astrology?

No, says Lakatos. The difference is that theories have to be seen as methodologies. The best are vibrant, open to change, and therefore often undergoing emendation. Lakatos refers to methodologies as research programs or problem shifts. He says that while research programs progressively change, they are worth keeping. When research programs are not progressively changing, when they are instead "degenerating," it is time for a new research program to be chosen. In the selection, we get a picture of a progressive program. A degenerating program would have few, if any, of the characteristics of a progressive program.

Examples of progressive research programs would be biochemical genetics, the germ theory of disease, and applying chaos theory to weather systems. Astrology would represent a degenerating research program. It has not changed at all since its inception. It has made no effort to deal with falsified predictions except to claim that if only the data were clearer, the predictions would be better. This claim is acceptable, but only for a short while. As fewer and fewer predictions come true, astrology should say, according to Lakatos, that it is time to revamp the theory, change the program.

Lakatos views research programs as made of core beliefs (the hard core) surrounded by less important beliefs. Every theory (research program) has a positive heuristic telling how to defend the hard core against counterevidence. Lakatos's "negative heuristic" is the specification of the hard core with the rule that we cannot allow for the refutation of the hard core. Falsified predictions usually strike only at the outer belt. That is why it is acceptable to change in the face of such falsification. It is not seeing theories in this way that led Popper to think that any single falsification should lead to the rejection of a theory.

Sometimes, however, an experiment (usually a set of experiments) will force attention into the core. They will show that there is something wrong at the very center of the theory. When that happens, the theory must be given up because the alternative "fixed" theory is just so clearly inelegant and unworkable and continues to lead to the same dead ends. This is what happened when the research program based on the belief that the genetic material was protein had to be given up in the face of many experiments over many years that made it hard to accept that the genetic material was not DNA. (On this, see the reading by Olby in Chapter 8.)

Notice that if one changes the core, by definition, the theory would have changed. Here we see where Lakatos and Kuhn are close. Kuhn would call such core-questioning experiments anomalies and then would go on to tell his version of what happens when anomalies occur. That is, research programs in Lakatosian terms serve the role of Kuhnian paradigms.

Falsification and the Methodology of Scientific Research Programmes

IMRE LAKATOS

... I have discussed the problem of objective appraisal of scientific growth in terms of progressive and degenerating problemshifts in series of scientific theories. The most important such series in the growth of science are characterized by a certain *continuity* which connects their members. This continuity evolves from a genuine research programme adumbrated at the start. The programme consists of methodological rules: some tell us what paths of research to avoid *(negative heuristic)*, and others what paths to pursue *(positive heuristic)*.[1]

(a) Negative heuristic: the "hard core" of the programme

All scientific research programmes may be characterized by their *"hard core."* The negative heuristic of the programme forbids us to refute the ... "hard core." ... We must use our ingenuity to articulate or even invent "auxiliary hypotheses," which form a *protective belt* around this core. ... It is this protective belt of auxiliary hypotheses which has to bear the brunt of tests and get adjusted and re-adjusted, or even completely replaced, to defend the thus-hardened core. A research programme is successful if all this leads to a progressive problemshift; unsuccessful if it leads to a degenerating problemshift.

The classical example of a successful research programme is Newton's gravitational theory: possibly the most successful research programme ever. ...

From Imre Lakatos and Alan Musgrave, (eds.), *Criticism and the Growth of Knowledge* (Cambridge: Cambridge University Press, 1981), pp. 132–138. © Cambridge University Press 1970. Reprinted with the permission of Cambridge University Press.

(b) Positive heuristic: the construction of the "protective belt" and the relative autonomy of theoretical science

Research programmes, besides their negative heuristic, are also characterized by their positive heuristic.

Even the most rapidly and consistently progressive research programmes can digest their "counter-evidence" only piecemeal: anomalies are never completely exhausted. But it should not be thought that yet unexplained anomalies—"puzzles" as Kuhn might call them—are taken in random order, and the protective belt built up in an eclectic fashion, without any preconceived order. The order is usually decided in the theoretician's cabinet, independently of the *known* anomalies. Few theoretical scientists engaged in a research programme pay undue attention to "refutations." They have a long-term research policy which anticipates these refutations. This research policy, or order of research, is set out—in more or less detail—in the *positive heuristic* of the research programme. The negative heuristic specifies the "hard core" of the programme which is "irrefutable" by the methodological decision of its protagonists; the positive heuristic consists of a partially articulated set of suggestions or hints on how to change, develop the "refutable variants" of the research-programme, how to modify, sophisticate, the "refutable" protective belt.

The positive heuristic of the programme saves the scientist from becoming confused by the ocean of anomalies. The positive heuristic sets out a programme which lists a chain of ever more complicated *models* simulating reality: the scientist's attention is riveted on building his models following instructions which are laid down in the positive part of his programme. He ignores the *actual* counterexamples, the available *"data."*[2] Newton first worked out his programme for a planetary system with a fixed point-like sun and one single point-like planet. It was in this model that he derived his inverse square law for Kepler's ellipse. But this model was forbidden by Newton's own third law of dynamics, therefore the model had to be replaced by one in which both sun and planet revolved round their common centre of gravity. This change was not motivated by any observation (the data did not suggest an "anomaly" here) but by a theoretical difficulty in developing the programme. Then he worked out the programme for more planets as if there were only heliocentric but no interplanetary forces. Then he worked out the case where the sun and planets were not mass-points but mass-*balls*. Again, for this change he did not *need* the observation of an anomaly; infinite density was forbidden by an (inarticulated) touchstone theory, therefore planets *had* to be extended. This change involved considerable mathematical difficulties, held up Newton's work—and delayed the publication of the *Principia* by more than a decade. Having solved this "puzzle," he started work on *spinning balls* and their wobbles. Then he admitted interplanetary forces and started work on *perturbations*. At this point he started to look more anxiously at the facts. Many of them were beautifully explained (qualitatively) by this model, many were not. It was then that he started to work on *bulging* planets, rather than round planets, etc.

Newton despised people who, like Hooke, stumbled on a first naive model but did not have the tenacity and ability to develop it into a research programme, and who thought that a first version, a mere

aside, constituted a "discovery." He held up publication until his programme had achieved a remarkable progressive shift.[3]

Most, if not all, Newtonian "puzzles," leading to a series of new variants superseding each other, were forseeable at the time of Newton's first naive model and no doubt Newton and his colleagues *did* forsee them: Newton must have been fully aware of the blatant falsity of his first variants. Nothing shows the existence of a positive heuristic of a research programme clearer than this fact: this is why one speaks of "models" in research programmes. A *"model"* is a set of initial conditions (possibly together with some of the observational theories) which one knows is *bound* to be replaced during the further development of the programme, and one even knows, more or less, how. This shows once more how irrelevant "refutations" of any specific variant are in a research programme: their existence is fully expected, the positive heuristic is there as the strategy both for predicting (producing) and digesting them. Indeed, if the positive heuristic is clearly spelt out, the difficulties of the programme are mathematical rather than empirical.[4]

One may formulate the "positive heuristic" of a research programme as a "metaphysical" principle. For instance one may formulate Newton's programme like this: "The planets are essentially gravitating spinning-tops of roughly spherical shape." This idea was never *rigidly* maintained: the planets are not *just* gravitational, they have also, for example, electromagnetic characteristics which may influence their motion. Positive heuristic is thus in general more flexible than negative heuristic. Moreover, it occasionally happens that when a research programme gets into a degenerating phase, a little revolution or a *creative shift* in its positive heuristic may push it forward again.[5] It is better therefore to separate the "hard core" from the more flexible metaphysical principles expressing the positive heuristic.

Our considerations show that the positive heuristic forges ahead with almost complete disregard of "refutations": it may seem that it is the *"verifications"*[6] rather than the refutations which provide the contact points with reality. Although one must point out that any "verification" of the $n +$ 1-th version of the programme is a refutation of the n-th version, we cannot deny that *some* defeats of the subsequent versions are always foreseen: it is the "verifications" which keep the programme going, recalcitrant instances notwithstanding.

We may appraise research programmes, even after their "elimination," for their *heuristic power:* how many new facts did they produce, how great was "their capacity to explain their refutations in the course of their growth"?[7]

(We may also appraise them for the stimulus they gave to mathematics. The real difficulties for the theoretical scientist arise rather from the *mathematical difficulties* of the programme than from anomalies. The greatness of the Newtonian programme comes partly from the development—by Newtonians—of classical infinitesimal analysis which was a crucial precondition of its success.)

Thus the methodology of scientific research programmes accounts for the *relative autonomy of theoretical science:* a historical fact whose rationality cannot be explained by the earlier falsificationists. Which problems scientists working in powerful research programmes rationally choose, is determined by the positive heuristic of the programme rather than by psychologically worrying (or technologically urgent) anomalies. The anomalies are listed but shoved aside in the hope that they will turn, in due course, into corroborations of the programme. Only those scientists have to rivet their attention on anomalies who are either engaged in trial-and-error exercises or who work in a degenerating phase of a research programme when the positive heuristic ran out of steam. (All this, of course, must sound repugnant to naive falsificationists who hold that once a theory is "refuted" by experiment (by *their* rule book), it is irrational (and dishonest) to develop it further: one has to replace the old "refuted" theory by a new, unrefuted one.)

NOTES

1. One may point out that the negative and positive heuristic gives a rough (implicit) definition of the "conceptual framework" (and consequently of the language). The recognition that the history of science is the history of research programmes rather than of theories may therefore be seen as a partial vindication of the view that the history of science is the history of conceptual frameworks or of scientific languages.

2. If a scientist (or mathematician) has a positive heuristic, he refuses to be drawn into observation. He will "lie down on his couch, shut his eyes and forget about the data." (Cf. my [1963–4], especially pp. 300 ff., where there is a detailed case study of such a programme.) Occasionally, of course, he will ask Nature a shrewd question: he will then be encouraged by Nature's *YES*, but not discouraged by its *NO*.

3. Reichenbach, following Cajori, gives a different explanation of what delayed Newton in the publication of his *Principia:* "To his disappointment he found that the observational results disagreed with his calculations. Rather than set any theory, however beautiful, before the facts, Newton put the manuscript of his theory into his drawer. Some twenty years later, after new measurements of the circumference of the earth had been made by a French expedition, Newton saw that the figures on which he had based his test were false and that the improved figures agreed with his theoretical calculation. It was only after this test that he published his law. . . . The story of Newton is one of the most striking illustrations of the method of modern science" (Reichenbach [1951], pp. 101–2). Feyerabend criticizes Reichenbach's account (Feyerabend [1965], p. 229), but does not give an alternative *rationale.*

4. For this point cf. Truesdell [1960].

5. Soddy's contribution to Prout's programme or Pauli's to Bohr's (old quantum theory) programme are typical examples of such creative shifts.
6. A "verification" is a corroboration of excess content in the expanding programme. But, of course, a "verification" does not *verify* a programme: it shows only its heuristic power.
7. Cf. my [1963–4], pp. 324–30. Unfortunately in 1963–4 I had not yet made a clear terminological distinction between theories and research programmes, and this impaired my exposition of a research programme in informal, quasi-empirical mathematics.

REFERENCES

Feyerabend, [1965]. "Reply to Criticism" in R. Cohen and M. Wartofsky (eds.), *Boston Studies in the Philosophy of Science*, II (The Netherlands: Reidel), pp. 223–261.
Lakatos, I. [1963–1964]. "Proofs and Refutations," *The British Journal for the Philosophy of Science*, vol. 14, pp. 1–25, 120–139, 221–243, 296–342.
Reichenbach, H. [1951]. *The Rise of Scientific Philosophy.* (Berkeley: Univ. of California Press).
Truesdell, [1960]. "The Program toward Rediscovering the Rational Mechanics in the Age of Reason," *Archive of the History of Exact Sciences*, Vol I, pp. 3–36.

ROBERT MATTHEWS, "SPOILING A UNIVERSAL 'FUDGE FACTOR' "

In this brief article from *Science*, we see how a respected science, cosmology, the part of astrophysics that tries to explain the origins of the universe, has followed a Lakatosian path. It added to its equations for gravity what is called the cosmological constant in order to make the equations it wanted to use match what is actually observed. The article describes a good example of how scientists react to problems with their theories. Is the cosmological constant *ad hoc*?

Spoiling a Universal "Fudge Factor"

ROBERT MATTHEWS

Even the most enthusiastic cosmologist will admit that current theories of the nature of the universe have some big holes. One such gap is that the universe seems to be younger than some of the objects contained within it. Another problem is that the observed universe just doesn't appear to have enough matter in it to explain the way it behaves now, nor the way theorists predict it will evolve.

To overcome these problems, many cos-

mologists have suggested that the equations of gravity should contain a number called the cosmological constant: a fudge factor that, if it has the right value, would make these bugbears disappear (*Science*, 5 November 1993, p. 846). But a new analysis of observations of gravitational lenses—galaxies whose gravity bends the light of more distant objects—shows that, if the constant does exist, it cannot be big enough to explain the anomalous age of the universe or the missing mass. "The lensing statistics really are becoming a problem for the cos-

From *Science* 265 (1994): 740. Courtesy of the author.

mological constant models," admits cosmologist George Efstathiou of Oxford University.

Estimates of the age of the universe center on observations of distant galaxies: how far away they are and how fast they are receding as the universe expands. These data let cosmologists put a date on the Big Bang, and the current estimates put the beginning of time at around 8 billion years ago. But models of stellar evolution suggest that some star clusters are at least 5 billion years older than that, a discrepancy that is difficult to explain.

The emptiness of space is arguably an even tougher problem. According to the simplest current theories of the very early universe, there should be just enough matter in the cosmos to allow it to expand forever; any more matter and gravity will be strong enough to halt the expansion and pull the universe back into a cosmic crunch. Cosmologists express this theoretical prediction by saying that the value of "omega"—a measure of the density of matter in the universe—is precisely 1. Observations of the real universe tell a different story, however: omega values of just 0.2 are typical.

Many cosmologists felt that something quite fundamental needed to be done, so they proposed restoring the cosmological constant, originally suggested by Albert Einstein in 1918. In a universe with a cosmological constant, all of empty space would be endowed with extra energy, gently pushing distant galaxies away from each other. This would make the universe appear younger than it really is, because it boosts the speed at which galaxies recede from one another. The constant can also help with the value of omega: Because of the equivalence of mass and energy defined in relativity theory, the energy that accompanies the constant's antigravitational effect is equivalent to an increase in the apparent density of matter in the cosmos. Theory predicts that the cosmological constant could solve both the age and missing mass problems if it adds enough energy to produce the equivalent of an omega value of 0.8.

But gravitational lens expert Chris Kochanek of the Harvard-Smithsonian Center for Astrophysics in Cambridge, Massachusetts, has now all but slammed the door on that possibility. When light from, say, a quasar passes by an intervening galaxy on its way to Earth, the galaxy's gravity bends the light like a lens, creating multiple images of the quasar. Astronomers have been scouring the sky for these strange objects and counting how many they see out to a specific distance. If the cosmological constant exists, its antigravitational influence has the effect of boosting the volume of space between two distant objects—and thus increasing the number of gravitational lenses caught by surveys that look out to a given distance. Unlike counting single objects, gravitational lens numbers reflect conditions at two locations—that of the quasar and of the galaxy—both affected by a cosmological constant.

For a cosmological constant equivalent to an omega of 0.8, Kochanek calculates that about 15 gravitational lenses should have been seen by current surveys. So far, only 6 have been found. With his current results, to be published later this year in the *Astrophysical Journal*, Kochanek can say with 90% certainty that the cosmological constant is less than 0.5 for current models of the universe. "A cosmological constant of 0.8 is more or less right out," he says.

Cosmologists have taken the news on the chin, but still cling to the hope that the result may be flawed. Princeton University cosmologist Jim Peebles, for instance, notes that the apparent dearth of lenses may be the result of their being obscured by dust. But Kochanek, unswayed, counters that dust does not explain other problems, such as the constant's failure to give the correct distance of individual gravitational lenses.

So what now? One possibility is to introduce a cosmological constant that varies with time—an idea investigated by Peebles himself. With suitable tweaking, this might get around the current problems. But many cosmologists would find this disturbingly reminiscent of the attempts of medieval astronomers to patch up their Earth-centered view of the solar system by devising more complicated celestial machinery to propel the planets.

LARRY LAUDAN, "DISSECTING THE HOLIST PICTURE OF SCIENTIFIC CHANGE"

According to Laudan, Kuhn's ideas entail too much relativity in science. This is a sign that Kuhn has probably made some errors. Science is just too objective for Kuhn to be correct.

Laudan critiques Kuhn on scientific change. A Kuhnian paradigm has three inextricably related parts:

A conceptual framework—ontological claims

Rules that specify methods and techniques

Cognitive goals or ideals—what we take to be well-founded knowledge

We do not shift all three at once, contrary to what Kuhn claims. Rationality is not as paradigm-relative as Kuhn believes. What were Kuhn's mistakes? (1) He does not accurately reflect the history of science. (2) Theories (conceptual framework), methodological rules (method), and cognitive goals (values) are logically separate, as history can show. That is, Kuhn's holism regarding science is, at best, oversimplified. (3) Closure (deciding to give up a paradigm) does not always require external factors.

Laudan suggests that there is an interrelation among the three parts of a paradigm. He calls this the reticulated view—a view that allows for negotiation about whether all three parts have to be dropped at once. Laudan wants us to reject Kuhn's uncompromising holism, which stresses the impossibility of giving up the hard core of the paradigm and the requirement that the three parts of a paradigm must stand or fall together. Laudan wants a careful reexamination of the history of science because he is sure that Kuhn's description of revolutions is shaped by Kuhn's insistence that there are no gradual changes in science.

Laudan insists that what appear to be large-scale and immediate paradigm shifts may have occurred piecemeal. For example, first some ontological claims may be revised, then some goals may be shifted, and then some methodological rules may have to change. All of this may be a gradual accommodation over a fairly long period of time. If we approach the history of science certain that the three are inextricably bound, then that is what we will find. We will miss the small changes and see only the result: what appears to be a Kuhnian-style paradigm shift. Where there is no rival paradigm, Laudan refers to changes as unitraditional. Where there is a rival, there is multitraditional change.

Laudan cites examples from the history of science to support his view that change in science is more gradual than Kuhn allows.

Kuhn said that there can be no change in values (what counts as well-founded knowledge) unless there is a revolution. Laudan offers examples to show that there have been such changes without full-scale revolutions.

In another example, Laudan points out that the early rules of inductive inference did not allow for the use of theoretical entities. By the middle of the nineteenth century, such entities were considered *de rigueur*. This is a shift in methodology across many different disciplines. (Would Hesse see any shift here?) Laudan can find no one revolution to go with this methodological shift. Laudan uses yet another example. Giving up the idea of certain knowledge and replacing it with probability is a shift in values—again, however, a shift with no scientific revolution.

In sum, some Kuhnian revolutions may have occurred, but scientific change in general is gradual as Laudan lays it out. There is always the possibility that scientists can use rationality to decide between rival explanations—at the very least by ruling out some answers.

Dissecting the Holist Picture of Scientific Change

LARRY LAUDAN

It is notorious that the key Kuhnian concept of a paradigm is multiply ambiguous. Among its most central meanings are the following three: First and foremost, a paradigm offers a conceptual framework for classifying and explaining natural objects. That is, it specifies in a generic way the sorts of entities which are thought to populate a certain domain of experience and it sketches out how those entities generally interact. In short, every paradigm will make certain claims about what populates the world. Such ontological claims mark that paradigm off from others, since each paradigm is thought to postulate entities and modes of interaction which differentiate it from other paradigms. Second, a paradigm will specify the appropriate methods, techniques, and tools of inquiry for studying the objects in the relevant domain of application. Just as different paradigms have different ontologies, so they involve substantially different methodologies. (Consider, for instance, the very different methods of research and theory evaluation associated with behaviorism and cognitive psychology respectively.) These methodological commitments are

From Larry Laudan, *Science and Values* (Berkeley: University of California Press, 1984), pp. 67–87. Courtesy of the author and the University of California Press.

persistent ones, and they characterize the paradigm throughout its history. Finally, the proponents of different paradigms will, according to Kuhn, espouse different sets of cognitive goals or ideals. Although the partisans of two paradigms may (and usually do) share some aims in common, Kuhn insists that the goals are not fully overlapping between followers of rival paradigms. Indeed, to accept a paradigm is, for Kuhn, to subscribe to a complex of cognitive values which the proponents of no other paradigm accept fully.

Paradigm change, on this account, clearly represents a break of great magnitude. To trade in one paradigm for another is to involve oneself in changes at each of the three levels defined in chapter 2 above.[1] We give up one ontology for another, one methodology for another, and one set of cognitive goals for another. Moreover, according to Kuhn, this change is *simultaneous* rather than *sequential*. It is worth observing in passing that, for all Kuhn's vitriol about the impoverishment of older models of scientific rationality, there are several quite striking similarities between the classical version of the hierarchical model and Kuhn's alternative to it. Both lay central stress on the justificatory interactions between claims at the factual, methodological, and axiological levels. Both emphasize the centrality of values and standards as providing criteria of choice between rival views lower in the hierarchy. Where Kuhn breaks, and breaks radically, with the tradition is in his insistence that rationality must be relativized to choices within a paradigm rather than choices between paradigms. Whereas the older account of the hierarchical model had generally supposed that core axiological and methodological commitments would typically be common property across the sciences of an epoch, Kuhn asserts that there are methodological and axiological discrepancies between any two

paradigms. Indeed (as we shall see below), one of the core failings of Kuhn's position is that it so fully internalizes the classical hierarchical approach that, whenever the latter breaks down (as it certainly does in grappling with interparadigmatic debate, or any other sort of disagreement involving conflicting goals), Kuhn's approach has nothing more to offer concerning the possibility of rational choices.[2]

For now, however, the immediate point to stress is that Kuhn portrays paradigm changes in ways that make them seem to be abrupt and global ruptures in the life of a scientific community. So great is this supposed transition that several of Kuhn's critics have charged that, despite Kuhn's proclaimed intentions to the contrary, his analysis inevitably turns scientific change into a nonrational or irrational process. In part, but only in part, it is Kuhn's infelicitous terminology that produces this impression. Notoriously, he speaks of the acceptance of a new paradigm as a "conversion experience,"[3] conjuring up a picture of the scientific revolutionary as a born-again Christian, long on zeal and short on argument. At other times he likens paradigm change to an "irreversible Gestalt-shift."[4] Less metaphorically, he claims that there is never a point at which it is "unreasonable" to hold onto an old paradigm rather than to accept a new one.[5] Such language does not encourage one to imagine that paradigm change is exactly the result of a careful and deliberate weighing-up of the respective strengths of rival contenders. But impressions based on some of Kuhn's more lurid language can probably be rectified by cleaning up some of the vocabulary of *The Structure of Scientific Revolutions*, a task on which Kuhn has been embarked more or less since the book first appeared.[6] No changes of terminology, however, will alter the fact that some central features of Kuhn's model of science raise serious roadblocks to a rational analysis of scientific change. The bulk of this chapter is devoted to examining some of those impedimenta. Before we turn to that examination, however, I want to stress early on that my complaint with Kuhn is not merely that he has failed to give any normatively robust or rational account of theory change, serious as that failing is. As I show below, he has failed even at the descriptive or narrative task of offering an accurate story about the manner in which large-scale changes of scientific allegiance occur.

But there is a yet more fundamental respect in which Kuhn's approach presents obstacles to an understanding of the dynamics of theory change. Specifically, by insisting that individual paradigms have an integral and static character—that changes take place only between, rather than within, paradigms—Kuhn has missed the single feature of science which promises to mediate and rationalize the transition from one world view or paradigm to another. Kuhn's various writings on this subject leave the reader in no doubt that he thinks the parts of a paradigm go together as an inseparable package. As he puts it in *The Structure of Scientific Revolutions,* "In learning a paradigm the scientist acquires theory, methods, and standards together, usually in an *inextricable* mix."[7] This theme, of the inextricable and inseparable ingredients of a paradigm, is a persistent one in Kuhn's work. One key aim of this chapter is to show how drastically we need to alter Kuhn's views about how tightly the pieces of a paradigm's puzzle fit together before we can expect to understand how paradigmlike change occurs.

When scientific change is construed so globally, it is no small challenge to see how it could be other than a conversion experience. If different scientists not only espouse different theories but also subscribe to different standards of appraisal and ground those standards in different and conflicting

systems of cognitive goals, then it is difficult indeed to imagine that scientific change could be other than a whimsical change of style or taste. There could apparently never be compelling grounds for saying that one paradigm is better than another, for one has to ask: Better relative to which standards and whose goals? To make matters worse— much worse—Kuhn often suggested that each paradigm is more or less automatically guaranteed to satisfy its own standards and to fail the standards of rival paradigms, thus producing a kind of self-reinforcing solipsism in science. As he once put it, "To the extent, as significant as it is incomplete, that two scientific schools disagree about what is a problem and what a solution, they will inevitably talk through each other when debating the merits of their respective paradigms. In the partially circular arguments that regularly result, *each* paradigm will be shown to satisfy more or less the criteria that it dictates for itself and to fall short of those dictated by its opponent."[8] Anyone who writes prose of this sort must think that scientific decision making is fundamentally capricious. Or at least so many of us thought in the mid- and late 1960s, as philosophers began to digest Kuhn's ideas. In fact, if one looks at several discussions of Kuhn's work dating from that period, one sees this theme repeatedly. Paradigm change, it was said, could not possibly be a reasoned or rational process. Kuhn, we thought, has made science into an irrational "monster."

The clear implication of such passages in Kuhn's writings is that interparadigmatic debate is necessarily inconclusive and thus can never be brought to rational closure. When closure does occur, it must therefore be imposed on the situation by such external factors as the demise of some of the participants or the manipulation of the levers of power and reward within the institutional structure of the scientific community. Philosophers of science, almost without exception, have found such implications troubling, for they directly confute what philosophers have been at pains for two millennia to establish: to wit, that scientific disputes, and more generally all disagreements about matters of fact, are in principle open to rational clarification and resolution. It is on the strength of passages such as those I have mentioned that Kuhn has been charged with relativism, subjectivism, irrationalism, and a host of other sins high on the philosopher's hit list.

There is some justice in these criticisms of Kuhn's work, for . . . Kuhn has failed over the past twenty years to elaborate any coherent account of consensus formation, that is, of the manner in which scientists could ever agree to support one world view rather than another. But that flaw, serious though it is, can probably be remedied, for I want to suggest that the problem of consensus formation can be solved if we will make two fundamental amendments in Kuhn's position. First . . . we must replace the hierarchical view of justification with the reticulated picture, thereby making cognitive values "negotiable." Second, we must simply drop Kuhn's insistence on the integral character of world views or paradigms. More specifically, we solve the problem of consensus once we realize that *the various components of a world view are individually negotiable and individually replaceable in a piecemeal fashion* (that is, in such a manner that replacement of one element need not require wholesale repudiation of all the other components), Kuhn himself grants, of course, that some components of a world view can be revised; that is what "paradigm articulation" is all about. But for Kuhn, as for such other world view theorists as Lakatos and Foucault, the central commitments of a world view, its "hard core" (to use Lakatos's marvelous phrase), are not revisable—short of rejecting the entire world view. The core ontology of a world

view or paradigm, along with its methodology and axiology, comes on a take-it-or-leave-it basis. Where these levels of commitment are concerned, Kuhn (along with such critics of his as Lakatos) is an uncompromising holist. Consider, for instance, his remark: "Just because it is a transition between incommensurables, the transition between competing paradigms cannot be made a step at a time . . . like the Gestalt-switch, it must occur all at once or not at all."[9] Kuhn could hardly be less ambiguous on this point.

But paradigms or research programs need not be so rigidly conceived, and typically they are not so conceived by scientists; nor, if we reflect on it a moment, should they be so conceived. . . .

. . . There are complex justificatory interconnections among a scientist's ontology, his methodology, and his axiology. If a scientist's methodology fails to justify his ontology; if his methodology fails to promote his cognitive aims; if his cognitive aims prove to be utopian—in all these cases the scientist will have compelling reasons for replacing one component or other of his world view with an element that does the job better. Yet he need not modify everything else.

To be more precise, the choice confronting a scientist whose world view is under strain in this manner need be nothing like as stark as Kuhn suggests. . . . (where it is a matter of sticking with what he knows best unchanged or throwing that over for something completely different), but rather a choice where the modification of one core element—while retaining the others—may bring a decided improvement.

In all these examples there is enough common ground between the rivals to engender hope of finding an "Archimedean standpoint" which can rationally mediate the choice. When such commonality exists, there is no reason to regard the choice as just a matter of taste or whim; nor is there any reason to say of such choices, as Kuhn does: there can be no compelling grounds for one preference over another. Provided theory change occurs one level at a time, there is ample scope for regarding it as a thoroughly reasoned process.

But the crucial question is whether change actually does occur in this manner. If one thinks quickly of the great transitions in the history of science, they *seem* to preclude such a stepwise analysis. The shift from (say) an Aristotelian to a Newtonian world view clearly involved changes on all three levels. So, too, did the emergence of psychoanalysis from nineteenth-century mechanistic psychology. But before we accept this wholesale picture of scientific change too quickly, we should ask whether it might not acquire what plausibility it enjoys only because our characterizations of such historical revolutions make us compress or telescope a number of gradual changes (one level at a time, as it were) into what, at our distance in time, can easily appear as an abrupt and monumental shift.

By way of laying out the core features of a more gradualist (and, I argue, historically more faithful) picture of scientific change, I will sketch a highly idealized version of theory change. Once it is in front of us, I will show in detail how it makes sense of some real cases of scientific change. Eventually, we will want a model that can show how one might move from an initial state of disagreement between rival traditions or paradigms to consensus about which one is better. But, for purposes of exposition, I want to begin with a rather simpler situation, namely, one in which consensus in favor of one world view or tradition gives way eventually to consensus in favor of another, without scientists ever being faced with a choice as stark as that between two well-developed, and totally divergent, rival paradigms. My "tall tale" . . . might go like this:

at any given time, there will be at least one set of values, methods, and theories which one can identify as operating in any field or subfield of science. Let us call this collective C_1, and its components, T_1, M_1, and A_1. These components typically stand in the complex justificatory relationships to one another; . . . that is, A_1 will justify M_1 and harmonize with T_1; M_1 will justify T_1 and exhibit the realizability of A_1; and T_1 will constrain M_1 and exemplify A_1. Let us suppose that someone then proposes a new theory, T_2, to replace T_1. The rules M_1 will be consulted and they may well indicate grounds for preferring T_2 to T_1. Suppose that they do, and that we thereby replace T_1 with T_2. As time goes by, certain scientists may develop reservations about M_1 and propose a new and arguably superior methodology, M_2. Now a choice must be made between M_1 and M_2. As we have seen, that requires determining whether M_1 or M_2 offers more promise of realizing our aims. Since that determination will typically be an empirical matter, both A_1 and the then prevailing theory, T_2, will have to be consulted to ascertain whether M_1 or M_2 is optimal for securing A_1. Suppose that, in comparing the relative efficacy of achieving the shared values, A_1, cogent arguments can be made to show that M_2 is superior to M_1. Under the circumstances, assuming scientists behave rationally, M_2 will replace M_1. This means that as new theories, T_3, T_4, . . . , T_n, emerge later, they will be assessed by rules M_2 rather than M_1. Suppose, still further along in this fairy tale, we imagine a challenge to the basic values themselves. Someone may, for instance, point to new evidence suggesting that some element or other of A_1 is unrealizable. Someone else may point out that virtually none of the theories accepted by the scientific community as instances of good science exemplify the values expressed in A_1. (Or, it may be shown that A_1 is an inconsistent set in that its component aspirations are fundamentally at odds with one another.) Under such circumstances, scientists may rationally decide to abandon A_1 and to take up an alternative, consistent set of values, A_2, should it be available. (Although I have considered a temporal sequence of changes—first in theory, then in methods, and finally in aims—which superficially corresponds to the justificatory order of the hierarchical model, it is crucial to realize how unlike the hierarchical picture this sequence really is. That model would countenance no rational deliberation of the sort represented by the transition from $T_2M_2A_1$ to $T_2M_2A_2$. Equally, the hierarchical model, as noted in earlier chapters, does not permit our beliefs at the level of theories to shape our views as to permissible methods, since justification in the hierarchical model is entirely downward from methods to theories.)

. . . Before I present the evidence needed for demythologizing my story, we have to add a new twist to it. As I pointed out above, this story concerns what I call a "unitraditional paradigm shift." It reveals how it might be possible for scientists, originally advocates of one tradition or paradigm, to come around eventually to accept what appears to be a very different view of the world, not to say a very different view of what science is. I call such a change unitraditional because it is not prompted or provoked by the availability of a well-articulated rival world view. If you like, the unitraditional picture explains how one could get paradigm change by developments entirely internal to the dynamic of a particular paradigm. More interesting, and more challenging, is the problem of multitraditional paradigm shifts, that is, basic changes of world view which arise from competition between rival paradigms. To deal with such cases, we need to complicate our fairy story a bit.

Here, we need to imagine two of our complexes already well developed, and radically divergent (i.e., with different ontologies, different methodologies, and different axiologies). If we ask under what circumstances it would be reasonable for the partisans of C_1 to abandon it and accept C_2, some answers come immediately to mind. Suppose, for instance, it can be shown that the central theories of C_1 look worse than the theories of C_2, even by the standards of C_1. As we have seen, Kuhn denies that this is possible, since he says that the theories associated with a particular paradigm will always look better by its standards than will the theories of rival paradigms.[10] But as we have already seen, there is no way of guaranteeing in advance that the methods and standards of C_1 will always give the epistemic nod to theories associated with C_1, since it is always possible (and has sometimes happened) that rival paradigms to C_1 will develop theories that do a better job of satisfying the methodological demands of C_1 than do the theories developed within C_1 itself. Alternatively, suppose someone shows that there is a set of methods M_3 which is more nearly optimal than M_1 for achieving the aims of C_1, and that those methods give the epistemic nod to the theories of C_2 rather than those of C_1. Or, suppose that someone shows that the goals of C_1 are deeply at odds with the attributes of some of the major theories of science—theories that the partisans of C_1 themselves endorse—and that, by contrast, the cognitive values of C_2 are typified by those same theories. Again, new evidence might emerge which indicates the nonrealizability of some of the central cognitive aims of C_1 and the achievability of the aims of C_2. In all these circumstances (and several obvious ones which I shall not enumerate), the only reasonable thing for a scientist to do would be to give up C_1 and to embrace C_2.

But, once we begin to play around with the transformations permitted by the reticulational model, we see that the transition from one paradigm or world view to another can itself be a step-wise process, requiring none of the wholesale shifts in allegiance at every level required by Kuhn's analysis. The advocates of C_1 might, for instance, decide initially to accept many of the substantive theories of C_2, while still retaining for a time the methodology and axiology of C_1. At a later stage they might be led by a different chain of arguments and evidence to accept the methodology of C_2 while retaining C_1's axiology. Finally, they might eventually come to share the values of C_2. As William Whewell showed more than a century ago, precisely some such series of shifts occurred in the gradual capitulation of Cartesian physicists to the natural philosophy of Newton.[11]

In effect, I am claiming that the solution of the problem of consensus formation in the multiparadigm situation to be nothing more than a special or degenerate instance of unitraditional change. It follows that, if we can show that the unitraditional fairy tale has something going for it, then we will solve both forms of the consensus-formation problem simultaneously. The core question is whether the gradualist myth, which I have just sketched out, is better supported by the historical record than the holistic picture associated with Kuhn.

One striking way of formulating the contrast between the piecemeal and the holistic models, and thus designing a test to choose between them, is to ask a fairly straightforward question about the historical record: Is it true that the major historical shifts in the methodological rules of science and in the cognitive values of scientists have invariably been contemporaneous with one another *and* with shifts in substantive theories and ontologies? The holistic account is clearly committed to an affirmative answer to the question. Indeed, it is a straightforward corollary of Kuhn's analysis that

changes in rules or values, when they occur, will occur only when a scientific revolution takes place, that is, only when there is a concomitant shift in theories, methods, and values. A change in values without an associated change in basic ontology is not a permissible variation countenanced in the Kuhnian scheme.[12] Nor is a change in methods possible for Kuhn without a paradigm change. Kuhn's analysis flatly denies that the values and norms of a "mature" science can shift in the absence of a revolution. Yet there are plenty of examples one may cite to justify the assertion made here that changes at the three levels do not always go together. I shall mention two such examples.

Consider, first, a well-known shift at the level of methodological rules. From the time of Bacon until the early nineteenth century most scientists subscribed to variants of the rules of inductive inference associated with Bacon, Hume, and Newton. The methods of agreement, difference, and concomitant variations were a standard part of the repertoire of most working scientists for two hundred years. These rules, at least as then understood, foreclosed the postulation of any theoretical or hypothetical entities, since observable bodies were the only sort of objects and properties to which one could apply traditional inductive methods. More generally . . . , thinkers of the Enlightenment believed it important to develop rules of inquiry which would exclude unobservable entities and bring to heel the tendency of scientists to indulge their *l'esprit de système*. Newton's famous third rule of reasoning in philosophy, the notorious "hypotheses non fingo," was but a particularly succinct and influential formulation of this trenchant empiricism.

It is now common knowledge that by the late nineteenth century this methodological orientation had largely vanished from the writings of major scientists and methodologists. Whewell, Peirce, Helmholtz, Mach, Darwin, Hertz, and a host of other luminaries had, by the 1860s and 1870s, come to believe that it was quite legitimate for science to postulate unobservable entities, and that most of the traditional rules of inductive reasoning had been superseded by the logic of hypothetico-deduction. Elsewhere I have described this shift in detail.[13] What is important for our purposes is both that it occurred and when it occurred. That it took place would be denied, I think, by no one who studies the record; determining precisely when it occurred is more problematic, although probably no scholar would quarrel with the claim that it comes in the period from 1800 to 1860. And a dating as fuzzy as that is sufficient to make out my argument.

For here we have a shift in the history of the explicit methodology of the scientific community as significant as one can imagine—from methods of enumerative and eliminative induction to the method of hypothesis—occurring across the spectrum of the theoretical sciences, from celestial mechanics to chemistry and biology. Yet where is the larger and more global scientific revolution of which this methodological shift was the concomitant? There were of course revolutions, and important ones, in this period. Yet this change in methodology cannot be specifically linked to any of the familiar revolutions of the period. The method of hypothesis did not become the orthodoxy in science of the late nineteenth century becuase it rode on the coattails of any specific change in ontology or scientific values. So far as I can see, this methodological revolution was independent of any particular program of research in any one of the sciences, which is not to say that it did not reflect some very general tendencies appearing across the board in scientific research. The holist model, which would have us believe that changes in methodological orientation are invariably linked to changes in values and ontology, is patently mistaken here. Nor, if one reflects on the nature of methodological discussion, should we have expected otherwise. ... Methodological rules can reasonably be criticized and altered if one discovers that they fail optimally to promote our cognitive aims. If our aims shift, as they would in a Kuhnian paradigm shift, we would of course expect a reappraisal of our methods of inquiry in light of their suitability for promoting the new goals. But, even when our goals shift not at all, we sometimes discover arguments and evidence which indicate that the methods we have been using all along are not really suitable for our purposes. Such readjustments of methodological orientation, in the absence of a paradigm shift, are a direct corollary of the reticulational model as I described it earlier; yet they pose a serious anomaly for Kuhn's analysis.

What about changes in aims, as opposed to rules? Is it not perhaps more plausible to imagine, with Kuhn, that changes of cognitive values are always part of broader shifts of paradigm or world view? Here again, the historical record speaks out convincingly against this account. Consider, very briefly, one example: the abandonment of "infallible knowledge" as an epistemic aim for science. As before, my historical account will have to be "potted" for purposes of brevity; but there is ample serious scholarship to back up the claims I shall be making.[14]

That scholarship has established quite convincingly that, during the course of the nineteenth century, the view of science as aiming at certainty gave way among most scientists to a more modest program of producing theories that were plausible, probable, or well tested. As Peirce and Dewey have argued, this shift represents one of the great watersheds in the history of scientific philosophy: the abandonment of the quest for certainty. More or less from the time of Aristotle onward, scientists had sought theories that were demonstrable and apodictically certain. Although empiricists and rationalists disagreed about precisely how to certify knowledge as certain and incorrigible, all agreed that science was aiming exclusively at the production of such knowledge. This same view of science largely prevailed at the beginning of the nineteenth century. But by the end of that century this demonstrative and infallibilist ideal was well and truly dead. Scientists of almost every persuasion were insistent that science could, at most, aspire to the status of highly probable knowledge. Certainty, incorrigibility, and indefeasibility ceased to figure among the central aims of most twentieth-century scientists.

The full story surrounding the replacement of the quest for certainty by a thoroughgoing fallibilism is long and complicated; I have attempted to sketch out parts of that story elsewhere.[15] What matters for our purposes here is not so much the details of this epistemic revolution, but the fact that this profound transformation was not specifically associated with the emergence of any new scientific paradigms or research programs. The question of timing is crucial, for it is important to see that this deep shift in axiological sensibilities was independent of any specific change in scientific world view or paradigm. No new scientific tradition or paradigm in the nineteenth century was associated with a specifically fallibilist axiology. Quite the reverse, fallibilism came to be associated with virtually every major program of scientific research by the mid to late nineteenth century. Atomists and antiatomists, wave theorists and particle theorists, Darwinians and Lamarckians, uniformitarians and catastrophists—all subscribed to the new consensus about the corrigibility and indemonstrability of scientific theories. A similar story could be told about other cognitive values which have gone the way of all flesh. The abandonment of intel-

ligibility, of the requirement of picturable or mechanically constructible models of natural processes, of the insistence on "complete" descriptions of nature—all reveal a similar pattern. The abandonment of each of these cognitive ideals was largely independent of shifts in basic theories about nature.

Once again, the holistic approach leads to expectations that are confounded by the historical record. Changes in values and changes in substantive ontologies or methodologies show no neat isomorphism. Change certainly occurs at all levels, and sometimes changes are concurrent, but there is no striking covariance between the timing of changes at one level and the timing of those at any other. I conclude from such examples that scientific change is substantially more piecemeal than the holistic model would suggest. Value changes do not always accompany, nor are they always accompanied by, changes in scientific paradigm. Shifts in methodological rules may, but need not, be associated with shifts in either values or ontologies. The three levels, although unquestionably interrelated, do not come as an inseparable package on a take-it-or-leave-it basis.

. . . The fact that the levels of agreement are sometimes insufficient to terminate the controversy provides no comfort for Kuhn's subjectivist thesis that those levels of agreement are never sufficient to resolve the debate. . . .

Kuhn . . . confusedly slides from (a) the correct claim that the shared values of scientists are, in certain situations, incapable of yielding unambiguously a preference between two rival theories to (b) the surely mistaken claim that the shared values of scientists are never sufficient to warrant a preference between rival paradigms. Manifestly in some instances, the shared rules and standards of methodology are unavailing. But neither Kuhn nor anyone else has established that the rules, evaluative criteria, and values to which scientists subscribe are generally so ambiguous in application that virtually any theory or paradigm can be shown to satisfy them. And we must constantly bear in mind the point that, even when theories are underdetermined by a set of rules or standards, many theories will typically be ruled out by the relevant rules; and if one party to a scientific debate happens to be pushing for a theory that can be shown to violate those rules, then the rules will eliminate that theory from contention.

What has led holistic theorists to misdescribe so badly the relations among these various sorts of changes? As one who was himself once an advocate of such an account, I can explain specifically what led me into thinking that change on the various levels was virtually simultaneous. If one focuses, as most philosophers of science have, on the processes of justification in science, one begins to see systemic linkages among what I earlier called factual, methodological, and axiological ideas. One notices further that beliefs at all three levels shift through time. Under the circumstances it is quite natural to conjecture that these various changes may be interconnected. Specifically, one can imagine that the changes might well be simultaneous, or at least closely dependent on one another. The suggestion is further borne out—at least to a first approximation—by an analysis of some familiar scientific episodes. It is clear, for instance, that the scientific revolution of the seventeenth century brought with it changes in theories, ontologies, rules, and values. Equally, the twentieth-century revolution in relativity theory and quantum mechanics brought in its wake a shift in both methodological and axiological orientations among theoretical physicists. But as I have already suggested, these changes came seriatim, not simultaneously. More to the point, it is my impression that the over-

whelming majority of theory transitions in the history of science (including shifts as profound as that from creationist biology to evolution, from energeticist to atomistic views on the nature of matter, from catastrophism to uniformitarianism in geology, from particle to wave theories of light) have not taken place by means of Gestalt-like shifts at all levels concurrently. Often, change occurs on a single level only (e.g., the Darwinian revolution or the triumph of atomism, where it was chiefly theory or ontology that changed); sometimes it occurs on two levels simultaneously; rarely do we find an abrupt and wholesale shift of doctrines at all three levels.

This fact about scientific change has a range of important implications for our understanding of scientific debate and scientific controversy. Leaving aside the atypical case of simultaneous shifts at all three levels . . . , it means that most instances of scientific change—including most of the events we call scientific revolutions—occur amid a significant degree of consensus at a variety of levels among the contending parties. Scientists may, for instance, disagree about specific theories yet agree about the appropriate rules for theory appraisal. They may even disagree about both theories and rules but accept the same cognitive values. Alternatively, they may accept the same theories and rules yet disagree about the cognitive values they espouse. In all these cases there is no reason to speak (with Kuhn) of "incommensurable choices" or "conversion experiences," or (with Foucault) about abrupt "ruptures of thought," for there is in each instance the possibility of bringing the disagreement to rational closure. Of course, it may happen in specific cases that the mechanisms of rational adjudication are of no avail, for the parties may be contending about matters that are underdetermined by the beliefs and standards the contending parties share in common. But, even here, we can still say that there are rational rules governing the game being played, and that the moves being made (i.e., the beliefs being debated and the arguments being arrayed for and against them) are in full compliance with the rules of the game.

Above all, we must bear in mind that it has never been established that such instances of holistic change constitute more than a tiny fraction of scientific disagreements. Because such cases are arguably so atypical, it follows that sociologists and philosophers of science who predicate their theories of scientific change and cognition on the presumed ubiquity of irresolvable standoffs between monolithic world views (of the sort that Kuhn describes in *Structure of Scientific Revolutions*) run the clear risk of failing to recognize the complex ways in which rival theories typically share important background assumptions in common. To put it differently, global claims about the immunity of interparadigmatic disputes to rational adjudication (and such claims are central in the work of both Kuhn and Lakatos) depend for their plausibility on systematically ignoring the piecemeal character of most forms of scientific change and on a gross exaggeration of the importance of rational considerations to bring such disagreements to closure. Beyond that, I have argued that, even if interparadigmatic clashes had the character Kuhn says they do (namely, of involving little or no overlap at any of the three levels), it still would not follow that there are no rational grounds for a critical and comparative assessment of the rival paradigms. In sum, no adequate support has been provided for the claim that clashes between rival scientific camps can never, or rarely ever, be resolved in an objective fashion. The problem of consensus formation, which I earlier suggested was the great Kuhnian enigma,[15] can be resolved, but only if we realize that science

has adjudicatory mechanisms whose existence has gone unnoticed by Kuhn and the other holists.

NOTES

1. The three levels are ontological, methodological, and cognitive goals [Ed. note].
2. It has been insufficiently noted just how partial Kuhn's break with positivism is, so far as cognitive goals and values are concerned. As I show in detail below, most of his problems about the alleged incomparability of theories arise because Kuhn accepts without argument the positivist claim that cognitive values or standards at the top of the hierarchy are fundamentally immune to rational negotiation.
3. Kuhn (1962).
4. Ibid.
5. Ibid., p. 159.
6. As Kuhn himself remarks, he has been attempting "to eliminate misunderstandings for which my own past rhetoric is doubtless partially responsible" (1970, pp. 259–260).
7. Kuhn (1962), p. 108; my italics.
8. Ibid., pp. 108–109.
9. Ibid., p. 149.
10. See above, p. 43.
11. See Whewell's remarkably insightful essay of 1851, where he remarks, apropos the transition from one global theory to another: "The change ... is effected by a transformation, or series of transformations, of the earlier hypothesis, by means of which it is brought nearer and nearer to the second [i.e., later]" (1851, p. 139).
12. Some amplification of this point is required. Kuhn evidently believes that there are some values that transcend specific paradigms. He mentions such examples as the demand for accuracy, consistency, and simplicity. The fortunes of these values are not linked to specific paradigms. Thus, if they were to change, such change would presumably be independent of shifts in paradigms. In Kuhn's view, however, these values have persisted unchanged since the seventeenth century. Or, rather, scientists have invoked these values persistently since that time; strictly speaking, on Kuhn's analysis, these values are changing constantly, since each scientist interprets them slightly differently.
13. See Laudan (1981).
14. For an extensive bibliography on this issue, see Laudan (1968).
15. See Laudan (1981).
16. See Chap. 1, above.

LARRY LAUDAN

REFERENCES

Kuhn, Thomas (1962). *The Structure of Scientific Revolutions* (Chicago: University of Chicago Press).
—— (1970). "Reflections on My Critics," in I. Lakatos and A. Musgrave, *Criticism and the Growth of Knowledge* (Cambridge: Cambridge University Press).
Lakatos, Imre (1978). *The Methodology of Scientific*
Research Programmes (Cambridge: Cambridge University Press).
Laudan, Larry (1968). "Theories of Scientific Method from Plato to Mach," *History of Science* 7: 1–63.
—— (1981). *Science and Hypothesis* (Dordrecht: Reidel).
Whewell, William (1851). "Of the Transformation of Hypotheses in the History of Science," *Transactions of the Cambridge Philosophical Society* 9: 139–147.

PAUL FEYERABEND, "AGAINST METHOD"

Feyerabend has argued that one of the important implications of Kuhn's work is that science should be considered just like any other source of knowledge. Western science has used one very basic and general paradigm since about the seventeenth century. Oracles, crystal balls, tarot cards, witches, and rain dances are based on other, competing paradigms. For example, what is often referred to as "scientific medicine" is just one among many ways to look at health problems. Herbal medicine, homeopathy, ayurveda, and Christian Science differ from scientific medicine and from one another. They recognize different sorts of diseases and use different kinds of cures. Each employs different standards of judging success, derived from their differing paradigms. On Kuhnian grounds, it would be unfair to claim that all forms of medicine must be judged against scientific medicine.

Why, then, is Western European–style science held in such great esteem? asks Feyerabend. He points out that it is not surprising that by using the criteria of science, which were created by science, one will be led to the conclusion that nothing surpasses science in gaining trustworthy knowledge. To Feyerabend, the use of such standards to ensure the greatness of science smacks of egomania and self-deception.

Even the question "What is science?" is more complicated than Western science would like to admit. One way to answer it is to do anthropological research into what is called science in different cultures. Of course, whether we study the members of the National Academy of Science or members of the local Psychic Society will affect our answer. Another answer uses logic as the arbiter. Such a method will show us what the ideal science would be. Since there is no ideal science in real life, the best we will be able to do is see which of our existing disciplines comes closest to the ideal. Often this requires reconstructing the real disciplines so that they can more readily be compared to the ideal discipline. This is the preferred method of many philosophers of science, according to Feyerabend. (Indeed, Hempel-Oppenheim and Carnap saw it as necessary to filling out their views, whereas Hesse saw it as unrealizable.) It is so untrue to history that Feyerabend rejects it.

The third way to answer "What is science?" takes the Kuhnian position to its limits. Feyerabend extends the notion of paradigms to include the entire way that

186

a culture looks at life. This is a reminder that knowledge itself is relative to cultural standards. Feyerabend once suggested that it is only a contemporary, Western prejudice to think that Hopi rain dances did not work. Failure to see this is the result of our inability to maintain a truly critical attitude. In other words, what Feyerabend once held was that anything could be science and that in answer to what is the best method for pursuing knowledge, Feyerabend answered, "Anything goes."

In later years, he softened this position a bit. Notice that in this selection, Feyerabend only points out that the Cuahuila Indians did much better living in the desert with their knowledge than contemporary Americans are able to do with all their vaunted science. Also, Feyerabend is now willing to say that scientific medicine did some things that tribal (nonscientific) medicine could not. Feyerabend is quick to point out that from this sort of success, it does not follow that tribal medicine should be considered worthless.

Feyerabend's conclusion is not surprising. Most philosophers of science, he would claim, are living in a dream world of uncriticized assumptions. They read Kuhn as if they were sleepwalking. The question "What is so great about science?" never gets a fair hearing. If it did get such a hearing, the answer, according to Feyerabend, would be a resounding "Nothing!"

Against Method

PAUL FEYERABEND

This book proposes a thesis and draws consequences from it. The thesis is: *the events, procedures and results that constitute the sciences have no common structure;* there are no elements that occur in every scientific investigation but are missing elsewhere. Concrete developments (such as the overthrow of steady state cosmologies and the discovery of the structure of DNA) have distinct features and we can often explain why and how these features led to success. But not every discovery can be accounted for in the

From Paul Feyerabend, "Introduction," in *Against Method*, rev. ed. (London: Routledge, Chapman & Hall, 1988), pp. 1–4. Reprinted with the permission of Verso Press.

same manner, and procedures that paid off in the past may create havoc when imposed on the future. Successful research does not obey general standards; it relies now on one trick, now on another; the moves that advance it and the standards that define what counts as an advance are not always known to the movers. Far-reaching changes of outlook, such as the so-called "Copernican Revolution" or the "Darwinian Revolution," affect different areas of research in different ways and receive different impulses from them. A theory of science that devises standards and structural elements for *all* scientific activities and authorizes them by reference to "Reason" or

"Rationality" may impress outsiders—but it is much too crude an instrument for the people on the spot, that is, for scientists facing some concrete research problem.

In this book I try to support the thesis by historical examples. Such support does not *establish* it; it makes it *plausible* and the way in which it is reached indicates how future statements about "the nature of science" may be undermined; given any rule, or any general statement about the sciences, there always exist developments which are praised by those who support the rule but which show that the rule does more damage than good.

One consequence of the thesis is that *scientific successes cannot be explained in a simple way*. We cannot say: "the structure of the atomic nucleus was found because people did A, B, C . . ." where A, B and C are procedures which can be understood independently of their use in nuclear physics. All we can do is to give a historical account of the details, including social circumstances, accidents and personal idiosyncrasies.

Another consequence is that *the success of "science" cannot be used as an argument for treating as yet unsolved problems in a standardized way*. That could be done only if there are procedures that can be detached from particular research situations and whose presence guarantees success. The thesis says that there are no such procedures. Referring to the success of "science" in order to justify, say, quantifying human behavior is therefore an argument without substance. Quantification works in some cases, fails in others; for example, it ran into difficulties in one of the apparently most quantitative of all sciences, celestial mechanics (special region: stability of the planetary system) and was replaced by qualitative (topological) considerations.

It also follows that *"non-scientific" procedures cannot be pushed aside by argument*. To say: "the procedure you used is non-scientific, therefore we cannot trust your results and cannot give you money for research" assumes that "science" is successful and that it is successful because it uses uniform procedures. The first part of the assertion ("science is always successful") is not true, if by "science" we mean things done by scientists—there are lots of failures also. The second part—that successes are due to uniform procedures—is not true because there are no such procedures. Scientists are like architects who build buildings of different sizes and different shapes and who can be judged only *after* the event, i.e., only after they have finished their structure. It may stand up, it may fall down—nobody knows.

But if scientific achievements can be judged only after the event and if there is no abstract way of ensuring success beforehand, then there exists no special way of weighing scientific promises either—scientists are no better off than anybody else in these matters, they only know more details. This means that *the public can participate in the discussion without disturbing existing roads to success* (there are no such roads). In cases where the scientists' work affects the public it even *should* participate: first, because it is a concerned party (many scientific decisions affect public life); secondly, because such participation is the best scientific education the public can get—a full democratization of science (which includes the protection of minorities such as scientists) is not in conflict with science. It is in conflict with a philosophy, often called "Rationalism," that uses a frozen image of science to terrorize people unfamiliar with its practice.

A consequence I did not develop in my book but which is closely connected with its basic thesis is that *there can be many different kinds of science*. People starting from different social backgrounds will approach the world in different ways and learn different things about it. People survived millennia before Western science arose; to do this they had to know their surroundings up to and including elements of astronomy. "Several thousand Cuahuila Indians never exhausted the natural resources of a desert region in South California, in which today only a handful of white families manage to subsist. They lived in a land of plenty, for in this apparently completely barren territory, they were familiar with no less than sixty kinds of edible plants and twenty-eight others of narcotic, stimulant or medical properties."[1] The knowledge that preserves the lifestyles of nomads was acquired and is preserved in a non-scientific way ("science" now being modern natural science). Chinese technology for a long time lacked any Western-scientific underpinning and yet it was far ahead of contemporary Western technology. It is true that Western science now reigns supreme all over the globe; however, the reason was not insight in its "inherent rationality" but power play (the colonizing nations imposed their ways of living) and the need for weapons: Western science so far has created the most efficient instruments of death. The remark that without Western science many "Third World nations" would be starving is correct but one should add that the troubles were created, not alleviated by earlier forms of "development." It is also true that Western medicine helped eradicate parasites and some infectious diseases but this does not show that Western science is the only tradition that has good things to offer and that other forms of inquiry are without any merit whatsoever. *First-world science is one science among many;* by claiming to be more it ceases to be an instrument of research and turns into a (political) pressure group. More on these matters can be found in my book *Farewell to Reason.*[2]

My main motive in writing the book was humanitarian, not intellectual. I wanted to support people, not to "advance knowledge." People all over the world have developed ways of surviving in partly dangerous, partly agreeable surroundings. The stories they told and the activities they engaged in enriched their lives, protected them and gave them meaning. The "progress of knowledge and civilization"— as the process of pushing Western ways and values into all corners of the globe is being called—destroyed these wonderful products of human ingenuity and compassion without a single glance in their direction. "Progress of knowledge" in many places meant killing of minds. Today old traditions are being revived and people try again to adapt their lives to the ideas of their ancestors. I have tried to show, by an analysis of the apparently hardest parts of science, the natural sciences, that science, properly understood has no argument against such a procedure. There are many scientists who act accordingly. Physicians, anthropologists and environmentalists are starting to adapt their procedures to the values of the people they are supposed to advise. I am not against a science so understood. Such a science is one of the most wonderful inventions of the human mind. But I am against ideologies that use the name of science for cultural murder.

NOTES

1. C. Lévi-Strauss, *The Savage Mind* (Chicago, 1966), pp. 4ff.
2. P. Feyerabend, *Farewell to Reason* (London, 1987).

PHILIP KITCHER, "DARWIN'S APPEAL TO BIOGEOGRAPHY"

Kitcher will offer what he terms a view with "old-fashioned virtues." We will see what he means by this. To him, confirmation is much simpler than philosophers have made it out to be. According to Kitcher, scientists try merely to find and eliminate inconsistencies, provide a unified account of their subject matter, and create workable laws, after which they consider their work confirmed.

Kitcher gives an extended example from Darwin to illustrate his point. He focuses on the strategy Darwin used in Chapter 12 of *The Origin of Species.* (The selection from Darwin appearing in Chapter 8 shows us Darwin himself struggling with the question of the laws of geographical distribution of species.) Darwin's goal is to show that his theory is better confirmed than a creationist account. Kitcher reconstructs Darwin's argument as follows.

Darwin raises four questions about the distribution of species. Darwin then argues that the creationist claim will not do. He does this by appealing to well-accepted facts showing that the creationist cannot answer all four questions consistently. Moreover, accepting the creationist line means rejecting already well-accepted views about geography. After showing that the creationist line is inadequate, Darwin goes on to show that his own views are not subject to the same criticisms as the creationist theory and that there are no other good, readily available competing theories. As for the latter, one must choose between some form of creationism or some form of descent with modification (Darwin's view). Darwin has shown that no form of creationism is consistent enough to work. Thus he has only to show that his theory is free from inconsistency and does in fact unify the subject matter. Indeed, this is the strategy that Darwin uses. Finally, when Darwin shows that glacial dispersal can explain certain biogeographical distributions, this can count as having found a law. The claim that G (the glacial story) explains B (biogeographical distributions) can be translated into a standard prediction: "If G, then B." This point harks back to positivist views about laws, prediction, and explanation. This makes it clear why Kitcher, with tongue in cheek, calls himself old-fashioned. He says in an earlier passage in his book (p. 9), "My attempts to combine what I take to be important (and currently unappreciated) insights of logical empiricism with the *apercus* (insight) of historians and sociologists will rest on a novel way" of looking at science and the philosophy of science.

Darwin's Appeal to Biogeography

PHILIP KITCHER

I hope to show that the kinds of inferences I have been discussing play a role within scientific decision making even at times of large modification of scientific practice and that they can be employed without risk of underdetermination. Previous chapters have offered both a characterization of the overall strategy of Darwin's argument for descent with modification (minimal Darwinism) and some suggestions about how the argument was transmitted, refined and accepted. . . . The present aim is to look at Darwin's reasoning at a much finer grain—as if, in our survey of his decision making, we were turning up the power of our microscope.

My discussion will be based on the most fully developed version of Darwin's reasoning, that presented in the *Origin*.[1] Darwin contends that the phenomena of biogeographical distribution offer strong support for the thesis that organisms of different species are linked through networks of descent with modification. We can start with the general problem of biogeographical distribution: Why are G's found in R (where G is some taxon and R is a geographical region)? Darwin and his contemporaries agree that answers to questions of this form should trace the histories of current ranges, explaining why organisms are where they are now in terms of their dispersal from where they used to be. There are two ways of conceiving such historical narratives: either they begin from the point at which the species was created, specifying the locus of creation, or they extend further

From Philip Kitcher, *The Advancement of Science: Science without Legend, Objectivity without Illusions* (New York: Oxford University Press, 1993), pp. 263–272. Copyright © 1993 by Philip Kitcher. Reprinted by permission of Oxford University Press, Inc.

back into the past, claiming that members of the species under discussion are modified descendants of an ancestral species. The latter option is, of course, Darwin's. The former can be attributed to characters whom we may reasonably call "creationists"—although it should not be assumed that such people share the ideas and misconceptions of contemporary "scientific" creationists.

Since the Darwinian account links species (or, more generally, taxa) to one another, it is hardly surprising that the crucial questions in biogeography, the ones that most sharply divide Darwin from the creationists, are those that turn on *comparisons*. Thus the relative merits of the two types of account are to be considered by asking questions of the form, Why are G's found in R and G*'s in R*? In Darwin's discussion there are several important versions of this general form of question.

(A) *The Neighborhood Problem*—Suppose that G and G* are anatomically and physiologically very similar, and that R and R* are relatively close (where proximity is defined by the dispersal powers of the organisms under discussion). Less pedantically: neighborhood problems ask why we find similar organisms in the same neighborhood.

(B) *The Barrier Problem*—Suppose that G and G* are anatomically and physiologically very similar, and that all paths between R and R* would lead through a region which no organism of the kinds G, G* could traverse (a *barrier* for short).

(C) *The Disconnected Range Problem*— Suppose that G = G* and that R and R* are disconnected. Less pedantically: a single species inhabits separate regions and does not live in the places between them.

(D) *The Displaceable Organisms Problem*— Suppose that R and R^* are disjoint, and when G^*'s are introduced to R they displace G's. Less pedantically: organisms not found in a region do better in that region than the native inhabitants.

Before we see how problems of these four forms play a role in Darwin's reasoning, it is important to identify the commitments of creationism. *Minimal* creationists would see their task, in issues of biogeography, as one of simply tracing the histories of ranges back to the initial creation of the species concerned. Minimal Creationist accounts start from claims to the effect that a species S was created at a place P. They immediately confront the question, Why was S created at P?, and this question can be exacerbated by posing the neighborhood problem (A). Given the wealth of instances in which similar species are found in geographically adjacent regions, there is pressure on creationists to go beyond the minimal version of their doctrine and to replace the host of disconnected facts about similar species in neighboring places with a more unified treatment.[2] Appealing to the principle of unification, we can argue cogently that minimal creationism is epistemically unsatisfactory, that we need a coherent account of why organisms are created where they are.

So it should hardly be surprising that Darwin's contemporaries moved beyond minimal creationism and offered an obvious explanation of the sites of initial creation. They suggested that there is a link between the character of the place and the traits of the organisms created in it. Assuming that the Creator acts through secondary causes, they could even think of the qualities of the site as calling forth, in some unspecified, mysterious, way, the types of organisms

that were created there. In any case, to whatever extent creationists involved or distanced the Creator in the epoch-to-epoch business of creation, they maintained a principle of well-adaptedness:

> (WA) The organisms created at P are well adapted for living in P.

(WA) admits of a strong and a weak reading. On the strong construal, well-adaptedness conforms to the idea that the Creator arranges for an optimal distribution of organisms to sites of Creation: among their contemporaries of the same type, the organisms created at P are the *best adapted* for living in P. The weak reading supposes merely that they do well in P, allowing for the possibility that some of their contemporaries might do even better.

Armed with the *strong* version of (WA), creationists can tackle (A)–(C). The treatment of the neighborhood problem begins from the idea that adjacent places are physically similar, and hence call for organisms with similar traits: the optimally adapted organism in P is likely to be akin to the optimally adapted organism in P^* if P and P^* are much alike. Both (B) and (C) can be handled by recognizing independent creations of the same, or of similar, species. However, the commitment to the strong form of (WA) introduces severe problems for the creationist, difficulties that will be highlighted by (D). Darwin's biogeographical argument begins with an acute diagnosis of why the strong form of (WA) is too strong.

Chapter XI of the *Origin* opens with a statement of the anticreationist thesis: "In considering the distribution of organic beings over the face of the globe, the first great fact which strikes us is, that neither the similarity nor the dissimilarity of the inhabitants of various regions can be accounted for by their climatal and other physical conditions" (346).[3] Darwin follows up with an array of examples: Old World environments find their counterparts in the New World, and yet the faunas and floras are quite different; South Africa, western South America, and Australia have three "utterly dissimilar" faunas, despite having extremely similar physical conditions. Much later, in discussing the distributions on oceanic islands, the attack is focused sharply as presenting conclusive objections to the strong version of (WA).

In St. Helena there is reason to believe that the naturalised plants and animals have nearly or quite exterminated many native productions. He who admits the doctrine of the creation of each separate species, will have to admit, that a sufficient number of the best adapted plants and animals have not been created on oceanic islands; for man has unintentionally stocked them from various sources far more fully and perfectly than has nature. (390)

The displaceable organisms problem spells doom for the strong version of (WA). Schematically, the creationist is faced with an inconsistent set of commitments: {G's were created in P, G*'s were created in P*, P and P* are distinct, G's and G*'s are contemporaries of the same type, organisms created at a place are better adapted for living there than any of their contemporaries of the same type, G*'s are better adapted for living in P than are G's}. Faced with the example of the plants and animals of St. Helena, creationists can consider lines of escape from this predicament. It is hardly attractive to suppose that the inhabitants of St. Helena were created somewhere else: How did they get there? What has happened to them at their original place of creation? Nor is there joy in supposing that the introduced aliens were, in fact, originally created on St. Helena: What happened to them after their original creation there? The facts of competition, including near or complete extermination, make it impossible to deny that the aliens are better adapted for life on St. Helena than are the natives.

Revisionist geography, that would question the thesis of disjointness, has nothing to recommend it, and it is similarly impossible to question the fact that the organisms that have competed on St. Helena are contemporaries of the same type. Under these circumstances, the escape tree is blocked in every direction but one. The strong version of (WA) has to go.

Now, however, we have to consider what happens to the general line of solution to comparative problems in biogeography. Initially, it seemed that the creationist would answer questions of the form, Why are G's and not G*'s created at P? by instantiating the following schema:

(1) G's are better adapted to life in P than contemporary organisms of the same type.

(2) G*'s are not better adapted to life in P than contemporary organisms of the same type.

(3) The organisms created at P are those which, among contemporaries of a particular type, are best adapted to life in P.

G's and not G*'s are created at P.

Unfortunately, (3) is equivalent to the strong version of (WA). In abandoning the strong version of (WA), creationists reopen a large class of explanatory problems. The challenge for them is to reformulate the preceding schema in a way that will deploy only a weak version of (WA).

The force of this challenge is best appreciated by noting that versions of (WA) sufficiently weak to circumvent the problems posed by (D) have to allow that there is a relatively broad class of "well-adapted" organisms that are candidates for creation at a particular place. The organisms actually created need not be the best adapted of the candidates. But now it is plain that none of the problems (A)–(C) can be solved by simply substituting a weak version of (WA).

Consider, for example, the neighborhood problem, (A). The weak form of (WA) licenses us in concluding that there is a pool of candidate organisms for creation at one place and another pool available for creation at nearby places. If organisms are simply drawn at random from these pools, then there is only a very small probability that they will be similar to one another. Each member of either pool has a counterpart in the other pool, but each is dissimilar to most of the members of the other pool. Thus the creationist fails to account for the similarity of organisms created in adjacent physical reasons.

Darwin has an alternative way of attacking the creationist attempt to solve the neighborhood problem. For similarities among neighboring organisms arise even when the environments in which they live are radically different.

On these same plains of La Plata, we see the agouti and bizcacha, animals having nearly the same habits as our hares and rabbits and belonging to the same order of Rodents, but they plainly display an American type of structure. We ascend the lofty peaks of the Cordillera and we find an alpine species of bizcacha; we look to the waters, and we do not find the beaver or musk-rat, but the coypu and capybara, rodents of the American type. Innumerable other instances could be given. (349)

With the observation that the similarities among neighboring organisms outrun the similarities of their environments, Darwin exposes the inadequacy of creationist solutions that trace similarities of form to similarities of environmental demand.

But elimination of the creationist program will only work as an argument for Darwin's own solution if he can show that there are no promising available alternatives and that his own proposal is not subject to kindred severe criticisms. We have already examined the case for the first point. For any given species, the options of

descent from a prior species or creation de novo appear to be exhaustive. Hence, we must choose between some version of descent with modification and some form of creationism. As I have already suggested, minimal creationism is untenable, except possibly as a position of last resort, a confession of ignorance in reaction to the failure of all positive efforts to explain the distributions of plants and animals. So the creationist must find some substitute for the idea of creation in response to environmental demand and the strong principle (WA) to which it gives rise. Lacking any clues about how to develop the needed account, it is hard to retain creationism as a live possibility—unless, of course, its rival is in trouble, and we find ourselves in the dismal situation of having eliminated *all* the initially promising candidates. The crucial issue, then, is the viability of Darwin's own account, and the bulk of chapters XI and XII is devoted to responding to problems and inconsistency predicaments. He faces apparently serious difficulties generated by problems (B) and (C).

We can begin to represent the inconsistency predicament generated by the barrier problem, (B), by noting that Darwin is committed to instances of statements of the following forms:

G's and G*'s show repeated similarities (homologies).

[H] Organisms with repeated similarities (homologies) are derived from a common ancestor.

G's are found in R and G*'s are found in R*.

R and R* are now mutually inaccessible for G's and G*'s.

If Darwin were to be forced to abandon [H], he would lose his successful solutions to the neighborhood problem (A), and much more besides. However, we do not yet have an inconsistency. To produce an inconsistent set of schematic sentences, we have to add the idea that present inaccessibility betokens past inaccessibility. More exactly, we would have to assume:

[PA]   If R and R^* are presently mutually inaccessible for G's and G^*'s then it would have been impossible for the common ancestor of G's and G^*'s, G_0, to radiate into both R and R^*.

In cases where he is committed to instances of the first four schematic sentences, Darwin can save his cherished principle [H] by denying the appropriate instance of [PA]. In other cases, he can resolve the threat of inconsistency by denying the claim of *present* inaccessibility. Pursuing both strategies in tandem, he turns back potentially damaging criticisms of his position based on the barrier problem.

After noting the difficulties posed by the presence of apparently impassable barriers, Darwin calls attention to the possibility that [PA] may be false.

But the geographical and climatal changes, which have certainly occurred within recent geological times, must have interrupted or rendered discontinuous the formerly continuous range of many species. So that we are reduced to consider whether the exceptions to continuity of range are so numerous and of so grave a nature, that we ought to give up the belief, rendered probable by general considerations, that each species has been produced within one area, and has migrated thence as far as it could. (353–354)[4]

Investigation of the hard cases will require Darwin to look both at the possibilities of geographical change and at the dispersal powers of organisms. On the former score, he canvasses various ways in which islands may become linked to continents, bodies of water joined, changes of climate have allowed a "high road for migration" (356). Yet, contrary to the enthusiasm of some of his contemporaries, Darwin demands that

hypotheses about past changes in geographical position must be firmly founded in hypotheses about presently acting geological processes (357).

The second part of Darwin's strategy, to which he devotes greater length, explores the ways in which *current* organisms can be transported. Focusing on the apparently difficult example of the dispersal of plants across sea water, he reports a series of experiments to test the ability of seeds to germinate after floating on sea water for various periods. The argument deserves quoting at some length.

It is well known what a difference there is in the buoyancy of green and seasoned timber; and it occurred to me that floods might wash down plants or branches, and that these might be dried on the banks, and then by a fresh rise in the stream be washed into the sea. Hence I was led to dry stems and branches of 94 plants with ripe fruit, and to place them on sea water. The majority sank quickly, but some which whilst green floated for a very short time, when dried floated much longer; for instance, ripe hazel-nuts sank immediately, but when dried, they floated for 90 days and afterwards when planted they germinated; an asparagus plant with ripe berries floated for 23 days, when dried it floated for 85 days, and the seeds afterwards germinated: the ripe seeds of Heliosciadium sank in two days, when dried they floated for above 90 days and afterwards germinated. Altogether out of the 94 dried plants, 18 floated for above 28 days, and some of the 18 floated for a much longer period. So that as 64/87 seeds germinated after an immersion of 28 days; and as 18/94 plants with ripe fruit (but not all the same species as in the foregoing experiment) floated, after being dried, for above 28 days, as far as we can infer anything from these scanty facts, we may conclude that the seeds of 14/100 plants of any country might be floated by sea-currents during 28 days and would retain their power of germination. In Johnston's Physical Atlas, the average rate of the several Atlantic currents is 33 miles per diem (some currents running at the rate of 60 miles per diem); on this average, the seeds of 14/100 plants belonging to one country might be floated across 924 miles of sea to another country; and when stranded, if blown to a favorable spot by an inland gale, they would germinate. (359–360)

Darwin apologizes for his "scanty facts," and indeed, if his task were to establish precise rates of dispersal of plant species, the trials he performed are obviously too crude. But the goal is the far more modest one of warding off the threatened inconsistency obtained by instantiating the schematic sentences presented earlier by taking the G's as species of plants and R and R^* as continent and oceanic island. To block the inconsistency it is enough to show that one of the contributing claims can be challenged, and Darwin's explorations permit him to cast doubts on the efficacy of the alleged barrier.

This is only the opening wedge of the argument. Sensitive to the point that the means of transport he has canvassed may be too tenuous—or that they may not allow for transport of the right species—Darwin indicates a number of other ways in which the threatened inconsistency could be removed. Stones embedded in the roots of trees may enclose portions of seed-bearing dirt and offer complete protection against being washed away; drift timber can thus serve as a vehicle for seeds. Birds can swallow seeds, which are excreted whole and which will germinate. Birds also carry dirt particles on their beaks or their claws. Icebergs "are known to be sometimes loaded with earth and stones" (363). When we recognize the variety of ways in which seeds can be dispersed, Darwin concludes, we should think it to "be a marvellous fact if many plants had not thus become widely transported" (364).

As I read this section of the *Origin*, Darwin has responded to a threat of inconsistency by sketching an escape tree with several open branches. He has not demonstrated that each of the problematic instances can be resolved. But he has pro-

vided grounds for thinking that the problems may not be insuperable, that there are resources within his recommended practice to find relief from inconsistency. By assembling his catalogue of potential modes of transport, Darwin indicates the lines along which solutions can be found and so provides *corrigible* grounds for thinking that solutions are available. Given his successes with other problems (for example with (A)), the existence of apparent barriers offers no block to the acceptance of his proposal for biogeographical explanation.

I shall close by considering Darwin's response to (C), the disconnected ranges problem, where his discussion focuses on a very particular example and thus supplements the general outlining of possible solutions with a concrete achievement. He begins by suggesting that the case he will treat poses an exceptionally severe challenge to his approach to biogeography.

The identity of many plants and animals, on mountain-summits, separated from each other by hundreds of miles of lowlands, where the Alpine species could not possibly exist, is one of the most striking cases known of the same species living at distant points, without the apparent possibility of their having migrated from one to the other. (365)

Darwin's predicament can be identified by the following set of schematic sentences:

> G's are found both in R and R^*.
>
> R and R^* are mutually inaccessible for G's.
>
> G's descend from a single ancestral population.
>
> [PA*] If R and R^* are presently mutually inaccessible for G's, then it would have been impossible for the ancestral population of G's, from which all current G's descend, to radiate into both R and R^*.

When we take the G's to be alpine species of plants and animals, there are numerous instantiations of these schematic sentences which commit Darwin to the first three claims. If he is to escape inconsistency, he must therefore challenge the relevant instances of [PA*].

This is carried out in the section "Dispersal during the Glacial Period" by adducing geological evidence for large changes in the earth's climate.

The ruins of a house burnt by fire do not tell their tale more plainly, than do the mountains of Scotland and Wales, with their scored flanks, polished surfaces, and perched boulders, of the icy streams with which their valleys were lately filled. So greatly has the climate of Europe changed, that in Northern Italy, gigantic moraines, left by old glaciers, are now clothed by the vine and maize. Throughout a large part of the United States, erratic boulders and rocks scored by drifted icebergs and coast-ice, plainly reveal a former cold period. (366)

During this previous cold period, Darwin claims, arctic species of plants and animals would have been able to extend their ranges throughout much of Europe and North America. But, as the climate grew warmer again, they would have been displaced from the new additions to their ranges by the return of temperate organisms, previously driven south by the advancing cold.

As the warmth returned, the arctic forms would retreat northward, closely followed up in their retreat by the productions of the more temperate regions. And as the snow melted from the bases of the mountains, the arctic forms would seize on the cleared and thawed ground, always ascending higher and higher, as the warmth increased, whilst their brethren were pursuing their northward journey. Hence, when the warmth had fully returned, the same arctic species, which had lately lived in a body together on the lowlands of the Old and New Worlds, would be left isolated on distant mountain-summits (having been exterminated on all lesser heights) and in the arctic regions of both hemispheres. (367)

So Darwin provides evidence against [PA*], while simultaneously giving an explanation of the apparently anomalous distribution.

Darwin follows up this basic story with some detailed discussions of particular instances of distribution, designed to show that the glacial dispersal story not only resolves the initial difficulty but also accounts for particularities of distribution that have appeared peculiar on extant accounts of biogeography (see, for example, 376–379 on the distribution of temperate organisms in mountainous regions of the tropics). Even without probing his further arguments, I think that enough has been said to show the prevalence of those modes of reasoning discussed in previous sections. Darwin's overall strategy is to proceed by eliminating rival hypotheses. In doing so, he formulates inconsistency predicaments for his opponents and shows how the escape trees from those predicaments are blocked. He also responds to the inconsistency predicaments that threaten his own account, either showing in some detail how there is a line of escape (the discussion of the alpine fauna and flora) or at least indicating the possibilities of amending the inconsistent set without epistemic loss (the treatment of methods of dispersal). Notice finally that there is no serious threat of underdetermination. Although there are logically possible rival hypotheses at any number of points in Darwin's argument, none of them has any plausibility, given the state of practice in natural history from which Darwin begins. Of course, one *could* suppose that the cases in which new arrivals have displaced native inhabitants involve some hushed-up conspiracy on the part of colonizing humans, or that the Welsh mountains were scored by the hand of God (or the devil), or that birds used to secrete digestive juices that would destroy any seeds they might swallow. One could suppose that an evil demon has contrived the distribution of plants and animals to deceive us. Part of Darwin's achievement is to set forth an argument that leaves extravagant hypotheses akin to extreme forms of skepticism as the only refuge for his opponents.

NOTES

1. This differs only in level of detail from that offered in the notebooks, so, in this instance, we need not worry whether we are scrutinizing his initial reasoning or a retrospective justification.
2. Here, of course, we see the force of Darwin's frequent appeals to the goal of unifying our account of geographical distribution, and of Huxley's desire to reduce the "fundamental incomprehensibilities" to the smallest possible number.
3. These numbers refer to pages in the facsimile reprint of Darwin's *Origin*, 1st ed. (Cambridge, MA: Harvard University Press, 1967).
4. It is worth noting that Darwin is here pursuing both problems (B) and (C) by effectively supposing that barrier problems can (often? always?) be tackled by recognizing a continuous range of the ancestral species on both sides of the region in which a barrier emerges. His remarks also contrast his own line of solution with creationist approaches to (C).

JOHN EARMAN, "NORMAL SCIENCE, SCIENTIFIC REVOLUTIONS, AND ALL THAT"

Of the philosophers we have read in this section, Popper, Kuhn, Lakatos, and Laudan are singled out by Earman for making two sorts of mistakes: (1) Each overemphasizes some aspect of science to the neglect of others and so yields a distorted picture of the scientific enterprise, and (2) there is no scientific method to find (just as there was no snark in Carroll's poem, "The Hunting of the Snark"*). On this, Feyerabend is right.

Looking for "the" scientific method is a mistake resulting from not separating three different aspects of science or being incorrect in one's characterization of one or all of them. What are the three different aspects? First, there is the fact (Earman thinks he has shown this earlier in his book) that whatever the valid rules of scientific inference might be, they must be probabilistic and derived from a formalization of the rules for probability. In other words, there is nothing very mysterious or hard to find about scientific rules of inference. Second, the activity of science is a function of the social organization of science. A different social organization might well have led to different methodologies. Again, the conclusion is that there is no one method of science. Third, choosing between theories is best seen as a practical decision about where to spend money and time.

Has Earman sacrificed objectivity in his account of science? His answer is that objectivity in science comes down to agreement within a community of scientists. But that agreement must be based on knowledge claims that are backed by evidence, filled out in terms of probabilistic scientific rules of inference. Objectivity that is consensual but forced by what might be called peer pressure is not an objectivity worth having.

*The snark, it turned out, was a boojum.

Laudan, Earman, and Kitcher reject the relativistic implications of the contemporary view of science that stresses (overstresses, according to Earman) the cultural aspects of science. If science must be seen as more of a cultural phenomenon than as an objective methodology in practice, incommensurability will reign supreme. This means that progress in science will make very little sense and that the claim that science gives us an objective look at the world must be either rejected outright or considered highly dubious. In the next chapter, "Realism and Antirealism," we will get a closer look at what is at stake.

Normal Science, Scientific Revolutions, and All That

JOHN EARMAN

The philosophy of science is littered with methodologies of science, the best known of which are associated with the names of Popper, Kuhn, Lakatos, and Laudan. . . . I have offered a critique of the Kuhnian version, and given the space, I would offer specific complaints about the other versions. But aside from the specifics, I have two common complaints. The first stems from the fact that each of these methodologies seizes upon one or another feature of scientific activity and tries to promote it as the centerpiece of an account of what is distinctive about the scientific enterprise. The result in each case is a picture that accurately mirrors some important facets of science but only at the expense of an overall distortion. The second common complaint is that these philosophers, as well as many of their critics, are engaged in a snark hunt in trying to find The Methodology of Science. The hunt is fueled by a conflation of three aspects of science and/or by a wrongheaded perspective on one or more of these aspects.

From John Earman, *Bayes or Bust* (Cambridge, MA: MIT Press, 1992), pp. 203–205. Copyright © 1992 Massachusetts Institute of Technology.

The first and, to my mind, the most interesting aspect is the epistemic one. I insist (in my Bayesian mode) that this aspect be explained in Bayesian terms. This implies that all valid rules of scientific inference must be derived from the probability axioms and the rule of conditionalization. It follows that there is nothing left for the methodologists to do in this area. Another implication is that the methodologists are wasting their time in searching for a demarcation criterion that will draw a bright red line between science and nonscience in terms of the methodology of belief formation and validation, for it is just all Bayesianism through and through, whether the setting is the laboratory or the street. What does demarcate science as it is now practiced is the professionalized character of its quest for well-founded belief.

This brings me to the social/institutional aspect of science, which is responsible for many of the characteristic features of scientific activity. Why, for example, do scientists display the Mertonian virtue of communalism, openly sharing information? Not because they also possess the other Mertonian virtue of disinterestedness and strive selflessly to advance scientific knowledge rather than their own agendas. On the contrary, communalism is explained by coupling the selfish desire for recognition, which obviously does motivate most scientists, with the current institutional arrangement that gives credit for a discovery to the person who first publishes it in a professional journal.[1] Such arrangements are clearly contingent, since the course of history might well have evolved a different set of protocols. And if it had evolved a very different set, science as currently practiced would not exist. Whether the practice that did evolve would deserve to be called science is a nice question that in general will not have a definite answer unless one believes, as I do not, that there are identifiable essences attached to the concept of science. I most certainly do not draw from this line of reasoning the conclusion that because they are contingent, the current social/institutional arrangements of science and the characteristics they foster are not worthy objects of study. But I do caution against trying to use the results of such a study to build an account of The Methodology of Science.

Finally, there are decisions about the tactics and strategies of scientific research, an aspect of science that the methodologists have taken as their main theater of operations. A typical issue here might (with only mild caricature) be posed thus: "My old paradigm has an impressive record of predictive and explanatory success. But lately it has been unable to generate any novel predictions that stand up to experimental test, and it has been unable to resolve several long-standing anomalies. Should I continue to tinker with it in the hope that its fortunes can be revived, or should I switch allegiance to a rival paradigm?" I suggest that this and similar issues should be seen as practical decisions about the allocation of intellectual and economic resources. From this perspective, there is nothing left for the methodologists to do except to repeat, perhaps in disguised form, the advice to choose the action that maximizes expected utility.

In sum, I agree with Feyerabend that there is no Methodology. But my reasons do not stem from an ideology of anarchism or Dadaism; nor do they rely on incommensurability and fellow travelers. A little Bayesianism and a lot of calm reflection are all that is needed.

It might be complained that the picture I have sketched leaves out the interactions among the three aspects of science I have identified. I agree that these interactions generate a number of unresolved problems. I have, for example, tried to highlight in this chapter and the preceding one the curious relationship between the epistemic and social aspects as regards the notion of scientific objectivity. A key component of scientific objectivity is agreement among members of the relevant scientific community. But an objectivity worth having requires an individualism: the consensus must emerge not from social pressures but from an evidence-driven merger of individual opinions operating under Bayesian strictures. The account I have given of the matter is far from complete, and I am unsure about what else is needed to complete the story. But I do not think that Methodology is the answer.

NOTE

1. As I learned from David Hull's lecture "Why Scientists Behave Scientifically," delivered in the Pittsburgh Series in the Philosophy of Science, September 1990. Philip Kitcher pointed out to me that Merton himself offered an explanation along these lines (see Merton, R.K. (1973). "The Normative Structure of Science," in *The Sociology of Science* (Chicago: University of Chicago Press).).

EXERCISES

1. Why would Carnap and Popper be characterized as positivists?
2. What are the major similarities in the views of Kuhn and Lakatos? How do they differ from Popper's?
3. Using Laudan's criticism of Kuhn, construct a Laudan-like criticism of Popper and Feyerabend.
4. Why doesn't the article by Matthews show that cosmology is a pseudoscience?
5. How do Kitcher and Earman differ from Kuhn and Popper? Exactly what is there in Kitcher that would make someone refer to his views as positivist? Does he have anything in common with Hempel-Oppenheim?

4

Realism and Antirealism

In Chapter 1, we saw that one sense for *realism* was the view that the world was just as it is experienced—put another way, that what we experience is literally true of the world. Realists in the philosophy of science hold that scientific theories tell us just what the world is like—that what scientific theories say is literally true about the world. This means that a realistic interpretation of science requires a belief in a world separate from ourselves, a world that exists independent of our observing it, with properties that likewise exist independently of our observing them. Put briefly, there is an objective, external world.

Realists will admit that much of scientific observation is theory-laden, but they point out that from this it does not follow that all scientific claims are totally subjective. Realists admit that there are social and cultural influences on science, but they go on to say that the scientific method, when properly applied, can wash out the bias of these influences, thereby getting us to knowledge of how the world really is. You should recognize in this characterization of scientific realism the positivist distinction between the context of justification and the context of discovery (where all social and cultural realism was a basic assumption of the positivist ideal of science progressing in the sense of getting closer and closer to the truth).

Realism and objectivity go together. One guarantees the other. So it is not surprising that the rejection of realism, the view called antirealism, goes with subjectivity. And with subjectivity comes relativity. The relativist, antirealist picture of science grows out of a stress on theory-laden observation, incommensurability of paradigms, holism, and the work of Kuhn (and, to a lesser extent, Feyerabend).

The debate between realists and antirealists concerns two major issues. One has to do with whether it makes sense to say that science tells us the literal truth about the world. The other concerns theoretical entities. Just about all theories make use of theoretical entities. They are theoretical in the sense that they are not observable (muon, black hole, gravity, ego) or significantly less observable (gene, atom, magnetic field) than objects such as onions, desks, and opossums. If we accept a theory, are we committed to saying that the theoretical entities mentioned in the theory exist? Positivists were less realistic when it came to the existence of theoretical entities.

It is worth distinguishing another kind of concern that grows out of the realist-antirealist debate. It results from an analysis of objectivity that is worth rehearsing here. There are arguments to the effect that science is not objective. But if it is not objective, then what? The usual reply is that it is subjective. If that means that it varies from person to person or from culture to culture or from epoch to epoch, then science can be considered *relative* to each scientist, culture, or epoch.

Now consider incommensurability, as Kuhn described it in Chapter 3. One reason for incommensurability can be cultural relativity. Two very different cultures may have two very different ways of looking at the world and two very different ways of explaining the world. They may also have two very different standards for what counts as a good prediction. This sort of relativism will obviously lead to incommensurability. In the relativist view, there would be no warranted way to say that one culture's science was better than another's.

A relativist view of science, then, has political implications. An example of the political implications would be how one acts toward and funds projects that are considered by the majority to be most likely wrong, such as cold fusion, or totally wrongheaded, such as the pyramids of Central America's having been built by visitors from outer space. The National Institutes of Health now fund research into nontraditional health care. This may show that standards of science, wrong and wrongheaded, may change. It may also show that politically organized science is subject to political pressure.

If we stretch relativism so that it covers both what we normally call science (which, as relativists point out, is basically Western European science) and what we normally call general worldviews (such as Native American beliefs), then we will never be able rationally to justify choosing science over some other very different, general worldview. For example, trying to convince an isolated tribe in New Guinea that floods are better protected against by levees than by special dances would, according to relativism, be pure presumption. What underlies such presumption is, of course, reminiscent of whatever justified colonialism and evangelizing. What acted as justifications for them? A set of values that included greed and pride.

One might be attracted to relativism in the philosophy of science because one has already found the politically implied views of relativism comforting. That is, it is all too easy to be politically oriented and so argue for relativism precisely to find science biased by the values one finds detestable. Conversely, one might find the logic of the arguments leading to relativism in the philosophy of science more convincing than the arguments leading to any of the other antirelativist positions.

In this case, one would have the choice to stretch the relativism or not. One would also have the choice to act on the political implications of the relativism.

In his discussion of realism and antirealism, Ian Hacking pays no attention to the relativism side of the family. He prefers to concentrate on the question "Must science be committed to the existence of theoretical entities?" In this way, he avoids all of the politically related questions about the nature of Western science. Larry Laudan, by contrast, is explicitly scornful of those who are led to relativism for political purposes. In Chapter 7, we will see feminists squaring off against what they see as the all-too-often ignored politically aggrandizing, self-interested nature of science.

Theories of truth are featured players in the realism-versus-antirealism debate. Before getting enmeshed in that debate, some background in truth will help.

We will look at three very traditional theories of truth. Here is a brief rundown of each.

The Correspondence Theory

A statement's truth lies in its correspondence to the fact that it is about. If a statement is not about a fact, it is incapable of being either true or false. Understanding the correspondence theory of truth requires careful analysis of the words *corresponds*, *fact*, and *about*. Many philosophers believe that as stated, the correspondence theory cannot deliver on the need for clarity in their meaning. In the correspondence theory, "snow is white" is true when and only when snow is white and false otherwise.

The Coherence Theory

A statement's truth consists in its fitting together with already accepted statements. The already accepted statements or truths make up one interlocking system. This should remind you of holism as it was discussed in Chapter 1. Antirealists often cite the strengths of holism in support of their views. There are two versions of coherence. In one version, the already accepted truths are *all* of the already accepted truths. In another version, the already accepted truths are limited to a few key truths at the core of the system of truths. Coherence has to fill out the concept of "fits together" and, in the second version, explain why the core of truths is accepted. The important difference between correspondence and coherence for the realism-antirealism debate is that coherence makes no mention of what the world is really like outside of our acceptances of statements. Coherence is the theory of truth favored by many antirealists. According to the coherence theory of truth, "snow is white" is true if and only if it fits with statements such as "ermine is usually white," "ice is cold," "water has many forms," and so on.

The Pragmatic Theory

Pragmatists—especially William James (1842–1910)—talk about the truth of ideas. For pragmatism, the truth of an idea is defined by whether or not acting on it puts us into a (more) useful relationship with the world. Pragmatism assumes an external world, but pragmatism does not assume that we can know precisely what that world is like except for how we wind up relating to it. According to this definition, there are degrees of truth. Some philosophers consider this a weakness. Pragmatism owes us a good analysis of usefulness. There is another traditionally cited weakness. *True* and *useful* just do not seem to be the same. Lots of ideas are useful—for example, in Nazi Germany, it would have been very useful to hold the idea that Hitler was right about the Jews. But that is not enough to make it true. According to the pragmatic theory of truth, "snow is white" is true when and only when I take that white stuff, treat it as I would treat snow and make a snowman, and do in fact get what I really want, namely, first prize in the snowman-making contest.

LARRY LAUDAN, "AGAINST RELATIVISM"

Laudan makes it plain that he rejects the view that "the way we take things to be is quite independent of the way things are." This slogan, he claims, is the basis of the relativist position. Some contemporary philosophy of science (e.g., the ideas of Kuhn and Feyerabend) supports this relativist contention. We have already seen Laudan critique Kuhn (Chapter 3), and now we will get a glimpse of his overall opinion of relativism.

Laudan tells us that a proper understanding of science will not support relativism. Incommensurability and underdetermination of theories by facts, both of which add credence to relativism, need much more analysis than their proponents have given them. We have already devoted much space to incommensurability in Chapter 3. Underdetermination of theories by facts means that no matter how many facts we have to support one theory, there will always be another theory consistent with those facts.

Laudan thinks that there is a reason that relativists do not actively pursue a better understanding of incommensurability and underdetermination. Relativism can be used to support various political and social agendas. He cites feminists and creationists as among those who have misused incommensurability and underdetermination to further their political agendas. You will be able to evaluate his charge in Chapter 7, which deals with feminist philosophy of science.

Laudan's book, written in dialogue form, tries to show the incoherence of the relativist view and the beginnings of a strong version of antirelativism, which we can call pragmatic realism. Laudan's strategy here in dealing with two competing philosophical theories is very much akin to what Kitcher described as the strategy used in science in his selection in Chapter 3.

Laudan, near the end of his book, offers a pragmatic-based challenge to the relativists. He asks, how else can we explain the success of science in allowing us to manipulate the world if not that our interaction with nature constrains what we believe? Laudan points out that his view is not a realist answer. The realist says that the answer to Laudan's question is that our successful theories are true. But Laudan thinks that our scientific theories are not true. Pragmatism, according to Laudan, gives us just enough objectivity to secure meaning for commensurability, progress, and objectivity in science.

Against Relativism

LARRY LAUDAN

My belief . . . is that strong forms of epistemic relativism derive scant support from a clearheaded understanding of the contemporary state of the art in philosophy of science. I am not alone in that conviction; most of my fellow philosophers of science would doubtless wholeheartedly concur. But that consensus within the discipline apparently cuts little ice with those outside it, who evidently believe that Kuhn or Quine or Feyerabend has discredited the traditional picture of scientific knowledge. More than that; in this new "post-positivist" era, many scientists (especially social scientists), literati, and philosophers outside of philosophy of science proper have come to believe that the epistemic analysis of science since the 1960s provides potent ammunition for a general assault on the idea that science represents a reliable or superior form of knowing.

Many of my fellow theorists of science, seeing how outsiders have misconstrued our discipline, are persuaded that epistemic relativism is just one of those episodic cul-

tural sillinesses that will wither and die of its own accord. They seem to think that if one either ignores the Kuhns and Feyerabends, or dismisses them with a quick reductio, it will not be long before the situation puts itself right. But, more than a quarter century after the first salvoes from the new wave hit the presses, relativism—about knowledge in general and science in particular—shows no signs of abating. Quite the contrary, the wider intellectual community comes increasingly to suppose that the claims of science to knowledge of the world, even fallibly construed knowledge, have been discredited or at least put in serious doubt. In case my observations about the rampant character of relativism may strike some readers as an exaggeration, I shall quote from a blurb sitting before me, publicizing a conference held in October 1989 at Gustavus Adolphus College, a Lutheran liberal-arts college in the American upper Midwest. The theme of the conference was "The End of Science?"; ironically, the conference itself was officially sponsored by the Alfred Nobel Foundation—the same one that awards the prizes for scientific achievement. The con-

From Larry Laudan, *Science and Relativism* (Chicago: University of Chicago Press, 1990), pp. viii–xi. Copyright © 1990 by The University of Chicago.

ference announcement opens with this statement:

As we study our world today, there is an uneasy feeling that we have come to the end of science, that science, as a unified, universal, objective endeavor, is over. . . . We have begun to think of science as a more subjective and relativistic project, operating out of social attitudes and ideologies—Marxism and feminism, for example.

Sober Lutherans have not spoken about science in such terms since Luther's point man, Melanchthon, tore into Copernicus in the sixteenth century. I do not know who the intended "we" is supposed to be in this passage; it certainly does not speak for most philosophers of science. In the face of claims of this sort (and this conference was, I fear, typical of what passes for "the humanities" these days), what is needed—or so it seems to me—is a careful analysis in nontechnical terms of what current work in philosophy of science does and does not permit us to say concerning the nature and limits of scientific knowledge. The issues need to be couched in language that makes them accessible to those outside of the philosophy of science proper but that still comes close to doing justice to the intricacy and structure of the arguments.

However, I did not write this work merely with the aim of setting the exegetical record straight. My larger target is those contemporaries who—in repeated acts of wish-fulfillment—have appropriated conclusions from the philosophy of science and put them to work in aid of a variety of social cum political causes for which those conclusions are ill adapted. Feminists, religious apologists (including "creation scientists"), counterculturalists, neoconservatives, and a host of other curious fellow-travelers have claimed to find crucial grist for their mills in, for instance, the avowed incommensurability and underdetermination of scientific theories. The displacement of the idea that facts and evidence matter by the idea that

everything boils down to subjective interests and perspectives is—second only to American political campaigns—the most prominent and pernicious manifestation of anti-intellectualism in our time. The purpose of this short volume is to explore whether the epistemology of science provides—as it is often alleged to—a grounding for such ideological laissez-faire. It is intended both as a purgative and as a prophylactic. A purgative, for those who have already succumbed to the wiles of relativism, mistakenly believing it to be a philosophically coherent position; a prophylactic, for those who—without having jumped one way or another—find themselves perplexed by the claims and counterclaims in the debate between relativism and its critics.

The dialogue form seems ready-made for such situations. When I began writing this book, it was literally a *dia*logue, with precisely two interlocutors—one speaking for the prevailing wisdom in philosophy of science and the other speaking for epistemic relativism. It quickly became obvious that such a two-way conversation could only mislead; for what has become clear since the early 1960s is that there is not one generic position within the philosophy of science but three or four. What all these positions share is a conviction that strong relativism fails to be convincing—even if they arrive at that conclusion from quite different premises. It seemed to me that in order to capture the complexity of that dialectic, I needed a dialogue between a positivist, a realist, and a pragmatist. Each of the first three of these characters is a *composite*. I daresay that there is no living philosopher who holds all the views I put in the mouths of my realist, relativist, and positivist. (By contrast, there is at least one person who hews to the line I have my pragmatist defending.) But I have gone to some pains to make sure that the general positions I attribute to the representative from each camp are actually espoused by one or another contemporary philosopher who sails under the appropriate flag.

The hardest task, at least the one I have labored over the longest, is that of finding a suitable voice for the relativist. I believe the relativist position to be profoundly wrong-headed; because I know that about myself and because I am not interested in cheap victories, I have tried my best to make this relativist clever and argumentatively adept. (I note in passing that I have not been helped very much in this task by the sorry state of the relativist literature.) Notwithstanding, I have cited chapter and verse for all the major doctrines that I have my relativist espousing and defending.[1] Those sympathetic to relativism will—*if* the dialogue is successful—disclaim being *that* sort of relativist. Well and good. Nothing would please me more than the discovery that no one is prepared to lay claim to the relativist heritage in this form. But against those who may think I have misconstrued that heritage, I am prepared to defend the claim that much of the literature of contemporary relativism is committed to most of the views under discussion here.

NOTE

1. I should note for the record that two of the thinkers who loom large in the conceptual universe of the relativist of my dialogue (Kuhn and Quine) disavow the relativist label. Both are serious and conscientious scholars, who can readily see many of the paradoxes of relativism; but intentions are less important here than consequences. Kuhn's and Quine's writings have unmistakable relativist implications, a fact that few card-carrying relativists have overlooked. One simply cannot address contemporary relativism and ignore how central Kuhnian and Quinean themes have become for that tradition.

IAN HACKING, "WHAT IS SCIENTIFIC REALISM?"

Hacking begins by defining realism and antirealism. He takes the debate to be over the question "Do the theoretical entities described by correct theories exist?" Realism answers yes; antirealism answers no. Hacking tells us about an experiment dealing with quarks. Part of the experiment requires spraying with positrons. "Well," thinks Hacking, "if you can spray it, it must exist." He spells this out to mean that where there are almost endless and successful manipulations of the theoretical, there must be something that is being manipulated. This makes Hacking a realist, since he could have stopped by noting the successes of the manipulation. If he had done this, he would be an instrumentalist.

Hacking goes on to distinguish between realism about theories and realism about entities. He could not avoid the issue of realism about theories because he talked about the theoretical entities of correct theories. Trying to understand what makes a correct theory will involve one in the realism-antirealism question. Realism about entities asks if theoretical entities exist. Realism about theories asks if theories are true. But we need even more distinctions. Hacking uses the work of W. Newton-Smith, who discusses scientific realism in three ways:

1. Ontologically: Whether a scientific theory is true or false depends on how the world is.

2. Causally: If a theory is true, the theoretical terms are the causes for our observations (when we deal with that theory).

3. Epistemologically: Our belief that theories are true can be justified, and our belief that theoretical entities exist can also be justified.

Antirealism can deny that theories are true or that we are justified in believing that theories are true. We have seen that instrumentalism denies that theories are true. Bas van Fraassen, who we will read next, denies that we can be justified in thinking that the parts of theories that describe theoretical entities are true but accepts a variation of contention 1, namely, that the part of any theory that describes observations can be true and is true in virtue of how the world is. Notice that when 1 or 3 is denied, 2 makes no sense.

How about Hacking? Where does he stand according to Newton-Smith's look at realism?

Hacking is a realist with respect to entities and theories. So his realism about theories is that they are true and made true by the world; hence we can be justified in thinking that theories are true and that their theoretical entities exist. His realism about entities is that we can be justified in our belief that they exist and that they cause our observations, but from this it does not follow that they are in any *theory*. They can be theoretical, not in the sense of being in a theory, but rather in the sense that they are unobservable but still existing. The entities might be far too complicated for any theory. Cartwright (Chapter 2) is committed to such a view by her claim that the universe at bottom is very untidy.

Hacking's final point is that if we talk about the realism-antirealism issue as it concerns scientific theory, we will be led in the direction of metaphysics because the concepts needing analysis are (among others) truth, meaning, and representation. Metaphysics is interesting, but the arguments are, as he puts it, not decisive. Hacking suggests that we focus on experimentation in science. This will keep us from metaphysics and antirealism.

What Is Scientific Realism?

IAN HACKING

Scientific realism says that the entities, states and processes described by correct theories really do exist. Protons, photons, fields of force, and black holes are as real as toenails, turbines, eddies in a stream, and volcanoes. The weak interactions of small particle physics are as real as falling in love. Theories about the structure of molecules

From Ian Hacking, *Representing and Intervening* (Cambridge: Cambridge University Press, 1988), pp. 21–31. © Cambridge University Press 1983. Reprinted with the permission of Cambridge University Press.

that carry genetic codes are either true or false, and a genuinely correct theory would be a true one.

Even when our sciences have not yet got things right, the realist holds that we often get close to the truth. We aim at discovering the inner constitution of things and at knowing what inhabits the most distant reaches of the universe. Nor need we be too modest. We have already found out a good deal.

Anti-realism says the opposite: there are no such things as electrons. Certainly there are phenomena of electricity and of inheritance but we construct theories about tiny states, processes and entities only in order to predict and produce events that interest us. The electrons are fictions. Theories about them are tools for thinking. Theories are adequate or useful or warranted or applicable, but no matter how much we admire the speculative and technological triumphs of natural science, we should not regard even its most telling theories as true. Some anti-realists hold back because they believe theories are intellectual tools which cannot be understood as literal statements of how the world is. Others say that theories must be taken literally—there is no other way to understand them. But, such anti-realists contend, however much we may use the theories we do not have compelling reasons to believe they are right. Likewise anti-realists of either stripe will not include theoretical entities among the kinds of things that really exist in the world: turbines yes, but photons no.

We have indeed mastered many events in nature, says the anti-realist. Genetic engineering is becoming as commonplace as manufacturing steel, but do not be deluded. Do not suppose that long chains of molecules are really there to be spliced. Biologists may think more clearly about an amino acid if they build a molecular model out of wire and coloured balls. The model may help us arrange the phenomena in our minds. It may suggest new microtechnology, but it is not a literal picture of how things really are. I could make a model of the economy out of pulleys and levers and ball bearings and weights. Every decrease in weight M (the "money supply") produces a decrease in angle I (the "rate of inflation") and an increase in the number N of ball bearings in this pan (the number of unemployed workers). We get the right inputs and outputs, but no one suggests that this is what the economy *is*.

IF YOU CAN SPRAY THEM, THEN THEY ARE REAL

For my part I never thought twice about scientific realism until a friend told me about an ongoing experiment to detect the existence of fractional electric charges. These are called quarks. Now it is not the quarks that made me a realist, but rather electrons. Allow me to tell the story. It ought not to be a simple story, but a realistic one, one that connects with day to day scientific research. Let us start with an old experiment on electrons.

The fundamental unit of electric charge was long thought to be the electron. In 1908 J.A. Millikan devised a beautiful experiment to measure this quantity. A tiny negatively charged oil droplet is suspended between electrically charged plates. First it is allowed to fall with the electric field switched off. Then the field is applied to hasten the rate of fall. The two observed terminal velocities of the droplet are combined with the coefficient of viscosity of the air and the densities of air and oil. These, together with the known value of gravity, and of the electric field, enable one to compute the charge on the drop. In repeated experiments the charges on these drops are small integral multiples of a definite quantity. This is taken to be the minimum charge, that is, the charge on the electrons. Like all experiments, this one makes assumptions that are only roughly correct: that the drops are spherical, for instance. Millikan at first ignored the fact that the drops are not large compared to the mean free path of air molecules so they get bumped about a bit. But the idea of the experiment is definitive.

The electron was long held to be the unit of charge. We use e as the name of that charge. Small particle physics, however, increasingly suggests an entity, called a quark, that has a charge of $1/3\,e$. Nothing in theory suggests that quarks have independent existence; if they do come into being, theory implies, then they react immediately and are gobbled up at once. This has not deterred an ingenious experiment started by La Rue, Fairbank and Hebard at Stanford. They are hunting for "free" quarks using Millikan's basic idea.

Since quarks may be rare or short-lived, it helps to have a big ball rather than a tiny drop, for then there is a better chance of having a quark stuck to it. The drop used, although weighing less than 10^{-4} grams, is 10^7 times bigger than Millikan's drops. If it were made of oil it would fall like a stone, almost. Instead it is made of a substance called niobium, which is cooled below its superconducting transition temperature of 9 K. Once an electric charge is set going round this very cold ball, it stays going, forever. Hence the drop can be kept afloat in a magnetic field, and indeed driven back and forth by varying the field. One can also use a magnetometer to tell exactly where the drop is and how fast it is moving.

The initial charge placed on the ball is gradually changed, and, applying our present technology in a Millikan-like way, one determines whether the passage from positive to negative charge occurs at zero or at $\pm 1/3\,e$. If the latter, there must surely be one loose quark on the ball. In their most recent preprint, Fairbank and his associates report four fractional charges consistent with $+1/3\,e$, four with $-1/3\,e$, and 13 with zero.

Now how does one alter the charge on the niobium ball? "Well, at that stage," said my friend, "we spray it with positrons to increase the charge or with electrons to decrease the charge." From that day forth I've been a scientific realist. *So far as I'm concerned, if you can spray them, then they are real.*

Long-lived fractional charges are a matter of controversy. It is not quarks that convince me of realism. Nor, perhaps, would I have been convinced about electrons in 1908. There were ever so many more things for the sceptic to find out: There was that nagging worry about inter-molecular forces acting on the oil drops. Could that be what Millikan was actually measuring? So that his numbers showed nothing at all about so-called electrons? If so, Millikan goes no way towards showing the reality of electrons. Might there be minimum electric charges, but no electrons? In our quark example we have the same sorts of worry. Marinelli and Morpurgo, in a recent preprint, suggest that Fairbank's people are measuring a new electromagnetic force, not quarks. What convinced me of realism has nothing to do with quarks. It was the fact that by now there are standard emitters with which we can spray positrons and electrons—and that is precisely what we do with them. We understand the effects, we understand the causes, and we use these to find out something else. The same of course goes for all sorts of other tools of the trade, the devices for getting the circuit on the supercooled niobium ball and other almost endless manipulations of the "theoretical."

WHAT IS THE ARGUMENT ABOUT?

The practical person says: consider what you use to do what you do. If you spray electrons then they are real. That is a healthy reaction but unfortunately the issues cannot be so glibly dismissed. Anti-realism may sound daft to the experimentalist, but questions about realism recur again and again in the history of knowledge. In addition to serious verbal difficulties over the meanings of "true" and "real," there are substantive questions. Some arise from an intertwining of realism and other philosophies. For example, realism has, historically, been mixed up with materialism, which, in one version, says everything that exists is built up out of tiny material building blocks. Such a materialism will be realistic about atoms, but may then be anti-realistic about "immaterial" fields of force. The dialectical materialism of some orthodox Marxists gave many modern theoretical entities a very hard time. Lysenko rejected Mendelian genetics partly because he doubted the reality of postulated "genes."

Realism also runs counter to some philosophies about causation. Theoretical entities are often supposed to have causal powers: electrons neutralize positive charges on niobium balls. The original nineteenth-century positivists wanted to do science without ever speaking of "causes," so they tended to reject theoretical entities too. This kind of anti-realism is in full spate today.

Anti-realism also feeds on ideas about knowledge. Sometimes it arises from the doctrine that we can know for real only the subjects of sensory experience. Even fundamental problems of logic get involved; there is an anti-realism that puts in question what it is for theories to be true or false.

Questions from the special sciences have also fuelled controversy. Old-fashioned astronomers did not want to adopt a realist attitude to Copernicus. The idea of a solar system might help calculation, but it does not say how the world really is, for the earth, not the sun, they insisted, is the centre of the universe. Again, should we be realists about quantum mechanics? Should we realistically say that particles do have a definite although unknowable position and momentum? Or at the opposite extreme should we say that the "collapse of the wave packet" that occurs during microphysical measurement is an interaction with the human mind?

Nor shall we find realist problems only in the specialist natural sciences. The human sciences give even more scope for debate. There can be problems about the libido, the super ego, and the transference of which Freud teaches. Might one use psychoanalysis to understand oneself or another, yet cynically think that nothing answers to the network of terms that occurs in the theory? What should we say of Durkheim's supposition that there are real, though by no means distinctly discernible, social processes that act upon us as inexorably as the laws of gravity, and yet which exist in their own right, over and above the properties of the individuals that constitute society? Could one coherently be a realist about sociology and an anti-realist about physics, or vice versa?

Then there are meta-issues. Perhaps realism is as pretty an example as we could wish for, of the futile triviality of basic philosophical reflections. The questions, which first came to mind in antiquity, are serious enough. There was nothing wrong with asking, once, Are atoms real? But to go on discussing such a question may be only a feeble surrogate for serious thought about the physical world.

That worry is anti-philosophical cynicism. There is also philosophical anti-philosophy. It suggests that the whole family of issues about realism and anti-realism is mickey-mouse, founded upon a prototype that has dogged our civilization, a picture of knowledge "representing" reality. When the idea of correspondence between thought and the world is cast into its rightful place—namely, the grave—will not, it is asked, realism and anti-realism quickly follow?

MOVEMENTS, NOT DOCTRINES

Definitions of "scientific realism" merely point the way. It is more an attitude than a clearly stated doctrine. It is a way to think about the content of natural science. Art and literature furnish good comparisons, for not only has the word "realism" picked up a lot of philosophical connotations: it also denotes several artistic movements. During the nineteenth century many painters tried to escape the conventions that bound them to portray ideal, romantic, historical or religious topics on vast and energetic canvases. They chose to paint scenes from everyday life. They refused to "aestheticize" a scene. They accepted material that was trivial or banal. They refused to idealize it, refused to elevate it: they would not even make their pictures picturesque. Novelists adopted this realist stance, and in consequence we have the great tradition in French literature that passes through Flaubert and which issues in Zola's harrowing descriptions of industrial Europe. To quote an unsympathetic definition of long ago, "a realist is one who deliberately declines to select his subjects from the beautiful or harmonious, and, more especially, describes ugly things and brings out details of the unsavoury sort."

Such movements do not lack doctrines. Many issued manifestos. All were imbued with and contributed to the philosophical sensibilities of the day. In literature some latterday realism was called positivism. But we speak of movements rather than doctrine, of creative work sharing a family of motivations, and in part defining itself in opposition to other ways of thinking. Scientific realism and anti-realism are like that: they too are movements. We can enter their discussions armed with a pair of one-paragraph definitions, but once inside we shall encounter any number of competing and divergent opinions that comprise the philosophy of science in its present excited state.

TRUTH AND REAL EXISTENCE

With misleading brevity I shall use the term "theoretical entity" as a portmanteau word for all that ragbag of stuff postulated by theories but which we cannot observe. That means, among other things, particles, fields, processes, structures, states and the like. There are two kinds of scientific realism, one for theories, and one for entities.

The question about theories is whether they are true, or are true-or-false, or are candidates for truth, or aim at the truth.

The question about entities is whether they exist.

A majority of recent philosophers worries most about theories and truth. It might seem that if you believe a theory is true, then you automatically believe that the entities of the theory exist. For what is it to think that a theory about quarks is true, and yet deny that there are any quarks? Long ago Bertrand Russell showed how to do that. He was not, then, troubled by the truth of theories, but was worried about unobservable entities. He thought we should use logic to rewrite the theory so that the supposed entities turn out to be logical constructions. The term "quark" would not denote quarks, but would be shorthand, via logic, for a complex expression which makes reference only to observed phenomena. Russell was then a realist about theories but an anti-realist about entities.

It is also possible to be a realist about entities but an anti-realist about theories. Many Fathers of the Church exemplify this. They believed that God exists, but they believed that it was in principle impossible to form any true positive intelligible theory

213

about God. One could at best run off a list of what God is not—not finite, not limited, and so forth. The scientific-entities version of this says we have good reason to suppose that electrons exist, although no full-fledged description of electrons has any likelihood of being true. Our theories are constantly revised; for different purposes we use different and incompatible models of electrons which one does not think are literally true, but there are electrons, nonetheless.

TWO REALISMS

Realism about entities says that a good many theoretical entities really do exist. Anti-realism denies that, and says that they are fictions, logical constructions, or parts of an intellectual instrument for reasoning about the world. Or, less dogmatically, it may say that we have not and cannot have any reason to suppose they are not fictions. They may exist, but we need not assume that in order to understand the world.

Realism about theories says that scientificic theories are either true or false independent of what we know: science at least aims at the truth, and the truth is how the world is. Anti-realism says that theories are at best warranted, adequate, good to work on, acceptable but incredible, or what-not.

SUBDIVISIONS

I have just run together claims about reality and claims about what we know. My realism about entities implies both that a satisfactory theoretical entity would be one that existed (and was not merely a handy intellectual tool). That is a claim about entities and reality. It also implies that we actually know, or have good reason to believe in, at least some such entities in present science. That is a claim about knowledge.

I run knowledge and reality together because the whole issue would be idle if we did not *now* have some entities that some of us think really do exist. If we were talking about some future scientific utopia I would withdraw from the discussion. The two strands that I run together can be readily unscrambled, as in the following scheme of W. Newton-Smith's.[1] He notes three ingredients in scientific realism:

1. An *ontological* ingredient: scientific theories are either true or false, and that which a given theory is, is in virtue of how the world is.
2. A *causal* ingredient: if a theory is true, the theoretical terms of the theory denote theoretical entities which are causally responsible for the observable phenomena.
3. An *epistemological* ingredient: we can have warranted belief in theories or in entities (at least in principle).

Roughly speaking, Newton-Smith's causal and epistemological ingredients add up to my realism about entities. Since there are two ingredients, there can be two kinds of anti-realism. One rejects (1); the other rejects (3).

You might deny the ontological ingredient. You deny that theories are to be taken literally; they are not either true or false; they are intellectual tools for predicting phenomena; they are rules for working out what will happen in particular cases. There are many versions of this. Often an idea of this sort is called *instrumentalism* because it says that theories are only instruments.

Instrumentalism denies (1). You might instead deny (3). An example is Bas van Fraassen in his book *The Scientific Image* (1980). He thinks theories are to be taken literally—there is no other way to take them. They are either true or false, and which they are depends on the world—there is no alternative semantics. But we have no warrant or need to believe any theories about the unobservable in order to make sense of science. Thus he denies the epistemological ingredient.

My realism about theories is, then, roughly (1) and (3), but my realism about entities is not exactly (2) and (3). Newton-Smith's causal ingredient says that if a theory is true, then the theoretical terms denote entities that are causally responsible for what we can observe. He implies that belief in such entities depends on belief in a theory in which they are embedded. But one can believe in some entities without believing in any particular theory in which they are embedded. One can even hold that no general deep theory about the entities could possibly be true, for there is no such truth. Nancy Cartwright explains this idea in her book *How the Laws of Physics Lie* (1983). She means the title literally. The laws are deceitful. Only phenomenological laws are possibly true, but we may well know of causally effective theoretical entities all the same. . . .

METAPHYSICS AND THE SPECIAL SCIENCES

We should also distinguish realism-in-general from realism-in-particular.

To use an example from Nancy Cartwright, ever since Einstein's work on the photoelectric effect the photon has been an integral part of our understanding of light. Yet there are serious students of optics, such as Willis Lamb and his associates, who challenge the reality of photons, supposing that a deeper theory would show that the photon is chiefly an artifact of our present theories. Lamb is not saying that the extant theory of light is plain false. A more profound theory would preserve most of what is now believed about light, but would show that the effects we associate with photons yield, on analysis, to a different aspect of nature. Such a scientist could well be a realist in general, but an anti-realist about photons in particular.

Such localized anti-realism is a matter for optics, not philosophy. Yet N.R. Hanson noticed a curious characteristic of new departures in the natural sciences. At first an idea is proposed chiefly as a calculating device rather than a literal representation of how the world is. Later generations come to treat the theory and its entities in an increasingly realistic way. (Lamb is a sceptic proceeding in the opposite direction.) Often the first authors are ambivalent about their entities. Thus James Clerk Maxwell, one of the creators of statistical mechanics, was at first loth to say whether a gas really is made up of little bouncy balls producing effects of temperature pressure. He began by regarding this account as a "mere" model, which happily organizes more and more macroscopic phenomena. He became increasingly realist. Later generations apparently regard kinetic theory as a good sketch of how things really are. It is quite common in science for anti-realism about a particular theory or its entities to give way to realism.

Maxwell's caution about the molecules of a gas was part of a general distrust of atomism. The community of physicists and chemists became fully persuaded of the reality of atoms only in our century. Michael Gardner has well summarized some of the strands that enter into this story.[2] It ends, perhaps, when Brownian motion was fully analysed in terms of molecular trajectories. This feat was important not just because it suggested in detail how molecules were bumping into pollen grains, creating the observable movement. The real achievement was a new way to determine Avogadro's number, using Einstein's analysis of Brownian motion and Jean Perrin's experimental techniques.

That was of course a "scientific," not a "philosophical," discovery. Yet realism about atoms and molecules was once the central issue for philosophy of science. Far from being a local problem about one kind of entity, atoms and molecules were the chief candidates for real (or merely fictional) theoretical entities. Many of our present positions on scientific realism were worked out then, in connection with that debate. The very name "scientific realism" came into use at that time.

Realism-in-general is thus to be distinguished from realism-in-particular, with the proviso that a realism-in-particular can so dominate discussion that it determines the course of realism-in-general. A question of realism-in-particular is to be settled by research and development of a particular science. In the end the sceptic about photons or black holes has to put up or shut up. Realism-in-general reverberates with old metaphysics and recent philosophy of language. It is vastly less contingent on facts of nature than any realism-in-particular. Yet the two are not fully separable and often, in formative stages of our past, have been intimately combined.

REPRESENTATION AND INTERVENTION

Science is said to have two aims: theory and experiment. Theories try to say how the world is. Experiment and subsequent tech-

nology change the world. We represent and we intervene. We represent in order to intervene, and we intervene in the light of representations. Most of today's debate about scientific realism is couched in terms of theory, representation, and truth. The discussions are illuminating but not decisive. This is partly because they are so infected with intractable metaphysics. I suspect there can be no final argument for or against realism at the level of representation. When we turn from representation to intervention, to spraying niobium balls with positrons, anti-realism has less of a grip. In what follows I start with a somewhat old-fashioned concern with realism about entities. This soon leads to the chief modern studies of truth and representation, of realism and anti-realism about theories. Towards the end I shall come back to intervention, experiment, and entities.

The final arbitrator in philosophy is not how we think but what we do.

NOTES

1. W. Newton-Smith, "The Underdetermination of Theory by Data," *Proceedings of the Aristotelian Society* 52 (1978): 72 [suppl.].
2. M. Gardner, "Realism and Instrumentalism in 19th Century Atomism," *Philosophy of Science* 46 (1979): 1–34.

BAS C. VAN FRAASSEN, "ARGUMENTS CONCERNING SCIENTIFIC REALISM"

The view that the aim of science is the construction of theories that are literally true of the world and that this truth extends to theoretical entities is called scientific realism. Thus to scientific realism, theories are not metaphors (Hesse). They are not mere instruments for prediction (instrumentalism). Nor should the existence claims of theories be reduced to observations by operational definitions (correspondence rules)—which is the positivist position. Neither can we decide by convention to construct one theory or another. Decision by convention (called conventionalism) may work, as when deciding whether a car is a sports car or merely a sporty coupe. But according to realism, conventionalism will not work in science. Van Fraassen does not see himself as realist, "metaphorist," instrumentalist, positivist, or conventionalist. How, then, does van Fraassen view theories?

Van Fraassen develops a view of science and theories such that we are not committed to the existence of theoretical entities. To do this, he turns to the question "Why do people accept theories?" Part of the reason is belief—what he terms the epistemic dimension. But there is also a pragmatic aspect to theory acceptance. In terms of belief, we only have to believe that the theory correctly describes what is observable—that is, that the theory "saves the phenomena." But any decent theory will do this. How do we choose between two competing theories when they both save the phenomena? Van Fraassen's sketch of an answer is that we appeal to the pragmatic aspects of the theory. Pragmatic aspects may be the deciding factors in acceptance, but they do not amount to evidence strong enough for believing that the theoretical entities exist. Van Fraassen emphasizes that the aim of science is to display empirically adequate theories. By this he means that everything the theory says *about what is observable* is true.

What some commentators have regarded as commitment to the (truth of the) existence of the unobservables mentioned in a theory van Fraassen says is merely commitment to use the method and models of a theory to deal with new findings. This commitment is the pragmatic aspect just mentioned.

Van Fraassen calls his antirealism "constructive empiricism." An important point of constructive empiricism is that acceptance of theories requires less belief than realists claim. Notice that van Fraassen has separated two concepts, truth and acceptance. Realists do not separate truth and acceptance. These two concepts were also separated by William James. Here is a brief rundown of what James says about truth and acceptance. (His pragmatism is a forerunner to van Fraassen's, and van Fraassen cites him approvingly when he responds to critics of constructive realism in the book *Images of Science*.)*

James, in his essay "The Will to Believe,"† says that there are two ways to understand the claim that we can find out the truth about the world, the empiricist way and the absolutist way. Absolutists claim that when we find the truth, we will know that we have found it and so will need no further search. Absolutism leads to a form of skepticism: Believe nothing until the whole truth is known—until all the evidence is in. Empiricists say that we can find the truth but may not know when we have it. We may think we have it and then discover that we are wrong. Empiricists reject the skepticism that allows for belief only

---

*Bas C. van Fraassen, *Images of Science*, ed. Paul Churchland and Clifford Hooker (Chicago: University of Chicago Press, 1985), p. 252.
†James, William, "The Will to Believe," in *The Will to Believe and Other Essays in Popular Philosophy* (New York: Dover Publications, 1956).

upon having the whole truth (full or total evidence). James says that science has been empiricist in its leanings. Science has adopted theories on less than full evidence.

According to James, there are two different "commandments." One is to know truth; the other is to avoid error. James counsels us not to raise avoiding error to a first principle of scientific method. Instead, he says that error is not so awful, nor can it be avoided. Evidence never yields a sure thing. So the fittest thing for an empiricist to do is to risk believing what may be false.

Van Fraassen would point out that it is only by getting full evidence (not a meaningful concept according to many philosophers of science) that we would be able to say that the theoretical entities of a theory actually do exist. Put another way, scientific realism, van Fraassen suggests, claims that it is wrong to accept a theory unless we have enough evidence to accept the existence of the theoretical entities. But to van Fraassen, this is the absolutist version of what it means to find out the truth about the world. But only the empiricist version makes sense.

The following quotation from *The Theory of the Gene*, first published in 1929, shows how its author, the geneticist T. H. Morgan, pictured scientific theory. His view is basically van Fraassen's.

> Between the characters that furnish the data for the theory, and the postulated genes, to which the characters are referred, lies the whole field of embryonic development. The theory of the gene, as here formulated, states nothing with respect to . . . this interval [from embryonic development to gene]. . . . The sorting out of the characters in successive generations can be explained at present without reference to the way in which the gene affects the development process.*

For another related example, go back to Mendel's first cross with peas. According to van Fraassen, the theory is true and worth accepting to the extent that the ratios are accounted for by the theory. But the data from the cross alone could not support the contention that there are factors of inheritance. How could they? The data are about ratios of tall to short pea plants. How could this ever support the claim that microscopic factors of inheritance exist somewhere in the plant?

Why is it important to choose between realism and antirealism? The answer for van Fraassen is that realism yields an unrealistic picture of science, a picture that forces us to examine all sorts of metaphysical issues. Trying to avoid the metaphysical issues is a strategy he shares with Hacking. Notice, however, that to van Fraassen, avoiding metaphysics leads to antirealism. To Hacking, avoiding metaphysics means looking to experimentation to justify realism. For van Fraassen, why science is successful, why scientific theories have made progress, and why we accept scientific theories can be answered simply by pointing to the fact that a good scientific theory must yield truths about what we experience.

---

*T. H. Morgan, *The Theory of the Gene* (New York: Hafner, 1964), p. 29.

Arguments Concerning Scientific Realism

BAS C. VAN FRAASSEN

The rigour of science requires that we distinguish well the undraped figure of nature itself from the gay-coloured vesture with which we clothe it at our pleasure.
Heinrich Hertz, quoted by Ludwig Boltzmann, letter to *Nature*, 28 February 1895

In our century, the first dominant philosophy of science was developed as part of logical positivism. Even today, such an expression as "the received view of theories" refers to the views developed by the logical positivists, although their heyday preceded the Second World War.

. . . I shall examine, and criticize, the main arguments that have been offered for scientific realism. These arguments occurred frequently as part of a critique of logical positivism. But it is surely fair to discuss them in isolation, for even if scientific realism is most easily understood as a reaction against positivism, it should be able to stand alone. The alternative view which I advocate—for lack of a traditional name I shall call it *constructive empiricism*—is equally at odds with positivist doctrine.

§1. SCIENTIFIC REALISM AND CONSTRUCTIVE EMPIRICISM

In philosophy of science, the term "scientific realism" denotes a precise position on the question of how a scientific theory is to be understood, and what scientific activity really is. I shall attempt to define this position, and to canvass its possible alternatives. . . .

§1.1 Statement of Scientific Realism

What exactly is scientific realism? A naïve statement of the position would be this: the

picture which science gives us of the world is a true one, faithful in its details, and the entities postulated in science really exist: the advances of science are discoveries, not inventions. That statement is too naïve; it attributes to the scientific realist the belief that today's theories are correct. It would mean that the philosophical position of an earlier scientific realist such as C. S. Peirce had been refuted by empirical findings. I do not suppose that scientific realists wish to be committed, as such, even to the claim that science will arrive in due time at theories true in all respects—for the growth of science might be an endless self-correction; or worse, Armageddon might occur too soon.

But the naïve statement has the right flavour. It answers two main questions: it characterizes a scientific theory as a story about what there really is, and scientific activity as an enterprise of discovery, as opposed to invention. The two questions of what a scientific theory is, and what a scientific theory does, must be answered by any philosophy of science. The task we have at this point is to find a statement of scientific realism that shares these features with the naïve statement, but does not saddle the realists with unacceptably strong consequences. It is especially important to make the statement as weak as possible if we wish to argue against it, so as not to charge at windmills. . . .

Truth must play an important role in the formulation of the basic realist position. They also show that the formulation must incorporate an answer to the question what it is to *accept* or *hold* a theory. I shall now propose such a formulation, which seems to me to make sense of the above remarks, and also renders intelligible the reasoning by realists which I shall examine below—without burdening them with more than the minimum required for this.

Science aims to give us, in its theories, a literally true story of what the world is like; and acceptance of a scientific theory involves the belief that it is true. This is the correct statement of scientific realism.

Let me defend this formulation by showing that it is quite minimal, and can be agreed to by anyone who considers himself a scientific realist. The naïve statement said that science tells a true story; the correct statement says only that it is the aim of science to do so. The aim of science is of course not to be identified with individual scientists' motives. The aim of the game of chess is to checkmate your opponent; but the motive for playing may be fame, gold, and glory. What the aim is determines what counts as success in the enterprise as such; and this aim may be pursued for any number of reasons. Also, in calling something *the* aim, I do not deny that there are other subsidiary aims which may or may not be means to that end: everyone will readily agree that simplicity, informativeness, predictive power, explanation are (also) virtues. Perhaps my formulation can even be accepted by any philosopher who considers the most important aim of science to be something which only *requires* the finding of true theories—given that I wish to give the weakest formulation of the doctrine that is generally acceptable.

I have added "literally" to rule out as realist such positions as imply that science is true if "properly understood" but literally false or meaningless. For that would be consistent with conventionalism, logical positivism, and instrumentalism. . . .

The second part of the statement touches on epistemology. But it only equates acceptance of a theory with belief in its truth.[1] It does not imply that anyone is ever rationally warranted in forming such a belief. We have to make room for the epistemological position, today the subject of considerable debate, that a rational person never assigns personal probability 1 to any proposition except a tautology. It would, I think, be rare for a scientific realist to take this stand in epistemology, but it is certainly possible.[2]

To understand qualified acceptance we must first understand acceptance *tout court*. If acceptance of a theory involves the belief that it is true, then tentative acceptance involves the tentative adoption of the belief that it is true. If belief comes in degrees, so does acceptance, and we may then speak of a degree of acceptance involving a certain degree of belief that the theory is true. This must of course be distinguished from belief that the theory is approximately true, which seems to mean belief that some member of a class centring on the mentioned theory is (exactly) true. In this way the proposed formulation of realism can be used regardless of one's epistemological persuasion.

§1.2 Alternatives to Realism

Scientific realism is the position that scientific theory construction aims to give us a literally true story of what the world is like, and that acceptance of a scientific theory involves the belief that it is true. Accordingly, anti-realism is a position according to which the aim of science can well be served without giving such a literally true story, and acceptance of a theory may properly involve something less (or other) than belief that it is true.

What does a scientist do then, according to these different positions? According to the realist, when someone proposes a theory, he is asserting it to be true. But according to the anti-realist, the proposer does not assert the theory; *he displays it*, and claims certain virtues for it. These virtues may fall short of truth: empirical adequacy, perhaps; comprehensiveness, acceptability for various purposes. This will have to be spelt out, for the details here are not determined by the denial of realism. For now we must concentrate on the key notions that allow the generic division.

The idea of a literally true account has two aspects: the language is to be literally construed; and so construed, the account is true. This divides the anti-realists into two sorts. The first sort holds that science is or aims to be true, properly (but not literally) construed. The second holds that the language of science should be literally construed, but its theories need not be true to be good. The anti-realism I shall advocate belongs to the second sort.

It is not so easy to say what is meant by a literal construal. The idea comes perhaps from theology, where fundamentalists construe the Bible literally, and liberals have a variety of allegorical, metaphorical, and analogical interpretations, which "demythologize." The problem of explicating "literal construal" belongs to the philosophy of language. In Section 7 . . . I shall emphasize that "literal" does not mean "truth-valued." The term "literal" is well enough understood for general philosophical use, but if we try to explicate it we find ourselves in the midst of the problem of giving an adequate account of natural language. It would be bad tactics to link an inquiry into science to a commitment to some solution to that problem. The following remarks, and those in Section 7, should fix the usage of 'literal' sufficiently for present purposes.

The decision to rule out all but literal construals of the language of science, rules out those forms of anti-realism known as *positivism* and *instrumentalism*. First, on a literal construal, the apparent statements of science really are statements, *capable of* being true or false. Secondly, although a literal construal can elaborate, it cannot change logical relationships. (It is possible to elaborate, for instance, by identifying what the terms designate. The "reduction" of the language of phenomenological thermodynamics to that of statistical mechanics is like that: bodies of gas are identified as aggregates of molecules, temperature as mean kinetic energy, and so on.) On the positivists' interpretation of science, theoretical terms have meaning only through their connection with the observable. Hence they hold that two theories may in fact *say the same thing* although in form they contradict each other. (Perhaps the one says that all matter consists of atoms, while the other postulates instead a universal continuous medium; they will say the same thing nevertheless if they agree in their observable consequences, according to the positivists.) But two theories which contradict each other in such a way can "really" be saying the same thing only if they are not literally construed. Most specifically, if a theory says that something exists, then a literal construal may elaborate on what that something is, but will not remove the implication of existence.

There have been many critiques of positivist interpretations of science, and there is no need to repeat them. . . .

§1.3 Constructive Empiricism

To insist on a literal construal of the language of science is to rule out the construal of a theory as a metaphor or simile, or as intelligible only after it is "demythologized" or subjected to some other sort of "translation" that does not preserve logical form. If the theory's statements include "There are electrons," then the theory says that there are electrons. If in addition they include "Electrons are not planets," then the theory says, in part, that there are entities other than planets.

But this does not settle very much. It is often not at all obvious whether a theoretical term refers to a concrete entity or a mathematical entity. Perhaps one tenable interpretation of classical physics is that there are no concrete entities which are forces—that "there are forces such that . . ." can always be understood as a mathematical statement asserting the existence of certain functions. That is debatable.

Not every philosophical position concerning science which insists on a literal construal of the language of science is a realist position. For this insistence relates not at all to our epistemic attitudes toward theories, nor to the aim we pursue in constructing theories, but only to the correct understanding of *what a theory says.* (The fundamentalist theist, the agnostic, and the atheist presumably agree with each other (though not with liberal theologians) in their understanding of the statement that God, or gods, or angels exist.) After deciding that the language of science must be literally understood, we can still say that there is no need to believe good theories to be true, nor to believe *ipso facto* that the entities they postulate are real.

Science aims to give us theories which are empirically adequate; and acceptance of a theory involves as belief only that it is empirically adequate. This is the statement of the anti-realist position I advocate; I shall call it *constructive empiricism.*

This formulation is subject to the same qualifying remarks as that of scientific realism in Section 1.1 above. In addition it requires an explication of "empirically adequate." For now, I shall leave that with the preliminary explication that a theory is empirically adequate exactly if what it says about the observable things and events in this world, is true—exactly if it "saves the phenomena." A little more precisely: such a theory has at least one model that all the actual phenomena fit inside. I must emphasize that this refers to *all* the phenomena; these are not exhausted by those actually observed, nor even by those observed at some time, whether past, present, or future. . . .

The distinction I have drawn between realism and anti-realism, in so far as it pertains to acceptance, concerns only how much belief is involved therein. Acceptance of theories (whether full, tentative, to a degree, etc.) is a phenomenon of scientific activity which clearly involves more than belief. One main reason for this is that we are never confronted with a complete theory. So if a scientist accepts a theory, he thereby involves himself in a certain sort of research programme. That programme could well be different from the one acceptance of another theory would have given him, even if those two (very incomplete) theories are equivalent to each other with respect to everything that is observable—in so far as they go.

Thus acceptance involves not only belief but a certain commitment. Even for those of us who are not working scientists, the acceptance involves a commitment to confront any future phenomena by means of the conceptual resources of this theory. It determines the terms in which we shall seek explanations. If the acceptance is at all strong, it is exhibited in the person's assumption of the role of explainer, in his willingness to answer questions *ex cathedra.* Even if you do not accept a theory, you can engage in discourse in a context in which language use is guided by that theory—but acceptance produces such contexts. There are similarities in all of this to ideological commitment. A commitment is of course not true or false: The confidence exhibited is that it will be *vindicated.*

This is a preliminary sketch of the *pragmatic* dimension of theory acceptance.

Unlike the epistemic dimension, it does not figure overtly in the disagreement between realist and anti-realist. But because the amount of belief involved in acceptance is typically less according to anti-realists, they will tend to make more of the pragmatic aspects. It is as well to note here the important difference. Belief that a theory is true, or that it is empirically adequate, does not imply, and is not implied by, belief that full acceptance of the theory will be vindicated. To see this, you need only consider here a person who has quite definite beliefs about the future of the human race, or about the scientific community and the influences thereon and practical limitations we have. It might well be, for instance, that a theory which is empirically adequate will not combine easily with some other theories which we have accepted in fact, or that Armageddon will occur before we succeed. Whether belief that a theory is true, or that it is empirically adequate, can be equated with belief that acceptance of it would, under ideal research conditions, be vindicated in the long run, is another question. It seems to

me an irrelevant question within philosophy of science, because an affirmative answer would not obliterate the distinction we have already established by the preceding remarks. (The question may also assume that counterfactual statements are objectively true or false, which I would deny.)

Although it seems to me that realists and anti-realists need not disagree about the pragmatic aspects of theory acceptance, I have mentioned it here because I think that typically they do. We shall find ourselves returning time and again, for example, to requests for explanation to which realists typically attach an objective validity which anti-realists cannot grant.

NOTES

1. *The Works of the Honourable Robert Boyle,* ed. Birch (London, 1672), vol. III, p. 13; I take the quotation from R. S. Woolhouse, *Locke's Philosophy of Science and of Language* (Oxford: Blackwell, 1971), which has an excellent discussion of the philosophical issues of that period and of Boyle's role.
2. I. Levi, "Confirmational Conditionalization," *Journal of Philosophy,* 75 (1978), 730–7; p. 737.

ARTHUR FINE, "THE NATURAL ONTOLOGICAL ATTITUDE"

Both realism and antirealism claim to offer the "correct" interpretation for science seen as a set of practices. But the approach is misguided, according to Fine. Asking for an interpretation of science is like asking for the answer to "What is the purpose of life?" It looks like an intriguing question and seems to promise an equally intriguing answer. But the question as posed has no answer because it must be posed more specifically (Fine uses the term *locally*). Do not ask, "What is the purpose of life?" or "What is the good life?" Instead ask, "Why take calculus and not art history?" or "Should I study tonight or watch TV?" With respect to understanding science, this means taking a certain stance or attitude toward it. Fine refers to this attitude as the natural ontological attitude (NOA).

To develop this attitude, one should keep three things in mind:

1. Science has a long history with no obvious and clear theme common to all the individual examples of science. (This is a point that was made by Feyerabend in Chapter 3.)

2. "Science" is not a blue-ribbon label awarded only to fine examples of something. There is no sharp line of demarcation between good science and bad science.

3. The concept of truth changes with science. There is no reason to look for or think that there is one way that science accepts hypotheses. There is no sure way to know how the world is now or how it will be viewed or understood in the future. One has to wait and see.

Fine's point about NOA made in terms of what Hacking calls entity realism would be that the rules that science uses for claiming that entities exist should also apply to philosophy. Philosophy is not, and cannot be, in a position to make special readings of statements such as "There are no monopoles." It is a conceit of philosophy to think otherwise.

The Natural Ontological Attitude

ARTHUR FINE

The "isms" [mentioned here] each derive from a philosophical program in the context of which they seek to place science. The idea seems to be that when science is put in that context its significance, rationality, and purpose, as it were, just click into place. Consequently, the defense of these "isms," when a defense is offered, usually takes the form of arguing that the favorite one is better than its rivals because it makes better sense of science than its rivals do.[1]

What are we to conclude from this business of placing science in a context, supplying it with an aim, attempting to make better sense of it, and so forth? Surely, it is that realism and antirealism alike view science as susceptible to being set in context, provided with a goal, and being made sense of. And what manner of object, after all, could show such susceptibilities other than something that could not or did not do these very things for itself? What binds realism and antirealism together is this. They see science as a set of practices in need of an interpretation, and they see themselves as providing just the right interpretation.

But science is not needy in this way. Its history and current practice constitute a rich and meaningful setting. In that setting questions of goals or aims or purposes occur spontaneously and *locally*. For what purpose is a particular instrument being used, or why use a tungsten filament here rather than a copper one? What significant goals would be accomplished by building accelerators capable of generating energy levels in excess in 10^4 GeV? Why can we ignore gravitational effects in the analysis of Compton scattering? Etc. These sorts of questions have a teleological cast and, most likely, could be given appropriate answers in terms of ends, or goals, or the like. But when we are asked what is the aim of science itself, I think we find ourselves in a

From Arthur Fine, *The Shaky Game: Einstein, Realism, and the Quantum Theory* (Chicago: University of Chicago Press, 1986), pp. 147–150. Copyright © 1986 by The University of Chicago.

quandary, just as we do when asked "What is the purpose of life?" or indeed the corresponding sort of question for any sufficiently rich and varied practice or institution. As we grow up, I think we learn that such questions really do not require an answer, but rather they call for an empathetic analysis to get at the cognitive (and temperamental) sources of the question, and then a program of therapy to help change all that.

Let me try to collect my thoughts by means of a metaphor (or is it an allegory?). The realisms and antirealisms seem to treat science as a sort of grand performance, a play or opera, whose production requires interpretation and direction. They argue among themselves as to whose "reading" is best.[2] I have been trying to suggest that if science is a performance, then it is one where the audience and crew play as well. Directions for interpretation are also part of the act. If there are questions and conjectures about the meaning of this or that, or its purpose, then there is room for those in the production too. The script, moreover, is never finished, and no past dialogue can fix future action. Such a performance is not susceptible to a reading or interpretation in any global sense, and it picks out its own interpretations, locally, as it goes along.

To allow for such an open conception of science, the attitude one adopts must be neither realist nor antirealist. It is the attitude of NOA, the natural ontological attitude. The quickest way to get a feel for NOA is to understand it as undoing the idea of interpretation and the correlative idea of invariance (or essence).

The attitude that marks NOA is just this: try to take science on its own terms, and try not to read things into science. If one adopts this attitude, then the global interpretations, the "isms" of scientific philosophies, appear as idle overlays to science: not necessary, not warranted, and in the end, probably not

even intelligible. It is fundamental to NOA that science has a history, rooted indeed in everyday thinking. But there need not be any aspects invariant throughout that history, and hence, contrary to the isms, no necessary uniformity in the overall development of science (including projections for the future). NOA is, therefore, basically at odds with the temperament that looks for definite boundaries demarcating science from pseudoscience, or that is inclined to award the title "scientific" like a blue ribbon on a prize goat. Indeed, the antiessentialist aspect of NOA is intended to be very comprehensive, applying to all the concepts used in science, even the concept of truth.

Thus NOA is inclined to reject *all* interpretations, theories, construals, pictures, etc., of truth, just as it rejects the special correspondence theory of realism and the acceptance pictures of the truthmongering antirealisms. For the concept of truth is the fundamental semantical concept. Its uses, history, logic, and grammar are sufficiently definite to be partially catalogued, at least for a time. But it cannot be "explained" or given an "account of" without circularity. Nor does it require anything of the sort. The concept of truth is open-ended, growing with the growth of science. Particular questions (Is this true? What reason do we have to believe in the truth of that? Can we find out whether it is true? Etc.) are addressed in well-known ways. The significance of the answers to those questions is rooted in the practices and logic of truth judging (which practices, incidentally, are by no means confined to acceptance or the like), but that significance branches out beyond current practice along with the growing concept of truth. For present knowledge not only redistributes truth-values among past judgments, present knowledge also reevaluates the whole character of past practice. There is no saying, in advance, how this will go. Thus there is no projectable sketch now of what truth signifies, nor of what areas of science (e.g., "fundamental laws") truth is exempt from—nor will there ever be. Some questions, of course, are not settled by the current practices of truth judging. Perhaps some never will be settled.

NOA is fundamentally a heuristic attitude, one that is compatible with quite different assessments of particular scientific investigations, say, investigations concerning whether or not there are magnetic monopoles. At the time of this writing the scientific community is divided on this issue. There is a long history of experimental failure to detect monopoles, and one recent success—maybe. I believe that there are a number of new experiments under way, and considerable theoretical work that might narrow down the detectable properties of monopoles. In this context various ways of putting together the elements that enter into a judgment about monopoles will issue in various attitudes toward them, ranging from complete agnosticism to strong belief. NOA is happy with any of these attitudes. All that NOA insists is that one's ontological attitude toward monopoles, and everything else that might be collected in the scientific zoo (whether observable or not), be governed by the very same standards of evidence and inference that are employed by science itself. This attitude tolerates all the differences of opinion and all the varieties of doubt and skepticism that science tolerates. It does not, however, tolerate the prescriptions of empiricism or of other doctrines that externally limit the commitments of science. Nor does it overlay the judgment, say, that monopoles do exist, with the special readings of realism or of the truthmongering antirealisms. NOA tries to let science speak for itself, and it trusts in our native ability to get the message without having to rely on metaphysical or epistemological hearing aids.

I promised to conclude these reflections by singing in praise of NOA. The refrain I had in mind is an adaptation of a sentiment that Einstein once expressed concerning Mozart. Einstein said that the music of Mozart (read "NOA") seems so natural that, by contrast, the music of other composers (read "realism" or "antirealism") sounds artificial and contrived.

NOTES

1. "However, there is also a positive argument for constructive empiricism—it makes better sense of science, and of scientific activity, than realism does and does so without inflationary metaphysics" (van Fraassen, 1980, p. 73). I think Van Fraassen speaks here for all the antirealists. While I cannot recommend this as a defense of antirealism, I think van Fraassen's own critique of the explanationist defenses of realism is very incisive, especially if complemented with the attack of Laudan (1984). . . . Such explanationist (or coherentist) defenses of realism are bound to fail.

2. This way of putting it suggests that the philosophies of realism and antirealism are much closer to the hermeneutical tradition than (most of) their proponents would find comfortable. Similarly, I think the view of science that has emerged from these "isms" is just as contrived as the shallow, mainline view of the hermeneuts (science as control and manipulation, involving only dehumanized and purely imaginary models of the world). In opposition to this, I do not suggest that science is hermeneutic-proof, but rather that in science, as elsewhere, hermeneutical understanding has to be gained *from the inside*. It should not be prefabricated to meet external, philosophical specifications. There is, then, no legitimate hermeneutical *account* of science, but only an hermeneutical activity that is a lively part of science itself.

REFERENCES

Laudan, Larry, "A Confutation of Convergent Realism," in *Scientific Realism*, J. Leplin (ed.) (Berkeley: University of California Press, 1984), pp. 218–249.
van Fraassen, B.C., *The Scientific Image* (Oxford: Clarendon Press, 1980).

MARTIN BUNZL, "SCIENTIFIC ABSTRACTION AND THE REALIST IMPULSE"

Bunzl begins by restating Fine's position in a way that stresses Fine's use of the concept of truth. Fine sees truth in science and truth in everyday life as being the same concept. There is no need, according to Fine, to make truth something "fancier" in science than it is in everyday life. Indeed, trying to do so is the mistake that leads to the realist-antirealist debate. What is Fine's idea of truth? Need it be correspondence to reality? Bunzl sees no reason to think so. He thinks that criticizing Fine for assuming a correspondence theory of truth, the theory held by realists, and so pointing out that Fine's NOA is really a realist-oriented position, is misguided.

But Fine's NOA is subject to criticism, according to Bunzl, because of a presupposed distinction Fine makes between what is internal to science and what is external to it. Fine claims that the NOA is internal to science and that both realism and antirealism are external. Bunzl asks why.

The answer, he proposes, is that Fine sees realism and antirealism as making claims about all of science—what Bunzl refers to as global claims. Seen in this way, realism and antirealism are external to science. But one can see realism and antirealism as making much more limited claims about instances of science—what Bunzl calls local claims. These would be claims about particular episodes within particular periods of history. If realism and antirealism are interpreted in this way, they might very well be internal to science and legitimate competitors for the NOA.

From our discussion of instrumentalism it is easy to see that instrumentalists are antirealists. It would be difficult to be an antirealist and answer the question "What are scientific theories about?" were it not for the instrumentalist reply: Scientific theories are not about anything—they are merely predictive devices.

However, Howard Stein, a philosopher of science, has argued that instrumentalism can be characterized so broadly that it actually turns into realism. Stein points out that if we take a scientific theory to be an adequate representation of reality, as opposed to a match of reality, then asking whether that representation also matches reality is totally unnecessary. For Stein, "adequate representation" can only be made sense of in terms of some version of instrumentalism, and yet still is close to realism.

Bunzl thinks that Stein has gotten away too easily. Bunzl points out that the realist view depends on truth separate from any kind of instrumentalist approach. Put another way, Stein has redefined truth in terms of "adequate representation," but this will never do for realists. A realist wants truth to be more than just adequate representation.

Stein was trying to show that the distinction between realism and antirealism may be bogus. As Bunzl goes on to tell us, Stein's major point is that the important aspect of science is its reliance on mathematics. The use of mathematics makes up the core of science. Bunzl uses this observation to make his own point about the bogus realist-antirealist dichotomy.

Realism is best seen, according to Bunzl, as a style of thinking, a way of reasoning. But it really works only with typical (macroscopic) objects and events such as hearts and livers—a heart not pumping properly, a liver not making the appropriate albumin. When a science has reached the point where most of its reasoning is at the mathematical level, realism will not be very helpful because of the abstract nature of mathematics.

Thus, taken locally, as Bunzl would put it, a scientific theory will be realist to the extent that it is not mathematical and antirealist to the extent that it is mathematical. But seeing the dichotomy as ever present no matter what the theory, for all science, is a mistake. There are not two opposing ways to see all science. Rather, there are two ways to think about particular aspects of the world.

Scientific Abstraction and the Realist Impulse

MARTIN BUNZL

In a series of important papers, A. Fine (1984a,b; 1986a,b) has developed and defended the view that the proper reading of scientific practice is neither realist nor antirealist. Instead, he argues that realism and antirealism both add something extra to a core position *which is neither*. In this discussion I reexamine his claim in the light of some criticisms. Fine's position contains an important insight, but to draw that point out requires shifting the way in which Fine poses the argument. I do so by examining an argument by H. Stein.

For Fine, the core position involves treating science as of a kind with common garden varieties of knowledge. That is, "true" in science ought to be taken as having no other connotation than it does in ordinary life:

What is it to accept the evidence of one's senses and, *in the same way*, to accept confirmed scientific theories? It is to take them into one's life as true, with all that implies concerning adjusting one's behavior, practical and theoretical, to accommodate these truths. (Fine 1984b, 95–96)

From *Philosophy of Science* 61 (1994): 449–456. Courtesy of the author and the Philosophy of Science Association.

Fine thinks this is where we should stop *without an elaboration of the concept of truth at work here* (ibid., 101). He suggests instead that, viewing science in historical context and as a human, social process, we take the scientist as operating with the same conception of truth that characterizes other human concerns (1986b, 172–173).

For Fine the core position is adequate to an account of science. Rather than thinking of realism and antirealism as full-blown alternatives to this core position, Fine thinks of them as each illicitly "inflating" the core position motivated by misguided hermeneutic commitments to "the global enterprise of 'making sense of science' " (ibid., 171).

In an engaging metaphor, Fine evokes the image of the realist looking outward from the core position in an attempt to ground science, while the antirealist looks inward (ibid.). The first tries to embrace a view that allows us to step outside language to provide a mapping from theories to the world. Here the unanalyzed concept of "truth" in the core position is given a correspondence reading. The second looks inward to restrict the domain of knowledge to the observable. What is grafted onto the core position, here, is a prescriptive restriction on the practice of science.

Both A. Musgrave (1989) and R. Miller (1989) have raised a technical objection to Fine's approach by arguing that its cogency hinges on how the notion of truth is understood. To the extent that Fine's position makes use of an ordinary conception of truth, it makes use of a notion of correspondence and hence is in effect a realist doctrine. I am unmoved by this line of criticism since truth and correspondence do not have to go hand-in-hand even on an ordinary conception of "truth": The ordinary conception of truth is well captured by Convention *T without any accompanying analysis of truth*. Convention *T* itself is compatible with both the correspondence definition and its coherentist and pragmatist competitors.

Still, this criticism notwithstanding, as Miller has argued, we can approach Fine's argument at another level. Fine's "Natural Ontological Attitude" (NOA) resists the idea of moving outside science in an attempt to provide a global characterization of it:

NOA thinks of science as an historical entity, growing and changing under various internal and external pressures. Such an entity can be usefully studied in a variety of ways, sociological, historical economic, moral, and methodological—to name a few. One can ask a variety of questions about particular developments in particular historical periods. Sometimes there will be a basis in the practice itself for answering such questions. Sometimes that basis will support several plausible answers. Sometimes it will be clear that there is no basis in science itself for addressing the question, and then one must judge for oneself whether it is worth adding attachments on to science so as to make a place for the question, or whether one should just let the issue drop. (1986b, 172–173)

For Fine, both realists and antirealists err in their failure to appreciate the characteristics of science as a social enterprise. Miller argues convincingly that whatever the weakness of the way in which Fine sets up the contrast between the NOA and both realism and antirealism, the central issue is that both feed on "scaffolding external to science" (1989, 235).

Of course there is "external" and "external." As Miller points out, Fine's account can turn out to be either conservative in insulating scientific practice from criticism, *or* implausible in its characterization of realism, including the idea that it is imperialist about the goals of science (ibid., 235–237). Though Miller does not put it this way, also at issue is what I call the globalism that Fine wants to assign to both realists and antirealists. That is, the realism and antirealism under discussion are to be understood as competing claims to be applied uniformly to science as a whole rather than as piecemeal theories about particular scientific theories. Indeed, such a view of the global reach of both realism and antirealism is not unreasonable given how debates about realism have progressed in the philosophy of science over the past twenty-five years. Yet it turns out to be central in allowing Fine to distinguish the NOA from its competitors.

Whether you take issue with Fine's distinction between the core position and its additions (both realist and antirealist), his argument rests heavily on the distinction between the NOA as internal to science and its opponents as external. But what makes realism and antirealism external? In fact, Fine gives no argument to exclude realism and antirealism as *internal*. Still, what does rule this out as plausible is the implicit treatment of realism and antirealism as global theories, for, if we follow Fine in treating "science as an historical entity, growing and changing under various internal and external pressures" (1986b, 172), such globalism while *possible* is certainly not necessary nor particularly likely. The core of such a historical view of science is its very openness to the potential for change, which is just the feature that renders *any* global claims we might make about the nature of science suspect.

If globalism is set as a characteristic of realism and antirealism, then the implausibility of globalism will infect the plausibility of claims about realism and antirealism themselves. They will stand or fall with their global nature. Suppose we renounce a priori globalism. Then in fact realism and antirealism begin to look like plausible internal candidates along with the NOA. For suppose we agree that "[s]uch an entity [i.e., science itself] can be usefully studied in a variety of ways, sociological, historical economic, moral, and methodological—to name a few," then, why can we not include questions of realism and antirealism on this list, so long as we remember that we are asking "questions about particular developments in particular historical periods"?

If we allow for nonglobal versions of realism and antirealism, no argument has been provided to show that practice alone could not support one or the other under particular circumstances. By allowing for the historical variability of science as a social enterprise, the claim that past practice has not supported realism or antirealism does not exclude its possibility in the future.

To exclude it in the future, we need to do something more to bolster Fine's argument. Short of a principled argument that would rule out realism and antirealism under any circumstances, a sensible strategy would be to place limits on the range of those circumstances. Such a strategy suggests itself from the work of Stein (1989). Like Fine, Stein thinks that both realism and antirealism (in the form of instrumentalism) are irrelevant to scientific practice. In one sense, like Fine, Stein thinks they have a common core, but Stein's approach differs from Fine's in two respects. First, Fine casts the

core position in terms of a homely and unanalyzed conception of truth. The realist wants to add to this while the antirealist wants to restrict its domain of application. On the other hand, Stein wants to eschew talk of truth altogether in the core position. His core commitment for a theory is just that theories of phenomena "afford . . . a representation [that is] . . . in a suitable sense correct, and in a suitable sense adequate . . ." (ibid., 50).

Like Fine, Stein thinks that if instrumentalism is taken to be nothing more than predictive adequacy, it is too narrow. However, given his construal of the "core," Stein thinks it is easy to provide an account of instrumentalism that is as broad as we like. Think of the instrumentalist as treating theory as an instrument and no more. That instrument can be thought of as being put to a variety of uses. One of those can be prediction but there can be others. So anything we do with theories can be assimilated into this framework (ibid., 49–52).

What about realism? Fine's realism is wider than his core and the same is true for Stein. The (traditionally conceived) realist wants to argue that judging theories to be correct and adequate in a suitable sense is not enough, for such a theory might be either true or false (unless "suitable sense" has been designed to coincide with "true"). Like Fine, Stein thinks this realist asks us to do the epistemically impossible—for, beyond representing phenomena correctly and adequately, "how in the world could we ever tell what the actual case is?" (ibid., 50). But what is left of realism if we give up such talk? Stein thinks the position becomes not importantly different from the expanded version of instrumentalism. Both hoe a row guided by theories judged by their correctness and adequacy as representations in the "suitable sense."

So here is a core position for scientific practice that supports both realism and instrumentalism—at least when they are suitably redefined. However, if Fine's core position was vulnerable to the problem of being too easy for realists to accept and too hard for antirealists in the eyes of his critics, in Stein's case things are the other way around. Stein paints the realist as one who wants to *add* truth as a condition on what is in a "suitable sense correct, and in a suitable sense adequate" for a theory to represent phenomena. Suppose we take "adequate" to be empirical adequacy. Still, for a realist, what counts is truth itself (suitably defined),[1] which is not something above and beyond an interest in empirical adequacy. The explanatory interests that drive realism render empirical adequacy as merely a means that can even sometimes be sacrificed to preserve explanatory power (as sometimes when one of two competing theories exhibits significantly greater explanatory power while the other exhibits greater empirical adequacy). As such, the real fight between realists and their opponents concerns what counts as the core of the scientific enterprise. *Yet no core position remains for the realist once you take truth away.*

Put that way, we do not seem much better off than before. We lack a general argument to show the irrelevance of realism and its competitors. Yet, though Stein's account may fail in its formulation, he, like Fine, has a general story to tell about science that is more important, revolving around the centrality of mathematics. Over time:

what tends to persist . . . [is] not the features most conspicuous in referential semantics: the substances or "entities" and their own "basic" properties and relations, but the more abstract mathematical forms. (Ibid., 58)

If science is viewed in this way, success becomes the development of a mathematical account that the world may be said to instantiate, which seems to merely relocate the debate between realists and antirealists.

Now the issue becomes how to understand "instantiation," but in this locus it is much easier to be indifferent between Stein's versions of "enlightened" realism and "sophisticated" instrumentalism. For if we think of the canon of correctness and adequacy, what are the choices for a "suitable sense" for these when it comes to the mathematical accounts? In response, the "unenlightened realist" wants to say "truth!" coupled with correspondence. But what counts as correspondence in this context? It is not that one cannot answer this question, but the answers will involve entities whose ontological status is highly problematic. Contrast this to the idea of realism applied to the garden-variety furniture of the universe. Of course the committed antirealist will claim that this distinction relies on nothing more than a prejudice about the furniture of the universe. It is at this juncture that realism and antirealism seem to clash most naturally and the debate becomes one about differing interpretations of the correspondence theory of truth. But I think we should resist the temptation to let the argument settle in at this point. I think that realism is properly understood as a "style of reasoning" that only engages in certain kinds of situations. The paradigms of these situations involve scientific accounts of macroscopic objects. Such accounts get judged as adequate and correct to the extent that they coincide with features of the world that we take for granted. Realism, on this view, is not a position that falls out of a theory, but rather a mode of reasoning we bring to bear in certain kinds of model building for which we already have antecedent realist commitments to the subject independent of our model. But such a mode of reasoning is hard to engage for mathematical accounts.

On the view that I am defending, realism is a picture that engages the imagination at the level of events and things, for at such a level, our model building is easily assimilated to a general view that judges our creativity by how well it coincides with the world. It is also a picture that engages when we think of science as providing insight into the *machinery* of nature. Unfortunately, this picture has no ready analog when it comes to the *mathematical* treatment of the world.

Should we accept Stein's gloss on the centrality of mathematics? On the above argument, to do so means underplaying the significance of our questions about events and things. That seems to me to be right with respect to science's future as well as its past. As such, it holds the potential for a general account of why the debate between realism and antirealism is not important given our scientific interests. Of course, as we saw in examining Fine's account, we cannot rule out the possibility that other prevailing interests might undermine this conclusion. On the argument so far, they would only have to be nonmathematical. However, I do not think that the issue simply counterposes concrete particulars and mathematics. Rather, our more general scientific interests in abstraction are involved, for the same problem of how to understand the distinction between realism and antirealism arises in nonmathematical contexts of abstraction as well.

The point is best illustrated in the notion of fitness in biological theory. To understand evolutionary history is to understand the machinery of just how it was that some biological attributes were disfavored over others. Such subject matter does not demand such a high degree of abstraction as to rob us of a leg to stand on outside of our model building—so we can bring realism to it as a style of reasoning. Yet, evolutionary history is not very interesting. The interesting questions of biology quickly reach beyond particulars. Given the variability of the particulars in the biological world, reaching beyond the particular forces us to generalize over that variability. The models that result are no longer models of the world, but models

of very narrowly circumscribed *abstracted* properties of the world. The result is that the idea of *correspondence* as a one-to-one relation between things in the world and in our theories loses most of its meaning. Thus, in the case of natural selection, at the level of individual reproductive units, the details of historical circumstances are exquisitely variable—so much so that no generalization can be made at this level of description. To generalize, we have to recharacterize to subsume this variability. Thus requirements for fitness can vary radically. The resulting theory, though it names a real property, produces no straightforward instantiations of fitness at the level of individual units (for more see Sober 1984, 47–51, 71).

J. Bigelow and R. Pargetter (1990) have recently argued that realism should be defended as prior to semantic considerations. They argue that antirealism only gets a foothold if the realist allows the debate to be shifted onto the semantic terrain. Whatever the final plausibility of their argument (and I am sympathetic to the initial thrust), Bigelow and Pargetter must talk about realism without inviting a semantic interpretation. They solve the problem by grounding talk of realism in common garden varieties of cases. They want to avoid the move to semantic ascent, but accomplishing this means that they must discuss cases that appeal to our intuitions. "We believe," write Bigelow and Pargetter, "that the world is stocked with such things as plants and planets, frogs and photons, phenotypes and genotypes, oxygen and kinetic energy, magnetic fields and tectonic plates" (ibid., 437). Having primed their "intuition pump" with an appeal to these relatively mundane features of the world, Bigelow and Pargetter want to extend this picture to a full-blown version of metaphysical realism about universals (including mathematics). The problem here is not the first step but its extension, for if I am right, we strongly resonate to the idea of approaching the world of plants and planets with a realist style of talk. The disanalogies between such worlds and the world of scientific abstraction, however, makes the extension of such a style of reasoning only seem plausible because of the very force of those initial intuitions.

NOTE

1. Of course the whole debate can be cast in terms of a debate about the suitable sense of "truth."

REFERENCES

Bigelow, J., and Pargetter, R. "From Extroverted Realism to Correspondence: A Modest Proposal." *Philosophy and Phenomenological Research* 50 (1990): 435–460.

Fine, A. "And Not Anti-realism Either." *Noûs* 18 (1984a): 51–65.
———. "The Natural Ontological Attitude." In *Scientific Realism*, ed. J. Leplin, pp. 83–107. Berkeley: University of California Press, 1984b.
———. *The Shaky Game: Einstein, Realism, and the Quantum Theory.* Chicago: University of Chicago Press, 1986a.
———. "Unnatural Attitudes: Realist and Instrumentalist Attachments to Science." *Mind* 95 (1986b): 149–177.
Miller, R. "In Search of Einstein's Legacy: A Critical Notice of Arthur Fine, *The Shaky Game: Einstein, Realism, and the Quantum Theory.*" *Philosophical Review* 98 (1989): 215–238.
Musgrave, A. "NOA's Ark: Fine for Realism." *Philosophical Quarterly* 39 (1989): 383–398.
Sober, E. *The Nature of Selection: Evolutionary Theory in Philosophical Focus.* Cambridge, MA: MIT Press, 1984.
Stein, H. "Yes, but . . . : Some Skeptical Remarks on Realism and Anti-realism." *Dialectica* 43 (1989): 47–65.

PETER KOSSO, "SCIENCE AND OBJECTIVITY"

As we have seen, one of the central sticking points in the arguments between the realists and the antirealists is the question of objectivity. Realists hold that science is objective, indeed, that the objectivity of the scientific method ensures that the claims of science refer to what is real about the world. The antirealists deny that science is objective in any sense important or strong enough to establish the claims of the realists.

Kosso establishes what he takes to be an important sense of objectivity—important enough to support the claim that science is objective. With such a sense established for objectivity, the road to realism is much smoother. (Kosso does not explicitly address the realism-antirealism debate.)

Kosso will try to show how theory-ladenness of observation (discussed and stressed by Kuhn and a favorite of the antirealists) does not entail a total lack of objectivity in science. Using the theory-ladenness of observation to establish the relativity (subjectivity) of science is a favorite tactic of the antirealists.

What Kosso will do is explain how objectivity can be guaranteed by what he calls epistemic independence. He turns to observation and the claim that it is always theory-laden. His first point is that the theory that is laden in our observation need not always be the theory we are trying to confirm. Kosso cites Ian Hacking, who has pointed out that science is made of many scientific branches that are disconnected (for example, quantum mechanics and ecology). This disunity of the sciences shows that we can even use one science to help with the testing of another without necessarily losing objectivity due to the theory-ladenness of observation.

Our own senses are considered independent. We test for visual hallucinations by trying to touch. We look to see if that smell is really roses. Kosso offers a number of clear examples where independence works to underwrite our claims to knowledge. The examples lead him to ask, "What is it to say that theories are independent?" We have seen the beginnings of an answer with genetics, where it was pointed out that cytology was used to establish the reality of the genes.

Kosso defines independence of theories as follows: Two theories are independent when the truth or falsity of one does not also establish (he says "force us to accept") the truth or falsity of the other. His point is that if one theory cannot be accepted without also accepting another, one cannot be used in the confirmation or disconfirmation of the other. When we are able to use one theory to help confirm another theory, the theories must be independent. When they are independent and one is used to confirm the other, the theory confirmed can be trusted as objective.

We use an electron microscope to confirm the structure of a DNA molecule. The theories that underlie the observation via the electron microscope are independent enough in Kosso's sense from the theories that underlie what we take to be molecular structure so that this confirmation is not ruined and made subjective by the theory-ladenness of observation.

Kosso then gives two other clear examples, one in which there is no question that the theories are independent (stones and acceleration) and one in which the two theories are almost totally dependent (caloric and ether). In most cases, the degree of independence would be somewhere in the middle of these two extremes. In these cases, we judge as best we can.

Science and Objectivity

PETER KOSSO

A central goal in doing epistemology of science is the validation of scientific knowledge, or at least an appraisal of the possibilities and attempts to validate scientific knowledge. This facet of philosophy of science seeks to answer the straightforward question, "Why believe what science claims about the world?" This is a question made more acute with the realization that science is largely a self-regulating system. Insofar as observation is theory-relative in the sense that theory influences not only what observations are to be made but also what those observations mean, the accountability of scientific claims is an internal affair and the reliability of science is self-proclaimed. So why should we believe science?

I. INTRODUCTION: OBJECTIVITY AND INDEPENDENCE

John Ziman articulates a common and reasonable answer in claiming, "[t]he primary foundation for belief in science is the widespread impression that it is *objective*."[1] Israel Scheffler makes a similar point in *Science*

From *The Journal of Philosophy* 86 (1989): 245–257. Courtesy of the author and *The Journal of Philosophy*.

and Subjectivity,[2] indicating that science pursues an ideal of objectivity and is credible to the extent that it nears that ideal. But what ex-actly is objectivity and how do we know when it is present? Ziman links objectivity to intersubjectivity, that is, agreement among many persons, in this case scientists. Scientific knowledge is believed to be reliable, because it is required to pass judgment by many disinterested (that is, objective) reviewers. Scheffler associates objectivity with a more epistemic notion of independence. Evidence is objective if its gathering is independent of that for which it serves as evidence.

These are provocative suggestions, though they are still vague. My plan here is to pursue the notion of epistemic independence by making it more precise and showing how it can function in assessing our warrant for belief in scientific claims. If we think of objectivity as requiring an independent appraisal, then it is desirable to characterize precisely the relevant notion of independence and to indicate how it can be recognized.

This kind of epistemic independence can be applied in a variety of situations of validating scientific knowledge. One such situation is that of observations. Science is reliable, we might think, because its claims must be tested against the objective facts of observation. But by now many philosophers have conceded to a certain amount of theory dependence in observation and its role as an objective standard is threatened. Yet even if we cannot have observation that is entirely theory-independent, we might at least have observation that is independent of the particular theory we are testing. That is, if some observation O is to be used in confirming a theory T, then a degree of objectivity is preserved if the theories on which O depends are more or less independent of that particular theory T. Objective evidence is evidence that is verified independently of what it is

evidence for. Ian Hacking, in discussions of observation, refers to this phenomenon as, "the disunity of science."[3] Science is disunified in the sense that it is composed of several independent branches. It is a healthy disunity, since the independent branches can assist in independent, objective testing of each other's claims.

The benefits of independence can be appreciated by considering our own human perceptual systems. We consider our different senses to be independent to some degree when we use one of them to check another. If I am uncertain whether what I see is a hallucination or real fire, it is less convincing of a test simply to look again than it is to hold out my hand and feel the heat. The independent account is the more reliable, because it is less likely that a systematic error will infect both systems than that one system will be flawed.

The independence of sensory systems is a physical kind of independence, in the sense that events and conditions in one system have no causal influence on events and conditions in another. But the independence relevant to objectivity in science is an epistemic independence between theories. A closer analogy to the epistemic concept is found in history. Ancient history in particular is fortunate to have available two independent sources of information, the literature of ancient texts and archeological artifacts. Interpretation of artifacts, their age, their use in trade, and the like, is credible insofar as it is consistent with interpretations of ancient texts. In this way, claims made by archeologists can receive an independent corroboration by the claims made by interpreters of ancient texts. But the precise degree to which the two sources, archeology and literature, are independent is an important question, and it is just this issue, in the context of the sciences in general, which will be pursued here.

There are plenty of good examples in the

physical sciences of independence functioning as a rational measure of belief in scientific claims. One of the best is in the experiments of Jean Perrin in the beginning of this century, experiments designed to measure the number of molecules in one mole of material, Avogadro's number.[4] Perrin measured the same physical quantity in a variety of different ways, thereby invoking a variety of different auxiliary theories. And the reason that Perrin's results are so believable, and that they provide good reason to believe in the actual existence of molecules, is that he used a variety of *independent* theories and techniques and got them to agree on the answer. The chances of these independent theories all independently manufacturing the same ficticious result is small enough to be rationally discounted. It is the independence that supports the credibility of the account. But what exactly does it mean to claim in this context that two theories are independent?

II. INDEPENDENCE OF THEORIES

The concept of independence of two theories which is relevant to objectivity must be applicable to epistemic justification. Circumstances of discovery of the theories, for example that they were first proposed by the same person or motivated by the same evidence, should not influence the evaluation of independence in this sense. If an Albert Einstein is clever enough to propose both the special theory of relativity and the quantum theory of light, this does not make the theories any less epistemically independent. One could still supply an objective, independent check of the other as long as the truth conditions of one do not influence the truth conditions of the other.

Given two scientific theories T_1 and T_2, T_1 is independent of T_2 in a way that makes T_1 a possible source of objective test of T_2, if our acceptance of T_1 as true (or rejection of

T_1 as false) does not force us to accept T_2 as true (nor to reject T_2 as false). If the truth or falsity of T_1 is insulated from the truth or falsity of T_2, then the two theories are independent in the relevant way. T_1 could function as an auxiliary theory in an observation in support of T_2 without our worrying that T_1 or T_2 is acting in its own self-interest. This is what is meant by objective testing. . . .

III. INDEPENDENCE OF AN ACCOUNT

To claim generally that observation is theory-dependent hides a great deal that is relevant to issues of epistemology and science. If observation is theory-dependent, on which theories does it depend and in what ways? The responses to these questions are necessarily case-by-case affairs. Different observations may depend on different theories and in ways that differ in epistemologically significant ways. It is only by describing the nature of specific cases of observation that one can appreciate the impact of the theory dependence of data.

Several such studies of specific cases of observation have been done. Dudley Shapere describes observations of the sun which depend heavily on the observer's theoretical background,[5] and Hacking explains how theory accounts for the information scientists claim to be getting through optical microscopes.[6] With greater emphasis on human perception and less on machine-aided observation, Jerry Fodor suggests an empirical approach to determining at least which theories in our conceptual background do *not* influence particular observations.[7]

In all of these examples, an observation will be theory-dependent in the sense that there is some collection of theories which account for the information one claims to receive in the observation, the information that functions as evidence in science. These theories influence the observation in that a change in the theories would force a change in the claim about the observational information. Thus, for any singular claim that is based on an act of theory-dependent observation, there will be a collection of theories which validate the claim. Call this the set $\{T\}$ of theories which account for the particular observation.

Sometimes the set $\{T\}$ is easy to identify. The examples by Shapere and Hacking demonstrate this feature. Take as our own example the observation with an electron microscope of a DNA molecule, which we will follow through the description of independence of an account. The accounting theories in this case are those which describe the interactive properties of electrons as they scatter off the specimen and are focused in the microscope and impart their energy to the viewing screen. This is a substantial set of sophisticated theories and it represents a major capitulation to the theory dependence of observation. But it need not compromise the objectivity of the evidence or the objective nature of the test it provides. The test, after all, is to be of some theory about the specimen, a theory of DNA, and a degree of independence in the account, that is, objectivity of the evidence, is preserved if the singular observational claim is supported by an account that is independent of the theory being tested. . . .

IV. EXAMPLES

In developing a concept such as independence of an account and its relevance to objectivity, one wants a characterization that agrees with intuitive assessment of easy examples so that we can use it with confidence as a guide to intuition in the difficult cases. That is, one wants a characterization of independence which gets a high score, indicating an objective test of theory, in cases that we are predisposed to believe as cases of objective testing and reliable information. And where we have antecedent rea-

son to disbelieve, cases of unreliable information, the measure of independence ought to get a low score. Only then will the notion of independence of an account be acceptable as a warrant for belief in cases where we have no other indication of reliability of information. . . .

The best case, in the sense of the most independence of an account, is the case where . . . no part of the theory-of-x is used in the account. Observation claims of what we unhesitatingly call observables are often of this degree of independence. Consider the observation claim that the stone is accelerating. The theories from which one would draw to corroborate this claim, that is, the scientific account of the reliability of the observation, would be theories of optics and perception. But no part of either geology or, more importantly, kinematics, appear in the account. . . . Thus, in this and other cases of perception of midsized objects, our pre-analytic intuition accepts the observation as reliable information and the analysis of independence concurs with a ruling of high independence indicating a relatively objective test.

The worst case, that is, the least independent account, results if . . . all and only the theory-of-x and the particular property putatively observed is used to account for the observational reception of the information about a particular x having this property. The second link in the equation, the "only" part of "all and only," is unlikely to occur in actual science. It is rare that no disinterested auxiliary theory, usually a theory of optics or perception, is used in accounting for the evidence. But as a case that comes close to the bottom of the scale of independence, consider a historical account of alleged observation of caloric fluids. More precisely, we should describe this as a claim of the acquisition of information about caloric.

Use as an observing apparatus some

solid object such as a block of metal. The particles of caloric which, according to the caloric theory, are present in the object will be distributed throughout the object as a result of the repulsive force between particles. The caloric particles will surround the particles of the object.[8] As more caloric is added to the object, the ether-cloaked object particles experience a repulsive force between themselves as the ether particles push for distance between each other. The more caloric, the greater repulsive force and the object responds by expanding.

In this way, the expanding block displays information about caloric fluid, namely, that caloric is flowing into the block. But the informational link between the appearance of a block of metal and properties of caloric is provided almost entirely by the caloric theory itself. In other words, the set . . . of accounting theories is constituted almost entirely of claims . . . drawn from ether theory. And any property of ether, its characteristics of flow or its effects on material particles, must be described in the theoretical account in order to support the observational account. To adapt a Wittgensteinian analogy, we are not even buying another copy of the newspaper to check its reliability; we are simply accepting the assuring words printed at the top of each page, "all this is true."

The moral of the story is that, even though the ether theorist can claim observational evidence for the ether theory, that evidence can be discounted on the basis of its lacking independence. It is not objective evidence. In this case, again, our intuition (that the ether evidence is unreliable) parallels the analysis of independence of the account.

The majority of evidential claims in science fall somewhere in between the best and worst and are not immediately decidable with respect to reliability. In these cases the independence of account is useful as a measure of warrant for belief. To demonstrate this we can resurrect the DNA molecule as imaged with an electron microscope which was considered above. The image by the electron microscope may reveal, for example, that the DNA is denatured (split). In this case, T_x1 is that part of the theory of DNA which discusses the causes and effects of the splitting of the molecule. T_x2 will not be empty, since there must be an account of the composition of the molecule to explain its differential absorption of stain and its properties of scattering electrons. But T_x2 in this case appears to be disjoint from T_x1. And, of course, T_x2 is not the only source of theoretical support for the observation, since a great deal of electron scattering theory and electromagnetic theory are invoked to trace the production of the image.

This demonstrates that subdividing the theory of DNA into the claims about shape of the molecule (T_x1) and claims about composition of the molecule (T_x2) reveals a degree of independence in the account of electron-microscopic observation of a DNA molecule. The image on the screen of the microscope can therefore be regarded as objective evidence for the theory of DNA. This assessment, though, is really only a first-order approximation. The fine structure of independence in this account could be described through a characterization of the varying degrees of independence as suggested in the appendix.

V. CONCLUSION

The point of this discussion has been to suggest a characterization of objectivity. It has been motivated by the claim that objectivity is what makes science believable and is in part what is scientific about science. An objective test, we assume, is one that is less likely to reproduce theoretical artifacts and propagate hidden systematic error. An objective test, that is, is a more reliable test than is one administered by the testee. External review is valued for its trustworthiness. And objectivity in this sense can be evaluated in terms of accessible features of a scientific report, namely, independence of an account. There is no reference to external, inaccessible features such as truth or facts of the matter, and, for this reason, independence, in its relevance to objectivity, is a valuable and workable standard for evaluating warrant for belief.

The relevant concept for this purpose is independence of an account. The application of this concept is specific to each case of putatively objective evidence and requires dividing the theory to be tested into a part that will directly benefit from the test and a part that participates in the testing. This approach then maps neatly on to many examples from actual science.

The discussion has been done with the realization that observation in science is informative only with the aid of theory. In terms of epistemic compromise and of threatening reliability, though, some theory dependences are worse than others. A theory/observation dichotomy (or an observable/unobservable dichotomy) is therefore of limited importance as a guide to belief, both because so many observations are so

intimately theoretical and because it hides the detail (namely, independence) that is significant in evaluating warrant for belief. My suggestion, then, is to replace the traditional theory/observation dichotomy with an independent/not-independent dichotomy (or spectrum) as an indication of what is epistemologically significant in scientific evidence.

NOTES

1. J. Ziman, *Reliable Knowledge* (New York: Cambridge University Press, 1978), p. 107.
2. I. Scheffler, *Science and Subjectivity* (Indianapolis: Bobbs-Merrill, 1967).
3. I. Hacking, *Representing and Intervening* (New York: Cambridge University Press, 1983), p. 183.
4. A thorough account of Perrin's accomplishment is to be found in M. Nye, *Molecular Reality* (London: Macdonald, 1972).
5. D. Shapere, "The Concept of Observation in Science and Philosophy," *Philosophy of Science* 49 (1982): 485–525.
6. Hacking, *Representing and Intervening*, chap. 11.
7. J. Fodor, "Observation Reconsidered," *Philosophy of Science* 51 (1984): 23–43.
8. This piece of caloric lore is adapted from a description in G. Cantor and M. Hodge (eds.), *Conceptions of Ether* (New York: Cambridge University Press, 1981), pp. 27–28.

EXERCISES

1. What are the issues at stake in the debate between realists and antirealists? Why would Kuhn be considered on the side of the antirealists? Where would Carnap and Hempel and Oppenheim fit?

2. Fine tries to defuse the issue between the realists and the antirealists. Does he find a true middle ground, or does he lean toward the side of the realists (as Stein claims)?

3. Try to make clear exactly in what ways van Fraassen is not an instrumentalist.

4. As we have characterized positivism, would positivism lean toward realism or antirealism?

5. Hacking wrote a famous article, "Do We See through a Microscope?" (*Pacific Philosophical Quarterly* 62: [1981] 305–322). What do you think his answer was? How would van Fraassen answer the question? How would Kosso answer it?

5

Can Medicine Be a Science?

The question "Can medicine be a science?" suggests that medicine may not be a science at all. In fact, it is often argued that medicine is much more an art than a science. However, it is just as often said that medicine is a mix of art and science—that it is some special hybrid discipline. Some writers have thought that medicine is inextricably bound up with values in a way that physics, for example, is not. To these thinkers, the presence of values ensures that medicine cannot ever be a science. Still other thinkers believe that what really separates medicine from other clear examples of science is the kind of entity with which medicine deals. Patients, disease, health, and suffering just do not lend themselves to the creation of scientific laws (even *ceteris paribus* laws).

Before we can begin to tackle these issues, we need a clear meaning for *medicine*. Medicine covers three related areas. Sometimes the term *biomedicine* is used as a way of showing that more is meant than just any one of the following divisions:

1. The basic biology, chemistry, and physics associated with the workings of living organisms

2. The sort of research that is done to discover that basic biology and to discover ways to control that biology (e.g., research into pharmacology)

3. Clinical medicine, the application of points 1 and 2, involving diagnosing problems, prescribing medications and performing procedures in an attempt to alleviate or eliminate problems, all of which requires dealing with patients in many different circumstances

Even if the basic biology is a science in a sense that would satisfy Hempel and Oppenheim, it might still be the case that 2 and 3 are so different from usual science that medicine as a whole must be considered a different sort of discipline, totally autonomous from other sciences. The very different claim that 2 and 3 are nothing more than an expanded version of 1 would be called reductionistic. To indicate the importance of 2 and 3—what some analysts would term the addition of human factors—medicine can be referred to as a practice instead of a discipline. Schaffner makes a point of discussing the idea of medicine as a practice in his article.

K. DANNER CLOUSER AND ARTHUR ZUCKER, "MEDICINE AS ART: AN INITIAL EXPLORATION"

Clouser and Zucker set up a framework for discussions of the nature of medicine. They distinguish among three aspects of medicine: diagnosing, prescribing, and dealing in general with patients. For each of these areas, they show where the art may be. They point out that what makes medicine an art also makes any science an art. They conclude that something else must be at play in our intuition that medicine is not a science in the way that physics is a science. They suggest that one crucial difference is that the number of variables in a medical problem is so large that no simple use of generalizations will help. Matching the known generalizations with the medical problem at hand is what requires the insight and experience that is labeled "art." Cartwright (Chapter 2) would refer to medicine as an area where laws intersect and where very little is tidy.

Clouser and Zucker identify another important difference between medicine and sciences such as physics. Medicine is theory-laden, just as all science is theory-laden. In medicine, much more so than in physics, chemistry, or geology, part of the theory contains values. The very terms basic to medicine, *health* and *disease*, are not just theory-laden; they are value-laden.

Medicine as Art: An Initial Exploration

K. DANNER CLOUSER AND ARTHUR ZUCKER

I

That medicine is an art (or at least partly an art) has long been regarded a truism. We do not wish to challenge this belief; we want only to understand it. To that end the present article is barely a beginning. It is comprised of only hints and clues. We are surface-scratching in the hopes of enticing others to puzzle more deeply and systematically over this issue. More generally, we even harbor hopes of provoking increased interest in the philosophy of medicine.

We suspect that some important aspects of medicine are signaled by the tendency to

From *Texas Reports on Biology and Medicine* 32 (1974): 267–274. Courtesy of the authors and the publishers of *Texas Reports on Biology and Medicine.*

call it an art. Pursuing this label, we would hope to arrive at some insights concerning the nature of medicine. We can readily agree with Dr. Alvan R. Feinstein in his *Clinical Judgment* (1967) on several issues: that art in medicine is not confined to bedside manner, that much of art (imagination, creativity, intuition) is in science, that much of science (discipline, rationality, logic) is in art and that there is much art and science in clinical medicine. But having said all this we are still no closer to an understanding of what it is we are calling "art" as it applies to medicine.

We shall begin by explicating what seems to be the most common meaning of "medicine as art." Then we will comment briefly on several implications of that analysis, and finally we will suggest a deeper understanding of the issue. The constraints of space lead us to aim more at being provocative than definitive.

II

It should be noted from the start that we are making no attempt to give a historical account of the concept of medicine as an art. This would surely be an informative pursuit, but we are confining ourselves to a suggestion as to how the concept is now generally regarded.

The assertion "Medicine is an art" usually occurs in a context that indicates medicine is basically science but that it is something else besides. "The practice of medicine is an art which depends on a sound scientific base," as one medical school brochure reads. And Feinstein clearly thinks that for all the scientific instrumentation that assists clinical decision-making, humans finally must make clinical decisions about other humans, and that is where the artistry is crucial and indispensable (Chap. 16). The implication seems to be that medicine must go *beyond* science, and that that "something more" is the art. Science seems not to be enough to accomplish the ends of medicine; a further step called "art" appears necessary.

Very generally, our suggestion is that to regard medicine as an art is to emphasize that there is more in reality than can be encompassed in our formulas. It is emphasizing the vast number of variables in any particular situation that cannot all be systematically related by formula or theory. Hence, a practitioner must rely on his "intuition" or his "sixth sense" in order, somehow, to take into account this disordered barrage of influencing variables (though he might not even be explicitly aware of them). In short, talk about the "art" of medicine seems to bespeak the need for a sensitivity to clues and factors that cannot *methodically* be taken into account.

But this notion needs elaboration. It will help to look at the issue from three points of view: diagnosing, prescribing, and dealing with the patient, since each of these is thought to have its artful aspects.

In diagnosis the suggestion would be that there is no foolproof way to discover the cause of the patient's complaint. There are, of course, established procedures for examining the patient, but these procedures cannot cover every possibility. That's where the "art" comes in—the skill or sensitivity to perceive clues that will lead to a diagnosis. These clues could be anything from a physiological phenomenon to a verbal expression, from an environmental factor to a mannerism of a patient's relative. These myriad manifestations of illness, along with the endless exceptions, cannot be isolated, listed, and included systematically in diagnostic routines. The sensitivity required to pick up these clues is what gets labeled "art."

Even lab tests and physiological responses need this "art" in order for their significance to be determined. That is, a quantitative reading is not the last word; the doctor, by this conscious or unconscious awareness of other factors and circumstances concerning the patient, gives these readings more or less significance. This interpretative element is part of the "art" of medicine, and again, it has to do with one's "sixth sense" or "intuition," because there can be no general formula significantly linking these innumerable variables.

Before reflecting on some of the implications of this concept of art in medicine, it would be advantageous to push on to look at the role of "art" in treatment and in interrelating with the patient. Having now described that aspect of medicine we are labeling "art," we can more quickly highlight it as it appears in these two other activities.

In prescribing treatment the "art" must

enter into the "intuiting" of all those influencing variables that cannot be quantitatively formulated and that perhaps are not even explicitly known. These variables could be physiological or they could be the moods, tolerances, values, and family relationships of the patient. These cannot be quantified, interrelated and entered into the *Physicians' Desk Reference*. Though facts (indications) and empirical guidelines form a strong basis for prescription of medicine, idiosyncratic reaction to drugs and treatment is well known. So perhaps even there, some room is left for what practitioners call "art."

The third aspect of medicine—the interpersonal relationship with the patient—is what is often thought to be the only place where art is manifested in medicine. This is the art of relating to another human, knowing when to say this or that, when to encourage or discourage, when to sympathize, chide, or challenge. It involves interpreting the other's words, gestures, and expressions, and empathizing with him. Bedside manner is thought by some to be the sum total of "art" in medicine. But notice that in principle the art in interpersonal relationship is no different from the sense we gave to "art" in diagnosis and prescription. Here also there is an abundance of variables that cannot be quantified or precisely interrelated, some of which we are probably not explicitly conscious of. Consequently there are no formulas; there are no systematic procedures for accomplishing our ends. This is not to say there are no guidelines or general formulas for dealing with other human beings. We do, of course, build on such general knowledge. But there are far more variables and kinds of circumstances than we could ever formulate into working theories. So we "sense" or "intuit" the appropriate factors and act accordingly—and therein is the "art."

III

Having drawn out what seems the main pattern in the activities of medicine that get labeled "art," we will focus on that pattern briefly, in order to make several observations.

a) We have talked a lot about "intuition" and "sixth sense." This is not the place to explicate these difficult concepts. We have been using these terms simply to identify a kind of experience with which we are all familiar; namely, when our judgment is influenced by numerous elements in a total situation, elements of which we might not even be explicitly aware or at least which we are so far unable to sort out and consciously weigh. Sensitivity and experience seem to inform our judgments without all the factors necessarily being brought before the mind for explicit consideration. It is not unlike the "touch" one develops in a tennis shot, which seems to take into consideration the speed of the approaching ball, its spin, its liveliness, the playability of the court, the wind, and the player's own constantly changing relationship to the ball. Not many—if any—of these factors get considered and weighed in the consciousness of the player. He just "intuits" it all. (In fact, explicitly considering any of these factors and trying to calculate and execute the correct body response, almost guarantees disaster!)

b) Note that this is nothing which *in principle* could not become science, if we could identify, quantify, organize, and interrelate all the factors that we now "intuit." It is the sheer abundance and the extremely complicated and barely understood interrelationships of these variables that keep us from reducing it to a science. Frequently in initial stages of an investigation we are working intuitively, until we can locate, quantify, and interrelate the relevant factors. We speak of "getting it down to a science." The introduction of roentgenography, endoscopy, electrocardiography and the like has certainly made pathological diagnosis more accurate than ever. As the variables that a physician once had to take into account intuitively become identified, quantified, and interrelated, instrumentation becomes possible that helps "get it down to a science." So what begins as "art" can—at least in principle—evolve into science.

c) All this might suggest that "art" is the name given to sheer guesswork. And, in fact, sometimes it is used in just that fashion, but not without condescending overtones. But if the role of "sixth sense" or "intuition" is understood, it will be seen that it is not *sheer* guesswork. Experience, theory, and a scientific base is the point of departure. It is with that background and in that context that one "intuits." It is not the absence of any guidelines for judgment—as is sheer guesswork—it is the lack of an articulated, systematic, and formulated consideration of these determining factors. If anything like guesswork, art is closer to what we call "educated guesses."

d) Perhaps originally the "art" of medicine referred simply to a manual skill, comparable to barbering, woodcarving, masonry, etc. Medicine was another such skill. But even this sense of "art" would be amenable to our analysis, since these skills were not formulatable into precise rules and methodical procedures, but depended on the "intuition" of innumerable determining factors. One developed a "feel" for wielding the knife or the chisel, just as with the swing of the tennis racket. So also one might have a "feel" for locating sickness, or for manipulating the patient's body or for mixing him a potion.

e) An important puzzle emerges from our analysis of the art aspect of medicine: namely, if "art" in this sense means having no foolproof, methodical, systematized way of discovering (and hence having to "intuit" one's way through the innumerable variables), then this is true of *all* science, not just medicine. But then why is it that medicine in particular gets singled out for its element of art? There must be a further difference we have not yet uncovered.

That difference might lie in the difference in kind between what each is trying to discover. Science is usually seeking that which is not known: new entities, new theories, new laws, or new relationships among them. On the other hand, clinical medicine is not seeking something new in that sense; it is rather trying to discover which already known disease entity or dysfunction is present in a particular case. That is, medicine is trying to account for the symptoms and signs in a particular instance in terms of causal factors identified in similar symptoms and signs in other instances. The practitioner is more like a detective; he is using what he already knows in general to see what happened in the *particular* case. Thus medicine's art would seem to operate in that interface where generalities (formulas, recipes, theories, laws) are either used or sought in the particular instance. The art is in fitting together the general and the particular: in finding a recognized disease or dysfunction among the clutter of variables in the particular case, and in tailoring known therapies to meet the individual needs of the particular case. This, then, connects with our basic explication of "art" in medicine: when variables are too plentiful (as in the highly particularized case) to be significantly interrelated by formula or theory, dealing thoughtfully with them gets labeled "art" or "intuition."

All these points (a through e) need considerable elaboration. However, for the present, they must be left on an impressionistic level.

6

IV

As a parting shot, we have a further suggestion. It is an attempt to give a more profound reason for medicine's aura of art, which reason is at the same time consistent with our preceding explication.

The suggestion is this: that value considerations pervade medicine, being part and parcel of its basic concepts, and hence (1) its theoretical base is more like art in that respect than are the other sciences, and (2) since values are, like myriad miscellaneous variables, notoriously difficult to identify, quantify, and interrelate, art (in our sense) would necessarily be involved in medicine. As always, this point is meant to be only suggestive. We will elaborate the point, but make no attempt at rigorous defense.

Our scientific and artistic activities are theory-bound. That is, our theories (whether explicit or not) "inform" or guide our thinking; they influence the assumptions we make, the questions we ask, what we count as facts, what we count as evidence and counter-evidence, and how we deal with our raw material. The artist's choice to imitate reality, instead of to symbolize it or to express his feelings about it, is made on the basis of an aesthetic theory held by him. The difference between an opera by Mozart and an opera by Wagner is due, among other factors, to their different ideas about the relation of music to drama. An artist's theory sets the problem (how to paint a gloomy-looking field; how to make music the handmaiden of drama), shapes its solution (the impressionistic painting; *The Ring*), and limits the legitimate forms of criticism (it becomes irrelevant to say, "But women don't really look like that" or "The music is secondary").

It is the same with science. Observations are theory-bound. Cuvier and Lamarck had the very same fossil data. Lamarck saw it as evidence for evolution, whereas Cuvier insisted on the immutability of species and geologic catastrophes. Lavoisier and Priestley did the very same experiment. One saw the new element oxygen and the other saw only "dephlogisticated air." Einstein saw indeterminism in quantum mechanics not as a great discovery, but rather as an admission of ignorance and defeat.

Neither do the problems themselves come labeled as such. They are recognized as problems only within a particular theoretical framework. For example, problems for a Darwinian are not at issue for a believer in Special Creation, nor do chiropractors and MD's face the same problems in making a diagnosis. Similarly, slavery is not seen as a social problem unless one holds some presuppositions about fairness, justice and human dignity. The point is that what counts as a problem—and even perhaps as a fact—is largely determined by the theoretical framework to which we subscribe.

Our artistic and scientific activities are alike in that both are "theory-laden." Why then is it that clinical medicine is more often considered art than is science?

One possibility (other than that given in III *e* above) lies in its basic theoretical concepts. We are suggesting that it is because many of the basic concepts indigenous to medicine, like those of art, have inherent value considerations. That is, these terms cannot be defined by facts alone; rather, they subtly count on value judgments. Such considerations as preference, goal, or social purpose *necessarily* enter into the use of these concepts. The concepts of *disease, normal, health, cure*, are more like concepts such as *beautiful, ugly, balance, expressive*, than they are like *mass, ion, species, continental drift*. The first two groups are more alike because facts alone are not sufficient for the proper use of the terms.

To justify a verdict of "healthy," more is considered than the man's physical well-being. For example, there must be an assumption about life expectancy. A 65-year-old and an 18-year-old could both be pronounced "healthy." Yet if the 18-year-old's physical state were exactly similar to the 65-year-old's, he would be judged in very bad health indeed. When the 65-year-old is declared "healthy," 70 or so is assumed as a good, average life. Also "normal" is notorious for hidden presuppositions as to purposes and preferences. Neither brain-damaged children nor geniuses are normal. Yet only the former are considered sick and in need of help. That is because we have in mind certain purposes, preferences, and assumptions about the "good life." Even setting "normal ranges" for lab measurements can have extra-factual influences. In short, not every abnormality is considered a disease or sickness, and it is instructive to note that facts alone are not determinative; purposes and preferences (i.e., values) play an important role in labeling.

Here, then, is where we are suggesting medicine distinguishes itself from other sciences. In physics, chemistry, biology, and geology, the basic theoretical terms are not as "value-laden" as they are in medicine. We do not mean to prejudge the question of ultimately reducing values to facts. It is sufficient for our point that there be only a strong *prima facie* difference between them. For whatever the final disposition of that difference, art and medicine nevertheless continue to share the *prima facie* difference.

We will conclude with two observations on this fleeting excursion into the value-ladenness of some basic concepts of medicine.

a) If the activities of a discipline are molded by the theory and hence by the basic concepts of that discipline, and if those basic concepts are value-laden, we might also expect to find the activities of the discipline pervaded by value considerations. Their presence would be manifested by the frequent need to rely on "intuition" because values are notoriously difficult to quantify and interrelate by formula and theory. This may be in addition to, and partially account for, the "barrage of variables" which we earlier claimed made "art" or "intuition" necessary in medicine.

b) Perhaps value in the basic concepts also partially accounts for so much concern with medical ethics. If value judgments are unwittingly being made under the guise of objective, factual determination, it is no surprise that ferment eventually bubbles to the surface. No malice need be involved. The intrusion of these values can be so subtle and so hidden by the factual content that not even the users are aware of the infiltration. Much would be gained by flushing out these value insinuations from the factual underbrush.

REFERENCE

Feinstein, Alvan R. *Clinical Judgment*. Baltimore: Williams and Wilkins, 1967.

SAMUEL GOROVITZ AND ALASDAIR MACINTYRE, "TOWARD A THEORY OF MEDICAL FALLIBILITY"

Gorovitz and MacIntyre see medical error as unavoidable. They want to explain why this is. They begin by drawing a distinction between internal and external norms. Internal norms are the rules that govern the pursuit of knowledge. These internal norms would govern what positivists have called the context of justification. External norms are the goals that one has in pursuing the knowledge—either why one is in a particular field or the uses one chooses for that particular field.

Pursuing knowledge assumes that there is partial ignorance. Partial ignorance means that error is always possible. This could conclude the argument of Gorovitz and MacIntyre, but they go on to argue that the subject matter of clinical medicine inclines it to necessary error. They make this further claim because they want to rule out even the theoretical possibility of achieving full medical knowledge. Gorovitz and MacIntyre also want to counter the view that mistakes in science must be due to one of two mutually exclusive reasons: neglect or limitations of present knowledge. They point out that the usual distinctions between pure and applied sciences and between either of these and technology will not do the job that they want, for these distinctions will not allow for a third cause of error.

For a third source of error, Gorovitz and MacIntyre turn to individuals. Individuals were the bane of the Hempel-Oppenhein model (Chapter 2). For the D-N model, knowledge is knowledge of kinds of things (universals). Gorovitz and MacIntyre, by stressing the role of particulars in medicine, are saying that the D-N model fails for clinical medicine. How does it fail? Some particulars—individuals—are so representative of all individuals like them that there is no problem with using them in laws for explanation and prediction. Some particulars are not like this. Some are so different from others that they cannot be subsumed so easily under laws.

What is needed for particulars to be subsumable under laws, according to Gorovitz and MacIntyre, is that the particulars be fully understandable in terms of (that is, reducible to) their component parts at any one time. With some individuals, the component parts at any time are not enough. Gorovitz and MacIntyre give the example of salt marshes and hurricanes. With particulars such as these, one also needs the history of the particular for complete understanding. Put baldly, they claim that no hurricane is quite like any other hurricane. This is due to the fact that a hurricane's properties at any one time are a complex result of the interaction of a vast number of factors. This is precisely the point made against the reasonability of the D-N model by Scriven in Chapter 2. As Scriven might say: No ink stain is quite like any other ink stain. We could never predict on the basis of one ink stain what the next ink stain would be like.

Clinical medicine deals with patients. Patients are like hurricanes, salt marshes, and Scrivenian ink stains. Thus totally precise and accurate prediction is impossible in clinical medicine. Therefore, mistakes must always be a part of clinical medicine.

Toward a Theory of Medical Fallibility

SAMUEL GOROVITZ AND ALASDAIR MACINTYRE

No species of fallibility is more important or less understood than fallibility in medical practice. The physician's propensity for damaging error is widely denied, perhaps because it is so intensely feared. Patients who suffer at the hands of their physicians often seek compensation by invoking the procedures of malpractice claims, and physicians view such claims as perhaps the only outcomes more earnestly to be avoided than even the damaging errors from which they presumably arise. Malpractice insurance rates soar, physicians strike, legislatures intervene, and, in the end, health care suffers from the absence of a clear understanding of what medical error is, how it arises, to what extent it is avoidable, when it is culpable, and what relationship it should bear to compensation for harm. It is to this cluster of questions that we direct our efforts.

We seek to provide the basic outlines of a theory of medical fallibility. Such a theory, to be accepted as adequate, must account for certain basic data. Those data include the fact that medical error not only occurs, but seems unavoidable; that some medical error seems innocent even when severely damaging, whereas other medical error seems culpable; that the harm that results from medical error seems sometimes but not always to warrant compensation; that the error that causes harm seems sometimes but not always to warrant sanctions; and, finally, that the relationships among culpability, harm, compensation, and sanctions are obscure. To succeed, our theory must increase our understanding of why medical error occurs and must help us distinguish between culpable and innocent error—it

From *Journal of Medicine and Philosophy* 1 (1976): 51–71.
© Kluwer Academic Publishers.

must diminish the obscurity surrounding the relationships among harm, culpability, compensation, and sanctions. Finally, and most importantly, it must thereby provide a basis for a more rational societal response to the reality of error in clinical practice.

Medicine as a practice is more opaque than we normally take it to be. We approach it too easily with already well formed categories devised for other purposes such as those reflected in the sociology of the professions, the philosophy of the natural sciences, and the law. By so doing we overlook a unique blending of epistemological and social factors in the practice of medicine. For example, lawyers apparently assume that legislators and the courts are competent to determine when medical error is culpable and, correspondingly, when harmed patients are entitled to compensation, merely by applying the general principles with which our legal system handles torts. The reaction of the medical profession has normally been to claim prerogatives of professional jurisdiction in response. Relevant as the attitudes of both the legal and medical professions have been, both parties seem to assume that we already have an adequate understanding of the types of error to which physicians are liable.

We wish to construct a theory of medical error which will challenge this assumption. In order to do this, however, we have to turn away from the conventional discussions which center immediately upon the notion of medical responsibility, usually with some help from sociological studies of professional responsibility, and examine instead certain more fundamental notions which derive not from medicine understood as a profession, but from medicine understood as a science.

SCIENTIFIC NORMS AND THE SOURCES OF ERROR

Natural scientists tend not to have an entirely clear view of the normative character of their own activity, of the values that guide, constrain, and inform their activities. But there is a good deal of evidence for their finding plausible a distinction between *internal* and *external* norms. Internal norms are those which derive from the essential character of scientific activity as a cognitive pursuit. External norms are those which govern motives either for participating in or for making use of the results of scientific activity. Internal norms are concerned with such factors as verifiability, truth, and reason; external norms are concerned with such factors as curiosity, ambition, and social utility.

The recognized norms which are internal to scientific practice are perhaps fourfold. There is that which prescribes attention to central rather than to peripheral problems of the science in question. There is that which prescribes the standards of scientific craftsmanship—in the design of experiments, for example, or in the criteria of confirmation that determine when a claim is well enough supported to be accepted into the body of scientific knowledge. There is that belonging to the mathematical element in natural sciences which prescribes elegance and simplicity as the aesthetic hallmarks of distinguished theorizing. And finally, dominating all, there is that which prescribes the search for truth, that is, the search for a theory which will mark a gain in respect of truth relative to currently accepted theory.

These norms all presuppose that at any given moment a scientist's standards are necessarily set by the present state of his discipline. For that state he or she clearly cannot be held accountable; and there will be limits to the extent to which even the greatest thinker can revolutionize a science. Indeed, should everything be known about a given area of science, all *scientific* activity in that area would cease, even though work might continue on the practical applications of that knowledge. Therefore, where there is scientific activity, there is partial ignorance—the ignorance that exists as a precondition for scientific progress. And since ignorance is a precondition of progress, where there is the possibility of progress there is the possibility of error. This ignorance of what is not yet known is the permanent state of all science and a source of error even when all the internal norms of science have been fully respected.

Among external norms of natural science are those which are relevant to personal motives for entering upon a scientific career or for doing science. One of these prescribes a certain kind of honesty: assiduous care in acknowledging debts to others, and, above all, in acknowledging priority of publication. Such a norm is not internal to the practices of natural science in the way that the norms governing experimental design or theory construction are. Natural science could remain essentially what it is now, even if the norms about priority of publication were somewhat different. Natural science might for example, if it had had a different cultural history, have adopted the ideals of anonymity and impersonality which informed medieval architecture: who precisely built what is for that architecture relatively unimportant, and vastly unimportant compared with who precisely built what in modern architecture or who discovered what in modern science. Modern science is thus a competitive race, although one could have an internally impeccable science without the competition.

Some of the other external norms of natural science have a good deal to do with this accidentally competitive aspect of its activities: that which warns young scientists against making premature claims or that which enjoins a certain kind of respect for the processes of election to a Fellowship of the Royal Society or to a Nobel Prize. But others concern the reasons which a particular scientist may have for doing this rather than that sort of science: such reasons as that inquiry, in some particular area, is likely to lead to socially useful discoveries. What some external norms prescribe may sometimes be at variance with what internal norms are held to prescribe. When, for good ecological reasons, Barry Commoner persuaded a distinguished colleague in chemistry to turn his attention to problems concerning the nitrates in agricultural soils, the other chemists in his department were disturbed because the problems involved are not central to chemical inquiry as presently understood. But the very nature of the disagreement exhibits the acknowledgment of the two sets of norms as distinguishable.

Note that it is *not* our contention that this classification of norms is good or bad, clear or confused, complete or incomplete, for any particular purpose; it *is* our contention that these norms, classified in this way, are as a matter of fact implicit in current scientific practice, and that practicing natural scientists will readily recognize them as distinguishable influences or pressures on their own behavior. What matters for our subsequent argument is that this understanding of the norms of natural science involves acceptance of one particular way of classifying scientific errors. For on this view all scientific error will arise *either* from the limitations of the present state of natural science—i.e. ignorance—or from the willfulness of negligence of the natural scientist—i.e. ineptitude. This classification is treated as exhaustive. Willfulness and negligence will arise when those motives which are to be restrained by the external norms of natural science—ambition, impatience, competitiveness, a great anxiety to

do good in the world—are allowed to override the internal norms. One function then of at least some external norms is to prevent extra-scientific matters from invading and corrupting scientific activity; they could be other than they are in some respects, but some such set of norms would always be necessary.

It is worth remarking at this stage that to the extent to which our account so far is successful—that is, in being a recognizable version of what scientists characteristically would acknowledge about their practice—it is likely to seem familiar and even trivial. But it is the unsurprising character of the account that itself invites surprise when we go on to claim that this view of the sources of error in science presupposes a mistaken view of natural science. What will the relevance of this argument be to medical science? This view of ignorance and ineptitude as the only sources of error has been transmitted from the pure to the applied sciences, and then, more specifically, from medical science to medical practice viewed as the application of what is learned by medical science. In order to understand this connection we must now examine the way in which the distinction between pure and applied science is customarily understood.

PURE VS. APPLIED SCIENCES

Applied sciences are commonly held to differ from pure sciences in two main respects. First, they are defined with essential reference to some practical aim, such as the building of bridges, the expansion of agricultural production, or the promotion of the health of men or of animals. Second, they are defined in terms of some subject matter which is identified in pre-scientific terms. Pure sciences, by contrast, are only accidentally related to practical aims, and they continually redefine their own subject matter. What physics is about it is for physicists to say. Further, there is a useful distinction to be drawn between an applied science and a technology. An applied science is, like a pure science, a body of theoretically-organized knowledge, even if the principle of organization points toward a practical goal. A technology is a series of devices for realizing certain ends. Engineers, agriculturists, and medical scientists are unlikely to be entirely innocent of technology, but not every one of them need be a technologist.

Just as the pure scientist can err from one of only two types of cause, so it is also with the applied scientist, on the view we are describing. If the physician prescribes a drug which turns out to have drastically unfortunate side effects on his patient, then *either* the limits of pharmaceutical and physiological knowledge are to blame *or* the physician was negligent, that is, he failed to act in accordance with the best knowledge available. On the assumption that the physician did not bring about the side effects from some willful intention, then one of these two causes must have been operative. Where a surgeon is concerned, lack of technological skill may also be a factor. But failures from lack of technological skill are themselves classified in terms of the view of the sources of error which we have identified. Either they spring from the general level of the art: the technology in question just has not advanced far enough—in which case lack of technological, say of surgical, skill compares to scientific ignorance; or else, assuming he is not willful, the particular technologist has been negligent in either acquiring or exercising the requisite available skill. Hence technologies, as ordinarily understood, do not provide a counter-example to the account of error which we have imputed to the natural scientist's characteristic understanding of his own activity. The complexity of that last phrase is not accidental. For what we are suggesting is not that natural science requires this

account, but only a particular dominant interpretation of natural science. What that interpretation is, why it is dominant, and what the alternative to it is are the questions to which we must turn next.

REINTERPRETING NATURAL SCIENCE

Natural science did not in the seventeenth century discard quite as much of Aristotelianism as its philosophical protagonists supposed. What it retained included an inability to give a plausible account of our knowledge of particulars, of individuals—an inability for which Aristotelianism is notorious. For natural science, on a modern physicist's view just as much as on Plato's or Aristotle's, the objects of knowledge are universals, that is, the properties of objects classified by *kinds*, and the generalizations that link those properties. The scientist looks for law-like relationships between properties; particulars occur in this account only as the bearers of properties, and the implied concept of a particular is of a contingent collection of properties. To explain the behavior of a particular is nothing else than to subsume its particular properties under the relevant law-like generalization; to predict is to use the same stock of law-like generalizations about the relevant properties. Notice that on this view, predictive failure in science can only have two sources: factual ignorance as to the relevant laws or as to just which properties are present in a situation; or inferential error, such as when conclusions are drawn carelessly from the laws and descriptions of properties. Thus, where we are not ignorant, any inadequacy in our predictive powers must be attributed to the predictor, to his willfulness or his negligence.

What is it about *particulars* that escapes notice on this view? To answer this question, we must first say what we mean by "a particular." It will not do, for our present purposes, to give a syntactic definition in terms of the specification of some class of expressions, such as denoting expressions of a particular kind. The class of particulars with which we are concerned includes neither the square root of minus two nor the horizon. It does include such varied items as salt marshes, planetary systems, planets, dolphins, snowflakes, hurricanes, cities, crowds, and people. A particular occupies a region of space, persists through time, has boundaries, has an environment, has peripheral and more central areas, and characteristically can split into two or more parts. Notice that in this use of "particulars," certain collectivities are particulars—states, herds, forests, crowds, and cities, for example. Every particular continues to exist and has the characteristics that it has only in virtue of the operation of some set of physical and chemical mechanisms. Some particulars—ice cubes and molecules are notable examples—are such that nearly everything that we might want to know about them can be explained simply by citing the relevant mechanisms. Further, the generalizations that describe their behavior are generalizations that we accept as impeccably reliable. Thus, roasted ice cubes melt, and we can predict with complete assurance that any particular ice cube that we roast will in fact melt. This is in large measure because there is little diversity—at least, of any sort that interests us—among ice cubes. Each example of the type is, roughly speaking, quite like any other. The basic mistake made by that interpretation of science which considers that all genuine scientific knowledge is of universals is to suppose that all particulars are of this kind. But this is clearly false. Many particulars—salt marshes, hurricanes, and the higher primates, for example—cannot be understood solely as the sum-total of the physical and chemical mechanisms that operate on them. What effects such mechanisms do have is

affected by the particular history of that specific particular with all its contingent circumstances, contingent that is, and even accidental, relative to the operation of the mechanisms. One cannot expect therefore in the case of such particulars to be able to move from a theoretical knowledge of the relevant laws to a prediction of the particular's behavior. The history of the law-governed mechanisms and of the particular which is their bearer is, so to speak, an intervening variable which may always to some degree elude us.

It may be objected that this is a familiar point made in a misleading way. To predict any outcome, the scientist must possess not only accurate formulations of the relevant laws, but also knowledge of the initial and boundary conditions. Are we not merely saying that in the case of some types of particular we do not possess adequate knowledge of these conditions? This way of putting matters is however itself highly misleading. For the whole vocabulary of laws, initial conditions, and boundary conditions, has application to situations where either we have a controlled and limited environment or else we have a natural environment resembling a controlled environment to a high degree, wherein the transition from one state to another by the operation of a specific mechanism is detached from its historical antecedents as well as from the interventions of environmental circumstance. There are indeed types of particulars whose past and future can be mapped entirely in these terms, such as the roasted ice cube, but there are also types of particulars with respect to which this is not so.

Hurricanes and salt marshes, for instance, interact continuously with a variety of uncontrollable environmental factors. No hurricane is quite like any other hurricane, and no salt marsh is quite like any other salt marsh. Certainly everything that occurs to and in a hurricane or a salt marsh is law governed, but because we never know what historically specific interactions may impact on such historically specific particulars—for example, because of melting icebergs, flocks of migrating birds, changes in the temperature of deep-sea waters, etc.—we never know in advance which lawlike generalizations will be relevant—even if we know them all—and which boundary conditions will be relevant. Indeed, in order to have such knowledge, we would need to know in detail what the behavior would be of each potential influence on the particular subject of our inquiry. To understand perfectly the behavior of a given hurricane, we would need to have perfect understanding of the polar ice cap and the Gulf Stream. But these, too, are particulars interacting with their larger environments, which include among other things the very hurricane we wish to understand. We thus cannot have perfect knowledge of our hurricane short of having a complete understanding of all the laws that describe natural processes and a complete state description of the world. In short, perfect knowledge of that one particular hurricane is unavailable except under conditions of omniscience. Thus, it is not so much ignorance either of the initial conditions or of the relevant laws, or even of both conjoined, that is in question; rather, it is ignorance of the contingencies of the environmental context, a context that differs from that of experiment more radically than has normally been allowed. Hence, no degree of theoretical meteorological knowledge will enable us in the context of actual practice to do more than score a certain degree, although perhaps a high degree, of predictive success with hurricanes.

This difference between types of particulars—ice cubes on the one hand and hurricanes on the other—in respect of our predictive powers is matched by a difference between the types of generalizations by

means of which we may reasonably aspire to describe their behavior. For that type of particular wherein the particular's history is crucial, wherein a theoretical knowledge of the mechanisms will by itself never be adequate for explanatory or predictive purposes, wherein the actual environment does not adequately match the conditions of the ideal environment presupposed by the theory (as it sometimes does), the generalizations by means of which we effectively grasp their behavior will not be genuine universal law-like generalizations, but rather generalizations prefaced by "Characteristically and for the most part. . . ." Of such generalizations it is true that when we are in possession of the best possible formulation, we may still meet with counter-examples and yet not be supplied thereby with any good reason, even any *prima facie* reason, for discarding or revising our formulation.

Consider the example of smallpox vaccination. One in 1200 will experience dangerous and perhaps fatal effects, as a reaction to the vaccination. Although there must *be* reasons why some individuals succumb—factors that distinguish them from the majority who are unharmed by the vaccination—we do not know what those factors are. We thus cannot accept as a *universal* generalization the claim that vaccinated individuals, even of a certain sort, will not thereby be harmed. But we can accept with confidence the claim that characteristically and for the most part, vaccinated individuals will suffer no adverse consequences. *That* generalization is not refuted by the illness or death of the occasional individual. What, then, are we to say of an individual about to be vaccinated? Of course, the effect of the vaccination on him will be determined by natural laws, his condition, and perhaps the way he interacts with his environment subsequent to vaccination. But we do not and cannot know all the relevant laws and conditions, thus our knowledge of this individual is limited and our predictive ability is constrained. We can have reasonable, empirically based expectations, accepted with a high degree of confidence. But no more is available to us than that. Yet more would be needed to eliminate entirely the possibility of causing harm by giving the vaccine.

One observation should be appended to the argument so far. When we have spoken of law-like generalizations we have intended this to refer to genuine law-like probabilistic generalizations as well as to non-probabilistic ones. For our purposes there are no relevant differences between these. From this it does not of course follow that, as in the case of smallpox vaccinations, we may not on occasion be able *de facto* to assign a number to the proportion of individuals in a population who escape our formulation. But such a statement of a *de facto* proportion must never be confused with the kind of law found in, for example, statistical mechanics.

What is true of hurricanes and salt marshes is thus also true of animals and people. This is an empirical claim. That is, it is a question of fact about a given class of particulars whether or not the empirical, inductively founded generalizations with which we describe their behavior for explanatory and predictive purposes in our practical transactions with them can be simply deduced from the law-like generalizations of the relevant part of theoretical science. Where this is not so, practical experience becomes relevant in a manner quite different from that in which practical experience is important in a laboratory. What is important to the theoretical or experimental scientist is experience in research, not experience of the distinctive features of the particular crystals or molecules or other entities which provide a subject-matter for the research. That is, the scientist does have an interest in those particular entities, but it is an interest in what they have in common that typifies the activities of research. Thus principles of crystal formation or solubility are inferred from the observable characteristics of diverse particular crystals, but the *differences* among such crystals are not to the point; it is their *similarities* that support generalization. In contrast, what is important to the meteorologist, navigator, or veterinary surgeon is an understanding of particular, individual hurricanes, cloud formations, or cows, and thus what is distinctive about them as particulars is what is crucially important. How such particulars differ from one another in their diversity thus becomes as important as the characteristics they commonly share. Experience of a single entity over time is necessary for an understanding of that entity as a particular in all its distinctiveness, for its individual characteristics will not typically be inferable simply from what is known about the general—that is, commonly shared—characteristics of the *type* of entity of which it is an instance.

Our thesis is then that . . . natural science, defined so that it is concerned exclusively with the knowledge of universals, blinds us to the existence of particulars as proper objects of knowledge. In the process, it blinds us to the role of a type of generalization that is different in crucial respects from those law-like generalizations that are usually treated as the characteristic genre of the natural scientist. This thesis could be developed in either a stronger or a weaker version. Its stronger version would involve a challenge to that whole picture of natural science which makes theoretical physics the most fundamental of disciplines and then ranks chemistry and biology before the applied sciences. For in this stronger version the thesis would insist that nature consists of nothing but more or less complex particulars, that theoretical physics is the most abstract kind of knowledge, and that it therefore always has to be based on our knowledge of particulars gained by means of sciences of the concrete. The most fundamental sciences on this view would be the disciplines concerned with our practical transactions with particulars: medicine, veterinary medicine, engineering, military and political sciences, and so on.

But this stronger version of the thesis is unnecessary for our present purposes. Even on the weaker version of our thesis— namely that the dominant interpretation of natural science must be revised so as to allow a place for our knowledge of particulars alongside our knowledge of generalizations—it is clear that those sciences which do deal with particulars require a view of error quite different from that which is derived from the dominant interpretation. To this topic we shall therefore have to return. But first, we must examine one more feature of our revised view of natural science. . . .

NECESSARY FALLIBILITY

Precisely because our understanding and expectations of particulars cannot be fully spelled out merely in terms of law-like generalizations and initial conditions, the best possible judgment may always turn out to be erroneous—and erroneous not merely because our science has not yet progressed far enough, nor because the scientist has been either willful or negligent, but because of the necessary fallibility of our knowledge of particulars. For it is characteristic of empirical, inductively founded "characteristically-and-for-the-most-part" generalizations, as we have already noticed, that they may be the best possible instruments of prediction about particulars, and yet lead on occasion to unavoidable predictive failure as the evolving environment interacts with the particular with which we are concerned. What types of particulars must be understood, at least partly, in terms of this kind of generalization is an empirical question; for that very reason it is also an empirical question to what degree of error we are liable in a given area. The nature of the gap between theoretically perfect predictive power and our actual predictive powers at their best is itself a notable subject for empirical enquiry, and the answers will certainly turn out to be very different in different areas. The necessary fallibility of the meteorologist may turn out to be of a very different degree than the necessary fallibility of the veterinary surgeon.

The recognition of this element of necessary fallibility immediately disposes of that two-fold classification of the sources of error which we have seen both to inform natural scientists' understanding of their own practices and to be rooted in the epistemology which underlies that understanding. Error may indeed arise from the present state of scientific ignorance or from willfulness or negligence. But it may also arise precisely from this third factor which we have called necessary fallibility in respect to particulars. . . .

KENNETH F. SCHAFFNER, "EXEMPLAR REASONING ABOUT BIOLOGICAL MODELS"

Schaffner appeals to Kuhn's notion of the exemplar to show the differences between medicine and sciences such as physics. By exemplars, Kuhn and Schaffner mean the relatively easy problems used to teach students how to go on to solve more difficult problems. Exemplars are always specific to a discipline or subdiscipline. If you have ever taken a math or science course, you have probably noticed that the problems at the end of a chapter get progressively more difficult. The strategy of the authors is based on the fact that once students catch on to how to do the easy problems, they will be able to do the more difficult problems. Schaffner refers to using exemplars in this fashion as exemplar reasoning. Using exemplars requires seeing analogies. The analogies represent the relationships between models. Schaffner means by model just what Hesse did in her article in Chapter 2.

The difference between medicine and, say, physics, chemistry, and some areas of biology, is this. With the theories of physics, chemistry, and some areas of biology, it is possible to structure the theories in a formal, mathematical manner so that it is clear what follows from what. Schaffner uses the example of Euclidean geometry. The scientific theories of physics and chemistry can be made to look just like Euclidean geometry:

Axiom: Two points determine a straight line.

Definition: A triangle is the figure resulting from the intersection of three lines.

Theorem: The interior angles of a triangle add up to 180 degrees.

Proof: Here is a proof sketch of the above theorem (given without justifications of the statements.) Consider the triangle shown here.

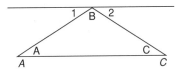

Draw a line parallel to base *AC*.

Angle 1 = angle A.

Angle 2 = angle C.

Angles 1 + B + 2 = 180 degrees.

Substitute angle A for angle 1 and angle C for angle 2.

Therefore, angles A + B + C = 180. (We used at least one axiom: Equals can be substituted for equals.)

When reformulated in this fashion, the structure "hidden" in the exemplars becomes obvious. One does not have to work problems to find the structure. One does not need exemplar reasoning if the theory's structure can be made explicit.

With medicine, the theories do not lend themselves to such formalization. Medicine cannot be formalized the way Euclidean geometry can. Thus there is no way to eliminate the need for exemplar reasoning in medicine. Hesse would point out that where exemplar reasoning is needed, metaphors and models are central to the science. Medicine would be a case where the use of metaphors is not just a heuristic device.

Unlike Gorovitz and MacIntyre, who think that medicine is a different kind of discipline from, say, physics, Schaffner thinks that the two disciplines differ more in degree with respect to the need for exemplar reasoning. Schaffner stresses the idea that in medicine there is a looser fit between generalization and instance than there is in physics or chemistry.

What does he mean by "looser fit"? Determining the boiling point of distilled water requires that we know the definition of *boiling,* how it relates to temperature, what counts as distilled water and how to get it, and how to set up an apparatus to boil water and measure its temperature throughout the heating process. The theory literally tells us that we can use this method to determine the boiling point for any sample of distilled water and for any liquid; if we were to reconstruct the theory to look like Euclidean geometry, it would be evident that this method will work for all liquids. We don't need analogies or models. In other words, exemplars are not required here. They might make things easier for us, but that is another issue, related to *our* abilities and not to the theory involved.

Diagnosing sudden infant death syndrome, battered-child syndrome, carpal tunnel syndrome, rheumatoid arthritis, sprained ankle, and most psychological problems and deciding whether to treat a toddler's middle-ear infection with antibiotics are quite different from answering "What is the boiling point of water?" The latter has a clear method that will lead to an answer. The medical questions lack such a clear method. There is no medical theory that will ensure that two children with the same injuries have both been battered, that two patients with the same sad story are clinically depressed, or that two toddlers with the same sort of earache ought to be treated in the same way. (There is a kind of test, an electromyelogram, that is used to help in diagnosing carpal tunnel syndrome. The test allows one to confirm that nervous conduction from upper arm to hand is being slowed at the wrist. Strictly speaking, it does not establish that the nerve running through the carpal tunnel is damaged.)

The medical questions require appropriate use of what physicians refer to as clinical impression. Clinical impression is a vague concept meant to express the fact that in making these sorts of diagnoses, physicians put together a total picture in a way that defies clear explication. Clinical impression is also a flag for the use of subjective judgments such as "This ankle looks more bruised than sprained" or "That is contact dermatitis, not a food allergy." Perhaps these judgments are just insightful uses of theory-laden observation. In any case, no one has yet determined just what makes the best physicians as good as they are at diagnostics.

Schaffner believes that pointing out the need and the role for exemplar reasoning is a more precise way of stating the point made by Gorovitz and MacIntyre that medicine is a science of particulars. Could medicine eliminate the need for exemplars? If we answer no, then we have discovered that medicine is a discipline autonomous (different in kind, not merely degree) from many scientific disciplines.

A no answer means no reduction of clinical medicine to biology, physics, and chemistry. If we answer yes, then we are saying that the need for exemplars in medicine is very much like the need for exemplars in physics. It is a psychological need due to weakness in our ability to teach and to learn medicine. If we answer yes, the laws of medicine will apply just like the laws of physics. If we answer yes, we are claiming that there is a structure to medicine, that we can restate medical theory so that it looks like Euclidean geometry, so that all the truths of medicine follow from definitions and axioms.

If we could eliminate the need for exemplars, if we could derive truly general laws of medicine, if we could lay out the structure of medical theory, then we would have reduced medicine to the ranks of the more theoretical biological sciences.

Exemplar Reasoning about Biological Models

KENNETH F. SCHAFFNER

EXEMPLARS, PRACTICES, AND THE STRUCTURE OF SCIENCE

Philosophy of science over the past two decades has often been preoccupied with the nature of the metascientific entities that would adequately represent structures of its first-order subject matter: science *per se*. The work of Kuhn (1962, 1970) on "paradigms," Toulmin on "ideals of natural order" (1961) and "disciplines" (1972), Lakatos (1970) on "research programmes," Shapere (1974) on "domains," and Laudan (1977) on "research traditions," among others, represent attempts to characterize in metascientific terms the entities that comprised the subject matter of science. Interest in multiplying metascientific entities seems to continue, Kitcher's recent concept of a "practice" (1983, 1984) being a case in point.

From Kenneth F. Schaffner, "Exemplar Reasoning about Biological Models and Diseases: A Relation between the Philosophy of Medicine and Philosophy of Science," *Journal of Medicine and Philosophy* 11 (1986): 63–80. © Kluwer Academic Publishers.

Philosophy of medicine in the past decade has been less concerned with analogues of these large scale units and more occupied with the *prima facie* peculiar ontological nature of medical science—specifically with the value-impregnated features of medicine's constitutive elements such as diseases, as well as with the "particularity" of medical concepts and reasoning. Grene (1976), Engelhardt (1975, 1976), Wartofsky (1976), and Whitbeck (1976) probed the former problem, and later debate between Boorse (1977) and Engelhardt (1985) has underscored both the centrality and the persistence of this issue in the philosophy of medicine. Gorovitz and MacIntyre (1976) introduced the notion of "medicine as a science of particulars" into the discipline. The notion of a special science of particulars, and the policy recommendations that might follow from it, were criticized by Martin (1977) and Bayles and Caplan (1978a, 1978b), with Gorovitz (1978) defending it against the latters' criticism. Minogue (1982) has also argued against Gorovitz and

MacIntyre's interpretation of the source of medical error as best located in the notion of a "science of particulars," and has had his position criticized by Brody (1982).

I want to suggest that a rather different perspective on the role of "particularity" is needed to resolve what Gorovitz and MacIntyre were seeking and to what their critics were objecting, at the same time these critics appeared to believe that a set of important questions were being raised. I want to begin from some comments made by Kuhn (1970) in the Postscript to the second edition of his extraordinarily influential [book] *The Structure of Scientific Revolutions* and elaborated somewhat in his (1974) [work] and then consider some recent proposals made by Kitcher (1983, 1984). With this as background, I will then reexamine the proposals of Gorovitz and MacIntyre on "particularity."

In *The Structure of Scientific Revolutions*, Kuhn attempts to further refine the concept of "paradigm" that is so central to the argument in the volume's first edition. The notion has, he claims, two interpenetrating but still rather different aspects, and Kuhn proposes that he use some new terminology, specifically the idea of a "disciplinary matrix," to clarify the earlier term "paradigm." The first aspect of "paradigm," which we may describe as a disciplinary matrix *per se*, is similar to what traditional philosophers of science had understood a scientific theory to be, namely, collections of (1) symbolic generalizations and (2) models. In his 1962 book, Kuhn makes a significant departure from traditional philosophy of science by introducing "values"—primarily of an epistemic sort—as an important component of a paradigm. This intrinsic value component is again reintroduced as element (3) of the disciplinary matrix in his volume's second edition (1970). A fourth component of the "disciplinary matrix," which Kuhn terms an "exemplar," was, however, viewed

by Kuhn as a *distinctly different sense of paradigm*. As Kuhn writes:

For . . . [the fourth sort of element in the disciplinary matrix] the term "paradigm" would be entirely appropriate, both philosophically and autobiographically; this is the component of a group's shared commitments which first led me to the choice of that word. Because the term has assumed a life of its own, however, I shall here substitute "exemplars." By it I mean, initially, the *concrete* problem solutions that students encounter as part of their scientific education, whether in laboratories, on examinations, or at the ends of chapters in science texts. To these shared examples should, however, be added at least some of the technical problem-solutions found in the periodical literature that scientists encounter during their post-educational careers and that also show them by example how their job is to be done. More than other sorts of components of the disciplinary matrix, differences between sets of exemplars provide the community fine-structure of science. (1970, pp. 186–187, emphasis added)

Kuhn adds that "the paradigm as shared example is the central element of what I now take to be the most novel and least understood aspect of *The Structure of Scientific Revolutions*," and, in the postscript (1970) and a later essay (1974), he elaborates further on the concept. For our purposes, I want to focus on the problem-solving aspect of exemplars, namely, the way in which individuals learning a discipline come to know how to apply the generalizations of the discipline to specific problematic situations. As Kuhn writes:

A phenomenon familiar to both students of science and historians of science provides a clue. The former regularly report that they have read through a chapter of their text, understood it perfectly, but nonetheless had difficulty solving a number of the problems at the chapter's end. Ordinarily also, those difficulties dissolve in the same way. The student discovers, with or without the assistance of his instructor, a way to see his problem as like a problem he has already

KENNETH F. SCHAFFNER

encountered. Having seen the resemblance, grasped the analogy between two or more distinct problems, he can interrelate symbols [constituting the law-sketch or scientific generalizations] and attach them to nature in the ways that have proved effective before. The law-sketch, say $f = ma$, has functioned as a tool, informing the student what similarities to look for, signaling the gestalt in which the situation is to be seen. The resultant ability to see a variety of situations as like each other, as subject for $f = ma$ or some other symbolic generalization, is, I think, the main thing a student acquires by doing exemplary problems. (1970, p. 189)

I believe that this is an important insight of Kuhn's and one that has largely gone unnoticed by most philosophers of science. One philosopher, Philip Kitcher, has, however, resonated with these suggestions and several others of Kuhn and has also taken a cue from some largely ignored proposals of Bromberger (1963, 1966). Kitcher has examined both the development of mathematical knowledge as well as classical and molecular genetics, and has proposed that a notion of a "practice" be utilized to capture scientific disciplines. Kitcher's "practice" bears important analogies to Kuhn's "paradigm" and also to other metascientific units such as Shapere's "domain" and Laudan's "research tradition," but I shall not attempt to examine those similarities and differences here. Rather the point is to suggest that continuing interest in such metascientific entities may well afford opportunities for synergistic interplay between philosophy of science and philosophy of medicine for reasons that I shall discuss in the following section. I will close this section by briefly outlining Kitcher's notion of a "practice" and illustrating some of these further possible points of interplay.

Kitcher introduced his notion of a "practice" in his volume *The Nature of Mathematical Knowledge* (1983), but I will confine most of my discussion to the manner in which he used the concept in connection with classi-

cal and molecular genetics. For our purposes, we are interested in (1) the structure of a practice, and (2) the manners to which it is put in scientific development and application.

In connection with classical genetics, a practice is characterized as follows:

There is a common language used to talk about hereditary phenomena, a set of accepted statements in that language (the corpus of beliefs about inheritance . . .), a set of questions taken to be appropriate questions to ask about hereditary phenomena, and a set of patterns of reasoning which are instantiated in answering some of the accepted questions; (also: sets of experimental procedures and methodological rules, both designed for use in evaluating proposed answers . . .). The practice of classical genetics at a time is completely specified by identifying each of the components just listed. (1984, p. 352)

It is the "pattern of reasoning" that I take to be most important for Kitcher's notion of practice. This idea is further elaborated:

A pattern of reasoning is a sequence of *schematic sentences*, that is sentences in which certain items of a nonlogical vocabulary have been replaced by dummy letters, together with a set of *filling instructions* which specify how substitutions are to be made in the schemata to produce reasoning which instantiates the pattern. This notion of pattern is intended to explicate the idea of a common structure that underlies a group of problem-solutions. (1984, p. 353)

Kitcher relates this account to what beginning students learn:

Neophytes are not taught (and never have been taught) a few fundamental theoretical laws from which genetic "theorems" are to be deduced. They are introduced to some technical terminology, which is used to advance a large amount of information about *special organisms*. Certain questions about heredity in *these organisms* are posed and answered. Those who understand the theory are those who know that questions are to be asked about *hitherto unstudied examples*, who know how to apply the technical language to the organisms involved in these *examples,* and who can apply the patterns of reasoning which are to be instantiated in constructing answers. More simply, successful students grasp general patterns of reasoning which can be used to resolve new cases. (1984, p. 354, emphasis added)

Though moving in the correct direction, I believe that Kitcher has understated the extent to which the nature of biomedical theorizing requires an increased emphasis on what might be called *prototype organisms* and on *analogical extension of biological knowledge.* In order to make this claim plausible, I need to rehearse my perspective on biological theorizing, more details and examples of which can be found in my article published elsewhere (1980).

EXEMPLARS, ANALOGY, AND THE STRUCTURE OF BIOMEDICAL SCIENCE

In my view, most, but not all, theories in the biomedical sciences are best construed as a *series of overlapping interlevel temporal models.* I distinguish this approach from the more traditional construal of theory structure that is largely patterned on theory structure in the physical sciences as seen through the lenses of logicism and the received view (see Suppe, 1974, 1977). Theory structure in the physical sciences illustrates what might be termed the "Euclidean Ideal"—a deductive systematization of a broad class of generalizations under a small number of axioms. . . .

Biologists—especially those biologists seeking a methodological unity with the physical sciences—and philosophers of biology, such as the early Ruse (1973), maintained that the laws and theories of biology has the exact same logical structure as did those of the physical sciences. This view is only supportable if one restricts one's attention to those few—but very important—theories in biology that in point of fact have a very broad scope and are characterizable in

their more simplified forms as a set of "laws" that admit of axiomatization and deductive elaboration. Certain forms of Mendelian genetics and of population genetics satisfy this characterization, but deeper analysis of even these theories will disclose difficulties with a strong methodological parallelism with the physical sciences (see Schaffner, 1980, and Kitcher, 1984). . . .

My position is that acquaintance with a number of shared exemplars is more important in the biomedical sciences than in the physical sciences because biomedical theories lack generalizations of broad scope, though there are some significant exceptions, such as the genetic code (which is almost universal, some codons in mitochondrial genes being different from the standard code) and some of the simpler forms of population genetic theories. Biomedical investigation focusses on an appropriate organism—often referred to as an "animal model" though perhaps the most widely examined organisms are the insect *Drosophila melanogaster* and the common intestinal bacterium *E. coli*—and articulates a "mechanism" (more accurately an interlevel, idealized, and usually temporal process) that explains *some* feature(s) of that organism. (A good example of such a "mechanism" is the operon model for genetic regulation in the *lac* region of *E. coli* K-12.) The organism (or component part of the organism) is construed to be a prototype, and to have similarities with other organisms (or parts of organisms)—and ultimately and hopefully with humans—that license the extension of the "mechanism" to a broader class of biological entities. Such extension is typically analogical, though after the new application has been made, it may be possible to isolate the common features and reconstruct the process so that it *appears* more like a deductive filling in of a general pattern.[1] . . .

The thesis advanced above, that exemplar thinking is more significant in the biomedical sciences than in the physical sciences, receives further confirmation in the clinical sciences. There the focus is the individual patient, and generalizations such as "diseases" are utilized to assist in prevention, prognosis, and therapy. The individual patient is the *clinical exemplar* of a (often multiple) disease or pathological process. Clinicians bring to the examination of individual patients a repository of classificatory or nosological generalizations, as well as a grounding in the basic sciences of biochemistry, histology, physiology, and the pathological variants of the "normal" or "healthy" processes. A theory in pathology can be construed as a family of models, each with "something wrong" with the "normal" or "healthy" process. Such a set of overlapping or "smeared out" models is then juxtaposed, often in a fairly loose way, with an overlapping or "smeared out" set of patient exemplars. This dual "smearedness"—one being in the basic biological models and the other in the patient population—typically requires that the clinician work extensively with analogical reasoning and with qualitative and at best *comparative* connecting pathophysiological principles. . . .

It is these loosely formulated pathophysiological principles that often constitute the *biomedical forms* of the "symbolic generalizations" described by Kuhn above. These generalizations articulate the shared similarities or *positive analogy* in a population and sometimes across a variety of organisms. Biological research as well as clinical problem-solving will require, if the view being developed [here] is correct, close experience with specific exemplars and analogical modeling of similar exemplars with the aid of the symbolic generalizations, utilizing largely qualitative and comparative reasoning of the type discussed. This is in contrast to the more precise mathematical

models and explicit qualitative reasoning widespread in the physical sciences. Such generalizations are, in spite of these differences, well-suited to provide explanations in the biomedical sciences.

The thesis developed to this point concerning the stress on exemplar thinking, along with a view of biological theories, clinical thinking, and associated analogical and comparative reasoning, permits me to take a somewhat different approach to particularity in medicine than have Gorovitz and MacIntyre.[2]

GOROVITZ AND MACINTYRE ON PARTICULARITY

The above discussion of the structure of medical science and the roles of exemplars is relevant for a reassessment of the issue of particularity in medicine. In their often cited, reprinted, and criticized essay, Gorovitz and MacIntyre (1976) sought to identify certain distinctive logical and epistemological features of medical science that they characterized as associated with an overlooked "science of particulars." Their position, briefly outlined, is as follows:

Our thesis . . . is that the Aristotelian inheritance of natural science, as a result of which natural science is defined so that it is exclusively concerned with the knowledge of universals, blinds us to the existence of particulars as proper objects of knowledge. In the process, it blinds us to the role of a type of generalization that is different in crucial respects from those lawlike generalizations that are usually treated as the characteristic genre of the natural scientist. (1976, p. 60)

Particulars are understood by Gorovitz and MacIntyre to

include such varied items as salt marshes, planetary systems, planets, dolphins, snowflakes, hurricanes, cities, crowds, and people. A particular occupies a region of space, persists through time, has boundaries, has an environment, has peripheral and more central areas, and characteristically can be split into two or more parts. (1976, p. 56)

They note that though some particulars are law-governed in a simple sense, such as are ice cubes vis-à-vis their melting property, other particulars are different. They write:

The basic mistake made by that interpretation of science which considers that all genuine scientific knowledge is of universals is to suppose that all particulars are of this [ice cube] kind. But this is clearly false. Many particulars—. . . hurricanes and the higher primates, for example—cannot be understood solely as the sum total of the physical and chemical mechanisms that operate on them. What effects such mechanisms have are affected by the particular history of that specific particular with all its contingent circumstances, that is, contingent and even accidental relative to the operation of the mechanism. (1976, p. 57)

Hurricanes, for example, are an instance of this type of particular and require for predictive purposes knowledge of an unmanageable amount of information about other particulars, such as the polar ice cap and the Gulf stream.

This leads Gorovitz and MacIntyre to their general thesis:

This difference between types of particular—ice cubes on the one hand and hurricanes on the other—in respect of our predictive powers is matched by a difference between the types of generalizations by means of which we may reasonably aspire to describe their behavior. . . . [T]he generalizations by means of which we effectively grasp their behavior will not be genuine universal law-like generalizations but rather generalizations prefaced by "Characteristically and for the most part. . . ." Of such generalizations it is true that, when we are in possession of the best possible information, we may still encounter counter-examples and yet not be supplied thereby with any good reason even any *prima facie* reasons, for discarding or revising our formulation. (1976, p. 48)

I believe that Gorovitz and MacIntyre have identified an important problem with their notion of a "science of particulars," but that they have not given sufficient reasons why more run-of-the-mill statistical generalizations cannot adequately represent their "generalization that is different in crucial respects from those lawlike genrealizations that are usually treated as the characteristic genre of the natural scientist" (1976, p. 60). This is a point that has troubled Bayles and Caplan in particular who note that "It is very difficult to determine exactly how . . . Gorovitz and MacIntyre believe these generalizations differ from statistical laws" (1978a, p. 174).

On the view elaborated . . . above, what makes generalizations in the biomedical sciences different from those typically found in the physicochemical sciences is their role as positive analogies tying together a family of overlapping models. This is not a strict difference in kind from the physicochemical sciences, but as argued above and at greater length in my article elsewhere (1980), it is an important difference in degree that affects training, research, and explanations in the biomedical sciences. In the physical sciences, specifically in the philosophy of the physical sciences, we tend to suppress this element of analogical connection by reformulating it in terms of the language of general laws and initial conditions. To illustrate this point, recall how one solves the problem of determining the velocity at the bottom of an inclined plane of a block of wood sliding down that plane. One draws a diagram that identifies the specific or initial conditions of the system: the angle of the plane (say, = 30 deg), the mass of the block of wood (say, = 5 kg), the initial position of the block of wood vis-à-vis the bottom of the plane (say, = 10 m), the initial velocity of the block (say, = 0), the coefficient of stationary and sliding friction for this block and this plane, and the like. A net force (or forces in the event of two coefficients of friction) is determined using the principles of vector addition. These values are then "plugged into" the general law, here, . . . f = ma, and the equation is [solved] with the use of the initial condition information (initial velocity = 0), to yield an answer.

One does not see the element of analogy in the inclined plane exemplar until, as Kuhn has argued, one tries to solve a similar problem, say a simple pendulum whose velocity is to the determined at the bottom of its swing. Then the existence of a family of "simple machines" becomes more evident, each bearing certain analogical relations with the others, with some generalizations such as $f = ma$ having such a broad scope that they are termed universal laws.

On the view I am defending, generalizations can fail to apply not only because they represent a stochastic process, i.e., are statistical generalizations, but also, and perhaps more often, because the generalizations represent only a partial fit due to individual or strain variation. The generalizations thus have a looser fit to their instances, which retain "particularity" or their own individual differences more so than do (most) entities in the physicochemical sciences. Thus one may use the phrase, "a science of particulars," to describe a science so characterized, but one is advised to recall that it is by virtue of that sciences' generalizations that it is a "science." This position that interprets a "science of particulars" as possessing distinctive characteristics because of analogical relations among its entities and a looser fit of its generalizations and explanatory principles has some similarity with Minogue's (1982) thesis that many medical judgments are "borderline," and that diseases and therapies should be considered not as having necessary and sufficient conditions associated with their definition and application, but rather should be viewed as like Wittgensteinian "family resemblance" concepts. . . .

NOTES

1. This view of the structure of the biological sciences has recently received further elaboration in a Report prepared by the National Academy of Sciences/National Research Council for the National Institutes of Health. In this Report (see National Academy of Sciences, 1985), Drs. Morowitz and Rosen develop the notion of a "matrix of biological knowledge" that appears to have the theoretical structure of collections of "middle range" theories. The Report raises significant issues of the difficulties of information transfer, and a Workshop held on May 29 and 30, 1985, in Washington D.C., made important advances in outlining biological database and artificial intelligence research to begin to solve these problems. An article by Dr. Morowitz summarizing that Workshop is in preparation.

2. It might be worth noting the additional point that if scientific theories are anything like what Kuhn terms paradigms or "disciplinary matrices" (or Kitcher "practices"), then concern with a *distinctive* value-ladenness of medical entities such as diseases may be largely misplaced, since *all* scientific theories may be conceived of as containing normative components. This is not an issue that I can pursue [here] however.

REFERENCES

Bayles, M., and Caplan, A. "Medical Fallibility and Malpractice." *Journal of Medicine and Philosophy* 3 (1978a): 169–186.

———. "A Response to Professor Gorovitz." *Journal of Medicine and Philosophy* 3 (1978b): 192–195.

Boorse, C. "Health as a Theoretical Concept." *Philosophy of Science* 44 (1977): 542–573.

Brody, H. "Commentary on 'Error, Malpractice, and the Problem of Universals.' " *Journal of Medicine and Philosophy* 7 (1982): 251–258.

Bromberger, S. "A Theory about the Theory of Theory and about the Theory of Theories." In *Philosophy of Science: The Delaware Seminar*, ed. W. L. Reese. New York: Wiley, 1963.

———. "Questions." *Journal of Philosophy* 68 (1966): 597–606.

Engelhardt, H. T., Jr. "The Concepts of Health and Disease." In *Evaluation and Explanation in the Biomedical Sciences*, ed. H. T. Engelhardt, Jr., and S. Spicker. Dordrecht, Netherlands: Reidel, 1975, pp. 125–141.

———. "Is There a Philosophy of Medicine?" In *PSA-1976*, vol. 2, ed. F. Suppe and P. Asquith. East Lansing, MI: Philosophy of Science Association, 1976, pp. 94–108.

———. *The Foundations of Bioethics*. New York: Oxford University·Press, 1985.

Gorovitz, S. "Medical Fallibility: A Rejoinder." *Journal of Medicine and Philosophy* 3 (1978): 187–191.

Gorovitz, S., and MacIntyre, A. "Toward a Theory of Medical Fallibility." *Journal of Medicine and Philosophy* 1 (1976): 51–71.

Grene, M. "Philosophy of Medicine: Prolegomena to a Philosophy of Medicine." In *PSA-1976*, vol. 2, ed. F. Suppe and P. Asquith. East Lansing, MI: Philosophy of Science Association, 1976, pp. 77–93.

Kitcher, P. *The Nature of Mathematical Knowledge*. New York: Oxford University Press, 1983.

———. "1953 and All That: A Tale of Two Sciences." *Philosophical Review* 18 (1984): 335–373.

Kuhn, T. *The Structure of Scientific Revolutions*. Chicago: University of Chicago Press, 1962, 1970.

———. "Second Thoughts and Paradigms." In *The Structure of Scientific Theories*, ed. F. Suppe. Urbana: University of Illinois Press, 1974, pp. 459–482.

Lakatos, I. "Falsification and the Methodology of Scientific Research Programs." In *Criticism and the Growth of Knowledge*, ed. I. Lakatos and A. Musgrave. Cambridge: Cambridge University Press, 1970, pp. 91–196.

Laudan, L. *Progress and Its Problems*. Berkeley: University of California Press, 1977.

Martin, M. "On a New Theory of Medical Fallibility." *Journal of Medicine and Philosophy* 2 (1977): 84–88.

Minogue, B. "Error, Malpractice, and the Problem of Universals." *Journal of Medicine and Philosophy* 7 (1982): 239–250.

National Academy of Sciences. *Models for Biomedical Research: A New Perspective*. Washington, DC: National Academy of Sciences, 1985.

Ruse, M. *Philosophy of Biology*. London: Hutchinson, 1973.

Schaffner, K. "Theory Structure in the Biomedical Sciences." *Journal of Medicine and Philosophy* 5 (1980): 57–97.

Shapere, D. "Scientific Theories and Their Domains." In *The Structure of Scientific Theories*, ed. F. Suppe. Urbana: University of Illinois Press, 1974, pp. 518–565.

Suppe, F. (ed.). *The Structure of Scientific Theories*. Urbana: University of Illinois Press, 1974, 1977.

Toulmin, S. *Foresight and Understanding*. London: Hutchinson, 1961.

———. *Human Understanding*, vol. 1. Princeton, NJ: Princeton University Press, 1972.

Wartofsky, M. "How to Begin Again: Medical Therapies for the Philosophy of Science." In *PSA-1976*, vol. 2, ed. F. Suppe and P. Asquith. East Lansing, MI: Philosophy of Science Association, 1976, pp. 109–122.

Whitbeck, C. "The Relevance of Philosophy of Medicine to the Philosophy of Science." In *PSA-1976*, vol. 2, ed. F. Suppe and P. Asquith. East Lansing, MI: Philosophy of Science Association, 1976, pp. 123–135.

ARTHUR L. CAPLAN, "EXEMPLARY REASONING? A COMMENT ON THEORY STRUCTURE IN BIOMEDICINE"

Caplan points out that what Schaffner refers to as biomedicine covers a wide territory, and it remains to be seen whether and how many of the theories within biomedicine have a clear structure. Moreover, even if some areas of medicine (and biology) are quite different from some areas of physics and chemistry, it does not follow that there are no general methodological principles that apply across the science board.

Caplan rejects the Gorovitz and MacIntyre view of medicine as the science of particulars. Caplan explains their view in terms of his own (just as Schaffner explained their view in terms of his own). According to Caplan, Gorovitz and MacIntyre focus on the idea that there are different kinds of individuals. Physics deals with one kind, and medicine deals with another. Physics deals with things like ice cubes and billiard balls. Medicine deals with things (patients) more like hurricanes and peat bogs. Caplan suggests that this distinction is an artifact of how examples are analyzed.

Philosophers of science use physics as the clearest example of science. They focus on Newtonian mechanics, astronomy, and relativity, not on civil engineering, hydraulics, or acoustics. If they did, they would get a different picture of physics, a different sense for "particular"—one that was close to medicine. Jane Flax, in Chapter 6, will make a similar point about Adolf Grünbaum's approach to psychology. What makes the difference? The answer is the need for practical solutions, often in as short a time as possible. Caplan says that what Schaffner and Gorovitz and MacIntyre have found is nothing more than the fact that when theory is applied to pressing practical problems, the resulting area of study (medicine and certain areas of engineering) will not look like the purely theoretical areas of physics.

Exemplary Reasoning? A Comment on Theory Structure in Biomedicine

ARTHUR L. CAPLAN

I. METHODOLOGICAL ESSENTIALISM AND DYNAMIC GRADUALISM

Physicians and scientists trying to follow current work in the philosophy of science find themselves confronting something of a fundamental dispute about the nature of science and scientific progress. There is a question on the extent to which we can account for and describe such progress. There is the question of the extent to which philosophers can do more than describe the activities of science and can in addition say how science ought to function or to progress.

A. Methodological Essentialism

One major thesis that has dominated philosophical analyses of science is what might be termed methodological essentialism. For many years philosophers of science have focused their attention on the laws and theories of the physical sciences as paradig-

From *Journal of Medicine and Philosophy* 11 (1986): 93–105. © Kluwer Academic Publishers.

matic examples of the structure and logic of science (Suppe, 1977). As a result of careful analyses of a few important theories in the physical sciences, many philosophers of science were led to espouse a general interpretation of all scientific theories, claiming that:

(a) all theories have a distinct and formalizable structure and logic. The elements of every theory can be arranged in an axiomatic hierarchy which are deductively related,
(b) this structure and logic is univocal; the same structure and logic can be used to characterize the constituent elements of all theories in science, both theoretical and applied, and to distinguish science from non-science or pseudoscience. (Caplan, 1978)

If methodological essentialism were true, it would have direct consequences for those working in the biomedical sciences. Many biomedical scientists and physicians are prone to feel more than a twinge of disciplinary envy when confronted with the pristine and elegant examples of theories in the physical sciences such as mechanics, thermodynamics, and quantum theory.

Very few theories in the biological and medical sciences exemplify the kind of mathematical precision, predictive accuracy, or explanatory utility associated with these theories. One is then led to ask why such differences exist.

Perhaps, those working in biology and medicine have not yet discovered the basic laws operating in these domains. They may simply be behind their brethren in the physical sciences in terms of time, cleverness or both.

Or perhaps the theories of biology and medicine differ in some more basic ways from those to be found in physics. This is the explanation Professor Schaffner (1986) offers in his exploration of the structure of theories in the biomedical sciences.

If Schaffner is correct, then, the differences to be found between the theories of physics and of the biomedical sciences are to be understood as a function of their subject matters rather than of the intellectual powers of those working in these domains. Indeed, if the theories of biomedicine are different structurally and logically from those of the physical sciences, biomedical scientists ought not to worry about any differences that exist between their theories and those manifest in other sciences. In fact, if Schaffner is correct, they would be misled by attending too closely to the kinds of theory structure and logic evident in the physical sciences in setting goals for their theoretical and practical labors.

B. Dynamic Gradualism

The second major concern of philosophers of science in recent years has been the analysis of the dynamics of theory change. The issue of how theories evolve over time and the closely related question of the rate and pace of theoretical evolution is one that has dominated philosophical discussion since Kuhn (1970, 1977) challenged philosophical orthodoxy on this matter. Whereas the previous generation of philosophers of science held that theory evolution was a slow and gradual process, Kuhn maintained that some theories evolve by leaps and bounds—the revolutionary paradigms so much in evidence in his work and in the writings of those who are his intellectual camp-followers (e.g., Gould, 1980).

The question of whether all scientific theories evolve slowly over time by means of the gradual accretion of facts, new hypotheses, and confirmations of these hypotheses or whether progress in science is sometimes (or, for radical dynamists, always) revolutionary in the sense that new theories represent radical breaks with pre-existing claims and hypotheses are issues with important implications for practicing scientists and clinicians.

If dynamic gradualism were universally true, then a strict requirement could be imposed upon every scientist to insure that new theories or, less grandiosely, new hypotheses, were at least logically and semantically consistent with previously existing beliefs in a particular area of inquiry. If dynamic gradualism is not universally applicable across all domains of science, those doing research or involved in the practical application of scientific ideas would then be well-advised to remind themselves that the views they hold need not be consistent with, or to put the matter baldly, might well be incommensurate with, existing knowledge and belief in a particular domain.

In part, the reason the analysis of the dynamics of theoretical evolution has come to prominence is that views about the adequacy of methodological essentialism have been understood as closely linked to dynamic gradualism.

Philosophers committed to methodological essentialism have been engaged in a rather fierce and occasionally nasty dispute with their intellectual cousins—the historians and sociologists of science. The latter have and continue to cast substantive and empirical aspersions upon dynamic gradualism by attempting to show that the actual practice of science, both now and in the past, totally undercuts the soundness of methodological essentialism and, as a result, dynamic gradualism (Bloor, 1980). As a consequence, *both* methodological essentialism and dynamic gradualism may be more prescriptive than descriptive. Both may involve saying what science *should* be, rather than simply what it is.

Most sociologists and historians of science view the continuing efforts of philosophers to locate the logical grail that will reveal the true essence of what makes a theory scientific with varying degrees of amusement and scorn. They believe that the evidence accumulated from the study of the actual practice of science, both in its contemporary forms and from historical cases, reveals the presence of a sufficient degree of politics, personal aggrandizement, bias, and plain luck to make the pursuit of a distinct, universal structure and logic of those theories that carry the label "science" at best a futile quest.

While most contemporary philosophers of science have found it necessary to acknowledge and even incorporate many of the insights of history and sociology in their inquires, many do so while still clinging to the desire to identity a univocal method or pattern of reasoning that will capture those aspects of inquiry that make science an intellectually distinct enterprise from other forms of intellectual activity such as religion, politics or ethics (Ruse, 1977; Rosenberg, 1980).

While personalities may appear to dominate much of the recent discussion in the philosophy of science, the adequacy or inadequacy of methodological essentialism and dynamic gradualism are important issues at the core of contemporary discussions. In order to see the relevance of Professor Schaffner's contribution to these major topics, one issue that further complicates the assessment of these theses must also be considered.

II. DESCRIPTION, PRESCRIPTION, OR BOTH?

In order to determine the validity of methodological essentialism or dynamic gradualism, most philosophers of science believe that they must engage in a process of reconstruction with respect to scientific theories (McMullin, 1986). Explanations, laws, and theories of the physical, biological and other sciences must first be isolated from historical accounts or identified from the literature of a particular science. They are then shorn of the "distorting" influence of personality, politics, and power. These suitably refined raw materials are then scrutinized, recast into terms that lend themselves to logical analysis, and then mined in order to ascertain their structure or logic in the hope of finding patterns that qualify the theories to be labelled as "scientific" in character.

Most philosophers of science, especially when talking to each other, readily admit that their goal is to do something more than accurately ascertain the structure and logic of science. The philosophy of science is, for many philosophers, not merely an exercize in post-hoc logical analysis but has as its purpose the aim of instructing the practitioners of science as to how to go about their business in a more efficient manner.

The discomfort that sometimes accompanies the reading of a good deal of the literature in the philosophy of science is not merely a result of prolonged exposure to an often-times prolix form of academic discourse. In part, it is a product of the uncertainty felt by many authors as to whom exactly they wish to have as their audience.

Description of the actual structure and logic of science is insufficient, for even those who proclaim this modest goal are often unwilling to limit themselves to it. Prescription lends itself to the concerns of scientists themselves and is surely what they want to hear, but most philosophers of science consider it immodest or foolhearty to publicly proclaim this as their intended outcome. The assessment of the utility of philosophical analyses of science, including Professor Schaffner's contribution, is made difficult whenever there is uncertainty as to whether description or prescription is intended—whether one is describing how science in fact functions, or how it should function. This question is as important for medicine in particular as it is for science in general. We are returned then to the opening questions. What is it to understand science and scientific method in medicine? Can we do more than simply describe the actual presentation of theories in the medical literature? . . .

Professor Schaffner notes that much of the work in the philosophy of science over the past two decades has been preoccupied with the analysis of theory evolution, what I have termed the thesis of dynamic gradualism, and the identification of the proper metascientific entities for analyzing this process. He also observes, correctly in my view, that the answers philosophers offer about both the appropriate units for analysis and the dynamics of scientific change are very much a function of what they take to be significant within the various domains of science. As Schaffner complains in bemoaning the relative paucity of actual case examples utilized by philosophers of biomedicine, philosophical thinking about both methodological essentialism and dynamic gradualism has been afflicted by a severe case of restricted vision.

Historically, philosophers of science have not been inclined to look outside the realm of the natural sciences for insights into the nature of laws, explanations, and theories of science or in order to ascertain the processes of theoretical evolution. Indeed, not only has the philosophy of science rarely looked outside the natural sciences to understand science, it has almost never looked outside the realm of "pure" science for the purposes of either description or prescription.

The focus on the natural sciences derives from a little-examined belief that the philosophy of science ought restrict itself to the purist forms of science. As a result, practical areas of scientific inquiry such as engineering, agriculture, and medicine, have been either ignored or slighted in favor of what are seen as the more important or basic aspects or components of scientific inquiry.

The omission of practical or applied inquiry is also a function of a kind of intellectual snobbery that views fields such as medicine or agriculture as just so much mindless, derivative drudgery. Most philosophers of science, at least if one is to take seriously the ommission of the practical sciences from nearly all philosophical discourse about science, appear to believe that applied science is not where the intellectual action really is. . . .

IV. HOW DIFFERENT ARE THE THEORIES OF BIOMEDICINE?

Professor Schaffner's paper, when viewed against the backdrop of arguments about methodological essentialism, dynamic gradualism, and ongoing ambivalence about the prescriptive or descriptive aims of the philosophy of science, can be seen to be raising issues of fundamental importance for both the philosophy and practice of biomedicine. Schaffner's paper, when viewed against these long-standing disputes within the philosophy of science, can be seen as a careful attempt to lay out the contributions the philosophy of medicine can make to the philosophy of science as well as to the practice of medicine. The following claims are at the heart of Schaffner's paper:

(1) Methodological essentialism is false. The structure of at least some theories in the biomedical sciences is fundamentally different from those to be found in the physical sciences.

(2) The key differences between the structure of theories in the biomedical sciences and those in the physical sciences are:

(a) theories in the physical sciences are best characterized as axiomatic hierarchies of laws and theorems of varying degrees of generality whereas at least some theories in biomedicine are best understood as utilizing exemplars to illustrate what Schaffner terms mechanisms of causal action, and

(b) the logic evident in the laws, principles, and claims of the physical sciences is best characterized as being deductive whereas the elements of at least some theories in the biomedical sciences are most accurately described in terms of analogical extensions from exemplars.

(3) The attempt by some philosophers of medicine, such as Gorovitz and MacIntyre, to argue for the distinctive particularity of medicine is best understood as an early effort to pinpoint the critical role played by analogical reasoning from exemplars in the theories of biomedicine.

(4) Disputes about the applicability of dynamic gradualism among philosophers of science have obscured the important role played by scientific practices in the evolution of scientific theories generally and in biomedicine in particular.

Professor Schaffner has done yeoman service for those interested in revitalizing the philosophy of medicine. His essay carries forward an interesting dispute within the recent philosophy of medicine, the claim that biomedical theories must grapple with the distinctive particularity associated with human beings, explain the effects of this particularity on biomedical theorizing, and use the theories of biomedicine to reveal a structure and logic that shows methodological essentialism to be inadequate as a claim about science generally.

If he is correct, the philosophy of medicine will contribute much of significance to both the philosophy of science and the practice of medicine. The study of the theories of biomedical science reveals the limited scope of methodological essentialism while, at the same time, highlighting the important role played by exemplars and analogy in a some areas of science. Those working in the realm of biomedicine might well be advised not to use the theories and explanations of the physical sciences as their exemplars and to seek instead to develop theories of the middle range.

There are really three questions that arise in considering Schaffner's rich menu of research items for future work in the philosophy of medicine:

(1) Has the case been made for at least suspecting that methodological essentialism is invalid as a result of the structural and logical peculiarities of theories in biomedicine?

(2) If the structure and logic of at least some theories in biomedicine are best characterized by means of analogical reasoning from exemplars, what bearing does this have on the thesis of dynamic gradualism?

(3) If the theories of biomedicine are in fact distinct from those of the physical sciences in terms of their structure and logic, why is this so?

At present, the case against methodological essentialism is tentative at best. Schaffner has provided a number of suggestive examples but further work to establish the prominence and prevalence of analogical reasoning utilizing exemplars needs to be done.

As Professor Schaffner notes, the evidential base supporting methodological essentialism is very narrow. However, narrowness is also a characteristic of the examples that dominate discussion about the philosophy of medicine. The paucity of examples is highlighted by the tendency, evident in Schaffner's paper, to lump vast areas of biology and medicine together under the general rubric of biomedicine. Further research will be necessary before sufficient support can be mustered in defense of the argument that all of the theories in biology and medicine rely upon exemplars and analogical reasoning.

Schaffner suggests that the generalizations drawn from textbooks of cardiology, pulmonary medicine, and endocrinology show the prominence of exemplar based reasoning in medicine. Similar illustrations are to be found, he argues, in such diverse fields as immunology, physiology, embryology, and the neurosciences.

Maybe so but, as Schaffner himself is well-aware, the structure and logic attributed to theories are strongly correlated with the examples chosen for analysis. The fact remains that philosophers of science in general and philosophers of medicine in particular have not taken a particularly long or hard look at the broad array of theories to be found in biology and medicine.

The theories that have been examined, at least in a preliminary way, have been elicited from either textbooks or influential articles in the periodical literature of science. Clinicians might well cringe at the thought that the essential structure and logic of the theories they use to guide their practice in the hospital or office are to be discerned by means of their presentation in textbooks intended for first or second year medical students. There is a real danger of confusing the medium with the message where textbooks and review articles provide the only windows upon scientific theorizing.

Nor should much be made of the discovery of counter-examples to the thesis of methodological essentialism. While it may be true that the hopes of an older generation of philosophers of science for finding a univocal structure and logic for all theories are doomed to be dashed on the exemplars of the biomedical sciences, it remains to be seen whether these counter-examples are really boulders or are merely pebbles. While a univocal structure and pattern of reasoning may not accurately characterize all theories, the set of structures and forms of reasoning manifest by theories may still be relatively small.

Schaffner is agnostic about the implications of the potential demise of methodological essentialism for the validity of dynamic gradualism. His agnosticism may be more a function of limitations of space than a carefully thought through position but agnosticism is the appropriate stance.

Critics of dynamic gradualism have tended to see an indivisible link between methodological essentialism and dynamic gradualism. If it can be shown that all scientific theories do not have a univocal structure and logic then, the critics conclude, the case for dynamic gradulism is also in jeopardy.

But the falsification of methodological essentialism by counter-examples drawn from the arena of biology and medicine has no bearing on claims about the tempo or mode of theoretical evolution in biomedicine or elsewhere. While the demonstration of the centrality of exemplar-based analogical reasoning in biomedicine has interesting implications for those committed to the reducibility of the theories of biology and medicine to the physical sciences, it says little or nothing about the validity of dynamic gradualism in describing theoretical evolution in the sciences.

The question of why biomedical theories differ in their structure and logic, if in fact they do, is fraught with the most interesting philosophical and practical implications. Are biology and medicine somehow different as subject matters from the phenomena addressed by physics or chemistry?

Gorovitz and MacIntyre, in their influential article of a decade ago (1976), suggested that there is something peculiar to the domains of biology and medicine that results in differences in the kinds of laws and theories found in biology and medicine. They argued that the particularity and teleology evident in human beings and other living creatures make it impossible to formulate deductive explanations in biology and medicine.

Schaffner suggests that their emphasis on particularity as the distinguishing feature of biomedical theorizing may be a result of the prominent role played by exemplars in biomedicine. However, it is not clear that Schaffner and Gorovitz and MacIntyre are referring to the same features in their talk of particularity and exemplars.

Gorovitz and MacIntyre argued that medicine ought not be viewed in the same conceptual light as physics and chemistry. They argued that ontological or metaphysical differences in the kinds of objects studied by medicine, what they termed particulars, made it unlikely that medicine would produce the same types of laws, explanations, and theories as are evident in the natural sciences.

Schaffner makes no such claim nor need he do so. Indeed, it is difficult to know whether he believes that such differences as may exist between the structure and logic of biomedical theories and other theories in science are due to the nature of the subject under examination, or are, rather, a function of the underdeveloped nature of inquiry in the biomedical sciences.

Is there any reason to posit ontological or metaphysical differences between the subject matters of biomedicine and the natural sciences? If methodological essentialism is not valid where biology and medicine are concerned, I believe it is less a function of the subject matter of these domains and more a matter of the practical or pragmatic goals that underlie research in these areas.

Most of the examples drawn from the natural sciences to support the validity of methodological essentialism (and dynamic gradualism) come from those areas of physics and chemistry that are more concerned with abstract properties and causal mechanisms than they are with application. One wonders whether an examination of theories in such areas as chemical engineering, hydraulics, metallurgy, aerodynamics, or navigation would not reveal a predominance of exemplar-based analogical theories of the middle range. If this is in fact so, then what Schaffner and other proponents of alternatives to methodological essentialism (Kitcher, 1984) have discovered is not, contrary to Gorovitz and MacIntyre, the structural and logical consequences of theory construction in an ontologically peculiar domain but, rather, the theoretical consequences of grappling with the practical application of scientific knowledge.

Those working in applied ethics have discovered that the practical application of moral theories to real world problems leads to a reliance on critical cases and analogical thinking about paradigmatic cases (Jonsen, 1980; Caplan, 1982). It may be that the differences that exist between the theories of medicine and those of physics are much more a function of the practical goals of some domains of science than they are of ontological differences between physical and biological phenomena.

The issue of whether the structure of theories in the biomedical sciences is different from those to be found in theories of the natural sciences may appear to lack relevance for the practice of medicine or even for the general philosophy of science. But, this is hardly the case. Schaffner's important contribution to the philosophy of medicine points directly to a set of critically important questions about the structure and logic of science, the aims and goals that ought to guide researchers in building theories, the aims and goals that ought to guide philosophers in analyzing theories, and, most importantly, the nature of the long-neglected relationship between theory and practice that surely must be given pride of place in future dialogues in the philosophy of medicine between physicians and philosophers.

REFERENCES

Bloor, D. *Knowledge and Social Imagery*. London: Routledge & Kegan Paul, 1980.

Caplan, A. "Testability, Disreputability and the Structure of the Modern Synthetic Theory of Evolution." *Erkenntnis* 13 (1978): 261–278.

———. "Mechanics on Duty: The Limitations of a Technical Definition of Moral Expertise for Work in Applied Ethics." *Canadian Journal of Philosophy* 8 (1982): 1–18.

Gorovitz, S., and MacIntyre, A. "Toward a Theory of Medical Fallibility." *Journal of Medicine and Philosophy* 1 (1976): 51–71.

Gould, S. *The Panda's Thumb*. New York: Norton, 1980.

Jonsen, A. "Can an Ethicist Be a Consultant?" In *Frontiers in Medical Ethics*, ed. V. Abernethy. Cambridge: Ballinger, 1980, pp. 157–172.

Kitcher, P. "1953 and All That: A Tale of Two Sciences." *Philosophical Review* 93 (1984): 335–373.

Kuhn, T. *The Structure of Scientific Revolutions* (2nd ed.). Chicago: University of Chicago Press, 1970.

———. "Second Thoughts on Paradigms." In *The Structure of Scientific Theories* (2nd ed.), ed. F. Suppe. Urbana: University of Illinois Press, 1977, pp. 459–482.

McMullin, E. "How Do Scientific Controversies End?" In *Scientific Controversies*, ed. H. T. Engelhardt, Jr., and A. Caplan. Cambridge: Cambridge University Press, 1986, pp. 49–92.

Rosenberg, A. *Sociobiology and the Preemption of Social Science*. Baltimore: Johns Hopkins University Press, 1980.

Ruse, M. "Is Biology Different from Physics?" In *Logic, Laws, and Life*, ed. R. Colodny. Pittsburgh, PA: University of Pittsburgh Press, 1977, pp. 89–128.

Schaffner, K. "Exemplar Reasoning about Biological Models and Diseases: A Relation between the Philosophy of Medicine and Philosophy of Science." *Journal of Medicine and Philosophy* 11 (1986): 63–80.

Suppe, F. (ed.). *The Structure of Scientific Theories* (2nd ed.). Urbana: University of Illinois Press, 1977.

E. A. MURPHY, "THE TACTICS OF THE DIAGNOSTIC PROCESS"

Murphy lays out quite clearly the structure of the diagnostic process. This falls somewhat short of a theory for all of biomedicine, but it is a start—a start that seems to support Caplan in his debate with both Schaffner and Gorovitz and MacIntyre.

Murphy lists axioms. Axioms 3 and 4 introduce matters of practicality into the process. With practicality comes the values that many philosophers are certain cannot be eliminated from any theoretical account of medicine. The axioms are consistent with any of four general approaches to diagnosis: gestalt, exhaustion, multiple branching, and steepest ascents.

The gestalt method is a variation of what cognitive psychologists call pattern recognition. Humans tend to see patterns more readily than we see discrete individuals. An everyday example is the ability to see a family resemblance and yet not be able to pick out individual features that the family members have in common. This method is the nonrational way that Kuhn thinks that we switch paradigms. First we see the world in one way, and then we see it in another way. After

273

much training, a dermatologist goes from seeing some light brown freckles to seeing a melanoma. This kind of seeing is what we called theory-laden observation.

The exhaustion method is really the Popperian method of falsification. Physicians refer to this as the method of "rule-outs." One creates a list of the most probable diseases (perhaps, as Murphy almost snidely suggests, by using a textbook with a very good index of symptoms) and then begins ruling them out one by one until only one is left.

Multiple branching makes one think of diagnosis as a flowchart. Any particular question ("When did you first notice the pain?") has many possible answers. The actual answer given leads, by the laws of physiology, to another question, the particular answer to which leads to yet another question, and so on, until one gets the solution, the correct diagnosis. Multiple branching is just a more complex version of what Murphy describes as the method of exhaustion.

Steepest ascents requires that one be able to represent one's problem as a mathematical function. The problem must be statable in the form of the dreaded "story problem" of calculus. Once so stated, the problem can be solved by using calculus. What is involved is finding the maximum or minimum value for something. Let us look at two simple examples.

1. You want to fence an area along a river to keep your grazing llamas safe from tourists. You need fence only three sides, since the river forms a natural barrier. You have 1,000 yards of fencing material. What dimensions of fence will maximize the area?

2. You live in Manhattan and want to get to Chicago to see your best friend. You must travel by automobile. You will want to get to Chicago as fast as possible in order to have as much time as possible to spend with your friend. How will you choose your route? You might not choose the shortest route if the roads along that shortest route were two-lane and known to be slow. You might also take the dangerousness of any route into account. In the winter, you might want a route that was well plowed in case of snow. One way to say all of this is that you are trying to maximize time in Chicago and that you will do this by minimizing time spent on the road.

Murphy reminds us of a problem with this method. Some functions have what is termed local maximum or minimum points. To use a metaphor, the maximum (or minimum) found is a peak (or valley) only within a certain part of the range. If one looked longer, one would find the real maximum (or minimum). In effect, this is a warning: Do not always accept the first good-sounding answer.

In a medical diagnosis, a physician can be seen as trying to minimize time, pain to the patient, cost to the patient, anxiety to the patient, and so on. Each hypothesis used along the way to a final diagnosis has a probability of giving a yes or no answer, and each answer comes at a price. Each yes or no answer helps determine to a certain degree what the next hypothesis to be considered ought to be. Although representing this method as a mathematical function is not easy, it can be done in some cases. Murphy's point is that we ought to strive to be able to do it in all cases.

In the example Murphy gives, where he shows how to distinguish between peptic ulcer and heart pain (angina pectoris), he is using a combination of multiple branching and steepest ascent. He is also appealing to rule-outs (falsification), as when he says that if the pain lasts less than ten minutes, it may be due to angina. This is just another way of saying that if the pain lasts less than ten minutes, the hypothesis "The cause of the pain is peptic ulcer" is very unlikely.

In general, Murphy is looking for a method that is systematic without being too inflexible and is also teachable. His criterion for this is that it must be able to be expressed in a computer language, which is to say representable as a mathematical function.

The Tactics of the Diagnostic Process

E. A. MURPHY

This is the most difficult aspect of the problem. In principle, anyone who can memorize facts and carry through the calculations can perform the analysis of the data: that aspect of diagnosis could be performed perfectly well by a computer and, indeed, much better than by any human brain. It is in the acquisition of the facts that real finesse is called for. This skill will be the last one to be captured in terms of logic and system.

THE AXIOMS

It is worthwhile to list some axioms that point up the special limits imposed on the process.

1. *The collection of facts is selective.* Whatever anybody may say (and there are

those who profess the contrary), it is totally impracticable to elicit all the facts about a patient before coming to a decision. A psychoanalyst seeing the patient two hours a week may take years to get all the facts he is interested in. Some of his facts may bear on any diagnosis; yet, obviously, the surgeon cannot put his patient through this process before doing some minor procedure. Even physical signs are examined selectively. A physician is not necessarily negligent because he could not swear, after having examined a patient, that he has not left-sided inattention on the soles of his feet or that the anvil sign is not present in the chest.

2. *The facts are evaluated in order.* Diagnosis is melodic not harmonic. This is not strictly true. A physician, while asking about a cough, may be noting whether the patient is blinking. But one cannot at the same time be asking about a cough and about appetite. Once this fact is admitted, the problem arises as to what the optimal

order of questions may be: in general, it will be different in one patient from what it is in another, and it could be argued with some plausibility that the order is unique for each patient. In a game of chess there is probably an ideal next move at a particular stage of the game. In diagnosis there is probably an ideal best inquiry to pursue next. The difficulty is to establish what it is.

3. *Diagnosis is a real-time problem.* By this we mean that decisions must be made within certain periods of time. The surgeon in the middle of a gastrectomy cannot go off to the library to read up on some point of interest. The physician cannot tell the patient with cancer to come back in fifty years time, when we know more about cancer. Thus, in practical situations it is commonly necessary to compromise between urgency and thoroughness of diagnosis.

4. *Diagnosis cannot go on indefinitely* even if there is no urgency. However many facts are known, we can always find more to collect. But at least three factors limit this approach.

a) Further facts may be irrelevant. An X-ray of the skull may be ordered on anyone, but it is unlikely to throw light on a patient's varicose veins. In probabilistic terms, the conditional probability of the diagnosis, given the result of a test not relevant to it, is the same as the unconditional probability.

b) Redundancy may be a limitation. A patient may be found to have a high serum globulin level and it would perhaps be a wise precaution to have it determined a second time to make sure there has been no error in the laboratory. We could also defend doing the test the following week to see if it is changing over time. But it seems doubtful that doing the measurement ten times a day is going to contribute anything further to the diagnosis. . . .

c) Cost is a serious consideration. This may first be understood in the crude monetary sense. Investigations cost money. They also strain economic resources. Hospital departments are designed not to take more than a particular load. There is further cost to the patient: having his serum globulin done ten times a day is going to get painful after a time. It exposes him to repeated (albeit small) risks of infection; it will eventually make him anemic; many patients will be made increasingly anxious at the apparent uncertainty of the physician.

5. *The patient may be suffering from a multiplicity of diseases.* They may be well-known associates (like tuberculosis and diabetes, or gout and arterial disease); they may reflect a common pattern (as measles and whooping cough do in childhood or dementia and osteoarthritis do in old age); they may be totally unrelated and their coexistence due to the fact that they confer no protection against one another. But it is the same patient who is experiencing them, and he is "broadcasting through a single channel." Part of diagnosis will be to separate the findings into groups, and it may be a formidable task. Many or all of these conditions may be important to recognize, but often, perhaps usually, there will be one of major importance, which the physician would want least to miss. We shall, therefore, call it the "global maximum" or (if unqualified) "maximum."

6. *It is not necessarily true that the point of departure, "the presenting symptom," has anything to do with the maximum.* Many a patient who comes complaining of a symptom due to a trivial disease has been found to be also suffering from some serious disease, which is, so far, symptomless. Clearly, no amount of inquiry into the details of the one will lead to the finding of the other. To antici-

pate, we might say that competent physical diagnosis has two aspects; an *ad hoc* inquiry and an undirected inquiry.

What, then, is the strategy by which a doctor arrives at a diagnosis? There are several theories about the process, which can be conveniently put in four groups.

Method 1: The Gestalt

This theory maintains that a doctor makes a diagnosis by having in his mind certain pictures associated with the various diseases. The diagnosis consists of ferreting among the facts until the clinician has built up a pattern for the patient, which conforms to one of these particular patterns of disease.

There are some areas of medicine in which the Gestalt is very important. In the early stages of Parkinson's disease, when no other abnormal signs may be present, the way in which the patient walks is, to the trained eye, quite distinctive. It is true, often, that the more closely the physician examines the patient the less he sees. One of the enemies of clinical acumen is the faculty for habituation, and from time to time first impressions about a patient may be most important. The Gestalt is important in many other diseases, notably those of the skin. However, this approach to diagnosis is not a very satisfactory one. It is difficult to teach. It is not sufficiently analytical in character to be put on a computer. And it can, on occasion, be disastrously misleading. It has a usefulness, but a limited one.

Method 2: The Method of Exhaustion

This method consists of painstakingly recording all the facts that can be elicited about a patient and then arguing that by means of the kind of decision procedures discussed previously a "most probable diagnosis" can be arrived at. It resembles the method of the man who wants to look up the word "myxedema" in a dictionary and feels sure that if he reads through painstakingly from "aardvark" to "zygote" he is bound to come across the word somewhere. It is a method that works if the patient and the diagnostician can stand it, but it is not a very efficient one. It is sometimes a method that works when all else fails.

The other two methods, which are closely related to one another, involve a process of selection and correspond to the kind of methods used in clinical practice. The patient is allowed to tell his story with no more irrelevancies than can possibly be helped; at every stage he should be encouraged to tell what his complaints are and dissuaded from saying what he thinks they are due to. But there comes a time at which the patient runs out of things to say, and further progress in diagnosis must be directed to certain questions, either in the history, the physical examination, or special investigations. From the standpoint of the theory of diagnosis, there is no need to distinguish among these three sources.

Method 3: The Multiple-Branching Process

This method supposes that the entire system of investigation can be represented by an elaborate branching system of invariable construction. Its structure is unmodified by the nature of the information that has already accumulated. The diagnostic process then consists of tracing one of a very large number of pathways through this system of branches. Each question gives an answer that automatically sets up the next question. With such a method it would be possible to put the whole system on a computer and have the computer conduct the questioning. This system is probably a fairly accurate representation of what goes on and, given certain circumstances, could be made to work very efficiently. It has been used in the study of certain kinds of diseases, such as congenital anomalies of the heart, or in certain limited fields, such as the blood disorders. The principal advantage of the method is that it is systematic; the principal disadvantage is that it is too rigid. I think that slightly better representation is given by the next method.

Method 4: The Method of Steepest Ascents

The argument is familiar to applied mathematicians. It is sometimes necessary to find those values of a variable or a set of variables that maximize some function of them. In some situations straightforward answers can be found by the methods of the calculus. But for higher order polynomials, or for transcendental or other complicated functions, it may be necessary to solve the problem by approximate means. . . . And one way of doing this efficiently is always to travel in the direction in which the ascent is steepest. Roughly speaking, this is done by following a line that cuts the present contour and the next contour upward at the same angle. Of course, when the maximum has been attained there is no direction in which the gradient is greater than zero.

This method works on the whole very efficiently. But it shares with the multiple branching method the disadvantage that there may be several local maximum points in the field, and there is no guarantee that the one attained by the method of steepest ascents is, in fact, the global maximum. In other words, it may be merely a local maximum. The analogy that this method bears to the diagnostic process is that it supposes the diagnosis in any particular case is the one that gives the maximum probability. . . .

One medical teacher . . . was continually depressed at the tendency that his students had for diagnosing the exotic; he used to say that if there are three birds sitting in a tree, they are much more likely to be sparrows than canaries. . . .

Granted, then, that the objective is to find a highest probability, the diagnostic process consists of attaining this maximum as quickly as possible. The diagnostician, however, must keep a weather eye open for the possibility of other peaks. It seems that the direction of steepest ascent at any time depends on the part of the diagnosis-space in which the clinician finds himself. This consideration calls for a great deal of flexibility in the form of the questioning—it may be, for example, that an accidental statement by a patient or an accidental finding by a radiologist on X-ray may move the position in the diagnosis-space to somewhere quite unexpected. This kind of flexibility is difficult to build into a multiple-branching model. . . .

Thus, a patient may have a pain over the lower part of the sternum. There will doubtless be more than this to the history, which may help to decide in what part of the diagnostic-space the inquirer is at some particular moment. But just to consider two possibilities, pain in this region could be due to heart disease or it could be due to duodenal disease. If it is due to heart disease, then a crucial question to explore is how long the pain lasts. If the pain lasts less than ten minutes, it may very likely be angina pectoris, due to narrowing of the arteries supplying the heart; whereas, the more it exceeds this duration the less likely it is to be due to this cause. Anything over half an hour makes the diagnosis unlikely. But if the patient had a peptic ulcer, the duration of the pain would not matter nearly so much, and the precise duration of the pain, therefore, would not be a crucial question. On the other hand, if it were thought that this pain was due to a duodenal ulcer, the relationship that it bore to meals would be an important point to pursue. Thus, it is clear that the most important question to ask next would really depend on what diagnosis the diagnostician had in mind.

This approach to the sequence of questions asked is oversimplified, and I think that a diagnostician departs from it in at least two ways. In the first place, when he receives an answer to a question that points away from some diagnosis that he has been entertaining, this does not immediately lead him to change direction. In aeronautical terms one would say there is a certain amount of "mush" in the diagnostic process, i.e., delay in responding. Too rapid a response to negative results is probably harmful. For one thing, there is a certain amount of variation in disease manifestations, and we cannot expect every patient to have all the typical findings in a high degree; so the diagnostician will perhaps pursue his original direction for another three or four inquiries before abandoning it in favor of some alternative diagnosis. The other point to be borne in mind is that patients sometimes have very confused notions about their symptoms—for example, they may have a vague idea of the duration of pain. Many of them have a poor vocabulary and a habit of using words imprecisely, so that even when they have a clear idea of what they are trying to say they may not express themselves very successfully.

The other way in which the experienced clinician departs from the simple scheme is that he allows his plan of inquiry to be modified by considerations of cost. He is anxious not to miss an important diagnosis, like coronary thrombosis, and, therefore, he will tolerate departures from the classical patterns and abandon the diagnosis more reluctantly than he would if the subject of consideration were a mere diagnostic curiosity of no prognostic or therapeutic importance. We could think of this cost in familiar terms as a kind of tilting of the diagnosis-space in such a way that the pathway to these more important diagnoses was made a little steeper.

We may summarize the rational approach to the diagnostic problem somewhat along the following lines. . . . Two activities are involved: to scan the diagnosis-space in search of peaks of interest and to pursue the clues thus turned up and those given by the presenting complaints. These have obvious analogies in the finding of the maximum values of a function.

We may find the maxima either by the method of steepest ascents, which is perhaps the surest, though not necessarily the fastest, way; or we may try to anticipate the direction in which the diagnosis is heading and short circuit the inquiry. Again, there are nice mathematical analogies. Finally, we are dealing, for the most part, not with smooth functions but with paths roughened with error and irrelevance—with "noise." It is as if we wished to find a maximum in a system that is not (in the mathematical sense) deterministic, but stochastic. An effective approach to the maximum, then, must depend on some kind of a "smoothing" function that will prevent excessive response to distracting influences.

GEORGE E. THIBAULT, "RARE × RARE"

The *New England Journal of Medicine* uses examples of diagnoses made by experts as a way of demonstrating how diagnosis should be done. Read through this case study and see if any of the principles discussed by Clouser and Zucker, Schaffner, Caplan, or Murphy are being used.

Each section of the report is numbered so that you can follow along more easily.

1. An elderly man has shortness of breath and chest pain when he exerts himself. What counts as exertion will vary from person to person, as will what is interpreted as shortness of breath and pain. What is the explanation? The first focus is the heart. Mechanisms are given that would explain how different sorts of heart problems would be the cause. Of course, there might be two problems, one with the heart and another with the lungs. Notice the comment "going with the percentages," showing how an initial hypothesis is chosen.

2. The history of the problems is given, and we are told that tests have ruled out problems with lungs and heart valves. A rare relationship between carpal tunnel syndrome (pain in the wrist due to a nerve rubbing against the sides of the carpal tunnel) and heart problems is not considered worth follow-up. Three things should jump out at you. The physician always offers causal mechanisms and appeals to the concept of "fitting the typical patient profile." This is an example of using exemplars. Also, the physician is using the simple rule-out method mentioned by Murphy.

3. Although there is some counterevidence for it, the man is diagnosed and treated for heart pain caused by constriction of the small arteries that feed the heart. This condition is called syndrome X. The counterevidence is that he does not fit the typical patient profile for this condition. The expression "consistent with" is used. The symptoms are sometimes caused by syndrome X, but not always. Conditions under medical study have many causes. Some are much rarer than others. Sometimes a set of symptoms that is usually caused by one disease entity is caused by two or three diseases. Going slow in assuming that there is one relatively simple cause for a problem is a feature of good clinical medicine.

4. The man's symptoms got worse over the next two years. This almost never happens with syndrome X. What else might be going on? The most usual cause is a problem with the tissue of the heart itself.

5. The symptoms got bad enough for a stay at the hospital. Tests were done. They showed anatomical evidence of problems with one of his heart valves, the one between the left ventricle and the left auricle. Now there is evidence for amyloidosis (abnormal deposition of amyloids, carbohydrates made in the body). This was a diagnosis put aside previously for lack of evidence. Again, the diagnosis is a hesitant one because this is not the usual picture of this problem. Amyloidosis *can* cause this man's problems; the question is, "In this case, does it?"

6. Tests are done with the idea of confirming the diagnosis of amyloidosis. The results of the tests confirm the diagnosis, but there are other possibilities. Another test is ordered. A biopsy of the heart tissue will show what the problem is.

7. The test showed that the heart tissue was the problem. Another test showed that there was very likely a problem with the lungs. There might be one cause (scleroderma, general thickening) for both lung and heart problems. Amyloidosis can cause such thickening in both heart and lungs. Another test is ordered.

8. Test results reveal that it is amyloidosis. A prediction is made. If this is amyloidosis, then the patient will get sicker and sicker and die relatively soon of congestive heart failure. He will also have problems with the electrical conduction system of his heart.

9. Unfortunately, the predictions were borne out.

The commentary on the case reviews in general terms the diagnostic strategy that was used. The comment "he astutely anticipated" points to what we have termed clinical impression. Notice that the author stresses the importance of not coming to "premature closure." This is Murphy's point about not being fooled by local minima or maxima. The disease was rare, and sometimes realizing this makes physicians work either from too large a list of rarities or without a set methodology—as if rarity of the condition should change the diagnostic process. This physician made neither of these mistakes and is praised for keeping to the straight and narrow.

Go back to section 5 in the case report. The doctor says, "The absence of pericardial fluid excludes . . . pericardial tamponade." We might rephrase this as "The hypothesis T will be confirmed by finding F." If we find that there is no F, we can assume that T is an incorrect hypothesis. This means that the hypothesis "If there is T, then there will be F" has been tested and falsified by the finding of no F. We have been able to substitute variables for the technical terms and see the underlying logic. If you found the technical terms daunting, try this procedure to highlight the problem-solving method being used.

Rare × Rare

GEORGE E. THIBAULT

1. A 70-year-old man was referred to a cardiologist for evaluation of exertional chest pain and dyspnea.

The first thing that comes to mind in a man

From *The New England Journal of Medicine* 327 (1992): 714–717. Reprinted by permission of *The New England Journal of Medicine*. Copyright © 1992, Massachusetts Medical Society.

in this age group with exertional chest pain and dyspnea is the possibility of myocardial ischemia, most probably due to coronary artery disease. The combination of exertional chest pain and dyspnea is an interesting one. Chest pain with effort is frequently angina; what about the dyspnea? Dyspnea can be one of the mainfestations of myocardial ischemia, secondary to an increase in left ventricular diastolic pressure and therefore elevation of the pulmonary venous pressure. In fact, some patients have dyspnea as a manifestation of coronary ischemia rather than classic anginal symptoms. So ischemic heart disease is something that would rank high in my mind.

Another situation that would explain exertional chest pain and dyspnea is a combination of cardiac disease and pulmonary disease. In patients who have chronic obstructive lung disease as well as coronary artery disease, dyspnea and angina may occur together, because even a slight elevation of left-sided pressures is likely to threaten marginal pulmonary reserve. Another possibility one would have to consider is valvular heart disease, particularly aortic stenosis in this age group. If the patient had mitral valve disease he would not have anginal symptoms unless he had associated coronary artery disease. He could have a combination of mitral regurgitation and coronary disease in which, with ischemia, the mitral regurgitation becomes much worse because of papillary-muscle dysfunction. There is a well-recognized syndrome, occurring predominately in older patients, of sudden severe mitral regurgitation and pulmonary edema secondary to myocardial ischemia. Cardiomyopathy, particularly hypertrophic cardiomyopathy, can also cause classic angina and dyspnea. Dilated cardiomyopathy is associated with chest pain, but that is usually not classic exertional angina.

Going with the percentages, I think the most likely possibility is ischemic heart disease due to atherosclerotic obstructive coronary artery disease. The dyspnea is probably secondary to ischemic left ventricular dysfunction (systolic or diastolic) or papillary-muscle dysfunction.

2. The patient has no known cardiac risk factors. He was well until four years

before evaluation, when he began experiencing classic exertional angina associated with shortness of breath. The symptoms resolved in one to three minutes with rest. Chest pain did not occur at rest, and he had no prolonged episodes. He reported no other symptoms, except numbness in his fingers, recently attributed to carpal tunnel syndrome. His earlier evaluations included two exercise tests (one with thallium and one without) that reproduced his symptoms but showed no evidence of ischemia. Two coronary arteriograms showed no important coronary artery disease. Left ventricular systolic function was normal on both noninvasive and invasive studies. Hemodynamics were normal on catheterization, with no valvular gradients. An extensive gastrointestinal evaluation was negative. The results of pulmonary-function studies were normal.

The normal coronary arteriograms make it very unlikely that his symptoms are due to obstructive large-vessel coronary artery disease. He also does not appear to have aortic stenosis or emphysema. Carpal tunnel syndrome doesn't tell me a great deal. There are obviously a few connections between carpal tunnel syndrome and cardiovascular problems, one of which is hypothyroidism. But I am not too concerned about that diagnosis, given the information I've received so far.

His symptoms are described as classic exertional angina. There has been no pain at rest to suggest the possibility of coronary artery spasm. So, what possibilities are left? He could have microvascular angina—angina with normal epicardial coronary arteries. Patients with this disorder are thought to have an "inadequate vasodilator reserve." He does not fit the typical profile of patients with this syndrome. For the most part, such patients are women and are under the age of 65. They frequently have classic angina, and they may have electro-cardiographic and metabolic abnormalities consistent with myocardial ischemia.

Pulmonary hypertensive disease can cause dyspnea and angina-like chest pain, but we are told that his hemodynamics were normal, so that rules out pulmonary hypertension. It would be unusual for a cardiomyopathy to present in this manner with normal hemodynamics. Constrictive pericarditis is associated with dyspnea, but angina is uncommon except in the presence of coronary artery disease. Also, there were apparently no hemodynamic abnormalities to suggest this diagnosis. An atrial myxoma can sometimes cause episodic dyspnea, but usually not chest pain. This diagnosis would probably have been made with the studies he has already had. Are there any clues on physical examination?

3. On physical examination he was a healthy-appearing man. Blood pressure was 120/78 mm Hg, pulse 72, and respirations 14. His examination was entirely normal. All routine laboratory studies were within normal limits. All the earlier studies were reviewed. The diagnosis of microvascular angina ("syndrome X") was made. He was treated with calcium-channel blockers.

The presence of classic angina with normal coronary arteriography and the absence of any other demonstrable cardiac abnormalities are features consistent with the diagnosis of idiopathic microvascular angina (syndrome X). Against this diagnosis are the facts that he is male and 70 years old. Another possibility that should come to mind is microvascular angina due to another cause, namely small-vessel coronary artery disease. Patients who have microvascular angina of the idiopathic type have anatomically normal small vessels, and their prognosis is generally quite good.

Patients who have anatomical disease of the small coronary arteries may have a very different course.

Amyloidosis may infiltrate the microvasculature. The principal cardiac manifestation of amyloidosis, however, is usually a restrictive cardiomyopathy. The normal hemodynamics and normal physical examination make it unlikely that a restrictive cardiomyopathy is present in this patient. It would be an unusual presentation for amyloidosis. The possibility of something else in the small coronary arteries must certainly be considered.

4. Over the next two years he became more symptomatic. His symptoms were made worse by both calcium-channel blockers and beta-blockers. He continued to have exertional chest pain responsive to rest, and he was progressively more limited by exertional dyspnea. A repeat exercise-tolerance test showed a marked reduction in exercise tolerance as compared with previous studies. The study was discontinued because of chest pain and dyspnea. His base-line electrocardiogram now had diffuse nonspecific ST-segment and T-wave changes that worsened at peak exercise. There were no perfusion abnormalities on the thallium scan.

The worsening of symptoms with calcium-channel blockers and beta-blockers does not tell us a great deal. Microvascular angina, or syndrome X, may be helped by beta-blockers, calcium-channel blockers, or nitrates, but not predictably. Patients with syndrome X frequently continue to have chest pain and may be disabled by their symptoms. Their long-term prognosis for survival is quite good, but ventricular dysfunction may develop over time. There is obviously something else going on in this man. The deterioration in exercise tolerance, with electrocardiographic changes, suggests that primary myocardial disease is the basis of his condition.

If this is syndrome X it would be a highly unusual case; in fact, it would be unique. It could be some sort of idiopathic small-vessel disease. It could be an infiltrative disease of the myocardium. Amyloidosis is still a possibility, although nothing else has pointed to that diagnosis. We do not have evidence of a restrictive component, nor are we told of diminution of the voltage on his electrocardiogram. At this point I would repeat his echocardiogram, perform another catheterization study, and carry out a myocardial biopsy.

5. He was hospitalized with severe shortness of breath, and for the first time there were radiographic changes consistent with left ventricular failure. His jugular venous pressure was elevated, and his electrocardiogram showed diffusely decreased voltage. Repeat echocardiography showed symmetrical left ventricular hypertrophy and an ejection fraction of 0.45. There was 2+ mitral regurgitation, and no pericardial fluid was present.

Heart failure with relatively well-preserved systolic function and decreased electrocardiographic voltage makes me think even more strongly about the possibility of amyloidosis, particularly in this age group. The absence of pericardial fluid excludes another important cause of this constellation of findings—namely, pericardial tamponade. No description is given of the quality of the myocardial echoes; a diffuse ground-glass appearance is sometimes seen in amyloidosis.

This six-year history with a major anginal component is an atypical presentation of amyloidosis. The more typical presentation is left- and right-sided heart failure.

Amyloidosis does involve the small vessels of the heart, and there may be a component of myocardial ischemia, but for the most part chest pain is not a prominent part of the syndrome. Nonetheless, I'm beginning to think this is the most likely diagnosis.

6. The patient was treated with diuretics and referred for cardiac catheterization. The findings were as follows: mean right atrial pressure, 9 mm Hg; right ventricular pressure, 44/12 mm Hg; pulmonary-artery pressure, 44/15 mm Hg; mean pulmonary-capillary wedge pressure, 21 mm Hg (V waves to 36 mm Hg); left ventricular pressure, 100/24 mm Hg; and cardiac index, 2.6 liters per minute per square meter. The left ventricle was not dilated; the ejection fraction was 0.5, and there was 2+ mitral regurgitation. Coronary arteriography was normal, and there was no coronary spasm with ergonovine.

The hemodynamic profile here involves elevated pressures on both sides of the heart, with a discrepancy between pulmonary wedge pressure and right atrial pressure. This is most compatible with a diagnosis of restrictive cardiomyopathy, and amyloidosis is certainly the principal consideration. In fact, there are not many other possibilities in this age group. There is a rare entity known as idiopathic restrictive cardiomyopathy, in which there is a diffuse increase in the fibrous tissue within the heart. This might also be seen in scleroderma. It might be seen in sarcoidosis as well, but that would be most unusual. I would like to know the results of a myocardial biopsy.

7. The diagnosis of restrictive cardiomyopathy was made. Additional study results were as follows: pulmonary-function tests revealed a marked restrictive defect, with the

diffusing capacity for carbon monoxide 30 percent of predicted; the hematocrit was 0.35; and the erythrocyte sedimentation rate was 15 mm per hour. The patient had normal blood urea nitrogen and serum creatinine, electrolyte, calcium, phosphorus, and iron levels and normal results on liver-function tests, urinalysis, and serum and urine protein electrophoresis.

I agree with the diagnosis of a restrictive cardiomyopathy. The pulmonary-function tests are certainly highly suggestive of independent lung disease, of which pulmonary fibrosis would be the most likely cause. It would be hard to explain these defects on the basis of left-sided heart failure alone. It raises the question of whether the same process is involving the lungs and the heart. Scleroderma involving only the heart and lungs is a possibility, although I think it unlikely. I still think that amyloidosis is the leading possibility; amyloidosis can involve the lungs as well as the heart. The normal serum and urine electrophoresis does not deter me from this diagnosis. I would order a biopsy of the myocardium.

8. An endomyocardial biopsy revealed extensive areas that showed apple-green fluorescence when stained with Congo red.

So it is amyloidosis involving the heart, and presumably the lungs. This is a long course for primary amyloidosis. Unfortunately, there is no treatment proved to be effective. There have been anecdotal reports of benefit with colchicine in the treatment of cardiac amyloidosis. I have used it in a few patients, one of whom is still alive six years after biopsy-proved amyloidosis of the heart. In general, such patients have a relentless downhill course once they are as symptomatic as this man. I anticipate that

progressive congestive heart failure will develop. He will probably also have conduction abnormalities, since patients with amyloidosis often have involvement of the sinus node and atrioventricular block. I expect that he will die of congestive heart failure or an arrhythmia.

9. He became progressively more limited during the next year and had cardiac arrest while driving his car. Resuscitation was unsuccessful. Postmortem examination revealed extensive amyloid deposits in the heart, lungs, and gastrointestinal tract and throughout the small and medium-sized arteries (including the intramyocardial coronary arteries). There was a renal infarct, but the glomeruli were normal.

This was a most unusual case. Even though everything appeared normal when the patient was first referred, I presume that, in fact, amyloidosis was present. I think his ischemic symptoms must have been due to amyloid small-vessel coronary disease.

COMMENTARY

This exemplary discussion indicates how logic and a systematic approach to the differential diagnosis of cardiac disease can, by a process of elimination, lead to the correct diagnosis. This process works even with an unusual presentation of a rare disease the clinician has not seen before. The discussant carefully presented a differential diagnosis at each step in the process. He first gave a brief and focused differential diagnosis of the combination of chest pain and shortness of breath and concluded that coronary artery disease was the most likely cause in a 70-year-old man. Once he learned that the large coronary arteries were normal he considered other cardiac diagnoses, including small-vessel coronary artery disease and car-

GEORGE E. THIBAULT

diomyopathy. As he further elaborated on
the possible causes of small-vessel coronary
artery disease, he mentioned amyloidosis.
The progression of symptoms and the new
evidence of primary myocardial disease
made him refocus his attention on the diagnosis of cardiomyopathy. Here, the intersection of his two differential diagnoses (for
small-vessel coronary artery disease and for
primary myocardial disease) led him to
amyloidosis as the leading diagnostic possibility. He asked for the results of a myocardial biopsy when he had considerably less
information than the clinicians caring for the
patient. In fact, he astutely anticipated the
hemodynamic abnormalities, the biopsy
findings, and the patient's clinical course.

At each step he tested a limited number
of hypotheses to see whether specific diagnostic entities fit the information that was
available. This process of diagnostic verification[1] left him appropriately in doubt until
more evidence of primary myocardial disease and corresponding hemodynamic
abnormalities emerged. He was skeptical
about the assigned diagnosis of idiopathic
microvascular angina because the demo-
graphic profile was wrong, and then he
became even more dissatisfied with that
diagnosis as the clinical course became
incompatible with his experience.[2] By avoiding premature closure,[3] he kept an open
mind until sufficient clinical data were available to allow him to conclude that one
hypothesis best fit all the information. He
wondered repeatedly whether there were
diagnoses he was missing, and he reassessed
previously rejected diagnoses to be sure that
he had not inappropriately excluded them.
He knew not to stray from a small list of
diagnostic possibilities, and even though the
patient had a rare presentation of a rare disease, an orderly process of inferential reasoning led him to the correct diagnosis.

In fact, even he missed some important
clues. The first was the association between

carpal tunnel syndrome and cardiac disease.
He mentioned only hypothyroidism as a
connection between the two, but amyloidosis is also such a connection. Up to 24 percent
of patients with primary systemic amyloidosis have carpal tunnel syndrome before or at
the time of diagnosis.[4] The response to treatment was another diagnostic clue.
Worsening symptoms of congestive heart
failure after treatment with calcium-channel
blockers, as in this patient, have been
reported in patients with amyloid heart disease.[5] The absence of increased myocardial
echogenicity on the echocardiogram should
not have deterred the discussant from the
diagnosis of amyloidosis, because the sensitivity of this finding has been reported to be
as low as 63 percent. Other echocardiographic findings, such as increased atrial sep-
tal thickness and a low ratio of electrocardiographic voltage to left ventricular
cross-sectional area, may have suggested the
correct diagnosis earlier.[6] Finally, the presentation of amyloid heart disease as angina
or myocardial ischemia has been reported on
several occasions.[7-9] In one autopsy series, 5
of 106 patients with cardiac amyloid deposits
had severe occlusive disease of the intramyocardial arteries, with extensive subendocar-
dial infarction as the sole manifestation of the
disease.[10] If we conclude, as the discussant
did in retrospect, that the patient's entire
symptomatic course was due to cardiac amyloid, then his survival for seven years after
the initial cardiac symptoms was unusual.
Five-year survival rates of 0 to 6.5 percent
have been reported in patients with cardiac
amyloid,[11] but most were patients who presented with congestive heart failure as the
first manifestation of their disease. This
patient's unusual longevity might be
explained if one hypothesizes that his amyloid was principally microvascular at first
and only became a diffuse tissue infiltration
later in the course of the disease.

What can we as clinicians take away

from this account? We can use this exercise to expand our own knowledge about the possible presentations of primary systemic amyloidosis. We can learn how to approach similar problems by applying the logical approach to differential diagnosis illustrated here. No clinician has ever seen all the possibilities there are to see, and we all continue to learn from our clinical experiences and those of others. Clinical reasoning improves not only with the sharpening of our logic but also with experience.[12]

REFERENCES

1. Kassirer JP, Kopelman RI. Learning clinical reasoning. Baltimore: Williams & Wilkins, 1991:187–91.
2. Pasternak RC, Thibault GE, Savoia M, DeSanctis RW, Hutter AM Jr. Chest pain with angiographically insignificant coronary arterial obstruction: clinical presentation and long-term follow-up. Am J Med 1980;68:813–7.
3. Voytovich AE, Rippey RM, Suffredini A. Premature conclusions in diagnostic reasoning. J Med Educ 1985;60:302–7.
4. Kyle RA, Greipp PR. Amyloidosis (AL): clinical and laboratory features in 229 cases. Mayo Clin Proc 1983;58:665–83.
5. Gertz MA, Falk RH, Skinner M, Cohen AS, Kyle RA. Worsening of congestive heart failure in amyloid heart disease treated by calcium channel-blocking agents. Am J Cardiol 1985;55:1645.
6. Falk RH, Plehn JF, Deering T, et al. Sensitivity and specificity of the echocardiographic features of cardiac amyloidosis. Am J Cardiol 1987;59:418–22.
7. Saffitz JE, Sazama K, Roberts WC. Amyloidosis limited to small arteries causing angina pectoris and sudden death. Am J Cardiol 1983;51:1234–5.
8. Saltissi S, Kertes PJ, Julian DG. Primary cardiac amyloidosis in a young man presenting with angina pectoris. Br Heart J 1984;52:233–6.
9. Barbour DJ, Roberts WC. Frequency of acute and healed myocardial infarcts in fatal cardiac amyloidosis. Am J Cardiol 1988;62:1134–5.
10. Smith RRL, Hutchins GM. Ischemic heart disease secondary to amyloidosis of intramyocardial arteries. Am J Cardiol 1979;44:413–7.
11. Gertz MA, Kyle RA. Primary systemic amyloidosis—a diagnostic primer. Mayo Clin Proc 1989;64:1505–19.
12. Patel VL, Groen GR. Knowledge-based solution strategies in medical reasoning. Cognitive Sci 1986;10:91–116.

EXERCISES

1. Which method of Murphy's would Gorovitz and MacIntyre think best fitted clinical medicine?
2. Is clinical medicine clinical primarily because it has not yet been reduced to its basic scientific components?
3. How would you reason through this question: Do I have a stomachache because I ate too much pizza or because I am afraid to take that calculus test tomorrow? Keep track of all of the philosophical aspects of your reasoning. For example, do you appeal to laws? How do you choose between competing hypotheses?
4. Is engineering just like clinical medicine, as Caplan suggests? Or is engineering closer to physics than medicine is to biology? How about architecture? Boxing? Cooking?
5. Can the values that Clouser and Zucker identify as central to the practice of medicine ever be reduced so that they play no role in clinical medicine?

6

Can There Be a Science of Dreams?

In Chapter 2, Brodbeck suggested that social sciences such as psychology used statistical generalizations in a way that allows us to say that they offer (or at least try to offer) deductive explanations. In this, she was in agreement with Hempel and Oppenheim. Basically, their position would be that even though psychology may not be quite the science that physics is, it may come closer and closer to physics, depending on how it develops. Indeed, many authors would point out that the strides made by psychopharmacology and neuroscience have made psychology more and more a biological science. Brodbeck, Hempel, and Oppenheim would see psychology reduced to one of the biological and neurological sciences if current trends continue.

Hesse would put it differently. To her, reduction is really just replacement of one metaphor (or model) by another. The replacement can come only after one metaphor has shown itself to be much more "fruitful" than another (in the Lakatosian sense of the term). Kuhn, like Hesse, would argue that once the shift in metaphors had been made, there would no longer be a way to compare the two disciplines. In this case, it is hard to see how one would be able to support the view that one had been reduced to the other except in the sense of "eliminative reduction": In the Kuhnian view, reduction is the elimination of one discipline (or part of a discipline) in favor of another. Still, this is not the typical reductionist story. In the traditional view, the process of reduction goes along slowly and with a direction. It is clearly rational in its method and goal. Yet, remember, for Kuhn, paradigm (metaphor) shifts are neither rational nor irrational. They just happen.

In other words, the question of whether psychology can be reduced to a science such as neurophysiology is complex. It is made even more complex by the claim that many psychological theories do not even deserve to be called theories; they are merely masquerading as theories. They are pseudoscience, no better than astrology, alchemy, or witchcraft. This was the view propounded in Chapter 3 by Popper. In this chapter, we will take a further look at his claim. We will ask for the scientific status of depth psychologies, those that look beyond our behavior and conscious reasoning to find explanations for what we do and what we think.

We will compare a small part of Freud's depth psychology to that of Adler's. These are the two mentioned by Popper. We will then look at how Freud (1856–1938) and Jung (1875–1961) interpret dreams. We will examine a contemporary attack on Freud's central contentions by Grünbaum, followed by a defense of Freud by Flax. We will follow this with two other approaches to dreams: neurophysiological (Hobson and McCarley) and philosophical (Malcolm).

SIGMUND FREUD, "THE WOLF MAN"

The "wolf man" was a patient of Freud's. Central to unraveling the case was a dream that Freud interpreted. Here is the dream as it was related to Freud by the "wolf man."

> I dreamt that it was night and that I was lying in my bed. (My bed stood with its foot towards the window; in front of the window there was a row of old walnut trees. I know it was winter when I had the dream, and night-time.) Suddenly the window opened of its own accord, and I was terrified to see that some wolves were sitting on the big walnut tree in front of the window. There were six or seven of them. The wolves were quite white, and looked more like foxes or sheep-dogs, for they had big tails like foxes, and they had their ears pricked like dogs when they pay attention to something. In great terror, evidently of being eaten up by the wolves, I screamed. . . .

Freud's task is to explain the dream. To Freud this means finding the latent content of the dream and relating it to whatever the problems of the patient may be. The latent content of a dream is what the dream means. The latent content is hidden. Each part of the dream, in effect, refers to something else. As Freud interprets the dream for us, he also gives us parts of his theory relating to dream analysis, trying to make plain why he gives the interpretations that he does. Notice that when Freud comes to the general explanation, the dream represents the "wolf man" as a child watching his parents having sexual intercourse, Freud expects disbelief in his readers. How can anyone believe this?

As has been noted by some of our authors, some philosophers (and scientists) have thought that scientific explanation is reduction to the familiar—showing how the old and well understood relates to the new, which is under consideration. Hesse's view is a variation of explanation as reduction to the familiar. Assuming for the moment that Freudian analysis is a kind of science, here is a case where the scientist offering the explanation realizes that there is no reduction to the familiar. He expects his readers to balk at the explanation. Now, about one hundred years later, the explanation in terms of sexuality—even if rejected for many reasons—sounds very familiar.

In his discussion of the case, Freud makes a comment about Adler's views. Freud says:

> I have never been convinced that [the motives of power are as important as Adler claims]. If I had not pursued my patient's analysis to the end, I [would have wound up agreeing with Adler]. The conclusion of the analysis unexpectedly brought up new material which . . . showed that the motive of power . . . [was only] a contributory cause . . . whereas the true underlying determination [was sexual in nature].

Here Freud might have been using Murphy's method of steepest ascents (see Chapter 5) to warn us not to give up explaining too early. Or he might have been stressing Kitcher's point about unification (Chapter 3). Of course, the question is "When is too early?" This is not easy to answer. Too often, the answer is, "Until I find something that will count in my favor." Many commentators have accused Freud, and all depth psychologists, of using this answer. In fact, we can interpret Popper as having said just this in his critique in Chapter 3. That is why Popper thought that falsification was superior to the simple forms of confirmation used by these psychologists.

Very briefly, here is Freud's general theory. In his view, what we see on the surface is a mere glimmer of how our unconscious has been processing our experiences. Something as simple as a dream turns into a complex discovery about a person's deepest anxieties. Something as simple as not remembering a foreign word (something we would just shrug off) turns out to be revealing. Here is how Freud explained this.

All of our experience is transformed into electrical energy, according to Freud. Freud modeled his theory on electrodynamics, which is modeled in part on hydrodynamics. The bits of energy Freud refers to as *cathexis*. Energy can be stored (as memory) or used and discarded (literally discharged). The storing takes at least two forms. It can be put where we can retrieve it, or it can be stored in such a way that we cannot retrieve it. To make it unretrievable requires that the original input be changed. This takes energy that would normally be used for something else. Also, to keep the changed input "hidden" requires energy that would normally be used to do something else. Thus every time information is stored in this nonretrievable fashion, our energy equilibrium is thrown off kilter.

On the conscious level, the retrievable energy is what we remember. The nonretrievable energy is what we cannot dredge up from memory. It is in our unconscious. The name for the mechanism for putting it there and keeping it there is repression. It turns out that on the mental level, we repress what we find unpleasant.

Combining the physical model and the mental version, we see what Freud meant when he said that repression is always a failure: The equilibrium will be thrown off, and this is felt as unease and will either find its way into consciousness and cause us emotional problems or, as is more frequent, find its way to the surface in our dreams. Because we do experience our dreams and the real content is unpleasant, the unconscious hides the true meaning of the dream from us. Thus we have Freud's distinction between the manifest and latent content of a dream.

The repression of sexual longings was often at the root of psychological problems, Freud believed. (At one time, Freud argued that the basic cause was often repressed sexual trauma, such as an incident of incest. Freud later decided that these memories of sexual trauma were really not memories at all. Rather, he came to believe that they were fantasies and that having these forbidden fantasies was what forced the repression.)

Freud appealed to many cases to substantiate his views. It is not clear which really came first, the cases, their solutions, and then his theory or the theory, the cases, and then the solutions to fit the theory. If the latter, Freud may well have led his patients to see exactly what he wanted them to see so that he could have confirmation of his theory. Of course, Freud would have done this unconsciously. Would Popper's method of falsification have been a better procedure for Freud?

The Wolf Man

SIGMUND FREUD

I have already published this dream elsewhere, on account of the quantity of material in it which is derived from fairy tales; and I will begin by repeating what I wrote on that occasion:

" '*I dreamt that it was night and that I was lying in my bed. (My bed stood with its foot towards the window; in front of the window there was a row of old walnut trees. I know it was winter when I had the dream, and night-time.) Suddenly the window opened of its own accord, and I was terrified to see that some white wolves were sitting on the big walnut tree in front of the window. There were six or seven of them. The wolves were quite white, and looked more like foxes or sheep-dogs, for they had big tails like foxes and they had their ears pricked like dogs when they pay attention to*

something. In great terror, evidently of being eaten up by the wolves, I screamed* and woke up. My nurse hurried to my bed, to see what had happened to me. It took quite a long while before I was convinced that it had only been a dream; I had had such a clear and life-like picture of the window opening and the wolves sitting on the tree. At last I grew quieter, felt as though I had escaped from some danger, and went to sleep again.

" '*The only piece of action in the dream was the opening of the window; for the wolves sat quite still and without making any movement on the branches of the tree, to the right and left of the trunk, and looked at me. It seemed as though they had riveted their whole attention upon me.—I think this was my first anxiety-dream. I was three, four, or at most five years old at the time. From then until my eleventh or twelfth year I was always afraid of seeing something terrible in my dreams.*'

"He added a drawing of the tree with the wolves, which confirmed his description

"Wolf Dream" from *The Collected Papers*, Volume 3 by Sigmund Freud. Authorized translation under the supervision of Alix and James Strachey. Published by Basic Books, Inc. by arrangement with the Hogarth Press, Ltd. and the Institute of Psycho-Analysis, London. Reprinted by permission of BasicBooks, a division of HarperCollins Publishers, Inc.

(Fig. 1). The analysis of the dream brought the following material to light.

"He had always connected this dream with the recollection that during these years of his childhood he was most tremendously afraid of the picture of a wolf in a book of fairy tales. His elder sister, who was very much his superior, used to tease him by holding up this particular picture in front of him on some excuse or other, so that he was terrified and began to scream. In this picture the wolf was standing upright, striding out with one foot, with its claws stretched out and its ears pricked. He thought this picture must have been an illustration to the story of 'Little Red Riding-Hood.'

"Why were the wolves white? This made him think of the sheep, large flocks of which were kept in the neighbourhood of the estate. His father occasionally took him with him to visit these flocks, and every time this happened he felt very proud and blissful. Later on—according to enquiries that were made it may easily have been shortly before the time of the dream—an epidemic broke out among the sheep. His father sent for a follower of Pasteur's, who inoculated the animals, but after the inoculation even more of them died than before.

"How did the wolves come to be on the tree? This reminded him of a story that he had heard his grandfather tell. He could not remember whether it was before or after the dream, but its subject is a decisive argument in favour of the former view. The story ran as follows. A tailor was sitting at work in his room, when the window opened and a wolf leapt in. The tailor hit after him with his yard—no (he corrected himself), caught him by his tail and pulled it off, so that the wolf ran away in terror. Some time later the tailor went into the forest, and suddenly saw a pack of wolves coming towards him; so he climbed up a tree to escape from them. At first the wolves were in perplexity; but the maimed one, which was among them and wanted to revenge himself on the tailor, proposed that they should climb one upon another till the last one could reach him. He himself—he was a vigorous old fellow—would be the base of the pyramid. The wolves did as he suggested, but the tailor

Figure 1

had recognized the visitor whom he had punished, and suddenly called out as he had before: 'Catch the grey one by his tail!' The tailless wolf, terrified by the recollection, ran away, and all the others tumbled down.

"In this story the tree appears, upon which the wolves were sitting in the dream. But it also contains an unmistakable allusion to the castration complex. The *old* wolf was docked of his tail by the tailor. The fox-tails of the wolves in the dream were probably compensations for this taillessness.

"Why were there six or seven wolves? There seemed to be no answer to this question, until I raised a doubt whether the picture that had frightened him could be connected with the story of 'Little Red Riding-Hood.' This fairy tale only offers an opportunity for two illustrations—Little Red Riding-Hood's meeting with the wolf in the wood, and the scene in which the wolf lies in bed in the grandmother's night-cap. There must therefore be some other fairy tale behind his recollection of the picture. He soon discovered that it could only be the story of 'The Wolf and the Seven Little Goats.' Here the number seven occurs, and also the number six, for the wolf only ate up six of the little goats, while the seventh hid itself in the clock-case. The white, too, comes into this story, for the wolf had his paw made white at the baker's after the little goats had recognized him on his first visit by his grey paw. Moreover, the two fairy tales have much in common. In both there is the eating up, the cutting open of the belly, the taking out of the people who had been eaten and their replacement by heavy stones, and finally in both of them the wicked wolf perishes. Besides all this, in the story of the little goats the tree appears. The wolf lay down under a tree after his meal and snored.

"I shall have, for a special reason, to deal with this dream again elsewhere, and interpret it and consider its significance in greater detail. For it is the earliest anxiety-dream that the dreamer remembered from his childhood, and its content, taken in connection with other dreams that followed it soon afterwards and with certain events in his earliest years, is of quite peculiar interest. We must confine ourselves here to the relation of the dream to the two fairy tales which have so much in common with each other, 'Little Red Riding-Hood' and 'The Wolf and the Seven Little Goats.' The effect produced by these stories was shown in the little dreamer by a regular animal phobia. This phobia was only distinguished from other similar cases by the fact that the anxiety-animal was not an object easily accessible to observation (such as a horse or a dog), but was known to him only from stories and picture-books.

"I shall discuss on another occasion the explanation of these animal phobias and the significance attaching to them. I will only remark in anticipation that this explanation is in complete harmony with the principal characteristic shown by the neurosis from which the present dreamer suffered later in his life. His fear of his father was the strongest motive for his falling ill, and his ambivalent attitude towards every father-surrogate was the dominating feature of his life as well as of his behaviour during the treatment.

"If in my patient's case the wolf was merely a first father-surrogate, the question arises whether the hidden content in the fairy tales of the wolf that ate up the little goats and of 'Little Red Riding-Hood' may not simply be infantile fear of the father. Moreover, my patient's father had the characteristic, shown by so many people in relation to their children, of indulging in 'affectionate abuse'; and it is possible that during the patient's earlier years his father (though he grew severe later on) may more than once, as he caressed the little boy or played with him, have threatened in fun to 'gobble him up.' One of my patients told me that her two children could never get to be fond of their grandfather, because in the course of his affectionate romping with them he used to frighten them by saying he would cut open their tummies."

Leaving on one side everything in this quotation that anticipates the dream's remoter implications, let us return to its immediate interpretation. I may remark that this interpretation was a task that dragged on over several years. The patient related the dream at a very early stage of the analysis and very soon came to share my conviction that the causes of his infantile neurosis lay concealed behind it. In the course of the treatment we often came back to the dream, but it was only during the last months of the analysis that it became possible to understand it completely, and only then thanks to spontaneous work on the patient's part. He had always emphasized the fact that two factors in the dream had made the greatest impression on him: first, the perfect stillness and immobility of the wolves, and secondly, the strained attention with which they all looked at him. The lasting sense of reality, too, which the dream left behind it, seemed to him to deserve notice.

Let us take this last remark as a starting-point. We know from our experience in interpreting dreams that this sense of reality carries a particular significance along with it. It assures us that some part of the latent material of the dream is claiming in the dreamer's memory to possess the quality of reality, that is, that the dream relates to an occurrence that really took place and was not merely imagined. It can naturally only be a question of the reality of something unknown; for instance, the conviction that his grandfather really told him the story of the tailor and the wolf, or that the stories of "Little Red Riding-Hood" and of "The Seven Little Goats" were really read aloud to him, would not be of a nature to be replaced by

this sense of reality that outlasted the dream. The dream seemed to point to an occurrence the reality of which was very strongly emphasized as being in marked contrast to the unreality of the fairy tales.

If it was to be assumed that behind the content of the dream there lay some such unknown scene—one, that is, which had already been forgotten at the time of the dream—then it must have taken place very early. The dreamer, it will be recalled, said: "I was three, four, or at most five years old at the time I had the dream." And we can add: "And I was reminded by the dream of something that must have belonged to an even earlier period."

The parts of the manifest content of the dream which were emphasized by the dreamer, the factors of attentive looking and of motionlessness, must lead to the content of this scene. We must naturally expect to find that this material reproduces the unknown material of the scene in some distorted form, perhaps even distorted into its opposite.

There were several conclusions, too, to be drawn from the raw material which had been produced by the patient's first analysis of the dream, and these had to be fitted into the collocation of which we were in search. Behind the mention of the sheep-breeding, evidence was to be expected of his sexual researches, his interest in which he was able to gratify during his visits with his father; but there must also have been allusions to a fear of death, since the greater part of the sheep had died of the epidemic. The most obtrusive thing in the dream, the wolves on the tree, led straight to his grandfather's story; and what was fascinating about this story and capable of provoking the dream can scarcely have been anything but its connection with the theme of castration.

We also concluded from the first incomplete analysis of the dream that the wolf may have been a father-surrogate; so that, in that case, this first anxiety-dream would have brought to light the fear of his father which from that time forward was to dominate his life. This conclusion, indeed, was in itself not yet binding. But if we put together as the result of the provisional analysis what can be derived from the material produced by the dreamer, we then find before us for reconstruction some such fragments as these: *A real occurrence—dating from a very early period—looking—immobility—sexual problems—castration—his father—something terrible.*

One day the patient began to continue with the interpretation of the dream. He thought that the part of the dream which said that "suddenly the window opened of its own accord" was not completely explained by its connection with the window at which the tailor was sitting and through which the wolf came into the room. "It must mean: 'My eyes suddenly opened.' I was asleep, therefore, and suddenly woke up, and as I woke I saw something: the tree with the wolves." No objection could be made to this; but the point could be developed further. He had woken up and had seen something. The attentive looking, which in the dream was ascribed to the wolves, should rather be shifted on to him. At a decisive point, therefore, a transposition has taken place; and moreover this is indicated by another transposition in the manifest content of the dream. For the fact that the wolves were sitting on the tree was also a transposition, since in his grandfather's story they were underneath, and were unable to climb on to the tree.

What, then, if the other factor emphasized by the dreamer were also distorted by means of a transposition or reversal? In that case instead of immobility (the wolves sat there motionless; they looked at him, but did not move) the meaning would have to be: the most violent motion. That is to say, he suddenly woke up, and saw in front of

him a scene of violent movement at which he looked with strained attention. In the one case the distortion would consist in an interchange of subject and object, of activity and passivity: being looked at instead of looking. In the other case it would consist in a transformation into the opposite; rest instead of motion.

On another occasion an association which suddenly occurred to him carried us another step forward in our understanding of the dream: "The tree was a Christmas-tree." He now knew that he had dreamt the dream shortly before Christmas and in expectation of it. Since Christmas Day was also his birthday, it now became possible to establish with certainty the date of the dream and of the change in him which proceeded from it. It was immediately before his fourth birthday. He had gone to sleep, then, in tense expectation of the day which ought to bring him a double quantity of presents. We know that in such circumstances a child may easily anticipate the fulfilment of his wishes. So it was already Christmas in his dream; the content of the dream showed him his Christmas box, the presents which were to be his were hanging on the tree. But instead of presents they had turned into—wolves, and the dream ended by his being overcome by fear of being eaten by the wolf (probably his father), and by his flying for refuge to his nurse. Our knowledge of his sexual development before the dream makes it possible for us to fill in the gaps in the dream and to explain the transformation of his satisfaction into anxiety. Of the wishes concerned in the formation of the dream the most powerful must have been the wish for the sexual satisfaction which he was at that time longing to obtain from his father. The strength of this wish made it possible to revive a long-forgotten trace in his memory of a scene which was able to show him what sexual satisfaction from his father was like; and the result was terror, horror of the fulfilment of the wish, the repression of the impulse which had manifested itself by means of the wish, and consequently a flight from his father to his less dangerous nurse.

The importance of this date of Christmas Day had been preserved in his supposed recollection of having had his first fit of rage because he was dissatisfied with his Christmas presents. The recollection combined elements of truth and of falsehood. It could not be entirely right, since according to the repeated declarations of his parents his naughtiness had already begun on their return in the autumn and it was not a fact that they had not come on till Christmas. But he had preserved the essential connection between his unsatisfied love, his rage, and Christmas.

But what picture can the nightly workings of his sexual desire have conjured up that could frighten him away so violently from the fulfilment for which he longed? The material of the analysis shows that there is one condition which this picture must satisfy. It must have been calculated to create a conviction of the reality of the existence of castration. Fear of castration could then become the motive power for the transformation of the affect.

I have now reached the point at which I must abandon the support I have hitherto had from the course of the analysis. I am afraid it will also be the point at which the reader's belief will abandon me.

What sprang into activity that night out of the chaos of the dreamer's unconscious memory-traces was the picture of copulation between his parents, copulation in circumstances which were not entirely usual and were especially favourable for observation. It gradually became possible to find satisfactory answers to all the questions that arose in connection with this scene; for in the course of the treatment the first dream returned in innumerable variations and new

editions, in connection with which the analysis produced the information that was required. Thus in the first place the child's age at the date of the observation was established as being about one and a half years.[1] He was suffering at the time from malaria, an attack of which used to come on every day at a particular hour.[2] From his tenth year onwards he was from time to time subject to moods of depression, which used to come on in the afternoon and reached their height at about five o'clock. This symptom still existed at the time of the analytic treatment. The recurring fits of depression took the place of the earlier attacks of fever or languor; five o'clock was either the time of the highest fever or of the observation of the intercourse, unless the two times coincided.[3] Probably for the very reason of this illness, he was in his parents' bedroom. The illness, the occurrence of which is also corroborated by direct tradition, makes it reasonable to refer the event to the summer, and, since the child was born on Christmas Day, to assume that his age was $n + 1\frac{1}{2}$ years. He had been sleeping in his cot, then, in his parents' bedroom, and woke up, perhaps because of his rising fever, in the afternoon, possibly at five o'clock, the hour which was later marked out by depression. It harmonizes with our assumption that it was a hot summer's day, if we suppose that his parents had retired, half undressed,[4] for an afternoon *siesta*. When he woke up, he witnessed a coitus *a tergo*, three times repeated;[5] he was able to see his mother's genitals as well as his father's organ; and he understood the process as well as its significance.[6] Lastly he interrupted his parents' intercourse in a manner which will be discussed later.

There is at bottom nothing extraordinary, nothing to give the impression of being the product of an extravagant imagination, in the fact that a young couple who had only been married a few years should have ended a *siesta* on a hot summer's afternoon with a love-scene, and should have disregarded the presence of their little boy of one and a half, asleep in his cot. On the contrary, such an event would, I think, be something entirely commonplace and *banal;* and even the position in which we have inferred that the coitus took place cannot in the least alter this judgment—especially as the evidence does not require that the intercourse should have been performed from behind each time. A single time would have been enough to give the spectator an opportunity for making observations which would have been rendered difficult or impossible by any other attitude of the lovers. The content of the scene cannot therefore in itself be an argument against its credibility. Doubts as to its probability will turn upon three other points: whether a child at the tender age of one and a half could be in a position to take in the perceptions of such a complicated process and to preserve them so accurately in his unconscious; secondly, whether it is possible at the age of four for a deferred revision of the impressions so received to penetrate the understanding; and finally, whether any procedure could succeed in bringing into consciousness coherently and convincingly the details of a scene of this kind which had been experienced and understood in such circumstances.[7]

Later on I shall carefully examine these and other doubts; but I can assure the reader that I am no less critically inclined than he towards an acceptance of this observation of the child's, and I will only ask him to join me in adopting a *provisional* belief in the reality of the scene. We will first proceed with the study of the relations between this "primal scene" and the patient's dream, his symptoms, and the history of his life; and we will trace separately the effects that followed from the essential content of the scene and from one of its visual impressions.

By the latter I mean the postures which he saw his parents adopt—the man upright, and the woman bent down like an animal. We have already heard that during his anxiety period his sister used to terrify him with a picture from the fairy-book, in which the wolf was shown standing upright, with one foot forward, with its claws stretched out and its ears pricked. He devoted himself with tireless perseverance during the treatment to the task of hunting in the second-hand bookshops till he had found the illustrated fairy-book of his childhood, and had recognized his bogy in an illustration to the story of "The Wolf and the Seven Little Goats." He thought that the posture of the wolf in this picture might have reminded him of that of his father during the constructed primal scene. At all events the picture became the point of departure for further manifestations of anxiety. Once when he was in his seventh or eighth year he was informed that next day a new tutor was coming for him. That night he dreamt of this tutor in the shape of a lion that came towards his bed roaring loudly and in the posture of the wolf in the picture; and once again he awoke in a state of anxiety. The wolf phobia had been overcome by that time, so he was free to choose himself a new anxiety-animal, and in this late dream he was recognizing the tutor as a father-surrogate. In the later years of his childhood each of his tutors and masters played the part of his father, and was endowed with his father's influence both for good and for evil.

While he was at his secondary school the Fates provided him with a remarkable opportunity of reviving his wolf phobia, and of using the relation which lay behind it as an occasion for severe inhibitions. The master who taught his form Latin was called Wolf. From the very first he felt cowed by him, and he was once taken severely to task by him for having made a stupid mistake in a piece of Latin translation. From that time on he could not get free from a paralysing fear of this master, and it was soon extended to other masters besides. But the occasion on which he made his blunder in the translation was also to the purpose. He had to translate the Latin word *filius*, and he did it with the French word *fils* instead of with the corresponding word from his own language. The wolf, in fact, was still his father.[8]

The first "transitory symptom"[9] which the patient produced during the treatment went back once more to the wolf phobia and to the fairy tale of "The Seven Little Goats." In the room in which the first sessions were held there was a large grandfather clock opposite the patient, who lay on a sofa facing away from me. I was struck by the fact that from time to time he turned his face towards me, looked at me in a very friendly way as though to propitiate me, and then turned his look away from me to the clock. I thought at the time that he was in this way showing his eagerness for the end of the hour. A long time afterwards the patient reminded me of this piece of dumb show, and gave me an explanation of it; for he recalled that the youngest of the seven little goats hid himself in the case of the grandfather clock while his six brothers were eaten up by the wolf. So what he had meant was: "Be kind to me! Must I be frightened of you? Are you going to eat me up? Shall I hide myself from you in the clock-case like the youngest little goat?"

The wolf that he was afraid of was undoubtedly his father; but his fear of the wolf was conditional upon the creature being in an upright posture. His recollection asserted most definitely that he had not been terrified by pictures of wolves going on all fours or, as in the story of "Little Red Riding-Hood," lying in bed. The posture which, according to our construction of the primal scene, he had seen the woman assume, was of no less significance; though in this case the significance was limited to the sexual sphere. The most striking phenomenon of his erotic life after maturity was his liability to compulsive attacks of falling physically in love which came on and disappeared again in the most puzzling succession. These attacks released a tremendous energy in him even at times when he was otherwise inhibited, and they were quite beyond his control. I must, for a specially important reason, postpone a full consideration of this compulsive love, but I may mention here that it was subject to a definite condition, which was concealed from his consciousness and was discovered only during the treatment. It was necessary that the woman should have assumed the posture which we have ascribed to his mother in the primal scene. From his puberty he had felt large and conspicuous buttocks as the most powerful attraction in a woman; to copulate except from behind gave him scarcely any enjoyment. At this point a criticism may justly be raised: it may be objected that a sexual preference of this kind for the hind parts of the body is a general characteristic of people who are inclined to an obsessional neurosis, and that its presence does not justify us in referring it back to a special impression in childhood. It is part of the fabric of the anal-erotic disposition and is one of the archaic traits which distinguish that constitution. Indeed, copulation from behind—*more ferarum*—may, after all, be regarded as phylogenetically the older form. We shall return to this point too in a later discussion, when we have brought forward the supplementary material which showed the basis of the unconscious condition upon which his falling in love depended.

Let us now proceed with our discussion of the relations between his dream and the primal scene. We should so far have expected the dream to present the child (who was rejoicing at Christmas in the prospect of the fulfilment of his wishes) with this picture of sexual satisfaction afforded through his father's agency, just as he had seen it in the primal scene, as a model of the satisfaction that he himself was longing to obtain from his father. Instead of this picture, however, there appeared the material of the story which he had been told by his grandfather shortly before: the tree, the wolves, and the taillessness (in the overcompensated form of the bushy tails of the putative wolves). At this point some connection is missing, some associative bridge to lead from the content of the primal scene to that of the wolf story. This connection is provided once again by the postures and only by them. In his grandfather's story the tailless wolf asked the others *to climb upon him.* It was this detail that called up the recollection of the picture of the primal scene; and it was in this way that it became possible for the material of the primal scene to be represented by that of the wolf story, and at the same time for the *two* parents to be replaced, as was desirable, by *several* wolves. The content of the dream met with a further transformation, and the material of the wolf story was made to fit in with the content of the fairy tale of "The Seven Little Goats," by borrowing from it the number seven.[10]

The steps in the transformation of the material, "primal scene—wolf story—fairy tale of 'The Seven Little Goats,' " are a reflection of the progress of the dreamer's thoughts during the construction of the dream: "longing for sexual satisfaction from his father—realization that castration is a necessary condition of it—fear of his father." It is only at this point, I think, that we can regard the anxiety-dream of this four-year-old boy as being exhaustively explained.[11]

After what has already been said I need only deal shortly with the pathogenic effect of the primal scene and the alteration which its revival produced in his sexual development. We will only trace that one of its effects to which the dream gave expression.

Later on we shall have to make it clear that it was not only a single sexual current that started from the primal scene but a whole set of them, that his sexual life was positively splintered up by it. We shall further bear in mind that the activation of this scene (I purposely avoid the word "recollection") had the same effect as though it were a recent experience. The effects of the scene were deferred, but meanwhile it had lost none of its freshness in the interval between the ages of one and a half and four years. We shall perhaps find in what follows reason to suppose that it produced certain effects even at the time of its perception, that is, from the age of one and a half onwards.

When the patient entered more deeply into the situation of the primal scene, he brought to light the following pieces of self-observation. He assumed to begin with, he said, that the event of which he was a witness was an act of violence, but the expression of enjoyment which he saw on his mother's face did not fit in with this; he was obliged to recognize that the experience was one of gratification.[12] What was essentially new for him in his observation of his parents' intercourse was the conviction of the reality of castration—a possibility with which his thoughts had already been occupied previously. (The sight of the two girls micturating, his Nanya's threat, the governess's interpretation of the sugar-sticks, the recollection of his father having beaten a snake to pieces.) For now he saw with his own eyes the wound of which his Nanya had spoken, and understood that its presence was a necessary condition of intercourse with his father. He could no longer confuse it with the bottom, as he had in his observation of the little girls.

The dream ended in a state of anxiety, from which he did not recover until he had his Nanya with him. He fled, therefore, from his father to her. His anxiety was a repudiation of the wish for sexual satisfaction from his father—the trend which had put the dream into his head. The form taken by the anxiety, the fear of "being eaten by the wolf," was only the (as we shall hear, regressive) transposition of the wish to be copulated with by his father, that is, to be given sexual satisfaction in the same way as his mother. His last sexual aim, the passive attitude towards his father, succumbed to repression, and fear of his father appeared in its place in the shape of the wolf phobia.

And the driving force of this repression? The circumstances of the case show that it can only have been his narcissistic genital libido, which, in the form of concern for his male organ, was fighting against a satisfaction whose attainment seemed to involve the renunciation of that organ. And it was from his threatened narcissism that he derived the masculinity with which he defended himself against his passive attitude towards his father.

We now observe that at this point in our narrative we must make an alteration in our terminology. During the dream he had reached a new phase in his sexual organization. Up to then the sexual opposites had been for him *active* and *passive*. Since his seduction his sexual aim had been a passive one, of being touched on the genitals; it was then transformed, by regression to the earlier stage of the sadistic-anal organization, into the masochistic aim of being beaten or punished. It was a matter of indifference to him whether he reached this aim with a man or with a woman. He had travelled, without considering the difference of sex, from his Nanya to his father; he had longed to have his penis touched by his Nanya, and had tried to provoke a beating from his father. Here his genitals were left out of account; though the connection with them which had been concealed by the regression was still expressed in his phantasy of being beaten *on the penis*. The activation of the primal scene in the dream now brought him

back to the genital organization. He discovered the vagina and the biological significance of masculine and feminine. He understood now that active was the same as masculine, while passive was the same as feminine. His passive sexual aim should now have been transformed into a feminine one, and have expressed itself as "being copulated with by his father" instead of "being beaten by him on the genitals or on the bottom." This feminine aim, however, underwent repression and was obliged to let itself be replaced by fear of the wolf.

We must here break off the discussion of his sexual development until new light is thrown from the later stages of his history upon these earlier ones. For the proper appreciation of the wolf phobia we will only add that both his father and mother became wolves. His mother took the part of the castrated wolf, which let the others climb upon it; his father took the part of the wolf that climbed. But his fear, as we have heard him assure us, related only to the standing wolf, that is, to his father. It must further strike us that the fear with which the dream ended had a model in his grandfather's story. For in this the castrated wolf, which had let the others climb upon it, was seized with fear as soon as it was reminded of the fact of its tail-lessness. It seems, therefore, as though he had identified himself with his castrated mother during the dream, and was now fighting against that fact. "If you want to be sexually satisfied by Father," we may perhaps represent him as saying to himself, "you must allow yourself to be castrated like Mother; but I won't have that." In short, a clear protest on the part of his masculinity! Let us, however, plainly understand that the sexual development of the case that we are now examining has a great disadvantage from the point of view of research, for it was by no means undisturbed. It was first decisively influenced by the seduction, and was then diverted by the scene of observation of the coitus, which in its deferred action operated like a second seduction. . . .

NOTES

1. The age of six months came under consideration as a far less probable, and indeed scarcely tenable, alternative.

2. Compare the subsequent metamorphoses of this factor during the obsessional neurosis. In the patient's dreams during the treatment it was replaced by a violent wind. *Aria* = "air."

3. We may remark in this connection that the patient drew only *five* wolves in his illustration to the dream, although the text mentioned six or seven.

4. In white underclothes: the *white* wolves.

5. Why three times? He suddenly one day produced the statement that I had discovered this detail by interpretation. This was not the case. It was a spontaneous association, exempt from further criticism; in his usual way he passed it off on to me, and by this projection tried to make it seem more trustworthy.

6. I mean that he understood it at the time of the dream when he was four years old, not at the time of the observation. He received the impressions when he was one and a half; his understanding of them was deferred, but became possible at the time of the dream owing to his development, his sexual excitations, and his sexual researches.

7. The first of these difficulties cannot be reduced by assuming that the child at the time of his observation was after all probably a year older, that is to say *two* and a half, an age at which he may perhaps have been perfectly capable of talking. All the minor details of my patient's case almost excluded the possibility of shifting the date in this way. Moreover, the fact should be taken into account that these scenes of observing parental intercourse are by no means rarely brought to light in analysis. The condition of their occurrence, however, is precisely that it should be in the earliest period of childhood. The older the child is, the more carefully, with parents above a certain social level, will the child be deprived of the opportunity for this kind of observation.

8. After this reprimand from the schoolmaster-wolf he learnt that it was the general opinion of his companions that, to be pacified, the master expected money from him. We shall return to this point later—I can see that it would greatly facilitate a rationalistic view of such a history of a child's development as this if it could be supposed that his whole fear of the wolf had really originated from the Latin master of that name, that it had been projected back into his childhood, and, supported by the illustration to the fairy tale, had caused the phantasy of the primal scene. But this is untenable; the chronological priority of the wolf phobia and its reference to the period of his childhood spent upon the first estate is far too securely attested. And his dream at the age of four?

9. Ferenczi, S., "Transitory Symptom-Foundations during Analysis." (Chapter vii, of Ferenczi, *Contributions to Psychoanalysis*, Boston, 1916.) Translated by Ernest Jones from "Über passagère Symptombildungen während der Analyse," *Zentralblatt für Psychoanalyse*, Bd. II., 1912.

10. It says "six or seven" in the dream. Six is the number of the children that were eaten; the seventh escaped into the clock-case. It is always a strict law of dream-interpretation that an explanation must be found for every detail.

11. Now that we have succeeded in making a synthesis of the dream, I will try to give a comprehensive account of the relations between the manifest content of the dream and the latent dream-thoughts.

    It was night, I was lying in my bed. The latter part of this is the beginning of the reproduction of the primal scene. "It was night" is a distortion of "I had been asleep." The remark, "I know it was winter when I had the dream, and night-time," refers to the patient's recollection of the dream and is not part of its content. It is correct, for it was one of the nights before his birthday, that is, Christmas Day.

    Suddenly the window opened of its own accord. That is to be translated: "Suddenly I woke up of my own accord," a recollection of the primal scene. The influence of the wolf story, in which the wolf leapt in through the window, is making itself felt as a modifying factor, and transforms a direct expression into a plastic one. At the same time the introduction of the window serves the purpose of providing a contemporary reference for the subsequent content of the dream. On Christmas Eve the door opens suddenly and one sees before one the tree with the presents. Here therefore the influence of the actual expectation of Christmas (which comprises the wish for sexual satisfaction) is making itself felt.

    The big walnut-tree. The representative of the Christmas tree, and therefore belonging to the current situation. But also the tree out of the wolf story, on which the tailor took refuge from pursuit, and under which the wolves were on the watch. Moreover, as I have often been able to satisfy myself, a high tree is a symbol of observing, of scopophilia. A person sitting on a tree can see everything that is going on below him and cannot himself be seen. Compare Boccaccio's well-known story, and similar *facetiae.*

The wolves. Their number: *six or seven.* In the wolf story there was a pack, and no number was given. The fixing of the number shows the influence of the fairy tale of "The Seven Little Goats," six of whom were eaten up. The fact that the number two in the primal scene is replaced by a larger number, which would be absurd in the primal scene, is welcomed by the resistance as a means of distortion. In the illustration to the dream the dreamer brings forward the number five, which is probably meant to correct the statement "It was night."

They were sitting on the tree. In the first place they replace the Christmas presents hanging on the tree. But they are also transposed on to the tree because that can mean that they are looking. In his grandfather's story they were posted underneath the tree. Their relation to the tree has therefore been reversed in the dream; and from this it may be concluded that there are further reversals of the latent material to be found in the content of the dream.

They were looking at him with strained attention. This feature comes entirely from the primal scene, and has got into the dream at the price of being turned completely round.

They were quite white. This feature is unessential in itself, but is strongly emphasized in the dreamer's narrative. It owes its intensity to a copious fusion of elements from all the strata of the material, and it combines unimportant details from the other sources of the dream with a fragment of the primal scene which is more significant. This last part of its determination goes back to the white of his parents' bedclothes and underclothes, and to this is added the white of the flocks of sheep, and of the sheep-dogs, as an allusion to his sexual researches among animals, and the white in the fairy tale of "The Seven Little Goats," in which the mother is recognized by the white of her hand. Later on we shall see that the white clothes are also an allusion to death.

They sat there motionless. This contradicts the most striking feature of the observed scene, namely, its agitated movement, which, in virtue of the postures to which it led, constitutes the connection between the primal scene and the wolf story.

They had tails like foxes. This must be the contradiction of a conclusion which was derived from the action of the primal scene on the wolf story, and which must be recognized as the most important result of the dreamer's sexual researches: "So there really is such a thing as castration." The terror with which this conclusion was received finally broke out in the dream and brought it to an end.

The fear of being eaten up by the wolves. It seemed to the dreamer as though the motive force of this fear was not derived from the content of the dream. He said he need not have been afraid, for the wolves looked more like foxes or dogs, and they did not rush at him as though to bite him, but were very still and not at all terrible. We observe that the dream-work tries for some time to make the distressing content harmless by transforming it into its opposite. ("They aren't moving, and, only look, they have the loveliest tails!") Until at last this expedient fails, and the fear breaks out. It expresses itself by the help of the fairy tale, in which the goat-children are eaten up by the wolf-father. This part of the fairy tale may perhaps have acted as a reminder of threats made by the child's father in fun when he was playing with him; so that the fear of being eaten up by the wolf may be a reminiscence as well as a substitute by displacement.

The wishes which act as motive forces in this dream are obvious. First there are the superficial wishes of the day, that Christmas with its presents may already be here (a dream of impatience) and accompanying these is the deeper wish, now permanently present, for sexual satisfaction from the dreamer's father. This is immediately replaced by the wish to see once more what was then so fascinating. The mental process then proceeds on its way. Starting from the fulfillment of this last wish with the conjuring up of the primal scene, it passes on to what has now become inevitable—the repudiation of that wish and its repression.

The diffuseness and elaboration of this commentary have been forced on me by the effort to present the reader with some sort of equivalent for the convincing power of an analysis carried through by oneself; perhaps they may also serve to discourage him from asking for the publication of analyses which have stretched over several years.

12. We might perhaps best do justice to this statement of the patient's by supposing that the object of his observation was in the first instance a coitus in the normal position, which cannot fail to produce the impression of being a sadistic act, and that only after this was the position altered, so that he had an opportunity for making other observations and judgments. This hypothesis, however, was not confirmed with certainty, and moreover does not seem to me indispensable. We must not forget the actual situation which lies behind the abbreviated description given in the text: the patient under analysis, at an age of over twenty-five years, was

putting the impressions and impulses of his fourth year into words which he would never have found at that time. If we fail to notice this, it may easily seem comic and incredible that a child of four should be capable of such technical judgments and learned notions. This is simply another instance of *deferred action*. At the age of one and a half the child receives an impression to which he is unable to react adequately; he is only able to understand it and to be moved by it when the impression is revived in him at the age of four; and only twenty years later, during the analysis, is he able to grasp with his conscious mental processes what was then going on in him. The patient justifiably disregards the three periods of time, and puts his present ego into the situation which is so long past. And in this we follow him, since with correct self-observation and interpretation the effect must be the same as though the distance between the second and third periods of time could be neglected. Moreover, we have no other means of describing the events of the second period.

CARL G. JUNG, "THE RELIGIOUS MAN"

Jung is a desexualized version of Freud. What Freud took to be sexual energy (the libido), Jung interpreted as a general life force. Jung is probably best known for his concepts of archetype and collective unconscious. They are both related to his dream analysis.

Dreams seemed almost to speak to Jung. Dreams were not shrouded in mysteries that needed sleuthing. They contained images that were rather obvious reflections of the ancestral and common experiences of people and other animals. These images as we experience them Jung called archetypes. Examples of archetypes are man, woman, aggression, and the feelings and emotions associated with what Freud called the Oedipus complex. In the archetype called the shadow, Jung put animal characteristics such as sex and aggression. Because we all share these archetypes, Jung referred to a "collective unconscious," the repository of the archetypes. Transference, so crucial to Freudian analysis, was the result of archetypes playing out against the backdrop of a current analytic experience, not, as Freud thought, a replaying of the past experiences in the life of the patient. There is much more to Jung's ideas, but this is enough to prepare us for his analysis of a dream.

The Religious Man

CARL G. JUNG

Dreams are the voice of the Unknown, that ever threatens with new schemes, new dangers, sacrifices, warfare and other troublesome things. . . . [How shall I] set about getting at those contents which form the root of any obsession[?] . . . Dreams will provide us with all the necessary information. We will take them as if they issued from an intelligent, purposive and, as it were, per-

From Carl G. Jung, "The Autonomy of the Unconscious Mind," in *Psychology and Religion* (New Haven: Yale University Press, 1938), pp. 21, 24–39, 118–120. Copyright © 1938 by Yale University Press.

sonal source. This is of course a bold hypothesis and at the same time an adventure, because we are going to give extraordinary credit to a discreditable entity, whose very existence is still denied by not a few contemporary psychologists as well as by philosophers. A famous anthropologist, to whom I had demonstrated my way of proceeding, made the typical remark: "That's all very interesting indeed, but dangerous." Yes, I admit, it is dangerous, just as dangerous as a neurosis. When you want to cure a neurosis, you have to risk something. To do something without risk is merely ineffectual, as we know only too well. A surgical operation for cancer is a risk too and yet it is what has to be done. For the sake of a better understanding I have often felt tempted to advise my patients to conceive of the psyche as of a subtle body, in which subtle tumors can grow. The prejudiced belief that the psyche is unimaginable and consequently less than air or that it is a more or less philosophic system of logical concepts, is so great that, when people are not conscious of certain contents, they assume that they do not exist. There is no confidence and no belief in a reliable psychical functioning outside consciousness, and dreams are thought to be only ridiculous. Under such conditions my proposal arouses the worst suspicions. And indeed I have heard every conceivable argument under the sun that man has ever invented used against the vague specters of dreams.

Yet in dreams we find, without any profound analysis, the same conflicts and complexes whose existence can also be ascertained by the association test. Moreover, those complexes form an integral part of the existing neurosis. We have, therefore, reason to believe that dreams can give us at least as much information about the content of a neurosis as the association test. As a matter of fact they give very much more.

The symptom is like the shoot above ground, yet the main plant is an extended rhizoma underground. The rhizoma represents the content of a neurosis; it is the matrix of complexes, of symptoms and of dreams. We have every reason, even, to believe that dreams mirror exactly the underground processes of the psyche. And if we get there, we literally get at the "roots" of the disease.

As it is not my intention to go further into the psychopathology of neuroses, I propose to choose another case as an example of how dreams reveal the unknown inner facts of the psyche and of what these facts consist. The dreamer is also an intellectual, of remarkable intelligence and learning. He was neurotic and was seeking my help because he felt that his neurosis had become overpowering and was slowly but surely undermining his morale. Fortunately his intellectual integrity had not yet suffered and he had the free use of his fine intelligence. On account of that I set him the task of observing and recording his dreams himself. The dreams were not analyzed or explained to him and it was only very much later that we began with their analysis. Thus the dreams I am going to demonstrate have not been tampered with at all. They represent an entirely uninfluenced natural sequence of events. The patient had never read psychology, not to speak of analytical psychology.

Since the series consists of over four hundred dreams, I could not possibly give an impression of the whole material; but I have published a selection of seventy-four of these dreams containing motives of a peculiar religious interest.[1] The dreamer, it should be said, is a Catholic by education, but he is no longer a practicing one, nor is he interested in religious problems. He belongs to those intellectuals or scientists who would be simply amazed if anybody should saddle them with religious views of any kind. If one holds that the unconscious mind is a psychical existence independent of consciousness, a case such as that of our dreamer might be of particular interest, provided we are not mistaken in our opinion about the religious character of certain dreams. And if one lays stress on the conscious mind alone and does not credit the unconscious with an independent existence, it will be interesting to find out whether or not the dream has really derived its material from conscious contents. Should the facts be in favor of the hypothesis which includes the unconscious, one can use dreams as sources of information about the possible religious tendencies of the unconscious mind.

One cannot expect that dreams will manifestly speak of religion as we know it. There are, however, just two dreams among the four hundred that obviously deal with religion. I will now give the text which the dreamer himself had taken down.

"There are many houses which have a theatrical character, a sort of stage scenery. Somebody mentions the name of Bernard Shaw. It is also mentioned that the play which is to follow refers to a remote future. One of the houses is distinguished by a sign-board with the following inscription:

This is the universal Catholic church.
It is the church of the Lord.
All those who feel themselves to be instruments of the Lord may enter.

And below in smaller letters:

The church is founded by Jesus and Paul.

—it is as if a firm boasted of its old standing. I say to my friend: 'Let us go in and have a look.' He replies: 'I do not see why many people should be together in order to have religious feelings.' But I say: 'You are a Protestant so you will never understand it.' There is a woman nodding approval. I now become aware of a bill posted on the wall of the church. It reads as follows:

Soldiers!
When you feel that you are under the power of the Lord avoid talking directly to him. The Lord is not accessible to words. We also recommend urgently that you should not indulge in discussions about the attributes of the Lord among yourselves. It would be fruitless, as anything of value and importance is ineffable.
Signed: Pope . . . (The name, however, is not decipherable.)

"We now enter the church. The interior resembles a mosque rather than a church, as a matter of fact it is particularly like the Hagia Sophia. There are no chairs, which produces a wonderful effect of space. There are also no images. There are only framed sentences on the walls (like those in the Hagia Sophia). One of these sentences reads: 'Do not flatter your benefactor.' The same woman who nodded approval to me before begins to weep and says: 'Then there is nothing left at all.' I reply: 'I think that it is perfectly all right,' but she vanishes.

"At first I am right in front of a pillar which obliterates the view, then I change my position and I see a crowd of people in front of me. I do not belong to them and I am standing alone. But I see them clearly and I also see their faces. They pronounce the following words: 'We confess that we are under the power of the Lord. The Kingdom of Heaven is within ourselves.' They repeat this thrice in a most solemn way. Then the organ plays a fugue by Bach and a choir sings. Sometimes it is music alone, sometimes the following words are repeated: 'Everything else is paper,' which means that it does not produce a living impression.

"When the music is finished the second part of the ceremony begins, as is the custom at students' meetings where the dealing with serious affairs is followed by the gay part of the gathering. There are serene and mature human beings. One walks to and fro, others talk together, they welcome each other, and wine from the episcopal seminary and other drinks are served. In the form of a toast one wishes the church a favorable development and a radio amplifier plays a ragtime melody with the refrain: 'Charles is now also in the game.' It is as if the pleasure concerning some new member of the society were to be expressed by that performance. A priest explains to me: 'These somewhat futile amusements are officially acknowledged and admitted. We must adapt a little to American methods. If you have to deal with big crowds, as we have, it is inevitable. We differ however on principle from the American churches in that we cherish an emphatically anti-ascetic tendency.' Whereupon I woke up with a feeling of great relief."

There are numerous works, as you know, concerning the phenomenology of dreams, but very few that deal with their psychology. This for the obvious reason that it is a most ticklish and risky business. Freud has made a courageous effort to elucidate the intricacies of dream psychology by the aid of views which he has gathered in the field of psychopathology.[2] Much as I admire the boldness of his attempt, I cannot agree with his method and its results. He explains the dream as a mere façade, behind which something has been carefully hidden. There is no doubt that neurotics hide disagreeable things, probably just as much as normal people do. But it is a serious question whether this category can be applied to such a normal and world-wide phenomenon as the dream. I am doubtful whether we can assume that a dream is something else than it appears to be. I am rather inclined to quote another Jewish authority, the Talmud, which says: "The dream is its own interpretation." In other words I take the dream for granted. The dream is such a difficult and intricate subject, that I do not dare to make any assumptions about its possible cunning. The dream is a natural event and there is no reason under the sun why we should assume that it is a crafty device to lead us astray. The dream occurs when consciousness and will are to a great extent extinguished. It seems to be a natural product which is also to be found in people who are not neurotic. Moreover, we know so little about the psychology of the dream process that we must be more than careful when we introduce elements foreign to the dream itself into its explanation.

For all these reasons I hold that our dream really speaks of religion and that it means to do so. Since the dream is elaborate and consistent it suggests a certain logic and a certain intention, that is, it is preceded by a motivation in the unconscious which finds direct expression in the dream content.

The first part of the dream is a serious statement in favor of the Catholic church. A certain Protestant point of view—that religion is an individual experience—is discouraged by the dreamer. The second, more grotesque part, is an adaptation by the church to a decidedly worldly point of view and the end is a statement in favor of an anti-ascetic tendency which would not and could not be backed up by the real church. But the dreamer's anti-ascetic priest makes it a matter of principle. Spiritualization and sublimation are emphatically Christian principles and any insistence upon the contrary would amount to a blasphemous paganism. Christianity has never been worldly nor has it ever cherished a friendly neighborliness with good wine and food, and it is more than doubtful whether the introduction of jazz music into the cult would be a particular asset. The "serene and mature" personalities, that peripatetically converse with each other in a more or less Epicurean style, remind one much more of an antique philosophic ideal, which is rather distasteful to the contemporary Christian. In the first as well as in the second part the importance of masses or crowds is stressed.

Thus the Catholic church, though it is strongly recommended, appears to be coupled with a strange pagan point of view which is irreconcilable to a fundamentally Christian attitude. The real irreconcilability does not appear in the dream. It is hushed up as it were by a "gemütliche" atmosphere, in which dangerous contrasts are blurred and blended. The Protestant point of view of an individual relationship to God is overpowered by mass organization and correspondingly collective religious feeling. The insistence upon crowds and the insinuation of a pagan ideal are peculiar parallels to things that actually happen in Europe. Everybody wondered about paganism in modern Germany, because nobody knew how to interpret Nietzsche's Dionysian experience. Nietzsche was but one case among thousands and millions of then future Germans in whose unconscious the Germanic cousin of Dionysos, that is, Wotan, developed during the Great War.[3] In the dreams of the Germans whom I treated then I could see clearly the Wotanistic revolution coming on, and in 1918 I published an article in which I pointed out the peculiar kind of new development which was to be expected in Germany.[4] Those Germans were by no means people who had studied *Thus Spake Zarathustra*, and surely those young people who started the pagan sacrifices of sheep did not know of Nietzsche's experience.[5] Therefore they called their god Wotan and not Dionysos. In Nietzsche's biography you will find irrefutable proofs that the god he originally meant was really Wotan, but, being a philologist and living in the seventies and eighties of the nineteenth century, he called him Dionysos. Looked at from a comparative standpoint, the two gods have indeed much in common.

There is apparently no opposition to collective feeling, mass religion and paganism in the whole dream of my patient, except the soon-silenced Protestant friend. There is only one curious incident deserving our attention: that is the unknown woman who first supports the eulogy of Catholicism and then suddenly weeps, saying: "Then there is nothing left at all," and vanishes without returning.

Who is this woman? She is to the dreamer a vague and unknown person, but when he had that dream he was already well acquainted with her as the "unknown woman" who had frequently appeared in previous dreams.

As this figure plays a great role in men's dreams, it carries the technical designation "anima,"[6] owing to the fact that since time immemorial man in his myths always manifested the idea of a coexistence of male and female in the same body. Such psychological intuitions were usually projected in the form of the divine Syzygia, the divine pair, or of the idea of the hermaphroditic nature of the creator.[7] Edward Maitland, the biographer of Anna Kingsford, relates in our own day an inner experience of the bisexual nature of the Deity,[8] then there is Hermetic philosophy with its hermaphrodite and its androgynous inner man,[9] the "homo Adamicus," who "though he appears in male form, always carries Eve, that is, his woman, with him, concealed in his body," as a medieval commentator of the *Hermetic Tractatus Aureus* says.[10]

The anima is presumably a psychical representation of the minority of female genes in a male body. This is all the more probable as the same figure is not to be found in the imagery of a feminine unconscious. There is a corresponding figure, however, that plays an equivalent role, yet it is not a woman's image but a man's. This male figure in a woman's psychology has been designated "animus."[11] One of the most typical manifestations of both figures is what has long been called "animosity." The anima causes illogical moods, and the animus produces irritating topics and unreasonable

307

opinions. Both are frequent dream figures. As a rule they personify the unconscious and give it its peculiarly disagreeable or irritating character. The unconscious in itself has no such negative qualities. They appear only when it is personified by those figures and they begin to influence consciousness. Being only partial personalities they have the character either of an inferior woman or of an inferior man, hence their irritating influence. A man experiencing this will be subject to unaccountable moods and a woman will be argumentative and will produce opinions which are beside the mark.

The wholly negative reaction of the anima to the church dream points out that the dreamer's feminine, that is, his unconscious, side disagrees with his attitude. The disagreement originates with the sentence on the wall: "Do not flatter your benefactor," with which the dreamer agrees. The meaning of the sentence seems to be sound enough, so that one does not understand why the woman should feel so desperate about it. Without delving further into this mystery, we must content ourselves for the time being with the fact that there is a contradiction in the dream and that a very important minority has left the stage under vivid protest and gives no more attention to the further proceedings.

We gather, then, from the dream, that the unconscious functioning of the dreamer's mind produces a pretty flat compromise between Catholicism and a pagan joie de vivre. The product of the unconscious is manifestly not expressing a point of view or a definite opinion, it is rather a dramatic exposition of an act of deliberation. It could be formulated perhaps in the following way: "Now what about this religious business? You are a Catholic, are you not? Is that not good enough? But asceticism—well, well, even the church has to adapt a little—movies, radio, spiritual five o'clock tea and all that—why not some ecclesiastical wine and gay acquaintances?" But for some secret reason this awkward mystery woman, well known from many former dreams, seems to be deeply disappointed and quits.

I must confess I find myself in sympathy with the anima. Obviously the compromise is too cheap and too superficial, but characteristic of the dreamer as well as of many other people to whom religion does not matter very much. Religion was of no concern to my patient and he certainly never expected that it would concern him in any way. But he had come to me because of a very serious experience. Being highly rationalistic and intellectual he had found that his attitude of mind and his philosophy forsook him completely in the face of his neurosis and its demoralizing forces. He found nothing in his whole Weltanschauung that would help him to gain a sufficient control over himself. He therefore was very much in the situation of a man deserted by his heretofore cherished convictions and ideals. It is by no means an extraordinary case that under such conditions a man should return to the religion of his childhood in the hope of finding something helpful there. It was, however, not a conscious attempt or a decision to revivify former religious beliefs. He merely dreamed it; that is, his unconscious produced a peculiar statement about his religion. It is just as if the spirit and the flesh, the eternal enemies in Christian consciousness, had made peace with each other in the form of a curious mitigation of their contradictory nature. Spirituality and worldliness come together in unexpected peacefulness. The effect is somewhat grotesque and comical. The inexorable severity of the spirit seems to be undermined by an almost antique gaiety, perfumed by wine and roses. The dream certainly describes a spiritual and worldly atmosphere that dulls the sharpness of a moral conflict and swallows up in oblivion all mental pain and distress.

If this was a wish fulfilment, it was surely a conscious one, for it was precisely what the patient had already overdone. And he was not unconscious about this either, since wine was one of his most dangerous enemies. The dream is, on the contrary, an impartial statement of the patient's spiritual condition. It is the picture of a degenerate religion corrupted by worldliness and mob instincts. There is religious sentimentality instead of the numinosum of divine experience. This is the well-known characteristic of a religion that has lost the living mystery. It is easily understandable that such a religion is incapable of giving help or of having any other moral effect.

The general aspect of the dream is surely unfavorable although certain other aspects of a more positive nature are dimly visible. It rarely occurs that dreams are either exclusively positive or exclusively negative. As a rule one finds both aspects, but usually one is stronger than the other. It is obvious that such a dream provides the psychologist with enough material to raise the problem of a religious attitude. If our dream were the only one we possess, we could hardly hope to unlock its innermost meaning, but we have quite a number of dreams in our series which suggest a strange religious problem. I never, if I can help it, interpret one dream by itself. As a rule a dream belongs in a series. As there is a continuity in consciousness, despite the fact that it is regularly interrupted by sleep, there is probably also a continuity of unconscious processes and perhaps even more so than with the events of consciousness. In any case my experience is in favor of the probability that dreams are the visible links in a chain of unconscious events. If we want any light on the question of the deeper reasons for the dream, we must go back to the series and find out where it has its position in the long chain of the four hundred dreams.

We find our dream wedged in between two important dreams of an uncanny quality. The dream before reports that there is a gathering of many people and that a peculiar ceremony is taking place, apparently of magic character, with the purpose of "reconstructing the gibbon." The dream after is occupied with a similar theme—the magic transformation of animals into human beings.

Both dreams are intensely disagreeable and very alarming to the patient. Whereas the church dream manifestly moves on the surface and exhibits opinions which in other circumstances could as well be thought consciously, these two dreams are strange and remote in character and their emotional effect is such that the dreamer would avoid them if possible. As a matter of fact, the text of the second dream literally says: "If one runs away, everything is lost." This remark coincides curiously with that of the unknown woman: "Then there is nothing left at all." The inference we draw from these remarks is that the church dream was an attempt at escape from other dream thoughts of a much deeper significance. Those thoughts appear spuriously in the dreams occurring before and after it.

NOTES

1. Jung, "Traumsymbole des Individuationsprozesses," *Eranos-Jahrbuch 1935* (Zürich, 1936). Although the dreams I quote are mentioned in this publication, they have been examined there from another angle. As dreams have many aspects, they can be studied from different sides.
2. Freud, *Traumdeutung* (Vienna, 1900). Eng. trans., *Interpretation of Dreams*. Herbert Silberer, *Der Traum* (1919), represents a more cautious and a more balanced point of view. Concerning the difference between Freud's and my own views, I refer the reader to my little essay on this subject in *Modern Man in Search of a Soul* (London, 1933), p. 132. Further material in *Two Essays on Analytical Psychology* (1928), p. 83 *et sqq.;* W. M. Kranefeldt, *Secret Ways of the Mind* (New York, 1932); Gerhard Adler, *Entdeckung der Seele* (Zürich, 1934); T. Wolff, "Einführung in die Grundlagen der Komplexen

Psychologie," *Die Kulturelle Bedeutung der Komplexen Psychologie* (Berlin, 1935), pp. 1–168.

3. Cf. the relation of Odin as a god of poets, seers and raving enthusiasts, and Mimir, the wise one, to Dionysos and Silenos. The word Odin has a root connection with Gall. οὐατεις, Jr. fäith, Lat. Vates, similar to μάντις and μαινομαι. Martin Ninck, *Wodan und germanischer Schicksalsglaube* (1935), p. 30 *et sqq.*

4. In *Über das Unbewusste* (Schweizerland, 1918).

5. In "Wotan," *Neue Schweizer Rundschau*, Heft 11 (1936).

   An abbreviated edition in *Saturday Review of Literature* (Oct. 16, 1937). The Wotan parallels in Nietzsche's work are to be found (1) in the poem of 1863–64 "To the Unknown God"; (2) in "Klage der Ariadne," *Also sprach Zarathustra*, p. 366; (3) *Also sprach Zarathustra*, p. 143 and p. 200; (4) The Wotan dream of 1859 in E. Foerster-Nietzsche, *Der werdende Nietzsche* (1924), p. 84 *et sqq.*

6. *Two Essays*, p. 202 *et sqq.*; *Psychological Types* (1923), pp. 588, 593 *et sqq.*; "Über die Archetypen des collectiven Unbewussten," *Eranos-Jahrbuch 1934*, p. 204 *et sqq.*; "Über den Archetypus mit besonderer Berücksichtigung des Animabegriffes," *Zentralblatt für Psychotherapie*, IX (1936), 259 *et sqq.*

7. *Zentralbl. f. Psychotherapie*, IX, 259 *et sqq.*

8. Edward Maitland, *Anna Kingsford, Her Life, Letters, Diary and Work* (London, 1896), p. 129 *et seq.*

9. The statement, concerning the hermaphroditic nature of the Deity in *Corpus Hermeticum*, Lib. I (ed. W. Scott, *Hermetica*, I, p. 118: ὁ δὲ νοῦς ὁ πρῶτοςἀρρενόθηλυς ὤν), is probably derived from Plato, *Symposium XIV*. It is questionable whether the later medieval representatives of the hermaphrodite are derived from the "Poimandres" (*Corp. Herm.*, Lib. I) since it was practically unknown in the West before it was printed by Marsilius Ficinus in 1471. There is a possibility, however, that a Greek scholar, though rare in those days, has gleaned the idea from one of the then existing codices graeci, as, for instance, the *Cod. Laurentianus 71*, 33 of the fourteenth century, the *Parisinus Graec. 1220*, fourteenth century, the *Vaticanus Graec. 237* and *951*, fourteenth century. There are no older codices. The first Latin translation by Marsilius Ficinus had a sensational effect. But before that date we have the hermaphroditic symbols of the *Cod. Germ. Monac.*, 598 of 1417. It seems more probable to me that the hermaphroditic symbol is derived from Arabic or Syriac Mss. translated in the eleventh or twelfth century. In the old Latin *Tractatulus Avicennae*, strongly influenced by Arabic tradition, we find: "(Elixir) Ipsum est serpens luxurians, seipsum impraegnans (*Artis Auriferae*, etc. [1593], T. I., p. 406). Although it is matter of a Pseudo-Avicenna and not of the authentic Ibn Sina (970–1037), he belongs to the Arabo-Latin sources of the medieval Hermetic philosophy. We find the same passage in the tractatus "Rosinus ad Sarratantam" (*Art Aurif.* [1593], I, 309): "Et ipsum est serpens seipsum luxurians, seipsum impraegnans, etc." "Rosinus" is an Arabo-Latin corruption of "Zosimos," the Greek neo-Platonic philosopher of the third century. His tract *Ad Sarratantam* belongs to the same class of literature and since the history of these texts is still completely in the dark, nobody can say who copied from whom. The *Turba Philosophorum*, Sermo LXV, a Latin text of Arabic origin, also makes the allusion: "compositum germinat se ipsum" (J. Ruska, *Turba Philosophorum. Quellen und Studien zur Geschichte der Naturwissenschaften und der Medizin* [1931], p. 165). As far as I can make out, the first text definitely mentioning the hermaphrodite is the "Liber de Arte Chimica incerti autoris," sixteenth century (in *Art. Aurif.* [1593], I, 575 *et sqq.*), p. 610: "Is vero mercurius est omnia metalla, masculus et foemina, et monstrum Hermaphroditum in ipso animae et corporis matrimonio." Of later literature I mention only: *Pandora* (a German text, 1588); "Splendor Solis" in *Aureum Vellus*, etc. (1598); Michael Majer, *Symbola aureae mensae duodecim nationum* (1617); *idem*, *Atalanta Fugiens* (1618). J. D. Mylius, *Philosophia Reformata* (1622).

10. The *Tractatus Aureus Hermetis* is of Arabic origin and does not belong to the *Corpus Hermeticum*. Its history is unknown (first printed in the *Ars Chemica*, 1566). Dominicus Gnosius has written a commentary to the text in *Hermetis Trismegisti Tractatus vere Aureus de Lapidis Philosophici Secreto cum Scholiis Dominici Gnosii*, 1610. He says (p. 101): "Quem ad modum in sole ambulantis corpus continuo sequitur umbra . . . sic hermaphroditus noster Adamicus, quamvis in forma masculi appareat semper tamen in corpore occultatam Evam sive foeminam suam secum circumfert." This commentary, together with the text, is reproduced in J. J. Mangeti, *Bibl. Chem.* (1702), I, 401 *et sqq.*

11. A description of both types in *Two Essays*, II, 202 *et sqq.* See also *Psychological Types*, Definition No. 48, p. 588 *et sqq.*; also Emma Jung, "Ein Beitrag zum Problem des Animus," in *Wirklichkeit der Seele* (1934) p. 296 *et sqq.*

ADOLF GRÜNBAUM, "THE LIABILITIES OF FREUDIAN PSYCHOANALYSIS"

Current criticisms of Freudian psychoanalytic theory are many. They range from Freud's lack of understanding of women and his own psychological infirmities to a highly questionable tendency to generalize from one or two instances and to glorify only temporary successes in therapy.

Grünbaum claims that Freud argued that each success in therapy was evidence that his general theory of personality was correct. To do this, Freud had to defend against two claims. One, any method of analysis might work as well. Two, since analysts lead their patients, there is no way to tell when the true cause of a problem has been reached—it may just be an answer agreed upon by the analyst and the patient. If this is so, then this is hardly confirmation of Freud's specific theory. Freud's defense, according to Grünbaum, is found in the following three theses held by Freud.

A necessary condition for a successful outcome in therapy is the patient's being led to see the actual hidden causes of his/her problems. It is necessary to use Freudian psychoanalysis to find these causes because no other method works. These causes not only seem true to the patient but are in fact true (or extremely close to true). Grünbaum refers to the first two theses as the necessary condition thesis (NCT). Grünbaum also finds what he calls the tally argument in Freud.

In one paper, Freud referred to interpretations that cured as "tallying with what is real." In other words, if one achieves a cure using the Freudian method, what is accepted as real by the patient must actually be what happened.

Grünbaum argues that because there is usually no independent way to verify a happening ferreted out through analysis and because there is no way to rule out a therapist's leading a patient to a conclusion, there cannot be a trustworthy way to say, "This is indeed what really happened." Moreover, whatever successes Freudian psychoanalysis has, other approaches also have successes. Thus psychoanalysis is not the only road to recovery. Also, there is no way to distinguish a success resulting from the therapy and one resulting from what is called the placebo effect. The placebo effect is the name given to the well-known fact that many cures in medicine can be attributed to patient expectations and not the treatment itself. A good example is the effectiveness of a parent's kiss in removing pain from a toddler's skinned knee.

Grünbaum thinks that he has totally undercut the scientific validity of Freudian psychoanalysis.

Grünbaum focuses his attention on Freud's term *übereinstimmen*. It is translated as "tally with reality," but in a broader sense, it can be translated as "agree" or "concur." This broader translation can be justified by looking at Freud in another way. In this other view, Freud is not committed to tallying the discoveries from therapy with truth. Rather, Freud and his patients are committed only to accepting those stories that have the ring of truth, that add up (in German, *stimmen*, "be in tune, be true"). On these grounds, what one looks for in analysis is a good and compelling story, one that is harmonious.

As the story approach makes more and more sense, so does the view that one can be more liberal with the translation of *übereinstimmen*. The problem with this interpretation of Freud is that he comes out less a scientist and more a novelist. To those who insist that psychoanalysis is a science and Freud its founder, this interpretation of Freud just will not do. However, to those who see psychoanalysis as a part of medicine and therefore at least partly an art, there is no problem with regarding Freud as a storytelling artist.

Some notes on Grünbaum's vocabulary are in order.

The word *probative* means "increasing the evidence for a claim's truth." Thus when he says, "Clinical data have no probative value for the confirmation of the psychoanalytic theory of personality," he means that clinical data add no evidence to strengthen the claim.

Psychoneuroses are the mental expressions of disturbances of sexual function. Actual neuroses are the direct expressions of the disturbances. Excessive and unrealistic fear of horses (the problem of Little Hans, another of Freud's early cases) would be a psychoneurosis according to Freud. Impotence would be an actual neurosis.

To *retrodict* (Brodbeck used the word *postdict*) is to predict on the basis of present evidence that something happened in the past. Astronomers often retrodict the positions of comets.

The *analysand* is the patient in psychoanalysis.

Veridical means "truthful."

Post hoc ergo propter hoc is Latin for "after this, therefore, because of this." If one assumes that B is the effect of A because B comes after A, then one is using the principle *post hoc ergo propter hoc*. The principle is fallacious. The rooster does not cause the sun to rise by crowing shortly before sunrise.

If you find that after reading the Grünbaum piece, you are still a bit confused, go on to the next article by Erwin, which summarizes Grünbaum's arguments. The article after Erwin's, by Flax, also contains a summary of Grünbaum's main points.

The Liabilities of Freudian Psychoanalysis

ADOLF GRÜNBAUM

A. ARE CLINICAL CONFIRMATIONS AN ARTIFACT OF THE PATIENT'S POSITIVE "TRANSFERENCE" FEELINGS TOWARD THE ANALYST?

Despite Freud's fundamental epistemic reliance on clinical testing, he did indeed acknowledge the challenge that data from the couch ought to be discounted as being inadmissably contaminated. Even friendly critics like Wilhelm Fliess charged that analysts induce their docile patients by suggestion to furnish the very clinical responses needed to validate the psychoanalytic theory of personality (Freud 1954: pp. 334–337). Freud himself deemed it necessary to counter decisively this ominous charge of *spurious* clinical confirmation. For he was keenly aware that unless the methodologically damaging import of the patient's compliance with his doctor's expectations can somehow be neutralized, the doctor is on thin ice when purporting to mediate veridical insights to his client rather than only fanciful *pseudo*insights persuasively endowed with the ring of verisimilitude. Indeed, if the probative value of the analysand's responses is thus negated by brainwashing, then Freudian therapy might reasonably be held to function as an emotional corrective *not* because it enables the analysand to acquire bona fide self-knowledge, but instead because he or she succumbs to proselytizing *suggestion*, which operates the more insidiously under the pretense that analysis is *non*directive.

After Freud had practiced analysis for

some time by communicating his interpretations of the patient's unconscious motivations, he felt himself driven to modify the dynamics of his therapy by according the role of a catalyst, vehicle, or icebreaker to the patient's positive feelings for the analyst. For Freud had to mobilize these positive feelings to overcome the analysand's resistances with a view to eliciting confirmation from the latter's memory, whenever possible (S.E.[1] 1920, 18: 18). And depending on whether the analysand's feelings toward his doctor were positive or negative, Freud spoke of the emotional relationship as a positive or negative "transference" (S.E. 1912, 12: 105). When thus acknowledging the vehicular therapeutic role of the positive transference relationship and attributing it to the doctor's authority qua parent surrogate, Freud knew all too well (S.E. 1917, 16: 446–447) that he was playing right into the hands of those critics who made the following complaints: clinical data have no probative value for the confirmation of the psychoanalytic theory of personality, and any therapeutic gains from analysis are *not* wrought by true insightful self-discovery but rather are the placebo effects induced by the analyst's suggestive influence. Thus, Freud gave ammunition to just these critics when he acknowledged the following: in order to overcome the patient's fierce resistances to the analyst's interpretations of his unconscious conflicts, the analyst cannot rely on the patient's intellectual insight but must decisively enlist the patient's need for his doctor's approval qua parental surrogate (S.E. 1917, 16: 445; 1919, 17: 159). In fact, Freud himself points out that precisely this affectionate help-seeking subservience on the part of the analysand "clothes the doctor with authority and is transformed into belief in his communications and explanations" (S.E. 1917, 16: 445). In this vein, Freud asks the patient to believe in the analyst's theoretical retrodictions of significant happenings in the client's early life when the patient himself is *unable to recall* these hypothesized remote events (S.E. 1920, 18: 18–19). For, as Freud tells us: "The patient cannot remember the whole of what is repressed in him, and what he cannot remember may be precisely the essential part of it. Thus he acquires no sense of conviction of the correctness of the construction that has been communicated to him" (S.E. 1920, 18: 18).

Thus, despite his best efforts, the analyst may well be stymied when seeking confirmation of his reconstructions of the patient's childhood by retrieving the latter's repressed memories. In such situations, Freud justifies his demand for the patient's faith in his retrodictions by the assumption that the analysand has a "compulsion to repeat" or re-enact prototypic conflictual childhood themes with the doctor: "He [the patient] is obliged to *repeat* the repressed material as a contemporary experience instead of, as the physician would prefer to see, *remembering* it as something belonging to the past" (S.E. 1920, 18: 18). The repeated themes are held to derive from infantile sexual yearnings once entertained by the patient toward his parents (S.E. 1925, 20: 43). Now the main evidence that Freud adduces for his repetition-compulsion postulate is that the adult realities at the time of the analytic transaction show the patient's positive feelings toward his analyst to be extravagant in degree as well as grotesque in character (S.E. 1914, 12: 150; 1917, 16: 439–444). Yet this very state of mind clearly heightens the patient's suggestibility via intellectual and psychological subordination to his doctor. . . .

. . . At the end of his 1917 lecture "Transference," which beautifully set the stage for the crucial next one, "Analytic

Therapy," Freud squarely addressed the portentous challenge of suggestibility as follows:

It must dawn on us that in our technique we have abandoned hypnosis only to rediscover suggestion in the shape of transference.

But here I will pause, and let you have a word; for I see an objection boiling up in you so fiercely that it would make you incapable of listening if it were not put into words: "Ah! so you've admitted it at last! You work with the help of suggestion, just like the hypnotists! That is what we've thought for a long time. But, if so, why the roundabout road by way of memories of the past, discovering the unconscious, interpreting and translating back distortions—this immense expenditure of labour, time and money—when the one effective thing is after all only suggestion? Why do you not make direct suggestions against the symptoms, as the others do—the honest hypnotists? Moreover, if you try to excuse yourself for your long detour on the ground that you have made a number of important psychological discoveries which are hidden by direct suggestion—what about the certainty of these discoveries now? Are not they a result of suggestion too, of unintentional suggestion? Is it not possible that you are forcing on the patient what you want and what seems to you correct in this field as well?"

What you are throwing up at me in this is uncommonly interesting and must be answered. [S.E. 1917, 16: 446–447]

This thoroughgoing recognition of the double bombshell of suggestibility *and* the careful 1917 argument Freud then offered in an attempt to defuse it stand in refreshing contrast to the manner in which typical contemporary analysts insouciantly ignore the heart of the matter or make light of it. . . .

B. FREUD'S RELIANCE ON THE HYPOTHESIZED DYNAMICS OF THERAPY AS A VINDICATION OF HIS THEORY OF UNCONSCIOUS MOTIVATION

Freud begins his 1917 "Analytic Therapy" lecture by recalling the question that he is about to address. As he puts it:

You asked me why we do not make use of direct suggestion in psycho-analytic therapy, when we admit that our influence rests essentially on transference [which amounts to the utilization of the patient's personal relationship to the analyst]—that is, on suggestion; and you added a doubt whether, in view of this predominance of suggestion, we are still able to claim that our psychological discoveries are objective [rather than self-fulfilling products of *unintentional* suggestion]. I promised I would give you a detailed reply. [S.E. 1917, 16: 448]

The careful reply he then proceeds to give falls into two parts.

First, he tries to explain meticulously that in *hypnosis,* suggestion serves the *pivotal* role of simply ceremonially *forbidding* the symptoms to exist, whereas in the dynamics of psychoanalytic therapy, the function of suggestion is that of being a *catalyst* or "vehicle" in the *educative* excavation of the repressed underlying etiology of the symptoms. And as he stressed nearly a decade later, "it would be a mistake to believe that this factor [of suggestion] is the vehicle and promoter of the treatment throughout its length. At the beginning, no doubt" (S.E. 1926, 20: 190). Second, far from begging the question by just *asserting* this epistemically wholesome role for suggestion in analysis, he justifies his assertion by enunciating the following premise: the veridical disclosure of the patient's hidden conflicts, which are the pathogens of his or her neurosis, is causally necessary for the durable and thoroughgoing conquest of his or her illness. But the disclosure thus requisite for therapeutic success will occur, in turn, *only* if incorrect analytic interpretations, spuriously confirmed by *contaminated* responses from the patient, have been discarded in favor of correct constructions derived from clinical data *not* distorted by the patient's compliance with the analyst's communicated expectations. In short, in the second part of his reply to the stated charge of contamination, Freud gives

an *argument* for deeming the therapeutically favorable outcome of an analysis to be adequate reason for attributing the following probative merit to such a successful analysis: "Whatever in the doctor's conjectures is inaccurate drops out in the course of the analysis" (S.E. 1917, 16: 452). . . .

Let us now articulate systematically the *argument* he uses to counter the charge of epistemic contamination of clinical data by suggestion, and his attempt to avert the ominous import of that charge. His counterargument does invoke *therapeutic* success. Hence, let us be mindful that the successful therapeutic conquest of the analysand's neurosis is held to consist in an adaptive restructuring of the intrapsychic personality dispositions such that there is concomitant lasting overt symptom relief without symptom substitution. The intrapsychic restructuring is deemed crucial to safeguard the quality and durability of overt symptomatic improvement.

Immediately after asserting that the doctor's theoretical stance, *if erroneous,* can persuasively affect the patient's intelligence but *cannot* dislodge his illness, Freud gives us the fundamental premise on which he rests this imperviousness of the patient's neurosis: "After all, his conflicts will only be successfully solved and his resistances overcome if the anticipatory ideas [i.e., interpretative depictions of analytic meaning] he is given tally [both objectively and subjectively] with what is real in him" (S.E. 1917, 16: 452). This bold assertion of the *causal indispensability* of psychoanalytic insight for the conquest of the patient's psychoneurosis is a terse enunciation of the thesis that Freud had previously formulated more explicitly in his 1909 case history of Little Hans, where he wrote:

In a psycho-analysis the physician always gives his patient (sometimes to a greater and sometimes to a less extent) the conscious anticipatory ideas by the help of which he is put in a position to recognize and to grasp the unconscious material. For there are some patients who need more of such assistance and some who need less; but there are none who get through without some of it. Slight disorders may perhaps be brought to an end by the subject's unaided efforts, but never a neurosis—a thing which has set itself up against the ego as an element alien to it. To get the better of such an element another person must be brought in, and in so far as that other person can be of assistance the neurosis will be curable. [S.E. 1909, 10: 104]

The assumptions that Freud actually invokes in this context can be stated as a conjunction of two causally necessary conditions as follows: (1) only the psychoanalytic method of interpretation and treatment can yield or mediate to the patient correct insight into the unconscious pathogens of his psychoneurosis, and (2) the analysand's correct insight into the etiology of his affliction and into the unconscious dynamics of his character is, in turn, *causally necessary* for the therapeutic conquest of his neurosis. I shall refer to the *conjunction* of these two Freudian claims as his "Necessary Condition Thesis" or, for brevity, "NCT." I have been careful to formulate this thesis with respect to the "psychoneuroses," as distinct from the so-called "actual" neuroses. For, as we shall see further on, Freud denied that NCT holds for the *actual* neuroses, and I ask that this important restriction be borne in mind even when I omit the qualification for brevity. Clearly, NCT entails not only that there is no spontaneous remission of psychoneurosis but also that, if there are any cures at all, psychoanalysis is *uniquely* therapeutic for such disorders as compared to any *rival* therapies. In view of the importance of NCT, I have also dubbed it "Freud's Master Proposition" (Grünbaum 1983: 17).

Armed with his daring NCT, Freud promptly uses it to legitimate probatively the clinical data furnished by psychoneurotic patients whose analyses presumably had been successful. Nay, upon asserting the existence of such therapeutically successful patients *P*, as well as Freud's NCT, *two* conclusions follow in regard to any and all patients *P* who emerged cured from their analyses:

Conclusion 1. The psychoanalytic interpretations of the hidden causes of *P*'s behavior given to him by his analyst are indeed correct, and thus—as Freud put it—these interpretations "tally with what is real" in *P*.

Conclusion 2. Only analytic treatment could have wrought the conquest of *P*'s psychoneurosis.

In view of Freud's use of the appealing phrase "tally with what is real," I have used the label "Tally Argument" for the argument whose two premises and two conclusions I have just stated. And this designation has since been adopted by other writers.

In view of capital importance to appreciate that Freud is at pains to employ the Tally Argument in order to justify the following epistemological claim: actual *durable* therapeutic success guarantees *not only* that the pertinent analytic interpretations *ring* true or credible to the analysand *but also* that they *are* indeed veridical, or at least quite close to the mark. Freud then relies on this bold intermediate contention to conclude nothing less than the following: collectively, the successful outcomes of analyses do constitute *cogent* evidence for all that general psychoanalytic theory tells us about the influences of the unconscious dynamics of the mind on our lives. In short, psychoanalytic treatment successes as a whole vouch for the truth of the Freudian theory of personality, including its specific etiologies of the psychoneuroses and even its general theory of psychosexual development.

As a further corollary, the psychoanalytic probing of the unconscious is vindicated as a method of etiologic investigation by its therapeutic achievements. Thus, this method has the extraordinary capacity to validate major causal claims by essentially retrospective inquiries, *without* the burdens of prospective longitudinal studies employing (experimental) controls. Yet these causal inferences are not vitiated by *post hoc ergo propter hoc* or other known pitfalls of causal inference. Magnificent, if true!

. . . I have called attention to *two* conclusions that follow from the premises of Freud's Tally Argument. One of them asserts the truth of the psychoanalytic theory of personality; the other claims unique efficacy for analytic therapy. . . . If psychoanalytic treatment does have the therapeutic monopoly entailed by the Tally Argument, then it can warrantedly take credit for the recoveries of its patients *without* statistical comparisons with the results from untreated control groups, or from controls treated by rival modalities (cf. S.E. 1917, 16: 461–462). Moreover, when analytic therapy does score remedial triumphs, these gains are *not* placebo effects. For if the second conjunct of NCT is to be believed, the working through of the patient's unconscious conflicts is the decisive remedial factor. And this quintessential therapeutic role is not compromised by the analyst's function as parent-surrogate and catalytic icebreaker in the earlier stages of treatment (S.E. 1926, 20: 1990). . . .

To gauge the probative value of his evidence, however, we must not overlook that he avowedly coaxed, coached, and even browbeat the patient in the quest for the theoretically expected data. Thus, as we saw, he relates just how he *"infallibly"* arrived at the purported early sexual traumata: "If the first-discovered scene is unsatisfactory, we tell our patient that this experience explains nothing, but that behind it there must be hidden a more significant, earlier experience; and we direct his attention by the same technique to the associative thread which connects the two memories—the one that has been discovered and the one that has still to be discovered" (S.E. 1896, 3: 195–196). Numerous other statements by Freud (e.g., S.E. 1895, 2: 293; 1898, 3: 269; 1905, 7: 58–59; 1909, 10: 179–180) show that he felt entitled on theoretical grounds to hector the patient relentlessly for not having retrieved the desired sort of memory. Indeed, as he reports (S.E. 1896, 3: 204), "Before they come for analysis the patients know nothing about these scenes. They are indignant as a rule if we warn them that such scenes are going to emerge." Clearly, the analysand is admonished beforehand as to what is expected of him. And this avowed brain washing is conducive to yielding only spurious confirmations of etiologic hypotheses. For Freud's inquisitorial methods could not even reliably authenticate the bare occurrence of the doctrinally desired early experience. But an event that never happened could hardly have been the pathogen. Yet patently, he thought that his ensuing findings were anything but bogus.

C. WAS FREUD'S ATTEMPTED THERAPEUTIC VINDICATION OF THE PSYCHOANALYTIC THEORY OF PERSONALITY SUCCESSFUL?

The capacity of Freud's 1917 Tally Argument to *warrant* the actual truth of its conclusions depends, of course, on the empirical tenability of its two premises. As noted before, NCT is the pivot that gave any therapeutic triumphs achieved by analysis the leverage to vouch for the authenticity of its clinical data. Hence, to the extent that Freud disavowed one or both of these premises in later years, he forfeited his erstwhile reliance on this argument to vindicate the psychoanalytic method of inquiry and/or the conclusions he had reached by means of it. Again, to the extent that anlaytic treatment nowadays continues not to effect real cures of neuroses, and NCT is rendered dubious by currently available empirical information, Freudian theory is now devoid of this vindication in the face of the remaining twin challenge from suggestibility. As we saw in Section *A*, Freud himself had acknowledged (S.E. 1917, 16: 446–447) that he must try to nullify the following two-fold indictment: Suggestion is at once the decisive agent in his therapy, and the cognitive bane of the psychoanalytic method of investigation.

For a number of decades, Freud did claim empirical sanction for both of the premises in his Tally Argument. But ironically, in his later years he himself undermined this argument by gradually renouncing or significantly weakening each premise. Thus, in an important 1937 paper (S.E. 1937, 23: 216–254), his disparagement of the quality and durability of actual psychoanalytic treatment outcome bordered on a repudiation of treatment success. As Freud reported ruefully, a satisfactory psychoanalysis is not even prophylactic against the recurrence of the affliction for which the analysand was treated, let alone immunizing against the outbreak of a different neurosis. Thus, far from holding out hope for cures, Freud essentially confined the prospects to palliation. But the import of this therapeutic pessimism is shattering. For, even if NCT were true, it would need the existential premise of documented cures in order to vouch for the etiologies inferred by means of free association. But even when Freud was not quite that pessimistic about the caliber of therapeutic outcome (S.E. 1926, 20: 265), he again said his erstwhile NCT in 1926 by conceding the existence of spontaneous remission as follows: "As a rule our therapy must be content with bringing about more quickly, more reliably and with less expenditure of energy than would otherwise be the case the good result which in favourable circumstances

would have occurred of itself" (S.E. 1926, 20: 154). Of course, the label "spontaneous remission" is to convey that gains made by an afflicted person were caused entirely by extraclinical life events rather than by professional therapists, not that these benefits were uncaused. Notably, Freud grants that neuroses yielding to analytic therapy would, in due course, remit spontaneously anyway. In this way, he demoted his own treatment from being therapeutically indispensable to the status of a mere expediter of otherwise expectable recoveries. Hence, even Freud's own evidence placed his NCT premise in serious jeopardy. And once that proposition became defunct, even spectacular therapeutic triumphs became probatively unavailing for the validation of his hypotheses by means of the Tally Argument.

Other analysts have likewise made concessions to spontaneous remission and have acknowledged that "all pervading" psychic improvements or cures can be effected without psychoanalytic insight by theoretically rival treatment modalities such as behavior therapy (Malan 1976: 172–173, 269, 147). It is to be understood that various treatment modalities are held to be "rivals" of one another in the sense that there is a divergence between their *theories* of the rationale, dynamics, methods, or techniques of the therapeutic process. Notably in psychoanalysis and behavior therapy, but perhaps also in some of the other modalities, the underlying theoretical rationale also comprises hypotheses pertaining to personality development, etiology, and the current dynamics of pathological behavior. Thus, the divergences between the rival therapies naturally extend to *these* causal hypotheses as well. Notoriously, there is a plethora of such rival therapeutic modalities, at least well over 125.

In recent decades, comparative studies of treatment outcome from rival therapies have failed to reveal any sort of superiority of psychoanalysis within the class of therapeutic modalities that exceed the spontaneous remission rate gleaned from the (quasi-)untreated controls (Smith, Glass, and Miller 1980; Rachman and Wilson 1980; Strupp, Hadley, and Gomes-Schwartz 1977). But, if analytic treatment is thus not superior to its rivals in the pertinent diagnostic categories, it becomes quite reasonable—though *not* compelling—to interpret its therapeutic achievements as placebo effects. And, if so, then the therapeutic successes of psychoanalysis are *not* wrought after all by the patient's acquisition of self-knowledge, much to Socrates' sorrow. In this vein, the psychiatrist Jerome Frank has contended that the analyst, no less than his competitor, heals neurotics by supportively counteracting their demoralization, not by excavating their repressions. Indeed, Frank's hypothesis even allows rival therapies to have differential effects in virtue of their differential abilities to mobilize agencies common to all of them. The shared techniques for such mobilization usually include well practiced rituals, a special vocabulary, a knowledgeable manner, and the therapist's charisma (Grünbaum 1980: 341–351). To be sure, it is still arguable that psychoanalytic treatment gains are *not* placebogenic. But, the damaging fact remains that NCT has become quite doubtful. Moreover, even the evidence for treatment gains from analytic and nonanalytic psychotherapy, which was adduced by Smith, Glass and Miller (1980), has just been deemed incapable of sustaining their conclusion. As Prioleau, Murdock, and Brody (1983) have pointed out, the findings used by Smith et al. do not show that the benefits from psychotherapy exceed those yielded by treatments designed to be placebos.

Ironically, in the case of some psychoanalytic theoreticians, the willingness to countenance the existence of spontaneous remission of full-fledged neuroses in *contravention* of NCT was prompted by the need to cope with a difficulty posed by behavior therapy for the *received* Freudian theory of the origin *and* maintenance of neurotic symptoms. To articulate the pertinent difficulty, note what would be expected to happen, according to this received account of symptom formation, when a symptom is extinguished by a direct attack on it, while its underlying neurosis is left intact. A neurotic symptom is held to be a compromise, *formed* in response to an unresolved conflict between a forbidden unconscious impulse and the ego's defense against it. The symptom is held to be *sustained* at any given time by a *coexisting*, ongoing unconscious conflict, which—as claimed by NCT—does not resolve itself without psychoanalytic intervention. Hence, if the repression of the unconscious wish is not lifted psychoanalytically, the underlying neurosis will persist, even if behavior therapy or hypnosis, for example, extinguishes the particular symptom that only *manifests* the neurosis at the time. As long as the neurotic conflict does persist, the patient's psyche will call for the defensive service previously rendered by the banished symptom. Hence, typically and especially in severe cases, the unresolved conflict ought to engender a *new* symptom. And incidentally, this expectation qualifies as a "risky" prediction in Popper's sense, since such rival extant theories as behavior intervention disavow just that expectation.

Thus, when Freud explained his disappointments with hypnotic therapy, he claimed, as we saw, that in every severe case he had treated suggestively, the patient either relapsed or developed *"some substitute"* for the original symptoms (emphasis added; S.E. 1905, 7: 261). But is such so-called "symptom substitution," which is the *replacement* of an extinguished symptom by a new one, in fact a normal

ADOLF GRÜNBAUM

occurrence? Fisher and Greenberg (1977: 370) have summarized empirical studies of the incidence of *new* symptoms, construed as "behaviors judged socially or personally maladaptive":

The evidence is consistent and solid that in many types of cases, symptoms can be removed by behavioral treatments with no indication that the patient suffers any negative consequences. . . . In fact, many of the investigations find signs of generalized improvement in functioning after the removal of an incapacitating symptom.

More recently, in a long-term follow-up of agoraphobic patients who had received behavior therapy, these patients were not only "much better at follow-up than they had been before treatment" but there was also no evidence of any symptom substitution (Munby and Johnston 1980: 418). This, then, is the difficulty posed for the analytic dynamics of symptom maintenance by behavioristic symptom extinction without relapse. . . .

Since the Tally Argument is thus gravely undercut, any therapeutic successes scored by analysts, even if spectacular, have become *probatively* unavailing to the validation of psychoanalytic theory via that argument. Indeed, as I took pains to show (Grünbaum 1980: 343–352), not only is NCT discredited but no empirically warranted *alternative* premise that could take its place and yield the desired sanguine conclusions seems to be in sight. Hence, currently no viable surrogate for the defunct Tally Argument appears on the horizon.

NOTE

1. All references to "S.E." (standard edition) are to Strachey et al. (1953–1974).

REFERENCES

Fisher, S., and Greenberg, R.P. *The Scientific Credibility of Freud's Theory and Therapy* (New York: Basic Books, 1977).
Freud, S. *The Origins of Psychoanalysis* (New York: Basic Books, 1954).
Grünbaum, A. "Epistemological Liabilities in the Clinical Appraisal of Psychoanalytic Theory." *Noûs* 14 (1980): 307–385.
———. "Is Object Relations Theory Better Founded than Orthodox Psychoanalysis? A Reply to Jane Flax." *Journal of Philosophy* 80 (1983): 46–51.
Malan, D.H. *Toward the Validation of Dynamic Psychotherapy* (New York: Plenum Press, 1976).
Munby, M., and Johnston, D. W. "Agoraphobia: The Long-Term Follow-up of Behavioural Treatment." *British Journal of Psychiatry* 137 (1980):418–427.
Prioleau, L., Murdock, M., and Brody, N. "An Analysis of Psychotherapy Versus Placebo." *The Behavioral and Brain Sciences* 6 (1983):275–285.
Rachman, S. J., and Wilson, G. T. *The Effects of Psychological Therapy.* 2d enlarged ed. New York: Pergamon Press, 1980.
Smith, M. L., Glass, G. V., and Miller, T. I. *The Benefits of Psychotherapy.* Baltimore: Johns Hopkins University Press, 1980.
Stannard, D. E. *Shrinking History.* New York: Oxford University Press, 1980.
Steele, R. S. "Psychoanalysis and Hermeneutics." *International Review of Psychoanalysis* 6 (1979): 389–411.
Strachey, J., et al. (eds.). *The Complete Works of Sigmund Freud* (London: Hogarth Press, 1953–1974).
Strupp, H. H., Hadley, S. W., and Gomes-Schwartz, B. *Psychotherapy for Better or Worse: The Problem of Negative Effects* (New York: Jason Aronson, 1977).

EDWARD ERWIN, "PSYCHOANALYSIS: HOW FIRM IS THE EVIDENCE?"

Here is another summary of Grünbaum's article.

Psychoanalysis: How Firm is the Evidence?

EDWARD ERWIN

There is a way of connecting clinical success to the theoretical claims of Freud. Grünbaum does this by means of the following "Tally" argument, which Freud himself apparently used.

Premise 1: The analysis of patient x was therapeutically successful.

Premise 2: Only psychoanalytic interpretations that "tally with what is real" in the patient can mediate veridical insight, and such insight, in turn is causally necessary for the successful alleviation of his neurosis.

Conclusion: The psychoanalytic interpretations given to x were veridical and seemed verisimilar to x.

Would the first premise of the Tally Argument be true if x were replaced by expressions referring to many different patients? That is, is psychoanalysis generally effective for patients having certain kinds of neurotic problems? As is well known, Eysenck (1952) raised important doubts about answering this question affirmatively. He reviewed 24 studies covering over 7000 cases and found no evidence that psychoanalysis was effective. He argued that the remission rate over a two year period for neurotics not receiving formal therapy was approximately 66% and that the psychoanalytic patients in the studies he reviewed did no better, and perhaps did worse. Eysenck's argument is now controversial for several reasons (Bergin & Lambert [1978]; Brown & Herrnstein [1975];

From Noûs 14 (1980): 443–456. Reprinted by permission of Blackwell Publishers.

Bergin & Suinn [1975]). First, it has been charged that Eysenck used an inflated spontaneous remission rate. Second, his interpretation of some of the studies reviewed has been challenged. Third, recent studies are said to provide new evidence for the effectiveness of psychoanalysis. I have recently reviewed these objections and have tried to show that Eysenck's argument can be rendered immune to these and other criticisms. The conclusion of that review is that there is still no firm evidence that psychoanalysis is therapeutically effective (Erwin [1980]). Because of the length of treatment, however, there are special practical and ethical problems involved in doing the kind of studies needed to demonstrate the effectiveness of psychoanalysis. A psychoanalyst, then, might argue that the failure to find evidence of effectiveness is to be expected even if the therapy does work: The right kind of studies simply have not been done. If this is right, then we cannot conclude that the first premise of the Tally Argument is false, but only that there is no reason to think that it is true.

What of the second premise? Is psychoanalysis, as the second premise implies, superior to other treatment? One view is that of Bergin and Lambert (1978): All of the psychotherapies that appear to work may do so primarily because of non-specific or placebo factors. In Grünbaum's terminology, these various psychotherapies, including behavior therapy, may be "inadvertant placebos". The main argument for this view is that recent comparison studies are said to show little difference in therapeutic outcome for different therapies. I have doubts about this argument. First as Kazdin and Wilson point out (1978: 100) in comparison studies between behavior therapy and other therapies, the behavior therapy proved superior in the majority of studies, and proved inferior in none of them. Second, the evidence for the effectiveness of various behavior therapy techniques comes partly from studies comparing treatment to no treatment (Erwin [1978], Kazdin & Wilson [1978]). However, even if the Bergin and Lambert view proves correct, this would not help the defender of the Tally Argument: Both their view and the view that some behavior therapy techniques are effective (and are not mere placebos) for certain sorts of problems imply that the second premise of the argument is false.

In short, I see no way to salvage the Tally Argument. There is no evidence for the first premise (Erwin [1980]) and there is a lot of evidence from the behavior therapy literature (Erwin [1978]); Kazdin & Wilson [1978]) that the second premise is false. At this point, a psychoanalyst might be wise to give up on the Tally Argument and look to other ways to support his theory. One option is to look for other types of clinical data. Grünbaum looks at some of the possibilities, but explains, to my satisfaction, why they are not promising.

REFERENCES

Bergin, A. E. & Lambert, M. J., "The Evaluation of Therapeutic Outcomes," in S. L. Garfield & A. E. Bergin (eds.), *Handbook of Psychotherapy and Behavior Change,* 2nd ed. (New York: Wiley, 1978).

Bergin, A. & Suinn, R., "Individual Psychotherapy and Behavior Therapy," *Annual Review of Psychology* 26 (1975): 509–56.

Brown, R. & Herrnstein, R., *Psychology* (Boston: Little, Brown, 1975).

Erwin, E., *Behavior Therapy: Scientific, Philosophical and Moral Foundations* (New York: Cambridge University Press, 1978).

———, "Psychoanalytic Therapy: The Eysenck Argument," *American Psychologist* (1980).

Eysenck, H. J., "The Effects of Psychotherapy: An Evaluation," *Journal of Consulting Psychology* 16 (1952): 319–24.

Kazdin, A. E. & Wilson, G. T., *Evaluation of Behavior Therapy* (Cambridge, MA: Ballinger, 1978).

JANE FLAX, "PSYCHOANALYSIS AND THE PHILOSOPHY OF SCIENCE: CRITIQUE OR RESISTANCE?"

Flax brings to light questionable assumptions made by Grünbaum as he argues the weaknesses of psychoanalysis. (She also takes Popper to task.) Grünbaum makes two very general assumptions. First, he is, she claims, a straightforward empiricist. By this she means that Grünbaum believes that there are brute facts that are independent from theory and that these facts can be used to settle questions about theories. Although she does not state it, Flax is a follower of Kuhn, who of course rejects this simple sort of empiricism. Second, Grünbaum uses a small part of physics as his model for science. This is, she claims, far too restrictive. Third, before disscussing any particular science, Grünbaum reconstructs it, putting it in logical form as if it were like Euclidean geometry. Whether this is possible for medicine was debated by Schaffner and Caplan.

Flax's claim is that in his reconstruction of Freud, Grünbaum has been unfair to the theory as propounded by Freud. Grünbaum's reconstruction of Freud distorts many of the important concepts for Freud. (Flax complains that Grünbaum does not pay enough attention to transference. This was in 1982. The selection we read from Grünbaum is from 1984 and shows that he took her point to heart.) Important and underplayed by Grünbaum is the unconscious. According to Flax, Grünbaum fails to capture the "battle that is analysis." Instead, he sees it as a rational working through of issues—perhaps much as he sees working through a physics problem with a student.

It is not surprising that what Grünbaum thinks are liabilities of psychoanalysis Flax sees as crucial to psychoanalysis. They are at loggerheads over this. Flax realizes this. She says, in effect, that the liabilities Grünbaum finds in psychoanalysis are what would be liabilities in physics. But they needn't on that account be liabilities for psychoanalysis. Suppose, she could have suggested, that physics had been based on medicine or psychology. Then might it not look as though physics had the liabilities? Caplan made the same sort of point when he suggested that medicine would look different to philosophy if philosophy had chosen acoustics as its model discipline and not theoretical physics.

Flax's final suggestion is a playful one. Perhaps the philosophy of science is so eager to discredit psychoanalysis because psychoanalysis makes it plain that all knowledge, including science, is always partly irrational.

Psychoanalysis and the Philosophy of Science: Critique or Resistance?

JANE FLAX

The debate over the status of psychoanalysis has focused on the criteria by which it claims to be a science should be adjudicated and on whether, given a specific set of criteria, psychoanalysis has met them. Karl Popper[1] claims that psychoanalysis cannot be falsified and, hence, that it is not a science. Adolf Grünbaum[2] argues that some psychoanalytic hypotheses can be falsified and thus that Popper's criteria should be abandoned for his more stringent "neo-Baconian" ones. By Grünbaum's criteria psychoanalysis has only an exceedingly weak warrant to claim scientific status.

In this paper I will argue that most of the really important and interesting questions

psychoanalysis raises for philosophy are either ignored or inadequately addressed by Popper and Grünbaum. Neither Popper nor Grünbaum offers an adequate philosophy of science by which psychoanalysis may be judged. Each writer's account of psychoanalysis is inaccurate. Furthermore, the splits that pervade Western philosophy—reason/unreason, mind/body, knowledge/feeling—suggest that a psychological depth analysis of philosophy itself may prove therapeutic.

I. THE POPPER-GRÜNBAUM DISPUTE

Popper evinces little interest in the actual content or practice of psychoanalysis. Nonetheless, he concludes that it is a nonscience. Popper's conclusion[3] rests on these arguments: (1) Psychoanalysis is irrefutable.

From *The Journal of Philosophy* 78 (1981): 561–569. Reprinted by permission of the Author and *The Journal of Philosophy*.

(2) The evidence offered in support of the theory is inadequate. (3) Analysts have never attempted to test correctly, i.e., falsify, psychoanalytic theory.

Popper's concern is not psychoanalysis *per se* but the problems of observation and induction. Psychoanalysis is used to exemplify the inadequacies of the inductive model of science. Popper argues that observation alone cannot be the basis of science, given its theory-laden character and the problems raised by Hume concerning causality and induction. Falsification is the tenable alternative basis for the demarcation between science and nonscience. Thus psychoanalysis is used by Popper as *evidence* for the need for his demarcation criteria and *proof* that these criteria can satisfactorily replace inductivist ones.

Grünbaum argues that by Popper's own criteria psychoanalysis *is* a science. Therefore the claim of psychoanalysis to be a science is not an adequate reason to abandon an inductivist methodology for a Popperian one. In fact, "the inductivist criterion of demarcation is more stringent than Popper's rather than less so" (1979, p. 132).

Grünbaum argues (most especially in 1982) that psychoanalysis lacks inductively supporting evidence. According to Grünbaum, there are (for Freud) two causally necessary conditions for overcoming a neurosis: the analyst must provide interpretations that "tally with what is real" in the patient, and the veridical insight that results from such interpretation must be causally necessary for therapeutic success (1982, p. 29, and 1980, pp. 321–323). In turn, therapeutic success allows Freud to infer that "psychoanalytic interpretations had been both objectively correct and subjectively verisimilar" (1980, p. 321).

Grünbaum attacks Freud's theory on the following grounds (most thoroughly in 1982): (1) The patient's "insights," free associations, even dreams, are hopelessly "epistemically contaminated" by the influence of the analyst. (2) Recent empirical tests (as reported in 1980, pp. 353–367) have thrown into question the accuracy or even possibility of self-observation and analysis. The development of rational insight through the analytic process as conceived by Freud is therefore not possible. (3) It follows from the "contaminated" nature of clinical evidence that it cannot be used to validate psychoanalytic theory, nor can the therapeutic success (if any) of psychoanalysis be used to validate the theory. (4) Extraclinical experiments must be devised to test psychoanalytic theory. Evidence from such experiments is either nonexistent or unsupportive.

II. ASSUMPTIONS AND LIMITATIONS OF THIS DEBATE

By either Grünbaum's or Popper's standards psychoanalysis is not now and may never be a science. However, what appears to both Grünbaum and Popper as solid ground for rejecting psychoanalysis is itself extremely problematic. The following are only some of the many problematic assumptions suppressed within this debate.

1. *The nature of science and what constitutes correct scientific methodology.* Neither Grünbaum's nor Popper's philosophy can provide an adequate account of the scientific process. Empiricism is simply untenable as a methodology or philosophy of science.[4] A datum is never observed as it is in itself. Even sensual experience is constructed a priori by the human mind in the light of a theory.[5] Thus fact and theory cannot be totally distinct. Empirical experience loses its special status as the most privileged and unproblematic evidence. Facts also cannot lead to propositions nor can a fact prove a proposition.[6] All data are "epistemically contaminated."

Popper's philosophy of science is equally problematic. He argues that all facts are theory-laden and thus that all knowledge is fallible. Yet his philosophy of science depends upon a notion of objective knowledge that is not falsifiable and is apparently infallible but unknowable.[7] In Popper's philosophy, like Kant's ethics, reason rests on a prior act of faith. This is hardly convincing to a rational agnostic.

Furthermore, a purely internal philosophical analysis of theories and theory shifts is not adequate.[8] Such analysis cannot explain why a theory is accepted as "credible"[9] or when this acceptance occurs. Arguments about the status of a theory never hinge solely on the "facts." At least equally important and under dispute is what counts as a fact, how data are to be interpreted and which data must be explained. Different sorts of theories may have their own methodological criteria and their own phenomenal domain which are intrinsic to the theory itself, and social factors may enter into (among other things) the determination of what seems most in need of explanation.

2. *The unitary model of science.* Both Popper and Grünbaum assume that there is a unitary model for science and that all knowledge may be simply classified as science or nonscience. Generally, one particular science serves as a model for all science, i.e., physics, specifically physics from the time of Newton to early quantum mechanics. This choice of models is itself rarely justified. "Science" would look quite different if biology had been taken as the model for scientific theory and practice. The history of biology demonstrates the ways in which social factors enter into scientific theory construction and acceptance far more clearly than does physics.[10]

3. *Rationalization and legitimation.* Some of the greatest weaknesses of both Popper's and Grünbaum's accounts of science stem from the attempt rationally and arbitrarily

to reconstruct and demarcate the nature of scientific practice. Integrally connected with rationalization is their claim to legislate legitimately what counts as science and evaluate how well it is done. Neither Popper nor Grünbaum gives a scientific or philosophic justification for this claim, and there are good philosophic grounds for questioning its validity.[11] The accuracy and meaningfulness of either rational reconstruction of science are also questionable. The importance of the "nonrational" aspects of the scientific process, that is, not only the influence of external social factors but the role of aesthetic sensibility, play and imagination, of "getting beauty in one's equations"[12] are well known to historians and scientists.

III. GRÜNBAUM'S RECONSTRUCTION OF FREUD

Why should the rational reconstruction of modern physics, in any of its varying forms, serve as the basis for evaluation of all claims to science? Grünbaum's treatment of psychoanalysis illustrates the serious distortions that occur when the rules and methods of one domain are imported into another. First he must transform the material so that it can be evaluated by empiricist methods. He limits psychoanalysis to Freud's writings, because otherwise analytic theory is too varied and unsystematic to be reduced to simple propositions (1980, p. 11). This is like confining a discussion of physics to Newton because contemporary physics is in such disarray and then throwing out physics because there are unresolved problems in Newton's theory.

After delimiting "psychoanalysis" Grünbaum then reconstructs it in a way that makes Freud's theories subject to disproof: in the process much of what Freud had to say is distorted or ignored. Freud's insistence on the centrality of transference, working through, and resistance[13] disappears in Grünbaum's account.

The analytic process is rationalized. Instead of an on-going battle[14] in which the analyst and patient are sometimes allies and sometimes enemies in a shifting constellation of forces (ego vs. id, id vs. superego, etc.) Grünbaum presents us with a "docile" patient who, like Locke's blank slate, will accept any imprint thrust upon her/him by an all-powerful analyst. Freud in fact stresses over and over again that insight has meaning or efficacy only within the transference relation.[15] In this relation, as any analyst can attest, the patient is far from docile. Patients can be remarkably resistant, insightful, infuriating, even terrifying.

Grünbaum rarely mentions the unconscious, which is absolutely central to Freud's theory and therapy. Despite Freud's own inclinations, the very notion of the unconscious drove him beyond empiricism and positivism. In the unconscious, psyche and soma interact; no longer is there an absolute demarcation between mind and body, reason and unreason.[16] Freud's notion of the superego, which suggests a self partially constituted in and through personal relations, and the evidence from hysteria that mental processes can be converted into somatic processes further undermined his determinist simplicity.

The notion of a superego also undermined Freud's narcissistic concept of the individual.[17] The idea of an internalized personal relation (termed an "object relation") suggests that the mind is not a private self-enclosed space but rather that the mind itself is socialized in its very constitution and content. External and internal and social and individual become as problematic as the distinction between mind and body.

In part because of the unresolved tensions between the determinist and the "object relations" aspects of his work,[18] Freud was unable to give a very good explanation of why analysts should be therapeutic. If we reconstruct Freud's theory through the lens of object-relation theory rather than empiricism, it looks as follows: biochemical/genetic vulnerability + inadequate object relation + other environmental stresses = psychological difficulties (and somatic ones as well). Different illnesses could be generated by differing combinations of these factors.

Psychoanalytic theory and therapy would thus be connected, not because Freud wanted to make an argument about the scientific status of his theory, but because the theory states that mental illness arises in part from human relationships. The only way to undo distorted relations with others is to reexperience them in a context in which the consequences of these relations are acted out, can be interpreted and worked through because there is another person present who has no interest in maintaining the past but rather is interested only in enabling the patient to emancipate her/himself from it.

Both transference love and rational insight are necessary for the patient's emancipation, but this rational insight is of a very special sort. It is necessarily intersubjective[19] and is more like a mutually agreed-upon reading of a text[20] than a solution to a problem in quantum mechanics. The patient has the particular experience that she/he is trying to remember and work through with the help of the analyst who has a general schema which is useful to both of them in explicating the meaning of the patient's experience past and present (especially transference phenomena). Their goal is not "truth" in the empiricist sense of what "really" happened to the patient, but rather *understanding* which includes a powerful affective and experiential component. The past is lived through in transference; it is not merely grasped intellectually.[21]

All the phenomena that Grünbaum

counts as the clinical liabilities of psycho-analysis on empiricist grounds—epistemic contamination (i.e., intersubjectivity), sug-gestion, the placebo effect, etc.—are essential parts of the analytic process. Far from being liabilities, they are evidence that object-relations theory is correct. As the evidence Grünbaum cites shows (in both 1980 and 1982), the single most important factor in the success of psychotherapy is the relation between therapist and patient. This is so because, as object-relations theory claims, we become who we are (neurotic or not) in and through our relations with others (plus our own innate constitution and vulnerabilities).

IV. IMPOLITE ANALYTIC QUESTIONS FOR PHILOSOPHY

The inadequacy of Grünbaum's account of psychoanalysis suggests that we turn the problem on its head and allow the patient (psychoanalysis) to ask some questions of the analyst (philosophy of science). The fol-lowing topics seem most problematic:

1. *The demarcation between reason and unreason.* Psychoanalysis suggests there is no absolute demarcation between reason and unreason, nor can all interaction between them be eliminated. Reason may be a defense against the "madness within";[22] sublimation enables us to harness its power. However, according to Freud, if the ego defends itself primarily by repression rather than sublimation, it will be distorted and weakened. The ego becomes rigid, and the person succumbs to the "compulsion to repeat."[23] The person unconsciously recon-structs present events into the shape of the past and then continually fights old battles on the now familiar terrain.

2. *The mind/body split.* Philosophy too is the victim of repression and its conse-quences. Mainstream Western philosophy has repressed "id" material; a particular

notion of mind has been developed, begin-ning with Plato and reaching perhaps its extreme with Descartes, in which mind is seen as completely other than, opposite to, and independent of "the body."

Philosophers are then left with the ques-tion: What is the relation between mind and body? This question has been endlessly repeated over the centuries without resolu-tion. Psychoanalysis suggests more fruitful questions: Why are mind and body regarded as distinct and separate entities? What defensive functions does this separa-tion serve? What sorts of object relations make this sort of distinction plausible, pos-sible and necessary?[24]

3. *Concepts of the self.* If the self is partially constituted by and through object relations with others, then it loses its privileged sta-tus as a private internal space. The mind can be neither a Lockean blank slate as required by neo-Baconian empiricism nor any vari-ety of monad (as envisioned by Kant, Spinoza, or Descartes, etc.). Radical indi-vidualism, e.g., according to Hobbes or Rousseau, also becomes untenable. Analysis suggests that at least some forms of self-knowledge are necessarily dependent on intersubjectivity, as is the growth of the self as a whole.[25]

4. *Reason and emancipation.* Reason is not only required for emancipation or critical discussion; it can also become the ally of unreason. In alliance with the superego, on behalf of present forms of authority, it can suppress demands for pleasure which could counteract dangerously aggressive tenden-cies within society.[26] Out of fear of a punitive superego, the ego may also learn to comply with the authorities (intellectual or political); it may even convince itself that in so doing it is pursuing truth. Much more investiga-tion is necessary into how reason is shaped by its struggle and interaction with the unconscious and under what social condi-

tions and specific forms of object relations reason becomes not the guarantor of freedom but rather an instrument of tyranny.

The same sorts of concern can be raised about science itself. To what extent are unconscious motives at work within science, and how do these shape the purposes and content of scientific theory and methodology? Does science serve defensive functions, such as overcoming the fear of death, acting out a desire to dominate nature out of fear of its power, or attempting to control the irrational within the self?[27] In what ways are these motives related to specific forms of object relations? Philosophy of science must necessarily ignore these irrational elements in the process of rationalizing science. To what extent does philosophy of science therefore become part of science's defensive system, and, as such, must it necessarily reject the cogency of psychoanalysis?

5. *Character of knowledge.* From a psychoanalytic perspective, it would appear that all knowledge, including science and philosophy, is "epistemically contaminated," by our own internalized object relations (which include not only parents but the parents as formed by and representative of the culture) and by the defensive functions that reason serves. An adequate account of a particular theory would require not only an internal account of the field under study and its location in a particular historical moment, but also an examination of apparently irrelevant factors such as family structure, relations between men and women, and ideologies regarding the body and sexuality.

V. CONCLUSION

I have suggested: (1) Psychoanalysis does not fit into existing philosophies of science. (2) Existing philosophies of science are themselves problematic. (3) Psychoanalysis raises fundamental questions about the Western philosophic tradition. (4) Until these issues

are clarified the question, Is psychoanalysis a science? can have no agreed-upon meaning, much less a definitive reply. (5) By focusing on the question of the scientific status of psychoanalysis philosophers have been able to take for granted much of what is in fact problematic in their account of science and epistemology. (6) Psychoanalysis is a simultaneously empirical, intersubjective, hermaneutic, and emancipatory process and form of knowledge. It makes manifest philosophy's repeated acts of repression and avoidance and the need for a reconstruction of their content.

NOTES

1. See especially *Conjectures and Refutations: The Growth of Scientific Knowledge* (New York: Harper & Row, 1963), pp. 37–38.
2. In a series of articles: "How Scientific Is Psychoanalysis?," in Raphael Stern, Louise S. Horowitz, and Jack Lynes, eds., *Science and Psychotherapy* (New York: Haven, 1977); "Is Freudian Psychoanalytic Theory Pseudo-scientific by Karl Popper's Criterion of Demarcation?" *American Philosophical Quarterly,* 16 (April 1979): 131–141; "Epistemological Liabilities of the Clinical Appraisal of Psychoanalytic Theory," *Noûs* 14 (September 1980): 307–385; "Can Psychoanalytic Theory Be Congently Tested 'on the Couch'?" in A. Grünbaum and L. Laudan, eds., *Explanation and Evaluation in Psychiatry and Medicine* (Berkeley: Univ. of California Press, 1982). References to these works of Grünbaum will be by date of publication.
3. *Conjectures and Refutations.*
4. As Popper, *ibid.,* pp. 97–119, and Imre Lakatos, "Falsification and the Methodology of Scientific Research Programmes," in Imre Lakatos and Alan Musgrave, eds., *Criticism and the Growth of Knowledge* (New York: Cambridge Univ. Press, 1970), pp. 91–109, convincingly argue.
5. Einstein was especially insistent on this point. See Paul Arthur Schlipp, ed., *Albert Einstein: Philosopher-Scientist* (New York: Cambridge Univ. Press, 1969).
6. As Popper argues in *Conjectures and Refutations* on pp. 40–55.
7. As Lakatos forcibly (and uncritically) argues in "Falsification," pp. 179–180. For some of the problems with Popper's theory, see Thomas Kuhn, "Logic of Discovery or Psychology of Research?" in Lakatos and Musgrave, *Criticism.*

8. Variants of this argument include Thomas Kuhn, *The Structure of Scientific Revolutions* (Chicago: Univ. of Chicago Press, 1962); Jerome Ravetz, *Scientific Knowledge and Its Social Problems* (Oxford: Clarendon Press, 1971); and Paul Feyerabend, *Against Method* (London: Verso, 1978).

9. Grünbaum (1979) argues that "credibility" should replace verisimilitude (Popper) as the basis for choosing between competing theories.

10. See Donna Haraway, "Animal Sociology and a Natural Economy of the Body Politic," *Signs* 4 (Autumn 1978): 21–60.

11. As Richard Rorty, *Philosophy and the Mirror of Nature* (Princeton, NJ: Princeton Univ. Press, 1979), has recently argued.

12. Dirac, quoted in Stephen G. Brush, "Should the History of Science Be Rated X?" *Science* 183 (March 22, 1974): 1166.

13. An examination of Freud's papers on psychoanalytic technique makes this centrality evident. The same themes recur from "On Psychotherapy" (1904) to "Constructions in Analysis" (1937). A number of these papers are collected in Philip Rieff, ed., *Therapy and Technique* (New York: Collier, 1963).

14. Freud uses this imagery frequently. See, for example, *The Question of Lay Analysis*, James Strachey, trans. (New York: Norton, 1959), pp. 61–62.

15. See note 13.

16. Robert C. Solomon argues in "Freud's Neurological Theory of Mind," in Richard Wollheim, ed., *Freud: A Collection of Critical Essays* (New York: Doubleday, 1974), that this is the most radical aspect of Freud's theory.

17. On primary narcissism, see Sigmund Freud, *An Outline of Psychoanalysis*, James Strachey, trans. (New York: Norton, 1949), pp. 5–8.

18. For an excellent discussion of these tensions, see Harry Guntrip, *Personality Structure and Human Interaction* (New York: International Universities Press, 1964), pp. 55–160.

19. On this point, see especially D. W. Winnicott, "The Use of an Object and Relating through Identifications," in *Playing and Reality* (New York: Basic Books, 1971).

20. Herbert Fingarette, *The Self in Transformation* (New York: Harper & Row, 1963), pp. 15–70, and Jürgen Habermas, *Knowledge and Human Interests* (Boston: Beacon, 1971), pp. 214–273, stress the hermaneutic aspect of psychoanalysis.

21. See Freud's essay, "Recollection, Repetition and Working Through," in Rieff, *Therapy and Technique*, on this point.

22. Norman Jacobson, *Pride and Solace* (Berkeley: Univ. of California Press, 1978), discusses the defensive uses of reason within political theory.

23. See Freud, *Inhibitions, Symptoms and Anxiety*, James Strachey, ed. (New York: Norton, 1959), pp. 79–80.

24. For a feminist-psychoanalytic answer to this question, see Evelyn Fox Keller, "Gender and Science," *Psychoanalysis and Contemporary Thought*, 1 (1978): 409–433, and Dorothy Dinnerstein, *The Mermaid and the Minotaur* (New York: Harper & Row, 1976).

25. I have argued this point more extensively in "Object Relations, Political Theory and the Patriarchal Unconscious," in Sandra Harding and Merrill Hintikka, eds., *Discovering Reality: Feminist Perspectives on Epistemology, Metaphysics, Methodology, Philosophy of Science* (Boston: Reidel, 1982). My argument rests on a theory of human development presented in Margaret S. Mahler, Fred Pine, and Anni Bergman, *The Psychological Birth of the Human Infant* (New York: Basic Books, 1975).

26. This is Freud's argument in *Civilization and Its Discontents*, James Strachey, ed. (New York: Norton, 1961). See also Herbert Marcuse, *Eros and Civilization* (Boston: Beacon, 1955).

27. On this point, see Evelyn Fox Keller, "Cognitive Repression in Contemporary Physics," *American Journal of Physics*, 47 (August 1979): 718–721, and Max Horkheimer and Theodor Adorno, *The Dialectic of Englightenment* (New York: Herder & Herder, 1972), pp. 3–119.

J. ALLAN HOBSON AND ROBERT W. MCCARLEY, "THE BRAIN AS A DREAM STATE GENERATOR"

This article gives evidence to support the view that dreams are the result of a basic biological process, one that is far less subject to the psychologies of the dreamer than Freud and other psychologists had assumed. Hobson and McCarley use cats as a model for studying the neurophysiological basis of dreaming in man. They defend the use of cats as a model even though they admit that cats may not dream.

329

What enables them to do this is an operational definition of dreaming in terms of the presence of a certain kind of sleep state. This sleep state has a clear duration that can be measured. Our next author, Norman Malcolm, will challenge the idea that dreams have a duration.

If Hobson and McCarley are correct, then, as they so delicately put it, serious doubt has been cast on the psychological significance of Freudian dream analysis. Their interpretation, however, may support a Jungian view of dreaming because what they take to be genotypic determination of imagery can be seen as the result of evolutionary processes. Thus the imagery, determined by evolution, may well be the record of ancestral past experiences. (Actually, Freud can be interpreted as having based his theory on evolution in such a way that for him, as well as for Jung, we retain ancestral fears.)

Hobson and McCarley assume the existence of mind-body isomorphism. What they mean is that whatever a psychological state is, it must have a physical cause. Obviously, if one believed that psychological states such as desiring and dreaming were totally different in kind from biochemical events in the body, the type of research pursued by Hobson and McCarley would make no sense. They point out that Freud himself was a believer in the isomorphism of the mind and body.

Hobson and McCarley tell us clearly what their view can account for and what it still cannot explain. They challenge us to reject mind-body isomorphism and still come up with an equally powerful theory of dreaming. They point out the simplicity of their theory. Hobson and McCarley know that many well-established psychologists and psychiatrists assume without question that dreams have meaning. They do not want to be seen as totally undermining this view, so they underplay the conflict between their findings and the usual dream theories of psychologists. They also say, "The new theory does not deny meaning to dreams."

Freud commented that dreams are the royal road to the unconscious. Hobson and McCarley say that dreams are the royal road to the brain. In short, the theory proposed by Hobson and McCarley seems to reduce psychology to brain physiology.

The Brain as a Dream State Generator

J. ALLAN HOBSON AND ROBERT W. MCCARLEY

Since the turn of the century, dream theory has been dominated by the psychoanalytic

From J. Allan Hobson and Robert W. McCarley, "The Brain as a Dream State Generator: An Activation-Synthesis Hypothesis of the Dream Process," *American Journal of Psychiatry* 134 (1977): 1335–1348. Copyright © 1977, The American Psychiatric Association. Reprinted by permission.

hypothesis that dreaming is a reactive process designed to protect consciousness and sleep from the disruptive effect of unconscious wishes that are released in sleep.[1] Thus dreaming has been viewed as a psychodynamically determined state, and the distinctive formal features of dream content have been interpreted as manifestations of a defensive transformation of the unconscious wishes found unacceptable to consciousness by a hypothetical censor. A critical tenet of this wish fulfillment-disguise theory is that the transformation of the unconscious wish by the censor disguises or degrades the ideational information in forming the dream imagery. We were surprised to discover the origins of the major tenets of psychoanalytic dream theory in the neutrophysiology of 1890 and have specified the transformations made by Freud in an earlier, related article.[2] In detailing the neurophysiological origins of psychoanalytic dream theory, the concept of mind-body isomorphism, denoting similarity of form between psychological and physiological events, was seen as an explicit premise of Freud's thought.

Sharing Freud's conviction that mind-body isomorphism is a valid approach, we will now review modern neurophysiological evidence that we believe permits and necessitates important revisions in psychoanalytic dream theory. The activation-synthesis hypothesis that we will begin to develop in this paper asserts that many formal aspects of the dream experience may be the obligatory and relatively undistorted psychological concomitant of the regularly recurring and physiologically determined brain state called "dreaming sleep." It ascribes particular formal features of the dream experience to the particular organizational features of the brain during that state of sleep. More specifically, the theory details the mechanisms by which the brain becomes periodically activated during sleep and specifies the means by which both sensory input and motor output are simultaneously blocked, so as to account for the maintenance of sleep in the face of strong central activation of the brain. The occurrence and character of dreaming are seen as both determined and shaped by these physiological processes.

The most important tenet of the activation-synthesis hypothesis is that during dreaming the activated brain generates its own information by a pontine brain stem neuronal mechanism, which will be described in detail. We hypothesize that this internally generated sensorimotor information; which is partially random and partially specific, is then compared with stored sensorimotor data in the synthesis of dream content. The functional significance of the brain activation and the synthesis of endogenous information in dreaming sleep is not known, but we suggest that state-dependent learning is at least as likely a result of dreaming as is tension reduction or sleep maintenance.

While we believe that the two processes emphasized in this paper—activation and synthesis—are major and important advances in dream theory, we wish to state explicitly and comment on some of the things that our theory does not attempt to do. The activation-synthesis hypothesis does not exclude possible defensive distortions of the value-free sensorimotor dream stimuli, but it does deny the primacy of any such process in attempting to explain *formal* aspects of dream content or the fundamental impetus to dreaming itself. The idea that dreams reveal wishes is also beyond the direct reach of our new theory, but some specific alternatives to this interpretation of several classic dream situations can be advanced.

The new theory cannot yet account for the emotional aspects of the dream experience, but we assume that they are produced by the activation of brain regions subserving affect in parallel with the activation of the better known sensorimotor pathways. Finally, the new theory does not deny meaning to dreams, but it does suggest (1) a more direct route to their acquisition than anamnesis via free association, since dream origins are in basic physiological processes and not in disguised wishes, (2) a less complex approach to their interpretation than conversion from manifest to latent content, since unusual aspects of dreams are not seen as disguises but as results of the way the brain and mind function during sleep, and (3) a broader view of their use in therapy than that provided by the transference frame of reference, since dreams are not to be interpreted as the product of disguised unconscious (transference) wishes. Dreams offer a royal road to the mind and brain in a behavioral state, with different operating rules and principles than during waking and with the possibility of clinically useful insights from the product of these differences. These points are discussed . . . elsewhere.[3]

WHAT IS A DREAM?

A dream may be defined as a mental experience, occurring in sleep, which is characterized by hallucinoid imagery, predominantly visual and often vivid; by bizarre elements due to such spatiotemporal distortions as condensation, discontinuity, and acceleration; and by a delusional acceptance of these phenomena as "real" at the time that they occur. Strong emotion may or may not be associated with these distinctive formal properties of the dream, and subsequent recall of these mental events is almost invariably poor unless an immediate arousal from sleep occurs.

That this technical jargon describes a universal human experience seems certain, since the five key points in this definition are easily elicited from both naïve and sophisticated individuals when they are asked to characterize their dreams. We leave aside the question of whether other less vivid and nonperceptual forms of mental activity during sleep should also be called "dreams" and confine ourselves here to the psychophysiology of the hallucinoid type of dream. In doing so, we not only simplify the immediate task at hand but may also gain insight into the mechanisms underlying the most florid symptoms of psychopathology. We mean, of course, the hallucinations and delusions of the psychotic experience, which have so often invited comparison with the dream as we have defined it here.

WHAT IS THE STATE OF THE BRAIN DURING DREAMING SLEEP?

The physiological substrate of the dream experience is the CNS in one of its three principal operating states: waking (W), synchronized sleep (S), and desynchronized sleep (D). These states can be reliably and objectively differentiated by recording the EEG, the electromyogram (EMG), and the electrooculogram (see Table 1). Hallucinoid dreaming in man occurs predominantly during the periodically recurrent phase of sleep characterized by EEG desynchronization, EMG suppression, and REMs.[4] We call this kind of sleep "D" (meaning desynchronized, but also conveniently denoting dreaming).

. . . This D brain state is characterized by the following "sensorimotor" properties: activation of the brain; relative exclusion of external input; generation of some internal

Table 1 Electrographic Criteria for Behavioral State Determination

State	Electromyogram	EEG	Electrooculogram
Waking	+	Low voltage, fast	+
Sleep			
Synchronized	+	High-voltage, slow	−
Desynchronized	−	Low voltage, fast	+

input, which the activated forebrain then processes as information; and blocking of motor output, except for the oculomotor pathway. In this model the substrate of emotion is considered to be a part of the forebrain; it will not be further distinguished here because we have no specific physiological evidence as to how this part of the system might work in any brain state. Memory is not shown but is considered to be a differentiated function of the brain that operates during the D state, such that output from long-term storage is facilitated but input to long-term storage is blocked. A highly specific hypothesis about dream amnesia has previously been derived[5] from the same evidence that we will now review in our attempt to account for the general sensorimotor aspects of the dream process.

ELECTROPHYSIOLOGY OF THE BRAIN DURING THE DREAM STATE

The three major electrographic features of the D state are of obvious relevance to our attempt to answer the following three questions about the organization of the brain in the dream state.

How is the forebrain activated in the D state? Since EEG desynchronization also characterizes waking, similar mechanisms of "activation" may be involved in both instances. Physiological evidence suggests that this is so: the reticular formation of the anterior brain stem is at least as active in D sleep as it is in the waking state. . . .

How is motor output blocked in the D state? Physiological evidence clearly shows that the profound EMG suppression of D sleep is a consequence of the direct inhibition of spinal cord motoneurons.[6] As a consequence, any organized motor patterns that might be generated during the intense brain activation of D sleep cannot be expressed.

That organized movement patterns are in fact generated, but not expressed, in normal

D sleep is dramatically demonstrated by cats with lesions of the anterodorsal pontine brain stem.[7] The animals show all of the major manifestations of D sleep except the atonia; instead of the fine twitches of the digits and the limb jerks that are normally present in D, these cats display complex motor behaviors including repetitive paw movements and well-coordinated attack and defense sequences that have no apparent relationship to the environment.

How is sensory imagery generated in the D state? In waking, a corollary discharge of the oculomotor system has been shown to suppress visual transmission during saccadic eye movements, possibly contributing to the stability of the visual field during that state.[8] The same mechanisms might underlie the hallucinoid dream imagery by inhibiting and exciting neurons of the lateral geniculate body[9] and the visual cortex[10] during D sleep, when retinal input is reduced and unformed.

The possibility that oculomotor impulses trigger visual imagery is particularly intriguing in view of the demonstrated quantitative correlation between eye movement intensity and dream intensity.[11] More specific correlations have also been reported to relate eye movement direction to orientation of the hallucinated gaze in dreams.[12] This finding has been interpreted as indicative of "scanning" the visual field—implying cortical control of the eye movements in dreaming sleep. An alternative, although not exclusive, hypothesis is that the oculomotor activity is generated at the brain stem level and that the cortex is then provided with feed-forward information about the eye movements. According to this view, we are not so much scanning dream imagery with our D sleep eye movements as we are synthesizing the visual imagery appropriate to them. We will return to the implications of this intriguing possibility in discussing the generation of eye movements in dreaming sleep, but we wish to stress here the general significance of this clue to the identity of an "internal information generator" operating at the brain stem level in the dreaming sleep state.

The eye-movement-related inhibition of sensory relays,[13] as well as the possible occlusion of exogenous inputs by internally generated excitation, may also contribute to the maintenance of sleep in the face of strong central activation of the brain. In this sense the dream process is seen as having a sleep maintenance mechanism built into its physiological substrate rather than a sleep guardian function operating at the psychological level.

A firm general conclusion can be reached at this point: the desynchronized phase of sleep is the physiological substrate of hallucinoid dreaming, as defined. This conclusion is of profound significance to psychophysiology, since we can now reliably and objectively characterize and measure many aspects of the brain when it is in the dream state. For example, one feature that emerges from the psychophysiological study of dreaming and one that was not at all evident from introspective, psychoanalytically oriented research, is that the brain enters the dream state at regular intervals during sleep and stays in that state for appreciable and predictable lengths of time. One clear implication of this finding is that dreaming is an automatically preprogrammed brain event and not a response to exogenous (day residue) or endogenous (visceral) stimuli. A second implication is that the dream state generator mechanism is periodic, that is, the dream state generator is a neurobiological clock.[14] Since the length of the sleep cycle and, by inference, the frequency of dreaming, is a function of body size within and across mammalian species,[15] the system controlling the length of the period must have a structural substrate. Thus we must account for size-related periodicity with our model of the dream state generator.

AN ANIMAL MODEL OF THE BRAIN DURING THE DREAM STATE

We said that the length of the sleep cycle varies "across species." Does that mean that nonhuman animals dream? Unfortunately we cannot know, but we are willing to assert that if they do so, it is when their brains are in the D sleep state. Because we have no direct evidence of any significant difference between the brain state of man and the brain state of other mammals in D sleep, we therefore feel justified in asserting that the brain state of our experimental animal, the cat, constitutes a reasonable subject for our study of the brain as a dream process generator, whether or not cats dream. This assertion seems justified since we are restricting our attention here to formal aspects of the dream experience; our experimental model need not dream or even possess "consciousness" to be useful as a source of physiological information. If we accept this argument and use the definition of dreaming offered above, then the presence of D sleep in cats[16] offers nothing less than an animal model in which to study the neurophysiological basis of a hallucinoid mental process in man. Such a model is as important in experimental psychiatry as it is rare. Let us now turn to the biological data upon which our sketches of the brain as a dream state generator are based.

LOCALIZATION OF THE POWER SUPPLY OR TRIGGER ZONE OF THE DREAM STATE GENERATOR

Lesion, stimulation, and recording studies pioneered by Jouvet[17] have strongly implicated the pontine brain stem as critical to the generation of the desynchronized sleep phase. . . . Important findings supporting this hypothesis include the following.

Large lesions of the pontine reticular formation prevent the occurrence of desynchronized sleep for several weeks in cats.[17] This suggests that the pontine reticular formation may be the site of an executive or triggering mechanism for desynchronized sleep. Prepontine transections and forebrain ablation have no effect upon periodicity or duration of the skeletal, muscular, and oculomotor manifestations of D sleep.[17] The data indicate that the trigger, the power supply, and the clock are pontine.

The pontine brain stem is thus implicated as the site of both the trigger and the clock. The periodicity of the D sleep clock in poikilothermic pontine cats lengthens as temperature declines, indicating orthodox metabolic mediation of the cycle, in contrast to the temperature independence of circadian rhythms. If we assume that the physiological substrate of consciousness is in the forebrain, these facts completely eliminate any possible contribution of ideas (or their neural substrate) to the primary driving force of the dream process.

Small lesions of the dorsal pontine brain stem, in the region of the locus coeruleus (LC), may eliminate the atonia but no other aspects of desynchronized sleep.[7] This suggests that inhibition of muscle tone is somehow dependent upon the integrity of the LC. The elaborate motor behavior that characterizes the D sleep of cats with LC lesions has been described as "pseudo-hallucinatory." Whether or not one accepts the sensory implications of that designation, the importance of motor inhibition in quelling the effects of central excitation during the dream state is clear.

This finding has an important bearing on mechanisms of dream paralysis and suggests that in the classic chase dream, the dreamer who has trouble fleeing from a pursuer is as much accurately reading the activated state of his motor pattern generator and the paralyzed state of his spinal neurons as he is "wishing" to be caught. This dream experience is so universal and the feeling of constrained motor action so impressive as to make its physiological basis in the descending inhibition of motoneurons seem to us inescapable. Conversely, this reasonable and adequate explanation of the paradox of the chase dream makes its interpretation as wish fulfillment less compelling. Other implications of the D sleep activation of various motor system pattern generators for movements and dream plots have been discussed elsewhere.[3]

The vestibular system, as classically established, integrates head position and movement with eye position and posture. . . .

Thus the central, automatic activation during sleep of the vestibular system may provide a substrate for endogenously generated, specific information about body position and movement. Flying dreams may thus be a logical, direct, and unsymbolic way of synthesizing information generated endogenously by the vestibular system in D sleep. In view of this reasonable and direct explanation, it seems gratuitous to "interpret" the sensual flying dream as sexual.

In accord with the isomorphism principle, the degree of neuronal activation in brain systems should parallel the frequency and intensity of dreams to these systems,[3] and the predominance of visual sensorimotor activity in both brain and mind supports this notion. Symbol formation and the often bizarre juxtaposition of sensations in the dream may be a reflection of the heightened degree of simultaneous activation of multiple sensory channels in dreaming as compared with waking.[3]

Long-term electrical stimulation of the pontine brain stem results in the earlier appearance of sleep episodes and in increases in the absolute amounts of desynchronized sleep, but it does not affect the periodicity of its occurrence.[18] By implication, the delivery of electrical energy accomplishes what most psychological and behavioral treatments fail to achieve: an increase in the duration of dreaming sleep. Testing the assumption that the generator neurons are cholinoceptive, our laboratory team has recently established that injection of the cholinergic agent carbachol into the pontine reticular formation produces prolonged enhancement of D-like sleep behavior.[19] In man the parenteral injection of the anticholinesterase agent physostigmine potentiates D sleep, and the pharmacologically induced episodes are associated with hallucinoid dreaming.[20] The time of occurrence and duration of dreams may thus be chemically determined.

In summary, these results support the hypothesis that the pontine brain stem is the generator zone for the D sleep state. The trigger mechanism for the whole system, including the eye movement generator, may be cholinoceptive and the executive zones are probably in the reticular formation. The LC is involved, possibly in a permissive or reciprocal way, and is especially important in mediating spinal reflex inhibition. Together, these two regions may constitute the clock. We will have more to say about the hypothesis of reciprocal interaction between them later in this paper.

Although the brain stem mechanisms mediating atonia remain obscure, it is clear from the work of Pompeiano[6] that both monosynaptic and polysynaptic spinal reflexes are tonically inhibited during D sleep. . . . In addition, during the bursts of REM, there is a descending presynaptic inhibition of the most rapidly conducting (group 1a) spinal afferent endings. Both presynaptic and postsynaptic inhibition appear to be of brain stem origin. Phasic presynaptic inhibition has also been shown to occur in sensory relays elsewhere in the

brain during D sleep.[6] Thus motor output is tonically damped throughout D and sensory input is phasically damped in concert with the REM bursts. In other words, we are not only paralyzed during our dreams, but the degree to which we are paralyzed fluctuates in concert with the intensity of the internally generated information and the degree to which we suppress exogenous input.

On the basis of this evidence, the systems terminology used earlier can be tentatively translated into . . . anatomical and physiological terms . . . ; and the activation-synthesis hypothesis of dreaming can be stated as follows: during D sleep, a cholinergic mechanism in the reticular formation of the pontine brain stem is periodically activated. The consequences of this activation are as follows:

1. The forebrain is tonically activated, probably via the midbrain reticular formation that is also responsible for its activation during waking. Thus the forebrain is made ready to process information.

2. The spinal reflexes are tonically inhibited, possibly via the bulbar reticular formation and LC; thus motor outflow is blocked despite high levels of activity in the brain, including the motor cortex.

3. The oculomotor and vestibular systems are phasically activated by the pontine reticular formation so as to produce eye movements. This circuitry, in its entirety, is an internal information source or generator that provides the forebrain with spatially specific but temporally disorganized information about eye velocity, relative position, and direction of movement. Information may similarly be derived from the brain stem generators of patterned motor activity.

4. At the same time that internal information feedback is being generated by the activation of various motor systems, extero-

ceptive input to sensory systems is phasically blocked. This may intensify the relative impact of the endogenous inputs to the brain, accounting for the intensity of dream imagery and preventing sleep disruption by the externally generated excitation.

This working sketch of the dream state generator, based on the classical localizing methods of experimental neurology, is intriguing but unsatisfying in that it fails to specify the mechanisms by which the pontine generator is turned on, kept active for a time, and then shut off. Further, it does not say anything about the mechanism of periodicity. To provide details about the anatomy and physiology of the periodic trigger mechanisms of the generator process, we will now turn our attention to the neuronal level of analysis. In doing so, we also come full circle in our reaffirmation of isomorphism since it was the neuron that Freud recognized as the physical unit of the nervous system on which he based his dream theory.[2]

PSYCHOLOGICAL IMPLICATIONS OF THE CELLULAR NEUROPHYSIOLOGY OF DREAM SLEEP GENERATION

Hallucinoid dreaming is regarded as the psychological concomitant of D sleep. Brain activity in the D state has been analyzed to account for activation of the forebrain, occlusion of sensory input, blockade of motor output at the spinal cord level, and the generation of information within the system. The evidence that the pontine brain stem contains a clock-trigger mechanism that contributes to activation of the forebrain, occlusion of sensory input, and the generation of internal information has been reviewed. The periodicity of the triggering mechanism is hypothesized to be a function of reciprocal interaction of reciprocally connected, chemically coded cell groups in the pontine brain stem.

The psychological implications of this model, which we call the activation-synthesis hypothesis of the dream process (schematically represented in Figure 1), contrast sharply with many tenets of the dream theory provided by psychoanalysis (also represented in Figure 1) in the following ways:

1. *The primary motivating force for dreaming* is not psychological but physiological since the time of occurrence and duration of dreaming sleep are quite constant, suggesting a preprogrammed, neurally determined genesis. In fact, the neural mechanisms involved can now be precisely specified. This conclusion does not, of course, mean that dreams are not also psychological events; nor does it imply that they are without psychological meaning or function. But it does imply that the process is much more basic than the psychodynamically determined, evanescent, "guardian of sleep" process that Freud had imagined it to be; and it casts serious doubt upon the exclusively psychological significance attached to both the occurrence and quality of dreams.

2. *Specific stimuli for the dream imagery* appear to arise intracerebrally but from the pontine brain stem and not in cognitive areas of the cerebrum. These stimuli, whose generation appears to depend upon a largely random or reflex process, may provide spatially specific information which can be used in constructing dream imagery; but the unusual intensity, intermittency, and velocity of the eye movements may also contribute to features of the dream experience which are formally bizarre and have been interpreted as defensive by psychoanalysis. Thus such features as scene shifts, time compression, personal condensations, splitting, and symbol formation may be directly isomorphic with the state of the nervous system during dreaming sleep. In other words, the forebrain may be making the best of a bad job in producing even partially coherent

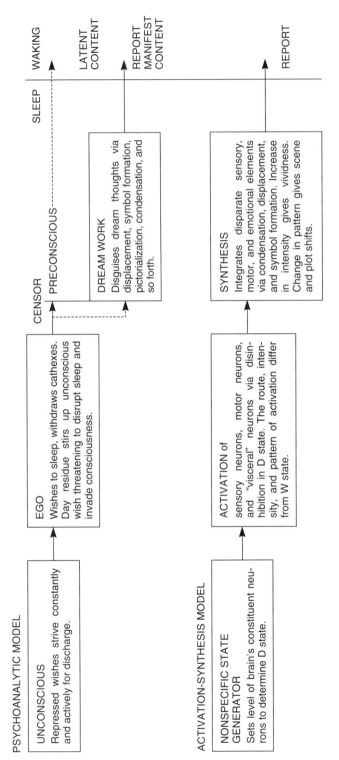

Figure 1 Two Models of the Dream Process

Note: In the psychoanalytic model the motive force of the process is the dynamically repressed unconscious wish that is released from control in sleep. The dream thoughts that emerge threaten consciousness and sleep; they are deterred by the censor. The "dream work" transforms the unconscious wish by the processes that are listed. The product, or manifest content, that becomes conscious thus contains only disguised elements of the original (latent) dream thoughts.

The activation-synthesis model is designed to contrast activation-synthesis theory with the guardian-censorship theory illustrated in the top portion of this figure. The motive force of the process is seen to be nonspecific neural energy or excitation hypothesized to arise from a nonspecific generator. This excitation affects the component systems of the forebrain represented in the upper box: sensory systems generate scene frames, structural fragments, and qualitative features; cognitive systems generate ideas that may be conscious (day residue thoughts) or unconscious (instinctually determined); emotion is also generated at this first stage. The dream report, easily obtainable if a state change to waking occurs, is seen as an accurate reflection of the integrated product of disparate, internally generated elements.

dream imagery from the relatively noisy signals sent up to it from the brain stem.

The dream process is thus seen as having its origin in sensorimotor systems, with little or no primary ideational, volitional, or emotional content. This concept is markedly different from that of the "dream thoughts" or wishes seen by Freud as the primary stimulus for the dream. The sensorimotor stimuli are viewed as possibly providing a frame into which ideational, volitional, or emotional content may be projected to form the integrated dream image, but this frame is itself conflict free. Thus both the major energetic drive for the dream process and the specific primary stimulus of the dream content are genotypically determined and therefore conflict free in the specifically psychodynamic sense of the term.

3. *The elaboration of the brain stem stimulus* by the perceptual, conceptual, and emotional structures of the forebrain is viewed as primarily a synthetic constructive process, rather than a distorting one as Freud presumed. Best fits to the relative inchoate and incomplete data provided by the primary stimuli are called up from memory, the access to which is facilitated during dreaming sleep. The brain, in the dreaming sleep state, is thus likened to a computer searching its addresses for key words. Rather than indicating a need for disguise, this fitting of phenotypic experiential data to genotypic stimuli is seen as the major basis of the "bizarre" formal qualities of dream mentation. There is, therefore, no need to postulate either a censor or an information degrading process working at the censor's behest. The dream content elaborated by the forebrain may include conflictually charged memories, but even this aspect of dream construction is seen as synthetic and transparent rather than degradative and opaque.

4. *With respect to the forgetting of dreams,* the normally poor recall is seen principally to reflect a state-dependent amnesia, since a carefully effected state change, to waking, may produce abundant recall even of highly charged dream material. There is thus no need to invoke repression to account for the forgetting of dreams. This hypothesis is appealingly economical, and in the light of the reciprocal interaction hypothesis dream amnesia can now be modeled in a testable way as the result of a different balance between cholinergic and aminergic neuronal activity and the resulting effects on second messengers and macromolecules.[5] Among its other surprising gifts to psychophysiology, dreaming sleep may thus also provide a biological model for the study of memory, and a functional role for dreaming sleep in promoting some aspect of the learning process is suggested.

SUMMARY AND CONCLUSIONS

Assuming that isomorphism, or identity of form, must characterize the simultaneous physiological and psychological events during dreaming, we have reviewed the general and cellular neurophysiology of dreaming sleep in search of new ways of accounting for some of the formal aspects of dream psychology. We have noted that the occurrence of dreaming depends upon the periodic activation of the forebrain during sleep. We have hypothesized that the activated forebrain synthesizes the dreams by fitting experiential data to information endogenously and automatically generated by reticular, vestibular, and oculomotor neurons in the pontine brain stem. A specific physiological and mathematical model of the pontine generator, based upon single cell recording studies in cats, is described: the model posits reciprocal interaction between inhibitory aminergic (level-setting) and excitatory cholinergic (generator) neurons.

Some of the "bizarre" formal features of the dream may directly reflect the properties of the brain stem neuronal generator mechanism. The physiological features of the generator mechanisms and their corresponding psychological implications include the following: the automaticity and periodicity of activation indicate a metabolically determined, conflict-free energetics of the dream process; the random but specific nature of the generator signals could provide abnormally sequenced and shaped, but spatiotemporally specific, frames for dream imagery; and the clustering of runs of generator signals might constitute time-marks for dream subplots and scene changes. Further, the activation by generator neurons of diffuse postsynaptic forebrain elements in multiple parallel channels might account for the disparate sensory, motor, and emotional elements that contribute to the "bizarreness" of dreams; the suppression of motor output and sensory input simultaneous with central activation of both sensory and motor patterns could assure the maintenance of sleep in the face of massive central excitation of the brain; and the change in the ratio of neurotransmitters affecting forebrain neurons might account for dream amnesia and indicate a state-dependent alteration of neural plasticity, with implications for the learning process.

NOTES

1. Freud S: The interpretation of dreams (1900), in The Complete Psychological Works, standard ed, vols 4 and 5. Translated and edited by Strachey J. London, Hogarth Press, 1966.
2. McCarley RW, Hobson JA: The neurobiological origins of psychoanalytic dream theory. Am J Psychiatry 134:1211–1221, 1977.
3. McCarley RW: Mind-body isomorphism and the study of dreams, in Advances in Sleep Research, vol 6. Edited by Fishbein W. New York, Spectrum, 1978.
4. Dement W. Kleitman N: The relation of eye movements during sleep to dream activity: an objective method for the study of dreaming. J Exp Psychol 53:89–97, 1957.
5. Hobson JA: The reciprocal interaction model of sleep cycle control: implication for PGO wave generation and dream amnesia, in Sleep and Memory. Edited by Drucker-Colin R. McGaugh J. New York, Academic Press, 1977, pp 159–183.
6. Pompeiano O: The neurophysiological mechanisms of the postural and motor events during desynchronized sleep. Res Publ Assoc Res Nerv Ment Dis 45:351–423, 1967.
7. Jouvet M. Delorme F: Locus coeruleus et sommeil paradoxal. Soc Biol 159:895, 1965.
8. Volkman F: Vision during voluntary saccadic eye movements. J Opt Soc Am 52:571–578, 1962.
9. Bizzi E: Discharge pattern of single geniculate neurons during the rapid eye movements of sleep. J Neurophysiol 29: 1087–1095, 1966.
10. Evarts EV: Activity of individual cerebral neurons during sleep and arousal. Res Publ Assoc Res Nerv Ment Dis 45:319–337, 1967.
11. Hobson JA, Goldfrank F, Snyder F: Sleep and respiration. J Psychiatr Res 3:79–90, 1965.
12. Roffwarg HP, Dement WC, Muzio JN, et al: Dream imagery: relationship to rapid eye movements of sleep. Arch Gen Psychiatry 7:235–258, 1962.
13. Pompeiano O: Sensory inhibition during motor activity in sleep, in Neurophysiological Basis of Normal and Abnormal Motor Activities. Edited by Yahr MD, Purpura DP. New York, Raven Press, 1967, pp. 323–375.
14. Hobson JA: The sleep-dream cycle, a neurobiological rhythm, in Pathobiology Annual. Edited by Ioachim H. New York, Appleton-Century-Crofts, 1975, pp 369–403.
15. Zepelin H. Rechtschaffen A: Mammalian sleep, longevity and energy metabolism. Brain Behav Evol 10:425–470, 1974.
16. Dement W: The occurrence of low-voltage fast electroencephalogram patterns during behavioral sleep in the cat. Electroencephalogr Clin Neurophysiol 10:291–296, 1958.
17. Jouvet M: Recherches sur les structures nerveuses et les mécanismes responsables des différentes phases du sommeil physiologique. Arch Ital Biol 100:125–206, 1962.
18. Frederickson CJ, Hobson JA: Electrical stimulation of the brain stem and subsequent sleep. Arch Ital Biol 108:564–576, 1970.
19. Amatruda TT, Black DA, McKenna TM, et al: Sleep cycle control and cholinergic mechanisms: differential effects of carbachol at pontine brain stem sites. Brain Res 98:501–515, 1975.
20. Sitaram N. Wyatt RJ, Dawson S, et al: REM sleep induction by physostigmine infusion during sleep. Science 191:1281–1283, 1976.

NORMAN MALCOLM, "TEMPORAL LOCATION AND DURATION OF DREAMS"

Malcolm details many now-famous findings concerning REM sleep and dreams. He does not dispute the science involved. His point is that one cannot assume from the data on rapid eye movements during sleep that dreams exist in space and time. Hobson and McCarley assumed a brain-dream isomorphism as part of their body-mind isomorphism; that is what makes their reductionistic theory feasible. Malcolm denies such isomorphisms and hence denies the reductionism of Hobson and McCarley.

Malcolm discusses what some philosophers would call the logic of dreaming discourse. He focuses on the criterion we have for saying that a dream was of a certain length and had certain content. The criterion is what we are told by the dreamer. There is no other way to check. This is not the sort of criterion that can be accepted by physical science. Physical science requires an objective check for the appropriate use of a term. Thus "content of a dream" and "duration of a dream" cannot be acceptable concepts in a science.

Sometimes dreams are affected by external events. We dream of loud noises and awake to discover that a thunderstorm is raging or a radiator is clanking. The noises affected the dreams, so the dreams must have taken place shortly after the sounds. Malcolm's reply is that what we associate here is the *report* of a dream and some noise. The dream itself is still unobserved in the sense required by physical science. We could stipulate that in these cases, the dream was close in time to the noise—but it would be just that, a stipulation (Malcolm says "convention"). It would not be anything new *discovered* about dreams.

But, dreams do occur during periods of sleeping and sleeping occurs in time, so dreams must occur in time. They must have a duration in the same sense that sleep does. Remember that this was the argument implicit in Hobson and McCarley. Malcolm replies that when we say, "Dreams occur in sleep," we are labeling a specific type of experience: A person wakes up, says that he or she dreamed something, and we know that what was dreamed did not actually occur. Again, Malcolm stresses, we have only the dream report to use as criterion that there was a dream and that it had a particular content. There is no way to connect the duration of the dream with anything until the dreamer is awake. This situation will never be objective enough to yield a scientific meaning for "dreams have duration."

What is the relation between REM states and dream duration? Malcolm's point is that there is no way to tell. We can stipulate that they are identical. But, again, that is a stipulation, not a discovery.

Malcolm realizes that we might want to change our current concept of dream and with it the way we talk about dreams. If we made such a change, we would have to admit that we had a new concept of dream. His point, then, is that our current concept of dream is such that it cannot be reduced to purely scientific terms. The reduction in Hobson and McCarley cannot be accomplished. Neither should it be assumed. There is just no way to translate from dream in our ordinary sense to dream as a brain state. We can change the concept and may well prefer to do so. But if we do make such a change, we should realize that we are now talking about something that is not a dream in our usual sense.

Temporal Location and Duration of Dreams

NORMAN MALCOLM

Since the notion of a dream as an occurrence that is logically independent of the sleeper's waking impression has no clear sense, it follows that the notions of the location and duration of a dream in physical time also have no clear sense. I mean that this is so if one keeps to the primary concept, where the sole criterion of the occurrence of a dream is the waking report. One may be easily tempted however to *give* a sense to these notions, as the following will illustrate.

A considerable amount of scientific work has had the aim of trying to establish correlations between dreaming and various physiological phenomena such as brain potentials, action currents, galvanic skin responses, and blood pressure. I will refer to one very recent study. The authors begin by saying:

The study of dream activity and its relation to physiological variables during sleep necessitates a reliable method of determining with precision when dreaming occurs. This knowledge, in the final analysis, always depends upon the subjective report of the dreamer, but becomes relatively objective if such reports can be significantly related to some physiological phenomena which in turn can be measured by physical techniques (Dement & Kleitman, p. 339).

The physiological phenomenon studied in their experiments was rapid eye move-

ments, recorded by sensitive instruments. The procedure was to waken the subjects from sleep during periods of rapid eye movements (abbreviated "REM") and also during periods when there were no rapid eye movements (abbreviated "NREM"), in order to find out whether they could recall dreams. With 9 subjects there were 191 awakenings during REM periods and 160 awakenings during NREM periods. The incidence of dream recall was high after the REM awakenings (152 out of 191) and low after the NREM awakenings (11 out of 160). It was observed that the duration of REM periods that were not terminated artificially by an awakening varied from 8 to 50 minutes with a mean of about 20 minutes. This was thought to suggest a measure of the duration of dreams. To test this the following experiment was performed: Subjects were awakened either 5 or 15 minutes after the beginning of REM's and "were required on the basis of their recall of the dream to decide which was the correct duration" of the dream. In 51 of the 5 minute awakenings the subjects decided in favour of 5 minutes a total of 45 times; in 60 of the 15 minute awakenings they decided in favour of 15 minutes a total of 47 times. The authors' conclusion is that all subjects, with one exception, "were able to choose the correct dream duration with high accuracy." They say of the one exceptional "inaccurate" subject that he "made most of his

From Norman Malcolm, *Dreaming* (London: Routledge, 1959), pp. 70–82, 121–123. Reprinted by permission.

incorrect choices by estimating 15 minutes to be 5 minutes." They add:

This is consistent with the interpretation that the dream was longer, but he was only able to recall the latter fraction and thus thought it was shorter than it actually was (p. 343).

They also say:

In addition to depending on the amount of actual dreaming, the lengths of the dream narratives were undoubtedly influenced by many other factors as, for example, the loquacity or taciturnity of S [the subject] (Ibid.).

An ingenious attempt was made to correlate the REM's with dream content. Sometimes the REM's were mainly vertical, sometimes mainly horizontal, sometimes a mixture of both. "It was hypothesized that the movements represented the visual imagery of the dream, that is, that they corresponded to where and at what the dreamer was looking." Only three cases of purely vertical movements were observed.

After each of these the dream content involved a predominance of action in the vertical plane. One S dreamed of standing at the bottom of a tall cliff operating some sort of hoist and looking up at climbers at various levels and down at the hoist machinery. Another S dreamed of climbing up a series of ladders looking up and down as he climbed. In the third instance the dreamer was throwing basketballs at a net, first shooting and looking up at the net, and then looking down to pick another ball off the floor. Only one instance of pure horizontal movement was seen. In the associated dream S was watching two people throwing tomatoes at each other (p. 344).

Twenty-one awakenings occurred after a mixture of movements and always the subjects reported that in their dreams they were looking at things close to them. Finally, the eye movements of subjects who were awake and were observing either distant or nearby occurrences, were recorded by the same apparatus. "The eye-movement potentials in all cases were comparable in both ampli-

tude and pattern to those occurring during dreaming."

The following are among the conclusions drawn by the authors: The experiments indicate that dreaming "occurred periodically in discreet episodes during the course of a night's sleep," that is to say, in periods of rapid eye movements. The few examples of dream recall when there were no eye movements "are best accounted for by assuming that the memory of the preceding dream persisted for an unusually long time. This is borne out by the fact that most of these instances occurred very close, within 8 minutes, after the end of REM periods" (p. 845). Some previous views about the duration and "progress" of dreams appear to have evidence against them:

There was nothing in the experiments reported in this paper to indicate that the dreams occurred instantaneously, or with great rapidity, as some have supposed. Rather, they seemed to progress at a rate comparable to a real experience of the same sort. An increment in the length of REM periods was almost invariably associated with a proportional increase in the length of the dream (p. 346).

Finally:

It seems reasonable to conclude that an objective measurement of dreaming may be accomplished by recording REM's during sleep. This stands in marked contrast to the forgetting, distortion, and other factors that are involved in the reliance on the subjective recall of dreams. It thus becomes possible to objectively study the effect on dreaming of environmental changes, psychological stress, drug administration, and a variety of other factors and influences (Ibid.).

These experimental findings would incline many people to want to employ the phenomenon of rapid eye movements as the *criterion* of the occurrence, temporal location and duration of dreams. If one consciously decided to do this one would then say of a person awakened during a period of these movements, who could recall no dream, that he had *forgotten* the dream (which undoubtedly occurred). One could say even that he had not been *aware* of the dream (just as it is often said that people are not always aware of their sensations); for what would be the difference here between saying that he had been aware of the dream but forgot it, and saying that he had not been aware of it when it occurred? The temptation to take the latter step would be nearly irresistible if a person who was awakened during an REM period insisted that he had *not* been dreaming. If someone had a "long" dream (as measured by the duration of the REM period) but could recall only a "short" dream (as measured by the number of words in his dream narrative and also by his impression that it was a "short" dream) then one would say that he remembered only a "fraction" of the dream, as Dement and Kleitman actually suggest. If a person who was awakened during a period of no eye movements related a dream, one would say (as Dement and Kleitman "assume") that his memory of the *preceding* dream had persisted.

I do not claim that Dement and Kleitman actually made the decision to use eye movements as their criterion of dreaming. If they had done so, deliberately and consciously, their conclusions would not be as tentative as they are. At the same time they are strongly drawn toward that decision, and this is understandable. They want to do *scientific* work on dreams and therefore they need "a reliable method of determining with precision when dreaming occurs" and exactly how long it lasts. This need is not filled by the criterion of "subjective reports" of dreams.

The interest in a physiological criterion of dreaming is due, I believe, to an error that philosophers, psychologists, physiologists and everyone who reflects on the nature of dreaming tends to commit, namely, of supposing that a dream *must* have a definite location and duration in physical time. (This is an excellent example of what Wittgenstein calls a "prejudice" produced by "grammatical illusions"). It might be replied that a dream is surely an *event* and that an event must have a definite date and duration in physical time. But this gets one nowhere, for what justifies the claim that a dream is an event in *that* sense? There can be only as much precision in the common concept of dreaming as is provided by the common criterion of dreaming. The testimony of the sleeper does sometimes determine *when* a dream occurred. A man may say that he was dreaming "just before" he awakened, or that he woke up "in the middle" of a dream, or that in his dream he jumped from a cliff "and then awoke." This testimony does not provide however a determination that would be satisfactory to physical science. One has no idea what "just before" the sleeper awakened would amount to on the clock: it is not *that* sort of determination. It is something he is *inclined to say* on waking up. It is no part of the concept of dreams to provide a translation of this impression into physical time.

There is however a feature of dream-telling that does appear to yield a determination in physical time. People often make connections between their dreams and physical events: e.g. "I dreamt it was thundering; the thunder grew louder and louder; finally I awoke and realized that it was the hammering of the radiator." It would seem that the dream is simultaneous with the physical event and therefore an exact time of occurrence by the clock can be fixed for both. Here the connection with a physical event was made directly by the testimony of the awakened person. But it might be established in a different way. It might be proved (and indeed there is considerable evidence for it—e.g. Ramsey, pp. 441–442) that the contents of dreams can be causally influenced by external stimulation of the sleeper (e.g. if his blankets were removed he would dream of snow, icebergs, and freezing cold). Then would it not be certain that the dream occurred at the same time as (or after) the physical event that causally influenced the content of the dream?

It would certainly be overwhelmingly natural for us to adopt this *convention*—for that is what it would be. No one would have directly observed any causal or temporal relation between dreams and physical occurrences (nor would it make sense to do so), but only between *reports* of dreams and physical occurrences. Since our usual criterion of the occurrence of a dream is the report, the natural step to take in assigning a location in physical time to a dream would be to say that the dream was simultaneous with the physical occurrence during sleep, if there was one, that influenced the waking account of the dream. This would be a definition and not a discovery. One is not *required* to give any sense to the location of dreams in physical time.

It might be said that since dreams occur *in* or *during* sleep, and since sleep is a phenomenon in physical time, therefore dreams must occur in physical time. But here one is being carried away by spatial imagery. The locution that dreams occur "in" sleep is used in this way: people declare on awaking that various incidents *took* place (past tense) which did not take place. We then say that these incidents were *dreamt* (past tense). This is merely how we label the above facts, which imply nothing about the occurrence of dreams in physical time.

The natural convention mentioned above would still have unsatisfactory features from the standpoint of physical science. It would still rely on the awakened person's report; it would provide no criterion for the temporal location of dreams whose content could not be connected with external stimulation during sleep; and it would provide no criterion of *duration*. Consider this last point. There is of course a familiar notion of the duration of dreams. In telling a dream one sometimes says it was a "short" or a "long" dream. This is one's waking impression. But this is not duration in physical time. Dream-telling cannot yield *that* concept. Here it becomes obvious how new convention—stipulation—must enter the scene if that concept is to be provided.

Dement and Kleitman speak of the "length" of a dream without realizing, apparently, that it has no clear sense and must be given one. They say that an increase in the length of the period of rapid eye movements was "almost invariably associated with a proportional increase in the length of the dream" (p. 346). But what is their criterion of the *length* of a dream? It should not be the duration of the associated REM period, for that would make nonsense of their assertion of a *proportional relation* between the two. Yet their article contains an indication that this *is* their criterion. In giving an account of their experiment with the "dream-duration estimates" of their subjects (where the latter were awakened after either 5 or 15 minutes of rapid eye movements and "required on the basis of their recall of the dream to decide which was the correct duration") they report that all subjects save one "were able to choose the correct dream duration with high accuracy" (p. 343). How is it decided what the correct dream duration was? Nothing explicit is said on this point in the article. The most plausible conjecture is that their criterion of the duration of a dream is the duration of the associated REM period. But if the duration of the two is identical then it is truly nonsense to say that an increase in the duration of the REM periods was "almost invariably associated with a proportional increase in the length of the dream" (p. 346).

These physiologists are in a muddle about the duration of dreams because, I think, they do not realize that in the familiar concept of dreaming there is no provision for the duration of dreams in physical time.[1] They assume that this provision is already *there*, only somewhat obscured and in need of being made more precise. The truth is that this notion does not belong to the common concept of dreaming at all. To see this is to realize that to bring it in is to create a new concept under an old label.

That Dement and Kleitman have an erroneous picture of the concept of dreaming comes out, I believe, in their choice of the phrase "the subjective report of the dreamer" (p. 339), and in their concluding remark that rapid eye movements would seem to provide "an objective measurement of dreaming" in contrast to the ordinary reliance on the "subjective recall" of dreams (p. 346). They take for granted that the distinction "subjective-objective" applies to dreams. This distinction is identical with the distinction of "appearance and reality." But if someone tells a dream or says he had one he is not making a "subjective" report which may or may not agree with "objective" fact. His waking impression is what establishes that he had a dream, and his account of his dream establishes what the content of his dream was. If he has a vague impression of his dream then it was a vague dream. If he is not certain whether he dreamt then there is an uncertainty in reality. His impression is the criterion of reality and therefore it cannot be characterized as "subjective." "Subjective" and "objective" are *one* in the case of dreams—which is to say that this distinction does not apply.

Without an adequate realization of what they are doing, Dement and Kleitman are proposing a new concept in which the notions of location and duration in physical time and the subjective-objective distinction will all have a place. We ought to consider the consequences of these stipulations and

ask ourselves whether it is appropriate to call this creation a concept of *dreaming*. If rapid eye movements during sleep became the criterion of dreaming one consequence is that if someone were to tell a dream it could turn out that his impression that he dreamt was *mistaken*—and not in the sense that the incidents he related had really occurred and so his impression was not of a dream but of reality. The new concept would allow him to be mistaken in saying he had a dream even if his impression that he had seen and done various things was false. Another consequence is that it would be possible to discover that a man's assertion that he had slept a dreamless sleep was in error: and here one would have to choose between saying either that he forgot his dreams or that he had not been aware of them when he dreamt them. People would have to be *informed* on waking up that they had dreamt or not—instead of their informing us, as it now is. It could turn out that there was a tribe of people among whom the phenomenon of telling a dream was quite unknown—and yet physiological experiments proved that all of them dreamt every night.

Consider how differently the new concept would be *taught*. As things are, a certain kind of narrative produced in certain circumstances is what we call "telling a dream," and we teach a child to preface such narratives with the word, "I dreamt." If the physiological criterion were adopted, telling a dream would be only a more or less reliable indication of dreaming. It would not be, as now, a matter of definition that someone who told a dream had dreamt. We should not be justified in teaching him to begin those narratives with "I dreamt." To teach him the new concept of dreaming we should have to explain the physiological experiment that provides the new criterion. If mankind should cease to tell dreams the physiological criterion of dreaming could still be employed with possible affirmative results. Much information about the "dreaming habits" of people might continue to be collected. But what were then called "dreams" would no longer be of interest to poets, psychoanalysts, philosophers, and to all of us, children and adults, who like a strange tale.

Considering the radical conceptual changes that the adoption of a physiological criterion would entail, it is evident that a new concept would have been created that only remotely resembled the old one. To use the name "dreaming" for the new concept would spring from confusion and result in confusion. All of this can be avoided by holding firmly to waking testimony as the sole criterion of dreaming. Physiological phenomena, such as rapid eye movements or muscular action currents, may be found to stand in interesting empirical correlations with dreaming, but the possibility of these discoveries presupposes that these phenomena are *not* used as the criterion of dreaming. The desire to know more about dreaming should not lead scientists into transforming the concept in such a way that their subsequent discoveries do not pertain to *dreaming*.

Appendix
DREAMS AND PSYCHIATRY

Some readers . . . may think that my views conflict with the conception of the nature and significance of dreaming commonly held by psychoanalysts, and that this is refutation enough. I am inclined to agree that when Freud thought about the place of dreams in the general theory of psychoanalysis, he pictured it in a way that is at odds with some of my conclusions. "The dream is the mind's reaction in sleep to the experience of the previous day" (Freud, p. 114). The dream is "the life of the mind during sleep," and "dreams are the reaction to a stimulus disturbing sleep" (*Ibid.*, pp. 79 and 82).

We have learnt that the function of dreams is to protect sleep; that they arise out of two conflicting tendencies, of which the one, the desire for sleep, remains constant, whilst the other endeavours to satisfy some mental stimulus; that they have two main characteristics, i.e. they are wish-fulfilments and hallucinatory experiences (*Ibid.*, p. 118).

On the face of it he seems to be supposing a number of things that I have rejected as nonsensical, e.g. that one could, while asleep, have an hallucination or "endeavour to satisfy some mental stimulus." If I am right then a good deal of Freud's theory of dreams needs to be rewritten.

On the other hand I believe that there is no conflict at all with his theory of the *practice* of psychoanalysis, as far as I understand it. I have emphasized the telling of a dream as the criterion of the occurrence and content of a dream. Dreaming is not to be conceived of as something logically independent of dream reports. Now Freud discovered that important information about his patients could be obtained by extending the technique of free association to their dream reports. In giving an account of his method of interpreting dreams he makes this interesting remark:

Any disadvantage resulting from the uncertain recollection of dreams may be remedied by deciding that exactly what the dreamer tells is to count as the dream, and by ignoring all that he may have forgotten or altered in the process of recollection (*Ibid.*, p. 76).

What he is saying, in effect, is that if one tries to conceive of a dream as a process or occurrence quite independent of the dream report, to which the latter may or may not correspond, then psychoanalytic practice has nothing to do with such a conception. The American psychiatrist, Harry Stack Sullivan, says the following:

For the purposes of my theory, one never, under any circumstances, deals directly with dreams. It is simply impossible. What one deals with in psychiatry, and actually in a great many other aspects of life, are recollections pertaining to dreams; how closely, how adequately these recollections approximate the actual dreams is an insoluble problem, because as far as I know there is no way to develop a reasonable conviction of one-to-one correspondence between recollections of dreams and dreams themselves (Sullivan, pp. 331–332).

There is a strong indication here of a philosophical muddle about the "one-to-one correspondence." But what is valuable in these remarks for the present point is the implication that psychiatry is not concerned with this "insoluble problem," and in its workaday therapy is content to use the recollection of a dream as the criterion of the occurrence and content of the dream.

NOTE

1. Empirical studies of dreaming have produced the most divergent estimates of the duration of dreams, some investigators holding that dreams rarely last more than 1 or 2 seconds; others believe that it is 1 to 10 minutes. Dement and Kleitman . . . think that dreams last as long as 50 minutes and that the average length is 20 minutes. These different estimates arise solely from the employment of different criteria of measurement. For an interesting survey of experimental work on dreams see Ramsey.

REFERENCES

Dement, W., and Kleitman, N., "The Relation of Eye Movements during Sleep to Dream Activity: An Objective Method for the Study of Dreaming," *J. Exper. Psychol.* 53 (1957): 339–346.

Freud, S., *A General Introduction to Psychoanalysis* (Garden City, 1943).

Ramsey, G., "Studies of Dreaming," *Psychol. Bull.* 50 (1953).

Sullivan, H. S., *The Interpersonal Theory of Psychiatry* (Norton, 1953).

Wittgenstein, L., *Philosophical Investigations* (Blackwell, 1953).

EXERCISES

1. Why were dreams so important to Freud's methodology? Is his analysis of the Wolf Man's dream believable? Should Freudian dream analysis (perhaps all dream analysis) be considered so theory-laden as to be unacceptable to all but believers of the theories?
2. What exactly is Grünbaum's charge against Freud? Does Flax reply adequately on behalf of Freud? What would it mean to be a realist with respect to dreams? An instrumentalist? A constructive empiricist (what are the phenomena to save)?
3. Evaluate Hobson and McCarley's claim not to have undercut Freud.
4. Carefully evaluate the claim that if dreams are reducible to brain states, then both Freud and Hobson and McCarley are right but Malcolm is wrong.
5. Are the methods used by Malcolm legitimate for the philosophy of science?

7

Science and Gender

This chapter is meant to present a different view of science and the philosophy of science, a feminist one. This is not to say that there is one feminist view on every topic within the philosophy of science. And it certainly is not to say that women in science and the philosophy of science all adhere to one party line. In fact, there are enough differing ideas within feminist philosophy of science that this chapter tries only to present a small selection from among those views.

One goal of feminist philosophy of science—indeed, feminist philosophy in general—is to make it plain where gender bias may be involved. What is gender bias? It is an unconsciously slanted look at the world that is at least in part a function of one's gender. (On some views, it is not really unconscious in the sense of extremely difficult to bring to consciousness.) Gender refers to the behaviors, roles, and expectations that society places on each of us on the basis of our bodies. Gender differs from sex, which classifies nearly all bodies into one of two categories. Sex is a biological trait, whereas gender is a social construction. Gender is not just looking a certain way. It is not just the result of one's genes or chromosomes or one's secondary sexual characteristics. Nor is it just with whom or how one acts sexually. Feminist philosophers of science ask (among other questions), "Does gender affect science in important ways?"

Feminists, such as Helen Longino, point out that science may be both gender-biased and "good" because there are times when the bias does not affect either the gathering of data or the reasoning from data to conclusions. Moreover, if one were to find science full of values where before it had been thought to be free of values, one might merely redefine *objective* to take this finding into account. In this way, science would not be as objective as originally thought but still might be more objective than other disciplines.

One of the tools of feminist philosophy is psychology. Given the characterization of gender, this should not be surprising. Gender bias itself results from a mix of psychological, economic, sociological, and political phenomena. It takes expertise in each of these areas to find it. Philosophical analysis alone—based as it is on the logic of concepts—will not do the job that feminists want done. A feminist would find it crucial to ask whether there is a connection between the traditional philosophy of science and the general psychological makeup of men. Feminists would expect to find a clear correlation; traditional philosophy would declare that correlation irrelevant. Here the feminist approach and the traditional approach would bump heads. This issue of relevance is the issue of whether there is and ought to be a distinction between the context of discovery and the context of justification. Obviously, feminists will deny the legitimacy of the distinction.

Just as there is no one philosophy of science and no one positivist philosophy of science, so there is no one feminist philosophy of science. We will concentrate on three claims made by some feminist philosophers of science.

1. Our scientific picture of the world is less an accurate portrayal of the world than it is a look at the world through the eyes of men.

2. The way that women tend to look at the world—even when studying it—is different, if only in emphasis, from the way that men tend to look at the world.

3. Male-dominated science is hostile to women, making it exceptionally difficult for women to succeed as scientists.

These views are consistent with a Kuhnian approach to understanding science. Feminist philosophers of science, as has been noted, are like Kuhn in denying the legitimacy of the distinction between the context of discovery and the context of justification. Scientific development can be understood only by dropping the two-contexts distinction. Ruth Ginzberg, in the article we will read, stresses Kuhn's talk of different paradigms creating different and incommensurable worlds. Alison Jaggar, whose work we will also read, agrees with Kuhn's dismissal of the two-contexts distinction because without it, emotions and feelings can be allowed into science. The general point is that when social relations, including those that lead to discovery, are excluded from the philosophy of science, the resulting understanding of science by philosophy is minimal. Leaving out the social nature of science is characteristic of most philosophy of science before the writings of Kuhn.

Note that May Brodbeck (in Chapter 2) stood firm on holding the two-contexts distinction and that Paul Feyerabend (in Chapter 3) insisted that science must be understood as a social phenomenon. This makes it clear that none of these views about science are limited by gender alone.

ALISON JAGGAR, "THE MYTH OF DISPASSIONATE INVESTIGATION"

Laudan represents a current reaction to the views of Feyerabend and to some others who agree with Feyerabend that the contention that science is objective is biased. Where Laudan is trying to find something of worth in the traditional view of science as objective, Jaggar takes what appears to be an extremist view on the nature of science. Looking at science as a feminist, she sees a male-dominated institution. She concludes that science has never been and could not be free of emotion. She mentions the work of Barbara McClintock (1902–1993).

McClintock often described herself as having a feeling for the organisms she researched. It was this feeling—a kind of empathy—that allowed her insights beyond those of her colleagues. Thus it was that she discovered the fact that genes "jump," or move on the chromosome. Genes are not positionally stable, as everyone had thought. Her views were at first rejected, but she turned out to be correct. (There will be more on McClintock in this chapter, in the selection by Keller.) Jaggar uses this example to support her contentions that emotions can direct our attention to new investigations and thence to new pictures of the world.

Jaggar interprets the positivist distinction between the logic of discovery and the logic of justification as a tool for keeping emotion out of science. For the positivists, science is what is found by examining the logic of justification. There, emotion is outlawed. Of course, we will find emotion in the logic (context) of discovery, for here "anything goes." Thus Jaggar will reject the two-contexts distinction. She appeals to Kuhn's arguments to do this.

With the two-contexts distinction eliminated, emotions can be considered part of science. What do we gain by doing this? Jaggar's claim is that we get a truer look at science because science, like all human activities, is shot through with emotions. How could it not be? Given that it is, we should not pretend that the two are mutually inconsistent.

Jaggar takes a feminist turn by pointing out that the two-contexts distinction, and its corollary that emotion and knowledge are mutually exclusive, serves a very important purpose. After all, who is traditionally considered intrinsically emotional and hence incapable of gaining true knowledge? Women. This is not surprising given who made the rules—men. Jaggar refers to this set of beliefs about emotion, the two contexts, and the emotional nature of women as ideological. In other words, these are beliefs that people want to hold whether they are defendable or not. Feyerabend used the same sort of language when he discussed science.

Jaggar goes further when she argues that the very use of words like *angry* or *sad* means that we are applying the standards of society because those standards govern how those words are used, what they mean, and what they presuppose. Social norms are therefore built into our vocabulary. Social norms always serve to perpetuate the people in power. Who has always been in power? Men. To hide this, many emotional responses are considered part of our character. This means that an unconventional response is unnatural, perhaps even indicative of a psychological problem.

These unconventional emotions or feelings Jaggar calls "outlaw emotions." They just do not fit with what we have been taught we should be feeling. They make us uncomfortable. Jaggar emphasizes that our response to such feelings is socially imbued and serves the interests of the men in power. Such unconventional emotions are needed to begin critical evaluations of what everyone else accepts. In Kuhnian terms, a revolutionary scientist will experience outlaw emotions.

Just as a Kuhnian revolution leaves us with a new way to picture the world, so Jaggar claims that outlaw emotions can lead us to see the world differently. But which are the appropriate outlaw emotions? After all, some emotions are so odd that even Jaggar would admit that they are pathological. Her answer is that the "right" outlaw emotions are those that, when acted on, lead to a just society. This is because outlaw emotions are often caused by injustice. Who is most likely to have such correct outlaw emotions? Whoever is oppressed by the people in power.

Jaggar has in mind, of course, women. So in her view, we should expect women scientists to be in conflict with their male counterparts over such emotions. More than that, Jaggar would expect women scientists with outlaw emotions as part of their science to turn out to be correct more often than their male colleagues would believe. Remember her example of McClintock. Jaggar would claim that McClintock's feeling for the organism was an outlaw emotion that led her to the truth, a truth to which the more traditional geneticists were blinded.

In brief, Jaggar reiterates a standard feminist claim that challenges the very heart of scientific objectivity: There is an interaction between who and what we are as people and how we understand the world.

The Myth of Dispassionate Investigation

ALISON JAGGAR

... Western epistemology has tended to view emotion with suspicion and even hostility.[1] This derogatory western attitude towards emotion, like the earlier western contempt for sensory observation, fails to recognize that emotion, like sensory perception, is necessary to human survival. Emotions prompt us to act appropriately, to approach some people and situations and to avoid others, to caress or cuddle, fight or flee. Without emotion, human life would be unthinkable. Moreover, emotions have an intrinsic as well as an instrumental value. Although not all emotions are enjoyable or

Reprinted from Alison Jaggar, "Love and Knowledge: Emotion in Feminist Epistemology," *Inquiry* 32 (1989): 161–176, with permission from Scandinavian University Press, Oslo, Norway.

even justifiable, as we shall see, life without any emotion would be life without any meaning.

Within the context of western culture, however, people often have been encouraged to control or even suppress their emotions. Consequently, it is not unusual for people to be unaware of their emotional state or to deny it to themselves and others. This lack of awareness, especially combined with a neopositivist understanding of emotion that construes it just as a feeling of which one is aware, lends plausibility to the myth of dispassionate investigation. But lack of awareness of emotions certainly does not mean that emotions are not present subconsciously or unconsciously, or that subterranean emotions do not exert a continuing influence on people's articulated values and observations, thoughts and actions.[2]

Within the positivist tradition, the influence of emotion usually is seen only as distorting or impeding observation or knowledge. Certainly it is true that contempt, disgust, shame, revulsion, or fear may inhibit investigation of certain situations or phenomena. Furiously angry or extremely sad people often seem quite unaware of their surroundings or even their own conditions; they may fail to hear or may systematically misinterpret what other people say. People in love are notoriously oblivious to many aspects of the situation around them.

In spite of these examples, however, positivist epistemology recognizes that the role of emotion in the construction of knowledge is not invariably deleterious and that emotions may make a valuable contribution to knowledge. But the positivist tradition will allow emotion to play only the role of suggesting hypotheses for emotion. Emotions are allowed this because the so-called logic of discovery sets no limits on the idiosyncratic methods that investigators may use for generating hypotheses.

When hypotheses are to be tested, however, positivist epistemology imposes the much stricter logic of justification. The core of this logic is replicability, a criterion believed capable of eliminating or cancelling out what are conceptualized as emotional as well as evaluative biases on the part of individual investigators. The conclusions of western science thus are presumed "objective," precisely in the sense that they are uncontaminated by the supposedly "subjective" values and emotions that might bias individual investigators (Nagel 1968: 33–4).

But if, as has been argued, the positivist distinction between discovery and justification is not viable, then such a distinction is incapable of filtering out values in science. For example, although such a split, when built into the western scientific method, generally is successful in neutralizing the idiosyncratic or unconventional values of individual investigators, it has been argued that it does not, indeed cannot, eliminate generally accepted social values. These values are implicit in the identification of the problems that are considered worthy of investigation, in the selection of the hypotheses that are considered worthy of testing, and in the solutions to the problems that are considered worthy of acceptance. The science of past centuries provides ample evidence of the influence of prevailing social values, whether seventeenth century atomistic physics (Merchant 1980) or nineteenth century competitive interpretations of natural selection (Young 1985).

Of course, only hindsight allows us to identify clearly the values that shaped the science of the past and thus to reveal the formative influence on science of pervasive emotional attitudes, attitudes that typically went unremarked at the time because they were shared so generally. For instance, it is now glaringly evident that contempt for (and perhaps fear of) people of color is implicit in nineteenth century anthropology's interpretations and even constructions of anthropological facts. Because we are closer to them, however, it is harder for us to see how certain emotions, such as sexual possessiveness or the need to dominate others, currently are accepted as guiding principles in twentieth century sociobiology or even defined as part of reason within political theory and economics (Quinby 1986).

Values and emotions enter into the science of the past and the present not only on the level of scientific practice but also on the metascientific level, as answers to various questions: What is science? How should it be practiced? And what is the status of scientific investigation versus nonscientific modes of enquiry? For instance, it is claimed with increasing frequency that the modern western conception of science, which identifies knowledge with power and views it as a weapon for dominating nature, reflects the imperialism, racism and misogyny of the societies that created it. Several feminist theorists have argued that modern epistemology itself may be viewed as an expression of certain emotions alleged to be especially characteristic of males in certain periods, such as separation anxiety and paranoia (Flax 1983; Bordo 1987) or an obsession with control and fear of contamination (Scheman 1985; Schott 1988).

Positivism views values and emotions as alien invaders that must be repelled by a stricter application of the scientific method. If the forgoing claims are correct, however, the scientific method and even its positivist construals themselves incorporate values and emotions. Moreover, such an incorporation seems a necessary feature of all knowledge and conceptions of knowledge. Therefore, rather than repressing emotion in epistemology it is necessary to rethink the relation between knowledge and emotion and construct a conceptual model that demonstrates the mutually constitutive rather than oppositional relation between reason and emotion. Far from precluding the possibility of reliable knowledge, emotion as well as value must be shown as necessary to such knowledge. Despite its classical antecedents and like the ideal of disinterested enquiry, the ideal of dispassionate enquiry is an impossible dream, but a dream nonetheless, or perhaps a myth that has exerted enormous influence on western epistemology. Like all myths, it is a form of ideology that fulfills certain social and political functions.

THE IDEOLOGICAL FUNCTION OF THE MYTH

So far, I have spoken very generally of people and their emotions, as though everyone experienced similar emotions and dealt with them in similar ways. It is an axiom of feminist theory, however, that all generalizations about "people" are suspect. The divisions in our society are so deep, particularly the divisions of race, class, and gender, that many feminist theorists would claim that talk about people in general is ideologically dangerous because such talk obscures the fact that no one is simply a person but instead is constituted fundamentally by race, class and gender. Race, class, and gender shape every aspect of our lives, and our emotional constitution is not excluded. Recognizing this helps us to see more clearly the political functions of the myth of the dispassionate investigator.

Feminist theorists have pointed out that the western tradition has not seen everyone as equally emotional. Instead, reason has been associated with members of dominant political, social, and cultural groups and emotion with members of subordinate groups. Prominent among those subordinate groups in our society are people of color, except for supposedly "inscrutable orientals," and women.[3]

Although the emotionality of women is a familiar cultural stereotype, its grounding is quite shaky. Women appear to be more emotional than men because they, along with some groups of people of color, are permitted and even required to express emotion more openly. In contemporary western culture, emotionally inexpressive women are suspect as not being real women[4] whereas men who express their emotions freely are suspected of being homosexual or in some other way deviant from the masculine ideal. Modern western men, in contrast with Shakespeare's heroes, for instance, are required to present a facade of coolness, lack of excitement, even boredom, to express emotion only rarely and then for relatively trivial events, such as sporting occasions, where the emotions

expressed are acknowledged to be drama-
tized and so are not taken entirely seriously.
Thus, women in our society form the main
group allowed or even expected to feel
emotion. A woman may cry in the face of
disaster, and a man of color may gesticulate,
but a white man merely sets his jaw.[5]

White men's control of their emotional
expression may go to the extremes of
repressing their emotions, failing to develop
emotionally, or even losing the capacity to
experience many emotions. Not uncommonly, these men are unable to identify
what they are feeling, and even they may be
surprised, on occasion, by their own apparent lack of emotional response to a situation,
such as a death, where emotional reaction is
perceived appropriate. In some married cou-
ples, the wife implicitly is assigned the job of
feeling emotion for both of them. White, col-
lege-educated men increasingly enter therapy in order to learn how to "get in touch
with" their emotions, a project other men
may ridicule as weakness. In therapeutic situations, men may learn that they are just as
emotional as women but less adept at identifying their own or others' emotions. In consequence, their emotional development may
be relatively rudimentary; this may lead to
moral rigidity or insensitivity. Paradoxically,
men's lacking awareness of their own emotional responses frequently results in their
being more influenced by emotion rather
than less.

Although there is no reason to suppose
that the thoughts and actions of women are
any more influenced by emotion than the
thoughts and actions of men, the stereotypes
of cool men and emotional women continue
to flourish because they are confirmed by an
uncritical daily experience. In these circumstances, where there is a differential assign-
ment of reason and emotion, it is easy to see
the ideological function of the myth of the
dispassionate investigator. It functions, obviously, to bolster the epistemic authority of

the currently dominant groups, composed
largely of white men, and to discredit the
observations and claims of the currently
subordinate groups including, of course, the
observations and claims of many people of
color and women. The more forcefully and
vehemently the latter groups express their
observations and claims, the more emotional
they appear and so the more easily they are
discredited. The alleged epistemic authority
of the dominant groups then justifies their
political authority.

The previous section of this paper argued
that dispassionate inquiry was a myth. This
section has shown that the myth promotes a
conception of epistemological justification
vindicating the silencing of those, especially
women, who are defined culturally as the
bearers of emotion and so are perceived as
more "subjective," biased, and irrational. In
our present social context, therefore, the ideal
of the dispassionate investigator is a classist,
racist, and especially masculinist myth.[6]

EMOTIONAL HEGEMONY AND
EMOTIONAL SUBVERSION

As we have seen already, mature human
emotions are neither instinctive nor biologically determined, although they may have
developed out of presocial, instinctive
responses. Like everything else that is
human, emotions in part are socially constructed; like all social constructs, they are
historical products, bearing the marks of the
society that constructed them. Within the
very language of emotion, in our basic definitions and explanations of what it is to feel
pride or embarrassment, resentment or contempt, cultural norms and expectations are
embedded. Simply describing ourselves as
angry, for instance, presupposes that we
view ourselves as having been wronged,
victimized by the violation of some social
norm. Thus, we absorb the standards and
values of our society in the very process of

learning the language of emotion, and those standards and values are built into the foundation of our emotional constitution.

Within a hierarchical society, the norms and values that predominate tend to serve the interest of the dominant groups. Within a capitalist, white supremacist, and male-dominant society, the predominant values will tend to be those that serve the interests of rich white men. Consequently, we are all likely to develop an emotional constitution that is quite inappropriate for feminism. Whatever our color, we are likely to feel what Irving Thalberg has called "visceral racism"; whatever our sexual orientation, we are likely to be homophobic; whatever our class, we are likely to be at least somewhat ambitious and competitive; whatever our sex, we are likely to feel contempt for women. The emotional responses may be rooted in us so deeply that they are relatively impervious to intellectual argument and may recur even when we pay lip service to changed intellectual convictions.[7]

By forming our emotional constitution in particular ways, our society helps to ensure its own perpetuation. The dominant values are implicit in responses taken to be precultural or acultural, our so-called gut responses. Not only do these conservative responses hamper and disrupt our attempts to live in or prefigure alternative social forms but also, and insofar as we take them to be natural responses, they limit our vision theoretically. For instance, they limit our capacity for outrage; they either prevent us from despising or encourage us to despise; they lend plausibility to the belief that greed and domination are inevitable human motivations; in sum, they blind us to the possibility of alternative ways of living.

This picture may seem at first to support the positivist claim that the intrusion of emotion only disrupts the process of seeking knowledge and distorts the results of that process. The picture, however, is not complete; it ignores the fact that people do not always experience the conventionally acceptable emotions. They may feel satisfaction rather than embarrassment when their leaders make fools of themselves. They may feel resentment rather than gratitude for welfare payments and hand-me-downs. They may be attracted to forbidden modes of sexual expression. They may feel revulsion for socially sanctioned ways of treating children or animals. In other words, the hegemony that our society exercises over people's emotional constitution is not total.

People who experience conventionally unacceptable, or what I call "outlaw," emotions often are subordinated individuals who pay a disproportionately high price for maintaining the status quo. The social situation of such people makes them unable to experience the conventionally prescribed emotions: for instance, people of color are more likely to experience anger than amusement when a racist joke is recounted, and women subjected to male sexual banter are less likely to be flattered than uncomfortable or even afraid.

When unconventional emotional responses are experienced by isolated individuals, those concerned may be confused, unable to name their experience; they may even doubt their own sanity. Women may come to believe that they are "emotionally disturbed" and that the embarrassment or fear aroused in them by male sexual innuendo is prudery or paranoia. When certain emotions are shared or validated by others, however, the basis exists for forming a subculture defined by perceptions, norms, and values that systematically oppose the prevailing perceptions, norms, and values. By constituting the basis for such a subculture, outlaw emotions may be politically (because epistemologically) subversive.

Outlaw emotions are distinguished by their incompatibility with the dominant perceptions and values, and some, though certainly not all, of these outlaw emotions are potentially or actually feminist emotions. Emotions become feminist when they incorporate feminist perceptions and values, just as emotions are sexist or racist when they incorporate sexist or racist perceptions and values. For example, anger becomes feminist anger when it involves the perception that the persistent importuning endured by one woman is a single instance of a widespread pattern of sexual harassment, and pride becomes feminist pride when it is evoked by realizing that a certain person's achievement was possible only because that individual overcame specifically gendered obstacles to success.[8]

Outlaw emotions stand in a dialectical relation to critical social theory: at least some are necessary to developing a critical perspective on the world, but they also presuppose at least the beginnings of such a perspective. Feminists need to be aware of how we can draw on some of our outlaw emotions in constructing feminist theory and also of how the increasing sophistication of feminist theory can contribute to the reeducation, refinement, and eventual reconstruction of our emotional constitution.

OUTLAW EMOTIONS AND FEMINIST THEORY

The most obvious way in which feminist and other outlaw emotions can help in developing alternatives to prevailing conceptions of reality is by motivating new investigations. This is possible because, as we saw earlier, emotions may be long-term as well as momentary; it makes sense to say that someone continues to be shocked or saddened by a situation, even if she is at the moment laughing heartily. As we have seen already, theoretical investigation is always purposeful, and observation is always selective. Feminist emotions provide a political motivation for investigation and so help to

determine the selection of problems as well as the method by which they are investigated. Susan Griffin makes the same point when she characterizes feminist theory as following "a direction determined by pain, and trauma, and compassion and outrage" (Griffin 1979: 31).

As well as motivating critical research, outlaw emotions may also enable us to perceive the world differently than we would from its portrayal in conventional descriptions. They may provide the first indications that something is wrong with the way alleged facts have been constructed, with accepted understandings of how things are. Conventionally unexpected or inappropriate emotions may precede our conscious recognition that accepted descriptions and justifications often conceal as much as reveal the prevailing state of affairs. Only when we reflect on our initially puzzling irritability, revulsion, anger, or fear, may we bring to consciousness our "gut-level" awareness that we are in a situation of coercion, cruelty, injustice, or danger. Thus, conventionally inexplicable emotions, particularly, though not exclusively, those experienced by women, may lead us to make subversive observations that challenge dominant conceptions of the status quo. They may help us to realize that what are taken generally to be facts have been constructed in a way that obscures the reality of subordinated people, especially women's reality.

But why should we trust the emotional responses of women and other subordinated groups? How can we determine which outlaw emotions we should endorse or encourage and which reject? In what sense can we say that some emotional responses are more appropriate than others? What reason is there for supposing that certain alternative perceptions of the world, perceptions informed by outlaw emotions, are to be preferred to perceptions informed by conventional emotions? Here I can indicate only the general direction of an answer, whose full elaboration must await another occasion.[9]

I suggest that emotions are appropriate if they are characteristic of a society in which all humans (and perhaps some nonhuman life too) thrive, or if they are conducive to establishing such a society. For instance, it is appropriate to feel joy when we are developing or exercising our creative powers, and it is appropriate to feel anger and perhaps disgust in those situations where humans are denied their full creativity or freedom. Similarly, it is appropriate to feel fear if those capacities are threatened in us.

This suggestion obviously is extremely vague and may even verge on the tautological. How can we apply it in situations where there is disagreement over what is or is not disgusting or exhilarating or unjust? Here I appeal to a claim for which I have argued elsewhere: the perspective on reality that is available from the standpoint of the oppressed, which in part at least is the standpoint of women, is a perspective that offers a less partial and distorted and therefore more reliable view (Jaggar 1983: chap. 11). Oppressed people have a kind of epistemological privilege insofar as they have easier access to this standpoint and therefore a better chance of ascertaining the possible beginnings of a society in which all could thrive. For this reason, I would claim that the emotional responses of oppressed people in general, and often of women in particular, are more likely to be appropriate than the emotional responses of the dominant class. That is, they are more likely to incorporate reliable appraisals of situations.

Even in contemporary science, where the ideology of dispassionate inquiry is almost overwhelming, it is possible to discover a few examples that seem to support the claim that certain emotions are more appropriate than others in both a moral and epistemological sense. For instance, Hilary Rose claims that women's practice of caring, even though warped by its containment in the alienated context of a coercive sexual division of labor, nevertheless has generated more accurate and less oppressive understandings of women's bodily functions, such as menstruation (Rose 1983). Certain emotions may be both morally appropriate and epistemologically advantageous in approaching the nonhuman and even the inanimate world. Jane Goodall's scientific contribution to our understanding of chimpanzee behavior seems to have been made possible only by her amazing empathy with or even love for these animals (Goodall 1986). In her study of Barbara McClintock, Evelyn Fox Keller describes McClintock's relation to the objects of her research—grains of maize and their genetic properties—as a relation of affection, empathy and "the highest form of love: love that allows for intimacy without the annihilation of difference." She notes that McClintock's "vocabulary is consistently a vocabulary of affection, of kinship, of empathy" (Keller 1984: 164). Examples like these prompt Hilary Rose to assert that a feminist science of nature needs to draw on heart as well as hand and brain.

SOME IMPLICATIONS OF RECOGNIZING THE EPISTEMIC POTENTIAL OF EMOTION

Accepting that appropriate emotions are indispensible to reliable knowledge does not mean, of course, that uncritical feeling may be substituted for supposedly dispassionate investigation. Nor does it mean that the emotional responses of women and other members of the underclass are to be trusted without question. Although our emotions are epistemologically indispensable, they are not epistemologically indisputable. Like all our faculties, they may be misleading, and their data, like all data, are always subject to reinterpretation and revision. Because emotions are not presocial, physiological responses to unequivocal situations, they are open to challenge on various grounds. They may be dishonest or self-deceptive, they may incorporate inaccurate or partial perceptions, or they may be constituted by oppressive values. Accepting the indispensability of appropriate emotions to knowledge means no more (and no less) than that discordant emotions should be attended to seriously and respectfully rather than condemned, ignored, discounted, or suppressed.

Just as appropriate emotions may contribute to the development of knowledge so the growth of knowledge may contribute to the development of appropriate emotions. For instance, the powerful insights of feminist theory often stimulate new emotional responses to past and present situations. Inevitably, our emotions are affected by the knowledge that the women on our faculty are paid systematically less than the men, that one girl in four is subjected to sexual abuse from heterosexual men in her own family, and that few women reach orgasm in heterosexual intercourse. We are likely to feel different emotions towards older women or people of color as we reevaluate our standards of sexual attractiveness or acknowledge that Black is beautiful. The new emotions evoked by feminist insights are likely in turn to stimulate further feminist observations and insights, and these may generate new directions in both theory and political practice. There is a continuous feedback loop between our emotional constitution and our theorizing such that each continually modifies the other and is in principle inseparable from it.

The ease and speed with which we can reeducate our emotions unfortunately is not great. Emotions are only partially within our control as individuals. Although affected by new information, they are habitual responses not quickly unlearned. Even when we come to believe consciously that our fear or shame or revulsion is unwar-

ranted, we may still continue to experience emotions inconsistent with our conscious politics. We may still continue to be anxious for male approval, competitive with our comrades and sisters and possessive with our lovers. These unwelcome, because apparently inappropriate, emotions should not be suppressed or denied; instead, they should be acknowledged and subjected to critical scrutiny. The persistence of such recalcitrant emotions probably demonstrates how fundamentally we have been constituted by the dominant world view, but it may also indicate superficiality or other inadequacy in our emerging theory and politics.[10] We can only start from where we are—beings who have been created in a cruelly racist, capitalist, and male-dominated society that has shaped our bodies and our minds, our perceptions, our values and our emotions, our language and our systems of knowledge.

The alternative epistemological model that I suggest displays the continuous interaction between how we understand the world and who we are as people. It shows how our emotional responses to the world change as we conceptualize it differently and how our changing emotional responses then stimulate us to new insights. The model demonstrates the need for theory to be self-reflexive, to focus not only on the outer world but also on ourselves and our relation to that world, to examine critically our social location, our actions, our values, our perceptions and our emotions. The model also shows how feminist and other critical social theories are indispensable psychotherapeutic tools because they provide some insights necessary to a full understanding of our emotional constitution. Thus, the model explains how the reconstruction of knowledge is inseparable from the reconstruction of ourselves.

A corollary of the reflexivity of feminist and other critical theory is that it requires a

ALISON JAGGAR

much broader construal than positivism accepts of the process of theoretical investigation. In particular, it requires acknowledging that a necessary part of theoretical process is critical self-examination. Time spent in analyzing emotions and uncovering their sources should be viewed, therefore, neither as irrelevant to theoretical investigation nor even as a prerequisite for it; it is not a kind of clearing of the emotional decks, "dealing with" our emotions so that they will not influence our thinking. Instead, we must recognize that our efforts to reinterpret and refine our emotions are necessary to our theoretical investigation, just as our efforts to reeducate our emotions are necessary to our political activity. Critical reflection on emotion is not a self-indulgent substitute for political analysis and political action. It is itself a kind of political theory and political practice, indispensable for an adequate social theory and social transformation.

Finally, the recognition that emotions play a vital part in developing knowledge enlarges our understanding of women's claimed epistemic advantage. We can now see that women's subversive insights owe much to women's outlaw emotions, themselves appropriate responses to the situations of women's subordination. In addition to their propensity to experience outlaw emotions, at least on some level, women are relatively adept at identifying such emotions, in themselves and others, in part because of their social responsibility for caretaking, including emotional nurturance. It is true that women (like all subordinated peoples, especially those who must live in close proximity with their masters) often engage in emotional deception and even self-deception as the price of their survival. Even so, women may be less likely than other subordinated groups to engage in denial or suppression of outlaw emotions. Women's work of emotional nurturance has

required them to develop a special acuity in recognizing hidden emotions and in understanding the genesis of those emotions. This emotional acumen can now be recognized as a skill in political analysts and validated as giving women a special advantage both in understanding the mechanisms of domination and in envisioning freer ways to live.

CONCLUSION

The claim that emotion is vital to systematic knowledge is only the most obvious contrast between the conception of theoretical investigation that I have sketched here and the conception provided by positivism. For instance, the alternative approach emphasizes that what we identify as emotion is a conceptual abstraction from a complex process of human activity that also involves acting, sensing, and evaluating. This proposed account of theoretical construction demonstrates the simultaneous necessity for and interdependence of faculties that our culture has abstracted and separated from each other: emotion and reason, evaluation and perception, observation and action. The model of knowing suggested here is non-hierarchical and antifoundationalist; instead, it is appropriately symbolized by the radical feminist metaphor of the upward spiral. Emotions are neither more basic than observation, reason, or action in building theory, nor secondary to them. Each of these human faculties reflects an aspect of human knowing inseparable from the other aspects. Thus, to borrow a famous phrase from a Marxian context, the development of each of these faculties is a necessary condition for the development of all.

In conclusion, it is interesting to note that acknowledging the importance of emotion for knowledge is not an entirely novel suggestion within the western epistemological tradition. The archrationalist, Plato himself, came to accept in the end that knowledge required a (very purified form of) love. It may be no accident that in the *Symposium* Socrates learns this lesson from Diotima, the wise woman!

NOTES

1. The positivist attitude toward emotion, which requires that ideal investigators be both disinterested and dispassionate, may be a modern variant of older traditions in western philosophy that recommended that people seek to minimize their emotional responses to the world and develop instead their powers of rationality and pure contemplation.

2. It is now widely accepted that the suppression and repression of emotion has damaging if not explosive consequences. There is general acknowledgement that no one can avoid at some time experiencing emotions she or he finds unpleasant, and there is also increasing recognition that the denial of such emotions is likely to result in hysterical disorders of thought and behavior, in projecting one's own emotions on to others, in displacing them to inappropriate situations, or in psychosomatic ailments. Psychotherapy, which purports to help individuals recognize and "deal with" their emotions, has become an enormous industry, especially in the U.S. In much conventional psychotherapy, however, emotions still are conceived as feelings or passions, "subjective" disturbances that afflict individuals or interfere with their capacity for rational thought and action. Different therapies, therefore, have developed a wide variety of techniques for encouraging people to "discharge" or "vent" their emotions, just as they would drain an abscess. Once emotions have been discharged or vented, they are supposed to be experienced less intensely, or even to vanish entirely, and consequently to exert less influence on individuals' thoughts and actions. This approach to psychotherapy clearly demonstrates its kinship with the "folk" theory of anger mentioned earlier, and it equally clearly retains the traditional western assumption that emotion is inimical to rational thought and action. Thus, such approaches fail to challenge and indeed provide covert support for the view that "objective" knowers are not only disinterested but also dispassionate.

3. E. V. Spelman (1982) illustrates this point with a quotation from the well known contemporary philosopher, R. S. Peters, who wrote "we speak of emotional outbursts, reactions, upheavals and women" (*Proceedings of the Aristotelian Society*, New Series, vol. 62).

4. It seems likely that the conspicuous absence of emotion shown by Mrs. Thatcher is a deliberate strategy she finds necessary to counter the public perception of women as too emotional for political leadership. The strategy results in her being perceived as a formidable leader, but as an Iron Lady rather than a real woman. Ironically, Neil Kinnock, leader of the British Labour Party and Thatcher's main opponent in the 1987 General Election, was able to muster considerable public support through television commercials portraying him in the stereotypically feminine role of caring about the unfortunate victims of Thatcher economics. Ultimately, however, this support was not sufficient to destroy public confidence in Mrs. Thatcher's "masculine" competence and gain Kinnock the election.

5. On the rare occasions when a white man cries, he is embarrassed and feels constrained to apologize. The one exception to the rule that men should be emotionless is that they are allowed and often even expected to experience anger. Spelman (1982) points out that men's cultural permission to be angry bolsters their claim to authority.

6. Someone might argue that the viciousness of this myth was not a logical necessity. In the egalitarian society, where the concepts of reason and emotion were not gender-bound in the way they still are today, it might be argued that the ideal of the dispassionate investigator could be epistemologically beneficial. Is it possible that, in such socially and conceptually egalitarian circumstances, the myth of the dispassionate investigator could serve as a heuristic device, an ideal never to be realized in practice but nevertheless helping to minimize "subjectivity" and bias? My own view is that counterfactual myths rarely bring the benefits advertised and that this one is no exception. This myth fosters an equally mythical conception of pure truth and objectivity, quite independent of human interests or desires, and in this way it functions to disguise the inseparability of theory and practice, science and politics. Thus, it is part of an antidemocratic world view that mystifies the political dimension of knowledge and unwarrantedly circumscribes the arena of political debate.

7. Of course, the similarities in our emotional constitutions should not blind us to systematic differences. For instance, girls rather than boys are taught fear and disgust for spiders and snakes, affection for fluffy animals, and shame for their naked bodies. It is primarily, though not exclusively, men rather than women whose sexual responses are shaped by exposure to visual and sometimes violent pornography. Girls and women

are taught to cultivate sympathy for others; boys and men are taught to separate themselves emotionally from others. As I have noted already, more emotional expression is permitted for lower-class and some nonwhite men than for ruling-class men, perhaps because the expression of emotion is thought to expose vulnerability. Men of the upper classes learn to cultivate an attitude of condescension, boredom, or detached amusement. As we shall see shortly, differences in the emotional constitution of various groups may be epistemologically significant in so far as they both presuppose and facilitate different ways of perceiving the world.

8. A necessary condition for experiencing feminist emotions is that one already be a feminist in some sense, even if one does not consciously wear that label. But many women and some men, even those who would deny that they are feminist, still experience emotions compatible with feminist values. For instance, they may be angered by the perception that someone is being mistreated just because she is a woman, or they may take special pride in the achievement of a woman. If those who experience such emotions are unwilling to recognize them as feminist, their emotions are probably better described as potentially feminist or prefeminist emotions.

9. I owe this suggestion to Marcia Lind.

10. Within a feminist context, Bernice Fisher suggests that we focus particular attention on our emotions of guilt and shame as part of a critical reevaluation of our political ideals and our political practice (Fisher 1984).

REFERENCES

Bordo, Susan R. 1987. *The Flight to Objectivity: Essays on Cartesianism and Culture.* Albany: State University of New York Press.

Fisher, Berenice. 1984. "Guilt and Shame in the Women's Movement: The Radical Ideal of Action and Its Meaning for Feminist Intellectuals." *Feminist Studies* 10: 185–212.

Flax, Jane. 1983. "Political Philosophy and the Patriarchal Unconscious: A Psychoanalytic Perspective on Epistemology and Metaphysics." In *Discovering Reality: Feminist Perspectives on Epistemology, Metaphysics, Methodology and Philosophy of Science,* ed. Sandra Harding and Merrill Hintikka. Dordrecht, Netherlands: Reidel.

Goodall, Jane. 1986. *The Chimpanzees of Bombe: Patterns of Behavior.* Cambridge, MA: Harvard University Press.

Griffin, Susan. 1979. *Rape: The Power of Consciousness.* San Francisco: Harper & Row.

Jaggar, Alison M. 1983. *Feminist Politics and Human Nature.* Totowa, NJ: Rowman & Allanheld.

Keller, Evelyn Fox. 1984. *Gender and Science.* New Haven, CT: Yale University Press.

Merchant, Carolyn M. 1980. *The Death of Nature: Women, Ecology, and the Scientific Revolution.* New York: Harper & Row.

Nagel, Ernest. 1968. "The Subjective Nature of Social Subject Matter." In *Readings in the Philosophy of the Social Sciences,* ed. May Brodbeck. New York: Macmillan.

Quinby, Lee. 1986. Discussion following talk at Hobart and William Smith Colleges, April 1986.

Rose, Hilary. 1983. "Hand, Brain, and Heart: A Feminist Epistemology for the Natural Sciences." *Signs: Journal of Women in Culture and Society* 9, 1: 73–90.

Scheman, Naomi. 1985. "Women in the Philosophy Curriculum." Paper presented at the Annual Meeting of the Central Division of the American Philosophical Association, Chicago, April 1985.

Schott, Robin M. 1988. *Cognition and Eros: A Critique of the Kantian Paradigm.* Boston: Beacon Press.

Spelman, Elizabeth V. 1982. "Anger and Insubordination." Paper presented to the Midwestern Chapter of the Society for Women in Philosophy, Spring 1982.

Young, Robert M. 1985. *Darwin's Metaphor: Nature's Place in Victorian Culture.* Cambridge: Cambridge University Press.

RUTH GINZBERG, "UNCOVERING GYNOCENTRIC SCIENCE"

Just as Jaggar claimed that science has always included emotion, so Ginzberg claims that there has always been gynocentric science, science characterized by what is distinct to women. Androcentric science is science characteristic of what is distinct to men. The dichotomy between androcentric and gynocentric is not a sharp one. Some men hold gynocentric views, and some women hold androcentric views. One can hold a position that contains some of each. Androcentric science is pretty much science as we now have it. It is science as described by the positivists. As both Ginzberg and Longino make clear, it is very difficult to describe precisely what gynocentric science would be because our only experience of science has been androcentric. Why hasn't this been noticed? Ginzberg's answer is that men have decided what will count as science. She refers to this decision as a political one made by men. Like all political decisions, it is made to enforce the standards of the people in power. Ginzberg knows that politics is seen as the art of compromise. Compromise, however, makes sense only when there is some real sharing of power. So Ginzberg assumes that between the genders, there has been little or no such sharing. It has all been one-sided.

What has really been gynocentric science, men have called "art." This does not dismiss areas such as cooking or midwifery as unimportant. It does, however, allow them to be classified as value laden and so as enterprises not quite as trustworthy as sciences, which are supposedly value free. Rudner, as we will see in the next reading, challenges the view that science can be value free.

Ginzberg gives four reasons why we have not noticed gynocentric science:

1. The word *science* is not descriptive. It is meant to convey a positive value of approval. It is an "honorific title" more than a simple description. It is no wonder that it has been reserved for whatever is in the mainstream, something that gynocentric science would not be.

2. Historians of science, in general, have never considered the areas that Ginzberg calls gynocentric as science. Thus we have no literal written history of such activities' being called science. There is only oral history. And the tradition in history has been to ignore much that is recorded orally.

3. Women tend not to see the world as hierarchical. They do not arrange their knowledge in this way (the biological classifications of Linnaeus are hierarchies), nor do they arrange their relations with each other in this way. Again, the result just does not look like traditional science.

4. There are simple reasons of vested interest that gynocentric science is demeaned by being called "art." Ginzberg's best example is the wresting away of authority in childbirth from midwives by the new specialty of obstetrics.

In her use of the midwifery example, notice that she appeals to Kuhn's notion of incommensurability of paradigms. Also notice that she uses scientific facts to support her thesis. Her most vivid defense of midwifery as science is the extended analogy whereby she discusses the origin of what might be termed "eating science." One of the interesting implications of her view is that activities such as cooking and "homemaking" can be considered science. She goes so far as to suggest that gossip is a reasonable way to get information about the world and so can be considered to have a methodology. We might have to admit the science of gossiping; or perhaps make it a branch of epistemology.

Uncovering Gynocentric Science

RUTH GINZBERG

Feminist philosophers of science have produced an exciting array of works in the last several years, from critiques of androcentrism in traditional science to theories about what might constitute feminist science. I suggest here another possibility: that gynocentric science has existed all along, then the task of identifying a feminist alternative to androcentric science should be a suitable candidate for empirical investigation. Such empirical investigation could provide a solid ground for further theorizing about feminist science at a time when that solid ground is looking rather necessary.

Recent feminist critiques of science have documented a wide variety of forms of androcentrism in traditional Western science (Griffin 1980; Merchant 1980; Bleier 1984; Keller 1985; Harding 1986; Birke 1986; Bleier 1986). There have been some attempts made to define a gynocentric conception of science; Evelyn Fox Keller (1983, 1985) for example, has suggested that we might find clues about gynocentric science by examining the work of women scientists like Barbara McClintock. But many feminist philosophers of science, including Keller, are still at a loss when asked to define what a truly gynocentric alternative might look like. Ruth Bleier articulates the question that many of us struggle with: "[H]ow can we even begin to conceptualize science as non-masculine . . . when most of written civilization—our history, language, conceptual frameworks, literature—has been generated by men?" (Bleier 1986, 15). Some have suggested that we are not yet in a position to identify a fully articulated feminist successor science (Fee 1983; Harding 1986; Rose 1986). On a Kuhnian model of scientific paradigms, a successor science that would follow the current andro-Eurocentric paradigm could not be fully articulated at this time, partly because of incommensurability and partly because paradigms are never fully articulated even in their own fullest maturity (Kuhn 1970). I would like to toss yet another suggestion into the realm of discourse about feminist science in partial response to Bleier's question: the suggestion that there has been gynocentric science all along, but that we often fail to recognize it as gynocentric *science* because it traditionally has not been awarded the honorific label of "Science."

Taking a cue from so many other feminist inquiries, I would like to reexamine women's actual activities in order to discover clues about gynocentric science. My hunch is that if there is such a thing as gynocentric science, it is unlikely that it is just now beginning. I suspect that there is such a thing, and that it has been practiced throughout history—just as other gynocentric traditions have existed throughout history—but that the androcentric record-keepers have failed to notice or record it. In the same way that feminists are beginning to recover some of our artistic, political, spiritual and social traditions, I believe that we can now recover some of the scientific traditions of our foresisters by reviewing history with a feminist eye.

For a start, it seems important not to confine our review of history to those activities which have been officially labeled "Science" until now. As Feyerabend (1975) has argued "Science" is—at least in part—a political term. If Feyerabend is correct about this, and

From *Hypatia* 2, no. 3 (1987): 89–105. Courtesy of the author and *Hypatia*.

I am convinced that he is, then it is imperative that we look beyond the "official" histories to correct for the political factors working against women. As is typical of oppressed groups, much of women's activity has been outside of the mainstream of Western culture. But that doesn't mean that these activities weren't occurring, or that they weren't valuable, nor does it necessarily mean that they weren't science. It only means that they weren't the subject of favorable attention from the members of the dominant cultures. What I am suggesting is that there are women's activities that haven't been called "Science" for *political* reasons, even when those activities have been model examples of inquiry leading to knowledge of the natural world. So my partial answer to Bleier's question is that we must look outside of the histories, conceptual frameworks, literature, and possibly even the language, that have been generated by men.

The question, then, becomes that of how to begin. I like Keller's approach as a starting point: She has examined carefully the life and work of a woman scientist who *has* been acknowledged for her scientific work, but who was often seen as a bit "odd" or "incomprehensible." These are hallmarks of the sort of paradigmatic incommensurability described by Kuhn (1970), and should serve as clues about the possible existence of another scientific paradigm. In her biography of Barbara McClintock, Keller (1983, 201) points to such things as "a deep reverence for nature, a capacity for union with that which is to be known," and a sort of holism of approach as being thematic in McClintock's work. There are hints of this sort of theme as well in the work of Rachel Carson, who introduced the concept of ecology to the American public. Anticipating some of the recent, more overtly feminist critiques, Carson wrote in the early 1960's that "The 'control of nature' is a phrase conceived in arrogance, born of the Neanderthal

age of biology and philosophy, when it was supposed that nature exists for the convenience of man." Arguing that we were poisoning the entire planet with pesticides in our efforts to "control" insects rather than learning to live along side them, Carson urged the world to halt "the chemical barrage [which] has been hurled against the fabric of life" (Carson 1964, 261).

In fact some sort of ecology of interconnection is a common theme articulated in feminist conceptions of knowledge (Daly 1978; Rich 1979; Griffin 1980; Merchant 1980; Lorde 1984; Keller 1985; Bleier 1986; Belenky et al. 1986). In the work of both McClintock and Carson, this epistemology of interconnection is expressed through their careful attention to the dynamics of living systems as pieces of a larger and more awesome natural world which is constantly responding to, and responsive to, itself. As Haunani-Kay Trask has found in her analysis of other work by feminist writers, "their work reverberates with two themes: love (nurturance, care, need, sensitivity, relationship) and power (freedom, expression, creativity, generation, transformation)." These themes are what she had identified as "twin manifestations of the 'life force' " which she names "the feminist Eros" (Trask 1986, 86). We are now in a position to formulate an hypothesis: the hypothesis is that this "feminist Eros" will be an identifying landmark in the epistemology of gynocentric science. Yet while the examination of the work of women who have been recognized as scientists is exciting, it is also unsatisfying; we see only a small fraction of the work that women have done in investigating the world around them from their own perspectives. Following our hypothesis, and Keller's suggestion that a feminist conception of the erotic might yield a fundamentally different conception of science than the one that Plato bequeathed to us, it seems reasonable to suspect that gynocentric science in its natural habitat might already exist, looking somewhat different from androcentric science because of the different conception of the nature and position of the erotic with respect to epistemology (Keller 1985). It is this hitherto unrecognized science that I would like to begin uncovering here.

In searching through women's activities outside of those that have been formally bestowed the label of "Science," I have come to suspect that gynocentric science often has been called "art," as in the *art* of midwifery, or the *art* of cooking, or the *art* of home-making. Had these "arts" been androcentric activities, I have no doubt that they would have been called, respectively obstetrical *science*, food *science*, and family *social science*. Indeed as men have taken an interest in these subjects they have been renamed sciences—and, more importantly, they have been reconceived in the androcentric model of science. There is no question that all of these activities as defined and practiced by women have had important aesthetic, affective, social and erotic dimensions which androcentric science does not acknowledge as Scientific. But that is exactly what our hypothesis predicts for feminist science: that it will be less isolated from other aspects of our lives, less fetishized about individualism, more holistic, more nurturing, more concerned with relations than with objects, perhaps more dialectic, because of the nature and position of the erotic with respect to its epistemology. It might be that the presence of these aesthetic or affective components in gynocentric science underlies some of the reasons that the masculist guardians of Science have not recognized these activities as science, at least not as they were conceived and practiced by women.

GYNOCENTRIC SCIENCE IN ITS NATURAL HABITAT

In particular, I would like to suggest that we reexamine midwifery as a paradigm example of gynocentric science. This idea is not originally mine; in 1973 Ehrenreich and English suggested that the "magic" of the 16th Century European witch-healer and midwife "was the science of her time" (Ehrenreich and English 1973, 14). However by no means do I believe that midwifery is the only possible example of gynocentric science. For example, there are good reasons to believe that women's knowledge of food and nutrition historically had to include some fairly sophisticated knowledge of botany and ecosystems, as well as of human nutritional needs. This knowledge undoubtedly was accumulated as women worked in their capacities as the food, nutrition and health experts in a culture that had no pesticides, supermarkets or agricultural extension agents. Food production and preparation were largely women's provinces—and far from being mere social pastimes, they were indispensable to the sustenance of life. Without adequate knowledge of botany and of ecosystems, the life-sustaining gardens maintained primarily by women could have fallen victim to parasites, diseases and the depletion of soil nutrients. The food cultivated for humans would have been eaten by rabbits and deer and the genetic pool of the seed stock could have deteriorated through inbreeding; the concentrated plant populations in women's gardens would have been vulnerable to destruction by parasites and disease. Knowledge about the differences between edible and inedible plants, knowledge about the prevention of spoilage and food poisoning, knowledge about companion planting and crop rotation undoubtedly would have been part of the gynocentric science. One wonders whether food science would have gained the status of a science much sooner (and in a much different way) if women had been defining the sciences.

Pharmacology is another area in which there probably was a substantial tradition of gynocentric science. In his often quoted and equally often ignored remark, Paracelsus— the "father" of modern pharmacology— attributed his entire knowledge of pharmacology to the wise women of his community. Paracelsus is an enigma in the history of science; modern androcentric historians of science don't know what to make of his mysticism and his holistic approach to the natural world. In the typically androcentric reconstruction of Paracelsus' work, his "Scientific" writings are unbundled from his "Unscientific" writings and packaged separately as Science, though we know that Paracelsus himself objected to this abuse of his own work. Given that he attributed his knowledge of pharmacology to a gynocentric tradition, it might be useful to us to reexamine *all* of what he did say, including that which is often omitted for being "unscientific," perhaps with the idea in mind of gaining clues to what gynocentric science looked like in his time.

But I doubt if gynocentric science is all from eras of long ago. In the twentieth century, for example, the androcentric social sciences have been granted the status of sciences, but the wisdom shared between and among women about the social fabric of their communities is still sneeringly labeled "gossip." Recently, however Belenky *et al.* (1986) have suggested that gossip is a paradigm example of what they call "connected knowledge," a way of knowing that their research has found to be highly developed in some women. It would be interesting to investigate the idea that women's traditional vehicles of gossip—garden clubs, sewing circles, coffee klatches, baby showers and backyard fence discussions—actually are part of a gynocentric social science tradition which is oral and dialectic in nature. Another gynocentric field which has emerged in the last century is the field of home economics. Although this field has suffered from the attempts of androcentric

educational administrators to turn its academic niche into vocational classes in cooking and sewing for future housewives, home economists undoubtedly have been concerned with home-based *economics*, a branch of economics that studies labor and production in the home. Additionally, there has been a very definite resurgence of gynocentric midwifery in the United States arising out of the women's health movement in the early 1970's. Often working outside of, or in opposition to, the law, lay midwives have organized schools, held conferences, published books and practiced midwifery in a way quite reminiscent of the midwives of the 16th and 17th centuries—who carried out their work in spite of the threat of the accusation of witchcraft for doing so (Ehrenreich and English 1973; Lang 1972; Arms 1975; Rich 1976; Gaskin 1978).

WOMEN'S KNOWLEDGE AND GYNOCENTRIC SCIENCE

If I am correct that gynocentric science has existed all along, then there ought to be reasons that it has remained hidden to us, and I think that there are:

First, there is our training, which teaches us that "science" is work that is done by people who have been awarded the title of Scientist, either by an institution from which they received a degree, or by history. Neither history nor degree-awarding institutions have been willing to award the title of Scientist to those who do not practice traditionally androcentric Western science, so it is to be expected that anyone who is practicing a different sort of science will not be included on the lists of certified Scientists. If we suspect that gynocentric science will be different in kind from androcentric science, even based in a fundamentally different epistemology, then it should be no surprise that gynocentric science would not be recognized as Science, and that gynocentric scientists would not have been labeled Scientists either by institutions or by history.

A second reason that it is easy to overlook gynocentric science is that the work of women has always been invisible in the recorded histories of androcentric Western culture. We are all familiar with the phenomenon of considering women's work to be non-work, as in "She doesn't work; she's a homemaker." Occasionally women scientists such as Marie Curie do make it into the recorded histories of science, but that is because Curie's work was spectacular and individualistic in nature, fitting it well within the model of what men think scientists do. If we are able to make out a case for two distinctly different scientific traditions, an androcentric tradition and a gynocentric tradition, we must not fall into the trap of believing that the practitioners within each of these traditions have been strictly divided along gender lines. Curie's work, though the work of a woman, was part of the androcentric tradition; the work of McClintock, Carson and Paracelsus probably was partially within each of the two traditions, as all three of these scientists seem to have been "claimed" to one extent or another as practitioners of both. Norman Casserley, a man prosecuted by the state of California for practicing midwifery in the early 1970's, probably was working within the gynocentric tradition (Arms 1975). The factors that identify a scientist as a member of one or the other tradition would be based in epistemological bases for inquiry, methodology, problem selection and scientific community—not in gender or sex. But the point is the same: not only women's activities, but all gynocentric activities, have been ignored by the androcentric recorders of history.

The third reason I would like to suggest is that throughout history the gynocentric sciences have been conducted primarily as oral rather than as written traditions. The accumulated wisdom and knowledge of midwives, for example, has been transmitted orally through personal contact and experiential apprenticeships. Midwives have not had professional journals in which they published their findings; they have not had heroes or methodological theoreticians who wrote treaties, nor have they had professional associations which held conferences and published their proceedings, and so on. Since Western androcentric science places such a premium on the written transmission of "results," any activity that has not included a large written component automatically has been excluded from consideration as a science. This undoubtedly is not unrelated to the fact that until very recently in Western history, literacy was much more available to White middle and upper class city-dwelling men than it was to women, the poor, Blacks, Native American tribes, rural families, and so on. Contrary to the usual assumption, which is that illiterate people don't do any science, I would like to propose that they probably do, but that their scientific traditions are oral and dialectic in nature rather than written.

A fourth reason, which is related to the third, is that women's knowledge, and its certification and transmission, may not have been organized hierarchically. The hierarchical organization of androcentric science was exquisitely described by Kuhn (1970) in his description of the socialization of young scientists into a scientific paradigm, and the rise and decline of particular paradigms. What he failed to realize, though Feyerabend (1975) did not, is that the hierarchical organization of both scientific knowledge and scientists is not a *necessary* feature of science, but rather simply a feature of Western science to which we have grown accustomed. While Feyerabend's epistemological anarchy might not provide a good description of the organization of gynocentric knowledge, it does provide the imagination with an alternative to the hierarchical organization of Western scientific knowledge.

A fifth reason, readily visible in the cases of midwifery and "gossip," is that there has been a concerted effort to suppress and discredit these bodies of gynocentric knowledge as being erroneous, based in superstition, and connected with harm or evil. More chillingly, history has recorded—although it attempts to forget—a violent campaign of torture and murder in the European witch-burnings which was both implicitly and explicitly directed at eradicating various gynocentric traditions (Ehrenreich and English 1973; Daly 1978; Edwards and Waldorf 1984). The influences of force and violence in establishing the Western andro-centric scientific tradition as the dominant one should not be underestimated.

SCIENCE AND BODILY FUNCTIONS

A look at the gynocentric approach and the androcentric approach to childbirth may provide a case study of one of the longest running disputes between—as Kuhn puts it—competing paradigms. The incommensurability between a gynocentric and an androcentric point of view is clearly visible in the differences between midwives' and scientific doctors' conceptions of childbirth. While medical science views childbirth as an abnormal state of health that has the potential to develop into a serious emergency, midwives have taken a much more holistic view of childbearing than has medical science; childbirth has been viewed as a normal physiological function during which a woman has an increased need for community support. This is not to say that midwives hold the naive view that life or health threatening emergencies never arise in the course of childbirth. Occasionally they do. But people also occasionally choke on food, drown in bathtubs, suffer strokes while playing golf and die of heart attacks during sex.

Science Fiction: Consider the following imaginary scenario: Suppose that, recognizing the many possible dangers associated with eating mishaps, the society decided to get much more scientific about the whole process. Federal funds were allocated for setting up elaborate hospital dining halls, and everyone who ate or served food was first urged, then required, to do so under proper medical supervision, "just in case." After all, one could never predict when a person might choke on, or have a sudden allergic reaction to their food. Additionally, experts in the eating sciences had become increasingly concerned about the lack of sterile conditions under which food was typically prepared in the home. Science had already well documented the large numbers of bacterial organisms found in virtually every home kitchen, and its increasing knowledge of the role of bacteria in disease made it obvious that untrained cooks, usually women, in bacteria-laden kitchens could no longer be trusted with the important responsibility of feeding the general population. There was particular concern about the health of children fed in the home. Young children could unknowingly be fed foods to which they might have a violent allergic reaction, and food scientists were alarmed about the numbers of children who were being exposed to the possibility of hives, asthma, lactose intolerance and digestive disturbances during home feeding. It was also suspected that Sudden Infant Death Syndrome and perhaps even some learning disabilities might be linked to unscientific feeding practices. But the dangers of home feeding were not confined to young children. It had long been recognized that eating practices were large factors in adult onset diabetes, heart disease, obesity, anorexia nervosa, diseases of the digestive system, cancer and possibly even drug abuse. At the hospital, each person could be carefully monitored for weight, calorie consumption, vitamin intake, and the percentage of fat and fiber in the diet. Special health problems could be discovered immediately, and each patient's blood and urine could be monitored regularly by the physicians who attended their eating sessions. High risk patients also might have their stomach secretions and peristaltic contractions electronically monitored during each meal at a central nursing station, and a computer controlled alarm would sound if any diner's digestive readings were outside the normal range for the type of meal that was being consumed. Some experts were even starting to suggest that all diners be electronically monitored while they were eating. If there was any indication of a developing eating problem, the patient would probably be admitted to the hospital for intravenous feeding until the problem had cleared up.

Science Reality: This is what androcentric science has done to childbirth.

HUMAN BIRTH: A REVIEW

As mammals, humans have always given birth to live young. Human pregnancy and childbirth, like eating, always have been biologically successful; that is, they have not been so hazardous or dangerous as to threaten the biological success of the human species. Unlike disease, which threatens the life or the fitness of individuals who suffer from it, pregnancy, childbirth and lactation normally do not threaten the fitness of either mother or child. If pregnancy, childbirth and lactation usually resulted in dead or unfit offspring, or in dead or incapacitated mothers, our species would not have survived. The fact is that the human species not only survives, it thrives with respect to reproduction, particularly when adequate nutrition, shelter and freedom from disease are available to mothers and their offspring. Studies have shown repeatedly that the vast majority of all human pregnancies would end with the birth of a healthy infant to a healthy woman even if she received no prenatal care or advice of any kind from any source (Lang 1972; Guttmacher 1973; Arms 1975; Rich 1976; Oxorn and Foote 1980). With social support, proper nutrition, adequate attention to physical fitness, and the elimination of habits detrimental to health such as smoking, drinking, and drug abuse, some studies have suggested that this figure may approach 95–98% or higher (Lang 1972; Guttmacher 1973; Arms 1975; Gaskin 1978; Edwards and Waldorf 1984). There is documented evidence, for example, that maternal mortality rates were approximately 0.4% in midwife-attended births in the American colonies during the eighteenth century— well before the introduction of modern antibiotics which could cure life-threatening infections (Wertz and Wertz 1979). Midwife-attended home births in Leslie County, KY, one of the poorest rural areas in Appalachia, with the highest birth rate in the country, had a maternal mortality rate of 0.091% from 1925–1955, compared to the national average of 0.34% for white women during the same time period (Arms 1975). This is consistent with the expected levels of health following birth in other species of mammals with typically single gestations. Often touted pseudo-explanations of Western women's difficulties in childbirth simply do not hold up under examination. Evolutionary biology, for example, does not support the idea that Western women could have "evolved" into a species with pelvic structures unsuited for childbirth in the dozen or so generations since androcentric doctors became interested in childbirth. It is possible that women's general levels of physical conditioning and nutrition could have deteriorated over this time period in such a way that the typical Western woman is in poor physical health throughout her childbearing years, but this is entirely environmental, not genetic.

It is also well documented that many of Western women's difficulties in giving birth are the result of the conditions imposed upon them by Western hospitals (Oxorn and Foote 1980; Arms 1975; Mendelsohn 1982). A prime example of this is the condition known as supine hypotensive syndrome. Oxorn and Foote describe the condition this way:

The clinical picture is one of hypotension when, in the late stages of pregnancy, the woman lies on her back. . . . Other symptoms include nausea, shortness of breath, faintness, pallor, tachycardia, and increased femoral venous pressure. . . . Reduced perfusion of the uterus and placenta leads to fetal hypoxia and changes in the fetal heart rate. (Oxorn and Foote 1980, 115)

This condition may occur to some extent or another in virtually all women who give birth in hospitals, or approximately 97.4% of all births in the United States. This is because hospital births are conducted with the laboring woman ("in the late stages of pregnancy") lying on her back in a bed or on a delivery table. The most common position, known as the lithotomy position, has the woman flat on her back with her legs up in the air in stirrups. Oxorn and Foote list as advantages of this position: more complete asepsis, easier for hospital personnel to monitor the fetal heartbeat without asking the woman to change position, easier for hospital personnel to administer three different kinds of drugs, easier for the doctor to see the birth, good position for the use of forceps and for performing the surgical procedure of episiotomy. As disadvantages they list: risk of supine hypotensive syndrome, sacroiliac or lumbosacral strain, possible thrombosis in the veins of the legs, possible nerve damage, and the danger of aspiration of vomitus (Oxorn and Foote 1980, 114). In contrast, they list the following advantages and disadvantages for women's and midwives' more traditionally preferred squatting position, which is almost never allowed by hospital regulations: Advantages: enlarges the pelvic outlet, enables laboring

woman to use her expulsive forces to the greatest advantage, eliminates risk of supine hypotensive syndrome; Disadvantages: difficult "for the accoucher to control the birth and to manage complications," impossible to administer certain types of drugs (Oxorn and Foote 1980, 113).

A feature of the lithotomy position not mentioned by Oxorn and Foote, perhaps because they couldn't decide whether it was an advantage or a disadvantage, is that it increases the amount of symptoms which are taken as indications for performing a cesarean section. The primary fetal indications for cesarean surgery are fetal hypoxia and changes in the fetal heart rate (Oxorn and Foote 1980, 667). These are exactly the fetal conditions that are part of the clinical picture of supine hypotensive syndrome. One would think that since Oxorn and Foote report "the risk of maternal death associated with cesarean section to be 26 times greater with vaginal delivery" (Oxorn and Foote 1980, 675) the avoidance of cesarean section would be an advantage. However they continually reassure the reader that cesarean section is a fine thing, a tribute to progressive technology. In fact, they advise against the cesarean operation only "when the fetus is dead or in such bad condition that it is unlikely to survive" because "[t]here is no point in submitting the patient to a needless serious operation" (Oxorn and Foote 1980, 669). One cannot help but suspect that physicians who have undergone nearly a decade of training in techniques of medical intervention find it boring and wasteful of their expertise *not* to engage in such interventions whenever possible.

Obviously in this case, when the laboring woman's physiological needs conflict with the convenience or the need for "control" on the part of the hospital staff, it is the woman's physiological needs that are sacrificed. One can hear echoes of Rachel Carson's protest about the "control of nature" and the dangerous effects of that approach in the critiques made by gynocentric investigators about androcentric conceptions of childbirth. Other factors may color androcentric science's research results as well. As Dr. Robert Mendelsohn put it in *Mal(e)practice*, "Doctors know that they can't afford to allow their patients to perceive childbirth as the normal, typically uncomplicated process that it really is. If they did, most women wouldn't need obstetricians" (Mendelsohn 1982, 130). One can almost imagine the same words being written by a dissident physician with respect to eating, in the years following the imaginary scenario in which androcentric science takes control of eating practices. These things are important to keep in mind as we compare gynocentric midwifery with androcentric obstetrical science.

MIDWIFERY AND OBSTETRICS AS COMPETING SCIENTIFIC PARADIGMS

Obstetrical science, for the most part, has adopted the view that midwifery is an incomplete, underdeveloped, less successful, and less scientific approach to the same scientific problems that it is attempting to solve. One cannot help but note the similarities between this view of midwifery and the now discredited psychoanalytic and philosophical theories that make out women to be incomplete, underdeveloped, less successful and less rational versions of men. A less biased description might be that midwifery and obstetrical science represent competing scientific paradigms which, like all competing paradigms according to Kuhn (1970), disagree not only about the list of problems to be resolved, but also about the theories, methodologies, and criteria for success that will be used to assess the results achieved.

If gynocentric science is, as I've suggested earlier, "less isolated from other aspects of our lives, less fetishized about individualism, more holistic, more nurturing, more concerned with relations than with objects, perhaps more dialectic, because of the nature and position of the erotic with respect to its epistemology," then these aspects of it should be evident in the work of gynocentric scientists practicing within their paradigm. On the other hand, the androcentric criteria for good science such as abstraction, reductionism, the determination to repress one's feelings to promote "objectivity" cited by Namenwirth (1986) should be evident in the work of androcentric scientists practicing within their paradigm. Consider these two examples:

MIDWIFERY AS GYNOCENTRIC SCIENCE

. . . I want to stress the importance of good continuous prenatal care. Without the knowledge of excellent health the risks of home birth increase for both mother and child.

To have a healthy pregnancy and good childbirth, certain aspects of existence on the physical, mental, and spiritual plane must be observed and trained to be in harmony with the forces within you, i.e., that of the creation of life.

You should be able to listen closely to everything your body is telling you about what's happening within, how your body feels about what goes into it, what comes out, and just how it feels organically.

As the pregnancy proceeds many things happen and a gradual process of training mind and body takes place.

Food may become a necessary discipline if a diet is not made normally of whole foods. Foods that have been flash grown, processed, refined, nutritionalized and put out as some predigested matter should be avoided.

. . . It's pretty easy to tell if you're doing the above correctly because you will be healthy organically and you can feel that through your entire body. —*Raven Lang*, Midwife

OBSTETRICS AS ANDROCENTRIC SCIENCE

Once the patient has carefully selected her doctor, she should let him shoulder the full responsibility of her pregnancy and labor, with the comforting knowledge that, no matter what develops, he has had similar cases and her health will be safeguarded by this background of experience.

Most obstetricians prefer to see their patients early in pregnancy, two or three weeks after the first menstrual period is missed. Many women look forward to this first interview with unnecessary dread. Perhaps a friend with previous experience has told them that it is a most embarrassing examination, and such questions! The patient is apt to forget that the doctor has examined literally thousands of women, and in the course of this experience has learned to impersonalize his attitude toward his patients.

At the first visit the obstetrician examines the woman completely from top to toe. It is essential that he determine the exact physical condition of his patient so that he may judge her ability to withstand the strain of pregnancy and labor.

—*Dr. Alan Guttmacher,*
Professor Emeritus, Department of
Obstetrics and Gynecology,
Mount Sinai Medical School, New York

If incommensurability is to be taken seriously, then we are faced with the ever present problem of theory choice. How are we to evaluate two competing scientific paradigms with respect to their successes at problem solving? "In the first place," wrote Kuhn "the proponents of competing paradigms will often disagree about the list of problems that any candidate for paradigm must resolve. Their standards or their definitions of science are not the same." Going on to explain linguistic incommensurability, he then comes to one of the most compelling observations in *The Structure of Scientific Revolutions:* "In a sense that I am unable to explicate further, the proponents of competing paradigms practice their trades in different worlds" (Kuhn 1970, 150). While the androcentric scientists scratch their heads in perplexed confusion about what Kuhn might possibly mean by this, many feminists smile with the pleasurable sensation of having encountered a clear

articulation of the obvious. Many of us are well acquainted with the feeling of dividing our time and attention between two different worlds. Carol Gilligan (1982) has suggested ways in which this plays itself out in ethics; Belenky *et al.* (1986) have recently done the same for epistemology. There is no reason for us to suspect that we can't do the same thing with respect to science. I don't for a minute want to claim to have demonstrated the existence of a gynocentric science here; what I have tried to do is to articulate an hypothesis that deserves further investigation. My hope is that some empirical investigation will yield fruitful results in this direction, and that these results—in the best of scientific traditions—can feed back into, and interact with, our growing body of theory about the nature of feminist science.

WHY CALL IT "SCIENCE"?

Well, why not?

Women *are* trapped in an androcentric world, as Bleier suggests, one in which language and meaning have been constructed around androcentric goals and enterprises. We've had troubles with language all along. As Marilyn Frye has pointed out, the very terms we use embed in them the connections and distinctions that *men* want to see (Frye 1983, 161). If the term "science" is to be construed only as a limited range of activities, conducted by properly certified people, under a limited range of circumstances, then perhaps the term "gynocentric science" is as much a self-contradiction as the term "military intelligence." But one of the projects of American feminists has been to claim our right to participate in the making of meaning. We have struggled, for example, to be able to apply the term "scholarship" to our work, even when much of that work didn't count as scholarship under the old androcentric language rules. For that matter, we've struggled for the right to apply the term "work" to many of our activities that were once considered not to be work. Feyerabend (1975) noticed, even without the benefit of a feminist perspective, that the distinction between science and non-science is political. And as Frye (1983, 105) pointed out, *"definition* is another face of power."

So maybe we are recreating the language a bit by calling midwifery or gossip or cooking "gynocentric science." But then, as members of the language-using community, we are entitled. The burden is not on us, but on those who object, to show that this is not a reasonable use of the term "science."

HESITATIONS

Even as I write this, I'm not completely convinced that tugging on the term "science" to fit gynocentric activities under its umbrella is necessarily the right thing to do. Perhaps, as Marion Namenwirth (1986) suggests, "abstraction, reductionism, the determination to repress one's feelings to promote 'objectivity' have not the same priority to women as they do men." Perhaps, as she doesn't suggest, these qualities are already so tied to the term "science" that we will choose to dissociate our work from the baggage of the term, and name our gynocentric work something else instead. I find that my own feelings about this waver. On the days when I'm hoping that feminism will make the world better for everybody, I want to tug at the meaning of science to get it to include gynocentric activities. On the days when I'm seeing science as the religion of advanced patriarchy, and philosophy as its theology, I want to withdraw from both entirely. But for those of us who, at least on some days, are struggling to find a feminist conception of science, I offer this suggestion: it's been around us all along. Our task now should be to research it; we need no longer merely fumble about for a theory of what it might be.

REFERENCES

Arms, Suzanne. 1975. *Immaculate Deception: A New Look at Women and Childbirth in America.* Boston: Houghton Mifflin.

Belenky, Mary, *et al.* 1986. *Women's Ways of Knowing.* New York: Basic Books.

Birke, Linda. 1986. *Women, Feminism and Biology: The Feminist Challenge.* New York: Methuen Press.

Bleier, Ruth. 1984. *Science and Gender: A Critique of Biology and Its Theories on Women.* Elmsford, NY: Pergamon.

———, ed. 1986. *Feminist Approaches to Science.* Elmsford, NY: Pergamon.

Carson, Rachel. 1964. *Silent Spring.* New York: Fawcett Crest.

Daly, Mary. 1978. *Gyn/ecology: The Metaethics of Radical Feminism.* Boston: Beacon Press.

Edwards, Margot, and Mary Waldorf. 1984. *Reclaiming Birth.* Trumansburg, NY: Crossing Press.

Ehrenreich, Barbara, and Deirdre English. 1973. *Witches, Midwives, and Nurses: A History of Women Healers.* Old Westbury, NY: Feminist Press.

Fee, Elizabeth. 1983. "Women's Nature and Scientific Objectivity." In *Women's Nature: Rationalizations of Inequality,* ed. M. Lowe and R. Hubbard, pp. 9–28. Elmsford, NY: Pergamon.

Feyerabend, Paul. 1975. *Against Method.* London: Verso.

Frye, Marilyn. 1983. *The Politics of Reality: Essays in Feminist Theory.* Trumansburg, NY: Crossing Press.

Gaskin, Ina May. 1978. *Spiritual Midwifery.* Summertown, TN: Book Publishing Company.

Gilligan, Carol. 1982. *In a Different Voice.* Cambridge, MA: Harvard University Press.

Griffin, Susan. 1980. *Woman and Nature: The Roaring inside Her.* New York: Harper & Row.

Guttmacher, Alan. 1973. *Pregnancy, Birth and Family Planning.* New York: Viking Press.

Harding, Sandra. 1986. *The Science Question in Feminism.* Ithaca, NY: Cornell University Press.

Keller, Evelyn Fox. 1983. *A Feeling for the Organism: The Life and Work of Barbara McClintock.* San Francisco: Freeman.

———. 1985. *Reflections on Science and Gender.* New Haven, CT: Yale University Press.

Kuhn, Thomas S. 1970. *The Structure of Scientific Revolutions.* Chicago: University of Chicago Press.

Lang, Raven. 1972. *Birth Book.* Ben Lomond, CA: Genesis Press.

Lorde, Audre. 1984. *Sister Outsider.* Trumansburg, NY: Crossing Press.

Mendelsohn, Robert. 1982. *Mal(e)practice.* Chicago: Contemporary Books.

Merchant, Carolyn. 1980. *The Death of Nature: Women, Ecology, and the Scientific Revolution.* New York: Harper & Row.

Namenwirth, Marion. 1986. "Science Seen through a Feminist Prism." In *Feminist Approaches to Science,* ed. Ruth Bleier. Elmsford, NY: Pergamon.

Oxorn, Harry, and William Foote. 1980. *Human Labor and Birth.* Englewood Cliffs, NJ: Prentice Hall.

Rich, Adrienne. 1976. *Of Woman Born: Motherhood as Experience and Institution.* New York: Norton.

———. 1979. *On Lies, Secrets, and Silence: Selected Prose, 1966–78.* New York: Norton.

Rose, Hilary. 1986. "Beyond Masculinist Realities: A Feminist Epistemology for the Sciences." In *Feminist Approaches to Science,* ed. Ruth Bleier, pp. 57–76. Elmsford, NY: Pergamon.

Trask, Haunani-Kay. 1986. *Eros and Power.* Philadelphia: University of Pennsylvania Press.

Wertz, Richard, and Dorothy Wertz. 1979. *Lying-in: A History of Childbirth in America.* New York: Shocken.

HELEN E. LONGINO, "CAN THERE BE A FEMINIST SCIENCE?"

In typical philosophical fashion, Longino distinguishes several senses of the question posed in the title. The question might be factual: "Are there feminists doing science?" Or it might be asking, "What are the characteristics of a uniquely feminist science, whether done by feminists or antifeminists?" It might even be asking, "What conditions in society and the profession of science itself would be most conducive to feminists' feeling comfortable doing science?"

Longino points out that feminism is an ideological stance about social and political conditions. At its core, she observes, is a desire to expand human potential. Because science is always taken to be the opposite of an ideology, "feminist science" therefore seems to be a contradiction. After all, ideologies are value laden. Science is supposedly value free. Longino will question this distinction. She will argue that science cannot be value free.

Longino divides science into its content and its practice. The content of a science is its theories. Feminist theories are holistic, are able to accept a complex basic level of explanation, and show, because they are the result of interaction, that interaction is basic to understanding the world. This is a reflection of the fact that in general, women tend to deal with the world by interacting with it (recall the research of Strum in Chapter 1), by taking a holistic stance toward it, by not being anxious to control the world. Women also tend to be comfortable with complexity. Since there is no way to interact with generalizations, women will pay attention to particulars. If the world is holistic and exceedingly complex, then women have the best chance for understanding it. Cartwright (Chapter 2), in arguing that the world may not be tidy and that all the laws of physics must be *ceteris paribus* laws, forcing attention on particular exceptions, was arguing along just these feminist lines. So were Gorovitz and MacIntyre.

The practice of science covers such things as how a laboratory is set up and the social and professional relations between scientists. The practice, according to Longino, includes scientific reasoning. Can the practice of science be feminist?

Longino says that whether one answers no because there is only one way to practice value-free science or yes because the present practice is too dominated by male values, an assumption is being made. The assumption is that science ought to be value free. Each side is claiming that the correct practice is the one that will lead to value-free methodology. Longino argues that science must be value laden and that both sides are wrong for not realizing this.

Her argument that science is value laden begins with a distinction between constitutive (internal) and contextual (external) values. Constitutive values are the origin of what is accepted as legitimate scientific methodology. Contextual values refer to broader preferences concerning what ought to be. For example, the desire to find cures for infertility rests on a contextual value judgment that infertility is a bad thing. Actually finding the cures will call into play the scientific method and its constitutive values, such as what counts as a scientific trial. Longino's distinction is basically the same as the one made by Gorovitz and MacIntyre between internal and external norms.

Longino claims that in the actual doing of science, there is rarely any way to separate these two sorts of values. Her argument is based on the underdetermination of theories. That is, no theory is ever fully confirmed. We have seen this thesis in Chapter 3. For every accepted theory, there is almost always another competing theory. The choice between such competing theories then will be, in part, a function of contextual values, since the underdetermination thesis really comes to the claim that constitutive values are not always sufficient to choose between theories.

None of this makes science, as Longino puts it, "shady." What the argument shows is that value commitments and "good science" can go together. Science, according to Longino, should be expected to be a product of the biases—values and metaphysics—of its society. This insight may not be as surprising as her claim that finding and critiquing these biases should also be considered a proper part of science.

Richard Rudner makes a point similar to Longino's.* The nub of his argument is as follows:

> I take it that no analysis of what constitutes the method of science would be satisfactory unless it comprised some assertion to the effect that the scientist as scientist accepts or rejects hypotheses.
>
> But if this is so then clearly the scientist as scientist does make value judgments. For, since no scientific hypothesis is ever completely verified, in accepting [or rejecting] a hypothesis the scientist must make the decision that the evidence is *sufficiently* strong [weak] or that the probability is sufficiently high [low] to warrant the acceptance [rejection] of the hypothesis. Obviously our decision regarding the evidence and respecting how strong is "strong enough" is going to be a function of the *importance*, in the typically ethical sense, of making a mistake in accepting or rejecting the hypothesis.

*Richard Rudner, "The Scientist qua Scientist Makes Value Judgments," *Philosophy of Science* 20 (1953): 2.

Can There Be a Feminist Science?

HELEN E. LONGINO

This paper explores a number of recent proposals regarding "feminist science" and rejects a content-based approach in favor of a process-based approach to characterizing feminist science. Philosophy of science can yield models of scientific reasoning that illuminate the interaction between cultural values and ideology and scientific inquiry. While we can use these models to expose masculine and other forms of bias, we can also use them to defend the introduction of assumptions grounded in feminist political values.

I

The question of this title conceals multiple ambiguities. Not only do the sciences consist of many distinct fields, but the term "science" can be used to refer to a method of inquiry, a historically changing collection of practices, a body of knowledge, a set of claims, a profession, a set of social groups, etc. And as the sciences are many, so are the scholarly disciplines that seek to understand them: philosophy, history, sociology, anthropology, psychology. Any answer from the perspective of some one of these disciplines will, then, of necessity, be partial. In this essay, I shall be asking about the possibility of theoretical natural science that is feminist and I shall ask from the perspective of a philosopher. Before beginning to develop my answer, however, I want to review some of the questions that could be meant, in order to arrive at the formulation I wish to address.

The question could be interpreted as factual, one to be answered by pointing to what feminists in the sciences are doing and saying: "Yes, and this is what it is." Such a response can be perceived as question-begging, however. Even such a friend of feminism as Stephen Gould dismisses the idea of a distinctively feminist or even female contribution to the sciences. In a generally positive review of Ruth Bleier's book, *Science and Gender,* Gould (1984) brushes aside her connection between women's attitudes and values and the interactionist science she calls for. Scientists (male, of course) are already proceeding with wholist and interactionist research programs. Why, he implied, should women or feminists have any particular, distinctive, contributions to make? There is not masculinist and feminist science, just good and bad science. The question of a feminist science cannot be settled by pointing, but involves a deeper, subtler investigation.

The deeper question can itself have several meanings. One set of meanings is sociological, the other conceptual. The sociological meaning proceeds as follows. We know what sorts of social conditions make misogynist science possible. The work of Margaret Rossiter (1982) on the history of women scientists in the United States and the work of Kathryn Addelson (1983) on the social structure of professional science detail the relations between a particular social structure for science and the kinds of science produced. What sorts of social conditions would make feminist science possible? This is an important question, one I am not equipped directly to investigate, although what I can investigate is, I believe, relevant to it. This is the second, conceptual, interpretation of the question: what sort of sense does it make to talk about a feminist sci-

From *Hypatia* 2, no. 3 (1987): 51–64. Courtesy of Professor Helen Longino.

ence? Why is the question itself not an oxy-moron, linking, as it does, values and ideo-logical commitment with the idea of imper-sonal, objective, value-free, inquiry? This is the problem I wish to address in this essay.

The hope for a feminist theoretical nat-ural science has concealed an ambiguity between content and practice. In the content sense the idea of a feminist science involves a number of assumptions and calls a num-ber of visions to mind. Some theorists have written as though a feminist science is one the theories of which encode a particular world view, characterized by complexity, interaction and wholism. Such a science is said to be feminist because it is the expres-sion and valorization of a female sensibility or cognitive temperament. Alternatively, it is claimed that women have certain traits (dispositions to attend to particulars, inter-active rather than individualist and control-ling social attitudes and behaviors) that enable them to understand the true charac-ter of natural processes (which are complex and interactive).[1] While proponents of this interactionist view see it as an improvement over most contemporary science, it has also been branded as soft—misdescribed as non-mathematical. Women in the sciences who feel they are being asked to do not better sci-ence, but inferior science, have responded angrily to this characterization of feminist science, thinking that it is simply new cloth-ing for the old idea that women can't do sci-ence. I think that the interactionist view can be defended against this response, although that requires rescuing it from some of its proponents as well. However, I also think that the characterization of feminist science as the expression of a distinctive female cog-nitive temperament has other drawbacks. It first conflates feminine with feminist. While it is important to reject the traditional dero-gation of the virtues assigned to women, it is also important to remember that women are *constructed* to occupy positions of social

subordinates. We should not uncritically embrace the feminine.

This characterization of feminist science is also a version of recently propounded notions of a "women's standpoint" or a "feminist standpoint" and suffers from the same suspect universalization that these ideas suffer from. If there is one such stand-point, there are many: as Maria Lugones and Elizabeth Spelman spell out in their tellingly entitled article, "Have We Got a Theory for You: Feminist Theory, Cultural Imperialism, and the Demand for 'The Woman's Voice,' " women are too diverse in our experiences to generate a single cog-nitive framework (Lugones and Spelman 1983). In addition, the sciences are them-selves too diverse for me to think that they might be equally transformed by such a framework. To reject this concept of a fem-inist science, however, is not to disengage science from feminism. I want to suggest that we focus on science as practice rather than content, as process rather than prod-uct; hence, not on feminist science, but on doing science as a feminist.

The doing of science involves many prac-tices: how one structures a laboratory (hier-archically or collectively), how one relates to other scientists (competitively or coopera-tively), how and whether one engages in political struggles over affirmative action. It extends also to intellectual practices, to the activities of scientific inquiry, such as obser-vation and reasoning. Can there be a femi-nist scientific inquiry? This possibility is seen to be problematic against the back-ground of certain standard presuppositions about science. The claim that there could be a feminist science in the sense of an intel-lectual practice is either nonsense because oxymoronic as suggested above or the claim is interpreted to mean that established sci-ence (science as done and dominated by men) is wrong about the world. Feminist science in this latter interpretation is presented as correcting the errors of masculine, standard science and as revealing the truth that is hidden by masculine "bad" science, as taking the sex out of science.

Both of these interpretations involve the rejection of one approach as incorrect and the embracing of the other as the way to a truer understanding of the natural world. Both trade one absolutism for another. Each is a side of the same coin, and that coin, I think, is the idea of a value-free science. This is the idea that scientific methodology guarantees the independence of scientific inquiry from values of value-related considerations. A science or a scientific research program informed by values is *ipso facto* "bad science." "Good science" is inquiry protected by methodology from values and ideology. This same idea underlies Gould's response to Bleier, so it bears closer scrutiny. In the pages that follow, I shall examine the idea of value-free science and then apply the results of that examination to the idea of feminist scientific inquiry.

II

I distinguish two kinds of values relevant to the sciences. Constitutive values, internal to the sciences, are the source of the rules determining what constitutes acceptable scientific practice or scientific method. The personal, social and cultural values, those group or individual preferences about what ought to be I call contextual values, to indicate that they belong to the social and cultural context in which science is done (Longino 1983c). The traditional interpretation of the value-freedom of modern natural science amounts to a claim that its constitutive and contextual features are clearly distinct from and independent of one another, that contextual values play no role in the inner workings of scientific inquiry, in reasoning and observation. I shall argue that this construal of the distinction cannot be maintained.

There are several ways to develop such an argument. One scholar is fond of inviting her audience to visit any science library and peruse the titles on the shelves. Observe how subservient to social and cultural interests are the inquiries represented by the book titles alone! Her listeners would soon abandon their ideas about the value-neutrality of the sciences, she suggests. This exercise may indeed show the influence of external, contextual considerations on what research gets done/supported (i.e., on problem selection). It does not show that such considerations affect reasoning or hypothesis acceptance. The latter would require detailed investigation of particular cases or a general conceptual argument. The conceptual arguments involve developing some version of what is known in philosophy of science as the underdetermination thesis, i.e., the thesis that a theory is always underdetermined by the evidence adduced in its support, with the consequence that different or incompatible theories are supported by or at least compatible with the same body of evidence. I shall sketch a version of the argument that appeals to features of scientific inference.

One of the rocks on which the logical positivist program foundered was the distinction between theoretical and observational language. Theoretical statements contain, as fundamental descriptive terms, terms that do not occur in the description of data. Thus, hypotheses in particle physics contain terms like "electron," "pion," "muon," "electron spin," etc. The evidence for a hypothesis such as "A pion decays sequentially into a muon, then a positron" is obviously not direct observations of pions, muons and positrons, but consists largely in photographs taken in large and complex experimental apparati: accelerators, cloud chambers, bubble chambers. The photographs show all sorts of squiggly lines and spirals. Evidence for the hypotheses of particle physics is presented as statements that describe these photographs. Eventually, of course, particle physicists point to a spot on a photograph and say things like "Here a neutrino hits a neutron." Such an assertion, however, is an interpretive achievement which involves collapsing theoretical and observational moments. A skeptic would have to be supplied a complicated argument linking the elements of the photograph to traces left by particles and these to particles themselves. What counts as theory and what as data in a pragmatic sense change over time, as some ideas and experimental procedures come to be securely embedded in a particular framework and others take their place on the horizons. As the history of physics shows, however, secure embeddedness is no guarantee against overthrow.

Logical positivists and their successors hoped to model scientific inference formally. Evidence for hypotheses, data, were to be represented as logical consequences of hypotheses. When we try to map this logical structure onto the sciences, however, we find that hypotheses are, for the most part, not just generalizations of data statements. The links between data and theory, therefore, cannot be adequately represented as formal or syntactic, but are established by means of assumptions that make or imply substantive claims about the field over which one theorizes. Theories are confirmed via the confirmation of their constituent hypotheses, so the confirmation of hypotheses and theories is relative to the assumptions relied upon in asserting the evidential connection. Confirmation of such assumptions, which are often unarticulated, is itself subject to similar relativization. And it is these assumptions that can be the vehicle for the involvement of considerations motivated primarily by contextual values (Longino 1979, 1983a).

The point of this extremely telescoped argument is that one can't give an a priori specification of confirmation that effectively

eliminates the role of value-laden assumptions in legitimate scientific inquiry without eliminating auxiliary hypotheses (assumptions) altogether. This is not to say that all scientific reasoning involves value-related assumptions. Sometimes auxiliary assumptions will be supported by mundane inductive reasoning. But sometimes they will not be. In any given case, they may be metaphysical in character; they may be untestable with present investigative techniques; they may be rooted in contextual, value-related considerations. If, however, there is no a priori way to eliminate such assumptions from evidential reasoning generally, and, hence, no way to rule out value-laden assumptions, then there is no formal basis for arguing that an inference mediated by contextual values is thereby bad science.

A comparable point is made by some historians investigating the origins of modern science. James Jacob (1977) and Margaret Jacob (1976) have, in a series of articles and books, argued that the adoption of conceptions of matter by 17th century scientists like Robert Boyle was inextricably intertwined with political considerations. Conceptions of matter provided the foundation on which physical theories were developed and Boyle's science, regardless of his reasons for it, has been fruitful in ways that far exceed his imaginings. If the presence of contextual influences were grounds for disallowing a line of inquiry, then early modern science would not have gotten off the ground.

The conclusion of this line of argument is that constitutive values conceived as epistemological (i.e., truth-seeking) are not adequate to screen out the influence of contextual values in the very structuring of scientific knowledge. Now the ways in which contextual values do, if they do, influence this structuring and interact, if they do, with constitutive values has to be determined separately for different theories and fields of science. But this argument, if it's sound, tells us that this sort of inquiry is perfectly respectable and involves no shady assumptions or unargued intuitively based rejections of positivism. It also opens the possibility that one can make explicit value commitments and still do "good" science. The conceptual argument doesn't show that all science is value-laden (as opposed to metaphysics-laden)—that must be established on a case-by-case basis, using the tools not just of logic and philosophy but of history and sociology as well. It does show that not all science is value-free and, more importantly, that it is not necessarily in the nature of science to be value-free. If we reject that idea we're in a better position to talk about the possibilities of feminist science.

III

In earlier articles (Longino 1981, 1983b; Longino and Doell 1983), I've used similar considerations to argue that scientific objectivity has to be reconceived as a function of the communal structure of scientific inquiry rather than as a property of individual scientists. I've then used these notions about scientific methodology to show that science displaying masculine bias is not *ipso facto* improper or "bad" science; that the fabric of science can neither rule out the expression of bias nor legitimate it. So I've argued that both the expression of masculine bias in the sciences and feminist criticism of research exhibiting that bias are—shall we say—business as usual; that scientific inquiry should be expected to display the deep metaphysical and normative commitments of the culture in which it flourishes; and finally that criticism of the deep assumptions that guide scientific reasoning about data is a proper part of science. . . .

NOTE

1. This seems to be suggested in Bleier (1984), Rose (1983) and in Sandra Harding's (1980) early work.

REFERENCES

Addelson, Kathryn Pine. 1983. "The Man of Professional Wisdom." In *Discovering Reality,* ed. Sandra Harding and Merrill Hintikka. Dordrecht, Netherlands: Reidel.

Bleier, Ruth. 1984. *Science and Gender.* Elmsford, NY: Pergamon.

Gould, Stephen Jay. 1984. Review of Ruth Bleier, *Science and Gender. New York Times Book Review,* August 12, p. 1.

Harding, Sandra. 1980. "The Norms of Inquiry and Masculine Experience." In *PSA 1980,* vol. 2, ed. Peter Asquith and Ronald Giere. East Lansing, MI: Philosophy of Science Association.

Jacob, James R. 1977. *Robert Boyle and the English Revolution: A Study in Social and Intellectual Change.* New York: Franklin.

Jacob, Margaret C. 1976. *The Newtonians and the English Revolution, 1689–1720.* Ithaca, NY: Cornell University Press.

Longino, Helen E. 1979. "Evidence and Hypothesis." *Philosophy of Science* 46 (1): 35–56.

———. 1981. "Scientific Objectivity and Feminist Theorizing." *Liberal Education* 67 (3): 33–41.

———. 1983a. "Beyond 'bad science.' " *Science, Technology and Human Values* 8 (1): 7–17.

———. 1983b. "The Idea of a Value-Free Science." Paper presented to the Pacific Division of the American Philosophical Association, March 25, Berkeley, CA.

———. 1983c. "Scientific Objectivity and Logics of Science." *Inquiry* 26 (1): 85–106.

Longino, Helen E., and Ruth Doell. 1983. "Body, Bias and Behavior." *Signs* 9 (2): 206–227.

Lugones, Maria, and Elizabeth Spelman. 1983. "Have We Got a Theory for You! Feminist Theory, Cultural Imperialism and the Demand for "the Woman's Voice." *Hypatia 1,* published as a special issue of *Women's Studies International Forum* 6 (6): 573–581.

Rose, Hilary. 1983. "Hand, Brain, and Heart: A Feminist Epistemology for the Natural Sciences." *Signs* 9 (1): 73–90.

Rossiter, Margaret. 1982. Women Scientists in America: Struggles and Strategies to 1940. Baltimore: Johns Hopkins University Press.

HELEN BERMAN, "RESTITUTION: A REVIEW OF *ROSALIND FRANKLIN AND DNA*"

Berman's review of Ann Sayre's book *Rosalind Franklin and DNA* requires some detailed background information concerning what has been termed the "race" to find the structure of DNA.

Rosalind Franklin (1921–1958), trained as a specialist in the physical chemistry of coal, came to work in Maurice Wilkins's laboratory at King's College in London early in 1951. Exactly who had charge of which research project was a bone of contention between Franklin and Wilkins. Perhaps because of this, the two never got on well.

Franklin delivered a paper on her DNA work in 1951, saying that DNA in one of its two forms was helical. Wilkins did not trust her results. He often repeated her experiments to check her results. Obviously, if there were a race between Cambridge (where Watson and Crick were working) and King's College, this would have given the edge to Cambridge.

Franklin and Wilkins, although not speaking, were just about to get the structure of DNA (in 1953) when Watson and Crick did. The Cambridge pair could not have done it (probably) without work from King's that Wilkins showed Watson, an X-ray diffraction made by Franklin.

Sayre's strategy is to present us with a picture of science in general so that we can compare the work of Franklin with the work of Watson and Crick. This picture is one of comparatively slow accumulation and convergence of bits and pieces of knowledge. The examples Sayre stresses most are Mendel's work with peas and Perutz's 27-year search for the structure of proteins. In general, then, she sees the processes of scientific research working against the "wunderkind" because there is so much to learn before creativity is possible.

She wants us to see the Watson and Crick discovery as part of the ongoing march of science and not as any kind of revolution. Sayre says that the discovery of the double helix was not really all that ingenious. She means to suggest that the data were pointing in that direction. Anyone with all the data and all the usual trappings of a biologically oriented research scientist would have realized that the structure of DNA was a double helix. Sayre views science as a positivist would.

The scientific method—which Sayre characterizes as logic versus guesses, with as few hastily drawn conclusions as possible—was Franklin's method. According to Sayre, Franklin showed commendable prudence with respect to unwarranted predicting of results. This contrasts with Watson and Crick, who, for example, proposed in September 1951 a triple helix that irked Franklin and Wilkins, who had come from London to see Watson and Crick's latest model.

Franklin continued to avoid using models. She did not oppose them in principle. She knew that they helped in determining structure only with appropriate information from X-ray diffractions and other sources. Franklin was only abiding by the scientific method when she refused to use models in her research.

More was involved in the discovery, however, than just the scientific method. What Franklin lacked was "the usual trappings" of the scientific life. What are the usual trappings? Friendly discussions over lunch with colleagues, sharp but not acrimonious debate, a general good feeling at work, and not least, some respect for confidences; these all fall into the category. Watson had all of these; Franklin had none. According to Sayre, Franklin's defeat in the race to determine the structure of DNA was not for any lack of scientific expertise but rather because of factors extrinsic to the actual practicing of science.

One might speculate that Watson had insight that Franklin lacked because he was a trained biologist. He would have been closer to his subject matter than Franklin. This sort of closeness might well be the feeling for the organism touted by Barbara McClintock. Perhaps Franklin was stymied by her insistence on what can only be termed a reductionist method of approach (X-ray diffraction).

Restitution: A Review of *Rosalind Franklin and DNA*

HELEN BERMAN

It is not really surprising or unusual that the credits for some aspects of a discovery as significant as the structure of DNA are often muddled; that often happens in science. Standard textbook accounts tell us that Watson and Crick proposed the structure on the basis of model building, Chargaff's discovery of base equivalence, and x-ray diffraction data obtained (variously in these accounts) by Wilkins, by Wilkins's group, or by Wilkins and Franklin. Rosalind Franklin is, perhaps, a dimly remembered figure in this episode. But with the publication of Watson's *The Double Helix*, she was indelibly characterized to us as "Wilkins's assistant," someone with a less than pleasant personality whose excellent set of x-ray photographs Watson had to obtain surreptitiously. Anne Sayre, a friend of Franklin's,

Reprinted with permission from *Science* 190 (1975): 665. Copyright © 1975 American Association for the Advancement of Science.

has been compelled to correct this impression and tells us, with considerable scholarship, about Rosalind Franklin the scientist and the person.

From the point of view of scientific documentation and history, the most important feature of *Rosalind Franklin and DNA* is the description of Franklin's research into the structure of DNA. Not only did she take "beautiful pictures," she also carefully interpreted the diffraction patterns. In a recorded oral presentation, which Watson attended in 1951, she described the structure of the B form of DNA as "helical with the phosphates near the outside." She was cautious and refused to commit herself to a helical structure for the more crystalline and less easily interpretable A form of DNA, but she was not, according to Sayre, "antihelical," as Wilkins called her. Franklin's stature as a scientist is evident from a remark by Crick that left on her own she would probably have arrived at the structure of DNA in "perhaps three weeks. Three months is likelier."

There is much more to this book than a description of Franlkin's research. Sayre in an attempt to replace the personality which she claims Watson "stole" reveals something about the family background and personal life of Franklin. We are told about a woman from a socially and politically active Jewish family who was educated at Cambridge during wartime and who had to face considerable challenge to establish and maintain her career in science. The book was not intended to be a biography, but what we are told is so fascinating that one wishes Sayre had given an even more complete picture.

Franklin was an intense person who expressed herself strongly; her home experience and her experience in Luzzati's laboratory in Paris encouraged that sort of behavior. Wilkins, a reserved person, who could have had several reasons to resent her, described her as "fierce." This "personality clash" was only one of Franklin's problems in the King's College laboratory. Before she came to London she had been in a congenial laboratory in Paris where she had learned diffraction after becoming an expert in the chemistry of carbon in England. She arrived at King's to find an ill-defined laboratory setup; the relationship that was meant to exist between Wilkins's and Franklin's research efforts on DNA in Randall's department was never clearly outlined to either of them. Moreover, she was not allowed to partake of the informal interchange at mealtimes because the men and

women had to eat separately and she had no female colleagues in the laboratory. It is not so surprising that, while she applied all her intelligence and characteristic dedication to the problem of DNA, very little of what she had to say about the results was heeded; there was a blank wall of "noncommunication." This is in marked contrast with her later experience in Birkbeck College, where she collaborated effectively with her colleagues on structural studies of tobacco mosaic virus.

In the last pages of her account, Sayre questions the effects of Watson's book on the morality of budding scientists. While it is true that the book may have served to perpetuate an overzealous competitiveness, it could also be said that Watson was simply reflecting what some of us regard as less desirable trends in science. It is unlikely that a serious student of science would change his or her way of approaching a research problem on the basis of a reading of Watson's book. The damaging aspect of Watson's book was the case he built against a person who figured prominently in a scientific discovery. His epilogue did not really correct the negative impression he left about Rosalind Franklin. Sayre has repaired the damage and has produced a book remarkable both for its content and for its readability.

REFERENCE

Sayre, Anne. *Rosalind Franklin and DNA*. New York: Norton, 1975.

EVELYN FOX KELLER, "A FEELING FOR THE ORGANISM"

Although many geneticists were studying the genetics of fruit flies, plants were the subjects of choice when McClintock arrived at Cornell, and she chose corn. It is important to Keller's thesis that McClintock was at Cornell and therefore able to research corn. To Keller, this suggests that the positivist distinction between internal and external factors must be questioned. After all, our very knowledge of genetics has depended on what McClintock found. She might not have found it if she had studied another organism.

Keller claims earlier in the book from which this selection is taken that 1944 was a pivotal year for genetics. In 1944, genetics turned from its macromethodology, crosses of relatively large organisms, to biochemical and microbial genetics. (Compared to bacteria and viruses, fruit flies and corn are rather large.) She sees this as a paradigm shift. We can characterize it as a shift to mechanism and reductionism. As we have seen, it was by linking Mendel's abstractions to real chromosomes that cytology provided this mechanistic and reductionistic shift. Such a shift would have been predicted by Merchant's account of the general development of science.

After 1944, any approach to genetics that was not in keeping with the new paradigm would be rejected. Briefly, what was McClintock's unorthodox approach to genetics? It was not that she did not use microtechniques. Indeed, she certainly understood and used biochemical methods. Rather, it was her philosophy that differed from that of most geneticists. To McClintock it was important to know your organism—to have a feeling for it. This could not be accomplished by knowing just the biochemistry. To have a feeling for the organism requires a holistic approach, a top-down approach. It requires subjective knowledge. One has to have a kind of sympathy for and empathy with the organism. All of this feeling for the organism conflicts with the traditional, positivist view of science as pure objectivity.

In detailing McClintock's feeling for the organism, is Keller just presenting an alternative method from which scientists may choose? If she sees science in a Kuhnian fashion, then she would be committed to saying that McClintock offers just one of many incommensurable ways of approaching science. Indeed, Keller sees feminist science as more open to differing approaches than traditional science. This, she claims, is a strength of the feminist viewpoint. Keller does stress that McClintock turned out to be right. Does this imply only that in this instance one scientist was vindicated? This is a reasonable interpretation. But there is another way to look at Keller's point. She says that McClintock saw "deeper and further into the mysteries of genetics." Did she see deeper and further only by luck? What of the possibility that McClintock saw deeper and further because she had the appropriate holistic approach?

Putting aside the finer points of analyzing Keller, we can say that if the traditional scientific method is androcentric and McClintock's approach is more closely related to a gynocentric point of view, then we have evidence that we should at the very least question traditional science and philosophy of science. Such questioning is in the spirit of any true pursuit of knowledge.

A Feeling for the Organism

EVELYN FOX KELLER

There are two equally dangerous extremes—to shut reason out, and to let nothing else in.
—Pascal

If Barbara McClintock's story illustrates the fallibility of science, it also bears witness to the underlying health of the scientific enterprise. Her eventual vindication demonstrates the capacity of science to overcome its own characteristic kinds of myopia, reminding us that its limitations do not reinforce themselves indefinitely. Their own methodology allows, even obliges, scientists to continually reencounter phenomena even their best theories cannot accommodate. Or—to look at it from the other side—however severely communication between science and nature may be impeded by the preconceptions of a particular time, some channels always remain open; and, through them, nature finds ways of reasserting itself.

But the story of McClintock's contributions to biology has another, less accessible, aspect. What is it in an individual scientist's relation to nature that facilitates the kind of seeing that eventually leads to productive discourse? What enabled McClintock to see further and deeper into the mysteries of genetics than her colleagues?

Her answer is simple. Over and over again, she tells us one must have the time to look, the patience to "hear what the material has to say to you," the openness to "let it come to you." Above all, one must have "a feeling for the organism."

One must understand "How it grows, understand its parts, understand when

something is going wrong with it. [An organism] isn't just a piece of plastic, it's something that is constantly being affected by the environment, constantly showing attributes or disabilities in its growth. You have to be aware of all of that. . . . You need to know those plants well enough so that if anything changes, . . . you [can] look at the plant and right away you know what this damage you see is from—something that scraped across it or something that bit it or something that the wind did." You need to have a feeling for every individual plant.

"No two plants are exactly alike. They're all different, and as a consequence, you have to know that difference," she explains. "I start with the seedling, and I don't want to leave it. I don't feel I really know the story if I don't watch the plant all the way along. So I know every plant in the field. I know them intimately, and I find it a great pleasure to know them."

This intimate knowledge, made possible by years of close association with the organism she studies, is a prerequisite for her extraordinary perspicacity. "I have learned so much about the corn plant that when I see things, I can interpret [them] right away." Both literally and figuratively, her "feeling for the organism" has extended her vision. At the same time, it has sustained her through a lifetime of lonely endeavor, unrelieved by the solace of human intimacy or even by the embrace of her profession.

Good science cannot proceed without a deep emotional investment on the part of the scientist. It is that emotional investment that provides the motivating force for the endless hours of intense, often grueling, labor. Einstein wrote: ". . . what deep longing to understand even a faint reflexion of the reason revealed in this world had to be alive in Kepler and Newton so that they could in lonely work for many years disentangle the mechanism of celestial mechanics?"[1] But McClintock's feeling for the organism is not simply a longing to behold the "reason revealed in this world." It is a longing to embrace the world in its very being, through reason and beyond.

For McClintock, reason—at least in the conventional sense of the word—is not by itself adequate to describe the vast complexity—even mystery—of living forms. Organisms have a life and order of their own that scientists can only partially fathom. No models we invent can begin to do full justice to the prodigious capacity of organisms to devise means for guaranteeing their own survival. On the contrary, "anything you can think of you will find." In comparison with the ingenuity of nature, our scientific intelligence seems pallid.

For her, the discovery of transposition was above all a key to the complexity of genetic organization—an indicator of the subtlety with which cytoplasm, membranes, and DNA are integrated into a single structure. It is the overall organization, or orchestration, that enables the organism to meet its needs, whatever they might be, in ways that never cease to surprise us. That capacity for surprise gives McClintock immense pleasure. She recalls, for example, the early post–World War II studies of the effect of radiation on *Drosophila:* "It turned out that the flies that had been under constant radiation were more vigorous than those that were standard. Well, it was hilarious; it was absolutely against everything that had been thought about earlier. I thought it was terribly funny; I was utterly delighted. Our experience with DDT has been similar. It was thought that insects could be readily killed off with the spraying of DDT. But the insects began to thumb their noses at anything you tried to do to them."

Our surprise is a measure of our tendency to underestimate the flexibility of living organisms. The adaptability of plants tends to be especially unappreciated. "Animals can walk around, but plants have to stay still to do the same things, with ingenious mechanisms. . . . Plants are extraordinary. For instance, . . . if you pinch a leaf of a plant you set off electric pulses. You can't touch a plant without setting off an electric pulse. . . . There is no question that plants have [all] kinds of sensitivities. They do a lot of responding to their environment. They can do almost anything you can think of. But just because they sit there, anybody walking down the road considers them just a plastic area to look at, [as if] they're not really alive."

An attentive observer knows better. At any time, for any plant, one who has sufficient patience and interest can see the myriad signs of life that a casual eye misses: "In the summertime, when you walk down the road, you'll see that the tulip leaves, if it's a little warm, turn themselves around so their backs are toward the sun. You can just see where the sun hits them and where the sun doesn't hit. . . . [Actually], within the restricted areas in which they live, they move around a great deal." These organisms "are fantastically beyond our wildest expectations."

For all of us, it is need and interest above all that induce the growth of our abilities; a motivated observer develops faculties that a casual spectator may never be aware of. Over the years, a special kind of sympathetic understanding grew in McClintock, heightening her powers of discernment, until finally, the objects of her study have become subjects in their own right; they claim from her a kind of attention that most of us experience only in relation to other persons. "Organism" is for her a code word—not simply a plant or animal ("Every component of the organism is as much of an organism as every other part")—but the name of a living form, of object-as-subject. With an uncharacteristic lapse into hyperbole, she adds: "Every time I walk on grass I feel sorry because I know the grass is screaming at me."

A bit of poetic license, perhaps, but McClintock is not a poet; she is a scientist. What marks her as such is her unwavering confidence in the underlying order of living forms, her use of the apparatus of science to gain access to that order, and her commitment to bringing back her insights into the shared language of science—even if doing so might require that language to change. The irregularities or surprises molecular biologists are now uncovering in the organization and behavior of DNA are not indications of a breakdown of order, but only of the inadequacies of our models in the face of the complexity of nature's actual order. Cells, and organisms, have an organization of their own in which nothing is random.

In short, McClintock shares with all other natural scientists the credo that nature is lawful, and the dedication to the task of articulating those laws. And she shares, with at least some, the additional awareness that reason and experiment, generally claimed to be the principal means of this pursuit, do not suffice. To quote Einstein again, ". . . only intuition, resting on sympathetic understanding, can lead to [these laws]; . . . the daily effort comes from no deliberate intention or program, but straight from the heart."[2]

A deep reverence for nature, a capacity for union with that which is to be known—these reflect a different image of science from that of a purely rational enterprise. Yet the two images have coexisted throughout history. We are familiar with the idea that a form of mysticism—a commitment to the unity of experience, the oneness of nature, the fundamental mystery underlying the laws of nature—plays an essential role in the process of scientific discovery. Einstein called it "cosmic religiosity." In turn, the experience of creative insight reinforces these commitments, fostering a sense of the limitations of the scientific method, and an appreciation of other ways of knowing. In all of this, McClintock is no exception. What is exceptional is her forthrightness of expression—the pride she takes in holding, and voicing, attitudes that run counter to our more customary ideas about science. In her mind, what we call the scientific method cannot by itself give us "real understanding." "It gives us relationships which are useful, valid, and technically marvelous; however, they are not the truth." And it is by no means the only way of acquiring knowledge.

That there are valid ways of knowing other than those conventionally espoused by science is a conviction of long standing for McClintock. It derives from a lifetime of experiences that science tells us little about, experiences that she herself could no more set aside than she could discard the anomalous pattern on a single kernel of corn. Perhaps it is this fidelity to her own experience that allows her to be more open than most other scientists about her unconventional beliefs. Correspondingly, she is open to unorthodox views in others, whether she agrees with them or not. She recalls, for example, a lecture given in the late 1940s at Cold Spring Harbor by Dick Roberts, a physicist from the Carnegie Institution of Washington, on the subject of extrasensory perception. Although she herself was out of town at the time, when she heard about the hostile reaction of her colleagues, she was incensed: "If they were as ignorant of the subject as I was, they had no reason for complaining."

For years, she has maintained an interest in ways of learning other than those used in the West, and she made a particular effort to inform herself about the Tibetan

Buddhists: "I was so startled by their method of training and by its results that I figured we were limiting ourselves by using what we call the scientific method."

Two kinds of Tibetan expertise interested her especially. One was the way the "running lamas" ran. These men were described as running for hours on end without sign of fatigue. It seemed to her exactly the same kind of effortless floating she had secretly learned as a child.

She was equally impressed by the ability that some Tibetans had developed to regulate body temperature: "We are scientists, and we know nothing basically about controlling our body temperature. [But] the Tibetans learn to live with nothing but a tiny cotton jacket. They're out there cold winters and hot summers, and when they have been through the learning process, they have to take certain tests. One of the tests is to take a wet blanket, put it over them, and dry that blanket in the coldest weather. And they dry it."

How were they able to do these things? What would one need to do to acquire this sort of "knowledge"? She began to look at related phenomena that were closer to home: "Hypnosis also had potentials that were quite extraordinary." She began to believe that not only one's temperature, but one's circulation, and many other bodily processes generally thought to be autonomous, could be brought under the influence of mind. She was convinced that the potential for mental control revealed in hypnosis experiments, and practiced by the Tibetans, was something that could be learned. "You can do it, it can be taught." And she set out to teach herself. Long before the word "biofeedback" was invented, McClintock experimented with ways to control her own temperature and blood flow, until, in time, she began to feel a sense of what it took.

But these interests were not popular. "I couldn't tell other people at the time because it was against the 'scientific method.' . . . We just hadn't touched on this kind of knowledge in our medical physiology, [and it is] very, very different from the knowledge we call the only way." What we label scientific knowledge is "lots of fun. You get lots of correlations, but you don't get the truth. . . . Things are much more marvelous than the scientific method allows us to conceive."

Our own method could tell us about some things, but not about others—for instance, she reflects, not about "the kinds of things that made it possible for me to be creative in an unknown way. *Why* do you know? Why were you so sure of something when you couldn't tell anyone else? You weren't sure in a boastful way; you were sure in what I call a completely internal way. . . . What you had to do was put it into their frame. Wherever it came in your frame, you had to work to put it into their frame. So you work with so-called scientific methods to put it into their frame *after* you know. Well, [the question is] *how* you know it. I had the idea that the Tibetans understood this *how* you know."

McClintock is not the only scientist who has looked to the East for correctives to the limitations of Western science. Her remarks on her relation to the phenomena she studies are especially reminiscent of the lessons many physicists have drawn from the discoveries of atomic physics. Erwin Schrödinger, for example, wrote: ". . . our science—Greek science—is based on objectification. . . . But I do believe that this is precisely the point where our present way of thinking does need to be amended, perhaps by a bit of blood-transfusion from Eastern thought."[3] Niels Bohr, the "father of quantum mechanics," was even more explicit on the subject. He wrote: "For a parallel to the lesson of atomic theory . . . [we must turn] to those kinds of epistemological problems with which already thinkers like the Buddha and Lao Tzu have been confronted, when trying to harmonize our position as spectators and actors in the great drama of existence."[4] Robert Oppenheimer held similar views: "The general notions about human understanding . . . which are illustrated by discoveries in atomic physics are not in the nature of being wholly unfamiliar, wholly unheard of, or new," he wrote. "Even in our culture they have a history, and in Buddhist and Hindu thought a more considerable and central place."[5] Indeed, as a result of a number of popular accounts published in the last decade, the correspondences between modern physics and Eastern thought have come to seem commonplace.[6] But among biologists, these interests are not common. McClintock is right to see them, and herself, as oddities. And here, as elsewhere, she takes pride in being different. She is proud to call herself a "mystic."

Above all, she is proud of her ability to draw on these other ways of knowing in her work as a scientist. It is that which, to her, makes the life of science such a deeply satisfying one—even, at times, ecstatic. "What is ecstasy? I don't understand ecstasy, but I enjoy it. When I have it. Rare ecstasy."

Somehow, she doesn't know how, she has always had an "exceedingly strong feeling" for the oneness of things: "Basically, everything is one. There is no way in which you draw a line between things. What we [normally] do is to make these subdivisions, but they're not real. Our educational system is full of subdivisions that are artificial, that shouldn't be there. I think maybe poets—although I don't read poetry—have some understanding of this." The ultimate descriptive task, for both artists and scientists, is to "ensoul" what one sees, to attribute to it the life one shares with it; one learns by identification.[7]

Much has been written on this subject, but certain remarks of Phyllis Greenacre, a psy-choanalyst who has devoted a lifetime to studying the dynamics of artistic creativity, come especially close to the crux of the issue that concerns us here. For Greenacre, the necessary condition for the flowering of great talent or genius is the development in the young child of what she calls a "love affair with the world."[8] Although she believes that a special range and intensity of sensory responsiveness may be innate in the potential artist, she also thinks that, under appropriate circumstances, this special sensitivity facilitates an early relationship with nature that resembles and may in fact substitute for the intimacy of a more conventional child's personal relationships. The forms and objects of nature provide what Greenacre calls "collective alternatives," drawing the child into a "collective love affair."

Greenacre's observations are intended to describe the childhood of the young artist, but they might just as readily depict McClintock's youth. By her own account, even as a child, McClintock neither had nor felt the need of emotional intimacy in any of her personal relationships. The world of nature provided for her the "collective alternatives" of Greenacre's artists; it became the principal focus of both her intellectual and her emotional energies. From reading the text of nature, McClintock reaps the kind of understanding and fulfillment that others acquire from personal intimacy. In short, her "feeling for the organism" is the mainspring of her creativity. It both promotes and is promoted by her access to the profound connectivity of all biological forms—of the cell, of the organism, of the ecosystem.

The flip side of the coin is her conviction that, without an awareness of the oneness of things, science can give us at most only nature-in-pieces; more often it gives us only pieces of nature. In McClintock's view, too restricted a reliance on scientific methodology invariably leads us into difficulty. "We've been spoiling the environment just dreadfully and thinking we were fine, because we were using the techniques of science. Then it turns into technology, and it's slapping us back because we didn't think it through. We were making assumptions we had no right to make. From the point of view of how the whole thing actually worked, we knew how part of it worked. . . . We didn't even inquire, didn't even see how the rest was going on. All these other things were happening and we didn't see it."

She cites the tragedy of Love Canal as one example, the acidification of the Adirondacks Lakes as another. "We didn't think [things] through. . . . If you take the train up to New Haven . . . and the wind is from the southeast, you find all of the smog from New York is going right up to New Haven. . . . We're not thinking it through, just spewing it out. . . . Technology is fine, but the scientists and engineers only partially think through their problems. They solve certain aspects, but not the total, and as a consequence it is slapping us back in the face very hard."

Barbara McClintock belongs to a rare genre of scientist; on a short-term view of the mood and tenor of modern biological laboratories, hers is an endangered species. Recently, after a public seminar McClintock gave in the Biology Department at Harvard University, she met informally with a group of graduate and postdoctoral students. They were responsive to her exhortation that they "take the time and look," but they were also troubled. Where does one get the time to look and to think? They argued that the new technology of molecular biology is self-propelling. It doesn't leave time. There's always the next experiment, the next sequencing to do. The pace of current research seems to preclude such a contemplative stance. McClintock was sympathetic, but reminded them, as they talked, of the "hidden complexity" that continues to lurk

in the most straightforward-seeming systems. She herself had been fortunate; she had worked with a slow technology, a slow organism. Even in the old days, corn had not been popular because one could never grow more than two crops a year. But after a while, she'd found that as slow as it was, two crops a year was too fast. If she was really to analyze all that there was to see, one crop was all she could handle.

There remain, of course, always a few biologists who are able to sustain the kind of "feeling for the organism" that was so productive—both scientifically and personally—for McClintock, but to some of them the difficulties of doing so seem to grow exponentially. One contemporary, who says of her own involvement in research, "If you want to really understand about a tumor, you've got to be a tumor," put it this way: "Everywhere in science the talk is of winners, patents, pressures, money, no money, the rat race, the lot; things that are so completely alien . . . that I no longer know whether I can be classified as a modern scientist or as an example of a beast on the way to extinction."[9]

McClintock takes a longer view. She is confident that nature is on the side of scientists like herself. For evidence, she points to the revolution now occurring in biology. In her view, conventional science fails to illuminate not only "how" you know, but also, and equally, "what" you know. McClintock sees additional confirmation of the need to expand our conception of science in her own—and now others—discoveries. The "molecular" revolution in biology was a triumph of the kind of science represented by classical physics. Now, the necessary next step seems to be the reincorporation of the naturalist's approach—an approach that does not press nature with leading questions but dwells patiently in the variety and complexity of organisms. The discovery of genetic liability and flexibility forces us to recognize the magnificent integration of cel-lular processes—kinds of integration that are "simply incredible to our old-style thinking." As she sees it, we are in the midst of a major revolution that "will reorganize the way we look at things, the way we do research." She adds, "And I can't wait. Because I think it's going to be marvelous, simply marvelous. We're going to have a completely new realization of the relation-ship of things to each other."

NOTES

1. Quoted in E. Broda, "Boltzman, Einstein, Natural Law and Evolution," *Comparative Biochemical Physiology* 67B (1980): 376.
2. Quoted in Banesh Hoffmann and Helen Dukes, *Albert Einstein, Creator and Rebel* (New York: New American Library, 1973), p. 222.
3. Erwin Schrödinger, *What Is Life?* (New York: Macmillan, 1946), p. 140.
4. Niels Bohr, *Atomic Physics and Human Knowledge* (New York: John Wiley and Sons, 1958), p. 33.
5. Robert J. Oppenheimer, *Science and the Common Understanding* (New York: Simon and Schuster, 1954), pp. 8–9.
6. See, for example, Fritz Capra, *The Tao of Physics* (Berkeley, Ca.: Shambhala, 1975), and Gary Zukov, *The Dancing Wu Li Masters* (New York: William Morrow, 1979).
7. The word "ensoul" is taken from Marion Milner, who wrote of her own endeavors as an artist: "I wanted to ensoul nature with what was really there." Marion Milner, *On Not Being Able to Paint* (New York: International Universities Press, 1957), p. 120.
8. Phyllis Greenacre, "The Childhood of the Artist: Libidinal Phase Development and Giftedness" (1957), reprinted in Phyllis Greenacre, *Emotion-al Growth: Psychoanalytic Studies of the Gifted and a Great Variety of Other Individuals* (New York: International Universities Press, 1971), p. 490.
9. June Goodfield, *An Imagined World: A Story of Scientific Discovery* (New York: Harper & Row, 1981), p. 213.

EXERCISES

1. How do the claims of Jaggar and Ginzberg affect the arguments of Kosso (Chapter 4) on objectivity in science?

2. Laudan rejects the relativism of feminism, claiming that the arguments are more political than philosophical. (See his article in Chapter 4.) Do the selections in this chapter support his contentions? How would Longino, Ginzberg, or Jaggar reply to Laudan?

3. Doesn't the whole issue of gender in science make it plain that one ought to keep to the distinction between what is internal to science and what is external to science?

4. Can one have something analogous to McClintock's "feeling for the organism" if one's subject matter is physics or chemistry?

5. Evaluate the following claim: What appear to be internal gender-related issues in science are really the result of external factors; in the future, these differences will no longer exist—and that is the proof that gender differences are only exter-nal. For example, women tend to have feelings for organisms in general because women are socially pressured away from developing a feeling for mathemat-ics. (Refer to Stein in the selection by Bunzl in Chapter 4.) Once this is changed, women will be just as mathematically (reductionistically) oriented as men.

8

Further Readings from Chemistry, Biology, Physics, and the Sociology of Medicine

These selections are meant to provide more detail on some of the scientific cases discussed in earlier chapters. They also provide you with an opportunity to apply what you have learned from the philosophy of science as you read some science and history of science. In a sense, these are exercises meant to help further develop your philosophical skills. In keeping with this, the selections are only briefly described here.

The first selection, by Henry Leicester, deals with phlogiston. It will make the articles by Kuhn and Laudan in Chapter 3 a bit clearer, for they both make mention of this issue. The other four selections are meant to offer more grist for the philosophy-of-science mill. As you read them, try to apply to them concepts discussed in earlier chapters.

Robert Olby demonstrates how a series of experiments that looks as though it should have led to the conclusion that protein was not the genetic material was reinterpreted according to a Lakatosian positive heuristic so that the thesis of protein as the genetic material did not have to be given up.

Charles Darwin (1809–1882) uses his theory of natural selection to explain the geographic distribution of organisms. His theory, like all theories, had weaknesses. He wanted to demonstrate a strength. As you read this selection, refer to Kitcher's article in Chapter 3.

John Williams, Frederick Trinklein, and H. Clark Metcalfe illustrate the differences between wave and corpuscularian theories of light. They show that choosing between the two theories was not easy until certain characteristics of light were discovered. They discuss these characteristics, interference and diffraction, in a much later chapter in their text. Remember that according to Kuhn, textbooks often present a slanted version of history.

The selection from Paul Starr's *Social Transformation of American Medicine* lays the foundation for his explanation for why American medicine has come to have the characteristics that it does today. He sees the roots in the nature of authority as well as in the nature of a profession.

Phlogiston and Affinity

HENRY LEICESTER

During the second half of the seventeenth century and throughout most of the eighteenth, the attention of chemists came more and more to be centered on the problems of the nature of combustion and the forces that held chemical compounds together. At the same time, practical chemistry greatly increased the knowledge of elements and compounds; quantitative methods came to be accepted as essential to chemical investigation; and the whole new field of the chemistry of gases was opened up. The combination of all these factors made possible the foundation of modern chemistry by Lavoisier and the French school at the end of the eighteenth century.

As this period opened, the old concept of expressing the nature of a substance in terms of its properties had by no means been abandoned, though the idea of atomism had been almost universally accepted. Applied to the ideas of combustion, these concepts led to a belief in atoms of fire substance, but did little to alter the age-old ideas of what happened when a substance burned. Theories of the nature of this phenomenon had from earliest times been based on direct observation of a fire. It seemed self-evident that this was one of the most important changes that went on in nature, and many Greek philosophers had made fire the central point in their cosmologies. The changes of material bodies in fire always interested the alchemists, whether mystical or practical. The importance ascribed to sulfur, the principle of combustibility in the sulfur-mercury theory

From Henry Leicester, "Theories of the Eighteenth Century: Phlogiston and Affinity," in *The Historical Background of Chemistry* (New York: Dover, 1956), pp. 119–129. Courtesy of the author and Dover Publications, Inc.

of metal composition, is sufficient evidence of this.

The most obvious fact in observing fire was that flame was escaping from the burning object. Something was being lost, and the relatively light ash left when an organic substance was consumed was further proof of this. Thus the inflammable principle, whatever it was, was naturally assumed to be escaping during combustion. This idea persisted as chemical theories grew more and more precise.[1]

The practical metallurgists of the Middle Ages knew quite well that when metals were heated they were converted to a heavier powder, the calx, but they probably did not bother to connect this with the burning of organic substances, since they were not interested in theoretical matters. They did not concern themselves with the conditions needed for combustion to take place.

Nevertheless, the idea gradually grew up that air was needed if combustion was to occur. The germ of this idea is found in the works of Paracelsus, who believed that air contributed something mysterious to life. This concept was made more specific by a Scottish alchemist, Alexander Seton (died 1604), called the Cosmopolite.[2] His book, *Novum Lumen Chymicum*, was published after his death by his follower, Michael Sendivogius (1556 or 1566–1636 or 1646), who added to it a tract, *De Sulphure*. In these works has been found the apparently specific source of the doctrine that air contains a vital spirit that nourishes life.[3] This vital spirit was identified with niter, by which was meant not the solid salt, but the essential spirit of niter that caused its violent reaction in gunpowder. This led directly into another ancient belief, stemming from the

Aristotelian doctrine of the two exhalations from the earth. It was supposed that, as sulfur and niter were needed to produce the explosion of gunpowder, so a spirit of sulfur and a spirit of niter produced such natural phenomena as thunder, lightning, and earthquakes.[4] These things were generally accepted by scientists of the seventeenth century and were responsible for some of the experiments of Boyle on combustion. Thus, he tried to burn sulfur in a vacuum[5] and failed, proving the need for air. This need was recognized even earlier by Jean Rey (c. 1575–1645),[6] in 1630. John Mayow (1641–1679) in 1674 and especially Robert Hooke in his *Micrographia* of 1665 expressed very clearly the idea that some part of the air was necessary for combustion, but not the whole. Hooke believed that the nitrous particles existed in niter, but Boyle thought that they were only trapped in this salt.[7] It is easy for the modern reader to see in all these works more than the writers intended, for their ideas of chemical combustion were very vague, and they thought of the removal of inflammable material as a sort of solution rather than as a combination in the modern sense. Even Rey, who believed that part of the air combined with a metal during calcination, considered the combination an absorption analogous to that of water on sand when the two are mixed. Nevertheless, if these ideas had been accepted and studied by the active laboratory workers of the eighteenth century, chemical progress might have been more rapid. In actual fact, these theories were little noted at the time, and another explanation came to be generally accepted. This was the phlogiston theory.

In France and England the atomistic theories had led to an attempt to explain the universe in purely mechanical terms. This was quite satisfactory to the physicists, but the chemists, confronted with a vast and growing mass of confusing and individualized compounds and reactions, could not

feel completely at ease in a clockwork universe. They did their best with the mechanical theories, but, when they were presented with a concept that grew out of the older chemical ideas of Van Helmont and that seemed to embrace many otherwise unrelated facts, they were quite ready to receive it. It was in Germany that the older ideas retained their greatest influence, and it was from Germany that the new theory emerged.

Johann Joachim Becher (1635–1682) resembled Van Helmont in many ways. He had similar, partly mystical ideas, and felt a great interest in organic compounds. To him, metals were only a by-product in the plan of the Creator, which was centered in organic life. Therefore, any explanation of combustion had to be based on the burning of organic substances. Becher accepted air, water, and earth as elements, but air, as Van Helmont had stated, could not take part in chemical reactions, and water had only its own specific properties. It followed, according to Becher, that the differences in chemical compounds resided in the different sorts of earth that composed them. He distinguished three kinds of earth: the vitreous, the fatty, and the fluid.[8] The first, corresponding to the Paracelsan salt, gave body to substances; the second, Paracelsan sulfur, gave combustibility; and the third, Paracelsan mercury, gave density and metallic luster. The second, or fatty earth, *terra pinguis*, was found particularly in animal or vegetable matter, and it left these bodies when they burned. It is clear that this theory of Becher was merely a restatement of older iatrochemical ideas, and by itself it would probably have exerted no more influence than many other contemporary theories.

It was, however, taken up by Becher's pupil, Georg Ernst Stahl (1660–1734), and made part of a unified theory that appealed greatly to other chemists. The explanation of combustion, at first merely a part of this generalized theory, eventually became the central doctrine of chemistry. As such it held sway until nearly the end of the eighteenth century.

Stahl was a physician, and mystically inclined, but he was also influenced by the strong metallurgical tradition of the German chemists which had been exemplified by the work of Agricola and Ercker. In his chemical theories he centered his attention on inorganic compounds rather than organic, as his master, Becher, had done.[9]

He accepted the existence of atoms, but, in addition to their mechanical properties, he endowed them with intrinsic ones. The particles of elementary substances were drawn to each other by a sort of Newtonian attraction. The resulting compounds were usually referred to as "mixts" at this period.[10] There were relatively few such simple mixts, and gold or silver were typical examples. The mixts could unite to more complex compounds, whose particles were still too small to be seen, and these compounds in turn could form aggregates whose particles were large enough to be visible.[11] The resemblance of these ideas to those of Boyle is clear.

The original elements could never be isolated, for they could not leave one mixt without entering another. Therefore, though each element had specific properties, these could be observed only in its compounds, and so the element could be known only by the effects it produced.[12] The elements of Stahl were the same as those of Becher. To the fatty earth, however, he gave the name phlogiston, from the Greek word for burned, or inflammable. The term had been used as early as 1606 by Hapelius, but not until the time of Stahl did it become common.[13]

Stahl, with his great interest in metals, centered more attention on phlogiston than Becher had done on his *terra pinguis*. He agreed with Becher that, when combustion occurred, the inflammable principle was lost. Thus, when a metal was heated, it lost phlogiston and was converted to the calx

(the oxide, in our terms). The metal was therefore a more complex substance than the calx. Regeneration of the metal occurred when the calx combined with phlogiston once more. This was not necessarily a simple matter. The phlogiston lost from a metal was dispersed throughout the air, which was essential as the medium to carry away the phlogiston. Air thus retained the character of a mere mechanical aid to combustion which had been assigned to it by Van Helmont, but the established need for air if combustion was to take place was explained. Plants could absorb phlogiston from the air once more, and animals could obtain it from plants. Thus plant and animal substances were rich in phlogiston and could react with metallic calces to restore the phlogiston and convert them to metals again. The most useful substance for this purpose was charcoal, which was considered extremely rich in phlogiston.[14]

Since phlogiston was an elementary principle, its nature could be known only from its effects. Stahl concentrated his attention upon the chemical phenomena of combustion. In this field, the phlogiston theory supplied an excellent explanation for the then known facts. All the facts that are now considered under the head of oxidation-reduction were involved in this theory, though the explanation was essentially the reverse of our own. Where we consider a substance, oxygen, to be taken up, Stahl considered a substance, phlogiston, to be given off. In either case, the concept is one of the transfer of something from one substance to another. It was essentially this concept of a transfer that made the theory so useful and made it possible to include so many facts under its heading. It was thus the first great unifying principle in chemistry.[15] Its success accounted for the importance it assumed for eighteenth century chemists.

The inconsistencies of the theory at first were mostly its failures to account for physical changes. To Stahl these were unimportant. The fact that, when an organic substance burned, the apparent products weighed less than the original substance, while calcination of inorganic substances, recognized as the same process, led to increased weight in the products, was of so little importance to Stahl that he did not even mention it. If he considered the matter at all, he probably believed that phlogiston was weightless.[16] Phlogiston, after all, was a principle that could not be known directly, not a definite physical substance as we conceive one. Therefore Stahl and many of his successors felt no inconsistency in disregarding facts that did not fit into the chemical picture. It was only later when the idea of a chemical substance as a physical entity became accepted by the chemists that this point became crucial for the phlogiston theory.

Stahl's theory did not at once achieve acceptance by all chemists. The most influential chemist of his time, Hermann Boerhaave (1668–1738), did not even mention it in his lectures or in his famous textbook, *Elementa Chymia,* published in 1732. In this work Boerhaave, professor of medicine, botany, and chemistry at Leiden, set the pattern for chemical instruction in the first half of the eighteenth century. Although he was not a phlogistonist, his ideas could be fitted into the pattern of the phlogiston theory, and the eventual fusion of the concepts of Stahl and Boerhaave, both drawing on the ideas of Van Helmont, Boyle, and other seventeenth century chemists, led to a chemical system from which Lavoisier could develop his brilliant new ideas.

Like Stahl, Boerhaave believed that air played only a mechanical part in chemical phenomena,[17] but he did not entirely exclude the possibility that it might, in some cases, play some part in certain reactions.[18] He thought of fire as a substance composed of fine particles that could penetrate other materials and alter the force of attraction that held them together.[19] He distinguished between fire as manifested in heat and fire manifested in combustion, a distinction not previously made. This opened the way for a consideration of fire as a material substance, a concept used by Lavoisier in developing his theory of caloric, and to later thermochemical ideas, such as Black's theory of latent heat.[20] Boerhaave believed that chemical reaction was essentially the same as solution. The solvent, or menstruum, usually a liquid, was composed of fine particles that pushed their way between the particles of dissolved substance. The atoms of each then remained suspended and related to one another as required by the affinities of each substance for the other.[21] Boerhaave here introduced the term affinity in the sense it retained for the next century.[22] From these ideas it was easy for Boerhaave to deduce that increased weight after calcination was due to the uptake of fire particles, which had weight, by the substance being calcined. This had been the explanation of Boyle, and its espousal by a second very influential chemist gave it great prestige. The idea that fire, heat, and light were material substances, originally suggested by the Cartesian idea of the ether and now supported by such strong authorities, became an accepted part of chemical thought until, in the nineteenth century, the concept of energy made it unnecessary.

The spread of the phlogiston theory and its almost complete acceptance by the middle of the eighteenth century coincided with a rapid accumulation of chemical facts. More and more chemists began to think of elements as substances just as material as any of the compounds with which they dealt in their laboratories. Both elements and compounds should obey the same laws, physical as well as chemical. It was no longer possible to think of abstract principles that could be made to fit any theory by disregarding inconvenient facts. It was thus impossible to ignore any longer the increase in weight of metals on calcination. As long as the part played by gases in chemical reactions was not understood, as long as air was assumed to be a substance that could not play a chemical role, the correct explanation of the increase could not be found. Nevertheless, a great amount of ingenuity was expended in attempts to find it.

The theory of Boyle and Boerhaave that fire particles were taken up during calcination satisfied many. Others confused density with absolute weight and assumed that the lower density of the calx actually indicated a loss of substance. Still others believed in the buoyancy of phlogiston, or assumed that it had a negative weight which caused an increase in weight of the calx when the phlogiston was lost. In the last days of the theory, when the part gases played in combustion was realized, it was sometimes assumed that, as phlogiston was lost, another substance with greater weight was taken up.[23] The disagreements among the phlogistonists, the accumulation of unsatisfactory theories, and the constant need to revise these theories as new facts were discovered made the fall of the phlogiston theory inevitable as soon as a more rational theory became available.

Side by side with the development of the phlogiston theory went the development of theories of affinity. The term itself dates back perhaps to Albertus Magnus, and crude, qualitative lists of the order of reactivity of metals toward various reagents had been given even in the writings of Geber,[24] but only when the occult forces of love and hate as an explanation of affinity had been banished by the mechanical theories of Boyle did it become possible for a more quantitative approach to give results. Even so, a further qualitative stage had to be passed, and the fundamental explanation of the actual cause of attraction between atoms remained unsatisfactory.

The wide acceptance of the physical theories of Newton could not but impress the chemists, and affinity began to be considered chiefly in terms of his ideas. Essentially, it was assumed that every particle of matter was endowed with a certain attractive force that uniquely caused all its chemical and physical reactions.[25] Although this theory was spectacularly successful when applied in astronomy and physics, it was in most cases too vague to apply to the special problems presented by individual chemical reactions.[26] The theories of Boerhaave on reaction and solution already discussed indicate how this concept of affinity was used to explain chemical behavior, but, in order to make the Newtonian concept generally useful, chemists felt the need to draw up tables of affinity that would express the reactivity of individual compounds toward each other, and that could, it was hoped, be used to predict the reactivity of other compounds in similar reactions. Such tables of necessity had to be based on actual experiments, and for this reason they were regarded with some suspicion by the atomic theorists of the period, who still felt it was better to reason abstractly than to test by experience.[27] Nevertheless, these tables typify the tendency of most chemists to use laboratory data as the true guide to further work, which became increasingly significant in the eighteenth century.

The first attempt to draw up such a table was made in 1718 by Etienne-François Geoffroy (1672–1731), usually called Geoffroy the Elder to distinguish him from his brother who was also a chemist. Geoffroy's basic idea was that "whenever two substances which have some disposition to unite, the one with the other, are united together and a third which has more affinity for one of the two is added, the third will unite with one of these, separating it from the other."[28] Geoffroy prepared a table with sixteen columns, each headed by the alchemical symbol for a chemical substance. In each column he listed the substances that were found by experiment to react with the substance at the head of the column. The order was such that each substance had a greater affinity for the parent material than any that stood below it in the column. Thus, in the first column, the heading was "acid spirits," and below were the symbols for fixed alkali salts (carbonates), volatile alkali salts (ammonium salts), absorbent earths (non-effervescing bases), and metallic substances.

The fixed alkali salts are placed in the column immediately below the acid spirits, since I know of no substance which will separate these, once they are united, and on the other hand whenever one of the three types of substance below is united to acid spirits, it abandons its place in favor of fixed alkali salts which when added combine directly with the acid.

This type of table became very popular and reached its culmination in 1775 in the elaborate compilation of the Swedish chemist, Torbern Bergman (1735–1784). Bergman had contributed greatly to the development of quantitative analysis, and so knew the difference in reaction of many compounds in the "wet way" (in solution) and in the "dry way" (by fusion). He prepared tables of affinity resembling those of Geoffroy for fifty-nine substances in each of these two methods of reaction. He distinguished between "attraction of aggregation" in homogeneous substances, which resulted only in an increase in mass, and "attraction of composition" in heterogeneous substances, which resulted in compound formation. He distinguished two main types of this attraction: "single elective attractions," which are displacements; and "double elective attractions," which are double decompositions. His terminology persisted for many years. The compilation of these tables became more difficult as the number of known chemical compounds increased. In fact, Bergman estimated that to determine all

the relations of the substances in his table would require over 30,000 separate experiments. A number of arbitrary assumptions were also needed. Bergman recognized that in some cases the amounts of reacting substances or the experimental conditions other than solution or fusion could affect the results of the reaction, but he thought that these differences were incidental and that the order of affinities was a true constant.[29]

The ideas of Bergman were popularized in the new dictionaries and encyclopedias of chemistry that began to appear in the eighteenth century, and that were probably the outgrowth of the wider interest in the science that developed from the work of such popularizers as Lémery in the previous century. In turn, these works still further widened the general knowledge of the science. The first of these, the dictionary of P. J. Macquer (1718–1784), appeared in 1766 and discussed affinity from the viewpoint of Geoffroy, but, in the second, enlarged edition of 1778, the discussion was in almost the same terms as those of Bergman.[30] Guyton de Morveau (1737–1816) wrote a long article on affinity for the *Encyclopédie méthodique* in 1786, again giving essentially the ideas of Bergman.[31] These ideas were, therefore, widespread at the end of the century.

Their qualitative nature was obvious, and, as the quantitative spirit developed during the century, it was natural that attempts should be made to measure accurately the affinities of various substances. As early as 1700, Wilhelm Homberg (1652–1715) tried to measure the amount of base required to neutralize various acids.[32] C. F. Wenzel (1740–1793) in 1777 tried to determine the relative rates of solution of metals in acids,[33] and Richard Kirwan (1733–1812) in 1781 believed that the weights of bases required to saturate a known weight of acid were a measure of the affinity of the acid for the bases,[34] a refinement of the idea of Homberg. None of these methods gave very accurate or reproducible results, but the principles that they used were subsequently employed by Cavendish, Richter, and Wollaston in establishing the theory of chemical equivalents.

NOTES

1. J. C. Gregory, *Combustion from Heracleitos to Lavoisier*, E. Arnold and Co., London, 1934, pp. 43, 45.
2. John Read, *Humour and Humanism in Chemistry*, G. Bell and Sons, London, 1947, pp. 37–51.
3. H. Guerlac, *Actes septième congr. intern. hist. sci.*, Jerusalem, 1953, pp. 332–349.
4. H. Guerlac, *Isis*, 45, 243–255 (1954).
5. Robert Boyle, *New Experiments Touching the Relation betwixt Flame and Air*, London, 1672.
6. Douglas McKie, *The Essays of Jean Rey*, E. Arnold and Co., London, 1951.
7. Douglas McKie, "Fire and the Flamma Vitalis," in *Science, Medicine and History: Essays on the Evolution of Scientific Thought and Medical Practice, Written in Honour of Charles Singer*, vol. 1, Oxford University Press, London, 1953, pp. 469–488.
8. Hélène Metzger, *Newton, Stahl, Boerhaave et la doctrine chimique*, Alcan, Paris, 1930, pp. 160–161.
9. *Ibid.*, p. 97.
10. *Ibid.*, p. 116.
11. *Ibid.*, pp. 121–124.
12. *Ibid.*, pp. 119–120.
13. J. H. White, *The History of the Phlogiston Theory*, E. Arnold and Co., London, 1932, p. 51.
14. Metzger, *Newton, Stahl, Boerhaave*, pp. 170, 177.
15. Walter Hückel, *Structural Chemistry of Inorganic Compounds*, translated by L. H. Long, vol. 1, Elsevier, New York, 1950, p. 8.
16. White, *History*, p. 56.
17. Metzger, *Newton, Stahl, Boerhaave*, pp. 240–241.
18. M. Kerker, *Isis*, 46, 36–49 (1955).
19. Metzger, *Newton, Stahl, Boerhaave*, pp. 223–224.
20. *Ibid.*, p. 228.
21. *Ibid.*, pp. 280–289.
22. M. M. Pattison Muir, *A History of Chemical Theories and Laws*, John Wiley & Sons, New York, 1907, p. 381.
23. J. R. Partington and Douglas McKie, *Ann. Sci* 2, 361–404 (1937); 3, 1–58 (1938); White, *History*, pp. 59–92.
24. P. Walden, *J. Chem. Educ.* 31, 27–33 (1954).
25. Metzger, *Newton, Stahl, Boerhaave*, p. 73.
26. *Ibid.*, p. 50.
27. Hélène Metzger, *Les doctrines chimiques en France du début du XVIIᵉ à la fin du XVIIIᵉ siècle*, vol. 1, Les presses universitaires de France, Paris, 1923, p. 418.
28. E. F. Geoffroy, *Mémoires de l'académie royale des sciences*, 1718, 202–212.
29. T. Bergman, *N. Actes d'Upsal 3* (1775).
30. L. J. M. Coleby, *The Chemical Studies of P. J. Macquer*, George Allen and Unwin, London, 1938, pp. 39–41.
31. Muir, *History*, pp. 289–290.
32. Metzger, *Les doctrines chimiques*, p. 413.
33. Muir, *History*, p. 383.
34. *Ibid.*, pp. 390–391.

The Nature of the Hereditary Material

ROBERT OLBY

When T. H. Morgan gave his Nobel lecture in Stockholm, in June 1933, he posed the question: "What are genes?"

Now that we locate them in the chromosomes are we justified in regarding them as material units; as chemical bodies of a higher order than molecules? Frankly, these are questions with which the

From Robert Olby, *The Path to the Double Helix* (Seattle: University of Washington Press, 1974), pp. 103–106. Courtesy of the author.

working geneticist has not much concerned himself, except now and then to speculate as to the nature of the postulated elements. There is no consensus of opinion amongst geneticists as to what the genes are—whether they are real or purely fictitious—because at the level at which the genetic experiments lie, it does not make the slightest difference whether the gene is a hypothetical unit, or whether the gene is a material particle. In either case the unit is associated with a specific chromosome, and can be localized there by purely genetic analysis. Hence, if the gene is a material unit, it is a piece of a chromosome; if it is a fictitious unit, it must be referred to a definite location in a chromosome—the same place as on the other hypothesis. Therefore, it makes no difference in the actual work in genetics which point of view is taken.

Between the characters that are used by the geneticist and the genes that his theory postulates lies the whole field of embryonic development. . . . (Morgan, 1933, 315)

One must remember that at this time little evidence of chemical differentiation along the chromosome was available. To be sure, the chromosome had been recognized as a row of deeply-staining chromomeres held together by a faintly-staining thread composed of a substance called "linin." But geneticists were justly unenthusiastic about the chemical basis for such vague distinctions. Their attitude began to change when E. Heitz advanced a new differentiation of the chromatin of the liverwort *Pellia* into two kinds of chromatin, morphologically sharply different—heterochromatin and euchromatin (Heitz, 1928), the former being stainable long after the latter had lost its stainability at the close of mitosis. Subsequently, he extended this discovery to *Drosophila* (Heitz, 1933). Even more compelling of the geneticists' attention was T. S. Painter's disclosure that the banding on salivary gland chromosomes of *Drosophila* was a constant and characteristic feature of them.[1]

In the euchromatic region of the X chromosome (see Fig. 1) he pictured more than 150 of the now well known bands, and gave the positions of breakage points and gene loci alongside them (Painter, 1933). Of this work Sturtevant remarked:

Here at last was a detailed correspondence in sequence between the crossover map and cytologically visible landmarks, and a technique that was capable of refinement to give the precise loci of genes in terms of recognizable bands. Instead of two or three landmarks per chromosome (the ends and centromeres), there were now hundreds, and there soon came to be thousands for the whole complex. (Sturtevant, 1965, 76)

Now if the genes could be located on specific sites of the chromosome the next step would be to analyse the chemical constitution of such chromosomal segments. The task of linking the geneticists' abstract units with the chemists' organic compounds now seemed worth attempting. This was not just another discovery. It was a landmark in bringing together the discoveries of the geneticists and those of the cytologists. And more, it opened up the way to the chemical exploration of the fine structure of chromosomes.

In his Nobel lecture in 1933, before Painter's work was published, Morgan showed a slide of the famous salivary gland chromosomes of *Drosophila* in which he demonstrated the transverse banding in material treated with strong acetic acid. One can well imagine how interested Hammarsten and Caspersson were in Morgan's slides. The group in Stockholm had developed a reagent which digested the protein of the chromosome and retained the nucleic acid fixed as a lanthanum salt. This enzyme–lanthanum reagent they used to search for a "protein structure in cell nuclei, especially in chromosomes" (Caspersson, Hammarsten, and Hammarsten, 1935, 367).

Figure 1 Painter's Camera Lucida sketch of the X chromosome of *Drosophila* as seen in the salivary gland after treatment with acetocarmine. Reprinted with permission from T. S. Painter, "A New Method for the Study of Chromosomes ..." *Science* 78 (1933): 586. Copyright © 1933 American Association for the Advancement of Science.

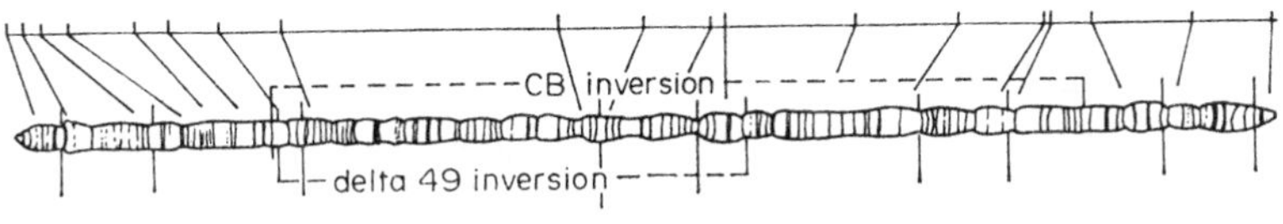

Their plan was to show by ultraviolet microphotometry a change in the pattern of ultraviolet absorption before and after treatment with the reagent. The absence of any conspicuous differences led them to doubt that a block-like packing of protein between nucleic acid bands existed in their material (*Stenobotrus* spp.) but they expected such an arrangement would be demonstrable in Morgan's material (*Ibid.*, 369). The strong acetic acid, they thought, had concealed a "negative" of protein concentration along the chromosome, the dark bands representing low protein content but high nucleic acid content.

When Hammarsten and Caspersson presented their report to the Faraday Society in London in 1934, their work was still in a preliminary stage. The ultraviolet microscope at their disposal was very imperfect and they used the double line of magnesium at 280 mμ for their light source. Later on, Caspersson greatly improved the quality of these microphotographs by using the cadmium light source which he passed through a monochromator to give 257 mμ—the portion of the ultraviolet spectrum most intensely absorbed by nucleic acids. The designer of the Zeiss ultraviolet microscope, August Köhler, had advocated the use of cadmium in 1904 when he published pictures he had obtained with it, the most striking of these were the larval gill bud cells of *Salamandra maculosa*. He saw the technique of ultraviolet microphotometry as a control on the results achieved by traditional staining techniques and as opening up a new field of research (Köhler, 1904, 302). Caspersson had taken slides to Köhler in Jena, probably in 1933, and had seen just what could be achieved with the Zeiss equipment there.

At long last, Köhler's toy was to prove its worth. Admittedly the hoped for duplication of resolving power at 275 mμ had not been achieved. An early attempt to use the microscope in the search for bacterial nuclei had brought disappointment (Schrötter, 1906), and Carl Zeiss only once demonstrated the instrument (1905). But when Caspersson used it on salivary gland chromosomes with Köhler's improved monochromator, what a wealth of detail was revealed! A new dimension in cytochemistry opened up which the Swedish scientists exploited to the full.

It was not that Caspersson was the first or the only one to use the ultraviolet microscope in the 1930's. There was Ralph Wyckoff at the Rockefeller and Muller and Prokofyeva in Russia, but the all important link between the absorption of ultraviolet light by the chromosomes and by nucleic acids was first seen by Caspersson. So here were these wonderful observations of chromosomes in the *living* cell as well as in the fixed cell, photographed under ultraviolet light, showing Painter's characteristic banded patterns. Was there after all a chemical morphology of which the genetic map was an expression? It seemed possible.

Having said all this, having urged the importance of the link between the genetic map and the distribution of nucleic acid, reluctantly we have to admit that the Hammarstens and Caspersson continued with the traditional assumption that the genes must be proteins. Referring to the proteins and nucleic acids as the "known substances" they wrote: "there are only the proteins to be considered, because they are the only known substances which are specific for the individual. *On that assumption a protein structure in chromosomes takes on a very great interest*" (Caspersson, Hammarsten and Hammarsten, 1935, 369). Consequently, their subsequent discovery of vigorous nucleic acid synthesis when chromosomes were thought to duplicate had to be turned on its head in order to preserve the protein version of the central dogma. What resulted we may term "The Nucleoprotein Theory of the Gene."

DNA SYNTHESIS AT THE ONSET
OF CELL DIVISION

Caspersson observed such a marked increase in ultraviolet absorption during meiosis that there was no shred of doubt in his mind that: "In the time between early leptotene, where scarcely any absorbing substance can be detected in the nuclei, and the development of the complete nucleic acid-rich tetrads, a genuine fresh synthesis must evidently have occurred" (Caspersson, 1936, 120). Interphase and ensuing prophase were correlated with loss and renewal of absorbing substances. The absorbing substance was nucleic acid: therefore, reasoned Caspersson, this substance is essential for chromosome duplication and hence for gene reproduction.

When Caspersson was joined by Jack Schultz in Stockholm, a correlation was found between nucleic acid content of certain bands in *Drosophila* salivary gland chromosomes and the variegated eye colour mutants discovered by Muller and attributed to "chromosomal displacements" (Muller, 1930, 299). Ultraviolet measurements in Stockholm showed that "the closer a given band is to the heterochromatic region, the greater the augmentation of its nucleic acid content" (Caspersson and Schultz, 1938, 295). A parallel increase in nucleic acid was noted when going from the eggs of XX females to those of XXY females. From their study of the salivary gland chromosomes, Caspersson and Schultz rightly concluded that the heterochromatin was not an inert region. Such regions of the chromosome, they argued, perform

a function also performed by all other genes—namely, the synthesis of nucleic acid. The relation of these regions to the variegation, taken together with the local appearance of nucleic acid in the chromosomes, suggests that the synthesis of nucleic acid is closely connected with gene reproduction. The structure-forming properties of thymonucleic acid, and its ability to form high molecular weight polymers, as well as

the correspondence of its X-ray diffraction pattern with that of the proteins, suggest a basis for this function.

These considerations have an especial interest in the case of the other self-reproducing molecules—the viruses and the bacteriophage—all of which have been shown to contain nucleic acid. Moreover, in the inactivation of the bacteriophage by ultraviolet light, the curve for the efficiencies of the different wavelengths does not agree completely with that of the bacteriophage, but does with the nucleic acid absorption spectrum. It seems hence that the unique structure conditioning activity and self-reproduction, possibly by successive polymerization and depolymerization, may depend on the nucleic acid portion of the molecule. It may be that the property of a protein which allows it to reproduce itself is its ability to synthesize nucleic acid. (Caspersson and Schultz, 1938, 295)

As we read this passage our excitement rises. Surely they will conclude that the genes *are* nucleic acids! But no—they turn the evidence on its head and in the last sentence we get a view into their inner thoughts. Sure enough, within two years Caspersson had made this conclusion the basis of a comprehensive scheme for the protein metabolism of the cell. Here protein synthesis in the cytoplasm was the equivalent of chromosome duplication in the nucleus. Both events involved the self-duplication of protein molecules in the presence of nucleic acids. Caspersson did not stop here. He sketched out the phylogenetic development of the nucleus, starting with simple RNA-containing plant viruses, going on to DNA-containing yeast and bacteria, and finally to the chromosomal nuclei of higher organisms. Here, the more primitive genetic material was located in the heterochromatin, where it produced histones. These accumulated in the nucleolus and were ultimately transferred to the cytoplasmic proteins; such a scheme appeared appropriate to Caspersson's observations of the nucleic acid content of actively secreting cells.

NOTE

1. Of course Painter was not the only contributor, the first to associate the banding with the genetic map being Kostoff (see Darlington, 1937, 175ff).

REFERENCES

Caspersson, T., 1936, "Ueber den chemischen Aufbau der Strukturen des Zellkernes," *Acta Med. Skand.* **73**, Suppl. 8, 1–151.

Caspersson, T., Hammarsten, E., and Hammarsten, H., 1935, "Interactions of Proteins and Nucleic Acids," *Trans. Faraday Soc.* **31**, 367–389.

Caspersson, T., and Schultz, J., 1938, "Nucleic Acid Metabolism of the Chromosomes in Relation to Gene Reproduction," *Nature* **142**, 294–295.

Darlington, C. D., 1937, *Recent Advances in Cytology*, Philadelphia: Blakiston's Son & Co.

Heitz, E., 1928, "Das Heterochromatin der Moose," *Jahrb. wiss. Bot.*, 69.

Köhler, A., 1904, "Mikrophotographische Untersuchungen mit ultraviolettem Licht," *Z. wiss. Mikroskopie* **21**, 129–165, 273–304.

Morgan, T. H., 1933, "The Relation of Genetics to Physiology and Medicine," in *Nobel Lectures . . . Physiology and Medicine 1922–1941*, Amsterdam: Elsevier, 1965, pp. 313–328.

Muller, H. J., 1930, "Types of Visible Variations Induced by X-rays in *Drosophila*," *Genetics* **22**, 299–334.

Painter, T. S., 1933, "A New Method for the Study of Chromosome Rearrangements and the Plotting of Chromosome Maps," *Science* **78**, 585–586.

Schrötter, H., 1906, "Beitrag zur Mikrophotographie mit ultraviolettem Lichte nach Köhler," *Virchow's Arch. path. Anat.* **183**, 343–376.

Sturtevant, A. J., 1965, *A History of Genetics*, New York: Harper & Row.

An Attempt to Explain the Laws of Geographical Distribution

CHARLES DARWIN

An attempt to explain the . . . laws of geographical distribution, on the theory of allied species having a common descent

First let us recall the circumstances most favourable for variation under domestication, as given in the first chapter—viz. 1st, a change, or repeated changes, in the conditions to which the organism has been exposed, continued through several seminal (i.e. not by buds or divisions) generations: 2nd, steady selection of the slight varieties thus generated with a fixed end in view: 3rd, isolation as perfect as possible of such selected varieties; that is, the preventing

From Charles Darwin, *The Foundations of the Origin of the Species: Two Essays Written in 1842 and 1844*, vol. 10 of *The Works of Charles Darwin*, ed. Paul H. Barrett and R. B. Freeman (New York: New York University Press, 1987), pp. 137–144.

their crossing with other forms; this latter condition applies to all terrestrial animals, to most if not all plants and perhaps even to most (or all) aquatic organisms. It will be convenient here to show the advantage of isolation in the formation of a new breed, by comparing the progress of two persons (to neither of whom let time be of any consequence) endeavouring to select and form some very peculiar new breed. Let one of these persons work on the vast herds of cattle in the plains of La Plata,[1] and the other on a small stock of 20 or 30 animals in an island. The latter might have to wait centuries (by the hypothesis of no importance)[2] before he obtained a "sport" approaching to what he wanted; but when he did and saved the greater number of its offspring and their offspring again, he might hope that his whole little stock would be in some degree affected, so that by continued selection he might /[3] gain his end. But on the Pampas, though the man might get his first approach to his desired form sooner, how hopeless would it be to attempt, by saving its offspring amongst so many of the common kind, to affect the whole herd: the effect of this one peculiar "sport"[4] would be quite lost before he could obtain a second original sport of the same kind. If, however, he could separate a small number of cattle, including the offspring of the desirable "sport," he might hope, like the man on the island, to effect his end. If there be organic beings of which two individuals *never* unite, then simple selection whether on a continent or island would be equally serviceable to make a new and desirable breed; and this new breed might be made in surprisingly few years from the great and geometrical powers of propagation to beat out the old breed; as has happened (notwithstanding crossing) where good breeds of dogs and pigs have been introduced into a limited country—for instance, into the islands of the Pacific.

Let us now take the simplest natural case of an islet upheaved by the volcanic or subterranean forces in a deep sea, at such a distance from other land that only a few organic beings at rare intervals were transported to it, whether borne by the sea[5] (like the seeds of plants to coral-reefs), or by hurricanes, or by floods, or on rafts, or in roots of large trees, or the germs of one plant or animal attached to or in the stomach of some other animal, or by the intervention (in most cases the most probable means) of other islands since sunk or destroyed. It may be remarked that when one part of the earth's crust is raised it is probably the / general rule that another part sinks. Let this island go on slowly, century after century, rising

foot by foot; and in the course of time we shall have instead [of] a small mass of rock,[6] lowland and highland, moist woods and dry sandy spots, various soils, marshes, streams and pools: under water on the sea shore, instead of a rocky steeply shelving coast, we shall have in some parts bays with mud, sandy beaches and rocky shoals. The formation of the island by itself must often slightly affect the surrounding climate. It is impossible that the first few transported organisms could be perfectly adapted to all these stations; and it will be a chance if those successively transported will be so adapted. The greater number would probably come from the lowlands of the nearest country; and not even all these would be perfectly adapted to the new islet whilst it continued low and exposed to coast influences. Moreover, as it is certain that all organisms are nearly as much adapted in their structure to the other inhabitants of their country as they are to its physical conditions, so the mere fact that a *few* beings (and these taken in great degree by chance) were in the first case transported to the islet, would in itself greatly modify their conditions.[7] As the island continued rising we might also expect an occasional new visitant; and I repeat that even one new being must often affect beyond our calculation by occupying the room and taking part of the subsistence of another (and this again from another and so on), several or many other organisms. Now as the first transported and any occasional successive visitants spread or tended to spread over the growing island, they would undoubtedly be exposed through several generations to new and varying conditions: it might also easily happen that some of / the species *on an average* might obtain an increase of food, or food of a more nourishing quality.[8] According then to every analogy with what we have seen takes place in every country, with nearly every organic being under domestication, we might expect that some of the inhabitants of the island would "sport," or have their organization rendered in some degree plastic. As the number of the inhabitants are supposed to be few and as all these cannot be so well adapted to their new and varying conditions as they were in their native country and habitat, we cannot believe that every place or office in the economy of the island would be as well filled as on a continent where the number of aboriginal species is far greater and where they consequently hold a more strictly limited place. We might therefore expect on our island that although very many slight variations were of no use to the plastic individuals, yet that occasionally in the course of a century an individual might be born[9] of which the structure or constitution in some slight degree would allow it better to fill up some office in the insular economy and to struggle against other species. If such were the case the individual and its offspring would have a better *chance* of surviving and of beating out its parent form; and if (as is probable) it and its offspring crossed with the unvaried parent form, yet the number of the individuals being not very great, there would be a chance of the new and more serviceable form being nevertheless in some slight degree preserved. The struggle for existence would go on annually selecting such individuals until a new race or species was formed. Either few or all the first visitants to the island might become modified, according / as the physical conditions of the island and those resulting from the kind and number of other transported species were different from those of the parent country—according to the difficulties offered to fresh immigration—and according to the length of time since the first inhabitants were introduced. It is obvious that whatever was the country, generally the nearest from which the first tenants were transported, they would show an affinity, even if all had become modified, to the natives of that country and even if the inhabitants of the same source (?) had been modified. On this view we can at once understand the cause and meaning of the affinity of the fauna and flora of the Galápagos Islands with that of the coast of S. America; and consequently why the inhabitants of these islands show not the smallest affinity with those inhabiting other volcanic islands, with a very similar climate and soil, near the coast of Africa.[10]

To return once again to our island, if by the continued action of the subterranean forces other neighbouring islands were formed, these would generally be stocked by the inhabitants of the first island, or by a few immigrants from the neighbouring mainland; but if considerable obstacles were interposed to any communication between the terrestrial productions of these islands, and their conditions were different (perhaps only by the number of different species on each island), a form transported from one island to another might become altered in the same manner as one from the continent; and we should have several of the islands tenanted by representative races or species, as is so wonderfully the case with the different islands of the Galápagos Archipelago. As the islands become mountainous, if mountain-species were not introduced, as could rarely happen, a greater amount of variation and / selection would be requisite to adapt the species, which originally came from the lowlands of the nearest continent, to the mountain-summits than to the lower districts of our islands. For the lowland species from the continent would have first to struggle against other species and other conditions on the coast-land of the island, and so probably become modified by the selection of its best fitted varieties, then to undergo the same process when the land had attained a moderate elevation; and then lastly when it had become Alpine. Hence we can understand why the faunas of insular mountain-summits are, as in the case of

Teneriffe, eminently peculiar. Putting on one side the case of a widely extended flora being driven up the mountain-summits, during a change of climate from cold to temperate, we can see why in other cases the floras of mountain-summits (or as I have called them islands in a sea of land) should be tenanted by peculiar species, but related to those of the surrounding lowlands, as are the inhabitants of a real island in the sea to those of the nearest continent.[11]

Let us now consider the effect of a change of climate or of other conditions on the inhabitants of a continent and of an isolated island without any great change of level. On a continent the chief effects would be changes in the numerical proportion of the individuals of the different species; for whether the climate became warmer or colder, drier or damper, more uniform or extreme, some species are at present adapted to its diversified districts; if for instance it became cooler, species would migrate from its more temperate parts and from its higher land; if damper, from its damper / regions, etc. On a small and isolated island, however, with few species, and these not adapted to much diversified conditions, such changes instead of merely increasing the number of certain species already adapted to such conditions, and decreasing the number of other species, would be apt to affect the constitutions of some of the insular species: thus if the island became damper it might well happen that there were no species living in any part of it adapted to the consequences resulting from more moisture. In this case therefore, and still more (as we have seen) during the production of new stations from the elevation of the land, an island would be a far more fertile source, as far as we can judge, of new specific forms than a continent. The new forms thus generated on an island, we might expect, would occasionally be transported by accident, or through long-contin-

ued geographical changes be enabled to emigrate and thus become slowly diffused.

But if we look to the origin of a continent; almost every geologist will admit that in most cases it will have first existed as separate islands which gradually increased in size;[12] and therefore all that which has been said concerning the probable changes of the forms tenanting a small archipelago is applicable to a continent in its early state. Furthermore, a geologist who reflects on the geological history of Europe (the only region well known) will admit that it has been many times depressed, raised and left stationary. During the sinking of a continent and the probable generally accompanying changes of climate the effect would be little, *except* on the numerical proportions and in the extinction (from the lessening of rivers, the drying of marshes / and the conversion of high-lands into low, etc.) of some or of many of the species. As soon however as the continent became divided into many isolated portions or islands, preventing free immigration from one part to another, the effect of climatic and other changes on the species would be greater. But let the now broken continent, forming isolated islands, begin to rise and new stations thus to be formed, exactly as in the first case of the upheaved volcanic islet, and we shall have equally favourable conditions for the modification of old forms, that is the formation of new races or species. Let the islands become reunited into a continent; and then the new and old forms would all spread, as far as barriers, the means of transportal, and the preoccupation of the land by other species, would permit. Some of the new species or races would probably become extinct, and some perhaps would cross and blend together. We should thus have a multitude of forms, adapted to all kinds of slightly different stations, and to diverse groups of either antagonist or food-serving species. The oftener these oscillations of level had taken place (and therefore generally the older the land) the greater the number of species [which] would tend to be formed. The inhabitants of a continent being thus derived in the first stage from the same original parents, and subsequently from the inhabitants of one wide area, since often broken up and reunited, all would be obviously related together and the inhabitants of the most *dissimilar* stations on the same continent would be more closely allied than the inhabitants of two very *similar* stations on two of the main divisions of the world.[13]

I need hardly point out that we now can obviously / see why the number of species in two districts, independently of the number of stations in such districts, should be in some cases as widely different as in New Zealand and the Cape of Good Hope.[14] We can see, knowing the difficulty in the transport of terrestrial mammals, why islands far from mainlands do not possess them;[15] we see the general reason, namely accidental transport (though not the precise reason), why certain islands should, and others should not, possess members of the class of reptiles. We can see why an ancient channel of communication between two distant points, as the Cordillera probably was between southern Chile and the United States during the former cold periods; and icebergs between the Falkland Islands and Tierra del Fuego; and gales, at a former or present time, between the Asiatic shores of the Pacific and eastern islands in this ocean; is connected with (or we may now say causes) an affinity between the species, though distinct, in two such districts. We can see how the better chance of diffusion, from several of the species of any genus having wide ranges in their own countries, explains the presence of other species of the same genus in other countries;[16] and on the other hand, of species of restricted powers of ranging, forming genera with restricted ranges.

As every one would be surprised if two exactly similar but peculiar varieties[17] of any species were raised by man by long continued selection, in two different countries, or at two very different periods, so we ought not to expect that an exactly similar form would be produced from the modification of an old one in two distinct countries or at two distinct / periods. For in such places and times they would probably be exposed to somewhat different climates and almost certainly to different associates. Hence we can see why each species appears to have been produced singly, in space and in time. I need hardly remark that, according to this theory of descent, there is no necessity of modification in a species, when it reaches a new and isolated country. If it be able to survive and if slight variations better adapted to the new conditions are not selected, it might retain (as far as we can see) its old form for an indefinite time. As we see that some sub-varieties produced under domestication are more variable than others, so in nature, perhaps, some species and genera are more variable than others. The same precise form, however, would probably be seldom preserved through successive geological periods, or in widely and differently conditioned countries.[18]

Finally, during the long periods of time and probably of oscillations of level, necessary for the formation of a continent, we may conclude (as above explained) that many forms would become extinct. These extinct forms, and those surviving (whether or not modified and changed in structure), will all be related in each continent in the same manner and degree, as are the inhabitants of any two different sub-regions in that same continent. I do not mean to say that, for instance, the present Marsupials of Australia or Edentata and rodents of S. America have descended from any one of the few fossils of the same orders which have been discovered in these countries. It is possible that, in a very few instances, this may be the case; but generally they must be considered as merely codescendants of common stocks.[19] I believe in this, from the improbability, considering the vast number of species, which (as / explained in the last chapter) must by our theory have existed, that the *comparatively* few fossils which have been found should chance to be the immediate and linear progenitors of those now existing. Recent as the yet discovered fossil mammifers of S. America are, who will pretend to say that very many intermediate forms may not have existed? Moreover, we shall see in the ensuing chapter that the very existence of genera and species can be explained only by a few species of each epoch leaving modified successors or new species to a future period; and the more distant that future period, the fewer will be the *linear* heirs of the former epoch. As by our theory, all mammifers must have descended from the same parent stock, so is it necessary that each land now possessing terrestrial mammifers shall at some time have been so far united to other land as to permit the passage of mammifers;[20] and it accords with this necessity, that in looking far back into the earth's history we find, first changes in the geographical distribution, and secondly a period when the mammiferous forms most distinctive of two of the present main divisions of the world were living together.[21]

I think then I am justified in asserting that most of the above enumerated and often trivial points in the geographical distribution of past and present organisms (which points must be viewed by the creationists as so many ultimate facts) follow as a simple consequence of specific forms being mutable and of their being adapted by natural selection to diverse ends, conjoined with their powers of dispersal, and the geologico-geographical changes now in slow progress and which undoubtedly have taken place. This large class of facts being thus explained, / far more than coun-

terbalances many separate difficulties and apparent objections in convincing my mind of the truth of this theory of common descent.

NOTES

1. This instance occurs in the Essay of 1842, p. [32] 24, but not in the *Origin;* though the importance of isolation is discussed (*Origin*, Ed. i, p. 104; vi, p. 127).
2. The meaning of the words within parenthesis is obscure.
3. The slashes indicate where the page breaks in the original manuscript occurred [Ed.].
4. It is unusual to find the author speaking of the selection of *sports* rather than small variations.
5. This brief discussion is represented in the *Origin*, Ed. i by a much fuller one (pp. 356, 383; vi, pp. 504, 535). See, however, the section in the present Essay, p. [168] 127.
6. On the formation of new stations, see *Origin*, Ed. i, p. 292; vi, p. 429.
7. *Origin*, Ed. i, pp. 390, 400; vi, pp. 543, 554.
8. In the ms. *some of the species . . . nourishing quality* is doubtfully erased. It seems clear that he doubted whether such a problematical supply of food would be likely to cause variation.
9. At this time the author clearly put more faith in the importance of sport-like variation than in later years.
10. *Origin*, Ed. i, p. 398; vi, p. 553.
11. See *Origin*, Ed. i, p. 403; vi, p. 558, where the author speaks of Alpine humming birds, rodents, plants, etc. in S. America, all of strictly American forms. In the MS the author has added between the lines "As world has been getting hotter, there has been radiation from high-lands—old view?—curious; I presume Diluvian in origin."
12. See the comparison between the Malay Archipelago and the probable former state of Europe, *Origin*, Ed. i, p. 299; vi, p. 438, also *Origin*, Ed. i, p. 292; vi, p. 429.
13. *Origin*, Ed. i, p. 349; vi, p. 496. The arrangement of the argument in the present Essay leads to repetition of statements made in the earlier part of the book: in the *Origin* this is avoided.
14. *Origin*, Ed. i, p. 389; vi, p. 542.
15. *Origin*, Ed. i, p. 393; vi, p. 547.
16. *Origin*, Ed. i, pp. 350, 404; vi, pp. 498, 559.
17. *Origin*, Ed. i, p. 352; vi, p. 500.
18. *Origin*, Ed. i, p. 313; vi, p. 454.
19. *Origin*, Ed. i, p. 341; vi, p. 487.
20. *Origin*, Ed. i, p. 396; vi, p. 549.
21. *Origin*, Ed. i, p. 340; vi, p. 486.

The Nature of Light

JOHN WILLIAMS, FREDERICK TRINKLEIN, AND H. CLARK METCALFE

It must have been evident to Newton and to other scientists in his day that only two general theories could explain the properties of light, since the transmission of energy from one place to another was involved.

A window pane may be shattered by a moving object, such as a baseball thrown from a distance, or by the concussion resulting from a distant explosion. In general, energy can be propagated either by particles of matter or by wave disturbances traveling from one place to another.

Arguments favoring both a particle (corpuscular) theory and a wave theory were plausible when applied to the properties of light observed in the seventeenth century. The principal advocate of the corpuscular theory was Newton, whose arguments were supported by the French mathematician, Laplace (1749–1827). The wave theory was upheld principally by Christian Huygens (1629–1695), a Dutch mathematician, physicist, and astronomer. He was supported by Robert Hooke of England. Because of the plausibility of both theories, a scientific debate concerning the nature of light developed between the followers of Newton and Huygens which continued unresolved for more than a century. Let us consider some of the arguments which support each of these classical theories of light.

———

Sir Isaac Newton believed that light consists of streams of tiny particles (which he called corpuscles) emanating from a luminous

source. Let us examine the arguments used by those who believed the particle theory best explained the various light phenomena known to them.

1. *Rectilinear propagation.* A ball thrown into space follows a curved path because of the influence of gravity. Yet if the ball is thrown with greater and greater speed, we know that its path curves less and less. We can easily imagine minute particles traveling at such enormous speed that their paths form essentially straight lines.

Newton experienced no difficulty in explaining the rectilinear propagation of light by means of his particle model. In fact, this property of light provided the supporters of the corpuscular theory with one of their strongest arguments against a wave theory. How, they asked, could waves travel in straight lines? A sound can easily be heard around the corner of an obstruction, but a light certainly cannot be seen from behind an obstruction. The former is unquestionably a wave phenomenon. How can the latter also be one?

The simple and direct explanation of rectilinear propagation provided by the particle model of light, together with the great prestige of Sir Isaac Newton, were largely responsible for the preference shown for the corpuscular theory during the seventeenth and eighteenth centuries.

2. *Reflection.* Where light is incident on a smooth surface such as a mirror, we know that it is regularly reflected. How do particles behave under similar circumstances? Steel ball bearings thrown against a smooth steel plate rebound in much the same way light is reflected. Perfectly elastic particles rebounding from a resilient surface, then,

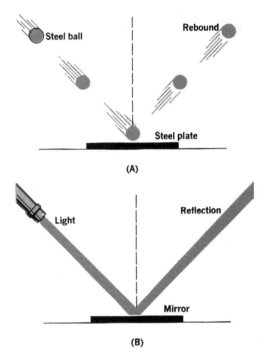

Figure 1 The rebound of a steel ball from a resilient surface resembles the reflection of light from a mirror surface. This example was used as an early argument to "prove" that light rays were streams of tiny particles.

could provide a suitable model for the reflection of light. See Fig. 1.

3. *Refraction.* Newton was able to demonstrate the nature of refraction by means of his particle model. We can duplicate this experimentally by arranging two level surfaces, one higher than the other, with their adjacent edges joined by an incline. . . . A ball may be rolled across the upper surface, down the incline, and across the lower surface. Of course, it will experience an acceleration due to the force of gravity while rolling down the incline and will move across the lower surface at a higher speed than it had initially.

Suppose the ball is set rolling on the higher surface toward the incline at a given angle with the normal to the edge. At the incline, the accelerating force exerts a pull on the ball causing it to roll across the lower surface at a smaller angle with the normal to its edge. Now if we think of the upper surface as representing air, the lower surface as an optically more dense medium like water, and the incline as the interface of the two transmitting media, the rolling ball behaves like particles of light being redirected, or refracted, as they pass from air into water.

By varying the grade of the incline while maintaining both constant rolling speed and constant angle with the normal on the upper surface, the refractive characteristics of different transmitting media can be illustrated by the rolling-ball model.

Newton believed that the water attracted the approaching particles of light in much the same way that gravity attracts the rolling ball on the incline. The rolling ball experiments imply, as they did to Newton, that light particles accelerate as they pass from air into an optically more dense medium such as water or glass. The corpuscular theory required that the speed of light in water be greater than in air. Newton recognized that if it should ever be determined that the speed of light is less in water than it is in air, his corpuscular theory would have to be abandoned. It was not until 1850, one hundred and twenty-three years after Newton's death, that the lesser speed in water was demonstrated experimentally by the French physicist Jean Foucault (1819–1868).

———

Christian Huygens is generally considered to be the founder of the wave theory of light. Although somewhat different in its modern form, Huygens' basic concept is still very useful to us in predicting and interpreting the behavior of light. Let us recall a familiar characteristic of water waves as an introduction to this important principle.

If a stone is dropped into a pool of quiet

water, it creates a disturbance in the water and a series of concentric waves travels out from the disturbance point. The stone quickly comes to rest on the bottom of the pool, so its action on the water is of short duration. However, wave disturbances persist for a considerable time thereafter and cannot reasonably be attributed to any activity on the part of the stone. It must be that the disturbances existing at all points along the wave fronts at one instant of time generate those in existence at the next instant.

Huygens recognized this logical deduction as a basic aspect of wave behavior and devised a geometric method of finding new wave fronts. His concept, published in 1690 and now recognized as *Huygens' principle,* may be stated as follows: *each point on a wave front may be regarded as a new source of disturbance.*

According to this principle, a wave front originating at a source **S** of Fig. 2(A) arrives at the position **AB.** Each point in this wave front may be considered as a secondary source sending out wavelets. Thus, from points **1, 2, 3,** etc., a series of wavelets develops simultaneously which, after a time, *t,* have a radius equal to *vt,* where *v* is the velocity of the wave.

The principle further states that the surface **A′B′,** tangent to all the wavelets, constitutes the new wave front. It is apparent from Fig. 2 that spherical wave fronts are propagated from spherical waves and plane wave fronts from plane waves.

The wave theory treats light as a train of waves having wave fronts perpendicular to the paths of the light rays. In contrast to the particle model discussed earlier, the light energy is considered to be distributed uniformly over the advancing wave front.

Figure 2 By Huygens's principle, every point on an advancing wave front is regarded as a source of disturbance.

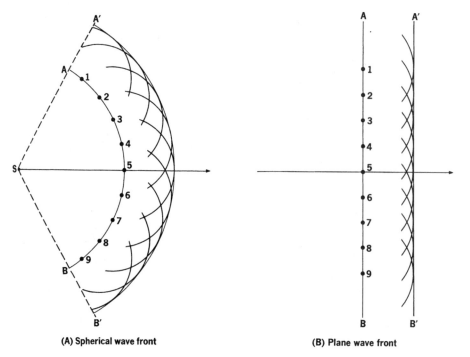

(A) Spherical wave front

(B) Plane wave front

Huygens thought of a ray merely as a line of direction of waves propagated from a light source.

The supporters of the wave theory were able to explain reflection and refraction of light satisfactorily, that of the latter requiring the speed of light in optically dense media such as water and glass to be *less* than in air. They had trouble, however, explaining rectilinear propagation. This was the primary reason why Newton rejected the wave theory.

Before the nineteenth century, interference of light was unknown, and the speed of light in such media as water and glass had not been measured. Diffraction fringes or shadows had been observed as early as the seventeenth century, but, in the absence of knowledge of interference, neither Newton nor Huygens attached much significance to them.

In 1801 the interference of light was discovered. This was followed in 1816 by the explanation of diffraction based on the interference principles. . . .

These two phenomena imply a wave character and cannot be explained satisfactorily by the behavior of particles. Thus, despite the great prestige of Sir Isaac Newton, the corpuscular theory was largely abandoned in favor of the wave theory. The final blow to the corpuscular theory came when Foucault found that the speed of light was less in water than in air. Through the remainder of the nineteenth century the wave concept supplied the basic laws from which came remarkable advances in optical theory and technology.

The Growth of Medical Authority

PAUL STARR

The rise of the professions was the outcome of a struggle for cultural authority as well as for social mobility. It needs to be understood not only in terms of the knowledge and ambitions of the medical profession, but also in the context of broader changes in culture and society that explain why Americans became willing to acknowledge and institutionalize their dependence on the professions. The acceptance of professional authority was, in a sense, America's cultural revolution, and like other revolutions, it threw new groups to power—in this case, power over experience as much as power over work and institutions.

In a society where an established religion claims to have the final say on all aspects of human experience, the cultural authority of medicine clearly will be restricted. But this was no longer the principal barrier to medicine in the early nineteenth century. Many Americans who already had a rationalist, activist orientation to disease refused to accept physicians as authoritative. They believed that common sense and native intelligence could deal as effectively with most problems of health and illness. Moreover, the medical profession itself had little unity and was unable to assert any collective authority over its own members, who held diverse and incompatible views.

Authority, as I've indicated, involves a surrender of private judgment, and nine-

From Paul Starr, *The Social Transformation of American Medicine* (New York: Basic Books, 1982), pp. 17–21. Copyright © 1982 by Paul Starr. Reprinted by permission of BasicBooks, a division of HarperCollins Publishers, Inc.

teenth-century Americans were not willing to make that surrender to physicians. Authority signifies the possession of a special status or claim that compels trust, and medicine lacked that compelling claim in nineteenth-century America. The esoteric learning, knowledge of Latin, and high culture and status of traditional English physicians were more compelling grounds for belief in a hierarchically ordered society than in a democratic one. The basis of modern professionalism had to be reconstructed around the claim to technical competence, gained through standardized training and evaluation. But this standardization of the profession was blocked by internal as well as external barriers—sectarianism among medical practitioners and a general resistance to privileged monopolies in the society at large.

The forces that transformed medicine into an authoritative profession involved both its internal development and broader changes in social and economic life. Internally, as a result of changes in social structure as well as scientific advance, the profession gained in cohesiveness toward the end of the nineteenth century and became more effective in asserting its claims. With the growth of hospitals and specialization, doctors became more dependent on one another for referrals and access to facilities. Consequently, they were encouraged to adjust their views to those of their peers, instead of advertising themselves as members of competing medical sects. Greater cohesiveness strengthened professional authority. Professional authority also benefited from the development of diagnostic technology, which strengthened the powers of the physician in physical examination of the patient and reduced reliance on the patient's report of symptoms and superficial appearance.

At the same time, there were profound changes in Americans' way of life and forms of consciousness that made them more dependent upon professional authority and more willing to accept it as legitimate. Different ways of life make different demands upon people and endow them with different types of competence. In preindustrial America, rural and small-town communities endowed their members with a wide range of skills and self-confidence in dealing with their own needs. The division of labor was not highly developed, and there was a strong orientation toward self-reliance, grounded in religious and political ideals. Under these conditions, professional authority could make few inroads. Americans were accustomed to dealing with most problems of illness within their own family or local community, with only occasional intervention by physicians. But toward the end of the nineteenth century, as their society became more urban, Americans became more accustomed to relying on the specialized skills of strangers. Professionals became less expensive to consult as telephones and mechanized transportation reduced the cost of time and travel. Bolstered by genuine advances in science and technology, the claims of the professions to competent authority became more plausible, even when they were not yet objectively true; for science worked even greater changes on the imagination than it worked on the processes of disease. Technological change was revolutionizing daily life; it seemed entirely plausible to believe that science would do the same for healing, and eventually it did. Besides, once people began to regard science as a superior and legitimately complex way of explaining and controlling reality, they wanted physicians' interpretations of experience regardless of whether the doctors had remedies to offer.

At a time when traditional certainties were breaking down, professional authority offered a means of sorting out different conceptions of human needs and the nature and meaning of events. In the nineteenth century, many Americans, epitomized by the Populists, continued to believe in the adequacy of common sense and to resist the claims of the professions. On the other hand, there were those, like the Progressives, who believed that science provided the means of moral as well as political reform and who saw in the professions a new and more advanced basis of order. The Progressive view, always stated as a disinterested ideal, nevertheless happily coincided with the ambitions of the emerging professional class to cure and reform. The cultural triumph of Progressivism, which proved more lasting than its political victories, was inseparable from the rise in status and power of professionals in new occupations and organizational hierarchies. Yet this was no simple usurpation; the new authority of professionals reflected the instability of a new way of life and its challenge to traditional belief. The less one could believe "one's own eyes"—and the new world of science continually prompted that feeling—the more receptive one became to seeing the world through the eyes of those who claimed specialized, technical knowledge, validated by communities of their peers.[1]

The growth of medical authority also needs to be understood as a change in institutions. In the nineteenth century, before the profession consolidated its position, some doctors had great personal authority and they pronounced on all manner of problems, by no means restricted to physical illness. Indeed, in the small communities of early American society, where the number of educated men was relatively small, some physicians may have possessed even broader personal authority than do most of their counterparts today. What I am talking about here, on the other hand, is authority that inheres in the status of physician because it has been institutionalized in a system of standardized education and licensing. The establishment of such a sys-

tem reproduces authority from one generation to the next, and transmits it from the profession as a whole to all its individual members. Before the profession's authority was institutionalized in the late nineteenth and early twentieth centuries, physicians might win personal authority by dint of their character and intimate knowledge of their patients. But once it was institutionalized, standardized programs of education and licensing conferred authority upon all who passed through them. The recognition of authority in a given doctor by laymen and colleagues became relatively unambiguous. Authority no longer depended on individual character and lay attitudes; instead, it was increasingly built into the structure of institutions.

"Built-in" dependence on professional authority increased with such developments as the rise of hospitals. I do not mean only the development of mental hospitals and procedures for involuntary commitment, though the asylum is obviously an important and radical form of institutionalized medical authority. Even the voluntary shift of seriously ill patients from their homes to general hospitals increases the dependent condition of the sick. At home, patients may quite easily choose to ignore the doctor's instructions, and many do; this is much more difficult in a hospital. For the seriously ill, clinical personnel subordinate to the doctor have, in effect, replaced the family as the physician's vicarious agent. They not only administer treatment in the doctor's absence, but also maintain surveillance, keep records, and reinforce the message that the doctor's instructions must be followed.

Other institutional changes have also made people dependent on medical authority regardless of whether they are receptive or hostile to doctors. As the various certifying and gatekeeping functions of doctors have grown, so has the dependence of people seeking benefits that require certification. Laws prohibiting laymen from obtaining certain classes of drugs without a doctor's prescription increase dependence on physicians. "The more strategic the accessories controlled by the profession," Eliot Freidson writes, "the stronger the sanctions supporting its authority."[2] In the twentieth century, health insurance has become an important mechanism for ensuring dependence on the profession. When insurance payments are made only for treatment given by physicians, the beneficiaries become dependent on doctors for reimbursable services. A doctor's authorization for drugs and prosthetics has become necessary for a host of insurance and tax benefits. In all these ways, professional authority has become institutionally routine, and compliance has ceased to be a matter of voluntary choice. What people think about doctors' judgments is still important, but it is much less important than it used to be.

In their combined effect, the mechanisms of legitimation (standardized education and licensing) and the mechanisms of dependency (hospitalization, gatekeeping, insurance) have given a definite structure to the relations of doctors and patients that transcends personalities and attitudes. This social structure is based, not purely on shared expectations about the roles of physicians and the sick, but on the institutionalized arrangements that often impose severe costs on people who wish to behave in some other way.[3]

The institutional reinforcement of professional authority also regulates the relations of physicians to each other. The doctor whose personal authority in the nineteenth century rested on his imposing character and relations with patients was in a fundamentally different situation from the doctor in the twentieth century whose authority depends on holding the necessary credentials and institutional affiliations. While lay-

men have become more dependent on professionals, professionals have become more dependent on each other. Both changes have contributed to the collective power of the profession and helped physicians to convert their clinical authority into social and economic privilege. . . .

NOTES

1. For an excellent account of the struggle for authority and its relation to changing social organization, see Thomas L. Haskell, *The Emergence of Professional Social Science* (Urbana, Ill.: University of Illinois Press, 1977).
2. Eliot Freidson, *Professional Dominance: The Social Structure of Medical Care* (New York: Atherton, 1970), 117.
3. Role expectations are the heart of what was once the most influential schema in the sociology of medicine—that of Talcott Parsons. According to Parsons, the social structure of medical practice can be defined by the shared expectations about the "sick role" and the role of the doctor. On the one hand, the sick are exempt from normal obligations; they are not held responsible for their illness; they must try to get well; and they must seek competent help. On the other, the physician is expected to be "universalistic," "functionally specific," "affectively neutral," and "collectivity-oriented." These complementary normative rules have a functional relation to the therapeutic process and the larger society.[4]

While useful as a point of departure for understanding doctor-patient relations, Parsons' model is open to severe objections as a model of medical practice. It fails to convey the ambivalence of doctor-patient relationships and the contradictory expectations with which each party must contend.[5] It also accepts the ideological claims of the profession—for example, to be altruistic ("collectivity-oriented")—and ignores evidence of contrary rules of behavior, such as tacit agreements to ignore colleagues' mistakes.[6] Parsons' approach concentrates almost entirely upon the system of norms in purely voluntary doctor-patient relations. That such relations are not wholly voluntary both because of dependency conditions and the historical process that lies behind professional dominance is a point Parsons simply overlooks. The distribution of power, control of markets, and so on do not enter significantly into his analysis. Parsons also neglects other relations important to medical practice, such as those among doctors and between doctors and organizations. The more important these collegial and bureaucratic relations become, the less useful Parsons' approach appears.

4. For Parsons' classic statement, see *The Social System* (Glencoe, Ill.: Free Press, 1951), Chap. 10.

5. See Robert K. Merton and Elinor Barber, "Sociological Ambivalence," in *Sociological Theory, Values and Sociocultural Change*, ed. Edward A. Tiryakian (New York: Free Press, 1963), 91–120.

6. See E. Freidson, *Profession of Medicine* (New York: Dodd, Mead, 1970), esp. Chap. 7.

EXERCISES

1. What was the role of reductionism in the development of the theories of phlogiston and affinity according to the account of Leicester? Is his account consistent with the history of science as it is related by Merchant? Using only the information provided in Leicester's account, develop a theory of confirmation; a theory of scientific explanation.

2. Olby says that Caspersson and Schultz "turn the evidence on its head" when they fail to conclude that genes are nucleic acids. What does he mean by this? Should what Olby terms "The Nucleoprotein Theory of the Gene" be considered a Kuhnian paradigm? Precisely how does (or doesn't) Olby's account of this incident from the history of genetics support Keller's views about the history of genetics?

3. What does Darwin mean by law; by explanation? What role do models play in Darwin's explanation? What is the model on which he relies? Darwin says that he is convinced of "the truth of this theory of common descent." What does Darwin mean by truth?

4. In "The Nature of Light," which is more important, confirmation or falsification? Why? Did Newton and Huygens use similar or different kinds of models in explaining the nature of light? How does the story of the overthrow of the corpuscular theory of light fit what Kuhn would tell us to expect from a textbook? If Kuhn is right, how would the wave theory have replaced the corpuscular theory?

5. Starr says that medicine revolutionized healing. How important is this, according to Starr, in the growth of medicine's authority in the United States? Would the growth of medicine's authority, as Starr defines it, be internal or external (as Gorovitz and MacIntyre use the terms) to medicine? Starr points out the importance of medicine's "organizational hierarchies." How does this fit with the feminist views of Merchant, Ginzberg, and Keller?